Bernard Shaw and the Actresses

Books by Margot Peters:

BERNARD SHAW AND THE ACTRESSES

UNQUIET SOUL: A BIOGRAPHY OF CHARLOTTE BRONTE

CHARLOTTE BRONTE: STYLE IN THE NOVEL

Bernard Shaw and the Actresses

—

Margot Peters

Doubleday & Company, Inc., Garden City, New York
1980

Photographs of Mrs. Jane (Jenny) Patterson (MSS. 50587, F. 22) and Janet Achurch (date unknown) (MSS. 50585, f. 100), and the letter from Ellen Terry to Bernard Shaw (previously unpublished), November 5 and 6, 1896 (MSS. 43,800, f. 172 and 173) have been reproduced by permission of the British Library Board.

Photograph of Florence Farr from *Pall Mall Budget* (April 19, 1894) is from the collection of the General Research and Humanities Division, The New York Public Library, Astor, Lenox and Tilden Foundations.

Book Design by Beverley Gallegos

ISBN: 0-385-12051-6
Library of Congress Catalog Card Number 79–7205

For Ray

Contents

List of Illustrations

following page 272

Nora Charrington.
Lillah McCarthy, Charlotte Shaw, and Harley Granville-Barker
  photographed by Shaw.
Lillah McCarthy in *Man and Superman*
Lillah McCarthy in *Fanny's First Play*.
Lena Ashwell in Tolstoy's *Resurrection*.
Ellen Terry in *Captain Brassbound's Conversion*.
Shaw rehearsing Lillah McCarthy in *Androcles and
  the Lion*.

following page 368

Mrs. Patrick Campbell.
Caricatures of Mrs. Patrick Campbell as Eliza Doolittle.
Stella Campbell photographed by Shaw.
Shaw and Molly Tompkins.
Shaw's London residence.
Shaw's Corner, Ayot St. Lawrence.
Charlotte Shaw's sitting room.
Dining room at Shaw's Corner.
Hatstand and stick rack.
Bernard Shaw.

Introduction

"UNLESS YOU CAN shew me in the context of my time, as a member of a very interesting crowd," Shaw once told his official biographer Archibald Henderson, "you will fail to produce the only thing that makes biography tolerable." Shaw made the assignment difficult, of course, first by being the Complete Outsider, then by creating the gigantic personality of G.B.S. to mask his alienation. Still it is possible to talk about Shaw and the Fabians; Shaw and transitional dramatists Pinero, Jones, Grundy, and Barrie; Shaw and theatrical critics such as Walkley, Archer, and Beerbohm, although Shaw tends to dominate such studies. He dominates this one, although the crowd he is placed among is a very interesting one in its own right. These are the actresses with whom, as a dramatic critic and struggling playwright, Shaw found himself writing for, competing with, courting for their influence, and often simply courting. They were important to his career, as this study attempts to demonstrate; for the New Drama was very much the drama of the New Woman: the emancipation of women on stage reflected the emancipation of women off it, and was fought for to a great extent by actresses struggling to free themselves from the bondage of traditional roles.

Shaw allied himself with these actresses, and wrote the kinds of parts they wished to play into his drama, from Blanche Sartorius in his first play *Widowers' Houses* to Candida, Ann Whitefield, Saint Joan, and Epifania Ognisanti di Parerga Fitzfassenden, the millionairess. To the casting of these roles Shaw devoted a considerable portion of his seemingly inexhaustible energies, the more so because he so often became personally involved with the actresses he sought to influence professionally. Of the thousands of letters Shaw "the writing machine" produced in his long life, a large portion were written to these actresses—Florence Farr, Janet Achurch, Elizabeth Robins, Alma Murray, Ada Rehan, Eleanor Robson, Ellen Terry, Gertrude Kingston, Lillah McCarthy, Lena Ashwell, Mrs. Patrick Campbell. They influenced his art; certainly he influenced their careers. "If actors were oftener given such lines to speak," said Ellen O'Malley, the actress who created Nora in *John Bull's Other Island*, "acting would soon become an easy matter." "Ann Whitefield made a new woman of me," said Lillah McCarthy. Gertrude Kingston, Shaw's Great Catherine, decided that G.B.S. helped more lame dogs over stiles than anyone else she knew. Sybil Thorndike thanked him not only for the opportunity of playing Saint Joan and the invaluable lessons in acting he gave her, but for strengthening her faith in God.

But the establishment of the new woman on stage and the careers of those actresses who wished to play her were not won without struggle. Elizabeth Robins, a feminist and the actress chiefly responsible for putting Ibsen on the London stage, was one who experienced the frustrations of the actress-manager in late Victorian England. "We had come to realize how essential to success some freedom of judgment and action are to the actor," she wrote retrospectively in *Theatre and Friendship* in 1932. "The strangulation of this rôle and that through arbitrary stage management, was an experience we had shared with men. But we had further seen how freedom in the practice of our art, how the bare opportunity to practise it at all, depended, for the actress, on considerations humiliatingly different from those that confronted the actor. The stage career of an actress was inextricably involved in the fact that she was a woman and that those who were masters of the theatre were men. These considerations did not belong to art; they stultified art." Behind Robins's veiled complaint lay the fact that the actress was still considered a loose woman by much of society and many of her colleagues, that her acting aspirations were not taken seriously, that her attempts at management were frustrated, that her salary did not match an actor's, and that she was seen as merely an appendage to the actor-manager, someone to set off his acting by never competing with it. The leading lady in leading strings, Elizabeth Robins called her.

When Shaw wrote in 1917 to a father anxious over his daughter's choice of career that "The stage is the only profession in which women are on equal terms with men," his reply measured the progress that had been achieved since the 1880s. As a new playwright he had agreed that the subordinate role of the actress stultified art, and fought vigorously for her emancipation in his drama, a fight which is largely the subject of this book. To begin the battle with his first play *Widowers' Houses*, however, would be to omit much of the campaign: one must begin with Shaw as a struggling young novelist in London, for three of the five "novels of his nonage"—*Immaturity* (1879), *The Irrational Knot* (1880),

and *Love Among the Artists* (1881)—turn the popular notion of the
debauched actress about by showing her as more honest, hard-working,
and fastidious than her respectable married sisters. Very early he had
concluded that marriage for property was prostitution, a career and economic independence the more honorable life for a woman. And to concentrate only on the plays would be to omit Shaw's campaign as a dramatic critic to liberate the theatre of the 1890s from the conservative
actor-manager mentality he believed held it in thrall. The actress would
be the first to benefit from that liberation, for, as Shaw argued in a preface to *The Theatrical "World" of 1894*, a glance at London theatres
showed that the higher artistic career was virtually closed to the leading
lady. Thus the ill-paid and unpopular group of actresses attempting to
bring to the stage real roles for women—roles in which women were
dignified by something more than the amorous attentions of the hero—
seemed to Shaw more enviable than Lyceum leading lady Ellen Terry, so
often condemned to merely "supporting" actor-manager Sir Henry Irving. As a critic he fought for the new actress and the types of roles she
wished to see performed. Hedda Gabler, Rebecca West, Nora Helmer,
and Mrs. Alving were not the charming heroines of male fantasy, but
even to show women as "unamiable human beings" was a great advance
over showing them eternally as "amiable imposters."

Shaw's alliance with the actress was not without friction, however. Established actresses like Ellen Terry and Mrs. Patrick Campbell resisted
his plays as long as they could. Willing and emancipated actresses like
Florence Farr and Janet Achurch often lacked the polished technique
Shaw demanded for his plays. And some actresses—notably Elizabeth
Robins—looked upon his feminism with suspicion. She did not believe
that Shaw liked women very well or portrayed them fairly in his plays.
Were Vivie Warren, Candida, Ann Whitefield, and Great Catherine, for
example, really human beings—or were they, after all, versions of Shaw's
very ambivalent feelings about women: Shavian stereotypes of the domi-
nant female rather than traditional stereotypes? Necessarily, therefore,
Bernard Shaw and the Actresses explores the wider question of Shaw's
attitude toward women, thus touching on his relationships with women
such as Alice Lockett, Jenny Patterson, May Morris, Annie Besant, and
Charlotte Payne-Townshend.

This study does not attempt comprehensiveness. A book could be
written on Shaw and Janet Achurch alone, for example, and later
actresses like Sybil Thorndike, Edith Evans, and Ellen Pollock are omitted in favor of the actresses important during the crucial years of
1892–1907 when Shaw was striving for recognition as a dramatist. I have
also chosen to emphasize the actresses who were important personally as
well as professionally to Shaw, thus considerably narrowing the field.
The portrait of Shaw is not rounded, nor intended to be, though hope-

fully none the less valid for that. There is little or nothing of Shaw the Fabian, Shaw the committee-man, Shaw the war critic, Shaw the platform speaker; there is a good deal of Shaw the "ladies' tailor," Shaw the philanderer, Shaw the lover, Shaw the feminist, Shaw the Tannhäuserian hero, Shaw the puritan. It was a Shaw from which his official biographer preferred to avert his gaze, not only, one supposes, because he often disliked Shaw's conduct with women and wished to obliterate it from the record, but because he considered the subject of women unimportant. Shaw fueled that idea with comments like "Women and love—the most tedious subjects on earth," yet devoted considerable time and energy to both, if only to attack the latter. Ultimately I have been concerned with the impact of women in general, the actress specifically, on Shaw's art. He himself rated that impact high. "I have just seen Mary Ann," he wrote Eleanor Robson in 1904, "and I am for ever yours devotedly. I have no interest in mere females; but I *love* all artists: they belong to me in the most sacred way and you are an artist. . . ." So might he have written to Janet Achurch, to Ellen Terry, to Mrs. Campbell. And finally I have tried to explore the importance of actresses like Florence Farr, Janet Achurch, Elizabeth Robins, Lena Ashwell, and Lillah McCarthy to the modern drama: to lift some of the shadow inevitably cast by the eminence of Shaw, and make a case for their contribution to what is now taken for granted: the presence of the emancipated woman on the stage.

Bernard Shaw and the Actresses

CHAPTER ONE

—◆—

1876-1880

ON THE LAST DAY of March 1876, when he was not yet twenty, George Bernard Shaw packed a carpetbag, boarded the North Wall boat, put his native Dublin behind him, and, in his own words, "plunged blindly into London." His step was made slightly less desperate by the fact that his mother and sister Lucy had preceded him in 1873, and were now established in a small way as a voice teacher and singer and living in a semi-detached villa at No. 13 Victoria Grove, West Brompton. To them he came, driving solemnly in a growler "through streets whose names Dickens had made familiar to me, London being at its spring best, which is its very best." Although confident of his genius, he had no certain notion of the form it would take. As we do not know the taste of water because it is always in our mouths, he did not think much about his innate gift for language.[1]

Shaw's half-comic, half-tragic accounts of his family life suggest that his welcome at Victoria Grove was not enthusiastic. His mother, said Shaw, "did not hate anybody, nor love anybody," going on to add with his extraordinary sense of justice: "Everybody had disappointed her, or betrayed her, or tyrannized over her. . . . Under all the circumstances it says a great deal for my mother's humanity that she did not hate her children." Nor, apparently, did she hate her husband, although she had left him to follow her music mentor George John Vandeleur Lee to London. As for his twenty-three-year-old sister Lucy: "Everybody loved her, and she loved nobody," said Shaw.[2]

Nevertheless, the young Shaw settled in rather comfortably at No. 13. If the Shaws did not love each other, they did not hate each other either. Shaw could joke with Lucy: "Your remarks are most offensive. Let my nose alone, better a bottle than a peony." He was not too intimidated to mischievously interfere in a dispute between his mother and sister, and laugh at the consequences: ". . . you may as well drop all your dignity with Lucy. You are basely betrayed. . . . I told her everything you said about her. . . . I told her all! ALL! ALL! . . . I know that you will love me as you never did before for my straightforward conduct. I feel that even now you are wishing you could kiss me."[3]

Some of the betrayals that had hardened his mother had already hardened him. He too had experienced "the hell into which [his] mother descended when she found out what shabby-genteel poverty with a drunken husband" was like. There had been the day, for instance, when his father playfully pretended to toss him into the canal and almost succeeded. "Mamma," said the boy when they got home, "I think Papa is drunk." "When is he anything else?" retorted his mother bitterly, stung at last into admission. Said Shaw, looking back at that awful discovery: "It is a rhetorical exaggeration to say that I have never since believed in anything or anybody; but the wrench from my childish faith in my father as perfect and omniscient to the discovery that he was a hypocrite and a dipsomaniac was so sudden and violent that it must have left its mark on me."[4]

This early loss of faith did mark Shaw in many ways. It created in the young boy a distrust of all motives and appearances. It inspired in him a compulsion to turn everything upside down: to jeer at the sacred and revere the unorthodox. And, since he had imbibed a sense of irreverent, anti-climactic humor from his father, he was able (in self-protection) to find the truth funny instead of tragic. Thus he could stand at the parlor window and watch the governor, "an imperfectly wrapped-up goose under one arm and a ham in the same condition under the other (both purchased under heaven knows what delusion of festivity), butting at the garden wall in the belief that he was pushing open the gate, and transforming his tall hat to a concertina in the process"—and find himself so overcome with laughter that he could hardly go to the rescue.[5]

Such sympathies as remained turned to his mother. He admired her stiff-backed refusal to be dragged down to her husband's level of amiable futility. He delighted in the music that she brought into the house: he hung about during the piano and singing lessons and amateur opera rehearsals, and was whistling Beethoven, Rossini, Donizetti, and Mozart when he was twelve. When she finally incorporated her singing master, Dublin musician Vandeleur Lee, into the household in an apparently platonic ménage à trois, the young boy found the situation improving. Perhaps the climax of his admiration for her came one summer day when they were walking together on Dalkey Hill high above the northern bend of Dublin Bay. His mother stopped and pointed to a small squared-off cottage. "Look," she said: "it is ours." It was, in fact, Lee having made the use of it a gift. The boy seized her hand and kissed it again and again, overcome with happiness. It is his only recorded demonstration of emotion toward her.

Unfortunately, the Spartan hardness Lucinda Shaw had acquired through a difficult childhood, adolescence, and marriage had left her incapable of expressing affection. She was not soured, said Shaw: "she never made scenes, never complained, never punished nor retaliated nor lost her superiority to spites and tantrums and tempers." Only, equally, she never sympathized, never protected, never rewarded, never forgave —never, apparently, lost her superiority to frail human impulses like tenderness and love. "From my mother I . . . learned that the wrath on which the sun goes down is negligible compared to the clear vision and criticism that is neither created by anger nor ended with it," said the clear-visioned Shaw.[6]

His relationship with his sister Lucy was less unhappy because less profound. Back in Dublin Lucy had been considered the brilliant member of the family. She was witty in company where Shaw was shy; aggressively handsome and dimpled while his plain face was distinguished chiefly by a sneer; admitted to her mother's musical circle by virtue of her pleasing soprano voice while Shaw hung about its edges. Lucy later accused her brother of triumphing at her expense: "George listens to all I say, and then he takes the good bits and writes them down as his own, and everybody laughs and thinks how clever he is."[7] There was a good deal of rivalry between them, therefore; and Lucy probably looked upon her brother's arrival with skepticism. *She* was already contributing something to the slender family finances by occasional singing engagements and a bit of writing. *He*, on the other hand, had thrown over a respectable clerkship in Dublin paying £84 a year and, convinced that he was born to greatness, had come to try their patience and their resources until he realized it. All very well, but he had not yet convinced her.

Shaw, however, did "nothing decisive" the first years of his life in London, although his later claim that he had come to London resolved never to do another honest day's work exaggerates as much as does his portrait of himself as a shameless sponger who threw his mother into the "struggle for life" and made her work for the next twenty-two years for his living. Fragments of diary he kept in 1876 show he made two unenthusiastic applications for work on recommendations given him by Vandeleur Lee and by his aunt Georgina, both applications, however, "without result."[8] In September he began a cram course with the intention of preparing himself for the Civil Service examination, although he gave up the effort in November when Lee came to his aid again by handing over his musical criticism column in an obscure publication called *The Hornet* for Shaw to ghost-write. A year later he has an introduction to the East India Docks, but that too proves "not worth anything." In

November of 1878 he is introduced to a Kretschmar of the Imperial Bank, South Kensington, "without result." In October of 1879, Shaw's cousin Mrs. Cashel Hoey, a writer of three-decker novels who "knew everybody" and was disposed to help Shaw, took Lucy to the theatre with Arnold White, secretary of the Edison Telephone Company. Shaw called on White almost immediately and asked him for employment, "Lucy having given a very favorable account of me." This lead was worth something: Shaw set to work collecting wayleaves—permissions to erect insulators, poles, and derricks on houseowners' roofs to carry the new telephone lines; then he found wayleave soliciting "a most distasteful business," resigned, was tempted back with £5 to quiet his complaints and a salary of £48 a year besides commission, and in February 1880 found himself wayleave manager at a salary of £80 a year plus commission.

Shaw thus tried the conventional gambit of the shabby-genteel young man—the Civil Service, the banks, the East India Company—while at the same time struggling desperately to save himself from the very work he applied for. He jumped at the chance, for example, to write music criticism for *The Hornet*, immediately abandoning thoughts of the Civil Service. But the move was premature: the job made him miserable, not only because his articles appeared with endless misprints, cuts, and garbled revisions, but because he did not know how to criticize, and was tortured with "the guilt and shame which attend ignorance and incompetence." Eleven months later he records, "Hornet finally abandoned."

He tried his hand at something more ambitious: he began a "profane Passion Play" in blank verse, making Mary a termagant and Joseph a shiftless carpenter, and throwing a good deal of himself into the character of Judas; but left it unfinished.

More seriously, he undertook (and finished) in 1878 a curious piece of writing that took the form of a long letter of advice to a female child of five. He was already good at giving instructions. "My Dear Lucy," he had written his sister from Dublin when he was all of eighteen: "The sum of my advice to you is, to cultivate of all things, serene philosophy. Never under any circumstances lose temper, and never let yourself be put out. . . . be immoveable, polite, generally amiable, and adamant."[9] *My Dear Dorothea* expanded on his letter to Lucy: Dorothea is instructed how to subvert and conquer the adult world by proving herself superior to the majority of its inhabitants. "Let your rule of conduct always be to do whatever is best for yourself," lectures Shaw. "Be as selfish as you can." Again, if Dorothea has the highest respect for herself, she "will be too proud to act badly." She must always be polite, particularly to those she dislikes, "because politeness is a mark of superiority." Dorothea must also "remember constantly this rule: the more you think for yourself, the more marked will your Individuality be. The more you allow others to think for you, the more you will resemble others."

It is the twenty-one-year-old Shaw preaching his mother's precepts to a female child to disguise the fact that he is bracing himself for the world. He was also bracing himself for a long stay in the same house with his mother. Dorothea's mother, Shaw imagines, has "long since exhausted the novelty of having a child of her own" and thinks of her only as a troublesome and inquisitive little creature. "For such a parent," Shaw advises, "you must be particularly careful not to form any warm affection. Be very friendly with her, because you are in the same house as she, and it is unpleasant to live with one whom you dislike. If you have any griefs, do not tell her of them."[10] Shaw was to keep this piece of advice for twenty-two years. *My Dear Dorothea* offers evidence of a mind born wise.

Although Shaw had coaxed his mother into teaching him the fundamentals of singing and music as soon as he arrived in London (having desperately missed the music she brought into his life when she left him behind in Dublin), and although he was studying harmony and counterpoint during 1878, *My Dear Dorothea* turned him down the path of writing. On the fifth of March 1879 he went out and bought sixpennorths of cheap white paper and, with the business-like habits acquired as a clerk in Dublin, began to fill five pages a day "rain or shine, dull or inspired." It was as much a business venture as anything else, the novel being the only kind of writing that could command immediate and substantial payment.

Undoubtedly, too, he was inspired to fiction by his new friendship with the novelist Elinor Huddart. This forty-year-old music pupil of his mother's evidently met Shaw at Victoria Grove, and began to correspond with him from Uplands, her home in Fareham, Hampshire. Shaw was to exhort and rail at Elinor for sixteen years until their correspondence died a natural death in 1894. Elinor, who had prayed as a child to be a boy and hated her sex, maddeningly combined talent and intelligence with insecurity and dilatoriness. She had broken into the publishing world with a novel, but her career launched, she seemed determined to destroy it. She hesitated, excused, refused to perfect—"I *cannot* revise"—and, too diffident about her shortcomings, constantly apologized to Shaw for weakness, illogicality, narrowmindedness, and imbecility. As he saw, however, her greatest crime was the fact that she never used the same pen name twice, therefore failing utterly to establish a name and reputation.[11] He perhaps did not recognize a classic Victorian case: the penniless Elinor felt forced to hide her literary activity from a rich, tyrannical father and relatives who would have disowned her had they learned she wrote novels. At first, however, the published writer strongly impressed the young man, and undoubtedly encouraged him to attempt fiction himself.

The result of his five pages a day rain or shine was *Immaturity*. As his hero Shaw created Robert Smith, like himself a slender, lathy, gray-eyed, sensitive young man; like himself a clerk who finds his profession the most contemptible in the world; and like himself, a son who is conscious of not being enthusiastically appreciated by his mother. Unlike himself, however, Robert Smith was decidedly dull.

Yet his relationships with women are interesting. He is strongly attracted to Harriet Russell, a good and humble dressmaker. After an emotional farewell at King's Cross Station, however, when Harriet gives him her hand for the first time, Smith's reaction to romance is to take himself off to the Alhambra music hall, which he has heard spoken of as a "wicked place." Here he is bored with the cigar smoke and the dissipated crowd until on stage a dark, flashing-eyed dancer emerges from a haystack as the Spirit of the Golden Harvest, clad in "blood-red poppy lightening into a gorgeous orange," cornflowers and golden ears of wheat twisted fantastically in her dark hair. Smith is spellbound by her dancing and infatuated in a moment. He runs home to pour out his intoxication in "Lines to a Southern Passion Flower," and in a week, although nearly penniless, he returns to see Signorina Pertoldi three times.

No sooner is Robert Smith bewitched, however, than the shame of being dominated by a sensuous attraction begins to torment him; and when he sees Harriet Russell again "her appearance in the morning sunlight made him feel as though he had just stepped from that vile-smelling midnight vision of gilt sheaves, painted skies, and electric radiance, into a real harvest field, full of fresh air, noisy birds, and sunshine." Yet Harriet Russell cannot satisfy Smith either: she will not be molded by him in his image: she is incurably pragmatic, will learn only what she likes or finds useful, cares nothing for speculation or philosophy, remembers what he gives her to read but makes not the slightest distinction between Bunyan and Walter Scott, and has no scientific curiosity. Smith craves a female friend who can match his intelligence and sensitivity. "Happily," concludes Shaw, "he found none such. The power to stand alone is worth acquiring at the expense of much sorrowful solitude . . . ."

On the surface nothing could be more trite than the good dressmaker and the wicked music hall dancer as representative Woman in the twenty-two-year-old Shaw's first novel. Or the egotism of the young man who decides after knowing all of two women that the female is inferior in chastity and philosophy to the male.

But Shaw did not stop there. The joke is on Robert Smith. As he feared, the voluptuous Signorina Pertoldi is not what she seems, but neither is she what Smith thought her—a painted wanton. The Signorina turns out to be "Old Biddy" from Wexford, forty-three years old, married to a builder named Muggins, mother of four grown children, and a prude who is "ready with her hands" against swells who try anything funny. Harriet Russell also surprises him. She turns into a successful business woman and fascinates the fashionable painter Cyril Scott. His set find her admirable, original, and absolutely terrifying.

The boating scene on the Thames shows why. Cyril reclines uneasily on the cushions, Harriet sculls vigorously: "I hate to sit idle and let another person do for me what I can do better for myself." Cyril hesitantly broaches plans for their marriage; Harriet overrides him: "Go tomorrow to wherever the proper place is; and get a license for the nearest date you possibly can. Not one of those expensive special licenses, though: there is no use in wasting fifty pounds to save a fortnight. Then—when we are married, I mean—to please you, we will go to some country place for a fortnight. By that time you will be in as great a hurry to come back as you are now to go. Don't interrupt me. We will stay in London as long as it is necessary to prepare for travelling; and then we will go as far round the world as we can afford time and money for . . . ." This settled, Harriet discovers that they are late for an appointment. "Get up and unship that big oar," she commands; "and we will pull back to the bridge. I am going to be stroke; so you must pass me; and pray do not capsize the boat, as you will if you attempt any nonsense."

It is Harriet who has the last word about the hero. "You are not a boy," she tells her would-be mentor; "and you are not grown-up. Some day you will get away from your books and come to know the world and get properly set. But just now there is no doing anything with you. You are just a bad case of immaturity."[12]

Shaw thus revealed a great deal in his first novel about his attitude toward women. He is strongly tempted to see them in stereotypes of the painted temptress and the good but ignorant girl: Robert Smith's revulsions against Signorina Pertoldi and Harriet Russell are very convincing. Having condemned them, however, Shaw seems deliberately to pull himself up: his precocious intelligence, sense of justice, and above all, his iconoclasm, tell him he is wrong. His answer is not to modify character, however; instead he turns it totally upside down. Biddy Muggins cannot simply be an ordinary person underneath the makeup: she must be a prudish, middle-aged mother of four. Harriet Russell cannot evolve from protégée into a moderately intelligent and independent woman: she must turn into the epitome of ruthlessly unemotional will. The result is refreshing—the rug is pulled out from under conventionality with a terrific jerk; but were Shaw's women finally any more real than the original stereotypes? More interesting, did Shaw believe they were?

As his diary proves, women were already important in Shaw's life. The year 1871 saw "The L *** Episode," which turned out to be "but food for mirth and mocking." In 1875 "the Calypso infatuation" begins and reaches a "catastrophe" or "indiscretion" about the beginning of August 1877. Fast on the heels of Calypso comes "the Terpsichorean episode" in 1876 and "also La Carbonaja." At the end of 1877, Shaw records "La follia della Carbonaja," the "eclipse of Calypso," and "Terpsichore in repose." All during 1878 La Carbonaja is "in the ascendant": she "flickers until the 11th" of 1879 when Terpsichore evaporates and "the star of Leonora gains the ascendant."

It is no great distance from the young Shaw's romantic vision of quite ordinary young ladies as Calypsos and Carbonajas in the pages of his notebook to the enchantment of Signorina Pertoldi as she dances under electric moonlight in *Immaturity*. And it is nothing new for shy young men to idealize young women. The twist—and it would become increasingly plain—is that temperamentally Shaw was himself the Calypso: the siren who lured women with seductive song, the tempter who promised and evaded. Signorina Pertoldi is a projection of Shaw as fascinator. At the same time, Shaw was unsentimental, fastidious, hard-driving, and high-minded—just as Pertoldi and Harriet Russell turn out to be. Ostensibly opposites, Shaw's siren and boss-woman have idealism and austerity in common: both find gratification chiefly in the exercise of their will. Asked in later life about the extraordinary knowledge of women he showed in his plays, Shaw explained: "I have always assumed that a woman is a person exactly like myself, and that is how the trick is done."[18] He employed the trick in *Immaturity*, arguably the tactic of a man who does not know women at all. But in paying women the compliment of considering them human—that is, male—like himself, Shaw hit upon a vein of truth that few male writers had discovered. Yet in ignoring the fact that women, given their upbringing, could not behave nor feel like himself, he initiated a long string of heroines who were so clearly Shaw in petticoats that they were scarcely credible—revolutionary though they might be.

With businesslike precision, Shaw recorded in his diary that he finished the manuscript on 28 September and began immediately to revise. The next month brought him the introduction to Arnold White of the Edison Telephone Company. Shaw limited his jottings to fact, but the drama is there. Faced with necessary but uncongenial employment, he speedily finishes the revision of *Immaturity* on 5 November, asks the publishers Hurst and Blackett to read it on the seventh, and sends them the manuscript on the eighth. Will they accept it? If they do, with decent terms, his career is made and the Edison Telephone Company can go to blazes. But Hurst and Blackett turn down the appropriately titled first novel on the twelfth; and the next day Shaw is forced to report to the Wayleave Department at Edison. Before he does so, however, he calls at the offices of another publisher, receives encouragement, and fires off a hurried note to Hurst and Blackett telling them to forward the manuscript immediately to Kegan Paul. He might still be saved.

He was not, however. The list of firms that eventually rejected *Immaturity* reads like a London publishing directory. Disappointed but still determined, Shaw wryly answered a polite refusal from Messrs. Bentley and Son in January 1880: "You cannot possibly regret the unfavorable result more than I do." Extreme diffidence tempered his determination: he had an abhorrence of imposing second-rate goods on anyone. "Should you earnestly believe that you can render me a real service by putting this unlucky book into the fire," he added, ". . . you are at liberty to do so." Similarly, he was warning potential publishers away from a short story he had written called "The Brand of Cain": "Indeed, I fear the story is too preposterous to be worth publishing" and, "I think the failure of the story is more radical than you suppose."[14] Disgusted by his father's bluff, Shaw steadily refused to try to put anything over on anyone.

Eventually he sent the novel to Elinor Huddart. He had criticized one of her female characters for being masculine and unreal when she was logical; what, one wonders, did he expect her to make of Harriet Russell? Elinor replied:

Immaturity is a work to be proud of. There is enough thought in it for a dozen novels, and not enough emotion in it for half a one. . . . But these people how they talk! . . . You have put too much of George Shaw's brain into their noddles. I hear you talking when I am meant to hear Scott, or Mrs. Scott, or Smith (Smith I believe to be yourself) or Lady Geraldine. . . . I don't like any of your women. Miss Russel repels me. She is a female prig. Can no one have self-control and independence without a demeanor of ice and insolence? . . . The love which you depict is chilling. . . . Their amatory sayings fall like snow-flakes.[15]

Elinor Huddart's opinion was shared by the publishers, and would become the standard reaction to all his works. It became necessary for Shaw to save himself from the business world. Opportunity came when the Bell Telephone Company bought out Edison. Shaw altered the application form for employment with the new company before signing it, refused to withdraw the altered form, quarreled with Arnold White and, as he noted in his diary, "made myself generally intractable being, in truth, sick of telephoning and anxious to get back to 'The Irrational Knot.' I left on the 5th June."

Free to write, Shaw again began to fill his quota of five pages a day rain or shine, forcing himself to the task and only occasionally throwing down his pen to go to the piano and pour out arias from *Carmen*, then new in London. In a little more than a year he had acquired a far more mature and subtle grasp of character, and—who knows how or where—

amazing insight into the complexities of a husband and wife relationship: the "irrational knot" is, of course, marriage. Robert Smith had been a shadowy figure. Edward Conolly is Shaw's version of the new aristocrat: the self-made electrical engineer, product of the new science; a pragmatist whose self-control and rationality make him seem inhuman to people who act from impulse—that is, to nine tenths of the human race. Shaw sees him as a hero,[16] yet sees at the same time how the strong can unintentionally destroy the weak. Conolly marries an heiress, Marian Lind, everybody's idea of charm, goodness, and talent. Pitting the forces of romantic conservatism against bourgeois realism, the novel records the near-annihilation of Marian Lind. Conolly is an ideal husband: he never quarrels, never chides, never denies, never restrains. It is only that Marian, faced with his superhuman rationality, justice, and self-sufficiency, crumbles. Her charm, her sympathetic conversation, her little musical talents, her romantic notions suddenly have no more potency than sticks hurled at a stone wall. She loses all confidence in herself, and runs off with a complete cad who wins her easily by simply offering what her husband withheld, flattery and superficial sympathy. Not quite twenty-four years old, Shaw had dissected one kind of marital relationship with great prescience.

Conolly's sister Susanna, however, is the most striking character in *The Irrational Knot*. In his second novel, Shaw pushes Signorina Pertoldi onto center stage as Lalage Virtue, an actress in opéra bouffe. Susanna, or Lalage as she is known professionally, is also a siren: the Reverend George Lind, Marian's brother, calling on business finds her "seated on an ottoman, dressed in wide trousers, Turkish slippers . . . a voluminous sash, a short Greek jacket, a long silk robe with sleeves, and a turban, all of fine soft materials and rare colors." Although over rather than underdressed, Susanna with her painted face, exotic costume, and long dark hair makes the clergyman feel "like St. Anthony struggling with the fascination of a disguised devil."

Despite the paint and harem silks, however, Susanna is brainy, fearless, independent, and, as Shaw is at great pains to show, more moral than her respectable society sisters who barter themselves in the marriage marketplace.

> *I* snap my fingers at society [she tells the bewildered Lind], and care as little about it as it cares about me. . . . I can support myself, and may shew Bob a clean pair of heels tomorrow, if I choose. I confess I shouldnt like to make a regular legal bargain of going to live with a man. I dont care to make love a matter of money; it gives it a taste of the harem, or even worse. Poor Bob, meaning to be honorable, offered to buy me in the regular way at St. George's, Hanover Square, before we came to live here; but, of course, I refused, as any decent woman in my circumstances

would. Understand me now, Doctor: I dont want to give myself any virtuous airs . . . . But dont you try to make me swallow any gammon about my disgracing you and so forth. I intend to stay as I am. I can respect myself; and I dont care whether you or your family respect me or not.

I must confess that I do not understand you at all [replies Lind, anticipating the publishers' response to this second novel]. You seem to see everything reversed—upside down. You—I—you bewilder me . . . .

Shaw thus used the actress to lash conventional morality in his first major pieces of writing: paradoxically Lalage Virtue *is* virtuous. But why the actress?

Ada Tyrrell, a neighbor of the Shaws in Dublin, remembers that she first saw "Sonny" Shaw as a pale, refined-looking child of ten or eleven "seated at a table, constructing a cardboard theatre."[17] As a boy, Shaw had found his way to the Theatre Royal, Dublin's main playhouse, enough times to have soaked up the atmosphere of the stage and developed a taste for drama. He had seen the famous Barry Sullivan as Hamlet, and the not yet famous Henry Irving making his mark as Digby Grant in *Two Roses*. More important here, he had seen three famous actresses: Adelaide Ristori as Maria Stuart, Madame Celeste in *The Woman in Red* and, as Wilkie Collins' "new Magdalen," Ada Cavendish, with whom he "fell wildly, madly, suddenly in love." During his early London years Shaw also gravitated conspicuously toward the theatre. His diary mentions operatic events like *Carmen, Don Giovanni,* and *Faust;* like the hero of *Immaturity* he too fell under the spell of a music hall dancer, and went home to write the "Lines to a Southern Passion Flower" that appear in the novel. And if his own experiences with the theatre were necessarily limited (he had little money for entertainment), then another member of the family could provide inspiration; for while George slaved away at his five pages a day, Lucy—or Miss Carr-Shaw, as she chose to be known professionally—was struggling to make her mark in the theatrical world.

Mrs. Shaw and Lucy had pursued their musical liaison with Vandeleur Lee in London, although Lee had descended from a reputable musical director in Dublin to a charlatan who bilked young ladies out of twelve guineas with promises to make them prima donnas overnight. In concerts arranged by Lee and her mother, Lucy appeared in *Ruy Blas* and in *Faust.* Mrs. Cashel Hoey, the cousin who "knew everybody," probably introduced her to the Wildes. By November of 1879, Lucy's naturally beautiful soprano and gold-leaf hair had charmed Oscar and Willie, paving the way for invitations for the rest of her family to Lady Wilde's famous soirees. Awkward and ill-clothed, Shaw forced himself to attend, heard his sister's singing captivate Lady Wilde's company, met the novelist Mrs. Lynn Linton "and others." (Lady Wilde, or "Speranza" as she chose to be known in artistic circles, did not captivate Shaw, nor did he take to Oscar.) A month later, as her brother recorded in his notebook, Lucy debuted as Primrose in the pantomime *Beauty and the Beast* at the Park Theatre, Camden Town, on Christmas Eve, 1879. Her career as a musical star seemed to be launched.

His sister Lucy, then, gave Shaw much of the raw material from which to create Edward Conolly's sister, Lalage Virtue. Love of paradox, of course, directed him to the actress, symbol *par excellence* of low morals and high living: he would outrage his readers by insisting that independent women who give themselves freely in sex have the moral edge over women who first demand the legal bond. If he needed confirmation, however, that glamorous theatrical stars were in reality rather pragmatic young ladies who lived with mothers and quarreled with brothers, there was Lucy. If he needed proof that society gave up for damned young women who chose the stage, he had the reaction of the Shaw relatives. "When starting her theatrical career," wrote Mabel Dolmetsch, "Lucy intended to use the name of Carr (a name on her father's side) in order to spare the Shaw relatives any embarrassment. But when she heard that they had been censuring her for 'going on the stage,' she defiantly clapped on the 'Shaw.' "[18] And if he needed confirmation that charming blond singers were in reality sharp, brainy women, there was Lucy also. Lucy complained that her brother picked up her own witty sayings and got himself applauded for being clever. Shaw put the same complaint in Lalage Virtue's mouth: "My cleverness was my ruin. Ned was not half so quick. It used to take him months to learn things that I picked up offhand, and yet you see how much better he has done than I."

At this point, the brother's success was more wish than fact. Did fraternal antagonism as well as Shaw's very ambiguous attitude toward the artificiality of the theatrical world inspire him to saddle Lalage with a less happy family trait? Clever and independent as the actress is, she cannot stay away from champagne and brandy: she dies a drunk, and Shaw undermines his own case by making *The Irrational Knot* both a defense and a condemnation of the life of an actress.

Immaturity had actually had near success: Blackwood had first accepted it and then changed their minds, and Macmillan's reader John (afterward Lord) Morley had called it "undoubtedly clever" and invited him to write for the *Pall Mall Gazette*, although when Shaw did, he rejected the articles. Shaw finished *The Irrational Knot* in December 1880 and started it on its rounds with Macmillan the fifteenth of that month; but his second novel—the best he was to write—found no favor. "Too conversational and destitute of dramatic interest," said the firm of Smith, Elder months later, "to achieve popularity."[19] Baffled by the rejection at the time, Shaw later came to understand the reason for this second failure and, in 1905, claimed "the first order" for *The Irrational*

Knot. It had, he saw, the quality that to his mind set Ibsen above Shakespeare as an artist: its morality was not ready-made. But Shaw's attack upon Victorian hypocrisy would only shock the good men who read the manuscript in the early 1880s: the novel was destined to fail.

A few weeks after Shaw completed the manuscript, the family left Victoria Grove because, as they told friends, the location proved inconvenient for Mrs. Shaw's music pupils, but actually because money was running low.[20] They took first-floor unfurnished rooms at 37 Fitzroy Street, a decided comedown from the semi-detached villa. With two failures to his credit, Shaw forced himself to sit down to a third novel, *Love Among the Artists*, on the nineteenth of May 1881.

These were years of desperate penny-pinching and humiliating poverty. ". . . I remember one evening during the novel-writing period," wrote Shaw later, "when nobody would pay a farthing for a stroke of my pen, walking along Sloane Street in that blessed shield of literary shabbiness, evening dress. A man accosted me with an eloquent appeal for help, ending with the assurance that he had not a penny in the world. I replied, with exact truth, 'Neither have I.' He thanked me civilly, and went away, apparently not in the least surprised, leaving me to ask myself why I did not turn beggar too, since I felt sure that a man who did it as well as he, must be in comfortable circumstances."[21]

Shaw did not turn beggar, but neither did he throw his whole heart into trying to find regular work, continuing to answer various advertisements "without success." His clothes grew shabbier: he began to trim his fraying cuffs with a scissors and sported a tall hat "so limp with age that I had to wear it back-to-front to enable me to take it off without doubling up the brim."[22] Gathering material for his novels, he was forced to prowl elegant Belgravia and Mayfair at night "owing to the too obvious decay of the morning wardrobe." Nor was his physical appearance prepossessing: he was tall, thin as a lath, virginal, gentlemanly, and underneath a brash self-confidence, painfully shy. His pale face was hairless and almost feminine: Richard Deck, an Alsatian émigré to whom Shaw went three nights a week to learn French and prune the Irish barbarisms from his speech, disliked the effeminacy and taught him to bank up his pale red hair in front instead of wearing it parted in the middle and plastered down smoothly like a woman. If his own conscience did not rebuke him for failing to bring in money—and surely it did—there were futile, protesting letters from his father in Dublin. "There is no use expressing my opinion that it would be well if you get something to do to earn some money," wrote Mr. Shaw in December 1882, having just posted a parcel to his twenty-six-year-old son containing "a splendid *new* coat & waistcoat, a present from your Aunt Cha." "It is much wanted by all of us. I enclose a PO order for 10 [shillings] which I hope will be acceptable. I wish it were for more."[23]

Yet Shaw refused to be intimidated by guilt, poverty, or rejection. These early years in London were also years of tremendous zest and hope and discovery. If Shaw's shabby linen and mortal shyness kept him from fashionable drawing rooms and entertainments, he was conspicuous elsewhere—talking vigorously at the homes of new acquaintances like Lecky, Beatty, Barton, the Lawsons, the Homes, and the Bells; hammering out piano accompaniments for his mother's voice pupils; bombarding magazines with "bushels" of articles; studying counterpoint, shorthand, French; debating Catholicism with Father Addis at the Brompton Oratory; politely rejecting ladies of the pavement in Piccadilly; getting up amateur musical performances with Lee; revising novels for a fee; reading and writing at the British Museum, now within easy walking distance: discovering, absorbing, growing.

Most important, perhaps, was the event recorded in his diary for 28 October 1880: "Began the practice of addressing audiences, at the Zetetical (debating) Society, which I joined immediately afterwards." Although Shaw's hand so shook with nervousness that he could scarcely guide the pen to sign the minutes, his determination to excel at public speaking effectually decided his career. He learned rapidly, joined another debating society, the Dialectical, the next year, and practiced on every soapbox he could find. He was to write five novels, but the challenge of public speaking would turn him away from the private writer-to-reader form of the novel to the public propagandistic form of the drama. When he eventually met a young dramatic critic named William Archer in the Reading Room of the British Museum and Archer proposed collaborating on a play, Shaw would be ready to synthesize his gifts of oratory and prose, and begin to find his range at last as a dramatist.

CHAPTER TWO

1881-1885

SHAW WAS A VICTIM of the smallpox epidemic of 1881, a circumstance that must have repelled his fastidious soul. He recuperated at Leyton, where his maternal uncle Walter John Gurly kept up a medical practice that had deteriorated along with the district—from visits to country estates with horse and trap to calls on foot to the small houses of clerks and laborers blighting the once-elegant parks of the rich. Here Shaw grew a red frizzing beard to hide the smallpox scars, revised a paper titled "On the Sacredness of Human Life" with which he intended to devastate the Zetetical Society as soon as he worked up courage enough to deliver it, worked at shorthand, met a young woman named Jane Lockett, and continued his third novel.

In *Love Among the Artists* Shaw utilized the experience of middle-class Bohemian circles that his one suit of evening clothes and ability to play piano accompaniments to the satisfaction of amateur singers opened to him. But these social experiences were decidedly few, Shaw being, as he himself said, no dancer and "a more dispiriting object in a drawing room than at a supper table." Again, therefore, he looked to Lucy's experiences for material. She was now on tour with the Carl Rosa Opera Company, and her example furnished the character of Madge Brailsford, the respectable girl who defies her father and runs away from home to go on the stage. Shaw devoted a long chapter to the rise of Madge from pantomime star to Shakespearean actress: she is the only true professional among the group of dilettante artists who people the novel. Again he emphasized the morality of the woman who supports herself and chooses her lovers: "She stood on her honor according to her own instinct, took no gifts, tolerated no advances from men whose affections were not truly touched. . . . She rather pitied her married colleagues, knowing perfectly well that they were not free to be so fastidious, reserved, and temperate as her instinct told her a great artist should always be." Again Shaw used the actress, the woman outside the pale of respectability, to attack Victorian morality: the marriage bed, symbol of sanctified procreation, was in reality no such thing, he urged, but a place where intemperate lust and slavery were licensed by the very society that called its Madge Brailsfords immoral. As a fastidious, reserved, temperate artist, Shaw identified with Madge; as the "complete outsider"—poor, uneducated (at least conventionally), powerless—he could identify with women, whose position in society was much the same.

He returned to London, finished the third novel in January 1882, delivered his paper successfully to the Zetetical Society, suffered a light attack of scarlet fever from drinking infected milk in February (Lucy, temporarily at home, suffered severely), and found himself back at Leyton convalescing a second time. During this visit Jane Lockett introduced him to her younger sister Alice Mary, and Shaw fell violently in love.[1]

Although Shaw recovered his health and thus lost an excuse for remaining at Leyton after the middle of March, he managed to get employment there in April during the election of Poor Law guardians, stayed a week, earned six guineas, and pursued Alice. It came to moonlight walks and heavy flirtation, although Alice was a very proper young woman. Alice, Shaw reported to Elinor Huddart on the seventeenth of April, thinks I am in love with her. She had every reason to believe it:

> When we speak I say "Miss Lockett";
> Now my courtesy I'll pocket
> And indulge myself by spelling
> "Alice," and not hear her telling
> Me to check my mad presumption,
> With an exquisite assumption
> Of offended dignity
> Which endears her more to me.
> Recklessly I dare again
> On this page with ink to rain
> Alice, Alice
> Alice, Alice, Alice
> Alice!
> Alice!
> Alice!
> Alice!
> Alice!
> Alice!
> Alice!

Alice!

Alice!

Alice!

Alice!

Alice!

Alice!

Darling Alice!!![2]

There had been other poems to other enchantresses: "Then farewell, oh bewitching Calypso," Shaw had written to an unidentified girl in Dublin who had captivated him the year before his departure: "Thou didst shake my philosophy well." Alice Lockett, however, was more than an infatuation.

Shaw was extremely vulnerable to women. His boyhood dreams had been violently colored by visions of beautiful maidens all in need of rescue by a chivalrous George Shaw. Woman was the Ideal, the sexless angel in floating skirts. The shattering of that Ideal could be traumatic. There was the day when a woman always in advance of the fashion dropped in to call. "Crinolines were going out," Shaw related much later; "and she had discarded hers. I, an innocent unprepared child, walked bang into the room and suddenly saw, for the first time, a woman not shaped like Primrose Hill, but with a narrow skirt which evidently wrapped a pair of human legs. I have never recovered from the shock, and never shall."[3] Shaw exaggerated his reaction; yet he apparently did have difficulty adjusting to the discovery that women were human and therefore sexual beings. He could sympathize with the ideal, for he himself had many characteristics that were traditionally feminine: physical modesty, narcissism, vanity, flirtatiousness, talkativeness, sensitivity.[4] Of course, his mother had taught him how false these cultural stereotypes could be: wasn't she the unemotional, practical, strong-minded parent, not his father? And his early-learned iconoclasm caused him to violently reject conventionality. Yet the violence of that rejection suggests how deeply certain ideals had impressed him, while his mother's behavior after all alienated more than assured him: her coldness left him extremely insecure where women were concerned and therefore in awe of their powers. It would be strange if, at the same time, Shaw did not secretly resent and fear the being to which he attributed such omnipotence. He approached Alice Lockett, it may be fairly said, in a state of high confusion.

In the love affair of Shaw and Alice Lockett two vulnerable egos were at stake. Alice protected hers with the defenses her Victorian young lady's upbringing provided: offended dignity, righteous anger, cold prudishness. Shaw protected his with brightly polished weapons of irreverence, wit, cruelty, frivolity. Fundamentally, they were opposites: he an iconoclastic genius, she a conventional bourgeois. Yet when Shaw met her, she was twenty-three, sick of her small world of Walthamstow, determined to forge an independent life for herself and already pursuing a nursing career. Shaw's energy, silver tongue, and London sophistication attracted her; her ambition, high spirits, beautiful complexion, and "beaux yeux" attracted him.

She arranged for singing lessons from Mrs. Shaw so they could see each other at least once a week. The Shaws had retrenched again, taking rooms on the second floor and a bedroom for Shaw on the third at 30 Osnaburgh Street. Here Alice appeared on Thursdays. A long courtship ensued consisting chiefly of the singing lesson, tea afterward, amorous sessions with Shaw at the piano ("Oh the infinite mischief that a woman may do by stooping forward to turn over a sheet of music!"); then a long ride to Liverpool Street Station, Alice sitting cozily beside him if they had not quarreled and like "a Chinese idol" opposite if they had; suspense—would the train be waiting or might it have just left, thus giving them more time together; a lingering or perhaps hasty farewell in the drafty terminus; and then the rush home to pen letters in which they attacked each other for the inevitable misunderstandings of the day.

Shaw had the advantage of her verbally and temperamentally. He instinctively defended himself by pretending to be cold. This is his ploy, for example, after one of their skirmishes at the station. She has let herself miss her train, he has congratulated her upon showing some heart at last, she has been wounded by his "presumption" and immediately sorry that she stayed behind. This new coldness wounds Shaw's ego, and thus he cannot help insisting upon his invulnerability while at the same time encouraging her to be generous with him:

> Heavens! to regret having dared at last to be frank and kind! Did you not see at that moment a set of leading strings fall from you and hang themselves upon me in the form of golden chains? The heart of any other man would have stopped during those seconds after you had slowly turned your back upon the barrier and yet were still in doubt. Mine is a machine and did not stop; but it did something strange. It put me in *suspense*, which is the essence of woman's power over man, and which you had never made me feel before—and I was always certain of what you would do until that question of the train arose. And I repaid you for the luxury by paining you. I did not intend to do so any more than you intended to please me, so forgive forgive forgive forgive forgive me.
>
> I cannot (or perhaps will not) resist the impulse to write to you. Believe nothing that I say—and I have a wicked tongue, a deadly pen, and a cold heart—I shall be angry with myself tomorrow for sending you this, and yet, when I next meet you, I shall plunge headlong into fresh cause for anger.[5]

It was Alice who was angry, retaliating with, "May I ask what was the object of your letter to me? Did you think it necessary to revive the pain caused by your words of last evening? All people are not machines: some are capable of genuine feelings. . . . Your letter proves what I have many times told you—that you are one of the weakest men I have ever met; and in spite of your cleverness I cannot help despising you."[6]

Shaw analyzed her as a split personality: Miss Lockett and Alice. Miss Lockett was prim, prudish, and proper—always tossing her head and defending her dignity and pretending to be sophisticated and worldly, but essentially a weak and cowardly person terrified of her better impulses. Alice was those better impulses: Alice was strong, generous, frank, and free. "Well, let Miss Lockett beware," warned Shaw, "for she is the dragon that preys upon Alice, and I will rescue Alice from her. I hate her with a mortal hatred. Already I have shaken her. I have (as she admits) power to pain her, and I have (as she presumes) the will to use that power. . . . I will shew Alice what she is, and Alice will abandon her forever."[7]

Understandably, however, Alice disliked her lover's pride in his wicked tongue, deadly pen, and cold heart. When she despised him, it was his vanity that galled her: correctly she diagnosed that it betrayed insecurity rather than strength. Had she known that he scribbled at length to Elinor Huddart about marriage, love, and kissing, she would have despised him more. "Marry, marry!" Elinor had answered Shaw's letter announcing that he had made a matrimonial "note" about "someone"—of course, Alice. "It is always your cry. I will not marry. Marry yourself and see how you like it. . . . What a flirt you are."[8] Telling his love was already a compulsion with Shaw, a symptom of insecurity, vanity, irrepressible talkativeness, and a positive delight in violating the traditions of chivalry. Elinor Huddart recoiled from this aspect of the correspondent she otherwise considered her only male friend. "If you hurt your friends' bodies the way you hurt their feelings," she told Shaw, "you would be voted bloodthirsty. I hate this trait in you."

Shaw recognized that his own contradictions played a part in his stormy love affair with Alice. "Have I not also a dual self," he admitted, "—an enemy within my gates—an egotistical George Shaw upon whose neck I have to keep a grinding foot—a first cousin of Miss Lockett?" This other self was more than egotistical: it was diabolical. "I am alone," he writes, "and yet there is a detestable, hardheaded, heartless, cynical, cool devil seated in my chair telling me that all this is insincere lying affection. But I defy him—it is he who lies. I have only sold my working hours to him. Hate and mistrust him as much as you will; but believe me too, and help me to snatch a few moments from his withering power."[9] Shaw's recognition of his own split personality, however, was not enough: the paradox of his demand that Alice be free and affectionate while he proclaimed heartless invulnerability was unsolvable: Shaw's devil and Miss Lockett could never be reconciled.

If Shaw's personal affairs at this time were turbulent, on the philosophical level he was experiencing a revolution that would crystallize his thinking on social issues for the rest of his life. On a Tuesday evening, the fifth of September 1882, he strolled casually into the Memorial Hall on Farringdon Street to hear the American economist Henry George speak on "Land Nationalization and Single Tax."

Before he walked in, as Shaw later explained, he was a born communist—that is, a gifted individual "ashamed of his poverty, in continual dread of doing the wrong thing, resentfully insubordinate and seditious in a social order which he not only accepts but in which he actually claims a privileged part," a person, that is, frustrated and angry with an unjust society but impotent to understand his plight. Henry George supplied the key that unlocked the mystery of the social order for Shaw: economics. Immediately the scales fell from his eyes. He saw that "Property is theft: respectability founded on poverty is blasphemy: marriage founded on property is prostitution: it is easier for a camel to go through the eye of a needle than for a rich man to enter the kingdom of heaven."[10]

Being a "born communist," Shaw had more than an inkling of this state of affairs before that Tuesday evening in 1882: in *The Irrational Knot*, for example, he had shown clearly that marriage founded on property is prostitution. His attack on social institutions in that novel, however, had been inspired more by a disillusioned iconoclasm and love of paradox than by any systematic analysis of society. He went home from Henry George's lecture to read his *Progress and Poverty*, and from there to the British Museum to search out Marx's *Das Kapital*. He emerged from the Reading Room a socialist: a man with a cause.

In February 1883 he spent sixpence to post a fourth heavy brown paper parcel on its rounds. *Cashel Byron's Profession* had been inspired by his friend Pakenham Beatty's enthusiasm for pugilism. Beatty had made a fan of Shaw, who attended bouts, tried his hand at sparring, and immediately went home to convert this new interest into fiction. Having just finished *Cashel* and now deep into Marx, Shaw sat down to formulate his new creed in still another novel, *An Unsocial Socialist*.

The plot of this new work mingled love, marriage, and socialist propaganda deliberately, but uneasily. Sidney Trefusis, the son of a wealthy self-made manufacturer like Dickens' Bounderby, has married Henrietta Jansenius, a conventional, romantic, middle-class young woman who has the bad grace to protest when her husband, suddenly converted to socialism, disappears one day without a word. She discovers him eventually masquerading as a country bumpkin in corduroys; explanations follow;

he sends her home. Henrietta dies; and after deflecting the passion of Gertrude Lindsay, who has fallen in love with him, Trefusis marries Agatha Wylie, a frank no-nonsense person who regards their union, as he does, as Eugenic Duty. "A bachelor is a man who shirks responsibilities and duties," says Trefusis, echoing the argument Shaw was having on paper with Elinor Huddart that winter over the obligation of marriage; "I seek them, and consider it my duty, with my monstrous superfluity of means, not to let the individualists outbreed me. . . . I wanted a genial partner for domestic business, and Agatha struck me quite suddenly as being the nearest approach to what I desired that I was likely to find in the marriage market . . . . I admire Agatha's courage and capability, and believe I shall be able to make her like me, and that the attachment so begun may turn into as close a union as is either healthy or necessary between two separate individuals."

An Unsocial Socialist leveled a three-pronged attack at Shaw's new social enemies: romantic love, individualism, and private property—or more broadly, at the system which breeds all three, capitalism. It is Henrietta's tragedy that she cannot see, as Trefusis does, that the end of human sympathy is not the private marital lovenest, but the pursuit of social good. "I only understand that you hate me," she says, "and want to go away from me." "That would be easy to understand," her husband tells her. "But the strangeness is that I *love* you and want to go away from you." Then, taking her in his arms where they are lying on the bank of a canal, and between kisses, Trefusis explains to his wife the capitalist profit system, his mission to liberate the Manchester laborers who are his father's slaves, and his preference for his corduroys and two-room cottage to "our pretty little house and your pretty little ways."

The scene aptly illustrated Shaw's own personal struggle between the clouds of romantic illusion Trefusis admits still cling and his newly conceived mission of social duty. He was, after all, poring over *Tristan und Isolde* at the British Museum, as well as *Das Kapital.* Perhaps he recognized the potential aridity of pure mission: he originally titled the novel *The Heartless Man,* although he probably meant it ironically. Shaw wrote Alice Lockett into the book as Gertrude Lindsay: "your dual entity made the foundation of the most sentimental part of my new book," he told her, referring to passages such as the following in which Trefusis says, "Miss Lindsay never to me, but only to those who cannot see through her to the soul within, which is Gertrude. There are a thousand Miss Lindsays in the world, formal and false. There is but one Gertrude." Yet the conflict Shaw was experiencing in his affair with Alice Lockett is not told so much in the Gertrude Lindsay episode as in the struggle between Trefusis and Henrietta. Henrietta dies of a chill and a broken heart, not having learned to love the masses more than her husband. It is not too fanciful to suggest that Shaw was trying to bury his own romantic self with her: the birthdate on her tombstone is his own: 26 July 1856.

The form he chose for his new socialistic creed created a conflict in itself. He wanted to show a man "turning with loathing from his egotist's dream of independence to the collective interests of society, with the welfare of which he now perceives his own happiness to be inextricably bound up." Yet he chose the novel, read and written, in his own words, for "half-educated women, rebelliously slavish, superstitious, sentimental," who consider "the infatuation of a pair of lovers as the highest manifestation of the social instinct"—and found himself enslaved to the very genre whose ideological capitalistic basis he wished to destroy.[11] He did not realize the paradox at the time. *An Unsocial Socialist*, according to his original design, was "only the first chapter of a vast work depicting capitalist society in dissolution, with its downfall as the final grand catastrophe. But when I had finished my chapter I found I had emptied my sack and left myself no more to say for the moment, and had better defer completion until my education was considerably more advanced." Yet the incompatibility of pouring socialist theory into a bourgeois mold baffled him enough to make him abandon the notion of becoming a successful novelist: although he made a start at one more novel, *An Unsocial Socialist* proved to be his last.

"Socialism very active this spring," Shaw recorded in his diary notes for 1883. He was selling more and more of his hours to the cool cynical devil in him who whispered that romance was a waste of time, a private indulgence, a false channel for emotion, and even, like the love of Tristan and Isolde, the way to death. More and more he mentally divided his life into the serious and the trivial: his work and Alice. He tells her that his head is in "a tumult with matters about which you do not care twopence"; he announces that he is full of serious business and does not know how she continues "to thrust herself in." He admits that her "corner is an adorable place in which to pass the evening of a busy day"; then he retracts even that complimentary insult. Her corner is not adorable, but frivolous. She does not deserve all the hours he has given her. She is a sensual—a fatal temptation. But Shaw the puritan will not be beguiled: "I snap your chains like Samson."

And yet he is full of remorse for the hard things he says to her. He does not want her, and yet he does. "If I had your heart, I know I should break it, and yet I wish I had it. Is not this monstrous? Take your lesson in the morning, so that I may never see you again, I implore you; and when you have done so, and I presently beg you to come in the evening, do not listen to me." He cannot quite give her up: "Write to me, and I will make love to you—to relieve the enormous solitude which I carry about with me. I do not like myself, and sometimes I do not like you; but there are moments when our two unfortunate souls seem to cling to the same spar in a gleam of sunshine, free of the other wreckage for a moment."[12] And yet in June 1883 he wrote Aileen Bell, one of his casual conquests, that his engagement was broken off.[13]

Alice Lockett's response to Shaw's consciously dramatized version of his inner struggle was unfortunately conventional. She became hard and high-handed. She sent him ten stamps, telling him she endured "a positive pain to feel that you have spent one penny on me"; she returned one of his letters with "This is not worth a penny stamp" scrawled across the envelope. Shaw in return became hard and angry, no longer finding her "assumption of offended dignity" exquisite or endearing. " 'Which yet my soul seeketh, but I find not,' " he retorted: " 'one man in a thousand have I found, but a woman among all those have I not found.' Farewell, incorrigible trifler: I am awake and in earnest at last."[14]

They parted forever; then she came to Osnaburgh Street and insisted he walk with her to Edgware Road. They agreed to meet at Liverpool Street Station the next time she was in town. Alice understood that they were to meet at eight-thirty. She arrived at the station, waited until eight thirty-two; then, as she wrote him that night, "distrust crept into my heart . . . and acting upon a nature at once imaginative and impulsive, I went straight home."

Shaw had understood only that she would leave the International Health Exhibition for the station at eight. He arrived at quarter to nine, sat in "their" waiting room, read a little, moped a little, hung about, watched the nine-thirty train depart, went back, slept, woke for the ten-ten train, and finally gave her up. He peremptorily dismissed her explanation when it arrived: "Mistrust did not creep into your heart . . . you have no heart, and you have mistrusted me (and, with more reason, yourself also) ever since we first met. . . . I am not offended: I am only furious. You were quite right to go by the 8.32. Had you waited, I should have despised you (or tried to, on principle); for I respect people who always act sensibly and are devoid of the weaknesses known as 'feelings.' You behaved like a prudent woman, like a lady, and like a flint-hearted wretch."[15]

She defended herself by pitying him. "Do you know that I feel very sorry for George Shaw," she wrote 28 October 1884; "he thinks he is all in all to himself—mistaken delusion. He has never known the streets of sympathy—insults his friends by telling them they have nothing to do with the serious part of his life." The affair dragged on into December. He is like an old dress with the color all washed out, she tells him; she has lost all respect for him; she has forgotten him. She ends one letter with a caustic parody of his columnar accountant's style:

Adieu!
My idol.
My hero.
My pattern.
My love.
My life.
My all.[16]

Shaw clung to affairs and friendships: since he never totally committed himself, perhaps he never felt the need to totally extricate himself; certainly he craved the security of female relationships. Elinor Huddart, for example, was one who wondered at his tenacity: "I can put forth no fresh leaves. Why begin [again] a correspondence that wearied and irritated you? I always wondered that you cared to continue it so long. Leave my ashes in peace. They can do you no good."[17] Now, however, even Shaw had evidently had enough. He had categorized Alice Lockett to his satisfaction. She was an amateur at letter writing, he a professional; he was a novice at lovemaking, she an expert. "If you have made me feel," he asked her, "have I not made you think?" Ideally, their disparate talents might have welded them into a harmonious whole. But Shaw had decided emphatically that her contribution did not equal his: feeling did not match brain and was even incompatible with it.

He wrote Alice to say that he had never been in love with her. She retaliated: "Dear Mr. Shaw . . . Nay! I know better. You always were—you are—and you always will be." Despite the bravado, she called an end on 27 December 1884 to what was already finished. "Let our correspondence close with the year," she wrote, and signed herself, "Yours truly, Alice M. Lockett."

Shaw's prodigious activity allowed him little time for backward glances. He had fingers in dozens of pies. He had started *An Unsocial Socialist* on its rounds with his usual honesty: R. Bentley and Son desired him not to send the manuscript, "since you yourself are of the opinion that the work is not one we should risk publishing." Then James Leigh Joynes and Belfort Bax, two acquaintances he had made through socialism, purchased a magazine called *To-Day*. Shaw offered them *An Unsocial Socialist;* they accepted it, and ran it serially through 1884: his last-written, most radical novel was his first in print. At the request of Shakespearean scholar F. J. Furnivall, Shaw then undertook to compile an index and glossary to the Hunterian Club's new edition of the works of Thomas Lodge for the sum of five guineas—a project which, he said, wasted the year deplorably. He set to work to edit Laurence Gronlund's *The Co-operative Commonwealth*, and was promised £5—if the book ever made money. He was turning out articles, speeches, letters, short stories on any and all topics. He made speeches at the Browning Society, delivered his first unwritten lecture at Woolwich, lectured on socialism at working men's clubs, revised *The Irrational Knot* for publication in Annie Besant's *Our Corner*, acted as accompanist and stage manager for some amateur performances of *Faust* and *Il Trovatore*, rehearsed *Don Giovanni* at Vandeleur Lee's place and fell in love "for a week or so" with Katie Samuel, who sang Donna Anna, regularly appeared at the New Shakespeare Society, attended revolutionist Charlotte Wilson's circle for reading Marx's *Kapital* in Hampstead, and joined the Fabian Society, a socialist group which appealed to Shaw more than the others he had sampled because its members belonged to the middle class, his class.

Shaw did much of his studying and writing those days in the Reading Room of the British Museum. It was inhabited by another young man, just Shaw's age, who later recalled his first impressions of the red-bearded eccentric studying next to him. "Far away back in the olden days," wrote William Archer, "while as yet the Independent Theatre slumbered in the womb of Time, together with the New Drama, the New Criticism, the New Humour, and all the other glories of our renovated world, I used to be a daily frequenter of the British Museum Reading Room. Even more assiduous in his attendance was a young man of tawny complexion and attire, beside whom I used frequently to find myself seated. My curiosity was piqued by the odd conjunction of his subjects of research. Day after day for weeks he had before him two books, which he studied alternately, if not simultaneously—Karl Marx's *Das Kapital* (in French), and an orchestral score of *Tristan und Isolde*. I did not know then how exactly this quaint juxtaposition symbolised the main interests of his life. Presently I met him at the house of a common acquaintance, and we conversed for the first time."[18]

The acquaintance ripened quickly into friendship, an extremely important one for Shaw. Archer already had a reputation as a journalist for the London *Figaro;* recognizing Shaw's great abilities as well as his pride and diffidence, he was prepared to help him establish a reputation of his own. Two apparently more incompatible men were hard to imagine: Archer a tall, well-built Scot—self-controlled, wooden-faced—to all appearances dour, puritanically rigid, and totally lacking in humor; Shaw Irish, strikingly flamboyant in appearance, spilling over with wit, paradox, and heresy, humming with energy—to all appearances comic, revolutionary, and more than slightly mad. Beneath the public image he was busy creating, however, remained the diffident, lonely, and unworldly Shaw. In turn Archer's wooden exterior concealed a romantic nature and "an unsleeping and incorrigible sense of humor." ". . . I interested him," said Shaw, ". . . by being so laughably free, not only from superstitions recognized by him as such, but from many conventions which he had never dreamt of challenging . . . I appealed irresistibly to him as an incarnate joke. . . . The way to get on with Archer was to amuse him: to argue with him was dangerous. The invaluable precept of Robert Owen: 'Never argue: repeat your assertion,' established me with Archer on the footing of a privileged lunatic, and made quarrels impossible."[19] And the two had many important qualities in common: seriousness of purpose, integrity, a passion for things of the mind, and indifference to "things of the body and of the pocket, as long as they stopped short of disablement and painful privation."

Shaw soon confided to Archer that in writing fiction construction was not his strong point, but that his dialogue was incomparable. Archer, who had "a certain hankering after the rewards, if not the glories, of the playwright," replied that he could not write dialogue at all, but that he considered himself a born constructor. In the autumn of 1884, therefore, Archer proposed, and Shaw agreed, to collaborate on a play. Archer thumbed through various plots he kept in stock and handed Shaw *Das Rheingold*, a play planned for two heroines, a rich one and a poor one, and a hero who was to prefer the poor one to the rich one, and in the end have his disinterestedness rewarded by the lucrative discovery that the poor one was really the rich one. "All this I gravely propounded to Mr. Shaw," said Archer, "who listened with no less admirable gravity. Then I thought the matter had dropped, for I heard no more of it for many weeks. I used to see Mr. Shaw at the Museum, laboriously writing page after page of the most exquisitely neat shorthand at the rate of about three words per minute; but it did not occur to me that this was our play. After about six weeks he said to me 'Look here, I've written half the first act of that comedy, and I've used up all your plot. Now I want some more to go with.' "[20] Shaw's version differed slightly; he recalled telling Archer that he had finished the first act and not yet come to his plot, and asked Archer to refresh his memory about it. Archer objected indignantly, until Shaw appeased him by pointing out that the well-made play never gets going until the second act, and that he had after all used Archer's Rhine setting for the meeting of the lovers. Mollified, Archer rehearsed his plot again for Shaw, who took it away with him only to return shortly with the announcement that he had indeed gotten to Act II, but now had used up all of Archer's plot and needed more to go on with. Archer, said Shaw, did not take this second crime against his constructional genius gracefully. He retired from the collaboration on the spot, convinced that Shaw was far less of a playwright and more of a lunatic than he had suspected. Shaw tucked the shorthand manuscript away in a drawer and, with it, his fleeting ambition to score as a playwright. The socialist revival, the Fabian Society, his developing powers as an orator, and his pressing need to earn a regular wage—all seemed far more important to him than fiddling with the drama.

"Father's death put [a] stop to 30/ a week he'd been sending," wrote Shaw in April 1885 in the daily diary he had begun to keep that year, "but we got nearly £100 by life insurance. We could do little more than pay off debts, replace worn-out clothes." Shaw's brisk letter to his uncle R. Frederick Shaw saying that he was rather sorry he had not means to cremate his father evoked an indignant response: "No one who knows you either personally or by report through your Father, ever doubted that in all the relations of private life and habits you are otherwise than you ought to be. . . ."[21] Mrs. Shaw was still teaching voice. Lucy was touring in the provinces; she was in fact in Dublin when her father died alone in a lodging house of congestion of the lungs, but she did not attend the funeral. Since his arrival in London nine years before, Shaw had managed to earn a grand total of six pounds by his pen. Paid journalism, now that the loyal but meager dribble of shillings from Dublin had stopped, became a necessity. On 16 May 1885, Shaw undertook his first salaried job as a writer: William Archer had found him a job reviewing books at two guineas per thousand words for the *Pall Mall Gazette*. Then the picture critic on the *World*, a paper for which Archer had begun to write theatrical news, died. The post could not be filled, Shaw was available: he became the *World*'s art critic at five pence per line. In June of that year Annie Besant began to employ him as art critic for her little magazine *Our Corner*. "Journalism," Shaw once said, "is the art of stating public problems brilliantly without ever having the time to solve them." He now found himself practicing that art.

CHAPTER THREE

1885 - 1887

MRS. SHAW'S PROFESSION put another woman in her son's way while he was still in love with Alice Lockett. Chiding Alice for her ill temper in a letter of 7 July 1884, Shaw warned her that he had had "for consolation a long walk with Mrs. Chatterbox." Jane (Jenny) Patterson—"Mrs. Chatterbox"—was a dark, voluptuous, well-to-do Irish widow some fifteen years older than Shaw, and a voice pupil of Mrs. Shaw's who had rapidly become a friend of the family. Increasingly in the winter of 1884–85, Shaw would find the attractive widow chatting with his mother over the teacups when he came home from the British Museum:

FEBRUARY 10. Mrs. Patterson here in the evening. Got a letter from V. L. [Vandeleur Lee] and went out late to see Mrs. P. to a bus, and to call on L.

FEBRUARY 13. Met Mrs. Patterson coming out of the house as I went in, and saw her to her bus.

FEBRUARY 15. Mrs. Patterson's at 18. At 19.15 went off to Perseverance Hall, and lectured to 21 people. Wet night.

FEBRUARY 16. Worked at the first installment of *The Irrational Knot*. Mrs. Patterson here when I returned. She went with Mother to see Mrs. Langtry in *The School for Scandal*.

FEBRUARY 17. Mrs. Patterson at home when I returned from the Avelings. Mother went off to theatre and left Mrs. P., G.[ordon] and myself together.

FEBRUARY 21. Found Mrs. Patterson here when I returned [from going to the Dramatic Review office with Archer]. Sat chatting and play-

ing and singing until past 21, when [I] put her into a cab with her
dog and went off to Barton's.

MARCH 16. Up late. Mrs. Patterson here in the morning for a lesson. . . .
Walked with Mrs. Patterson to Marshall and Snelgrove's.

MARCH 21. Did not go to Museum. Went to Bach Festival, then to Mrs.
Patterson.

Jenny Patterson was soon violently infatuated with Shaw. He fascinated and bewildered her. One minute he scintillated with charm, gallantry, outrageous flattery; the next found him aloof, evasive, cold. He
could chatter to her as sympathetically as a woman; he could be ar-
rogantly masculine and insulting. He could harangue her man to man
about socialism and the Fabians and the great and wonderful freethinker
William Morris whose famous Kelmscott House at Hammersmith he had
begun to frequent, treating her just as though she were a human being
with a mind. Elinor Huddart prized this quality in him: "You are the
only man friend I have ever made. Men do not interest themselves in
women as a rule, unless they find in them the gratification of their vanities, or their passions. I am content to be your friend and no man's
wife."[1] The next minute would find him hostile and denouncing women
as frivolous and unworthy of his time or thought.

His sexual passivity attracted and maddened Jenny. The more eager he
was to put her safely into a cab, the more eager was she to pull him in
beside her and carry him off to her house in Brompton Square. Yet her
love for him was not only physical. His mental fireworks dazzled her.
When he strode in where she sat with his mother he brought with him
fresh winds from the world of affairs—the real world of socialist debate
and revolutionary fervor, of the newest picture in the gallery and the latest *Nozze di Figaro* at Drury Lane, of working-class riots and strikes, of
the hottest current controversies—vegetarianism, vivisection, vaccination.
He was full of what Sidney Webb had said, and what Morris had said,
and Eleanor Marx Aveling, and Archer and Annie Besant. His activity
made her head spin: he was always just breezing in or dashing off. Music
seemed the only cultural card she had to play: he would spend an evening quite contentedly at the piano singing to her. How else could she
win his attention? She mused, and began to contemplate becoming a
socialist.[2]

Shaw, however, was not immune to Jenny Patterson's physical attrac-
tions. In April his father died and the event, besides providing a little
ready cash so that he could spend £11/11 at Jaegers for an all-wool suit,
new woolen trousers, black coat and vest ("the first new garments I have
had for years"), undoubtedly had the effect of triggering some kind of
psychosexual release.[3] By July the tempo of his relationship with Mrs.
Patterson had accelerated considerably:

JULY 4. At about 20.20 called at Mrs. Patterson's. She was out. . . . Then went to Mrs. Patterson and stayed there until 1. Vein of conversation decidedly gallant.

JULY 10. Found Mrs. Patterson here when I came home. Walked to her house with her by way of the park. Supper, music and curious conversation, and a declaration of passion. Left at 3. *Virgo intacta* still.

JULY 17. Mrs. Patterson came. Saw her for a few moments. Blush etc. Spoke at the Fabian in the evening and walked with Mrs. Besant to her gate. Sat up to write to Mrs. Patterson.

JULY 18. Went to Inventions . . . and thence to J. Patterson's. Forced caresses. Thence to Lady Wilde's . . . . Thence to Barton's . . . . called at Brompton Square on way back, but she had not come in yet, and I did not wait.

JULY 19. Went to Brompton Square, but was too late to see JP who was going to bed, so walked home. Wrote to her.

On the afternoon of 25 July Shaw went around to the International Inventions Exhibition at South Kensington to cover a musical program, and from there walked to Brompton Square, where he found Jenny Patterson and his mother in the sitting room. They declared their interest in the Inventions. He walked back with them to South Kensington, left them at the door of the Exhibition, and went on to his friend Barton's to kill time until he could go back to Brompton Square. He met his mother and Jenny as he was returning. "We walked along the Brompton Road looking for a bus, but they were all full, so, on the corner of Montpelier St. Mother went on by herself, and I returned to the Square with JP, and stayed there until 3 o'clock on my 29th birthday which I celebrated by a new experience. Was watched by an old woman next door, whose evil interpretations of the lateness of my departure greatly alarmed us." The evening plunged Shaw into an affair with Jenny Patterson that would in turn please and revolt him, and would nearly succeed in driving her mad.

Clearly, Shaw's mother knew the situation and approved it, as much as she concerned herself with any of her son's affairs. She had tolerated his conduct with Alice Lockett: upon Shaw's explaining once that he had not been at the Museum but with Alice, Mrs. Shaw had been at first outraged and then, after a moment's reflection, resigned: "She is old enough to take care of herself." Jenny Patterson was more than old enough to take care of herself; she was, in fact, sufficiently well-to-do to take good care of Shaw if he would let her. She was besides a close friend of Lucinda Shaw's and Lucy's, obviously because the intimacy gave her access to Shaw, but also, it seems, because she genuinely liked them. It is unlikely that "Mrs. Chatterbox" did not confide her hopes and fears about Mrs. Shaw's son to Mrs. Shaw during their tea-taking, or their excursions to concerts, galleries, and the shops. Mrs. Shaw, therefore, collaborated in the affair by constantly putting Mrs. Patterson in her son's way. As for Lucy, she followed its progress with interest, especially since Shaw carelessly left his mistress's love letters lying about his cluttered study in exactly the same spirit that he compulsively talked about his love affairs to anyone who would listen. *"Do* not leave this for Lucy to read," Jenny is forced to plead. "She will look for it I know." Georgina Shaw, living in London, also participated. *"Dont* leave this about for your aunt to read," begs Jenny. "Think of *her* morals."

If Jenny Patterson thought her birthday gift to Shaw would secure his affections, she was to be sharply disillusioned. She was not wholly the pursuer in the affair: "Went to JP" is a frequent entry in his diary. Many nights he lingered in Brompton Square looking at her dark windows, having arrived after a meeting or an evening with friends too late to knock at her door. And, as Shaw later confided to Frank Harris, he "preferred women who knew what they were doing." She was passionate, both in love and in temper: a relief after the offended dignity of Miss Lockett and the impassivity of a mother who "never made scenes, never complained, never punished nor retaliated nor lost her superiority to spites and tantrums and tempers." In a sense, too, she was his fictional moral woman: the economically independent woman who bestowed herself only where she chose. He pursued the relationship, therefore, with some enthusiasm. He could tell her, "Be faithful to me or I will kill you by mere intensity of hate." And she could speak truth when she wrote him, "You will not believe me I know but it is absolutely true that often my body has been an unwilling minister to you. In many of your letters have not you threatened me with your desertion if I did not love you passionately." It was not the "love" that she loved, Jenny told him, but her lover. She had awakened his sensuality. "I will not be tired on my return," she writes. "Be as ardent as you were last week. It is your [place] to be so. I adore to be made love to like that. It takes my breath away at the time & leaves oh such a memory behind! Your ardor makes me feel not half ardent enough, but I think you find me warm enough?"[4]

"Someday a pair of dark eyes, a fierce temperament and a woman will obtain you body and soul," Elinor Huddart had warned him. Jenny Patterson's dark eyes, fierce temperament, and womanliness had certainly obtained Shaw's body. But for Shaw, the more physical the relationship, the more violent eventually his guilt and disgust. If he had berated himself for wasting time on Alice Lockett, eventually painting her into an unimportant corner of his life, his affair with Jenny Patterson, which lacked the romance of sexual denial, would cause him deep revulsions. At his kindest in this mood he would argue for a platonic relationship: platonic, at least, unless *he* desired sex. Sometimes Jenny resisted this ascetic mood: "I don't believe in platonics and saints," she protested. Sometimes, made desperate by his neglect, she pleaded for mere friendship: "My

Saint: Come and see me in a purely platonic way soon—to play to me & talk to me." At his cruelest Shaw answered her ardors with cold post-cards or with torrents of abuse; dropped round to Brompton Square on his way to a speaking engagement and left ten minutes later; complained rudely when bread and fruit and his special Van Houten's cocoa were not served up promptly; woke her out of a sound sleep returning from the Fabian meeting or Hammersmith or from seeing Annie Besant to her gate; taunted her with accounts of the other women he currently held under his spell. Or, he simply avoided her: "With regard to the 'à bien-tôt' at the end of your note," he wrote her on 10 March 1886, "I may say that my diary presents an unbroken array of engagements right up to the 23rd."

Perhaps because Jenny Patterson's wholehearted submission gave him a sense of power he had never felt before, Shaw accelerated his conquests of women in these years to a frenetic tempo. As if to make up for a child-hood and adolescence of his mother's neglect, he now craved to see him-self reflected in every female eye. He did not, apparently, win them with good looks. "Shaw was not, in those early days, very attractive," mused the fastidious Max Beerbohm many years later: "—dead white, and his face was pitted by some disease. The back of his neck was especially bleak—very long, untenanted, dead white. His hair was like seaweed. In those days, you were lucky not to see G.B.S. from the back."[5] For the type of woman who preferred gallantry in a man instead of aggression, however, words instead of deeds, intelligence rather than physicality, playfulness rather than solidity—Shaw was irresistible.

There was Eleanor Marx Aveling, daughter of Shaw's idol Karl Marx: feminist, freethinker, socialist, translator of Flaubert's *Madame Bovary*, Ibsenite, and common-law wife of Edward Aveling, professor of science, journalist, and translator of Marx's *Kapital*. Shaw got to know both of them well in January of 1885—Eleanor was just thirty—when they re-hearsed and performed a comedy called *Alone* for the benefit of the Socialist League. Actually he had been struck with admiration for Eleanor months before: "Of course," retorted Elinor Huddart sarcas-tically 28 April 1884, "I remember, you are to marry Eleanor Marx—And you are not yet personally acquainted." Soon Shaw was hurrying across the street when he emerged from the gates of the British Museum to knock at the Avelings' door at 55 Great Russell Street. He usually managed to find Eleanor alone. Had Aveling been there, however, Shaw would not have been a bit disconcerted. After years of observing Vandeleur Lee's success as the third of the Shaw household triangle, Shaw now found the role congenial for his own temperament. The Pakenham Beattys, for example, with whom he spent most Sunday eve-nings: was he not on the friendliest terms with Edith Beatty, writing her notes of advice about her son "Bismarck's" clothes, diet, and doctor? It was a gratifying role: dynamic genius descends into the lives of a talented couple who are at best rather bored with, at worst sick to death of each other. Dynamic genius talks public affairs with husband, amorous blarney to the wife, ingratiates himself with both, who are ready to kiss him for suddenly sparking their humdrum existence. Of course, the line must be trod delicately: wives could grow suddenly intense and husbands jealous; but Shaw balanced expertly on that tightrope, sowing his gallantry thickly with the names of other women, playing the buffoon, and insisting upon a frank camaraderie with the husband. The triangle gave him what he craved: it duplicated a domestic pattern in which he played the eternal child (as he had never been), coddled by the woman-mother, tolerated and half-feared by the male-father. And since he was not bent on seduction (having great vanity but not a strong genital drive), the married woman proved curiously satisfactory. He did not feel obliged to seduce her since that would be ungrateful; yet at the same time, what more gratifying to the ego than winning the affections of a woman already pledged to another? The challenge was irresistible. As he had once boasted to Alice Lockett, "When you return I will make you fall in love with me merely to shew you how clever I am."

He perhaps did not succeed with Eleanor, who bestowed upon Edward Aveling the intensity of love that in some women can only be elicited by an unscrupulous and philandering man. Certainly Shaw consoled her for Aveling's conduct, which was notorious: "As a borrower of money and a swindler and seducer of women," observed Shaw, "his record was unimpeachable." The often-deserted Eleanor was soon writing to ask him to come and save her "from a long day and evening of tête-à-tête with myself."[6] If Shaw did not admire Eleanor's "pungent armpits" and heavy cigarette smoking, he certainly could admire her fine black eyes and curly black hair, her sensitive, emotional disposition, her exceptionally musical voice, her vivacity, her lively intelligence. She aroused his interest in a play called *Nora* by the Norwegian dramatist Henrik Ibsen; she talked Shakespeare and theatre with him, and he encouraged her to follow her original dream of becoming an actress. And she was in the center of the socialist activity Shaw so energetically pursued.

There was also Edith Bland. As a fellow Fabian, Shaw of course knew her husband Hubert Bland, one of the founders of the Society and its treasurer. Under the name E. Nesbit, Edith wrote novels, extremely successful children's books, and poetry. Since Shaw was a fellow artistic spirit at Fabian meetings, Edith Bland quickly grew partial to him. She teased him into sitting next to her, where she observed him, finding him "very plain" and "the grossest flatterer," yet, of course, fascinating. Not able to capture enough of his attention at the Friday night Fabian gatherings, Edith pursued her quarry to his favorite haunts, the Reading Room and the Wheatsheaf, a vegetarian restaurant in Rathbone Place off Tottenham Court Road where he took dinner every day at two or three o'clock. There were long walks in Regent's Park and tea at Osnaburgh Street with Mrs. Shaw. Like Eleanor Marx, Edith Bland suffered the notoriety of her husband's woman-chasing: her handsome, monocled, essentially conservative husband conducted his affairs hardly less scrupulously than the dubious Aveling. Unlike Eleanor, Edith adjusted to them rather well, eventually submitting to one of her husband's mistresses and illegitimate children living under her own roof. It is no wonder, however, that this tall, engaging, restless, moody woman (as H. G. Wells described her) rapidly fell in love with Shaw's "maddening white face."

On the morning of 26 June 1886, Edith Bland appeared in the Reading Room and found Shaw as usual. This time, however, they did not part. "The whole day was devoted to Mrs. Bland," Shaw recorded. They dined together at the Wheatsheaf, had tea together, and then Shaw went home with her to Wald Hall, Eltham, a moated house with a walled garden. There they sang and played the piano, and there Edith Bland declared to Shaw that she had become passionately attached to him. At length her husband came in from volunteer work and Shaw said good night. "A memorable evening!" he noted.

After that evening, Shaw looked up more and more often from his work in the Reading Room to find Edith Bland bearing down upon him with plans for his day. "She would not be denied coming here to tea," he wrote in September. On 25 October she asked Shaw to meet her at King's Cross Station in the evening and go for a walk. "It rained," Shaw recorded. "She insisted on going to Enfield [north London]. I insisted on going 3rd class for the sake of company [sic]. . . . When we got to Enfield it was very wet. I got her some hot whiskey and water to prevent her catching cold. . . . Got home just after 1 in the morning. Hot whiskey and water for Mrs. B at Enfield 3d." They met again and walked along Camden Road, Caledonian Road, and into Barnsbury Square, where they went to look at the house she lived in as a girl. On 6 December Edith was again at the Museum. This time, however, Hubert Bland also put in an appearance. He was looking, Shaw observed, "rather sulky."

He need not have, for by now Shaw himself was wearying of the chase. In 1887, he noted in his diary, he was forced to give up working at the British Museum because acquaintances constantly came to chat with him. The chief intruder, evidently, was Edith Bland. Finally he took a stand. On 11 May 1887 Edith insisted on returning home with him as they left the Museum together, although Shaw objected. They found Mrs. Shaw out. Using this circumstance as a weapon, Shaw quarreled, and "she went away after an unpleasant scene caused by my telling her that I wished her to go, as I was afraid that a visit to me alone would compromise her." Shaw's transparent excuse for getting rid of her effectually quenched Edith Bland.

There was May Morris. Like Eleanor Marx she was the daughter of a man Shaw revered; and Shaw was prepared to romanticize May as part of the Morris mystique: Morris himself, craftsman, poet, utopian socialist; Kelmscott House in Hammersmith overlooking the Thames, with its exquisite green, blue, and pink "Lily" Wilton carpet, the blue and gold "Bird" tapestry, the Chaucer wardrobe which Burne-Jones had decorated with "The Prioresses Tale" in rich reds and golds and blacks, the fruit-and-flower thick wallpapers, the massive oak tables, the tall black overarching settle painted with Morris's sunflower design; Jane Morris, the wife, famed for her night-colored hair, pouting bee-stung mouth, and long swelling throat already immortalized in Dante Gabriel Rossetti's painting "The Blue Dress." May Morris, called "my maiden" by her father, was also revered as an aesthetic object: Violet Hunt called her "simply, to my eyes, the most beautiful creature I ever saw." Yet her haunting dark eyes and thick black hair were May's chief ornaments: her face could not live up to Pre-Raphaelite standards. Perhaps realizing this, May took to creating beauty instead of idly embodying it, becoming known for her embroidery and calligraphy, and taking pupils at Kelmscott House.

May Morris played the role of Maude Trevor in *Alone*, the same benefit production which starred the Avelings, and Shaw as Stratton Strawless. Writing to fellow socialist Mary Grace Walker 23 January 1885, Shaw claimed that he had not "rehearsed a play with Miss Morris without some damage to my self-possession. I do not love her—I have too much sense for such follies; but I hate and envy the detestable villain who plays her lover with all my soul."[7] May had not been equally impressed with Shaw. "Your conduct towards the theatrical society company is quite disgraceful," she wrote, "tho' it seems to give you great pleasure to think that you are causing them trouble & annoyance. There is a [rehearsal] call for 11 a.m. tomorrow . . . . I shall be much surprised if you turn up. Yours in anger, May Morris." Six months later, however, May was finding Shaw's antics highly amusing, and deploring the thought of his missing one of their entertainments: "My intellect is enfeebled this morning by too much laughing at you last night. I repeat, you must come to us on Thursday—How incomplete were a Social Entertainment without the critical smile & quiet sneer of George Bernard Shaw."[8]

By September that year, the simple "her" of Shaw's letter to Mary Grace Walker had become "Her." Reporting to Edith Beatty about William Morris's arrest on 21 September in a shoving match in court with a policeman, and his subsequent release and appearance at the Socialist League meeting, Shaw said, "I was relieved to see Morris, and delighted to see Her. [Henry Hyde] Champion had to speak twice, and was much occupied. I, between following the proceedings and watching the divine profile of the most beautiful of women, soon became utterly indifferent to everything else."⁹ Shaw was not too indifferent, however, to throw himself into this latest struggle over the right to free speech: he pledged himself "to speak next Sunday, to get arrested, to refuse to pay the fine, and to do the month." He was as good as his word: Shaw, Aveling, Henry Hyndman, and the Reverend Stewart Headlam all arrived to martyr themselves at the corner of Dod Street and Burdett Road in Limehouse near the East India Docks, the most popular site for open-air meetings with the East London Radical Club and now for the socialists. This time, however, public protest and indignation over previous arrests had made the government wary: under orders the police held back, not daring to tackle the huge crowd of between thirty and fifty thousand that had gathered to demonstrate for Free Speech, and Shaw awaited arrest in vain. After the meeting he traveled all the way across town to Hammersmith. "Went there," reports his diary, "to see May Morris."

There were many places Shaw might see May Morris. He might find her at the Socialist League offices at 13 Farringdon Road; he might coax her to a Friday evening Fabian meeting, although first she had to overcome her shyness of the Fabians—"they are all so gruesomely respectable"; he might walk her to her train afterward, and travel as far as the next station with her or even all the way to Hammersmith. She had begged him to join the Socialist League Choir: she hoped he would find her at their practices. He might take her to a Heckman Quartet concert with tickets given him by Jenny Patterson. He might find her at Walham Green or Weltje Road holding the Socialist League banner while her father addressed an audience on the evils of capitalism, or standing in the Hammersmith Broadway handing out her father's paper *The Commonweal* to passersby, an experience "trying and even humiliating," May complained, "for anyone who has not the talent for that form of martyrdom." Chiefly he saw her Sundays at Kelmscott House, where socialists like Emery Walker, Andreas Scheu, Belfort Bax, and Henry Halliday Sparling gathered for supper around the massive oak table after lecturing at open-air meetings morning and afternoon. Sometimes there would be only Morris, May, and Shaw at table: Jane Morris, herself from the working classes and immune to their charms, refused to have anything to do with her husband's "Comrades" when they invaded Kelmscott. Sometimes a lecture would be canceled, and then Shaw would follow May upstairs to one of the "queer little rooms above for larking" where they would talk and play duets and flirt until it was time for Shaw to make a dash for the last train back. Oddly enough, Shaw made part of a triangle in this relationship too: May adored and devoted herself to her barrel-chested, curly-bearded father, though of his "maidens" the elder sister Jenny was his favorite.

Clearly Shaw respected May's feelings: at least he made a resolution at the beginning of their acquaintance "not to make love," a resolution May dryly called "most judicious and worthy of all praise." His awakening interest in May coincided with the acceleration of his involvement with Jenny Patterson: he was content, therefore, that May be the spiritual Ideal, since Jenny was so obviously the sexual Real. He handled May with caution, never outrageously philandering with her, partially perhaps out of respect for the great William Morris. He tried to convince her that he was utterly shallow, a tack unfortunately guaranteed only to draw forth cries of disbelief; he tried equally to convince her of his "innate vulgarity"—she would not hear of it. His sarcasms baffled her. She was a plain person with little subtlety; she did not understand his fantastic whims and poses. Hers, she admitted, was "a morbid and dreary spirit," most likely to end "before the age of 70 in the pleasures of melancholia."

Certainly she was odd-woman-out at Hammersmith in a household that contained "the father" (as she called him), beloved and reverenced prophet of socialism; the beautiful, silent, legendary mother; the favored sister Jenny. She was uncertain about her role: conscious that in blindly admiring the proletariat and hating the bourgeoisie (as Shaw accused her of doing), she played the hypocrite; conscious that in loathing the dreary East End holes and corners to which her father carried the socialist doctrine, she proved herself an elitist; conscious that people scoffed at her for posing as "the aesthetic socialist." She served "the father." Perhaps the quality she most admired in Shaw was his gift as an orator: he surpassed Morris by far, both in wit and cool-headedness. "I don't know if you are aware that our audiences love you much," she told him: "their faces always broaden with pleasure when we promise them that if they are good Bernard Shaw shall be their next teacher." After almost a year and a half, however, Shaw still baffled her: "I don't believe I know you a bit better now than when we were first acquaint. Inscrutable man! I suppose this is *your* form of vanity—for shallow you cannot be."[10]

There were Geraldine Spooner, Grace Black, and Grace Gilchrist, all socialists and all sudden frequenters of the British Museum Reading Room. Eventually angered by his evasiveness, Grace Black wrote to tell him that he did not believe in or care enough for people to be an effective socialist. Shaw coolly retorted that this only meant he didn't care enough for her. She answered him: "I guessed you would think I was in love with you. So I am . . . . of course, of course, I do not mind whether you care about me or not. I can't imagine you doing so; & if you did I shᵈ be unhappy." Grace Gilchrist minded Shaw's indifference more. "I have felt myself these last few weeks socially estranged from you. I wish I had not parted so abruptly from you after that walk home . . . I am sure it was all a misunderstanding: I was wrong to give way to childish jealousy of other women . . . I know I have everything to learn in socialism: my faults are not my destiny, though sometimes indeed one's faults create an adverse destiny for one."[11]

There was Annie Besant. In the early eighties Shaw had gone to hear the famous Freethinker and orator deplore the fact that "sexual intercourse was made the occasion of great anxiety instead of a pleasure," decry the "miserable subterfuges" women were forced into when they found themselves pregnant, and urge the necessity of birth control. He followed her career, although his uncle Walter Gurly sent him newspapers that denounced Mrs. Besant and her platform partner, the atheist Charles Bradlaugh, as "that bestial man and woman who go about earning a living by corrupting the young of England." In his first speech before the Zetetical Society, however, Shaw denounced Mrs. Besant himself; at least he defended the state's action in awarding her daughter Mabel to her clergyman husband in the famous court case that took place in May of 1876, not long after Shaw had stepped off the boat from Dublin.

Annie Besant first saw Shaw in May 1884 when he spoke as a socialist against the Freethought Party. He began his address by describing himself—in his usual provocative way—as a loafer. Annie Besant, earnest, zealous, and therefore intensely humorless, swallowed the bait, and went home to attack him sharply in print. "I was fairly astounded at the audacious confession that he led so shameful a life," she reported in Bradlaugh's paper, the *National Reformer*: ". . . Mr. Shaw's description of himself is, I am inclined to think, pretty accurate, and explains a thing that has often puzzled me, why he should be so marvellously shrewish and 'crooked' in discussion. It must be a very sad thing to be a 'loafer' in a world where there is so much to be done . . . ."[12]

Less than two weeks later, having received of course an irresistibly charming letter from the "loafer," Mrs. Besant retracted her criticism in the same paper. Looking back at the beginning of this momentous relationship in her *Autobiography*, she described her conversion to Shaw: "At this time I also met George Bernard Shaw, one of the most brilliant of Socialist writers and most provoking of men; a man with a perfect genius for 'aggravating' the enthusiastically earnest, and with a passion for representing himself as a scoundrel. On my first experience of him on the platform at South Place Institute he described himself as a 'loafer,' and I gave an angry snarl at him in the *Reformer*, for a loafer was my detestation, and behold! I found that he was very poor, because he was a writer with principles and preferred starving his body to starving his conscience; that he gave time and earnest work to the spreading of Socialism, spending night after night in workmen's clubs; and that 'a loafer' was only an amiable way of describing himself because he did not carry a hod. Of course I had to apologise for my sharp criticism as doing him a serious injustice, but privately felt somewhat injured at having been entrapped into such a blunder."[13]

Their first face-to-face encounter did not occur until 21 January 1885 when Annie Besant came to hear Shaw lecture on "Socialism" at the Dialectical Society, although she had asked for *The Irrational Knot* for her sixpenny monthly *Our Corner* two days before.[14] During the preceding year, the militant Freethinker had privately discovered "that the case for Socialism was intellectually complete and ethically beautiful"; the public still knew her, however, as a foe who denounced socialism as just a fashion, "as aestheticism had been a few years ago."

> I was warned on all hands that she had come down to destroy me [Shaw later wrote], and that from the moment she rose to speak my cause was lost. I resigned myself to my fate, and pleaded my cause as best I could. When the discussion began everyone waited for Mrs. Besant to lead the opposition. She did not rise; and at last the opposition was undertaken by another man. When he had finished, Mrs. Besant, to the amazement of the meeting, got up and utterly demolished him. There was nothing left for me to do but gasp and triumph under her shield. At the end she asked me to nominate her for election to the Fabian Society, and invited me to dine with her.[15]

Shaw had made an important if temporary convert to socialism and Fabianism: for the far-reaching influence of her oratory and pamphleteering, Annie Besant would be the Fabian Friedrich Engels respected most.

The dinner took place ten days later on 31 January at Annie's house "Oatlands" in St. John's Wood. Present, besides Shaw and Elizabeth Cracknell, a contributor to *Our Corner*, was John Mackinnon Robertson. Robertson, just Shaw's age and therefore sixteen years younger than Annie Besant, was a socialist, an assistant on her magazine, her current protégé, her boarder, and her deeply attached friend. Shaw had found another household to invade.

Shaw revised *The Irrational Knot* for an April 1885 first installment, and in March received a welcome two pounds, fifteen shillings from Mrs. Besant in payment. By June he had ousted Elizabeth Cracknell as contributor to the "Art Corner" in Besant's magazine. That year their meetings coincided chiefly with the Friday night Fabian session, after which he sometimes put her into a cab or sometimes walked her home. He began to write her letters. Her political causes had bound Annie Besant emotionally to other men: her instructor in the new science, Edward

Aveling, had inspired a passion; she was extremely intimate with her partner in Freethought, Charles Bradlaugh. Socialism brought her Bernard Shaw. By 1886 Annie Besant was in love with him.

Perhaps he came close to loving her. That year, two nights after he had spent the evening with Annie, he went to Jenny Patterson and for the first time in his diary entered the word "revulsion." That year, too, Henry Sparling told him as they were returning on the same train from Hammersmith of his intention to marry May Morris. Shaw was evidently taken by surprise. Not that he intended to marry May himself, but the Morris mystique had seduced him, and he even liked to play fancifully with the notion that he had pledged himself to May the moment their eyes first met in a kind of "Mystical Betrothal." Now the real event had temporarily distracted May's attention from him. And then Edith Bland was becoming a decided problem. Of course, he continued to juggle all his romances: "Mrs. Bland came to Museum. Walked with her to Charing Cross and bought two toads on the way. . . . saw May Morris in the window of the Socialist League [headquarters] and went in for a few minutes. JP here when I returned. Hurried off to Mrs. Besant's"—so ran a not atypical day. Even Alice Lockett could still attract him: she paid a call, he walked with her to the station, and "they were on the old footing in no time at all." But he began to spend more and more time with Annie Besant.

Fabian affairs brought them together often. Then on 19 March 1886 they were both elected—along with Sidney Webb, Edward Pease, Frank Podmore, Hubert Bland, and Charlotte Wilson—to the Fabian Executive, and were thrown together almost daily. And then Annie decided to do an article for *Our Corner* on how London amuses itself in the West and East Ends. For the East End she took along a notebook and Shaw. They went to the music halls: the Variety in Pitfield Street, hot, crowded, and stuffy, and the rough Sebright's in Hackney Road with its muscled bouncers ready for trouble. They stopped to watch a pathetically bad "Penny Gaff" in Mile End Road featuring a young performer who divided her time between the stage, a piano-organ, and a baby that slept despite the bang-banging of the organ in its ear. One Saturday evening they walked "from Commonwealth Road, Whitechapel, down Leman Street along the Ratcliffe Highway, through Limehouse, Stepney, and Poplar." They found their excursion along Ratcliffe Highway, as the notorious main thoroughfare to the docks was once called, disappointingly peaceful, except for the exoticism of the foreign sailors and foreign shop signs, the smell of salt water, the drunks and their curses, and the ominous fact that the policemen patrolling the fetid courts walked only in pairs. They passed a public house where a dance was going on, paused to read the sign "No females admitted without hats, and unless respectably attired," then stayed to watch "two hatless and otherwise improperly attired" girls kicking up their heels outside the door to "the thrum-thrum of the music." "And as we walked down Wellclose Court," wrote Annie in the August issue, "my companion told me that one day passing through he saw dancing in one of the rooms, with the window open, three men and three women, without a rag upon them; and that two girls, for a wager, raced each other round Wellclose Square stark naked and not ashamed." Having bravely passed on Shaw's story to her readers, the ex-Freethinker added hastily: "Let us drop the curtain. In such fashion, in the nineteenth century, does part of a city that is called civilised amuse itself."

Jenny Patterson possessed a volatile and vulgar temper. With Edith and Grace and Emma and May and Geraldine and Eleanor and Annie variously occupying Shaw's time—to say nothing of lecturing, concert, play and gallery going, journalism, and the Fabian—it is not surprising that she lost it rather often. She tried many ploys to win his attention. Although a vegetarian and fastidious, Shaw liked food. She had in the past invited him to "eat and make love." She had tempted him with "brown bread, cocoa, strawberries & cream and any other fruit I can get." She had humbly apologized for not feeding him at once, promising "all shall be on the table waiting so that you shall not have even the shadow of an excuse to be displeased." Now she perfected herself in the art of making his favorite Van Houten's cocoa; she promised, "I will have any amount of good things for your *other* appetite which is as arant almost as 'the' other." She took a cottage at Broadstairs on the coast of Kent where she tried to lure him on 25 July 1887 with promises of "vegetarian food, a piano, Mozart, fresh air"—if he would only come. Unfortunately, Shaw was playing duets that Sunday with Annie Besant. She wept and threatened, and then apologized abjectly: "My tears & unhappiness are for my own ill behaviour & my rage all against myself (with one little exception) . . . for one like myself who has never been educated or controlled, in fact a savage. But you must give me a trial . . . not cut me off from you or your friends or 'Boycott' me in any way."[16]

She tried to make his friends her friends. She came to the Fabian meetings, often with his mother and Lucy, and especially when he lectured. She joined the Hammersmith socialist group, and turned up at the Morris's table on Sunday evenings with May and Shaw. Doing so, she exposed herself to speculation and malicious gossip, for her infatuation could not be hidden. May Morris was one of the kinder ones. "What a fascinating & charming lady your friend Mrs. Paterson is!" she wrote on 12 February 1886. "I wonder why you professed to be reluctant to introduce me to her. Did you think I sh^d bore her so much? I mean to find out whether she joined our Branch because a Socialist at heart, or because —you persuaded her to 'join first & learn later.'"

May was wrong on both counts: Jenny Patterson joined the socialist ranks because her lover was to be found there. Her worst enemy in her struggle to become part of his circle, however, was Shaw himself. He wrote back to May Morris expressing utter disbelief that she could find Jenny Patterson charming. May replied: "In good faith I thought her charming & amusing, tho' I confess to somewhat doubting her pretensions to the new-acquired name of Socialist (w^h the serious consider not to be lightly taken up) . . . . Are you not rather a disloyal friend? I confess I sh^d much hate to be scoffed at behind my back as you profess to scoff at Mrs. Patterson. But then you know my atrociously sentimental mind, & its utter incapacity for having a joke."[17] Shaw replied immediately, assuring her that he would never scoff at her, and telling her plainly that he wished to "cultivate" her. At the same time, he reported to Jenny that May Morris doubted her political sincerity. This hurt and angered Jenny. "I am just as good a socialist as you and May Morris," she retorted.

Shaw continued to make mischief for Jenny, repeating ill-natured remarks that the gossipy Belfort Baxes had made about her so that the next time they met, Jenny tossed her head and treated the Baxes contemptuously and even let her tongue go and spoke ill of Mrs. Bax—but only, as she tearfully tried to explain to Shaw later, because he himself had run them down. Shaw in turn jeered at his socialist friends for Jenny's benefit; to her credit, this did not appease her. "You talk about his [Bland's] wife in a way that is not right," she chided. "You have no business to say to any one (not even me) the things you do about her even tho' they are in fun."[18] But such table-turning was not the rule: pathetically enough Jenny Patterson invited only the gossip and ridicule of both Shaw and his friends when she tried to follow him into his socialist sphere.

In Annie Besant she had her most formidable antagonist. How could she hope to compete with this famous, powerful, and prestigious woman; how could she dare to quarrel with her? She could not; she could only watch and rage inwardly. On 7 July 1886, for example, she and Lucinda Shaw went out to hear the Sunday afternoon lectures at Hammersmith, and all were invited to stay on for supper at Kelmscott House. A pleasant day, except that Mrs. Besant was there too and engaging a great deal of Shaw's attention. The four of them took the train back. If Jenny had expected Shaw to get off at South Kensington and escort her home, she was mistaken. He went on to Baker Street with Mrs. Besant and walked with her along Regent's Park to her home in Avenue Road. Tricks like this taught Jenny to be more tenacious. After one Fabian meeting, Shaw reported, both Mrs. Besant and Jenny came away with him. "At last I had to leave JP in Piccadilly and go up Bond St. with Mrs. B. whom I put into a bus at the corner of Orchard St. Then I found that JP had been following us." What passed between them may be imagined. Shaw hurried Jenny to Brompton Square—and then went home to write to Annie Besant.

Jenny Patterson's jealousy of Annie Besant reached new heights in 1887. This is paradoxical, for according to Shaw's diary note, "The intimacy with Mrs. Besant alluded to last year reached in January a point at which it threatened to become a vulgar intrigue, chiefly through my fault. But I roused myself in time and avoided this. I however frequently went to her house on Monday evenings and played pianoforte duets (mostly Haydn symphonies arranged) with her." Shaw's statement suggests that what came after January 1887 was under control. January was indeed a climax of some sort: between the nineteenth and the twenty-sixth he wrote Annie five letters; and on the twenty-seventh, after meeting her at the Museum, they ate dinner together and then walked to the magazine office at 63 Fleet Street. Perhaps this was the moment that she presented him with a formal contract setting forth the terms on which she would be willing to live with him as, since she was still married, common-law man and wife. Shaw read the document through with mounting alarm. "Good God!" he remembers himself as saying. "This is worse than all the vows of all the Churches on earth. I had rather be legally married to you ten times over."[19] If this proposal was the "vulgar intrigue" Shaw referred to, then this too must have been the moment he realized his danger and called a halt. Highly displeased, Annie argued seriously for the arrangement; Shaw only laughed. "Scene with her," he records in his entry for that day.

Perhaps Annie Besant now understood the limits of Shaw's feelings for her, but their relationship by no means tapered off. Shaw's days and nights were full of Mrs. Besant: "went to JP's where I wrote to Mrs. Besant"; "did nothing at Mrs. B's but talk, though we intended to play duets"; "after the Fabian Mrs. Besant and I walked to Oxford St. where I put her into a bus. Squabbled about an umbrella of which she wished to make me a present" (he later paid her 10/6 for it); "Mrs. Besant came here and had tea with me after Champion's lecture. Mother out. Sweetmeats 2d"; "call for Mrs. Besant at Fleet St. at 18-½"; "got a telegram from Mrs. Besant in the morning to go over and see her. Went across eagerly. Sentimental nonsense only; no business of real importance."

Little wonder that Jenny Patterson nearly went mad with jealousy. "You are really a very black villain," she writes from Broadstairs on 2 May. "No matter—that *one* act of unfaithfulness is as bad as a hundred. *How* could you? ? ? And after such lips & kisses as mine! Faugh!" By 30 September she was temporizing: "Any way if you are unfaithful to me (but you mustn't be!) let it be with someone *nice* not a horrid looking woman. I feel sure that she is at it again out of pure cussedness against *me*—she resents your being faithful to me. . . . but she must not poach on my preserve. You belong to me." By 18 October, she seemed to be (at least temporarily) resigned: "All right my love . . . I really must take a back seat where Mrs. B is concerned. . . . She'll be a worse habit than me. You may commit Bigamy or Trigamy or as many 'gamies' as you like . . . of course I am an idiot to pay for the compliment of being jealous of you."

Given Shaw's ubiquitousness, of course, it is possible that Mrs. B is not Annie Besant at all, but Mrs. Bland, Mrs. Bax, Mrs. Beatty—or any other Mrs. B. Yet Annie Besant is the likely candidate. Sixteen years older than Shaw, her once-attractive face and figure grown coarse and stout, she might have qualified as "horrid looking"; certainly Annie Besant was the woman who dominated Shaw's attention that year and was the cause of Jenny's jealousy. On 15 November, for example, they had "a tedious quarrel about Mrs. Besant." And yet the "act of unfaithfulness" does not square with Shaw's avowal in his diary that he avoided a vulgar intrigue with Annie. Shaw was not apt to lie to himself, however, although he might well lie to Jenny. Perhaps he was unkindly teasing her: perhaps the act of unfaithfulness was something as dastardly as a kiss.

In effect, the affair was over. On 23 December Annie Besant gave Shaw back his letters. (Perhaps Shaw's prudent retreat from the violence at Trafalgar Square on 13 November—Bloody Sunday—while she pushed on in the face of mounted police and the military, had finally alienated her.) The next day, Christmas Eve, he returned hers, taking them to the offices of *Our Corner* in Fleet Street and then, finding her gone, walking with Sidney Webb to Avenue Road and leaving them at Oatlands. Upon returning home, he discovered that his den had been invaded: his letters to Annie, which predictably he had left lying about, had been rifled and nine were missing. The thief needed no naming. As it turned out, Jenny had come for the bird she had promised Mrs. Shaw to care for in her absence; had on impulse run up the stone steps to Shaw's study; had discovered instead of Shaw a heap of his letters to her rival, and evidently a few of the rival's to him; had seized a handful and had fled with the incriminating documents and the bird.

At 2 A.M. Christmas morning she sat down to write her lover in no Christian spirit:

> I make no excuse for taking the letters. I don't ask you to excuse me either. I should do exactly the same again under the same conditions. When I read *her* letters I felt that she must have had great encouragement . . . . I am ill & numb. I feel as if I had had a blow on the head . . . in the morning all the pain will be back again & my loneliness almost unbearable. . . . To flatter your own vanity & this woman's you have humiliated me. . . . No better "than a woman of the streets." . . . I know

that a woman who places herself in the position I have with a man has no claims on him. I have paid dearly for my folly.

Waiting until there were cabs to be had, Jenny descended upon Shaw Christmas Day, knocking at his door until he got out of bed and answered. "She had come about the letters," he noted unnecessarily. Evidently he had already destroyed the bulk of Annie's letters; now he wrested the nine away from her and destroyed those too. But Jenny, endlessly forgiving of Shaw's philandering and expecting (vainly) to be forgiven her jealousy in return, could not stay angry long. "My dear love," she wrote him three days later. "Come if it is only for a minute the last of this old year. I promise I won't ask you to stay a second only to kiss me good luck & happiness."

Enough, one would think, to soften a hardened criminal. Shaw, of course, was not without regrets. "Reading over my letters before destroying them," he confessed, "rather disgusted me with the trifling of the last two years or so about women." He also wrote: "a good deal of laziness, late rising and" (perhaps in connection with his philandering) "remorse towards the end of the year."

He was interested enough in his compulsive behavior with women to explore it in a short story he wrote in the summer of 1887, titled "Don Giovanni Explains." The character of the Don had fascinated him since adolescence; Mozart's *Don Giovanni* he believed the greatest opera ever written. Shaw's Don Giovanni bears some resemblance to Mozart's, but far more to Shaw himself:

In my youth and early manhood [explains the Don], my indifference to conventional opinions, and a humorously cynical touch in conversation, gained me from censorious people the names atheist and libertine; but I was in fact no worse than a studious and rather romantic freethinker. On rare occasions, some woman would strike my young fancy; and I would worship her at a distance for a long time, never venturing to seek her acquaintance. If by accident I was thrown into her company, I was too timid, too credulous, too chivalrously respectful, to presume on what bystanders could plainly perceive to be the strongest encouragement; and in the end some more experienced cavalier would bear off the prize without a word of protest from me. At last a widow lady at whose house I sometimes visited, and of whose sentiments towards me I had not the least suspicion, grew desperate at my stupidity, and one evening threw herself into my arms and confessed her passion for me. The surprise, the flattery, my inexperience, and her pretty distress, overwhelmed me. I was incapable of the brutality of repulsing her; and indeed for nearly a month I enjoyed without scruple the pleasure she gave me, and sought her company whenever I could find nothing better to do. It was my first consummated love affair; and though for nearly two years the lady had no reason to complain of my fidelity, I found the romantic side of our intercourse, which seemed never to pall on her, tedious, unreasonable, and even forced and insincere except at rare moments, when the power of love made her beautiful, body and soul. Unfortunately, I had no sooner lost my illusions, my timidity, and my boyish curiosity about women, than I began to attract them irresistibly. My amusement at this soon changed to dismay. I became the subject of fierce jealousies: in spite of my utmost tact there was not a married friend of mine with whom I did not find myself sooner or later within an ace of a groundless duel.[20]

The passage seems at first glance to paint an exceptionally accurate self-portrait. The essence of Shaw's Don Giovanni is passivity: women want him, he does not want women: his unsolicited affairs have only embittered his existence. We remember that Jenny Patterson seduced him, that Edith Bland pursued him, that Annie Besant had tried to bind him with a marriage contract. Yet passivity is not really the word to describe Shaw's behavior. He constantly visited Brompton Square, often finding Jenny out and cooling his heels in her sitting room until she returned. He dashed off dozens if not hundreds of provocative letters to women. He boasted about his entanglements to Archer, to Webb, and to all his female victims. He faithfully recorded in his diary his day-to-day progress with women.

Puritanism, therefore, seems the better word to describe Shaw's affliction. Intellect and passion were violently split in him: he could not integrate them. He recognized this psychic chasm: "Women tend to regard love as a fusion of body, spirit and mind," he told Stephen Winsten. "It has never been so with me." What he did not add, but what is so far evident in both his writing and behavior, is the fact that he viewed "body" like the puritan: that is, he felt it disgusting, feared its vitiating powers, and subconsciously associated it with death. (Little wonder that Shaw's eventual vision of human immortality would exclude body altogether, reducing life to a vortex of pure thought.) Finding sex wrong, he thus found it incredibly fascinating; and then, hating its hold upon his imagination, deplored it the more. His basic disgust with physical passion and his divorce of it from the qualities of spirit or mind explain why his conduct is nearly irreproachable when his intellect is engaged, and often petty or even despicable when sex came into question: matters of passion did not demand better conduct from him. Thus in a letter to Annie Besant he can call Jenny Patterson—who called *him* "my dear love"— "no better than a woman of the streets." For the same reason, he could generously describe Annie Besant's benevolence and courage in later years; yet when asked whether she had ever attracted him physically, say brutally: "She had absolutely no sex appeal." So too he could look back and say, "Women have never played an important part in my life. I could always discard them more readily than my friends. . . . Women have been a ghastly nuisance"[21]—when more accurately he might have said, "Women have always played an important if not obsessional part in my life; but because I associate them with romantic nonsense and sex, I can dismiss them as insignificant." Shaw's puritanism explains too the curious unreality of many of the characters who inhabit his novels, for when he created his admirable men and women he omitted emotion and passion, fashioning unromantic, asexual creatures of pure intellect and will.

Of course, the women that Shaw became involved with during these years were intelligent, cultured, and "spiritual": Alice Lockett had been his only conventional conquest. Because his sexual passivity aroused their aggressiveness, however, Shaw formed the distorted view that women were sexually insatiable: the pursuers in the mating game. He made distinctions, of course: he saved his deepest contempt for the sexually generous Jenny Patterson, thinking of her only, she complained, "as a sucking baby does of its Mar when it is hungry!"[22] In Annie Besant he had found a woman whose energy, productivity, sense of duty, and passion for reform rivaled his; yet she too, he found to his dismay, was romantic. Yet he paid her the tribute of attempting to halt the relationship before she was too deeply involved.

Naturally he was not quick enough. Annie Besant had swept the boards for Shaw, allowing John Robertson to go abroad and sacrificing her intellectual intimacy with Charles Bradlaugh. She wanted to become his common-law wife. It is reported that after she returned Shaw's letters and destroyed her own, her dark hair suddenly turned gray, and she thought of suicide.

CHAPTER FOUR

1887-1889

Upon the bankruptcy of their landlord, Shaw and his mother had been forced to clear out of Osnaburgh Street 4 March 1887. They moved east to Fitzroy Square off the Tottenham Court Road, where they took the second and third floors. Shaw turned a second-floor room overlooking the square into a little studio for himself, a room that rapidly filled with a litter of books, letters, papers, manuscripts, stationery, duet books, pens, inkstands, blotters, proof sheets, stray apples, and empty cocoa cups.

There had been changes in the family circle. On 25 November 1886 Lucy had brought a young man named Harry Butterfield to visit her mother with the express purpose of announcing that she was engaged—not to Harry, but to his brother Charles, a fellow actor whom she had met on tour.

Then five days later Lucy brought news that Vandeleur Lee was dead. The announcement apparently created little sensation. Mrs. Shaw had rejected the man who in Dublin had helped her to lead a meaningful life apart from her husband: not only had he finally resorted to making money by letting out his rooms for "entertainments," but had made himself obnoxious in latter years by dangling after Lucy. Shaw, however, had kept up contact with Lee as late as August 1886. Now he went around to Lee's place in Park Lane to verify the news, and was told that Lee had been found dead of apparent heart disease on the morning of the twenty-ninth. Shaw reported his findings to his mother, and also to Annie Besant, who told him that she too had heart disease. Although Shaw recorded the fact soberly in his diary, Annie must have been speaking metaphorically, for nothing more was heard of her affliction. The Shaws ignored Vandeleur Lee's funeral.

A month later Lucy was having the kind of success she had long sought. *Dorothy*, Alfred Cellier's incredibly popular comedy opera, opened at the Prince of Wales Theatre 20 December with Marie Tempest as Dorothy and Miss Carr-Shaw playing Phyllis Tuppitt. Shaw was not on hand for his sister's opening night: a Fabian meeting evidently had the stronger claim. Given the Shaw family's penchant for ignoring ceremonious occasions, Lucy perhaps did not expect him to come. She was tough and elastic and apparently did not bear a grudge; in fact, she continued to attend her brother's lectures on Sunday, the only day she had off from work. When *Dorothy* went on tour in March 1887, Lucy was promoted to lead role, exciting critics to call her "a fascinating 'Dorothy,' full of innocent frolic and fun" and "a consummate success." Shaw finally got around to seeing the production in August when he showed up at a London dress rehearsal preparatory to the cast's second autumn tour. He was suffering from one of his rather frequent colds, which the chill, drafty theatre did nothing to improve; his opinion of Lucy's performance is unrecorded. Two years later, however, hearing that *Dorothy* was still alive and well and playing in Greenwich, Shaw and Archer, drawn by morbid curiosity and journalistic opportunity, traveled out to see it. From a precarious perch in the crowded balcony, Shaw observed "the condition to which 788 nights of Dorothying" had reduced H. J. Leslie's unfortunate "No. 1 Company":

As might have been expected, a settled weariness of life, an utter perfunctoriness, an unfathomable inanity pervaded the very souls of "No. I." The tenor, originally, I have no doubt, a fine young man, but now cherubically adipose, was evidently counting the days until death should release him from the part of Wilder. . . . The baritone had been affected the other way: he was thin and worn; and his clothes had lost their lustre. . . . the gentleman who understood [the comic part] addressed a comic lady called Priscilla as Sarsaparilla during his interludes . . . with a delight in the rare aroma of the joke, and in the roars of laughter it elicited, which will probably never pall. But anything that he himself escaped in the way of tedium was added tenfold to his unlucky colleagues, who sat out his buffooneries with an expression of deadly malignity. I trust the gentleman may die in his bed; but he would be unwise to build too much on doing so. . . . The ladies fared best. The female of the human species has not yet developed a conscience: she will apparently spend her life in artistic self-murder by induced Dorothitis without a pang of remorse, provided she be praised and paid regularly. . . . The chorus, too, seemed happy; but that was obviously because they did not know any better. . . .

The cherubically adipose tenor was, unfortunately, Charles Butterfield; the conscienceless female engaged in artistic self-murder, Lucy. Shaw, however, was comparatively generous with his sister, going on to write in his *Star* column:

Dorothy herself, a beauteous young lady of distinguished mien, with an immense variety of accents ranging from the finest Tunbridge Wells English (for genteel comedy) to the broadest Irish (for repartee and low comedy), sang without the slightest effort and without the slightest point, and was all the more desperately vapid because she suggested artistic gifts wasting in complaisant abeyance.[1]

After two acts Shaw roused Archer, who had the unfortunate, or perhaps fortunate, habit for a dramatic critic of sleeping through most of a production, and they fled.

Lucy laughed when she read Shaw's strictures in the *Star*, and called his attack "a typically fraternal—Irish fraternal—act."[2] Perhaps she saw the truth: that Shaw's witty stab was aimed not so much at the performers as at the institution of the old-fashioned stock company, "a criminal waste of young lives and young talents." As usual Shaw's review intended reform, in this case the establishment of a sane repertory system with at least a half-dozen works and a revolving cast. And yet Lucy should not have laughed. Shaw was right: she was still an amateur. Singing came easily for her. She learned and sang her parts with little effort, refusing to struggle for perfection, relying on her looks and charm and the adequacy of her voice. As a result, her reviews were usually— adequate. "Able and captivating," said the critics, "looks charming and sings in fine style." But they never raved, and Lucy never achieved a success of the first rank. Shaw, who had to fight a disposition to laziness in himself with alarm clocks and diary resolutions, saw Lucy's natural talent as her bane. Things had always come easily for her, while he had been forced to whet his skills against the hard stone of rejection. Shaw's review was not kind and brotherly, only true.

At this 789th performance of *Dorothy*, Lucy and Charles Butterfield did not even have the charm of courtship to stimulate them: they had been married 17 December 1887 at the Parish Church of St. John, Fitzroy Square. With typical Shaw *esprit du corps*, neither brother nor mother had attended the Saturday ceremony. Shaw had actually helped prepare refreshments at home for the small wedding party; then he "went off to dine at the Wheatsheaf as usual and did not get to the church until the ceremony [was] way over." Of course, Shaw was notoriously absentminded, arriving when meetings were rising to adjourn, missing trains, turning up on a Friday instead of a Monday, forgetting appointments altogether. Yet this absence in one year from Lee's funeral, Lucy's debut in *Dorothy*, and her wedding could hardly be accidental. Rather, Shaw the rebel detested sentimental convention, and Shaw the idealist demonstrated this contempt no matter whose feelings were involved. This time, according to one friend of Lucy's at any rate, Shaw's absence "made a crack in his sister's heart."[3]

Shaw's own career during these early years at 29 Fitzroy Square accelerated rapidly. Four of his five novels had now appeared in print and, although they attracted few readers, they had elicited both irritation and admiration. Robert Louis Stevenson's reaction became the most famous. "I have read your friend's work with singular relish," he wrote Archer, who had sent him *Cashel*. ". . . As a whole, it is (of course) a fever dream of the most feverish. . . . It is all mad, mad and deliciously delightful . . . . and I believe in his heart he thinks he is laboring in a quarry of solid granite realism."[4] He was becoming something of a celebrity. His reputation as a verbal pugilist grew: in 1888 the drama critic A. B. Walkley was begging him as "the great Impolite Letter Writer of the day" to contribute something to his new theatrical column.[5] In 1886 Archer had expressed his belief that Shaw was the best music critic in London. In March 1889 Shaw launched in the *Star* under the pseudonym "Corno di Bassetto" a weekly series of critiques that would prove some of the most brilliant music criticism ever written. The fact that these articles were scribbled in trains, under lampposts, on park benches, or between the acts of the opera he was reviewing only seemed to add to their vitality. And always, because the world of art and music (like the world of romance) threatened to degenerate into a mere "fools' paradise," he vigorously pursued the Real: his activities on the platform, on street corners, and in meetings for socialism.

Financially too Shaw had at last begun to prosper. Entries of money borrowed from and repaid to his mother disappear from his journal. Journalism paid him £150 in 1888, £197 in 1889, £252 in 1890, £310 in 1893.[6] Since, as he himself pointed out, a clerk with a family and appearances to keep up could scrape by on fifteen shillings a week (£39 a year), Shaw clearly could have left Fitzroy Square now had the relationship with his mother been an uncomfortable one.[7] But apparently Shaw was quite content to share quarters with the Mar. They spent evenings playing Mozart and Haydn symphonies together on the new piano they got on the hire system, or singing *Lucrezia Borgia* and Gounod's *Messe Solennelle*, or playing cards with Georgie Shaw. Lucinda Shaw often accompanied him to the concert or opera, or used his complimentary press tickets. Henry Salt, a former Eton master, writer, social drop-out, vegetarian, and new friend of Shaw's in 1888, met Mrs. Shaw at Fitzroy Square and reported that "Mrs. Shaw was a charming old lady, full of vivacity and wit; and it was evident that G. B. S. in spite of the levity of his talk, was very fond of her."⁸ But let us not conjure up too rosy a picture of domestic bliss. When Shaw's socialist friend James Leigh Joynes announced to her that her son was undoubtedly a great genius, she dismissed the notion. "Great geniuses grow on every bush in Ireland!" she scoffed.

Although diverted now into music criticism, Shaw still slowly advanced square by square toward a confrontation with his destiny, drama. In 1880, in response to John Morley's request for an article, Shaw had sent him a review of Henry Irving's Lyceum production of *The Merchant of Venice:* "a glance into it will give you an idea of what . . . I can do as a dramatic critic." Two years later he wrote two acts around Archer's *Rheingold* plot, but laid it aside. He had been caught up in the enthusiasm that swept Eleanor Marx's circle at the appearance of an English translation of Ibsen's *A Doll's House,* although when pressed into a play reading at the Marx-Aveling lodgings 15 January 1886 (Eleanor playing Nora, Aveling Torvald Helmer, and May Morris Kristine Linden), Shaw declared that he impersonated Nils Krogstad "with a very vague notion of what it was all about."⁹ He was more certain about the current state of the English stage: "The safe and usual course in theatres," he complained in *Our Corner* for January 1886, "is to present the public with nothing above the mental capacity of children, although the incidents may be beyond childish experience." Chief among offenders was the Lyceum, where the subtle and sardonic Henry Irving created virtuoso roles in elaborately upholstered productions of mutilated classics, and where leading lady Ellen Terry's costumes were often far more impressive than her lines. Perhaps it was the contrast between the rioting of the unemployed in the West End 8 February 1886 and the lavish archaism of Irving's *Faust* the same day that made Shaw find the performance "very dull, except for the stage effects":¹⁰ in the swirling tides of economic depression, unemployment, and socialist agitation, the palatial Lyceum seemed to Shaw to stand isolated and dreaming of the past. But the Lyceum was not the only culprit. On what London stage could one be confronted by the burning social issues of the day? On none.

Then in the autumn of 1887 (prompted, perhaps, by Lucy's success in *Dorothy* which he had witnessed in August), Shaw dug out the two acts of dialogue he had written around Archer's *Rheingold* plot, transcribed the shorthand, left it at Archer's house in John Street, and sent after it an apparently confident letter:

> The central notion is quite perfect; but the hallucinations with which you surrounded it are absent: you will have to put them in yourself. . . .
> You will perceive that my genius has brought the romantic notion which possessed you, into vivid contact with real life.
> I should prefer the St Jas's Theatre [continued Shaw bravely, citing the

star performers of the day], with Mrs Kendal as Blanche, Hare as Sartorius, Mackintosh as Lickcheese, Arthur Cecil as Cokane, and Kendal as Trench. Or Ellen Terry as Blanche, Wilson Barrett as Sartorius, George Barrett as Lickcheese, Irving as Cokane, and Gardiner as Trench. Harry Nicholls or Edward Terry might understudy Cokane; and Alma Murray might in extremity be allowed to play Blanche. What is your opinion? I think, by the bye, that the title Rheingold ought to be saved for a romantic play. This is realism.[11]

Two days later Shaw called on Archer after tea and read him the manuscript. Archer did not capitulate in the face of Shaw's dramatic genius: he resented Shaw's throwing his well-made plot to the winds, and found the dialogue inartistic and undramatic. "A long argument ensued," Shaw recorded in his diary, "Archer having received it with great contempt."

Archer's scorn daunted Shaw. Writing to the actress Alma Murray a few months later to ask her to lecture on acting to the Bedford Debating Society of which he was a member, Shaw appeared humbled:

I wish I could write you a real play myself; but unfortunately I have not the faculty. I once wrote two acts of a splendid play, and read them to an eminent dramatic critic. He laughed the first to scorn, and went asleep in the middle of the second; so I made him a present of the MS (to his intense indignation) and set to work to destroy the society that makes bad plays possible. What a career you will have when that work is completed![12]

Alma Murray declined to lecture, and finally on a "horribly cold and cheerless" day in February 1889 when he was "out of spirits," Shaw himself delivered a lecture to the Church and Stage Guild on "Acting, By One Who Does Not Believe in It." He vigorously defended the actor against the critics' charge that he is a fraud—"a fellow that fights without courage, dares without danger, is eloquent without ideas, commands without power, suffers without self-denial, loves without passion," claiming that acting is metaphysical self-realization, not shamming, and therefore Real. He poured scorn instead upon dramatic criticism, labeling it "the quintessence of art criticism, which is itself the essence of human folly and ignorance," and lashing out at artistic dilettantes who keep up "a Fools' Paradise in order to save themselves the trouble of making the real world any better." He, Shaw, had not run away from social duty, but had vigorously pursued the Real, first through attempting self-realization in art and then through incessant lecturing on socialism. The speech (so Shaw reported) drew a volley of questions from the socialist contingent—Edith and Hubert Bland, Stewart Headlam, Belfort Bax, and May Morris, from dramatic critic William Archer, whom Shaw had obviously been baiting, and from dramatist Oscar Wilde. Alma Murray, to whom he sent the speech, admired it but could not wholly agree with his views.[13]

Shaw was "out of spirits" much of the early part of 1889: nervous, depressed, and in bad health with fever, sweating, and sore throat. He eventually sought relief in a trip to the Continent with Sidney Webb. They left 17 April by train from Liverpool Street Station (intensely familiar to Shaw) and arrived in Antwerp the morning of the eighteenth. "My worst forebodings have been realized," Shaw wrote Archer glumly from the Hôtel de Vienne, Brussels. "I have seen nothing that I was not already tired of except the Musée Plantin at Antwerp, which nobody seems to care about, and which is worth a dozen such whitened dogholes as the Cathedral. . . . The weather has been magnificent; but Nature conspires with you in vain to palm off the Continent on me as a success."[14] Yet on the twenty-first in Amsterdam, Shaw saw something he was not already tired of: a production of Ibsen's *A Doll's House* in Dutch which he called "very successful."

Back in London he still felt very ill, his nerves "pretty much on the stretch"; he set about curing "a knocked-up throat" by diligently practicing scales and singing in the morning. But an event was on the horizon that would rouse his spirits; would indeed influence the course of his career, turning him into one of England's foremost champions of Ibsen, and spurring him to enter the lists as a dramatist at last. That event was the first London stage production of *A Doll's House*.[15]

In 1880, except to a handful of people, Ibsen was unknown in England. That year William Archer, who had translated *The Pillars of Society* in 1877, and vainly tried to interest people in the Norwegian dramatist, staged a single morning performance 15 December at the Gaiety Theatre. Although *Pillars of Society* impressed the small audience and won an enthusiastic notice from the *Athenaeum*, the morning of the sixteenth saw Ibsen no better known in London than had the evening of the fourteenth. In 1888, however, Walter Scott brought out a volume of three Ibsen plays: Archer's revised translation of *Pillars of Society*, Archer's revision of Henrietta Frances Lord's translation of *Ghosts*, and Eleanor Marx Aveling's translation of *An Enemy of the People*. This volume, prefaced by editor Havelock Ellis's illuminating commentary, scored an immediate success: Ibsen had "arrived" in England. A young and obscure pair of married actors, Janet Achurch and Charles Charrington, read the plays with mounting excitement. Ibsen, they discovered, was their kind of playwright. They were determined to produce him, only arguing over which would be the better play, *Ghosts* or *A Doll's House*. They sought Archer's advice: he promised to help them if they did *A Doll's House*. Archer then sat down to translate the play for them, but with only pessimism for the production's success. Ibsen on the English stage, he believed, was impossible. English playgoers would not tolerate didacticism for their entertainment: certainly they would not stand for Ibsen's morality—or immorality, as they were bound to call it. To succeed in England, Archer was convinced, Ibsen had to be trivialized—and he did not intend to trivialize *A Doll's House*.

The penniless Charringtons had scraped together enough money to run the play for a week. Janet Achurch would, of course, play Nora; Charrington undertook the funereal Dr. Rank; Herbert Waring was engaged for Torvald Helmer. Waring read the play through the first time with effort, finding no interest in "the frivolous and mendacious heroine," "the commonplace and pragmatical husband," and particularly disliking "the morbidly amorous and hereditarily afflicted" Dr. Rank. He found the dialogue "bald and trivial," and had already guessed the usual happy ending when he came to the final conversation between Nora and Helmer. The reversal electrified him. "Stimulated by a new hope," said Waring, "I read the play through again from beginning to end, and I can honestly say that never before or since have I experienced so much pleasurable excitement . . . . The uninteresting puppets became endowed with an intense actuality; the dialogue which I had previously thought so dull and unimaginative became the cogent and facile medium for the expression of individual and diverse character. Every word of the terse sentences, seemed to have a value of its own, and to suggest some subtle nuance of feeling. . . . Nora and Rank and Helmer were living and breathing entities."[16]

The Charringtons could afford only the Novelty Theatre in Great Queen Street. "Who does not know the forlorn and furtive enterprises undertaken at 'unlucky' theatres, with afternoon sunlight coming in through the side windows, at which Ibsen's masterpieces have been exposed to the adoration of the few and the laughter of the many," the theatre critic of *The Academy* remembered in March 1901. "These must remain among the bitterest memories of all who care for dramatic art . . . ." The dingy theatre, the dubiousness of the enterprise intimidated the cast: "The play was rehearsed at the forlorn Novelty Theatre in a spirit of doubt, with frequent lapses into despondency," Waring recalled. The keen enthusiasm of the Charringtons failed to ignite the players. They awaited opening night with dread. Would they "ever get safely to the end of the second act, or would the audience rise in its wrath at the terribly dangerous conversation between Nora and Rank, and denounce them as shameless interpreters of a wantonly pornographic dramatist"?

On the wet evening of 7 June 1889, Shaw, his mother, and Archer took their places with the rest of the rather dingy audience at the Novelty, few of whom must have realized, as the young American actress Elizabeth Robins enthusiastically put it, that they were "on the threshold of an event that was to change lives and literature." Shortly after eight-thirty the curtains parted on "a room, comfortably and tastefully, but not expensively furnished." Presently the outer door of the flat is heard to open, then Nora Helmer enters in a homemade fur cap and slightly shabby clothes, humming gaily, her arms filled with Christmas packages which she deposits on a table. Beckoning the porter to carry in the Christmas tree, she tips him lavishly, then dismisses him, and taking from her pocket a bag of macaroons, furtively but pleasurably nibbles one, crossing to the door of her husband's study, listening and then beginning to hum again. "Is that my lark twittering there?" calls Helmer from his room. "Yes, it is," cries Nora, hovering with childish delight over her parcels.

To Elizabeth Robins, every person in the cast seemed heaven-appointed for their roles, but particularly Janet Achurch. "I never knew before or since," she said, "anybody strike so surely the note of gaiety and homeliness as Janet Achurch did in that first scene. You saw her biting into one of the forbidden macaroons, white teeth flashing, blue eyes full of roguery, her entire *Wesen* inviting you to share that confidence in life that was so near shipwreck. . . . the famous lines . . . for all time they should be said just as they were first said, and by just that person."[17] To Archer's utter horror, one famous line did not get spoken that opening night. "I feel it my painful duty to record that in the first performance of 'A Doll's House' an unfortunate failure of memory caused me to omit the line, 'No man sacrifices his honour, even for one he loves,'" recalled Herbert Waring, "thereby precluding Nora's immortal reply, 'Millions of women have done so.' For this momentary lapse, the accomplished and erudite [Archer] has, I firmly believe, never quite forgiven me."[18]

After Nora had made her astounding exit from Torvald's life and the reverberation of a heavy door closing had died away, the audience did not rise in outrage, but greeted the cast with quite normal first-night enthusiasm. Shaw had seen Janet Achurch act before in the summer of 1888 as Hester Prynne in Edward Aveling's dramatization of *The Scarlet Letter*, a production whose brooding power had deeply impressed him. He walked out of the Novelty that night conscious that he had seen a greater performance, and that he had taken part in an epoch-making event, the production of a play that "gave Victorian domestic morality its death-blow."[19] As for Mrs. Shaw, she had looked the tawny-haired actress over intently and announced with the conviction possible to one who has slammed her own door: "That one is a *divil*."

This first performance of unadulterated Ibsen in London raised a storm of critical controversy that focused less on the play's artistic merits than on the burning moral question: is a woman who can leave husband and children a monster or a heroine? Anti-Ibsenites thundered abuse, Ibsenites parried. Clement Scott, dean of London critics and a former progressive back in the days when Robertsonian cup and saucer comedy seemed a realistic antidote to melodrama, had in recent years been stranded by the shifting tide of drama on a conservative shore. Now he launched into abusing Nora with vigor: "She is a wife no longer; the atmosphere is hideous, for he is a 'strange man.' Her husband appeals to her, but in vain. He reminds her of her duty; she cannot recognize it. . . . He recalls to her the innocent children; she has *herself* to look after now! It is all self, self, self! This is the ideal woman of the new creed . . . . a mass of aggregate conceit and self sufficiency, who leaves her home and deserts her friendless children because she has *herself* to look after. . . . Why should the men have it all their own way, and why should women be bored with the love of their children when they have themselves to study?" In the same 1 July issue of *Theatre* R. H. Hervey countered: "That many women are dissatisfied with their social position, and that more become so every day, is an undoubted fact; and of their dissatisfaction Ibsen has made himself the mouthpiece"; but such temperate comment could not divert the outrage of the anti-Ibsenites. Critics suddenly found themselves sharply divided into the Old and the New; but while the Old spoke for the majority, the New spoke for that small band of progressives who ultimately are the voices that matter.

The next month for Shaw was dominated by *A Doll's House* and by the twenty-five-year-old actress who overnight had made Nora a symbol of the new woman. Immediately after the performance he went off to the *Manchester Guardian* offices to write the notice for that paper in place of Archer, who, as translator, did not feel he could review himself. The next day Shaw was "dead beat"—both from reaction to the play and from staying up until three in the morning dashing out his own review article for the *World*. He found even writing two letters a failure and only picked up when after dinner he called on Archer, found him in bed with his clothes on, also recovering, and sat down with him to talk over the *Doll's House* "for a long time." On 11 June, he did not wake till twelve, found his throat still bad, practiced scales in an attempt to cure it, and began a reply to Robert Buchanan's attack on Ibsen in the *Pall Mall Gazette*.

That evening Archer, Shaw, and several others went again to *A Doll's House;* this time Shaw sat in the fourth row of the pit. The audience still may have been dingy, as Elizabeth Robins noted, but many of Shaw's socialist friends were there: Charlotte Wilson, Edith Bland, May Morris, Henry Sparling, and the Russian nihilist Sergius Stepniak. Shaw viewed the performance this time with a cooler eye and "noticed a good many shortcomings tonight that escaped me before & that ought to be remedied somehow." The situation in the second act, for example—Nora's idea that Helmer will take the forgery on himself—was not clear; moreover, several lines were lost over the footlights, causing him to sympathize with a fellow pit-ite who impatiently cried, "Speak up!" The company in general, Shaw thought, was slackening off: "They are all relapsing into their ordinary stage tricks now that they are at their ease & the strain of the first night off," he complained to Archer. "Miss A actually bowed to the applause on her entrance, a proceeding which so ruined the illusion—she was the only one who did it—that I have resorted to the 'last device of a coward,' an anonymous letter, begging her not to do it again. If she shews it to you—mum!"[20]

Three days later on 14 June, Shaw went down to the Novelty for a third time, intending to see *A Doll's House* again, but changed his mind and went to the Gaiety instead, where he saw Coquelin in *Les Surprises de Divorce*. On the sixteenth, however, Shaw let a sore throat and generally run-down condition keep him from his regular Sunday speaking engagements for the first time in years; he went instead to a celebratory dinner with the *Doll's House* cast in the upstairs saloon of the Novelty Theatre. Coincidentally he sat next to Janet Achurch at dinner. The fact that she smoked a great deal and carelessly emptied her wine glass as often as it was filled did not deter him; on the contrary, he declared at once that he loved her.[21]

If Shaw allowed Janet to get a word in edgewise, he may have learned that she was from Manchester, where her grandparents had once been managers of the Theatre Royal, that she was connected on her father's side to the great Sarah Siddons, and that she made her stage debut with Geneviève Ward's company at the Olympic when she was nineteen. Since then she'd toured with F. R. Benson's company in 1885, playing Lady Macbeth, Desdemona, and Ophelia when she was scarcely twenty-one, played melodrama at the Adelphi, and done well with Herbert Beerbohm Tree at the Haymarket. But *A Doll's House* was her and Charlie's first real success. They'd had to scrape and beg to get enough money for a few performances; their own household furnishings had provided most of the props. In fact, they'd been forced to sign for a joint engagement to tour the Antipodes for two years at £25 a week, just so they could mortgage that salary for this production. And now the play was going so well and bringing such acclaim for their acting—if only they could get out of going to Australia, but their managers were saying absolutely no. And this was confidential, but did he know that Henry Irving himself had contributed £100 to the enterprise? Of course, she hadn't actually mentioned Ibsen when she'd asked him for the money; she'd told him that she wanted the Novelty for *Clever Alice*. But then after the first-night success, she'd asked him to come and see the play, and the great Irving had actually appeared, although she had no idea what he'd thought about it.[22]

Shaw was well aware of London's foremost actor-manager's conservatism in choosing plays for the Lyceum, and could have guessed Irving's opinion of Ibsen. "If that's the sort of thing she wants to play," Irving had said coldly, "she'd better play it somewhere else."[23] Neither Shaw nor Janet, however, had any way of knowing that it was only through Ellen Terry's urging that Irving had been persuaded to lend the virtually unknown Charringtons a hundred pounds for their experiment. A pity, for Ellen's credibility, that they would never get around to paying the money back.[24]

Shaw went home after the dinner full of Ibsen and the New Woman and especially of Janet Achurch. She had fascinated him, although his diary entry—"Interesting young woman"—was laconic. The next day he sent her *Cashel Byron's Profession* ("supposed to be my classic—my masterpiece—my one complete work of art"), *An Unsocial Socialist*, and his lecture on acting, which, he told her, had been "received with inexpressible indignation" by all the actors present (there are none on record). Then he sat up until 2 A.M. writing her a letter. Sunday after Sunday he had lectured, he explained, getting old and hackneyed at the job, until yesterday—"and then imagine the effect of being suddenly magnetized, irradiated, transported, fired, rejuvenated, bewitched by a wild and glorious young woman who, fortified against all reprisals, by a happy prior attachment, simply amuses herself by ruthless and careless manslaughter. Under such circumstances the wisest man presents a miserable spectacle of infatuation; and I therefore plead for an indulgent construction of my motives and character. In short, though I shall always be happy to talk any quantity of insincere nonsense to amuse you, yet I, too, have histrionic powers, and can play the serious man on occasion, if no better actor is to be had."[25]

Shaw's Achurch fever did not abate in the following weeks. On Thursday, 20 June, he went to the play for the fourth time, sitting in Frances Archer's box with her and annoying her unspeakably by rattling on and on about his new infatuation. That very day he had received a letter from Janet, and though wanting to answer immediately, he was afraid of writing "extravagantly," so he slept on it. The next day he "spent all the forenoon writing to Janet," but sleep had hardly cooled his ardor:

> The world has vanished: the gardens of heaven surround me. I thought I was old—that youth was gone—that I should never be in love again in the starry way of the days before the great Disillusion; and lo! it is all back again, with the added wisdom to know my own happiness. I desire nothing: I hope for nothing: I covet nothing: I possess, enjoy, exult: the coward rejoices and is brave: the egotist loves and is not jealous. Come: set me some hard, squalid, sordid drudgery—twenty years of it to gain an inch of ground. Away with you to Australia—for ever, if you will. See

whether that prospect will dash me one jot! I have drunk the elixir of life —twice—a quarter to nine and a quarter past eleven; and now Time is vanquished. Change, fade, become a mere actress, spoil, wreck yourself, lose yourself, forget yourself: I shall still possess you in your first perfection. I have enjoyed: now let me work for the rest of my life.

All this by kind permission of Charles Charrington Esquire, the burden bearer and harvest reaper: lesser than Macbeth, & greater: not so happy, yet much happier.

She had invited him to call; she must let him know when she planned to be out, so that if he came he might not arrive too late "and be driven to walk straight down to the bridge and over the parapet." He concluded with a sudden sincere tribute to her acting powers, while denying their legitimacy: "The worst of this adulation is that it is all true: I never saw such an impersonation in my life, though I utterly refuse to give you the smallest credit for it. Avaunt sorceress! Charrington should really interfere."[26]

On Sunday Archer called for him in the morning and the two of them walked down to the *Manchester Guardian* offices and then along the Embankment to Blackfriars, talking about Ibsen and "about some unlucky offense I had given Mrs. Archer by going on about Miss Achurch." The incident only further convinced Shaw that in marrying, Archer had sacrificed his freedom and career as a playwright to the whims of a conventional woman; it would continue to rankle with him.[27] The next day, 24 June, he paid his first call on the Charringtons. His appointment was for four o'clock; after dinner he went to St. James's Park and sat on a bench correcting proofs of the *Fabian Essays*[28] until it was time for him to put in an appearance.

He found them at 10 Oakley Street, one of a row of modest look-alike dwellings in Chelsea between the King's Road and Cheyne Walk. Details of the visit are unrecorded. Shaw may have heard that Janet was married once before, briefly, to a young playwright named St. Aubyn Miller, and that Charles Charrington was really Charles Martin, who, but for a sudden and shocking passion for the stage, would have followed his respectable family's footsteps to the bar. He may have heard how the Charringtons had met when Janet was playing the Fairy Queen in the pantomime, and how they had gone on tour together playing Wilkie Collins' *New Magdalen,* and "what a treat" Janet had been in the mad scene in *Lady Audley's Secret.* He may have heard that Constance Benson admired Janet's brain power and beautiful blue eyes and her performance as Lady Macbeth; he probably did not hear that F. R. Benson's wife also found Janet a very trying roommate on tour for her self-centeredness and constant recitals of the sorrows and difficulties of her life. Certainly he heard that although they had offered Williamson, Garner, and Musgrove anything in reason if they would let them stay and realize the remarkable success of *A Doll's House*, the firm had refused to let them off, and now they were doomed to leave England the first week in July. The foothold they had secured in London would be lost: others would certainly capitalize on the new Ibsen craze in their absence, and in two years they would be forgotten.[29] Could anything be more frustrating? Nothing could, although, as Shaw would discover, it was a typical Charrington predicament.

Shaw felt quickly at ease with this couple: Charrington, handsome with light brown center-parted hair and a fine jaw; a quiet, rather scholarly man, very keen about the new drama and reforming the theatre, but terribly at sea about money matters and actually rejoicing that they had only lost £77 on *A Doll's House* instead of the hundreds he'd anticipated. And Janet herself, with her wild honey-colored hair and free laugh and warm throaty voice laced with just a trace of Lancashire and the lovely modeling of the brow above her deep-set blue eyes. Shaw loved a triangle, and here was one after his own heart: the husband adoring of his wife and carelessly generous with the amount of adoration he would tolerate from others; the wife gloriously unconventional, but fortified against his lovemaking by "a happy prior attachment."

The next day Shaw "clean forgot the Fabian Executive" for the second time in a row. Two days later on 27 June, Annie Besant telegraphed to say that she had tickets to spare for *A Doll's House*, and he dropped by for a moment to collect them. Shaw took Jenny Patterson that Thursday evening—his fifth visit to the Novelty; but the performance was a disappointment: "It was badly played," said Shaw; "they all seemed out of sorts, and did not catch the right pitch." Shaw went to Brompton Square with Jenny after the play. No doubt she was forced to hear a great deal about Janet Achurch.

If the cast had been out of sorts, certainly there was good reason: they were now forced to cut short an enterprise that had brought both critical acclaim and the prospect of mining the whole Ibsen lode: at this moment Ibsen in England belonged to Janet Achurch, Charles Charrington, and William Archer. For Janet Achurch the sacrifice was particularly severe. The critics had been unanimous in praise of the acting, but her Nora had been far and away the sensation of the performance. "The character presented enormous difficulties," praised R. H. Hervey in *Theatre*, "all of which she triumphantly overcame. Throughout she played with the utmost intelligence, subtlety, intensity, and truth." The *Pall Mall Gazette* called her performance "a splendid triumph"; another critic "so remarkable as to render it a subject of regret that the actress is leaving England for Australia." The exacting Archer noted that no actress for years had made such a success.[30] Shaw himself would pronounce Janet Achurch the "only tragic actress of genius we now possess." And now in leaving England she was forced to throw away everything that she had just gained.

On 29 June, Shaw began to map out a play inspired by the "Achurch-Archer incident." *The Cassone* was to pit B, a bachelor and friend of A, against Y, A's pretty but conventional wife, who, B feels, has clipped A's wings. Never finished, the play contained a theme that would become a favorite of Shaw's: the struggle between man the artist and woman the domesticator. About this time, Shaw went so far as to tell Archer that "Mrs. Archer was spoiling him, and that he would be a lost man unless he broke loose." In reply Archer told Shaw that he must not appear at their house while he entertained opinions so disparaging to Mrs. Archer.

On 30 June, after speaking for an hour and a half in Regent's Park for the St. Pancras Branch of the Social Democratic Federation, Shaw wrote Janet again. But the time for the Charringtons' departure for Australia was imminent. On Friday, 5 July, Shaw went to Charing Cross Station for a final leave-taking before their train pulled out at eleven. Although intending to make *A Doll's House* the main attraction of their tour, they were not even taking the complete manuscript along with them, having carelessly decided that it would not be needed. Their optimism and enthusiasm were incorrigible; and Shaw may have promised them a play from his own pen when they returned. So they said their farewells, little dreaming how disastrous their three years away from England would prove.

Janet Achurch's impact on Shaw is understandable. Although Jenny Patterson still occupied much of his time, Shaw had been caught between gallantries when Nora Helmer walked onto the stage of the Novelty that night in June and into his life—and Shaw was a man who needed gallantries as he needed air to breathe. But Janet was not just another woman: she was the New Woman incarnate, the woman who, in closing the door behind her, had struck a death-blow to the middle-class morality Shaw loathed. Nora Helmer seemed to have acted on the precept he had preached eleven years before in *My Dear Dorothea:* "Let your rule of conduct always be to do whatever is best for yourself. Be as selfish as you can"—a precept that he as artist had determinedly followed. Seven years before, he had experienced a similar shock of excitement when he discovered *Das Kapital:* Marx, he declared, had made a man of him. Ibsen excited him in much the same way: he provided him with another cause, this time the drama of social realism. Janet Achurch in her person, therefore, fused for the moment in Shaw the two estranged facets of his nature: the intellectual and the romantic. He could admire her intellectually as the symbol of the new morality, and at the same time worship her as a fascinating but unavailable woman. *A Doll's House* had been for its audiences "a strangely moving success," one of those rare events that change lives. Certainly it had changed Shaw's.

CHAPTER FIVE

1890-1891

IN THE LATE 1880s Shaw attached himself to another couple when he began to visit Henry and Kate Salt at their cottage "at a hole called Tilford" deep in the Surrey countryside.[1] He pretended to hate the country with "its uneven, ankle-twisting roads, the ditches with their dogs, rank weeds and swarms of poisonous flies" and "groups of feeble-minded children torturing something." In reality, he unwound there from the hectic London pace: washing dishes, making his own bed, going for long walks, and playing with Cosy the cat. Armed with his most killing amorous weapon, a book of pianoforte duets, he thundered out the secondo to Kate's primo or, alone at the big noisy grand, played for her the *Walküre* or *Parsifal* or *Siegfried* of his newer idol Wagner, and the *Don Giovanni* of his old.[2] And again, although (or because) Kate's sexual preference was for women, Shaw thoroughly charmed her: Kate loved me, said Shaw, as far as she could love any male creature. On 14 October 1889 Shaw stayed at the Salts' until past one, "for as Mrs. Salt was very curious about my sincerity as to women I thought it best to tell her—without mentioning names—about JP."

Jenny Patterson had at the moment several rivals for Shaw's attention. "The fair and fluffy Geraldine," as May Morris called Miss Spooner, was taking singing lessons from Mrs. Shaw, as had Elinor Huddart, Alice Lockett, and Jenny herself—with strikingly similar results. A far more serious rival was Janet Achurch, who continued to cast her spell over Shaw from nine thousand miles away. Jenny did her best to vilify Janet, muttering terrible things about lovers, about debts, about champagne. Shaw greeted this slander with loud derision, yet secretly believed every word.[3]

Yet he was not to be deterred. His new interest in Ibsen kept the Charringtons very much alive, just as the Charringtons stimulated his interest in Ibsen. He was reading *The Lady from the Sea, The Wild Duck,* and *Rosmersholm.* Then in January 1890, in a valiant attempt to counter the insidious influence of Nora's exit upon the morals of England, Sir Walter Besant (Annie's brother-in-law) published a sequel in the *English Illustrated Magazine* that soberly set forth the consequences. In "The Doll's House—and After" Besant's Nora has become a wealthy and high-living novelist; her husband, however, is now a drunkard, her son a forger, and her daughter Emmy a slavey who supports the family by stitching garments from morning till night. Nora returns to town one day, but ignores her family. Emmy's one hope is a match with Krogstad's son; Krogstad, however, breaks off the match, and Emmy kills herself. Nora leaves town in a satin gown, stopping only to complain because the men bearing the body of her drowned daughter momentarily block her carriage.

Most Ibsenites gave Walter Besant's sequel the attention it deserved; it struck Shaw, however, "as being of enormous importance as a representative middle class evangelical verdict on the play." Meeting Edward Aveling that January at a bookseller's in Holborn, he promised to write him a sequel to Besant's sequel for *Time.* "Besides which," he told Charrington in a letter of 28 January, "the ball must be kept rolling on every possible pretext, so that by the time you come back, everybody who has not seen the Doll's House will feel quite out of it, especially in the provinces."[4]

In "Still After the Doll's House," Shaw shows Nora at fifty, a calm, practical woman who hears of Emmy's suicide with detachment but compassion. She turns the guilt for her daughter's death around, and pins it firmly upon Krogstad, who has sacrificed Emmy to his respectability. Yet she sympathizes with Krogstad because he has betrayed his own potential by adjusting his spirit to his wife's narrow values. "That is the worst of marriage, Krogstad," says Nora: "it always either sacrifices one of the couple to the other or ruins both. Torvald was a success as long as I remained a failure. But it is not always the woman who is sacrificed. Twenty years ago, when I walked out of the doll's house, I saw only my own side of the question. . . . I did not see that the man must walk out of the doll's house as well as the woman. . . . the dolls are not all female."[5] Shaw's Nora echoed the message of *The Cassone,* and revealed a deepening conviction that in marriage it is the female who threatens to clip the wings of the male.

"The worst of it is," he continued to Charrington, "that my sequel is declared to be beneath the level even of Besant's—to be slosh, rubbish, dull dreary Philistine stuff &c &c &c. It is 'not even comic' they say. They are all wrong: it is first rate . . . ." Eleanor Marx Aveling disliked it heartily, and began a parody called "A Doll's House Repaired" which professed to restore Ibsen's obvious first intention—Nora's re-education as a good and proper wife by being denied her husband's bed and access to her children.[6] Archer too disliked "Still After the Doll's House," begging Shaw for the sake of his reputation not to publish. But then Archer was an incorrigible pessimist, actually convincing himself that *A Doll's House* had run for three nights "amid a hail of dead cats, sixteen-a-shilling eggs, brickbats & ginger-beer bottles" and the fourth to empty seats.

In the same letter to Charrington, Shaw tantalizingly waved Ibsen under the exiled couple's noses. "Rosmersholm & the Lady from the Sea have been published here. Rosmersholm was written expressly by Providence for you & your wife. You were created & brought together for no other end than that you should play it. Others could do this bit well & that bit cleverly; but you alone can sustain the deep black flood of feeling from the first moment to the last. . . . Never read any criticism but this: it is the only one that really concerns you." He also put up an elaborate pretense of indifference to Janet ("Miss—Miss—Miss—I forget the name: the lady who played Nora to your Dr. Rank at the Novelty"), and made a point of announcing that although he had put aside a guinea for the new deluxe edition of *A Doll's House* just for the sake of Janet's photograph, he had finally pledged his sovereign to the East End dock strikers instead. The sacrifice cost him not a pang. "Women are nothing to me. This heart is a rock: they will make grindstones for diamonds out of it when I am dead." Still protesting too much, he ended: "'Cashel Byron' was reported a failure in October last. . . . I cannot do novels now: I have grown out of it. My next effort in fiction—if I ever have time to make one—will be a play. Someday I shall write a piece for you and Janet Rehan—or is it Ada Achurch?—my memory is a wreck." Having repudiated any desire for Janet's photograph, he nevertheless bought one, and on 3 July spent one shilling ninepence having it framed at the Army and Navy Stores.

Jenny Patterson's doom was sealed not by Janet Achurch, however, but by another young woman Shaw encountered among the aesthetic socialist faction. Alice Lockett had engaged his heart, Jenny his body, Annie Besant his mind, and Janet had tantalized all three before disappearing—leaving Shaw as vulnerable as he could be to a new love affair. Florence Farr Emery was twenty-nine, educated, financially independent, separated after four years of marriage from actor Edward Emery, an actress herself, and a member of the Yeats-Paget-Todhunter circle of Bedford Park, a quiet, inexpensive, tree-lined, red brick London suburb swarming with Bohemians and, unfortunately, cockroaches.[7]

Florence had already met William Butler Yeats. Yeats could not remember who first brought him to the old stable next to Kelmscott

House where the Socialist League held their Sunday evening debates; but like Shaw he was soon one of the group who stayed afterward to supper, not for the socialism (a workman there told Yeats he talked more nonsense in one evening than he had heard in his whole life), but because, having discovered Morris's spontaneity and joy, he had made him his "chief of men."[8] If Florence had not met Yeats at Kelmscott House, she was sure to meet him at the Bedford Park homes of her sister Henrietta's husband, artist Henry Paget, or at the neighboring home of Dr. John Todhunter, or perhaps at 3 Blenheim Road itself. There in the late 1880s Yeats's father and mother, brother, two sisters, and himself, all newly arrived from Dublin, had settled in the red brick house with a balcony and "a little garden shadowed by a great horse-chestnut tree."

Florence's father Dr. William Farr had been a nearly eminent Victorian, a statistician and sanitary reformer who had worked closely with Florence Nightingale, and an advocate of equal education and professional rights for women. Yet Florence had found home life with seven siblings (five survived), a mother who died when she was fifteen, and a father whose intellect gradually evaporated as he sank into senile paralysis of the brain, an experience not to be repeated. She managed to escape to college, doing well in English and French, yet coming to the conclusion that the whole purpose of a university seemed to be the sterile acquisition of factual knowledge for examinations. So she gradually gave up on Queen's College, letting attendance slide from "very regular" in 1877 to "regular" to "irregular" in 1878 when she stopped taking courses for credit before she finally drifted away in 1880. Casting her horoscope, she decided that her move had been "good."

She tried teaching without success; then gravitated toward the theatre, equipped with a melodious speaking voice, a face at once boyish and soulful, and no formal training at all. The voice and face were enough, however; and soon she was appearing as Mary Lester in minor parts at Toole's Playhouse in King William Street, where on Friday the supporting players ran through for the first time the play that they presented to the public on Saturday, at which time both public and cast got their first glimpse of the star. But Florence liked theatrical life little better than collegiate life, and showed her uncertainty by hesitating between Mary Lester and Florence Farr as stage names until she solved her dilemma by appearing as Florence at matinees and Mary in the evening. Perhaps boredom with the emancipated life made marriage with Edward Emery an attractive alternative. They were married 31 December 1884 at Chiswick during a provincial tour. But for Florence the union turned out to be four long years of increasing disillusionment. If a lover was polite and considerate, marriage was sure to blunt his manners. If love could be ecstasy, marriage might be relied upon to kill it. If sex was pleasurable at first, forced repetition soon made it loathsome. If a fiancé was terribly amusing, a husband proved the dullest dog on earth. And Edward Emery himself may have had reason to complain, for his wife could not hide her dislike of the "ungraceful gestures" of lovemaking, avoided housekeeping assiduously, intimated often that she found him weak and unexciting, retreated into herself, and when the money ran low spent days in bed to avoid hunger pangs, undoubtedly casting her horoscope and finding Edward Emery not in her stars.

They separated in 1888, a "very bad year" for Florence. Edward sailed for America, where he became a successful actor; and Florence was left to reappraise her life and to forget Edward—an apparently effortless task. She decided that since she was free she would stay that way: she would love where she chose, but remain as emotionally detached as possible. She also decided to abandon the commercial stage for the time being, and search for meaning and beauty in life.

About this time Yeats persuaded John Todhunter to write a deliberately artistic play about shepherds and shepherdesses with an eye to their own Bedford Park audience who would not mind if the characters spoke verse and avoided melodrama. The result was *A Sicilian Idyll*, a play Yeats did not rate high as poetry but very high on another account. "I made through these performances a close friend and a discovery that was to influence my life," he wrote in his *Autobiography*. "Todhunter had engaged several professional actors with a little reputation, but had given the chief woman's part to Florence Farr, who had qualities no contemporary professional practice could have increased. . . . Heron Allen and Florence Farr read poetry for their pleasure. While they were upon the stage no one else could hold an eye or an ear. Their speech was music, the poetry acquired a nobility, a passionate austerity that made it akin for certain moments to the great poetry of the world. . . . Florence Farr lived in lodgings some twenty minutes' walk away at Brook Green, and I was soon a constant caller, talking over plays that I would someday write her."[9]

Among the first-night audience at the Bedford Park Clubhouse on 5 May 1890 with Yeats, Alma Murray, Winifred Emery, Cyril Maude, Selwyn Image, and May Morris was Shaw, who arrived an hour early for the nine o'clock curtain. He was in the mood to be charmed by a new woman: the night before he had gone to Jenny's "but found her so fractious" that he had soon "shook the dust off" his feet and come away. No two Irishmen could have been more unlike: Shaw the socialist, Yeats "in all things Pre-Raphaelite"; Shaw the anti-romantic, Yeats the archromantic; Shaw the revolutionist, Yeats the mystic; Shaw energetic, brash, witty, seemingly shallow; Yeats in those years naive, moody, excitable, indolent. Yet both were struck with Florence, though they judged her performance very differently. Shaw the persuader believed in forceful athletic speech uttered with a full consciousness of meaning, and although there were moments when Florence's performance rose to his standards, sometimes her words were lost through poor projection, lack of timing, or ineffectual gesture.

Florence now began to appear more and more at the Morrises', where she was studying the art of embroidery with May. Eventually she turned up at Merton Abbey, Morris's factory across the river in Sussex on the Wandle River, where he was making aesthetic history with the weaving, dyeing, and printing of his own carpets, tapestries, textiles, and wallpapers. Here one day at a picnic in the old-fashioned garden bright with hollyhocks and sunflowers and loud with the rushing of the clear stream down to the Wandle, Florence met Shaw and, as he later reported to Janet Achurch, "astonished me by asking me would I play the Stranger in the Lady from the Sea if she succeeded in getting up a performance. She said that as I had a red beard she thought I would look the part in a pea jacket. I pleaded ineptitude and declined . . . ."[10] But he was much struck again by "the magnetic young lady" who confronted him so frankly and easily. Many years later, Shaw remembered their meeting more cynically, and on a different occasion. "She acted in an entertainment at the house on the Mall; and on this occasion I made her acquaintance, and had no difficulty in considerably improving it. She set no bounds to her relations with men whom she liked, and already had a sort of Leporello list of a dozen adventures, none of which, however, had led to anything serious."[11]

She had "something" certainly for both Shaw and Yeats. Yeats described it as "a tranquil beauty like that of Demeter's image near the British Museum reading-room door, and an incomparable sense of rhythm and a beautiful voice, the seeming natural expression of the image." But there were destructive forces in Florence, thought Yeats without understanding them, that compelled Florence to deny her natural beauty and poeticism. He deplored her irony and deprecation. "She would dress without care or calculation as if to hide her beauty and seem contemptuous of its power. If a man fell in love with her she would notice that she had seen just that movement upon the stage or had heard just that intonation and all seemed unreal. If she read out some poem in English or in French all was passion, all a traditional splendour, but she spoke of actual things with a cold wit or under the strain of paradox. . . . I formed with her an enduring friendship that was an enduring exasperation . . . ."[12]

While Yeats thus sought in Florence "traditional sanctity and loveliness," Shaw was drawn to the modern woman, the renegade who had "given home and family as much trial as seemed necessary" and rejected both. Florence's irony, her emotional detachment, her indifference to sexual attractiveness lured Shaw since they matched qualities of his own, and also promised that Florence would not make traditional romantic demands upon him. Nothing revealed Florence's divided nature more than the fact that she could be two such different persons to two such different people as Shaw and Yeats.

Florence first appears in Shaw's diary on 11 October 1890. That evening he met her by appointment at the train and took her to the first Saturday concert of the season at the Crystal Palace. Afterward Florence made it clear that she was not to be dismissed chivalrously into a cab, and Shaw went with her on the train to her lodgings at 123 Dalling Road, Ravenscourt Park, where he discovered that she had a talent for playing the piano and, of more interest, that she very much wanted to return to professional acting, particularly in Ibsen's *Lady from the Sea*. But Shaw preferred *Rosmersholm*,[18] and delivered "so powerful a discourse" on its merits that Florence presently told him that "she was resolved to create Rebecca or die." No matter that he had told the Charringtons that *Rosmersholm* had been created expressly by Providence for them, or that from her uneven performance in *Sicilian Idyll* he could hardly believe Florence to have the power to "sustain the deep black flood of feeling from the first moment to the last." Excited by his own power to influence Ibsen careers in London, and aware that a young American actress named Marion Lea wanted to do *The Lady from the Sea*, he now steered Florence toward the part of Rebecca West, a passionate, radical, opportunistic woman whom the gentle Florence, however, could have little success in portraying.

The relationship progressed rapidly. Five days later Shaw went to Jenny at Brompton Square. Striding into her sitting room angry and upset, having just interfered in an altercation outside between a young couple and a watchman evidently intent on blackmail, he found her angry and upset about another matter: Florence Farr Emery. "So the day ended unpleasantly," said Shaw in his diary. But meetings with Jenny *were* often unpleasant now. Annie Besant had been a formidable enough rival; but Florence had youth, beauty, and talent, and Jenny, at least fifty now with nothing new to offer Shaw except increasingly inventive fits of temper and tears, felt decidedly oppressed.

Shaw and Florence began to meet everywhere, either by appointment or because she began to gravitate toward places where he could be found. At piano recitals, at picture galleries, at a second Crystal Palace concert, at Paderewski's recital at St. James's Hall, at the Aerated Bread Shop at Oxford Circus, a vegetarian restaurant where Shaw could drink cocoa and she sip tea—they were constantly together. If they did not meet in town he took the underground to Dalling Road, where he stayed until he had to make a dash for the last train back. Sometimes he missed it. Although he recorded punctiliously on 4 December that he lost the last train home "through my watch being slow," a better reason was "through the pleasure of her company"; and when he missed the train in future he did not feel compelled to offer a slow watch as the excuse. On the fifteenth of November they had their "first really intimate conversation."

It is difficult to know how much Shaw's iconoclasm encouraged the cold wit in Florence that Yeats deplored or, conversely, how much Florence's unconventionality shaped Shaw's ideas about women. When he wrote in 1898 in his Preface to *Plays Unpleasant* that "nobody has yet done justice to the modern clever Englishwoman's loathing of the very word Home," he had certainly heard about this loathing from Florence Farr. In that first really intimate conversation Florence may well have confessed her hatred of domesticity, her dislike of marriage, her loathing for the mind of one dull man. She could not shock Shaw. He had already accepted these attitudes in his mother. But when he came to write that "home is the girl's prison and the woman's workhouse," he had certainly heard the complaint from Florence Farr.

On sexual matters they were also in agreement. Florence once wrote that she looked back on the episode of matrimony with "as much disgust as if she had awakened from a pigsty." Shaw had already shuddered at the incontinent sexuality of marriage in *Love Among the Artists*. Indeed in the character of Madge Brailsford, the young woman from a good middle-class Victorian home who defies her family to go on stage, he had already portrayed a woman very much like Florence. He had even foreseen her attitude toward sex. "She stood on her honor according to her own instinct," he had written of Madge and might have written of Florence, "took no gifts, tolerated no advances from men whose affections were not truly touched"; she pitied married friends who were not free to be so fastidious, reserved, and temperate as she. Wary of romantic feeling and, like Shaw, prone to separate it from sex, Florence sought to control her relations with men, rather than let them control her. Cynically sure that all men wanted the physical relation, or at least a kiss, she made a habit of grasping those more reticent adorers she could tolerate by the wrists, pulling them smartly into her arms, and commanding "Let's get it over."[14] But she seldom allowed them more. It was this kind of pragmatism that the idealistic Yeats deplored. He fell in love with Maud Gonne instead, the woman who looked like the sybil he wished Florence to play, the woman for whom Virgil's "she walks like a goddess" was meant. Besides, as he later complained rather contradictorily to Henrietta Paget, Florence would not make love with him. This sexual fastidiousness which was satisfied with only occasional encounters appealed to Shaw; the aloof man had found the aloof woman and was narcissistically fascinated with her.

The "happy evening" he records on 30 December need not, therefore, have meant an evening of sexual pleasure. There is good evidence that Florence was asexual; that her appeal to men lay in the very detachment that made them feel they could say anything to her. Then too Florence disliked women, an attitude that men often find congenial. Chiefly she appealed to men with "advanced" ideas who admired daring in a woman as long as it did not seriously threaten them. "She plays with her life like a child with a toy, but she's a good pal and a brave woman," said York Powell, a friend who was intrigued by the gypsy in Florence. For Shaw, who was always trying to break out of the iron shell of his vaunted coldness and "become as a little child again," the pal and the child in Florence would have been irresistible.

The next evening, New Year's Eve, he went to Brompton Square. Five years ago, a new lover, he had also come to the Square on New Year's Eve to watch the old year out with Jenny; that night, however, her windows had been dark, and he had lingered instead in the winter-bare park to watch the other residents spill onto their doorsteps at the sound of midnight church bells. Other years she had begged him to come: "I would like my last look for the old year to be for you & to kiss you for the dawn of the new one—just for luck's sake nothing else in the world I swear"[15]—and often he had complied. This year he perhaps came without coaxing, for Jenny was to leave on a long journey to the Near East for the rest of the winter, and he could go to say goodbye. Jenny, however, could not let him off so easily. Returning to Fitzroy Square a week later after consulting Archer about a newly announced production of *A Doll's House,* he found her waiting for him. She was leaving on the ninth. They had a "long parting talk"; but she could have been under little illusion about who would occupy his time in her absence.

Jenny would have been deeply injured had she known that Shaw had "made holiday" the day before, spending the whole morning, afternoon, and evening writing to Janet Achurch in flights of poetic reverence that she, his mere mistress, had not the slightest chance of commanding. Shaw had received Janet's photograph. He should have been delighted, he protested, except for the discovery that she had left instructions to have it sent before she left, proving that she had not thought of him since. He was strongly tempted to tear it up—

And indeed I should have done so if it had shewn me nothing of you but your eyes and mouth and hair and the other commonplaces of which your devotees rave. But the cunning Cameron had just caught your profile so as to give that noble and beautiful outline of your brow which I can never remember without imagining myself lost at sea in the night, and turning for refuge toward a distant lighthouse, which, somehow, is you. Why a man of my years and sense should thus worship at the temple of Perversity I do not know; but it is so, all the same. And it was as impossible to destroy the photograph as to throw stones at the lighthouse, wherefore it survives, framed and glazed, tossing among the billows of dusty papers on my table.

He went on to tease her with news that "The nibblings at Ibsen are becoming more and more frequent here." He told her rather heartlessly that *Rosmersholm* was hung up, "not for want of Janet (for I have some hopes of the magnetic Miss Farr, whose conceptions of life I am kindling for the purpose by every wile in the Shaw repertory) but for want of Charrington, who seems to be irreplaceable." Archer was being extraordinarily difficult—one day insisting Ibsen couldn't be played, the next day coming with suggestions for a Farr performance. "Happily for her," said Shaw (and unhappily for Janet), "she has Mephistopheles Shaw at her elbow, and manages him perfectly. . . . All the frostbound seeds in him have been germinating like mad ever since your sun shone into his soul."

As for his private life, he told her, it was not free from frustrations. Now that he had abandoned Corno di Bassetto, leaving "all the foes of musical light as dead as a pen can kill them," he wished for the sake of Ibsen that he could get a crack at dramatic criticism. He was not yet married, nor likely to be. Some lightweight champion named Martin had married the woman he loved; another young woman, the one so like Janet, had married a stockbroker. "And I am getting middle-aged and uninteresting," complained Shaw, now thirty-four. "Political drudgery has swamped my literary career altogether. Still, as all the follies of love and ambition fall off from me, my soul burns with a brighter flame; and I grow ever more impenetrably conceited."

He concluded, however, with a resolve not to yield his higher ambitions to the necessity of making his living, and with encouragement for the exiled Janet:

I want the noblest poetic beauty in sights, sounds, relations. . . . Not that I will not face the inevitable squalor as hardily as ever; but I will not be reconciled to it. Consequently, my last word tonight shall be said to you, with whom I have no ignoble or unlovely associations. But indeed I have nothing to say: it is only to look at you. And I see you quite distinctly— on the stage of the Novelty, not as Nora, but as Janet Achurch, acknowledging the demonstrations of kind friends in front at the end of the play. This is unusual; for I never think of you with such mildewy surroundings as those of the Great Queen St upholstery, but always in a vast desert, or walking on the waters of a great sea, at a great distance from me, but the only other person there besides myself. Take courage, then; for if you can cast these magic spells on a man thousands of miles away, after years—centuries—of absence, what can you not do to those only separated from you by a row of footlights, with Ibsen to help you?[16]

CHAPTER SIX

1891

HAVING PERSUADED FLORENCE to do *Rosmersholm*, Shaw then had to discourage the opposition. "They tell me you have designs on Rosmersholm," he wrote Alma Murray. "Well, Miss Florence Farr, who lately played in Todhunter's Sicilian Idyll, is going to do Rosmersholm with Waring as Rosmer; and I am the one who persuaded her thereto. . . . since Miss Achurch has 'created' Nora, and Miss Farr will 'create' Rebecca, why do you not set to at once to get up a performance of The Lady from the Sea, and 'create' Ellida?"[1]

Failure to find money for a theatre of her own, rather than Shaw, forced Alma Murray to give up her designs on *Rosmersholm;* and Florence, backed by Dr. Todhunter, leased the Vaudeville Theatre for a series of matinees to begin in February 1891. Shaw felt the weight of responsibility. One way to make Florence's venture a success was to "keep the ball rolling" for Ibsen. To this end he had written a letter to the *Pall Mall Gazette* on 8 January complaining about West End managers who would not allow their actors to play in Ibsen matinees, and on 17 February he stepped up the attack by beginning an article for the *Gazette* on *Rosmersholm* and then appearing at the Playgoers' Club where he vigorously denounced Clement Scott as "God Almighty" and stupidly hostile to Ibsen.

He began to work with Florence on her part, on 6 February going over the first few scenes and becoming so involved with either Rebecca West or Florence that he did not get to the Fabian meeting until quarter to nine. On the eleventh he went out to Dalling Road again and stayed all evening, "playing, singing, trying on Rosmersholm dresses, going over her part etc." It was perhaps the height of his love for her. He would look back to these days when he, a beggar, "came into his great fortune"; when he, "an unscrupulous egotist with a remorseless will," had been "moralized" and had his backbone "sweetly stolen away."[2] On 19 February, however, the sudden realization that Florence was no Siddons or Bernhardt—nor likely to be by curtain time—sobered them both, and they spent the evening "in a most worried frame of mind." Archer's constitutional pessimism did not help. The rehearsals had so disheartened him that Shaw was having a terrible time persuading him to show up for a performance. Finally even the dauntless Shaw began to admit that he was absolutely terrified at having thrust Florence into such an adventure. Two days before opening he was in "very low spirits"; then after dining with the dramatist Comyns Carr and friends, he cheered up so completely that he went out to Florence at nine that evening in high spirits to prophesy a victory.

The first performance of *Rosmersholm* in England took place on the afternoon of Monday, 23 February. The audience at *A Doll's House* had been a rather shabby lot. Now the critic of the *Illustrated Sporting and Dramatic News* looked over the house and decided that never before, not even at an asylum concert or hospital treat, had he seen so many pale, sad, and deformed faces. Were these theatregoers? or outpatients waiting for the doctor? As Shaw had feared, both Florence's voice and actions lacked certainty and grip but, as he later told the Charringtons, "she got through it by dint of brains and a certain fascination and dimly visible originality." The second act was a decided success, and the last act, "though it was an utter staggerer, silenced the scoffers, the curtain falling amid a curious dumfounderment." He was too flattering: Frank R. Benson as Rosmer and Florence had merely spoken their lines: this *Rosmersholm* could scarcely be called a performance.

After the play he went with Florence and another couple to Gatti's "to feed"; then he and the still excited Florence strolled about the Embankment in the fog until it was time to go to the Playgoers' Club, where he spoke, after which they went to Rule's for some supper and then he went as far as St. James's Station with her on her way home. "N.B.," he added parenthetically in his letter to Charrington, "I am in love with Miss Farr; but for Heaven's sake do not tell Mrs. Charrington. Quand on ne peut avoir ce qu'on aime, il faut aimer ce qu'on a."[3]

The press was predictably caustic; and according to Shaw, the cast crept through the performance very humbly the next afternoon and did better as a result. Critics agreed that Frank Benson as Rosmer was weak and that Florence had intelligence but lacked the force to stamp the character of Rebecca West firmly enough. Still stinging from Shaw's attack on him at the Playgoers' Club, Clement Scott lauded Florence to the skies, however; and there was a general impression that again a theatrical event of moment had taken place. All enthusiasm over Florence's acting in *A Sicilian Idyll,* Yeats felt deeply divided about her Ibsen venture. He had hated *A Doll's House.* "I resented being invited to admire dialogue so close to modern educated speech that music and style were impossible. . . . As time passed Ibsen became in my eyes the chosen author of very clever young journalists . . . ." And yet, as he admitted, he could not escape Ibsen because, although he and Ibsen did not have the same friends, they had the same enemies. Florence aggravated his ambivalent feelings, for she was his ideal poetic woman thrown away now on a playwright he was forced to accept on principle—just as he was forced to accept Shaw because they too had the same enemies. "Florence Farr," he noted grudgingly, "who had but one great gift, the most perfect poetical elocution, became prominent as an Ibsen actress and had almost a success in *Rosmersholm,* where there is symbolism and a stale odour of spilt poetry."[4] He did not thank Shaw for his part in the matter. For his part in this almost success, Todhunter lost ten pounds, Benson got about twenty guineas, and Florence "got nothing but her dresses and the kudos."

1891 would prove to be the year for Ibsen in England, with six London performances of his plays. That year J. T. Grein founded the Independent Theatre, a group numbering among its first members Thomas Hardy, George Meredith, George Moore, Henry Arthur Jones, and Arthur Wing Pinero; the I.T. gave the new drama its first organized, if financially uncertain, support. With its production of *Ghosts* at the Royalty Theatre a storm of fury broke over the heads of Grein, his supporters, his actors, all Ibsenites, and of course the absent Master. Shaw and Florence went to the opening night of *Ghosts* on 13 March and witnessed, according to Shaw, "a most terrible success." The applause was tremendous after the first act; a third of the applauders were struck dumb at the end of the second; after the third, four fifths of the house sat in awed silence. "It's *too* horrible!" cried a voice from the gallery when the nervous Grein came out to make his speech, and was immediately greeted by the sarcastic shout, "Why don't you go to the Adelphi!" Clement Scott went "stark raving mad" the next day in the *Daily Telegraph,* producing a lead article in which he called an Ibsen play "a dirty act done publicly" and, with mounting hysteria, "bestial, cynical, disgusting, poisonous, sickly, delirious, indecent, loathsome, fetid, and crapulous."[5] Most of the press followed suit, and the Royalty management intimated a distinct reluctance to let Grein have the theatre again. Of course Shaw reported all the fun to the poor Charringtons.[6]

The previous summer Shaw had read an Ibsen paper at a Fabian gathering at the St. James Restaurant, Annie Besant as president in the chair. She had suggested that he develop his Ibsen paper into something longer. Now the hysteria of the press set Shaw to work on 16 March preparing a long Ibsen essay for the press which he counted on to inflame discussion

75

just as interest would be falling off. Giving up his Easter holiday to the task, he finished exactly a month later "in great excitement."

In the brilliant[7] *Quintessence of Ibsenism* Shaw set out to explain Ibsen to the Norwegian's puzzled, angered, repulsed, or enthusiastic audience by summarizing and interpreting the plots of his plays. What emerged, however, was a vigorous attack on ideals and idealists in the course of which he set up Ibsen (and himself) as one of the realists of society—one of those rare pioneers who have the courage to throw off slavery to Duty, and live and be free and do duty to the self, for in duty to the self true selflessness resides. And here Shaw's polemic took an unusual turn, for, influenced by *A Doll's House* and *Rosmersholm*, he saw woman and her repudiation of duty as the main force in the battle of the realists against the idealists. Had not woman been the chief victim of the ideals invented by a male society? Was not every woman still enslaved to the ideal of the "Womanly Woman," that poor dupe whose soul finds its supreme satisfaction in sacrificing for a lover, husband, or child? This ideal woman is the woman who does everything that men like and nothing else. She is not an end in herself like Man, but solely a means of ministering to his needs and appetites. Most abominable of all, this self-sacrifice is forced upon her under the pretense that she enjoys it. When infrequently she dares to rise up and declare that she does not, she is immediately branded "no true woman." And yet her only salvation is to rise up, to repudiate her duty to others, and before all else embrace her duty to herself. Surely Ibsen agreed, for in play after play all his "really vivid and solar figures" were women struggling toward selfhood.

And, Shaw argued, women were not only a potentially vital force for demolishing rotten ideals, they were also anti-rationalists, and therefore a long step ahead of men, who still clung to a rationalism which had been totally discredited by the recognition that human beings live not by reason but by will. The first blow to rationalism had been dealt by the discovery that although nothing could persuade women to adopt it, their impatience of reasoning no more prevented them from arriving at the right conclusions than the masculine belief in reason saved men from arriving at the wrong ones. When woman stoops to reason, warned Shaw, the sole result is that she falls into all the errors that men are just learning to distrust. In woman's instinctive anti-rationalism and in her revolt against the ideal of duty, therefore, the hope of society lies.

The Quintessence of Ibsenism proved to illuminate Shaw more than Ibsen: his hatred of middle-class morality; his distrust of the masculine "rationality" which had created it; his sympathy for the "unwomanly woman" since he in his distaste for war, sport, whisky, cigars, competitiveness, womanizing, and hard facts was certainly an "unmanly man"; his loathing of marriage as an unnatural slave state for men and women; his view of sex as a degrading appetite which, of all tyrannies, uses woman most brutally as a means to an end. Astute female readers might object to being labeled anti-rational, of course, and might suspect that Shaw was using women chiefly as a stick with which to beat the patriarchal system; yet few could deny that the *Quintessence* was, as Shaw later claimed, a feminist document. And after all, virtually every woman Shaw had known had taught him the falsity of the feminine ideal. When he claimed that wifehood and childraising were no more natural to women than soldiering was natural to men, he had the examples of his mother, Lucy, Eleanor Marx, Edith Bland, May Morris, Annie Besant, and Janet Achurch before him. And Florence Farr. Without subtracting anything from Shaw's document, it is still possible to sense the presence of Florence behind the *Quintessence*. As a woman who had left her family, refused to do housework or bear children, divorced her husband, chose her own attachments, and pursued a career, she was Shaw's realist par excellence.

Shaw's antipathy to sex in the *Quintessence* was strong, and encouraged some critics to ignore his revolutionary statement that woman must repudiate her servitude to man, with all its economic and political implications, and smear Ibsen admirers with *ad hominem* attacks upon their sexual status. "Unwomanly" quickly came to mean not liberated, but sexually unnatural. "The sexless . . . . The unwomanly woman, the unsexed females, the whole army of unprepossessing cranks in petticoats. . . . Educated and muck-ferreting dogs. . . . Effeminate men and male women. . . . doing not only a nasty but an illegal thing"—these were your Ibsenites, and they were the scum of society: so raged the conservative press.[8] For Shaw the fighter the shrieks of outrage were wonderfully intoxicating.

Since "the really vivid and solar" parts in Ibsen's anti-idealist plays were women, it was not surprising that many Ibsen pioneers were women. Sometimes without Shaw's perception that the revolt of women on the stage signaled the revolt of women in society, intelligent actresses saw in the creation of parts like Nora, Ellida, Mrs. Alving, Rebecca, and Hedda their only chance to play challenging roles. For the same reason, no actor-manager in London would touch Ibsen. One of the more enlightened of these, Herbert Beerbohm Tree, actually read *Ghosts*, then laid it down in astonishment saying, "But this is a woman's play. There's no part for me." While providing actresses with their best roles since Shakespeare, Ibsen as a "woman's" dramatist was inevitably relegated to second-class status, just as women were second-class citizens.

One day in March Shaw was visiting Archer when two of these pioneers rang at his door. They were Americans, two young actresses named Marion Lea and Elizabeth Robins, the latter a striking woman whose black widow's weeds only enhanced her luminous beauty. Elizabeth had come to London via Norway and had felt her superiority when, at a party in the summer of 1889 after the success of *A Doll's House,* she had been able to say to the new Ibsen enthusiasts that she had known about him for nearly a year. Janet Achurch's Nora had turned the tide of Elizabeth Robins's career: after that vivid performance traditional female roles had suddenly seemed ridiculously tame. Elizabeth therefore accepted the small part of Martha Bernick in the 1889 production of *The Pillars of Society;* then began to read more Ibsen in the original. "And so, all new-born into that tonic air, I received full in my face the piercing blast from Ghosts—shrank, shuddered," she recalled. "I found it terrible and revolting. But I could not stop there."

For an actress who wanted to play Ibsen, the next step, since Beerbohm Tree had refused her challenge to play *Ghosts,* appeared to be William Archer's acquaintance. Accordingly, Elizabeth had asked him to meet her at Gatti's in June of 1890 to discuss the possibility of a production. Elizabeth arrived with her dresser in tow as chaperone to ensure that the discussion of the dangerous play would be properly conducted; but Archer—"tall and dark, looks about thirty but probably thirty-eight, with big honest eyes that win confidence and friendliness" (so she remembered him at that first meeting)—proved to be most courteous.[9] The chaperone was superfluous, and did not prevent Archer from taking a deep interest in Elizabeth Robins.

That production of *Ghosts* had not materialized. It was Marion Lea who had first seen the possibilities of *Hedda Gabler* and convinced Elizabeth that she must play Hedda. Where to find the money? Marion owned a jeweled bracelet, Elizabeth "a small treasure": with these securities they borrowed three hundred pounds. They had taken the Vaudeville Theatre for a series of matinees beginning 20 April, and had come to consult Archer about a more speakable version of Edmund Gosse's translation. Shaw was not in on this discussion for at the entrance of Elizabeth and Marion he had fled.

Of course he was at the opening three o'clock matinee of *Hedda Gabler,* which was crowded with Ibsenites, including a large Fabian contingent. That evening between the acts of *La Traviata* he did not write his opera review as usual, but a letter to Elizabeth Robins. In his inimitable style, he criticized the actors' inaudibility, articulation, tone, and her unforgivable altering of the line "Do it beautifully" to "Do it gracefully." Had she said "Do it beautifully," the line would by now be a catchword all over London, worth a thousand pounds in advertising. Yet he allowed that she could safely accept all the compliments she was bound to receive on the play and on her part. He did not complain to her as he did later to Archer that actresses wanted to play Nora, Rebecca, and Hedda "with Ibsen left out"—omitting all the jars, the discords, the unpleasantnesses, the comic touches, and playing only an idealized version. In his opinion, all the Ibsen performances of late had signally lacked moral courage.

Both actresses and actors had "shirked pretty nearly everything that could be shirked."[10]

But Elizabeth Robins had not heard the last from Shaw. On 30 April, having seen the performance again, he scribbled hastily in his notebook where he sat over cocoa in the Aerated Bread Shop in the Strand:

Thank you for the stalls: I brought my mother, and gratified myself at the same time by going to see Hedda giving Lövborg the pistol with love in her eyes—a thing which has haunted me ever since Monday week. However, no living woman shall turn my head as you have turned Archer's: I have infinite fault to find. I declare before high heaven that you are guilty in the blackest degree of playing more and more up to the conventional villainess conception of Hedda. The first Act to-day was perfect Richard III. all through; and in the third act you did not give him the pistol with love in your eyes worth a cent: I wanted my money back. I demand the following modifications of your play. . . .

Shaw listed them, paid for his cocoa, caught the underground train, and took out his notebook once more. "I still protest vehemently against 'Do it gracefully.' . . . I maintain that a woman who would alter that passage would do anything . . . ."[11] Yet she must realize that the only reason he protested at all was that the performance had been so near excellence. Judging from the way the audience had fallen upon the single anti-Ibsenite who had hissed at the end of the first act that day, she had nothing to fear from the opposition.

The press generally praised. The *Athenaeum* applauded Elizabeth and Marion, "two clever, courageous and persevering young actresses" who, "in the face of opposition scarcely short of persecution" made "a gallant fight and have enabled a large number of playgoers to judge for themselves of a work that has caused one of the keenest controversies of the day." Elizabeth's Hedda was generally commended as subtle, picturesque, convincing, and, by Archer, diabolically feline; and on 29 April Ibsen himself wrote from Munich thanking William Archer for writing to tell him that *Hedda Gabler* had "met with a unanimously favorable reception at its first appearance in London." Finally the play was transferred to the evening bill for the entire month of May, a signal mark of success for an Ibsen drama. For those critics and theatregoers who still shuddered over Ibsen—"How should men understand Hedda on the stage when they didn't understand her in the persons of their wives, their daughters, their women friends?" asked Elizabeth scornfully.[12]

It was evident that Elizabeth Robins, not Charrington, was now the name to reckon with in Ibsen drama, and that Ibsen was a playwright to be reckoned with in London. A change was coming over the theatrical world which the hysterics of the anti-Ibsen press simply confirmed, a change that of course had its impetus in the social change of the eighties. Henry Irving at the Lyceum felt it, and was baffled. His sumptuous *Macbeth* in 1889, the year of *A Doll's House*, had still been received with enthusiasm. Ellen Terry's knee-length magenta braids, her heather velvet cape trimmed with flaming griffons, her gown crocheted out of soft green silk and blue tinsel, trimmed at the edges with diamonds and rubies and—spectacularly, breathtakingly—sewn all over with hundreds of real green beetle wings which shot forth a metallic dazzle at the slightest movement of her limbs—this Lady Macbeth had been perhaps the most sensational costuming effect in theatrical history, and *Macbeth* had run for 150 nights. Yet something new was in the air. Now, during the run of *Hedda Gabler*, Irving invited rival actor-manager Beerbohm Tree to meet the Prince of Wales at one of his famous suppers in the Beefsteak Room. Replied Tree: "My wife and I will be delighted to come to you on Tuesday night—we have no deep-rooted aversion to Princes, though the etiquette towards Serene Highnesses has occasionally caused me a sleepless night. It is, however, only through stress of this kind that one emerges a man of the world."[13] Surely Tree's reply left something to be desired? The Prince of Wales and Henry Irving in the Beefsteak Room were serious matters. What was happening to reverence and manners and custom?

Meanwhile, the Charringtons, whose *Doll's House* had started it all, had fallen upon evil days. The tour had begun inauspiciously when they had to rewrite the play from Janet's memory, having forgotten to bring along a copy. Yet at first *A Doll's House* had gone successfully: not only in the capitals of Australia and New Zealand, but in the bush towns business was often first-rate. Of course there were typical Charrington fiascoes. "It may interest you to know," Charrington wrote Shaw years later of one performance, "babes that we were—[that] although there was record opening night & great booking we forgot all about fees. They would have paid big ones. Our only desire was to get the play done without any Bowdlerizing . . . our innocence tempted their greed."[14] But the zeal to spread the word of the Master was strong and audiences generally enthusiastic and performances such as one in Sydney when the curtain was rushed down after Nora's exit in the last act to hisses and howls rare.

But the Charrington timing was poor; and Janet was forced to let out her stage dresses more and more as the tour progressed, for she was pregnant. The physical hardship of the tour drove her to rely on the brandy bottle ever more frequently as a source of stamina. By the time she went into labor in Melbourne in May 1890, she was in serious straits: perhaps now she received heavy doses of morphia to kill the pain. They named the daughter that was born Nora, after Janet's great success. Heaven had obviously signaled its disapproval of Charrington's liberties with the

Bernard Shaw in the 1890s.

Bernard Shaw in the 1890s.

Annie Besant in 1885.

Mrs. Jane (Jenny) Patterson.

Janet Achurch.

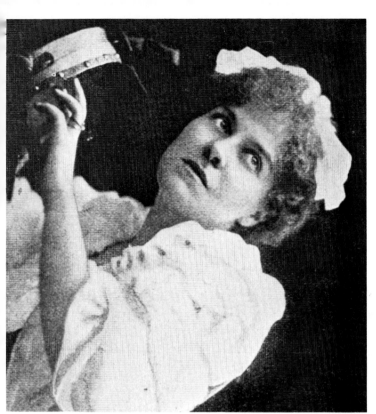

Janet Achurch on tour in Australia.

Charles Charrington.

Shaw the platform orator. Photograph of a copy of the painting by Bertha Newcombe done in February and March 1892.

Florence Farr as Louka in ARMS AND THE MAN.

Elizabeth Robins.
September 1891.

Florence Farr
publicity photograph for
ARMS AND THE MAN

Ahenobarbus
at Rehearsal.

Shaw rehearsing ARMS AND THE MAN *at the Avenue Theatre, April 1894. Drawing by J. Bernard Partridge for* THE SKETCH.

woman he loved, said Shaw when he heard the news, by giving his baby Shaw's red hair.

They moved on then to New Zealand, Java, Ceylon, and Calcutta, Janet in poor health and doping steadily as well as drinking. In Calcutta she was "frightfully bad" and acting only with the help of drugs. The day before their last performance Charrington opened a newspaper and read with all the indignation of guilt that Janet's unsteadiness on stage and her collapse after the fall of the curtain had been attributed to the proper cause. That night he came in front of the curtain at the Corinthian Theatre to attempt to salvage his wife's reputation. "During the past two weeks of our season," he explained:

> Mrs. Charrington has been very ill, suffering terrible agony from an abscess in the mouth, which rendered her work almost an impossibility. She has been at times almost delirious with pain. . . . Yet through all this she has persisted in continuing her work without interruption, and nothing I could say would persuade her to give it up. (Applause.) . . . But happening this evening to take up a copy of to-day's *Statesman*, I was astonished at finding in it a gross, cowardly and clumsy libel . . . so grossly insulting to Mrs. Charrington and myself, that I was compelled personally to take notice of it . . . . I am sure the performance will tonight proceed with more spirit and less imperfection than hitherto. (Cheers and applause.)[15]

Shaw meanwhile kept them current with news of past and projected Ibsen performances, with the result that Janet was wild to get back to London to try another Nora. But Shaw warned them away. The Ibsen boom, as he saw it, consisted of novices playing "at scratch matinees" on shoestring budgets. The turn of the skilled and polished actor would come. If he were Charrington, he would sacrifice London and Ibsen for the chance to perfect himself as an actor so that he could play everything as masterfully as Irving, for example, played Charles the First. Granted, Janet's talents were now fully ripe, and London would be in her interest; but the hard work of a tour could only help Charrington, since the consummation of a man's powers was "so much slower and later than a woman's." Hopefully Shaw weighed his advice well, for the Charrington commitment to Williamson, Garner, and Musgrove had ended after their first stop in Melbourne: Charrington had been in management for himself since 1890, and could have returned to London at any time.[16]

Shaw continued his killing pace of lectures, Fabian meetings, platform speeches, concertgoing, journalism, and letter writing—often dashing back to Fitzroy Square to dine hastily on bits of brown bread and cheese between assignments and meetings. A different traveler had returned from the East. On 27 April he went around to Brompton Square to welcome Jenny Patterson home, but had instead a frightful scene about "F.E." that kept him in the toils until three in the morning explaining why he had been too occupied evenings not to come to welcome her before. Scenes with Jenny now became increasingly more frequent, more violent, more absurd. On 7 May she appeared in his study to berate him about Florence, and although Shaw escaped to *Don Giovanni*, the opera was "rather spoilt in consequence." When he got back after midnight, he found her wandering distractedly about Fitzroy Square. There was only one course. He hailed a hansom, took her home in it, walked back, and fell into bed, dead tired, in the early hours of the morning.

She was increasingly ill and hysterical. He went to her, found her "very wretched," spent a trying evening, and did not get home until nearly two. In August she went to Boulogne and there was temporary relief; but then she was back too soon on the twenty-fourth, and the next day Shaw recorded "Much depressed. JP and FE." In October he was struggling with a very weighty paper called "The Difficulties of Anarchism" to be delivered to the Fabians on the sixteenth. There were interruptions. October 12: "Could get no work done as JP came in the morning and made terrible scenes all day. I went out before dinner to the Museum and to Archer's to avoid her; but she was there when I returned." October 16 itself: "Another desperate day finishing the paper amid intercourse and scenes from JP. Very tempestuous whilst I was at tea. At last pretended to throw her out of window. Went into Regents Park after dinner hoping that she would not be there when I came back." This time Shaw was very angry; and although Jenny dared to come back with him and Sydney Olivier to Fitzroy Square for tea after the Fabian meeting, she took her tea in another room with Mrs. Shaw and did not venture to leave it. On 4 December, however, Shaw was working amid his clutter at a Mozart article for the *World* when Jenny descended upon him again and made a Walkürean rather than Mozartean scene. "I got out of the room by main force and went to the Museum, telegraphing on my way to Mother to get the house cleared before I came back. . . . The scene upset me much."

He raged to Florence. "At this moment," he wrote on 1 May after Jenny had been with him for tea, "I am in a contemptuous fury & vehemently assert that your Christmas estimate of [the Patterson affair] was the right one. Not for forty thousand such relations will I forego one forty thousandth part of my relation with you. Every grain of cement she shakes from it falls like a block of granite on her own flimsy castle in the air, the work of my [her?] own imagination. The silly triumph with which she takes, with the air of a conqueror, that which I have torn out of my own entrails for her, almost brings the lightning down upon her. Imagine being told—but I cannot write it. Damnation!

triple damnation! You must give me back my peace. If you are disen-
gaged tomorrow afternoon, will you come to Prince's Hall (*not* St.
James's, mind) on the enclosed ticket. The hart pants for cooling
streams."[17]

But Jenny's behavior only "almost" brought the lightning down on her
head. Tannhäuser still did not break away. He took, perhaps, something
of a masochistic pleasure in his bondage; and then, under his hard-driving
verbal aggressiveness, he was strangely passive and hard to goad to anger.
He found relief instead in Florence's sympathetic companionship, so
much so that he could actually call her "my other self—no, not my other
self, but my very self." He went to her as often as possible, on 4 May
sending his mother to the opera, persuading a colleague to break an appointment, giving one meeting the slip, and leaving the Fabian early just
so he could spend a peaceful evening at Dalling Road. This time, however, she was not there since she had not expected him, and he went
home, irrationally disappointed, to rail: "Miserable, ill starred woman,
what have you done? When my need was at its highest, my weariness at
its uttermost, my love at its holiest, I found darkness, emptiness, void. I
cannot believe now that we shall ever meet again. . . . Wretch! selfish,
indifferent, heartless wretch! A million reproaches on you for ever and
ever. . . ."[18] His diary entry was rather less dramatic: "Went out to FE;
but found the place in darkness. Wandered about disappointed for a time
and then came home."

Yet there were deeper causes for disappointment in Florence. Another
performance of Todhunter's *Sicilian Idyll* on 15 June had exposed
Florence's shortcomings quite brutally, although the tepid amateurism of
the performance had not been solely her fault. Even Yeats, who had to
go out and hunt up people to fill the empty Vaudeville, had been forced
to regret her lack of vitality. Archer, whose presence at the first performance terrified Florence, recommended in his courteous way more
"decision of manner" and "crispness of attack," for she was "apt to seem
a little purposeless at times." Shaw was less tactful: he told her that a
hard grind was absolutely essential and began to drill her with *Rosmersholm*. Florence did not always take his criticism in spirit. His
overwhelming assurance made her defensive; her defensiveness maddened
him. "There is nothing that drives me to such utter despair," he groaned
after one hard session, "as when I make some blundering & unsuccessful
attempt to make you see some technical point that my mother can teach
to any idiot in a few lessons; and you shrink as if I were disparaging
your artistic gifts." He was only, he assured her, trying to make her realize *all* her potential, instead of just seven eighths or nine tenths. And at
the same time, he wanted to help her realize all her potential as a woman
too, for her ability to act must only be a consequence of her ability to
live. "You are so real to me as a woman," he assured her, "that I cannot

think of acting being to you anything more than a technical accomplishment which I want to see carried to a high degree of perfection."[19]

Taking a break from the lessons at the Salts' cottage in Surrey, he continued to exhort from afar. "Prithee persevere with the speaking," he wrote from where he was lying at the moment "among thistles & bees on the brink of a sandpit": ". . . You have reached the stage of the Idiotically Beautiful. There remain the stages of the Intelligently Beautiful & finally of the Powerfully Beautiful; & until you have attained the last you will never be able to compel me to recognize the substance of that soul of which I was shown a brief image by Nature for her own purposes."[20] Yet he was continually afraid that his brash confidence would alienate her; quite obviously needed her approval; could not forget for long those friendless days before he met her when disappointment seemed his "inevitable and constant lot." From Birmingham, where he had gone to hear William Morris speak on the Pre-Raphaelite painters at the opening of an exhibition, he sent her a testimony of love:

> This is to certify that you are my best and dearest love, the regenerator of my heart, the holiest joy of my soul, my treasure, my salvation, my rest, my reward, my darling youngest child, my secret glimpse of heaven, my angel of the Annunciation, not yet herself awake, but rousing me from a long sleep with the beat of her unconscious wings, and shining upon me with her beautiful eyes that are still blind.
>
> Also to observe incidentally [added Shaw, unable to forgo the protection of anti-climax] that Wednesday is the nearest evening that shews blank in my diary.[21]

The year drew to a close with an energetic fight with Archer over the Ibsen essay which had appeared and created much more of a stir than Shaw expected. Archer responded with an open letter to the *New Review* which attacked, among other failings, Shaw's repudiation of reason and separation of intellect and will. Since Shaw's *Quintessence* was reasoned closely from beginning to end, Archer argued, he had not gotten rid of reason at all. He sent the review to Shaw, who hurled back a reply, advising him to burn the notice at once before he ruined his reputation entirely. Dealing in rational ideas did not make one a Rationalist. Was he, Archer, a Positivist because he dealt with positive facts? Was he a Chiropodist because he had corns? If Archer went ahead and printed the article, he could also print this answer to his gross stupidities: "Oh William Archer, William Archer: where are your brains?"[22]

"I have always said you would end by being Pope, & now I'm sure of it," replied Archer imperturbably. "Better order your triple crown at once"—and sent his article for publication.

But brainlessness was not Archer's only crime. In a discussion of dramatic criticism in the *Fortnightly Review* he then innocently claimed that, unlike most reviewers, Ibsenite critics like himself were free from corruption. No one ever tried to "chicken and champagne" him to get a favorable notice. Down came Shaw's lightning upon his head again: "When I see you posing as the incorruptible Archer, assuring the public with an air of primeval simplicity that you would not know how to set about getting half a crown for a notice if you wanted to, and that no monk knows less of teas with pretty actresses than William the Anchorite, I really feel a moral revulsion. How if I were to tell the world that I have hardly once dropped in on you unexpectedly at Queen Square without disturbing a tete-a-tete between you and some pretty actress or another; so that your stock excuse became that I did it on purpose, having got wind of the appointment? Marion la bionda today: Elizabeth la bruna tomorrow. . . . Why, man alive, there is not an ambitious actress in London whose first move is not to get at William Archer."[23]

The reason for Shaw's fleeing Queen Square at the appearance of Elizabeth Robins and Marion Lea was now clear: he was disgusted at still another exhibition of Archer being "got at," as he thought; he wished to scotch any suspicion that he had come on purpose to meet them; he knew he was perfectly prone to pretty actresses himself; and he disliked the signs of an Ibsen coalition that might eliminate *his* actresses, Florence and Janet, from competition. For the Joint Management of Robins and Lea was steaming ahead vigorously. Elizabeth had already got publisher William Heinemann to write a letter for her to Henrik Ibsen in which she urged Heinemann's claims as sole British publisher, with the understanding, of course, that the eagerly awaited plays from Norway would pass into her hands before those of any other actress. A project was also on foot to produce *Twelfth Night* in strict Elizabethan style with restored text, minimal scenery, rich costumes, and authentic music. Elizabeth had won the affection and admiration of Henry James, and the lead in his play *The American* that fall in addition to engagements at the Adelphi and with Charles Wyndham at the Criterion. While Shaw had been struggling to improve Florence's "grip," Robins and Lea seemed to have grasped control of Ibsen remarkably fast. And so Shaw could not resist an injudicious taunt at "la bruna" herself:

Have you read Archer's article in the Fortnightly, where he declares that HE knows nothing about all this wicked corruption of critics—that HE, all the 12 years that he has been a critic, has never been "got at" by a pretty actress even to the extent of a cup of afternoon tea? What do you think of that, you, who put him in your pocket with one flash of your dark eyes so ridiculously easily that I blushed for him? *Do* write an article entitled "How to get at William Archer: by one who has done it." The editor of the Fortnightly will pay you golden guineas for it.[24]

Elizabeth Robins was furious. "No better instance of an outrageousness too outrageous even to be shown to W.A. than Shaw's own 9th Nov.," she wrote angrily on the letter. She had attracted Sir Herbert Tree as she had James and Archer; yet she had never stooped to seek advancement, she claimed, although "to ask for work, to pursue work, was a totally different matter": this Elizabeth Robins would do, and do aggressively and cleverly. But to use her charms sexually to advance herself, like so many other actresses did? To even hint it was an abomination.

Sexual advances from men were in themselves abomination. She had early learned that "a woman's first business in life was to please"; yet she "had to live out her youth in fear of the results of pleasing." Had this fear brought her marriage in 1887 to actor George Richmond Parks to its grotesque conclusion? Although they both acted for the Boston Museum Company, they had apparently seen little of each other after their marriage; and alone in Boston in June of that same year, George Parks had made an end by throwing himself into the Charles River clad in a full suit of stage armor. His motive was uncertain—too many bills, perhaps. Or had Elizabeth Robins's obsessive fear of sexuality turned her into *la belle dame sans merci?* Had there been a pregnancy? Abortion? A refusal to cohabitate? Lesbianism? From the enigmatic beauty in black whose luxurious chestnut hair was so heavy, so wearisome to coil, such a weight upon her slender neck that simply to wash and brush it was doing penance, few answers were forthcoming, although hints abounded.

There were unscrupulous men at her lodging house in Duchess Street, for example: she lived in fear of them. But then there was danger everywhere, even in places one would least expect it, like church or the open street. One day two gentlemen had helped her across a busy street in broad daylight. They had seemed like gentlemen, at any rate, until they gained the other side, when they began to say "things that frightened her." She had only shaken them off with great difficulty. Well before this she had learned to be afraid even in daytime of being followed. What life was like for the millions of infinitely better-looking young women, she did not pretend to know. . . . One was not safe in St. Paul's Cathedral. A disgusting old man. . . . She had changed her seat, "nearly faint with apprehension." Finally there had been a terrible experience at Duchess Street—a proposition, a midnight invasion of her room. Burning with shame and terrified that the landladies might think her at fault, she had fled with her few possessions from Duchess Street forever. She had brought a "duenna" along to chaperone her first meeting with

Archer. She had perfected herself in the cold, "Sir, you are wasting your time."[25] And now a notorious philanderer was casting aspersions on her conduct with a public figure and a married man. She answered Shaw in a cold fury, commanding that from now on he keep a dignified silence. Irrepressible, Shaw answered at length:

> . . . I did not mean that you deliberately went on the warpath and took his scalp. I never thought of you as one of the people who do such things. But I assure you the scalp went, all the same—walked spontaneously off his head and hung itself to your belt without the least help from you or consciousness on his part. And that is the way these things really happen. The reason I laugh at Archer is because he tells the public so solemnly that they never do happen—that criticism is unbiassed, incorruptible. . . . How is it possible for you to call on Archer and talk to him for half an hour without biassing him—"getting at him," to use his own phrase? . . . His implied declaration that his criticism of Hedda Gabler would have been word for word the same if he had never seen you before you stepped on the stage in the first act, is a piece of self-deception. . . .

"Do not mind my touch of coarseness more than you can help," Shaw added in a postscript. "I am an Irishman, and can understand a woman's delicacy without having a trace of it myself."[26] He was fussing so much about the matter, he told himself, because Archer's writing was getting "unscrupulous & careless" lately. It was blind to pretend he did not trim his work to suit his public and his paper. Even he, Shaw, prostituted himself as honestly as he could, but was "bought and sold for all that." Yet this time in challenging his friends to meet his standards, he had made an enemy in Elizabeth Robins.

The year ended with a hard frost. Shaw tried to take advantage of it by going to Holborn and buying a pair of skates and taking them to Hyde Park for a trial run. But the Serpentine was closed to skaters, and skidding on sleet-frozen streets when he tried to venture out Christmas Day was an unpleasant substitute. On 28 December he wrote a long letter to Jenny Patterson, who had left for Australia, and went to Florence in the evening. New Year's Eve he spent alone.

Florence had not been the only woman behind the *Quintessence of Ibsenism:* Jenny had been there too. Shaw had strongly attacked romantic idealists who insist upon self-surrender "as an indispensable element in true womanly love." "The extreme instance," he continued, "is the reckless self-abandonment seen in the infatuation of passionate sexual desire. Everyone who becomes the object of that infatuation shrinks from it instinctively. Love loses its charm when it is not free . . . it becomes valueless and even abhorrent, like the caresses of a maniac." The shudder here at the Venusberg of Brompton Square is very strong. If Florence Farr had been his model for the liberated "unwomanly woman," Jenny was his model for the glutting extremes of the "womanly woman." Certainly it was only a matter of time before he would break free.

CHAPTER SEVEN

1892

NOTHING COULD BETTER testify to Florence Farr's amiability than her refusal to make a fuss over Shaw's still-vital attachment to Jenny Patterson,
or her willingness to accept his energetic flaying of her artistic shortcomings. But under an unruffled surface lay dissatisfaction. She had other
friends, alien to Shaw, to undermine his influence with her: her Bedford
Park circle; Yeats, her companion in aestheticism and the occult; the
members of her secret society, the Golden Dawn. Alternately invigor-
ated by the cold north wind of Shaw's energy and lulled by the more be-
nign south wind of poetic mysteries, she was beginning to be a little restive under the former. "Analysts" had hinted that there might be "base
ingredients" in Shaw's regard for her. Personal ambition? Exhibitionism?
Mere sexual attraction? She confronted him with these possibilities, concluding with the challenge: "You best know what you are." Hurt by her
defection, Shaw hurled back a reply:

Now listen to me, will-less girl. When you tell me that I best know what
I am, I assent, not with humility, but with towering head striking against
every star and raising great bumps on them; so that astronomers reel
amazed from their telescopes. Cubits high and fathoms deep am I the noblest creature you have yet met in this wood of monkeys where I found
you straying. Some of them thought you a pretty female ape; others
thought you a goddess: the first asked you to play with them; the second
asked to be allowed to worship you: you could not say No to either.
Then come I, the man, and make you my woman on your stopping me as
I wandered lonely through the forest and asking me to look earnestly at
you. For many years had I wandered alone, sufficient to myself: I will, at

a word, wander on again alone. But what will you do—return to the monkeys? It is not possible: self-sufficient must you also become or else find no less a man than I to be your mate.[1]

Perhaps the temporary flare-up had its roots in the turn Florence's career had taken. Shaw wanted her to excel: to slough off amateurism—that genteel tradition that rewarded women for doing a little music, a little art work, a little reciting—and polish her talents to the hardest luster. Florence was satisfied evidently with less. In February 1892 she took a role in *Breezy Morning*, a slight curtain raiser at the Comedy Theatre. Shaw saw it on 3 March and was unhappy. "I wish to see you an accomplished actress," he persisted. ". . . I will not face the judgment bar at the end of my life with you if I am unable to meet the question, 'Why did you suffer her to do her work badly?' "[2]

He continued to promote Florence's career, sometimes unwisely. It is true that when the Shelley Society commissioned him to find a cast for a centenary performance of *The Cenci*, he first appealed to Alma Murray. With her refusal, however, he embarked on "the desperate course" of asking Beerbohm Tree to lend the Haymarket and to play Cenci to Florence's Beatrice. Tree was dubious about Florence: the part of Beatrice Cenci required several Bernhardts rolled into one, and "dear gentle Miss Farr" was anything but that. Besides, he could not imagine any audience enjoying the endless bestiality of Shelley's *Cenci* unless they were "impotent old men and nymphomaniac spinsters."[3] While Tree hesitated, Shaw devoted much energy trying to drive Florence up to the mark, taking the train out to Ravenscourt Park on 13 March, for example, and going over the part before walking her over to Todhunter's house, where F. J. Furnivall, Henry Salt, and J. T. Grein waited to hear her recite. Florence was approved, and Tree was on the point of lending the fashionable Haymarket when morality interfered. E. F. S. Pigott, licenser of plays at the Lord Chamberlain's Office, made it clear to Tree that any attempt to stage the play of the notorious atheist, socialist, and vegetarian would get him into trouble with the censor; and Tree withdrew his offer.

The Independent Theatre was similarly threatened, and *The Cenci* was finally offered in July 1892 at the red-brick Bedford Park Clubhouse. Florence again made a kind of esoteric success with her beauty and a certain originality, but the rest of the cast proved hopelessly amateurish. Struggling to maintain an "honorable gravity," Shaw barely managed to sit through the play; and reported to Alma Murray that "The Cenci performance collapsed most disgracefully."

His frustration with shoestring performances of great drama in dreary halls by third-rate casts accelerated. He had chafed at the arrangements for *The Cenci*, telling Alma Murray that the idea of waiting until the hot weather of July set in and then taking their luck in some deserted theatre with a last-minute cast under no particular discipline was extremely uninviting. If a calamity "can be brought about by any mortal means," he complained, "the Independent Theatre may be relied upon to achieve it." It galled him to see the efforts of Elizabeth Robins and Marion Lea, for example, hidden away in unfashionable theatres, while in the West End indifferent plays acted by mediocre but popular personalities flourished. He had attacked the West End establishment in the *Quintessence*—particularly, since Ibsen offered so much to the actress, "the senior generation of inveterately sentimental actresses, schooled in the old fashion if at all . . . quite out of the political and social movement around them . . . intellectually naive to the last degree." To these stars of the old school, said Shaw, the new generation of intellectual actresses say, "You cannot play Ibsen because you are ignoramuses." It was not a way of endearing the new actresses to the old, of course; but it did perhaps express the frustrations of the newcomers, who were finding that having brains on their side was (as usual) a meager consolation. The new drama needed popular theatres, efficient management, polished casts, money.

Then in June Shaw happened to receive a commission from one of the "ignoramuses," or rather from not just one of them, but from the leading English actress of the day. Ellen Terry had asked the fashionable weekly the *World* to send its music critic to the concert of her protégée F. Elvira Gambogi; Edmund Yates passed the assignment on to Shaw. Shaw seized the opportunity, partly out of a mischievous delight in having the interests of the leading lady of Henry Irving, whose antipathy had been aroused by the *Quintessence*, temporarily in his hands. He posted a note to Ellen Terry announcing his assignment (it immediately antagonized her), then went to the Lyric Club, where he listened to Miss Gambogi sing and concluded that she lacked execution and that "intense grip" that compels the interest of an audience. Of course, she had charm and grace, but those very qualities were drawbacks; for Shaw had observed (with an eye on his own awkward youth) that when nature intended anyone to be a great artist, she usually goaded them on by condemning them to "fiendishness or loutishness" until they had fulfilled her intention. And then Ellen Terry herself—tall, blond, ineffably graceful though largely made, with that strangely appealing wistful face that turned all others commonplace by comparison—Ellen Terry came on stage and recited "Monk" Lewis's "The Captive"; and Shaw, "morbidly alive" to the absurdities of the poem, nevertheless found his eyes brimming with tears at the sheer beauty of her execution. It was his whole claim as a critic of art —that he could be touched by artistry in that way. Miss Gambogi had not caused one vibration; and, in fact, after Ellen Terry's recitation, he left the Lyric Club hastily, unable to face anti-climax. He told Miss

Terry all this in a long letter of 24 June, which he begged her not to answer, or at least to say no more to than "Thank you for nothing" on a
postcard.⁴ He appeared naively anxious for a reply.

Ellen Terry read through this second letter at her pleasant house at 22
Barkston Gardens, Earl's Court, which was also occupied by her twenty-
two-year-old daughter Edith, three female servants, her companion Miss
Harries, an old nurse, and her son Teddy, twenty. It impressed her
differently from the first, and she sat down to answer it:

> I am exceedingly obliged to you for troubling yourself so much about
> my little friend. Your letter saddened me very much, for I do care for
> the girl, and long and long to help her. She's so alone, and so very, very
> little assertive. She *has* individuality; and I learn every day from her sim-
> plicity. . . .
> But I see a peep-hole in your words for Blessed Hope. I will work to
> get her a few lines on the stage for a few shillings a week and at least
> then she will know the great happiness of occupation.
> I didn't like you when you first wrote to me. I thought you unkind,
> and exceedingly stiff and prim. Now I beg your pardon most heartily.
> Although of course it matters no jot to you what I think, I must yet ask
> you to take my very bestest thanks for your long last splendid letter, and
> believe me most gratefully yours
>
> Ellen Terry⁵

The brief letter revealed a great deal. It said something, for example,
about Ellen Terry's generosity, as well as about her rather patronizing attitude to the many "little friends" (female) who hung about her. Very
revealing too was the phrase "the great happiness of occupation," for
Ellen's work was her religion to which everything else was ultimately
sacrificed. Perhaps most revealing of all was the fact that she did not
mind revealing herself. Secure in the love of her public and friends, she
gave to the stranger Shaw just as she gave nightly to her audience, without the least compromising her dignity or privacy.

Shaw appreciated her frank admission that at first she had not liked
him. He had feared much worse, for the *Quintessence* (surely she must
know it?) had established him as the inveterate enemy of the Lyceum.
Supposing she had been outraged by the attentions of a seditious wretch
who had once called her an ignoramus, and had complained to Edmund
Yates. But Ellen Terry had been happily oblivious of the career of this
desperado, and received the news of his sedition with sunny calm. "*Did*
you call me an 'ignoramus'?" she asked in a second note of 4 July. "Well,
I forgive you for speaking the truth. But I must ask Mr. Irving to tell me
all about it. It delights me to be able to tell you that the signorina cleared

£100 by that concert, the first money the poor girl has ever had. . . . Thank you. Thank you. *Thank* you for all your beautifulness. If you *could* ask me to do a little thing for you some day, I would do it, or I'd try to."[6]

Beguiled, Shaw responded with another letter ("positively the last") and a copy of the *Quintessence*. "When I wrote the book," he challenged, "I had a terrible grudge against you, and I have it still. . . ."

> One day I went into an afternoon performance, and found a poor un-gifted, dowdy, charmless young woman struggling pathetically with Ib-sen's Lady from the Sea. She was doing her best; and I thanked my stars that I was not a dramatic critic, and had not to go home and tell her that after all her study and toil she had done far more harm than good. That was the first act of my little experience. Act 2 was another visit to an-other theatre. There I found the woman who OUGHT to have played the Lady from the Sea—the woman with all the nameless charm, all the skill, all the force, in a word, all the genius—playing—guess what? Why, a charade the whole artistic weight of which would not have taxed the strength of the top joint of her little finger. And the silly public delight-edly applauding. Worse than that, traitors calling themselves critics were encouraging her—allowing their brains and consciences to be cajoled away by her beauty—talking fatuously of her child's play as if it had been the best she was capable of. I was furious. If I had been a god, and had created her powers for her, I should have interrupted the performance with thunder, and asked in a fearful voice why she was wasting the sa-cred fire of which I had made her trustee. But I knew that she had made her powers for herself, and could be called to account by nobody for the use she made of them. So I sat helpless, and went off in impotent rage. Since then I have never heard Nance Oldfield praised without vowing vengeance.

As if this were not abrasive enough, Shaw then declined to sympathize with Miss Gambogi, who had after all made a hundred pounds. "Do you hear that," he apostrophized, "oh Rosmersholm Rebecca, ruined by two enormously successful Ibsen matinees, and now honestly buckling-to at six lines in a *lever de rideau* to pay for your lodgings? Think of it, oh Hedda-Gabler-Karin, staring gloomily at the bank book that registers the cost of your courage and skill. What would you give for the half of it just now, oh cleaned-out and invalided, but still indomitable Nora? And you, oh vanished and forgotten Ellida, I wonder have *you* a hundred pounds to bless yourself with? And you, Nance Oldfield, what have you done to set against the records of these hardly used ones? Why (says you) created my incomparable self, sir. True, irresistible Ellen, quite true. That silences me. Farewell."[7]

Not surprisingly, it silenced Ellen Terry also, making her quite aware of the chasm between the worlds of the socialist street-corner orator and Ibsenite and the prima donna of the Lyceum. Yet Ellen had her own dissatisfactions with London's most prestigious theater. She had not liked her last role, the Katharine of Aragon she had played to Irving's Cardinal Wolsey and William Terriss's Henry the Eighth. Despite the usual lavish "Lyceum treatment" given this Shakespeare, Ellen had confessed: "I am not interested in it, or in my part."

Shaw had awaited the return of the Charringtons with intense interest, for the memory of Janet's Nora and of Janet herself was still green. They had returned in the spring of 1892, given out interviews about the great success of the tour, and taken the Avenue Theatre for a revival of *A Doll's House*, Charrington switching roles from Dr. Rank to Torvald Helmer and Marion Lea playing Mrs. Linden. Shaw was there for the first performance on 19 April and came down to earth with a crash. Gone was the original Nora's playfulness, her lightness of touch, her simplicity, her control. In their place was a restless and tempestuous actress whose "Hyde Parkian" voice exploded into fortissimos, lapsed into sibilant whispers, and ground out words harshly with a scandalous indifference to beauty of tone. It had taken, Shaw assured her, scribbling a letter hastily in a train compartment after the performance, "the united strength of my three companions, the *ouvreuse*, the acting manager, the fireman, and a commissionaire" to hold him down and restrain him from hurling an opera glass at her head. "I refuse to tolerate any Nora who tightens her lower lip like an india rubber band," he raged, "and then speaks by main force, exulting in the strength of her youth. I am not to be propitiated by any increase in tragic power, however striking. Anybody can be tragic if they are born so; but that every stroke shall be beautiful as well as powerful, beautiful to the eye and ear; that is what I call art."[8] But Shaw did not mention what must have been his chief shock: the all too obvious fact that Janet was acting with the help of "stimulants." Clement Scott had curtly remarked it in a *Daily Telegraph* review that raked her acting over the coals; but Shaw assured Janet that Scott could be ignored as long as she listened to him. His covert message to her then was this: I have noticed that you were rather intoxicated; I refrain from mentioning it—but we both know what caused your boisterousness on stage today, and that it is fatal to art.

Yet he added, curiously, that his admiration was "in nowise abated"; and this was clear in the unfeigned enthusiasm of his response to her note of 6 May asking him to call:

Death & distraction, it is midnight; and your letter has only just reached me. I could kill you—I could almost kill myself. You must have known that I had to go out at five: this is your revenge for the train letter. Never was there anything so heartless. I will complain of you to Charrington—I will have satisfaction—I will tear up by the roots all the fibres you have ever stirred in me—I will throw away my heart & soul and have my inside fitted with brass machinery and millstones.

Let me be calm: why should I care. I DONT care. I am perfectly composed—indifferent. I regret extremely that an engagement should have deprived me of the pleasure of answering your kind letter in person. I trust you are well—and Mr. Charrington—and your daughter. The weather is cold, but fine; and the crops are well advanced.

I must go to a concert tomorrow at three. I have an engagement in the evening. I am Laocoon in the toils. From four to five, from seven to eight, from five to seven, would it be of any use my calling then?[9]

Janet replied that the next afternoon would find her at home, and Shaw consequently turned up on 7 May. He had been appalled at her stridency on stage; Janet Achurch in person was hardly less disturbing. She was, as he would tell Ellen Terry, financially and physically cleaned out: the strenuous tour had broken her health and the Charrington purse. He knew about the alcohol; he now discovered that morphia was a way of life for her also. Yet except for the usual torrent of abuse from the anti-Ibsenite Clement Scott, her performance as Nora had again drawn praise, with only Shaw seeming to realize that more flamboyance was less art.

As usual the main question was financial backing so that the Charringtons could establish themselves again as serious competitors for serious plays. Shaw urged *Hedda Gabler*, both because it had proved the most popular Ibsen in London after *A Doll's House*, and because the Charringtons had Marion Lea, the original Thea, under engagement. But *Hedda Gabler* was in the hands of the clever, energetic Elizabeth Robins. Would the Charringtons make an ally of her? or an enemy.

Altogether, Shaw perhaps did not realize how three years had changed Janet: he found her as "indomitable" as ever. Yet after the seven weeks' run of *A Doll's House*, she collapsed. On 30 June Shaw visited her and they had a long conversation interrupted only by her doctor, until some visitors arrived, and he left. But her condition worsened steadily. Ellen Terry, goaded perhaps by Shaw's reference in his letter of 5 July to the "cleaned out and invalided, but still indomitable Nora," came to the Charrington lodgings and offered to take the two-year-old Nora, having heard that it was all up with Janet.[10] But the indomitable rallied, and was sent to Clacton-on-Sea in Essex to convalesce. Too restless to do anything else, Shaw spent an entire day in late July writing in hopes of amusing her and passing the time. They were beginning to be, as he would later describe it, on terms of complete intimacy.

Having less and less of Shaw to stay in London for, Jenny Patterson had been traveling abroad more and more. On 16 June, coming home from a concert at Steinway Hall, Shaw had found Jenny waiting for him. It was their first meeting since she had left for Australia in December, six months before. On 27 July he finally got around to paying her a visit at Brompton Square. The days when she would return to find him waiting in her parlor must have seemed remote indeed. She had come back to find him daring to write to the great Ellen Terry and sending her (ominous portent) a copy of his book. Two old rivals were flourishing: Janet Achurch and May Morris, who, now that she was safely Mrs. Henry Sparling, appeared to be exerting some of her old enchantment over Shaw. And there was a new name that her lover tossed rather frequently into the conversation.

Shaw had begun to sit for his portrait to a Chelsea artist named Bertha Newcombe at her studio at Cheyne Walk on 24 February 1892. As the portrait progressed so, inevitably, did the painter's fascination with the sitter. On 27 February Shaw gave her a sitting until nine-thirty in the evening and dined with her afterward—she could not let him go home to forage at Fitzroy Square. On this occasion, however, Shaw annoyingly ate and ran—to Florence at Dalling Road. On 2 March, however, he spent the entire day at Cheyne Walk, breaking for tea in the afternoon and also for a session at the piano, where he played and sang a few songs for her. His endurance as a sitter became increasingly impressive: four hours, five hours, or a whole morning and afternoon, after which they sang and played and Bertha fed him. The portrait was to be submitted by 1 April to the New English Art Club exhibition. As the deadline approached, Shaw gave up still more time to the sittings. Nearly all the last week of March was devoted to Cheyne Walk and all day of 31 March as Bertha Newcombe hurried to complete the portrait. And finally the reason for Shaw's monumental sacrifice became clear. Bertha Newcombe had succeeded beyond all expectation in capturing her sitter. The hand-on-hip stance was easy yet alert, the eyes alive and challenging, the moustaches on the *qui vive*, the upper lip drawn back, the mouth ready with a devastating riposte. This was the Shaw Yeats could delight in: "the formidable man" who could "hit my enemies and the enemies of all I loved, as I could never hit, as no living author that was dear to me could ever hit." Yet it was also a Shaw Yeats perhaps did not know, for Bertha Newcombe had lit the face with humor and kindliness. Shaw was impressed, and of course Bertha Newcombe was now in love with Shaw.

He continued to be much occupied with Florence. They gadded about as usual that summer of 1892, going for long walks along the towpath from Hammersmith to Putney, or across Wormwood Scrubs. They lounged in the grass on Putney Heath or Hampstead Heath on fine days. They spent a day together at Oxted with the Salts, and another visiting

Kew Gardens which, however, was spoiled for Florence because Shaw met John Burns, head of the trade unionists' Progressive Party, and immediately forgot all about her, leaving her to wander disconsolately around the flower beds while he launched into an animated discussion about the coming elections. Shaw got out of the situation by immediately taking the offensive and accusing her of being too shy to come up and be introduced (it was a favorite platform technique); and they were friends again before they were halfway back to Hammersmith. Friends, yes; but their relationship was changing. Shaw was "going out to FE in the evening" less, meeting her for excursions in public places more. What was undermining the closeness of their relationship?

The mysteries of the Golden Dawn, the secret occult society for the study and practice of magic to which Yeats ("Damon Est Deus Inversus") had introduced Florence two years before in June 1890, were, of course, secret. Florence would not have revealed to Shaw her personal mantra or motto, S.S.D.D.: Sapientia Sapienti Dono Data: "Wisdom is given to the wise as a gift."[11] But she could hardly hide her occult pursuits from Shaw in the closet along with her robes and magic paraphernalia, even had she wanted to. Her constant visits to the Golden Dawn headquarters in Clipstone Street, only a few blocks west of Fitzroy Square, would have to be explained away when they conflicted with their meetings. Her researches into the occult in the Reading Room of the British Museum occupied her more and more. The oriental draperies, the paintings of Egyptian gods and goddesses she executed in the Museum and hung on her walls, the esoteric musical instruments scattered about, the heaps of books on psychic and hermetic studies—all proclaimed an interest far removed from the extroverted social activism of Shaw.

Yet Shaw had experience enough with the "flight from reason" which, as one form of rebellion against the Victorian establishment, made him an uneasy ally since he too was in rebellion.[12] Despite her no-nonsense imperturbability, Mrs. Shaw had taken to the ouija board for messages from her dead Agnes and Vandeleur Lee, which, coincidently, she always seemed to receive. While this might be dismissed as an aging and lonely woman's folly, the flights from reason of Edward Carpenter, Henry Salt, Edith Bland, Hubert Bland, W. B. Yeats, and Conan Doyle—to name a handful—demanded more serious attention. Shaw himself had fled from reason in the *Quintessence*, of course; not to spirits, fairies, and gurus, however, but to Will. One flight from reason had thus severely jolted him. One day in June 1889, when he was in the throes of Ibsen and his first fascination for Janet Achurch, he had dropped by the *Star* office of its editor H. W. Massingham, casually picked up a handful of proofs, and noted a title: "Sic Itur ad Astra; or, Why I Became a

Theosophist." Curious, since Theosophy had been much in the air in recent years, he looked for a signature and found the name Annie Besant.

> Staggered by this unprepared blow [wrote Shaw], which meant to me the loss of a powerful colleague and of a friendship which had become part of my daily life, I rushed round to her office in Fleet Street, and there delivered myself of an unbounded denunciation of Theosophy in general, of female inconstancy, and in particular of H. P. Blavatsky, one of whose books—I forget whether it was "The Secret Doctrine" or "Isis Unveiled"—had done all the mischief.[13]

The mischief-maker had been *The Secret Doctrine*, sent to Annie to review by William T. Stead, editor of the *Pall Mall Gazette*—although Annie's interest in spiritualism had prompted Stead to choose her as the reviewer. While Annie was writing Stead, "I am immersed in Madame B! If I perish in the attempt to review her, you must write on my tomb, 'She has gone to investigate the Secret Doctrine at first hand!'" Shaw was having his own fling with the occult. At Belfort Bax's house, he reported on 16 February 1889, "we began spirit rapping and table turning, and in the excitement of it I forgot the last train. I cheated from the first, and as soon as Massingham detected me he became my accomplice and we caused the spirits to rap out long stories, lift the table into the air, and finally drink tumblers of whiskey and water, to the complete bewilderment of Bax. . . . I have not laughed so much in years."

Annie Besant would not have been amused. The next month she went with Herbert Burrows, socialist, visionary, and constant companion whom Shaw always met when he now infrequently dropped around to call, "in the soft spring evening" to the house of the "old Russian savage" Madame Blavatsky at 17 Lansdowne Road. At the sight of the coarse, masculine figure in the wheelchair, the eyes like burning coals in the yellow bloated face, Annie felt an immediate and overwhelming leap of attraction and then as strong a shrinking and rebellion, "as of some beast when it feels a mastering hand." Yet at the end of the meeting, when Madame said in a deep yearning voice, "Oh, my dear Mrs. Besant, if you would only come among us!" Annie had to fight a nearly uncontrollable desire to bend down and kiss her. Two months later Annie Besant shed her socialist skin to emerge as a Theosophist.

Flinging down the proofs, then, and rushing to her Fleet Street office, Shaw turned on Annie his formidable battery of argument, persuasion, and charm. But he had failed her before. Like socialism itself, he had not been able to satisfy her emotional craving. He now found her serene, polite, immovable. She listened to his ravings, her face kindly and amused; when he had finished she excused herself on the plea that the vegetarianism he had persuaded her to had perhaps softened her mind.

For the first time she was able to play with him as he had played with her, and he rightly interpreted the sign: his influence with her was finished. "Mrs. Besant, you may not have heard," Yeats wrote to a friend that September, "has turned Theosophist and is now staying with Madame Blavatsky." Two years later in 1891 Madame Blavatsky died, having passed her mantle to her disciple Annie Besant, who thereafter led the London Theosophical Society.

In the same way now, he felt his influence with Florence Farr subtly eroding. "What will you do," he had asked in exasperation: "return to this wood of monkeys where I found you straying?" He was no rationalist himself, yet secret societies which prostrated the human will before "mysteries" all too ridiculously human in origin could not claim his sympathy. His investigations into spiritualism had ended in laughter: he marveled at the credulity of people like Belfort Bax and Kate Salt. He could only view Florence's increasing involvement with the Golden Dawn with alarm, and try to rescue her from such a devious path.

He proposed to do this with a play. Although threatening Archer from time to time with finishing their play begun in 1884, he had evaded the job for eight years. Mrs. Shaw called him a dreadful procrastinator; but Archer's scorn, the necessity for earning a wage, and the lack of a manager to undertake the kind of play he intended to write had all discouraged him from considering himself a dramatist. Then in August of 1892, too exhausted from the general election business to do anything but leaf through old papers, he came across *Das Rheingold*. It so tickled him on rereading that he sat down then and there to continue it. On 20 October, after a walk with May Morris, he went to Dalling Road, found Florence out, but went in to wait and work on the play, which he decided to call *Widowers' Houses*. He effectually finished the play that day, and J. T. Grein accepted it for the Independent Theatre.

The role of the tempestuous Blanche Sartorius, partly inspired by Jenny Patterson and her infinite capacity for making scenes, seemed better fitted for Janet Achurch than Florence Farr; but the Charringtons had joined forces with Elizabeth Robins and taken *A Doll's House* and *Hedda Gabler* to Brighton. Shaw did not follow, but Archer was there and so was Elizabeth's mentor Henry James. James deplored the performance of *A Doll's House* to his and Elizabeth's friend Mrs. Hugo Bell as "born under the evil stars of flatness and feebleness. The Achurches (it sounds like bad grammar) are of a badness and dreariness so désespérant that our admirable friend, charming and interesting as she is as the melancholy Linden, has no picture to fit into—no ensemble to compose with—remains a lonely, stranded figure, ploughing through Charringtonian sands. . . . The houses are good and quiet and dull—this last to match the performance; for a more woeful slowness and sleepiness—like the casual murmurs of incoherent dreams—than the fearsome Charringtons manage to achieve, between them, in their scenes together, is not to be said or sung."[14] Then at a charming little supper with Elizabeth, the Archers, and the "Achurches" the next night after a "vastly better Hedda," James discovered that the somnambulistic Charringtons of the previous evening had both been on morphia—he overdosed on twelve grains by his own wife for neuralgia, she for the usual reasons. And indeed Janet as Thea had played so brilliantly in the first act of *Hedda* that James had actually begun to hope for a coup; but then she had disintegrated swiftly "in lemon-colored satin (!!!) and staginess"—so that James had been forced to dismiss her again. Altogether Brighton Ibsen was a disappointment, for even Elizabeth played indifferently.

Shaw's enthusiasm for Janet continued almost unabated, yet his chief allegiance was still to Florence. Besides, he perhaps did not think of himself yet as a playwright of Janet Achurch's caliber. He clearly considered himself a maverick. Attending a meeting of playwrights at Terry's on 8 November to discuss the formation of a Society of British Dramatic Authors, he had emphatically resolved to have no part of it. The role of leading lady, therefore, went to Florence Farr.

That late autumn, ostensibly because the drains were up at Fitzroy Square, he had moved in with May and Henry Sparling at 8 Hammersmith Terrace, "a quiet little house, with an embroidery factory cumbering the drawing-room from nine to five, on the river near this end of the Chiswick Mall." May had not been able to move any great distance from "the Father." Shaw had always been attracted to May; now, when he could play third in her household, the attraction was strong indeed, especially when there were intimations from May that she was not very happy with Sparling. Perhaps too the revived interest in May was a defense against Florence's increasing restlessness under his program for the reform of her life and art. He had made it clear that a true artist lives cleanly as well as creates cleanly: he was insistent about this: there had been a brief quarrel when he found her trying to cure a headache Achurch style with a spoonful of brandy. Thus his time during the weeks before the production of *Widowers' Houses* was much occupied with May and duets at the piano. One day, in fact, she dismissed her embroidery pupils early so that they could get to the piano and play Mendelssohn's *Scotch Symphony*, which she had bought for a duet. Another night he spent the whole evening singing to her—"Shouted away till past midnight"—whereupon he went to his own room in her house with who knews how many teasing protestations of reluctance. Yet always, to May's chagrin, there was "FE"; and the next morning, 24 November, Shaw was up and on his way to pick up Florence for a twelve-thirty rehearsal of *Widowers' Houses* at the Mona Hotel near the Royalty Theatre.

Grein had scraped together a cast: T. W. Percyval for Sartorius, W. J.

Robertson for the hero Trench, Arthur Whittaker as Cokane, Kate Phillips for the housemaid, and of course Florence for the heroine Blanche Sartorius. To Shaw's relief they managed to have "something like a real rehearsal at last," although the cast was unable to get through the second act. Most discouraging was the lack of an actor to play Lickcheese, the slum rent collector: the cast had to stumble around the considerable holes left by his unfilled part. The next day, however, fortune smiled. James Welch, a considerable actor of character roles, wandered innocently into the Mona Hotel on his way to somewhere else. He was immediately pounced upon by a tall, red-bearded, fanatic-looking man in snuff-colored wool Jaegers and red wool scarf who shoved a script into his hand and commanded him to start reading; and before he quite knew what was happening, Welch found himself acting Lickcheese in the first play of an unknown playwright.

Or rather, not unknown, for Shaw's platform pyrotechnics, his brilliant reviewing, and his natural volubility had by now turned him into a Personality. "Everybody in London knows Shaw," said the *Sunday World* in 1891, "Fabian Socialist, art and musical critic, vegetarian, ascetic, humourist, artist to the tips of his fingers, man of the people to the tips of his boots. The most original and inspiring of men—fiercely uncompromising, full of ideas, irrepressibly brilliant—an Irishman."[15] And Shaw made sure that *Widowers' Houses* would not go unnoticed, concocting an "interview" for the *Star* calculated to outrage, amuse, but at any price *notice* the new socialist playwright.

Under the impression that the play is titled *Wendover's Horses*, the "interviewer" approaches Fitzroy Square warily, having been warned that Shaw will talk his head off on every subject but the play. After performing on the Shaw doorbell for twelve minutes in vain and "concluding with a five minutes' fantasia on all the other bells," the interviewer is let in by a char, mounts some "desolate stone steps" to the second floor, and finds the author clad in gray collar and sandals sitting with a typewriter before him at a table that completely blocks the narrow space between the fire and the wide-open window of the small room. The interviewer is dismayed at the spectacle: dusty heaps of letters and papers in utter disorder mixed up with stationery, inkstands, *Stars, Chronicles*, butter, sugar, stray apples, knives, spoons, a full breakfast cup of cocoa, and a plate which Mr. Shaw is just filling with great spoonfuls of porridge out of a saucepan on the hob. If the interviewer is embarrassed, his host certainly is not, and he sits his visitor in a chair by the open window with complete affability.

The interviewer begins conventionally. To what genre does his play belong—comedy, tragedy, farce, melodrama? "To none of them," announces Shaw. "To Humanity solely. That is the only genre I recognize." In that case the interviewer ventures to hope that the play will not be too didactic. "Sir, it will be nothing else than didactic. Do you suppose I have gone to all this trouble to *amuse* the public?" Can he give a brief sketch of the plot? "There is no plot," replies the playwright pitilessly. "The hero, who has no conventionally heroic qualities, loves the heroine, who has no conventionally amiable ones." May the public in any case anticipate some of his unrivaled touches of humor? "Certainly not. I have removed with the greatest care every line that could possibly provoke a smile. . . . I am simply a propagandist." He is, of course, a follower of Ibsen? On no account, Mr. Shaw assures him: since he began this realist play in 1885 and wrote an Ibsenite novel at twenty-four, Ibsen is a follower of *his*. Shakespeare is then his model, perhaps? At the suggestion, Shaw explodes: "Shakespeare! stuff! Shakespeare—a disillusioned idealist! a pessimist! a rationalist! a capitalist! If the fellow had not been a great poet, his rubbish would have been forgotten long ago. Molière, as a thinker, was worth a thousand Shakespeares. If my play is not better than Shakespeare, let it be damned promptly." Refusing Shaw's offer of a few carrots and a glass of water as refreshment, the interviewer finally extricates himself and staggers down the steps, convinced that the author of *Widowers' Houses* is the most voluble egotist he has ever interviewed.[16]

The next day, 29 November, Shaw and Florence had "great fun over the interview in the Star." Had Florence read attentively, however, she would have found herself virtually marked for failure; for although Shaw praised her intelligence as an actress, her lively sense of humor, and her personal grace, he went on to call the part of Blanche Sartorius "a specially hazardous and disagreeable one"—and thus hardly within the range of (so he labeled her) "a quite unassuming member of Mr. Hawtrey's company at the Comedy Theatre." But persuaded by Shaw and with her "lively sense of humor," she perhaps enjoyed the prospect of playing Jenny Patterson on stage too much to pass it by. She would have heard of his latest contretemps on 5 November when, having taken tea at Brompton Square and been treated to a highly disagreeable scene with Jenny, who knew he was simply on his way to Dalling Road, he had indeed fled to her. On 3 December Shaw went over Florence's part with her, trying to inspire in her the color and passion needed if Blanche Sartorius were not to seem simply a shrew. He was not comforted. Act I was a difficulty. It required Florence to modulate gradually from mild pique at a misunderstanding with her fiancé, to growing anger at his seeming rejection, to intense passion as she rejects him, to a monumental rage in which she falls upon her maid, seizing her by the hair and throttling her, to a trembling subsidence after her father interrupts the tantrum, to a final collapse on her father's breast. The cast at rehearsal had been absolutely appalled at the scene (or so Shaw advertised in the *Star*); but the audience *would* be appalled unless Florence could successfully project Shaw's idea of passionate beauty.

By 5 December Shaw had been banished from rehearsals. James Welch was particularly annoyed at the novice's interference in stage matters of which, Welch concluded, he knew little. The "color" Shaw kept insisting upon came second; lines came first—and with Shaw interrupting, objecting, exhorting, and demonstrating, who could learn them? Shaw finally agreed to keep away so that they could learn their words. Two days later the cast went through a dress rehearsal at the Royalty Theatre, Dean Street, Soho—another unlucky theatre which had changed hands and names half a dozen times since its opening in 1840, although Ellen Terry had played there at fourteen, and Ada Cavendish, the actress with whom in Dublin days Shaw had fallen "wildly, madly, suddenly in love," had made her London debut on its stage. It was fitting, however, that Shaw, bringing the first of his strong women to the stage in *Widowers' Houses*, should have opened in a theatre managed by a woman, Kate Santley, who had the courage to play both Ibsen and Shaw and hear critics rave that her license should be revoked on account of it—but then the new drama in London was turning out to be in many ways a woman's movement.

Shaw watched the dress rehearsal anxiously. Florence's quite gorgeous costume changes from scarlet and jet fringe to heliotrope velvet to lemon satin under transparent gauze did not compensate for her lack of dramatic range. The other actors seemed to have scarcely better grasps on their parts. Welch went through the whole thing with an air of disbelief, never having quite agreed that he was acting in a genuine play. Shaw went away in despair. The rehearsal had been so "atrociously bad" that he could think of nothing else all evening, and sat down to write Grein and Florence last-minute letters of instruction. The next day there was a late rehearsal, and the next evening at eight-thirty the curtain would go up.

Shaw's diary entry for the momentous ninth of December was as brief as ever. "Production of Widowers' Houses by the Independent Theatre at the Royalty. 20½," he noted. "I forget what I did today, except—Oh, I remember. I went over to FE at about noon and stayed there for some hours. Then I walked into town. Made a speech at the end of the play. Spent the night at Fitzroy Square." Florence undoubtedly went home to brood. She had played Blanche as "a female cat," a sort of English Hedda Gabler, but according to Shaw her performance had been "painfully amateurish."

Yet the evening, like the evening of 7 June 1889 at the Novelty, had been an event. Lacking Ibsen's poetic feeling and psychological depth of characterization, Shaw had nevertheless created an important play. Fabians and Ibsenites had cheered, traditionalists booed, but, as Grein declared, the important point was that *Widowers' Houses* was recognized immediately as the first real English manifestation of the New Drama.

The buzzing of the critics, the discussions among the avant-garde were deafening. One paper reported at length on the socialist speech Shaw made before the curtain, then remembered absently that a play had preceded it. One critic called the work "a ridiculous abortion." But they were talking, as Shaw had wanted them to talk: he spent much of the next days reading reviews, and on 22 December "set to work making an album of all the press notices of the play."

Of course most critics, whether hostile or friendly, had misunderstood. They dismissed Sartorius, the man of business, as a "sophistical villain," whereas Shaw had meant him as a sweeping indictment of the capitalist class. "My portraiture of Lickcheese, the slum rent collector, an effective but quite common piece of work," wrote Shaw in a Preface to the published play three months later, "pleased better than any of the rest"—a tribute not only to Shaw, of course, but to the disaffected Welch. "My technical skill as a playwright sustained many attacks, all based on the assumption that the only admissible stage technique is the technique of plot construction . . . . It was further objected that my play, being didactic, was therefore not a work of art—a proposition which, if examined, will be found to mean either that the world's acknowledged masterpieces are not works of art, or else exactly nothing at all." Yet in claiming *Widowers' Houses* a work of art, Shaw felt compelled to make "a melancholy reservation." Nobody, he warned, "will find it a beautiful or lovable work. It is saturated with the vulgarity of the life it represents: the people do not speak nobly, live gracefully, or sincerely face their own position: the author is not giving expression in pleasant fancies to the underlying beauty and romance of happy life, but dragging up to the smooth surface of 'respectability' a handful of the slime and foulness of its polluted bed, and playing off your laughter at the scandal of the exposure against your shudder at its blackness. I offer it as my own criticism of the author of *Widowers' Houses* that the disillusion which makes all great dramatic poets tragic has here made him only derisive; and that derision is by common consent a baser atmosphere than that of tragedy."

The reservation was both humble and defiant. It recalled the young Shaw who, introduced to the beauties of Kelmscott House and the beautiful May, had tried to warn her of his innate vulgarity and his unconquerable penchant for derision. It recalled the more recent conflict of the Shaw who told Janet Achurch that he would face the inevitable squalor as bravely as ever, yet hungry for the noblest poetic beauty, would not be reconciled to it. Still Shaw asked that although *Widowers' Houses* had been created by a mind gorged with the problems of slums and poverty, his readers judge it not as a social pamphlet but as a work of art.[17]

William Archer could not do so; and it is a tribute to Shaw's amiability that the two continued to be friends after Archer's "It's a pity that

Mr. Shaw should labour under a delusion as to the true bent of his talent. . . . A man of his power of mind can do nothing that is altogether contemptible. We may be quite sure that if he took palette and 'commenced painter,' or set to work to manipulate a lump of clay, he would produce a picture or a statue that would bear the impress of a keen intelligence, and would be well worth looking at. That is precisely the case of *Widowers' Houses.* It is a curious example of what can be done in art by sheer brainpower, apart from natural aptitude. For it does not appear that Mr. Shaw has any more specific talent for the drama than he has for painting or sculpture."[18]

Another matinee was scheduled on 13 December before the players, not yet paid and not to be paid, disbanded. Shaw again made a little speech before the curtain. Afterward Jenny, Shaw's aunt Georgina, Lucy, and May Sparling came to Fitzroy Square to tea. Shaw did not mention his mother having attended either performance. That night he took the train out to Hammersmith. The next day he answered a letter from Charrington, who had written to demand why he had not approached him and Janet with his play:

> If you have seen 'Widowers' Houses' you will understand that it was altogether too experimental to be put on anywhere except at the I.T., least of all at the theatre of any manager for whom I had a ray of personal regard. . . . However, I have proved myself a man to be reckoned with. I have got the blue book across the footlights. I have made Welch's reputation and blasted Florence Farr's. . . . And I have spent so much time at rehearsal that I am stark ruined, and am ruefully asking myself whether a continental trip for my health would not have been far more economical than all this theatrical glory. For of what value was it to me when J. A. C. was not there to see. . . .[19]

He spent Christmas Eve and Day at Hammersmith with Morris, May, and Sparling. A hard frost had set in; the trees were soon "covered with hoar frost to the very tops, bright sunshine, very pretty." "Shaw is happy," Morris observed, "because (as he sleeps with his window wide open) his water-jug is frozen deeper than any one else's."[20] He was happy too with three offers to publish *Widowers' Houses;* he was correcting and fitting the play with a Preface, and still sifting through more than one hundred and thirty press notices.

The last day of the year S.S.D.D. called at the precincts of the Golden Dawn in Clipstone Street at one o'clock. In lieu of public success, she sought there private fulfillment, perhaps escaping into one of the magic rituals by entering the vault or private chamber, remaining in silence and contemplation for several minutes, rising and performing the Qabalistic Cross and prayer, then proceeding to the contemplation of some object such as a Tarot trump . . . .[21] That night when Shaw went around to Dalling Road to give her greeting for the new year there was no light in her window. She has gone to the theatre, he concluded; and took himself back to Hammersmith to be petted and adored by May.

CHAPTER EIGHT

1893

Shaw continued with the Sparlings at Hammersmith in the early days of January 1893, finding himself blessed in the charm of the house, for May had inherited her father's sense of beauty and proportion. And at first Sparling seemed glad to have him, for Shaw kept his wife in good humor, "and produced a cuisine that no mere husband could elicit." Eventually, however, the vegetarian dishes concocted especially for Shaw, his endless sessions at the piano with May, the animated tête-à-têtes, the skating excursions to Grove Park, Chiswick, the Irishman's irrepressible flirtations—all quite suddenly began to pall. The guest had become the center of the household, and it was quite obvious that, given to choose, May preferred Shaw. Considering the ménage à trois innocent and beneficial himself, Shaw suddenly found himself confronted by an irate husband who unaccountably did not find him either innocent or beneficial; who, in fact, considered his marriage broken. And by a wife who now considered that she rather belonged to Shaw.

There were several choices. According to Shaw, the mystic bond he had once felt with May now asserted itself irresistibly, making the situation very difficult. "To begin with," he explained much later, "the legal husband was a friend whose conduct towards me had always been irreproachable. To be welcomed in his house and then steal his wife was revolting to my sense of honor and socially inexcusable; for though I was as extreme a freethinker on sexual and religious questions as any sane human being could be, I was not the dupe of the Bohemian Anarchism that is very common in socialist and literary circles. I knew that a scandal would damage both of us and damage the Cause as well. It seems easy in view of my later position to have sat down together as three friends and arranged a divorce; but at that time I could not afford to marry and I was by no means sure that he could afford to be divorced. Besides, I hated the idea of a prosaic and even mercenary marriage: that, somehow or other, was not on the plane of the Mystic Betrothal."

But Shaw's reasoning here was specious. There was scandal enough in his having moved in with the Sparlings in the first place. And since socialists were commonly Bohemian Anarchists, would a divorce have damaged the Cause? And then he had stolen Sparling's wife already, whether intending to or not. The truth was, Shaw did not want to marry May, or anybody. To consummate was to kill illusion and desire or, as he put it, to fail to rise to the plane of the Mystic Betrothal. Meanwhile the atmosphere at 8 Hammersmith Terrace thickened. "The more I reasoned about the situation the worse it was doomed to appear," said Shaw. "So I did not argue about it. I vanished."[1]

But his seemingly infinite entanglements with women went on. On 26 January Jenny Patterson came to the Square, but he had little time for her since he was on his way to the Athenaeum on Tottenham Court Road for a private performance of *Ghosts* in which a beauteous young actress appeared named Mrs. Patrick Campbell, a name that would be known all over London in three months. At the performance he met May, and brought her back to Fitzroy Square, where they found no one home and no fire to make tea, until Mrs. Shaw finally appeared and stopped May just as she was leaving. She could not stop Shaw, however; he went to Dalling Road, leaving May with his mother, and read Walt Whitman with Florence, and was so happy that he had "a desperate run to catch the train." It was one of the more peaceful moments in his frenetic existence.

On Saturday, 4 February, at five o'clock, Shaw climbed the seventy-four steps that led to Elizabeth Robins's rooms at 28 Manchester Square Mansions, behind Wigmore Street. Since the previous November, quires of a yet unnamed new play by Ibsen had been arriving sporadically from Norway as fast as they were printed, generating the most intense interest among the three privileged to receive them—Edmund Gosse, William Archer, and Elizabeth Robins—and among those who were not. Would the new play be a woman's play, Elizabeth prayed, or a man's, like *An Enemy of the People* and *Brand?* If a woman's play, would it be her kind of role, or something she found impossible? It might be the chance of a lifetime; it might be nothing. The first pulls were a bitter disappointment. The main character was a man, an elderly architect, a "fearfully *charmless*" creature, thought Henry James, reading the pulls over Elizabeth's shoulder, as it were; and then there was a young girl, with a knapsack and sailor hat—some kind of strong-minded female pedestrian. Nothing for Elizabeth at all: clearly, said James, she must play the old man! But by the time the last batches of play had arrived, Elizabeth realized that the part of Hilda Wangel was made for her.

Shaw thus came to interview Elizabeth about the production of *The Master Builder* scheduled for 20 February at the Trafalgar Square Theatre, and found her alone. His "getting at Archer" letter still rankling, Elizabeth assumed her best "Sir!" attitude, and at the first hint of familiarity from Shaw, insisted that her co-producer Herbert Waring be present before she would say a word. Irrepressible, Shaw then dared to accuse her of attempting to corrupt *him* with "her lustrous eyes," promising that he would print the whole story the next day. This was too much for Elizabeth. "If you do, I will shoot you!" she cried, and pointed dramatically: "The revolver is there!" Shaw had been enraptured with Elizabeth's Hedda handing Lövborg the pistol with love in her eyes, but this kind of love-death was to be avoided at all costs, and he beat a retreat back down the seventy-four steps without his interview.[2] Beerbohm Tree had called Elizabeth "a destroying angel in a bonnet," and Shaw had met the pure, the destroying, and the ladylike head on.

He sought refuge by taking the underground out to Dalling Road, where Florence's good-natured calm would be sure to soothe his ruffled spirits. And so it did, until late that evening when Jenny Patterson—maddened by the Hammersmith affair, the recent sittings to Bertha Newcombe, the flourishing adoration of Janet, the continued visits to Florence, and who knows what other iniquities—suddenly burst into the room. The lovers sprang apart. "There was a most shocking scene," reported Shaw, obviously shaken at last; "JP being violent and using atrocious language. At last I sent FE out of the room, having to restrain JP by force from attacking her." As constitutionally incapable of physical brutality as of fidelity, Shaw was a good *two hours* getting Jenny out of Florence's place—coaxing, bullying, and soothing her as he might a bad child. "I did not get her home to Brompton Square until near 1," he recorded, "nor could I get away myself until 3." During these hours he made Jenny write a letter to him, "expressing her regret and promising not to annoy F.E. again," which he gave May the next day to deliver to Florence. "I was horribly tired and shocked and upset," he concluded; "but I kept patience and did not behave badly nor ungently. Did not get to bed until 4; and had but a disturbed night of it."

The next day he was comforted by a note from Elizabeth Robins informing him that their conversation had not been an interview, that no public use must be made of it, and that in view of his attitude the whole idea of an interview must be dropped altogether. "I am sorry to have been the occasion of your wasting so much time," she ended icily.[3] Imperturbable, he replied, "Will you just look at this rough sketch of the interview you were good enough to give me on Saturday, and say what you think of it":

SENSATIONAL HEADINGS ad. lib.
LUSTROUS EYES
IBSEN'S MASTERPIECE
IF YOU DO, I WILL SHOOT YOU
THE REVOLVER IS THERE

"Never in my life have I had such a professional success," he chafed. "You were clay in the hands of the potter. I have interviewed beautiful women before; but none of them were ever so noble as to threaten to shoot me. It would make any ordinary man's fortune." After full instructions on how to conduct interviews in the future, he finally offered an explanation: "I could never have convinced you of the impolicy of your frightful and quite undeserved mistrust of me except by mystifying you as I have done. Now select a nice rehearsal for me and let us have a talk with Waring; and I will promise not to play any more pranks on you."4

But Elizabeth did not unbend. "Dear Mr. Shaw," she replied 6 February. "Your kind advice has I'm afraid little bearing upon an informal 5 o'clock visit. Still I may find one at least of your suggestions of service *when* I am interviewed."5 Two very similar personalities had met and clashed. Shaw assumed the guise of a brash eccentric, Elizabeth the sensibilities of a lady. Underneath, both were hard-working, crusading, idealistic, squeamish about sex, and preferred to fascinate rather than gratify. Evidently they did not recognize one another.

Shaw had, however, more pressing personal matters than Elizabeth's fury to contend with. He had written Jenny in the aftermath of her raid upon Dalling Road. She returned his letter with a denial that she had read it. Shaw returned her letter and his along with it. In the midst of this bother, he had retreated to May at Hammersmith Terrace, Florence having walked him there as far as the top of St. Peter's Park. He and May played for a while and then, quitting the piano, had "a conversation about old ties—rather an emotional one." As a result, in symbolic gesture, he stayed the night at the Terrace. But there were other scenes ahead. On 15 February he went to report a concert at the Albert Hall. During the interval Bertha Newcombe came and sat beside him. She had come, Shaw discovered, to quarrel: "and we had a scene, as far as that was possible in so public a place, about our recent correspondence," before Bertha left angrily in the middle of the second half. To make things worse, Florence had left for the country, leaving him, as he complained to Janet, "bereft of the solace of female society, all the rest of her sex having no notion of a man except as something to fall in love with and make scenes at, a habit of mind which makes the world unfit to live in for an interesting person like myself, or, as applied to my own sex, for a lovely person like you. I am up to my weary temples in sordid work, and would give anything to be able to fly to a desert island and write that play for you."[6]

Thinking to restore his faith in the female sex, Janet invited him the next day to go for a morning hansom ride. But Shaw the puritan never gave up his forenoons to folly. "No," he replied: "when I go for a hansom ride with you it shall be in the darkest night, with a phantom horse and a spectral driver in an utterly lonely country." He could not help romancing, yet was in no mood for adventures. "All this to flatter you," he added; "yrs insincerely GBS."[7]

He was more interested in promoting the Charringtons' latest struggle: the inauguration of a repertory season at the Royalty beginning with Janet's translation from the German of Richard Voss's *Alexandra*. They had asked Shaw to do an interview with them about the venture, but with their usual resistance to advice, were slow to co-operate, and Shaw ended by concocting the interview himself. He was doubtful about their choice of plays. Why did they not do *Rosmersholm*, as he had urged? Elizabeth Robins had made a stunning success in *The Master Builder*, which he had seen on 20 February at the opening matinee. It was now Janet's turn to re-establish herself as an Ibsen actress in the part of Rebecca West. Meanwhile, he was trying to write a play for Janet himself, a tragedy: "our play, the heroine of which must be clean, dry, strong and straight," he told her, with an implicit rebuke for the "stimulants" which he could never forget or condone.[8]

Elizabeth Robins had indeed triumphed as Hilda Wangel. "A marvellous effort," the *Theatre* of 1 April raved. "From beginning to end there is not the faintest trace of Miss Robins—Miss Robins of the musical low voice, love of the minor chords, somewhat lackadaisical manner, and crushed and broken expression. . . . in their place is as radiant, vigorous, determined, buoyant a girl as one could well conceive. The stage is lighted by her presence. . . . The study is cleverer than her Hedda Gabler, cleverer than Miss Achurch's first Nora Helmer." A former colleague of Elizabeth's was there to see her success, the dark and beautiful Mrs. Patrick Campbell. The two had played villainess and heroine against each other in 1891 in the roaring melodrama *The Trumpet Call* at the Adelphi; but Elizabeth's heroine had been quite overshadowed on opening night (and after) by a titillating incident—a sudden flash of "limbs" when Mrs. Campbell's ragged black gypsy skirt had inexplicably fallen down around her feet. Now Mrs. Campbell marveled at the swiftness with which Elizabeth succeeded in sending thought across the footlights, and delighted in her seriousness and cleverness and intelligence, safe in the knowledge that one dropped skirt on a London stage was worth any amount of brains. As for Shaw, he expressed the deepest admiration for Elizabeth's noble and beautiful performance, but denied a personal truce.

". . . I hasten to relieve you from any sense of being disarmed against your will," he wrote her after the performance on 3 March, "by assuring you, in our personal, non-artistic and non-critical relations, of my unmitigated defiance, and resentment of the wounds you have dealt to my justifiable vanity."⁹

That same day Shaw attended the dress rehearsal of *Alexandra*. Back at Fitzroy Square he wrote to Janet:

> I cry off the tragedy: I can write nothing beautiful enough for you. And I can no longer allow myself to be in love with you: nobody short of an archangel with purple and gold wings shall henceforth be allowed to approach you. . . . I am actually less enamoured than before, because my admiration elbows out the commoner sentiment. I speak as a critic, not merely as a miserable two legged man. It was a masterpiece of conception in that *genre*, and a masterpiece of execution both for beauty of style and success of expression. Do not read the papers . . . . Do not let Archer put you out of conceit with your curious punctuation: it is all right—your internal music is not at fault: *I* say that everything was beautiful, and that you are the sufficient justification of all the shortcomings of the play. . . . Now for Rosmersholm. I will stand no more of that wretched old Doll's House. There is no going back now.¹⁰

The love talk was perhaps automatic; the criticism genuine, for to Charrington after the first night on 4 March he wrote, "It seems to me that the night left J. A. beyond all question at the head of her profession. Make her follow it up by something new."¹¹ The critics did not agree with Shaw—or at least while they praised the acting, they doomed the play. Bertha Newcombe was finishing a drawing of Janet that Shaw had persuaded her to do at the Charrington place in Onslow Square when Charrington came bursting in with an armful of newspapers and read out the various verdicts—"slated" here, "slated" there. The *Times* objected that the company for the most part took themselves very seriously. And Archer, a critic they needed on their side, complained in the *World* that *Alexandra* lacked the two main ingredients of the higher modern drama —analysis and irony—and proclaimed that he could really take no interest in anything so heavy.

And the Charringtons did not go forward, as Shaw had wisely urged. Except for a few performances of *The Lady from the Sea*, they fell back on *A Doll's House* again and began rehearsing Brandon Thomas's *Clever Alice* (Janet had begged money from Irving for it years before) and "the old stalking horse" *Adrienne Lecouvreur*. "I take the gloomiest view of the prospects of Clever Alice," Shaw told Charrington on opening night, 6 April. It was obvious to him that Janet merely wanted to dress up in a fancy tinsel costume and torment him by wearing an awful golden wig. And indeed, he informed her husband after the performance, the brazen curls had broken his heart.[12]

Adrienne Lecouvreur was worse. Florence Farr had joined the Charrington company again to play the Princess; and it was upon her head after the dismal first night that Shaw vented a tirade of invective that surpassed his considerable accomplishments in that line. The "unspeakable absurdity" of the performance had only been surpassed by the "unparalleled blastedness" of the play. The last act had been "simply ridiculous" and Janet "transcendently bad." The antics of the rest of the cast had been "ghastly and ridiculous." As for Florence, her wig was "only fit for a Salvation Army drumstick," her acting in the first scene had been "insufferable," her diction unintelligible, her carriage contorted. After this inventory of horrors, Florence must have been astonished to read that after all she had "rather scored off" the play. He was itching to go over her part with her, but Friday, Saturday, and Sunday were jam full, and after all, "The sooner the play disappears, the better for the reputation of the Charringtons & their enterprise."[13] To the certain disaster of the Charrington bank account, *Adrienne Lecouvreur* did disappear after a few performances. Florence did not so much mind not getting paid, but did resent Charrington's obvious contempt for her ability and his open reminders that he had only taken her on because he could get no one else.

The Charringtons were now broke; and Shaw chided, telling them that the money they had wasted on *Clever Alice* and *Adrienne* might better have been spent on advertising *Alexandra*, which had displayed Janet's talents so effectively. Useless to rehearse what might have been. Charrington could not seem to find the proper setting for his diamond, and Janet contemptuously refused to stoop to practical methods of finding money and patronage.[14] Shaw fretted: the idea of her not having plenty of money rankled; even the sight of a little hole in her glove gave his heartstrings a deadly twitch. He had little money to lend himself, but was not above lamenting the Charrington case with sympathetic souls, with the result that he was able to send Janet one day a loan of ten pounds from May Morris with the innocent instruction that if she was offended, she must take it out on him, not May. "Damn the whole monetary system!"[15]

Meanwhile, the actress who cordially detested him was continuing her triumphant progress through Ibsen with repeat performances of *Hedda Gabler*, *The Master Builder*, and *Rosmersholm* at the Opéra Comique—triumphs, Shaw felt, that should have belonged to Janet. Having Archer, Gosse, and Ibsen on one's side was clearly more profitable at the moment than having Shaw. And yet Elizabeth Robins had just forfeited her chance for a West End success. Inspired by Ibsen, Arthur Wing Pinero had written a seemingly frank play about a woman-with-a-past and sent it to George Alexander, actor-manager of the St. James's Theatre. Despite its daring, Alexander decided to produce *The Second Mrs. Tanqueray*. The only problem was the actress: she must be exotic, a little dangerous, very modern, quite neurotic, yet appealing. Remembering *Hedda Gabler*, Alexander felt that Elizabeth Robins was a distinct possibility; yet he sent his wife and Graham Robertson on a round of London theatres to scout the talent. Eventually they ended at the home of melodrama, the Adelphi, where they were bored immeasurably until the villainess of the piece entered, a young woman "almost painfully thin, with great eyes and a slow haunting utterance"; not beautiful, perhaps, but "intensely interesting and arresting." The scouters rushed to tell Alexander that Mrs. Patrick Campbell was his Paula Tanqueray. She was contacted, she accepted; then was refused release by the Adelphi management, which just days before had fired her. In the interim, Elizabeth Robins signed a contract with Alexander to play Paula. When a distracted Mrs. Campbell came to plead with him, he offered his apologies. Pinero, however, would not accept defeat: Mrs. Campbell *was* his Paula Tanqueray. To settle the impasse, Alexander and Pinero decided to put the case to Elizabeth Robins and accept her decision.

"I suppose Mr. Alexander has told you of what occurred Sunday and yesterday," Elizabeth wrote Stella Campbell. "I congratulate you upon your splendid fortune in having *The Second Mrs. Tanqueray* to play. From what I heard read of the part, it is the kind of thing that comes along once in an actress's lifetime, seldom oftener, and that it has come to *you* is my best consolation for having lost it myself. You will play it brilliantly, and your loyal service in less congenial *rôles* will find its reward in this glorious new opportunity. There is to my mind no woman in London so enviable at this moment, dear savage, as *you*."[16] Elizabeth never mentioned the incident again in public, but Mrs. Campbell remembered, as well she might, how Elizabeth "resigned the part to me without a murmur, in the most unselfish manner imaginable. Wasn't it sweet of her? I shall never forget her action, for it proves that women can be chivalrous to one another in spite of all that is said of them."[17] *The Second Mrs. Tanqueray* opened on 27 May. The dazed leading lady rushed home immediately after the curtain fell, sure that she had failed; and woke to find herself the most celebrated actress in London.

Shaw went with May to watch Hedda hand Lövborg the pistol with love in her eyes once more on the evening of 5 June, then went home to woo this strange woman who had failed to capitulate to his charm. What, after all, had been his crimes? She had snapped her fingers and said, "Dog: come here!" and he had gone, only to be threatened with a gun. He had found her a cab (did she remember that day a year ago?) and got in with her to drive with her home, only to have her suddenly remember some other appointment and fling him out again into the mud.

Granted he was odious—did she not see that he could be made use of? "You are too exacting," he accused. "I have flattered you beyond the utmost appetite of the next vainest woman in the world, heaping up praises that would have sounded exaggerated if divided among the Virgin Mary, Duse, and Cleopatra. But you always find I crumple one of the million roseleaves, and turn and rend me for it. . . ." But now he had a more tempting bait than reviews to dangle. "I have finished another play," he concluded, "with four good parts for men and three for women—the chief of the three a superb one. Aha! I do not know how to write for the stage, do I not? We shall see, injurious Elizabeth, we shall see."[18]

The play was not the tragedy for Janet Achurch with its clean, dry, strong, and straight heroine. Given Shaw's frantic activities during these months with May, Jenny, Florence, Elizabeth, Janet, Bertha, and even one day at Bertha's a Nellie Erichsen who attracted him considerably, how much more natural that he had sat down to write something called *The Philanderer*. The play consolidated the frustrations of eight years with Jenny Patterson's possessiveness. It was all there: Jenny's pathetic attempts to keep up with Shaw's advanced ideas and friends; Jenny's desperate attempts to prove that she was Shaw's new "unwomanly woman" just as much as Florence or Janet; her rages; her childish passions; her spying through wastebaskets for letters; her pretending to return letters unread; even her descent upon Dalling Road, for Shaw began his play with "Julia" bursting in on a pair of surprised lovers and the tirade, "Dont cast me off without a thought of all I have at stake. I could be a friend to you if you would only let me; if you would only tell me your plans; give me a share in your work; treat me as something more than the amusement of an idle hour. Oh, Leonard, Leonard, youve never given me a chance: indeed you havnt. I'll take pains; I'll read; I'll try to think; I'll conquer my jealousy I'll—Oh, I'm mad: I'm mad: youll kill me if you desert me."

The play is thus an exposure of the old ways of love: the secrecy, the "honor," the demands for fidelity, the forced chivalry, the lies—a condemnation, in short, of the outworn concepts of manliness and womanliness. And there are many effective stabs at the old ways: new woman Grace Tranfield's scornful reply to Julia, "I will not give myself to any man who has learnt how to treat women from you and your like"; or the philandering Charteris's "Advanced people form charming friendships; conventional people marry"; or Charteris's denunciation of Julia: "I accuse you of habitual and intolerable jealousy and ill temper; of insulting me on imaginary provocation . . . and then representing yourself as an ill used saint and martyr wantonly betrayed and deserted by a selfish monster of a man." Philanderers, Shaw tried to show, are not born but made by the artificial relations society enforces between men and women.

And yet the character of the philanderer half defeats Shaw's case for new and honorable relationships between the sexes, because Charteris emerges as that timeless misfortune: the person who evokes deep feeling while remaining immune to it him- or herself. And his actions are often crooked. He tries to convince Julia Craven, for example, that marriage would betray "their" advanced Ibsenist views, knowing all the while that she has only adopted those views to please him, and meanwhile proposing marriage to the genuinely modern Grace Tranfield. He is brash (as well as amusing), reading aloud the love letters of Julia and Grace to their fathers and announcing that they both want him ("May I ask, Mr. Charteris, is this the New Humor?" Grace's father demands). And he is callous, remaining "amused and untouched" even in the last minutes of the play when the others are awed by Julia's sorrow. He is condemned out of Julia's mouth when she cries, "I know you now, Leonard Charteris, through and through, in all your falseness, your petty spite, your cruelty and your vanity. . . . You fraud! You humbug! You miserable little plaster saint!" And he both condemns and redeems himself when he tells her: "Oh, what I have learnt from you! from you! who could learn nothing from me! I made a fool of you; and you brought me wisdom: I broke your heart; and you brought me joy: I made you curse your womanhood; and you revealed my manhood to me. Blessings for ever and ever on my Julia's name!"[19]

The Philanderer was thus a bitter-comic drama, with a heroine too understated to win the cause for the New Woman, a "heavy" too sympathetic to dash the case against the Old, and a hero who cannot be trusted with either. It is as ambiguous as Shaw's own feelings about the duel of sex, and its interest stems not so much from its topical case against sexual politics as from its unresolved tension between the woman who wants and the man who eludes. Shaw seemed to begin with the idea of Jenny Patterson as good copy, and ended by making her the most compelling figure in the play: four good parts for men, as he told Elizabeth Robins, and a superb one for a woman. Exaggeration aside, *The Philanderer* turned out to be both a stab at Jenny and his apology to her. For although "Tannhäuser may die in the conviction that one moment of the emotion he felt with St Elizabeth was fuller and happier than all the hours of passion he spent with Venus," wrote Shaw in the *Quintessence*, ". . . that does not alter the fact that love began for him with Venus. . . ." "I learnt more from the first stupid woman who fell in love with me," he would tell Ellen Terry more simply, "than ever [brains] taught me." But *The Philanderer* was also his farewell.

The drama finished, Shaw looked about for a company to play it. The Independent Theatre could not be trusted, he felt, to bring off the high comedy and "dressed, easy, and refined" atmosphere he wanted, even if Grein had admired the play—which he did not. Shaw looked wistfully toward the West End, where Charles Wyndham, actor-manager of the Criterion, could have played Leonard Charteris superbly: the only actor in England who could strike the nice balance between caddishness and sensibility that the part required. But the West End dealt in sexuality only when it could be insinuated or punished; and *The Philanderer*'s open and therefore unpleasant sexual theme was unthinkable, even if Shaw had connections in the West End—which he did not. Archer was frankly appalled by the play, and further convinced that the privileged lunatic was no playwright. Indeed no one seemed to like the play, and Shaw was required to put his second effort aside.

Florence undoubtedly appreciated *The Philanderer*. She was at work at the same time on a novel about a cad which she titled less severely *The Dancing Faun*.[20] Essentially good-natured and unpossessive, Florence felt nevertheless understandable frustration with Shaw's quixotic behavior. She revenged herself on paper by portraying George Travers, half man, half goat, a philanderer compounded perhaps of other men, but with a great deal that was recognizably Shaw. She too could turn the adventures of the past few months into copy, and must have taken some pleasure in having Lady Geraldine, the woman Travers philanders with behind his wife Grace's back, take up a pistol at the news he intends to desert her, and shoot him. On 11 May, a day that Shaw told Archer that he'd all but finished *The Philanderer*, "quite as promising a failure as Widowers' Houses, but a step nearer to something more than talk about what plays ought to be," Florence read him parts of *The Dancing Faun*. Shaw did not record his opinion of this glimpse of hostility.

He was finding Florence out when he called at Dalling Road more and more frequently. Her destination these days was often the premises of the Golden Dawn in Clipstone Street. She would make at least seventy visits in 1893, usually without bothering to tell him she would be out, else he hardly would have made so many futile trips to Ravenscourt Park. Yeats and the members of the Golden Dawn were more and more in the picture, the occult more and more prominent in her conversation. Of course they still gadded about together, meeting on the run for tea at the Orange Grove or at Crystal Palace concerts, spending the evening at the Earl's Court Exhibition and going down "the water shoot," stopping to listen to an extraordinary performance by a nightingale near Ealing, or in fine weather walking in Regent's Park. On 19 August they both took the afternoon off, meeting at the Finchley Road Station and walking to Hampstead Heath, buying some fruit on the way, and then settling down among the ferns not far from Spaniards Inn to read the papers and doze in the sunshine. Dead beat as usual from his fast pace, Shaw fell asleep and woke as the setting sun was turning a bank of clouds on the horizon into such a likeness of mountains with sun on them that he thought he must be asleep and dreaming of Switzerland, instead of awake with Florence on Hampstead Heath.

In the ferns he found a pencil that he had lost the day before, one that he had perhaps used in haphazardly jotting down ideas for still another play he had begun to think about almost as soon as finishing *The Philanderer*. This new play was far removed from Florence's and Yeats's pursuits at the Golden Dawn, but close to his intent in *The Philanderer* to show "the grotesque sexual compacts made between men and women under marriage laws . . . which 'advanced' individuals are therefore forced to evade." The impetus for this third drama had come from Janet Achurch, who had read Maupassant's *Yvette* and seen a play in it. "It being hopeless to get me to read anything," Shaw remembered (a boast: he had recently read *The Pilgrim's Progress, The Wandering Jew, Moll Flanders, All's Well That Ends Well, Twelfth Night,* and *Les Miserables*), "she told me the story, which was ultra-romantic. I said, 'Oh, I will work out the real truth about that mother some day.' "[21] Meanwhile, he suggested that since the Charringtons had perennial difficulty finding new plays and Janet was clever with her pen, she do her own version of *Yvette*.

At the end of August he was making a third with Sidney and Beatrice Webb at their cottage called the Argoed at Monmouth in the valley of the Wye and, as he informed Archer, had finished the first act of his new play, in which he had "skilfully blended the plot of The Second Mrs. Tanqueray with that of the Cenci." And indeed he had begun with the notion of making the fallen mother, like Paula Tanqueray, the central character in a conflict with a virtuous daughter, like Pinero's Ellean. Here, however, Beatrice Webb ("whose knowledge of English social types is as remarkable as her command of industrial and political questions," said Shaw) put in a word. "She suggested that I should put on the stage a real modern lady of the governing class—not the sort of thing that theatrical and critical authorities imagine such a lady to be." Shaw was always alert for ideas ("I am a crow who has followed many ploughs"), and seemed particularly open to suggestions from women who, in this age of social upheaval, seemed both right at the heart of things and, because they had not been allowed men's mistakes, right. He now retrained the emphasis of this third play, "and the result was Vivie Warren . . . Mrs. Warren herself was my version of the heroine of the romance narrated by Miss Achurch."

The heroine of Guy de Maupassant's "romance" is Mme. Obardi, a brothel-keeper who accepts her calling and, when not bored with her customers, enjoys falling in love with them. Shaw borrowed heavily from her defense against her innocent daughter's shocked discovery of her profession:

I'm a harlot, it's true, and I'm proud of it; I'm worth a dozen of your honest women. . . . If I weren't a harlot, you'd be a kitchenmaid today, as I was once, and you'd work for twenty sous a day, and you'd wash the dishes, and your mistress would send you out on errands to the butcher's, d'you hear, and kick you out if you were idle; whereas here you are, idling all day long, just because I *am* a harlot. There! When you're only a poor servant girl with fifty francs of savings, you must get away from it somehow if you don't want to rot in the workhouse; and there's only one way for women, only one way, d'you hear, when you're a servant! We can't make our fortunes on the stock exchange or at high finance. We've nothing but our bodies, nothing but our bodies.

Mme. Obardi does not convince her daughter, who tries to commit suicide by inhaling chloroform. The chloroform does not kill Yvette, however, but sends her into a rosy trance, so that when the roué she has resisted for so long leans over her bed to try to revive her, she opens her arms and yields at last to her mother's profession. The mother is relieved, the roué triumphant, and Yvette trapped immediately by the chloroform, but ultimately by her helplessness to escape the disreputable life to which she was born and raised.

Shaw rejected both the sensuality of the mother and the fatalism of the daughter's fall, making his brothel-keeper a businesswoman, and pulling her daughter out of the brothel and sending her to Newnham: Maupassant was content to describe the harlot with delicate cynicism; Shaw wished to reform the society that made her. He notified Janet of his progress on 4 September: "The play progresses bravely; but it has left the original lines. I have made the daughter the heroine, and the mother a most deplorable old rip (saving your presence). The great scene will be the crushing of the mother by the daughter. . . . The second act is half finished and wholly planned. How does your version progress?"[22] *Mrs. Warren's Profession*, he had decided, would be just the thing for the Independent Theatre.

Shaw's third play—the best he had written and one that would rank among his best—merged the themes of social corruption from *Widowers' Houses* and sexual corruption from *The Philanderer* in an explosive combination. Shaw intended first to "draw attention to the truth that prostitution is caused, not by female depravity and male licentiousness, but simply by underpaying, undervaluing, and overworking women so shamefully that the poorest of them are forced to resort to prostitution to keep body and soul together"; and second, "to expose the fact that prostitution is not only carried on without organization by individual enterprise in the lodgings of solitary women, each her own mistress as well as every customer's mistress, but organized and exploited as a big international commerce for the profit of capitalists like any other commerce, and very lucrative to great city estates, including Church estates, through the rents of the houses in which it is practised."[23] That was all: an intention no more unpalatable than his attempt in *An Unsocial Socialist* to indict the whole capitalist system. And if prostitution was not enough to shock, Shaw tossed in the incest theme from *The Cenci* by suggesting that Vivie Warren's marriage to either the old roué Crofts or young Frank Gardner might involve marrying a father or a brother; made his brothel-keeper a hideous parody of middle-class respectability; and created a shockingly cold heroine who rejects both mother and lover to return with gusto to her accounting business and cigars.

Back in London, "in rougher and coarser health" from his holiday, Shaw began the search for a cast, although the play was still unfinished. He intended the part of Vivie Warren for Janet, and went to the Charringtons' on 11 October to read her two acts. The "deplorable old rip" would be something of a problem. Meanwhile, he worked at Act III in his peripatetic way, strolling about the Mall under the lamps on the sixteenth until it was time to go to the Criterion, and on the eighteenth sitting on Primrose Hill, but not getting on as well as he expected. On 30 October he met Elizabeth Robins at Mrs. W. K. Clifford's, and had a long talk with her about playing Mrs. Warren, for which (after a detour past Florence's dark windows) he went home to apologize as usual. He had not been responsible for his actions that afternoon, he told her: he had been exhausted from work on the Fabian Manifesto and the resulting storm of abuse on its publication. "I was in quite a childish state when you arrived and magnetised me as usual; and if you had petted me, bought me some candy, and wheeled me home in a perambulator, I should have considered it as most kind and appropriate to my condition. As it was, you were an ineffable consolation to me—it was black ingratitude to try to let you in for this villainous play, which is quite unworthy of you."[24]

Meanwhile, he approached friends and acquaintances with the play. The result was not encouraging. As a heroine, Vivie Warren "laid William Archer's intellect in ruins." He read the play to Mrs. Theodore Wright, who had played Mrs. Alving in the notorious *Ghosts* and might be expected to welcome a challenging part. On hearing the play, however, the actress "rose up; declared that not even in her own room could she speak the part to herself, much less in public to a younger woman."[25] By mid-November he was again appealing to Elizabeth Robins. " 'Heilige Elisabeth, *Bitte für mich*': I am at my wit's end about this unlucky play of mine." He desperately needed someone to play Mrs. Warren, a woman between forty and fifty, to Janet's Vivie. "The play is not an *immoral* one," he assured her, "and the right woman ought to have the courage for it."[26] And indeed "Holy Elizabeth, pray for me," the repentant Tannhäuser's dying words, should have disarmed suspicion.

Enraged, Elizabeth showed Shaw's note to Archer, who, although one of Shaw's closest friends, could not always be accused of acting sympathetically toward him, especially where Elizabeth Robins was concerned. He wrote a reply which Elizabeth copied and sent Shaw along with his note: "Dear Mr. S. I think I ought to tell you that I have no appreciation for the style of German exemplified in the enclosed letter-card. If at any time you should want to write me on business I must ask you to use the usual forms of address; & in the mean time please don't take the trouble to answer this."[27]

Amazed at the touchiness of this actress who could not be persuaded to take his flattery as anything but a slight, Shaw viewed her eventual suggestions of Frances Ivor or Olga Nethersole, two "intellectual" actresses who might be tempted by the part, as a mockery and an attempt to ruin him: and supposed that in order to get her to act for him he would have to write a play with an inflated lead and all other parts about six lines long.[28] He seemed strangely obtuse in his method of treating her, not seeming to realize that she did not like his patent brand of flattery and wished to be treated like a professional, not like a pretty woman. Shaw considered her standoffish attitude mere ladylike hypocrisy, which he loathed, and tried to puncture her pretenses with coarseness and familiarity. She considered that she was making a stand for dignity in a profession which had too long been associated with prostitution. He did not consider her liaison with the infatuated Archer above suspicion. She knew his suspicions and considered them beneath contempt.

Although he believed *Mrs. Warren's Profession* just the thing for the I.T., Shaw was certain by the time he actually approached Grein that there was not the least chance of the play being licensed by the censor. It was partly cast—Janet for Vivie, Bernard Gould as Frank Gardner, Charrington to play Crofts; but there was no Mrs. Warren. "I should be content, myself, with Mrs. Patrick Campbell," Shaw told Grein, hopefully with irony since the actress was now the most sought-for commodity in London. "The part is a vulgar one; but unless the vulgarity is the artistic vulgarity of a refined actress, just as the immorality must be the artistic immorality of a woman whom the audience respects, the part will be unendurable. . . . There is a reputation to be got out of the part."[29]

Eventually, however, Shaw realized the extent of his audacity. "I could not have done anything more injurious to my prospects at the outset of my career," he wrote in the Preface. "My play was immediately stigmatized by the Lord Chamberlain . . . as 'immoral and otherwise improper for the stage.' Its performance was prohibited, I myself being branded by implication, to my great damage, as an unscrupulous and blackguardly author. . . . the injury done me, now admittedly indefensible, was real and considerable . . . ."

So Mrs. Warren's profession, the profession that Mrs. Patrick Campbell as Mrs. Tanqueray could suggest on a West End stage as long as she looked exquisitely genteel and committed suicide at the end of the play, could not stand the kind of social analysis that Shaw brought to it; and he put his play to rest along with the unacceptable *Philanderer*. Beaten into tough elasticity by years of rejection, however, Shaw could not be discouraged. Three weeks after completing his third play on 2 November 1893, he was writing a fourth.

CHAPTER NINE

1893-1894

LATE IN 1893 it became clear that Florence Farr, who had been treated shabbily by the Charringtons over *Adrienne Lecouvreur,* had found money for a theatrical venture of her own. On 7 November Shaw heard by letter that she had been offered £500 to produce *The Wild Duck;* that evening at six they took a short walk together, and Shaw began to steer her right back to his favorites, the always impoverished Charringtons. As a result, he went to the Charringtons in Onslow Square on 21 November to talk over their plan of doing a tour with Florence on the strength of the capital that had been promised her for the theatrical venture. There was talk of *The Vikings at Helgeland* as well as of the old standby, *A Doll's House.* With grand tactlessness, however, Janet made it clear that she was to have the best roles even though Florence put up the money. With Shaw on 23 November at the Albert Hall for Handel's *Israel in Egypt,* Florence quite naturally complained; and Shaw was forced to pen a quick warning to Janet: "F. must play Hiordis in The Vikings for the simple reason that she has the £500. How many people would find money for a tour and play Mrs. Linden to your Nora? Besides Farr couldnt play the other part [Dagny] in TV. Dont be greedy."[1] And yet if there were ever a part unsuitable to Florence's range, surely it was Hiordis.

The Golden Dawn had proved profitable for S.S.D.D. Among the practitioners of magic was Annie E. F. Horniman, thirty-three-year-old granddaughter of the founder of the Horniman tea company. Upon his death in 1893, Annie came into a substantial sum of money. She had always been fascinated with the theatre—secretly fascinated, for her puritanical family deplored the wicked world of the stage. Now she had met

Florence, an experienced actress with connections to the theatrical world, the New Drama, and the new playwright and publicist Bernard Shaw. Anonymously she would back Florence, who must decide about a company, the plays, a manager. Although *The Wild Duck* had been mentioned, Florence could do anything she liked.

Florence considered Ibsen and the Charringtons, and rejected both. Instead she asked Shaw for a play, with the result that on 26 November, after fleeing Fitzroy Square to avoid Jenny Patterson, who called ostensibly to cheer his sick mother, he was able to return and spend the evening playing the piano and beginning a romantic drama for Florence. Two days later, waiting for Florence at Dalling Road, he worked at the play until past four. On 2 December, advising Janet, who had always wanted to hear him lecture, that he would be speaking in her neighborhood on "How We Became Atheists," Shaw added, "I have made a desperate attempt to begin a real romantic play for F.F. in the style of Victor Hugo. The first act is nearly finished; and it is quite the funniest attempt at that style of composition ever made."[2] Having reminded himself what an amusing job he was making of it, he could not resist going over to the Charringtons' lodgings at Battersea Park to read them *Alps and Balkans*, as he had titled the play. The evening turned into a bout of play reading: Janet read him as much as she had written of her play—the original Mrs. Warren, now titled *Mrs. Daintree's Daughter*. Charrington came in later and read from the second act of his play (*Sister Helen?*), and then it was Shaw's turn—"an orgy of play-reading over which we all made merry."

Florence had another literary friend to turn to. At Christmastime she brought Yeats to her sister's Christmas party at Number Three The Orchard in Bedford Park. "She asked me to write a one-act play that her niece, Miss Dorothy Paget, a girl of eight or nine, might make her first stage appearance," Yeats remembered, "and I, with my Irish Theatre in mind, wrote *The Land of Heart's Desire*, in some discomfort when the child was theme, for I knew nothing of children, but with an abundant mind when Mary Bruin was, for I knew an Irish woman whose unrest troubled me."[3]

By January 1894 Florence was searching for a theatre, holding up the completion of a poster by Aubrey Beardsley, a young artist just rising to fame, until she decided upon the Avenue Theatre on Northumberland Avenue near the Embankment. She chose C. T. H. Helmsley for her manager ("Why is Florence no friend of yours?" Shaw would apostrophize Charrington: "Why had you not the handling of that Avenue season? . . . solely because you hated her, humiliated her"), and pressed Shaw for the play he had promised her. But *Arms and the Man*, as Shaw's fourth effort was now called, was not ready despite Florence's reproaches. She was forced to begin her season with John Todhunter's new play *A Comedy of Sighs* and Yeats's *Land of Heart's Desire*.

Todhunter's last play, *The Black Cat*, had provoked Archer to turn upon the New Drama with a snarl after opening night on 8 December. Todhunter, wrote Archer, had "treated the weird but scanty audience of long-haired atheists, sexless socialists, agnostics, Ibsenites, Anarchists and egotists to a demonstration in morbid anatomy so appalling and sickening as to delight their carrion-loving souls." But this verdict sounded so like Clement Scott's screams over Ibsen that it only convinced the avant-garde that Todhunter was the playwright of the moment.

A Comedy of Sighs opened 29 March. In compliance with Florence's tastes, Todhunter had written a Modern Woman play, emphasizing character development and dialogue rather than plot and situation in the Ibsen manner, but without Ibsen's genius. The play was full of Florence's distaste for marriage, and provided her with bravado lines like "Why should a girl be persecuted into marriage before she has time to live?" and "Didn't you find marriage rather a horrid experience when it came?" and "Don't you think a man's love is rather hard to bear?"[4] Accused in the past of apathy and lack of grip, Florence now determined to play Lady Brandon for every last ounce of shock value she was worth. The Avenue season would open with éclat.

Yeats and Shaw were of course both there for opening night. George Moore was there also, though he had always abused Florence's acting and called her "the woman with the big nose." Tonight he was unimpressed with *The Land of Heart's Desire*, and overcome with violent antipathy at his first sight of Yeats, whom he watched stride to and fro at the back of the dress circle, "a long black cloak drooping from his shoulders, a soft black sombrero on his head, a voluminous black silk tie flowing from his collar, loose black trousers dragging untidily over his long, heavy feet."[5] Yeats had invited Paget to share the anxieties of opening night with him, but the poet, suffering either from a cold or emotion, trumpeted unceasingly into his handkerchief, causing Paget to retort when Yeats leaned over to ask whether he could hear the actors, "Perfectly, if you would stop blowing your nose."[6]

Yeats's little play went quite well. *A Comedy of Sighs*, however, produced rather a different effect. "For two hours and a half, pit and gallery drowned the voices of the players with boos and jeers that were meant to be bitter to the author who sat visible to all in his box surrounded by his family, and to the actress struggling bravely through her weary part," Yeats recalled. Todhunter, at the best of times "a sallow, lank melancholy man," grew lanker and sallower act by act. He sat on to the end, continued Yeats, "listening to the howling of his enemies, while his friends slipped out one by one, till one saw everywhere their empty seats, but nothing could arouse the fighting instincts of that melancholy man. . . . He shared the superstition still current in the theatre, that the public wants sincere drama, but is kept from it by some conspiracy of managers or newspapers, and could not get out of his head that the actors were to blame."[7]

The pit and gallery then went home, according to Yeats, "to spread the lying story that the actress had a fit of hysterics in her dressing room." Poor Florence. She could have done any play she liked, but had wanted to "do something" for the stage by advancing the New Drama. What she had done was bring a hail of criticism down upon her and Todhunter's heads. Shaw's diary note was as noncommittal as ever, only mentioning that Todhunter's play "failed rather badly, owing to a lot of unlucky circumstances." He expressed himself more plainly to Elizabeth Robins, who had also witnessed the disaster:

> Oh my Saint Elizabeth, holy and consoling, have you ever seen so horrible a portent on the stage as this transformation of an amiable, clever sort of woman into a nightmare, a Medusa, a cold, loathly, terrifying, grey, callous, sexless devil? What madness led Todhunter to write her a part like that?—what idiocy has led me to do virtually the same thing in the play which I have written to help her in this hellish enterprise? Did you hear those damns and devils, meant to be pretty—did they not sound like the blasphemes of a fiend? Had she been able to give full effect to herself, the audience would have torn her to pieces. I lay under harrows of red hot steel; and I waited afterwards because I knew by instinct that you would come and be kind to me. For that divine comfort I kiss your beautiful hands and your healing eyes: you are my wonderful good fortune, my treasure, my one utterly fulfilled desire, my ennobler and my darling. I ask nothing more: it is enough: now let the world work me like a dog until it wears me out: I have had my pay and am content.
>
> Forgive me—I shall be sensible & brutal and cynical again in the morning. I have so little heart that when it kindles for ten minutes once a year I hasten to cry out what I feel, lest I should die without having once done anything to save life from emptiness.[8]

Is it possible that Elizabeth Robins had cut Shaw once again, and that his effusions were ironic? Certainly in addressing her again as his holy Saint Elizabeth, he was rubbing salt into the wound.

Noting the dismal circumstances which had turned *A Comedy of Sighs* into A Comedy of Groans, Archer's notice in the *World* cited the bad acoustics of the Avenue: "I, for one, heard only about half the dialogue, and that imperfectly and with a painful strain." He was mild with Florence: "Miss Florence Farr was (not inexcusably) panic-stricken from the outset; but at best one does not see that she possesses either the physique or the art for such a character. It is overwhelmingly difficult, and one is tempted to add, with Dr. Johnson, 'Would to heaven, madam, it were impossible.' "[9] On his part, Yeats had always known that Florence had a destructive urge against her own poetical gift and her own "Demeter-like face in the mirror." He could not understand why she tried to deny her femininity, to jeer at sentiment and love. He argued with her, but only got responses like, "It's no use doing what nobody wants," or "I want to show I can do what the others did." He darkly attributed her behavior to the journalistic mentality of the Ibsenites with their cold taste for realism—and to her diabolical mentor, Bernard Shaw.

It was to Shaw that Florence turned after the disaster. She read the press notices as they appeared the next day; that evening she telegraphed Shaw to come to the theatre immediately. "Went down," said Shaw, "and found FE and Helmsley [the acting manager] with *Widowers' Houses* open before them, contemplating its publication in despair. I dissuaded them from that and after some discussion took my new play out on to the Embankment Gardens and there and then put the last touches to it before leaving it to be typewritten." He was not sanguine about *Arms and the Man* restoring Florence to favor. Janet had severely criticized the third act, after which he had seen nothing for it but to virtually start over again and make a new act (so he claimed) according to her instructions. That same day, 6 March, he had told Elizabeth Robins that he prayed Todhunter's play might not fail, since his second string to Florence's bow would surely give the Avenue enterprise its coup de grâce. Certainly he had produced to date, as far as female characters went, a controversial lot: Blanche Sartorius, a high-willed young woman who beats her maid; Grace Tranfield, a New Woman; Julia Craven, a passionate beauty who falls upon her rivals with her fists; Mrs. Warren, a brothel-keeper; and Vivie Warren, a cigar-smoking female who prefers the office to home.

Despite his protests, however, *Arms and the Man* was a pleasant play; and it was now Shaw who feared that Florence, after her decidedly unpleasant performance in *A Comedy of Sighs*, would damage him. So, although he had begun the part of Raina for her, he went home after handing over the manuscript for typing to ask Alma Murray whether she would be willing to play his heroine in the event he could persuade Florence to give up the lead and play the servant girl, Louka. Or had he, as his comment on Florence's part to Elizabeth Robins suggests, always intended her for Louka? The amiable Florence relinquished her part; Alma Murray accepted it; and *Arms and the Man* went into rehearsal on 11 April.

In the next days Shaw drafted one of his "interviews" to forestall the anticipated question: "Why not Miss Farr for the heroine, since it is her theatre?" Had the *Star* "interviewer" any tact, sense, manners, or discretion, he would not pose the question, of course; now that he had, Shaw could only say that Miss Farr had so consummately demonstrated her powers to be unpleasant that he had positively hated her for days after *A*

Comedy of Sighs—and it was evident that critics had shared his feelings. Miss Farr had laughed heartily at his reaction; yet did not propose that he "should court Dr. Todhunter's doom" by casting her for a sympathetic role when there was an unsympathetic part far more congenial to her. "Now your maladroit question is answered fully," Shaw rebuked the "interviewer." "Had you not better leave before you commit yourself again?"[10]

Behind the scenes, Shaw was less authoritative. Having called on the Charringtons at their third new address in several months and found them out, he took pen and paper and sat down to write from 21 Elm Park Road, Chelsea, little Nora, left with the servant, hanging on his arm and chattering irrepressibly. "I want to know what terms I should exact from the mysterious management at the Avenue," he asked Charrington. ". . . I want to drive a fair bargain, as on the one hand I do not want to use my influence with F. F. to get more than my due; and on the other I do not want to blackleg dramatic authordom by taking too little & running down prices. Being new to the trade and its customs I should like to have your opinion (which ought to be an exceptionally judicial one as that of an author-actor-manager) as to what I should propose. . . ."[11]

Todhunter's unlucky drama was taken off 14 April; on 11 April the *Arms and the Man* cast assembled at the Avenue with ten days to rehearse before opening night. Florence, Helmsley, and Shaw had rounded up a good cast: Alma Murray, Yorke Stephens, Mrs. Charles Calvert, Bernard Gould, and James Welch, who had survived *Widowers' Houses* and was present this time by design, not accident. And Shaw as producer was everywhere again—onstage, backstage, out front—humming with energy, wit, enthusiasm, instructions. Bernard Gould, better known offstage as Bernard Partridge the illustrator, found time to draw the tall, lean figure standing erect and alert, one hand on his hip, the script balanced open in the other, drilling the cast with an eagle eye for the slightest lapse of intelligibility or grip. If he could not drive his points home sufficiently at the theatre, there were letters to be scratched off hurriedly from Fitzroy Square. "Dear Miss Alma Murray," he wrote on 16 April after the cast had rehearsed from eleven in the morning until seven at night: "The Wagner concert tomorrow will prevent my attending the rehearsal; so I had better let you have a couple of points that struck me this evening. . . ."

But these were not the depressing rehearsals of a bluebook play in an unlucky theatre that had so discouraged the cast of *Widowers' Houses*. *Arms and the Man* had color, romance, atmosphere, sparkle, heroism, the dash of opéra bouffe. Being Shavian, the play of course laughed at heroism and romantic ideals. But Shaw did not jeer: the wit was broad, not corrosive; the characters—their ideals exposed for delusions—not odious but pleasantly human; the audience would not leave the theatre stricken with their own guilt (the purpose of his first three plays), but encouraged by the essential decency of human nature. The only possible difficulty was Shaw's thesis that war was folly, heroism sheer accident, and soldiering best done by realistic cowards who could get the thing over as expediently as possible. Such a notion might well enrage a few British imperialists.

Shaw prepared for the opening with the strategy of a general. He sent Helmsley orders for complimentary boxes or good seats for people who would "add lustre to the first night"—Sergius Stepniak and Esper Aleksandrovich Serebryekov, the Bulgarian admiral who had provided Shaw with local color for his setting; Sydney Olivier, Graham Wallas, and Sidney Webb, who might bring along a cabinet minister if he had a box; playwrights Oscar Wilde, George Moore, and Henry Arthur Jones; William Archer, Henry Norman, H. W. Massingham, Ernest Parke, and Jules Magny of the press. "If there are *three* decent seats left after all this," he added, "they might be sent to Hubert Bland . . . Mrs. Bland will be worth a thousand posters in Blackheath, & they are both active journalists." Among the first names on his list were the Charringtons: two tickets had gone to still another address at 9 Overstrand Mansions, Battersea Park, and instructions to Helmsley to put Mrs. Charrington somewhere "where her beauty will not be lost."[12] He had been amused at his own family's possessiveness about theatre tickets in the past, warning Janet to keep mum about his giving her a stall, for "they would sit out anything sooner than allow a stall to go out of the family."[13] Presumably Mrs. Shaw, Georgina, Kate Gurly, now living at Fitzroy Square, and even Uncle Walter Gurly were not forgotten.

Yeats awaited opening night with interest. "My little play *The Land of Heart's Desire* is . . . considered a fair success," he wrote to John O'Leary, Irish nationalist and mentor, "and is to be put on again with the play by Shaw which goes on next week. . . . The whole venture has had to face the most amazing denunciations from the old type of critics. They have however been so abusive that a reaction has set in which has brought a rather artistic public to the theatre. The takings at the door rose steadily but not rapidly enough to make it safe to hold on with Todhunter's play which was really a brilliant piece of work. If Shaw's play does well a new play of mine will be put on—a much more ambitious play than anything I have yet done. It will give you some notion of the row that is going on when I tell you 'chuckers out' have been hired for the first night of Shaw. They are to be distributed over the theatre and are to put out all people who make a row. The whole venture will be history anyway for it is the first contest between the old commercial school of theatrical folk and the new artistic school."[14]

Between rehearsals Shaw kept up his usual pace, attending a Fabian Committee meeting and a meeting of the Executive afterward on 20

April, for example, and then dashing over to the final dress rehearsal at seven. There he got a demonstration of what might well happen the next night. He had deliberately begun his play with a cliché—an escaped soldier forcing his way into a young woman's bedroom and threatening her with a pistol if she cries for help—and then, having beguiled the audience into believing they were witnessing melodrama, suddenly turned the whole situation into comedy. "At the dress rehearsal," said Yeats, "a dramatist who had his own quarrel with the public, was taken in the noose; at the first laugh he stood up, turned his back on the stage, scowled at the audience, and even when everybody else knew what turn the play had taken, continued to scowl, and order those nearest to be silent." What confusions would opening night bring?

Shaw arrived at the Avenue the next night at eight-thirty, well into Yeats's curtain raiser, which had begun at eight. His "Chocolate-Cream Soldier" was due to march on at ten minutes to nine. The audience, as Shaw had intended, fell immediately into the trap. Again Yeats: "On the first night the whole pit and gallery, except certain members of the Fabian Society, started to laugh at the author and then, discovering that they themselves were being laughed at, sat there not converted—their hatred was too bitter for that—but dumbfounded, while the rest of the house cheered and laughed." The cheering and applause were loud at the final curtain, and there were cries of "Author." Shaw strode onstage. In the silence that fell a single "Boo!" rang out from the gallery. Shaw's pale eyes glittered. "My dear fellow, I quite agree with you," he said suavely; "but what are we two against so many?" The now-immortal reply brought down the house.[15] "And from that moment," Yeats reluctantly admitted, "Bernard Shaw became the most formidable man in modern letters."

Would Archer now admit that the eccentric red-bearded young man he had found studying Wagner and Marx ten years before at the British Museum could write a play? He could, but reluctantly, grudgingly. *Arms and the Man*, he declared in his review, the substance of which he conveyed to Shaw before presstime, was "a fantastic, psychological extravaganza, in which drama, farce, and Gilbertian irony keep flashing past the bewildered eye." Shaw immediately dashed off a rebuttal. He was not at all like Gilbert, a "paradoxically humorous cynic" who accepted conventional ideas implicitly and then, when people did not live up to them, declared pessimistically that life was a farce. He, Shaw, took quite the opposite stand: he did not accept conventional ideas at all, and showed in his play that when people could not live up to them, their best qualities emerged and flourished. "It is this positive element in my philosophy that makes Arms & The Man a perfectly genuine play about real people, with a happy ending and hope & life in it . . . . But my chief object in writing this letter," he concluded, "is to call your attention to the fact that last night, whether it leads to a commercial success or not, totally shatters your theory that I cannot write for the stage."

But Archer did not agree that Shaw's philosophy was positive; and Shaw found that the full notice of 25 April in the *World* contained these further strictures: "Mr. Shaw is by nature and habit one of those philosophers who concentrate their attention upon the seamy side of the human mind. . . . To look at nothing but the seamy side may be to see life steadily, but is not to see it whole. As an artist, Mr. Shaw suffers from this limitation. . . . He not only dwells on the seamy side to the exclusion of all else, but he makes his characters turn their moral garments inside out and go about with the linings displayed, flaunting the seams and raw edges and stiffenings and paddings." But Shaw only chided Archer briskly for bringing up "the good old seamy side." The notice, he jeered, might have been written by a Bulgarian idealist. And indeed, it was strange that Archer could call *Arms and the Man* seamy after Ibsen.

But Archer's opinion really did not matter. Shaw suddenly found himself at thirty-eight, eighteen years after coming to London, a literary success. He was approached almost immediately for the American rights and, after hastily consulting a few writer friends, showed in his bargaining the shrewdness and integrity that would become his trademark in business negotiations. On 9 June 1894 he signed a self-drafted contract with the American-based actor and manager Richard Mansfield for a one-year license at "£10 per centum of the gross receipts." A few days later he was contacted by a representative of the Neues Theatre, who, laboring under the delusion that *Arms and the Man* had been the hit of the season, wanted it for Berlin, and complimented the author on his strong resemblance to Jesus Christ. Shaw felt obliged to disabuse him: he got out the papers and told him where to go to see the really successful plays by the really successful authors. Then Charles Wyndham came around to call, showing "a very proper sense" of his gifts; and Shaw seized the occasion to read him the play that only Wyndham could do, his unlucky *Philanderer*. The fact that Wyndham found it impossible did not cancel the fact that a West End manager had come in search of him.

His popularity spread. "You have all seen him," the *Workman's Times* reported. "A tall, lean, icy man, white faced, with a hard, clear, fleshless voice, restless grey-blue eyes, neatly-parted fair hair, big feet, and a reddish, untamed beard." Shaw had always been ubiquitous, but now he was the author of a controversial yet entertaining play. The Prince of Wales and the Duke of Edinburgh came to the Avenue, and although the Duke of Edinburgh muttered abuse so loudly that the whole stalls were party to his displeasure, the amiable Prince of Wales (who knew something about failing to live up to noble ideals, the subject of *Arms and the Man*) was "very pleasant" and "got the Duke of Edinburgh away as soon as possible." They asked for the manager, and Helmsley came, all flushed and triumphant at the presence of royalty. The Prince of Wales courteously asked who Mr. Shaw was and "what he meant by it," but the Duke of Edinburgh only repeated again and again, "The man is mad, the man is mad."[16]

It was perhaps madness for Shaw now to resign his position as music critic on the *World*, and yet on 30 May he sent a letter asking whether it would cause "any serious inconvenience" if he dropped the post. "You dont intend to spend the rest of your life reviewing for the P. M. G., do you?" he had frequently demanded of Archer; and now he renounced the profession he had accepted with reluctance because he needed the money but carried on brilliantly. Unfortunately, money was not pouring in from the Avenue Theatre. By 11 June *Arms and the Man* had drawn as much as half the cost of sending up the curtain only twice, and during Whitsuntide week and a cab strike the takings went down to £14 a night. Shaw got only 5 per cent when receipts did not exceed £100—a common occurrence. Little, however, was enough. "As the production of *Arms and the Man* for the moment put me in possession of some spare money," he noted in the diary which he had kept with fair regularity since 1885, but this year abandoned as a record of his daily movements and expenditures, "I was able to venture on the step of giving up my position as musical critic."

Meanwhile the performance itself needed to be kept up to the mark. Alma Murray herself told Shaw that it was time he came to a performance and pulled them together. When he dropped around on 11 May he found that his leading lady was playing as Archer had described her—bloodlessly, cynically, without the passion and beauty that made Raina enchanting and her conversion dramatic. "What—oh what has become of my Raina?" he cried. "How could you have the heart to play that way for me—to lacerate every fibre in my being? Where's the poetry gone—the tenderness—the sincerity of the noble attitude and the thrilling voice? Where is the beauty of the dream about Sergius, the genuine heart stir and sympathy of the attempt to encourage the strange man when he breaks down? Have you turned cynic, or have you been reading the papers and believing in them instead of believing in your part? I have no reproaches deep enough for you. . . . Here is my heart, stuck full of swords by your cruel hands.—yours, agonised G. Bernard Shaw."[17] Alarmed, Alma Murray invited him to call and talk the part over; but Shaw returned to the Avenue on 1 June and then retracted, murmuring that it was quite impossible that she had ever played other than beautifully. It was the first of his struggles to maintain his vision on the stage. This time (and often in the future) he bowed to the actor's interpretation: she had made Raina her own: he found he could appreciate that transformation objectively, like anyone else in the audience.

During the first weeks Yeats was in the theatre almost every night, vexing his actors with the new lines he kept adding to his *Land of Heart's Desire*. Although he came to see how his own play went, he often stayed for Shaw's. ". . . I listened to *Arms and the Man* with admiration and hatred," said the poet many years later. "It seemed to me inorganic, logical straightness and not the crooked road of life, yet I stood aghast before its energy as to-day before that of the Stone Drill by Mr. Epstein or of some design by Mr. Wyndham Lewis. He was right to claim Samuel Butler for his master, for Butler was the first Englishman to make the discovery, that it is possible to write with great effect without music, without style, either good or bad, to eliminate from the mind all emotional implication and to prefer plain water to every vintage, so much metropolitan lead and solder to any tendril of the vine. Presently I had a nightmare that I was haunted by a sewing machine, that clicked and shone, but the incredible thing was that the machine smiled, smiled perpetually."[18]

Florence's way home was Yeats's also part of the way, and after the performance they often talked about Shaw, and the poet's deeply divided feelings about the mechanical man who was at the same time so formidably brilliant. Sometimes Florence would share Yeats's distaste, for like him she was strongly drawn to the poetic, illogical, mystic, crooked road of life. But not always; for she knew that underneath Shaw's hard surface lived a certain longing for the poetry, the tenderness, the nobility, and the "beauty of the dream" that he had cried out for in Raina—and had not trusted her to achieve. Yeats perhaps recognized the longing; but he saw more that Shaw created his great and beautiful poetic moments only to deflate them in a burst of laughter. It was this he could not bear—just as he could not bear Florence's cynical disparagement of her poetic nature. Ironically, Shaw had rejected her as his heroine for the same reason. What had he thought of her Louka? His comments were made privately; years later, however, he assured Alma Murray that the part played itself.

Shaw had for some time been urging Florence to divorce Edward Emery for the practical reason that if she did not he could show up at any moment with inconvenient legal claims. He had perhaps no personal motive for urging the divorce; what Florence made of his motive is uncertain. She let herself be persuaded, however; and on 30 July was escorted by her brother-in-law Henry Paget to court. She agonized over the brief though unpleasant routine, finding herself obliged to accuse Edward Emery of adultery when incompatibility should have been sufficient grounds, and hating to have to reveal in public "subjects no innocent person would care to mention in private." Did she expect Shaw to be waiting in the wings with a marriage proposal? Undoubtedly not. She had measured his temperament in *The Dancing Faun* (published that summer and winning from the *Athenaeum* the dubious praise that "Miss

Farr might not have been so effective if she had been more intelligible");
for her own reasons—her love of independence, emotional aloofness,
asexuality—she may not have desired marriage at all. Besides they were
drifting further and further apart. Two days after her divorce, it was not
Shaw who came to Dalling Road but Henrietta, Yeats, and "some
mediumistic chemist's assistant." Curtains were drawn, magical paraphernalia brought out, and wonders undoubtedly performed.

Of course they continued to see each other; and Shaw would talk and
talk and Florence would laugh and laugh like the good pal she was. But
there had been something symbolic as well as practical in Shaw's decision
that Florence could not be his heroine in *Arms and the Man,* for she was
losing that place in his affections too.

The play ran for fifty performances. "I have made £90 and your acquaintance," Shaw wrote C. T. H. Helmsley. "This is handsome payment, thanks to the latter item, which will, I hope, long outlast the former.
When you take a theatre of your own, just bring me pen and ink, a ream
of paper, a bottle of ginger beer, and a few beans, and you shall have the
most brilliant play of the century to open with."[19] To his old friend
from Dublin, Matthew Edward McNulty, he wrote that the play had
been "manufactured into a London success at a net loss of about
£4,000." He concluded on a rare sober note. "I have taken the very serious step of cutting off my income by privately arranging to drop the
World business at the end of the season; and now, if I cannot make
something out of the theatre, I am a ruined man; for I have not £20
saved; and Lucy and Kate Gurly (my mother's half sister) are now
members of the family. I am about to begin the world at last."[20]

CHAPTER TEN

1894 - 1895

MEANWHILE THE FORTUNES of the Charringtons rapidly declined. Unpopular plays, a mediocre company, unimpressive mountings, and insufficient advertising of the Royalty venture had canceled any effect that Janet and Charrington achieved as actors. Searching for better, but still serious, plays by current writers, they had taken Terry's Theatre in June 1893 for a quintuple bill, producing James M. Barrie's *Becky Sharp*, A. Conan Doyle's *Foreign Policy*, *Bud and Blossom*, a farce by Lady Colin Campbell, Mrs. W. K. Clifford's *The Interlude*, and *The Three Wayfarers* by Thomas Hardy. The Charringtons found the farce by Lady Colin Campbell, the writer-journalist who had taken Shaw's place as art critic on the *World*, too trivial for their serious purpose; and although they had counted most on Barrie, *Becky Sharp* proved once again that Thackeray would not do on the stage. Conan Doyle's *lever du rideau* was brilliant, however; and as for Hardy, "Mr. Hardy proved, what everybody was prepared to believe, that unaided and unhampered his work would *march* on the stage, more easily and more triumphantly than the work of any English dramatist of modern times. He is the *rara avis*—the born dramatist, and we would rather have produced 'The Three Wayfarers,' short as it is, than any work of the year."[1] Despite praise for the acting of both Charringtons, however, the quintuple bill closed after a week.

"Then," as Charrington told Shaw, "smash!" The couple packed up their furniture, reduced as it was by visits to the pawn shops, with which Charrington was becoming intimate, and began their wandering from cheap to cheaper lodgings. Charles and Janet both worked desperately at short stories, plays, translations—anything that might bring in a little cash. Janet got a few acting jobs, replacing Marion Terry, for example, in an Adelphi melodrama, *The Cotton King.* "We were nearly right," Charrington insisted to Shaw years later; "—only one Crawshay played us false." But "one Crawshay" was not to blame for the debts, the drinking, the shifty business maneuvers, the self-pity. Little Nora acquired a wisdom beyond her years. Upon a visitor's pulling out his watch to amuse her, she took it, examined and advised: "You could get ten shillings at the pawn shop for that!"

The missed chance with Florence's Avenue season; the always cheerful Shaw working away at a play for Florence, not for them; his theatrical triumph; her lack of work—all pitched Janet into the depths of depression. The night after *Arms and the Man* opened, she went to hear Shaw debate "Criticism, Corruption and the Remedy" at the Playgoers' Club. He gave a striking performance, impressive enough to make a disciple out of R. Golding Bright, the solitary dissenter at the Avenue the night before. But Janet made a far different impression upon the audience: she stood up; she spoke bitterly: she called herself a failure. Two days later she received a rebuke from Shaw: "This is a most private letter," he wrote. "It refers, as your conscience will have already told you, to your wicked exploit at the Playgoers' Club on Sunday night. If what you had said had been in any sense true, it would have been extremely painful: as it was, it was shocking." Publicly to display a want of reverence for her own genius—it was a far worse thing than showing a want of reverence for her own person, which she did every time she blurred the fine edge of her beauty for the sake of a miserable glass of whisky and soda. What would she say if he, Shaw, stood up and called himself a failure? And yet until just the other day, he had failed, and failed, and failed.

Of course her lot was harder than his—he understood that. He was active, she had been cut off from her field of action. "This, however, is your own fault," he continued. "You dont believe in yourself enough. You are not yet good enough for your own destiny. You will never convince the world except in masterpieces; and you lack the severity of taste and thought for them as yet." Worse, her constant sacrifice of time to everything but her art was nothing but sheer self-indulgence. She had been "jealously, defiantly, obstreperously altruistic" when she should have displayed "the iron egotism, the ruthless sacrifice of self which makes the ruthless sacrifice of everyone else to art a matter of course, which marks the fully nerved and concentrated artist. . . . Suppose I married a literary woman, do you think I would let her interfere with my work as you interfere with Charrington's and he with yours? . . ." She had played Nora; ironically, she did not have the courage to slam her own door.

"I have two sorts of feeling for you," Janet read, "one valuable to you and the other worthless. The worthless one is an ordinary man-and-woman hankering after you—the word is not a nice one; but I do not want to give the feeling any fine airs just now. As you know, you are very handsome and clever, and rich in a fine sort of passionate ardor which I enjoy, in an entirely selfish way, like any other man. When the play was over the other night, and the strain suddenly removed . . . I wanted to rest myself with you, simply as the most luxurious piece of spiritual upholstery at hand." But all that was not worth a snap of her fingers. The only really useful thing about him was his high opinion as an artist and trained critic of her ability as an actress. He wanted to see her powers in action, preserved, not wasted. If she could use him as a kind of spiritual stiffening, then he would be happy.[2]

Janet had now replaced Florence as the center of Shaw's emotions. Ostensibly the unstable, heavy-drinking actress seemed an unlikely candidate for the ascetic, rigorously disciplined Shaw. In reality she touched him deeply. She was articulate, intelligent, "clever with her pen," as well as (he believed) a great actress, so that he could admire her intellectually. Her powerful, rather heavy beauty drew him. Her fine, passionate ardor stirred his cooler nature, while her marriage and apparent fidelity to Charrington saved him the awkwardness of having to consummate with her the desire she aroused. She remained an ideal: the "hankering" tantalizingly unsatisfied: the temptation constant, so that he might flex his virtue against it and always triumph. Her drinking, her improvidence touched him: he had seen both in his father, and the sympathy that had not come then could be turned now upon her. They gave her that touch of the Bohemian which he half admired even while vigorously repudiating. Finally, she roused the reformer in him: the possibility that he might rescue her from dissipating her powers and raise her up as a great actress appealed to him irresistibly.

Since 1892 Shaw had been thinking about "their" play, their tragedy with its "clean, dry, strong and straight" heroine. On 2 October 1894, having during the summer and autumn become more and more deeply involved with Janet, he sat down to write it. The tragic was not his mode, but he would create for her a heroine who was strong and beautiful. Janet would become her part: would re-create herself: free herself from sensual pleasure, wipe the illusions from her eyes, rise to the plains of heaven. She had inspired him: he would inspire her. She would play Candida nobly, beautifully: success would be hers at last.

Writing *Candida*, Shaw set up his favorite dramatic situation, the triangle. Very roughly, he blocked in the three central characters along familiar lines: Morell, the rather pompous minister whose strength really comes from his wife; Marchbanks, the young poet who invades the household, falls in love with the wife, and, worshiping her, is appalled at the domestic drudgery that demeans her nobility; and Candida the wife, caught between the husband who needs and the young poet who idolizes her. The drama of Candida was very much the current drama of the Charringtons and Shaw.

But in writing the play a curious thing happened. Shaw had done his straying in the wood of monkeys, where, as he told Florence, he had found her. His philandering was notorious; yet eight years with Jenny Patterson had produced only revulsion, his once fresh love for Florence had palled, his attraction to Janet harassed him. In conceiving her play, therefore, a different feeling gradually came over him, lifting him beyond sensual desire to a more exalted enthusiasm for her. Perhaps not becoming a saint "at once," as he told Janet, Shaw found that the process of idealizing their relationship in *Candida* re-created *him*, transporting him to a plane of religious emotion. His ecstasy was so keen that Janet herself seemed to be caught up in it; and for a time began "to draw on rich stores of life," became "beautiful," "real," "almost saintly"—looked at him with eyes that had "no glamor of morphia in them." But was her transfiguration permanent? Shaw knew better. "The question is," he concluded his confession of newborn sainthood, "how am I to make Janet religious, so that she may recreate herself and feel no need of stimulants. That is the question that obsesses me."[3]

By 27 November Shaw had written through the first half of the third act, spurred on by the Charringtons' disastrous financial situation and his new exaltation. Janet had received another invitation to tour; she saw no other solution than to sign. Shaw spurned the idea impatiently. "Damn Australia! How is it possible to look on such an offer otherwise than in fury and despair? Janet will be bored out of her senses: she will quarrel with the management; she will drink; she will inject morphia with a garden syringe; she will ruin her style flinging melodrama at the colonials; she will come back a wreck." This tirade over, however, Shaw began to consider the situation. The tour would pay off their creditors. They could come back and start again—but *not* by taking a theatre. But above all, Charrington and Janet must work separately. Together they generated an impossible friction which hindered both their chances for engagements. Having reversed himself completely, Shaw concluded: "Therefore my advice is dont let the Australian engagement slip by making your inclusion a sine qua non. This need not prevent your going with her if nothing turns up to keep you here. Mine is the only heart that need be broken."[4] But he would much have preferred to see Janet go alone. He was convinced that Charrington was destroying her career, and had gone so far as to slip money into her pocket secretly in hopes of provoking a quarrel between them.

That same day, 4 December, Shaw accepted the job of dramatic critic on the *Saturday Review* at a weekly salary of £6, a position, he told Archer, "fairly forced on him" by its editor, Frank Harris. Although he had opened a bank account on 6 November for the first time in his life with a deposit of £187 from the American royalties of *Arms and the Man*, he knew his plays were not commercial properties: though critically acclaimed, *Arms and the Man* had run for only sixteen performances in New York. Moreover, he was extremely reluctant to put himself into a position of depending upon managers, preferring to turn his hand to any work that would allow him to hold back his plays until he could educate the public to want them. Then, too, the number of semi-dependents at Fitzroy Square had multiplied. Lucy was home, her stage career flickering out, her marriage to Charles Butterfield gone sour. "LOVE, my Con," she wrote to a Dublin relative during these months, "is dead sea fruit, whether it is parental, fraternal or marital, and anyone who sacrifices their all on its altar plays a game that is lost before it is begun."[5] Down on fraternal love, Lucy was on good enough terms with her brother to do him occasional service. A friend remembers her "chugging away at a small typewriter" and, when asked what she was doing, replying, "I am typing George's play called *Arms and the Man*." Certainly she reveled in his famous connections. "There goes Mrs. Sparling," she whispered to a companion at a Dolmetsch concert. "She's just divorced her husband, because she wants to marry George."[6] At Fitzroy Square too was Kate Gurly, Mrs. Shaw's hunchbacked half sister, drowning her unhappiness in heavy drinking. Clearly Shaw's mother, now sixty-four and still singing mistress at the North London Collegiate School for women, had enough financial burdens without her son's. Back to journalism, therefore, Shaw went.

The *Saturday Review* appointment did not begin until the new year, and he was able to finish *Candida* on 7 December. Three days later he told Janet, "I am struggling with an almost overpowering temptation to burn The Philanderer. Verstehst du?"[7] And Janet would have understood, since she had partaken of his rapture. And yet the bottle of wine or the needle of morphia was so much easier than the strait gate Shaw proposed. She was trying, but Charlie, who should have helped her, could so easily be persuaded to run to the chemist's—and in fact believed that the rough life of the stage made stimulants a virtual necessity. And friends poured wine so generously. And life was so very cruel. And was the play Shaw had written really for her after all?

He had intended to model a strong and free woman, a character that would inspire Janet to rise above petty domestic embroilments, throw off her improvident and uxorious husband—or at least separate their interests —stiffen her courage to attack the world and win the place on the stage that she deserved. By a curious twist, however, he had ended by showing that the doll in the house is not always the woman, but in this case the childishly dependent Morell. And thus, although he claimed that *Candida* asserted strongly the difficult position of the domestic woman whose unpaid services are taken as a matter of course,[8] he made his domestic Candida such a strong woman that he directed the sympathy, if not to the poet-lover, to the man she overpoweringly coddles. Candida does not change, as Shaw believed Janet must. She is at the end of the play what she was at the beginning, the mother-sister-nurse-wife of her boy husband Morell, trapped by the very altruism that Shaw was trying to root out of Janet so that she could put her herself and her art first. It is Eugene Marchbanks who experiences the metamorphosis from sensuality to spirituality and artistic dedication. Looking upon the suffocating commonplaces of the Morell household, he concludes that domesticity, security, and love are inferior ends compared with the sublime and lonely renunciation of the artist. Shaw thus washed his hands of Janet, leaving her model at home and giving to the poet the exit line he should have given her—and that she had spoken as Nora: "Let me go now. The night outside grows impatient." Shaw the artist closed the door on Janet Achurch with the secret he had meant to tell her unspoken.

He almost immediately contacted George Alexander, actor-manager of the St. James's Theatre, who had had the imagination to produce *The Second Mrs. Tanqueray*, inviting him to make him an offer for six matinees with Janet "as a *sine qua non*." Alexander listened while Shaw read, but shook his head, seeing immediately that it was Marchbanks' and Candida's play. He would produce it if he could get down to Marchbanks' age, but as for playing Morell, he had done that kind of part so often that people were saying he couldn't act. He needed a play, Henry James's *Guy Domville* having failed, but wanted to act the part of a clever man for a change. Shaw pricked up his ears. He had a play about a very clever man; and returning to Fitzroy Square he posted off the unburned *Philanderer* on the spot, but with no better luck than before.

Candida behind him, Shaw left London for Folkestone on the Kentish coast. Here he tried desperately to keep his foothold on the hills of heaven but, like Sergius, found it very fatiguing to sustain the "higher love." "I shall begin a new play presently," he wrote Janet on 22 December from the West Cliff Hotel. "The last having been so happily inspired by you, I look about Folkestone for some new inspiratrice, but in vain: every woman in the place either strikes me cheerfully prosaic at a glance, or else makes me boil with ten-philander-power cynicism." There was only thin air between the heights and the depths for Shaw. ". . . Convinced as I am that love is hopelessly vulgar and happiness insufferably tedious to those who have once gained the heights, I nevertheless find that these material heights—these windswept cliffs—make me robustly vulgar, greedy and ambitious. If you by any chance tumble off the heights yourself ever, you will understand how vigorously despicable I am under these circumstances. The ozone offers an immense opportunity to any thoroughly abandoned female who would like to become the heroine of a play as black as 'Candida' is white. . . . I am, as you will observe, in an entirely worthless humour. That is the result of health, fresh air, plenty of food, early rising, long walks and the rest of the bracing delusions."[9]

Visiting Janet when Shaw's letter arrived was Sydney Olivier, eminent Fabian whom Shaw had once described to Janet as an odd mixture of sensibility with remnants of "a mastiff-like county family breed," and a man who put his mild wife in the "position of a pigeon married to a condor." Olivier had found Janet draped in a counterpane in order not to be found in nothing at all. She tore Shaw's letter open eagerly, read it aloud, and sat down immediately to answer it, smoking cigarettes furiously as she dashed down page after page. She then declaimed her answer to Olivier. He was enchanted with the whole performance. "She can act anything," he wrote Shaw enthusiastically; "she even has brains."[10]

Shaw returned from Folkestone in high spirits, optimistic about placing *Candida,* ready to tackle theatre criticism, and still inspired by his new feeling for Janet. Under its impetus he asked her to share his stall at the Garrick for his first critical assignment, Sydney Grundy's *Slaves of the Ring.* Janet met him there on New Year's Day. She had dyed her hair a heartbreakingly false yellow, and could not disguise the terribly familiar signs of unsteadiness and belligerence. Shaw's spirits sank. While he scribbled notes on his knee, deciding that leading lady Kate Rorke turned her emotions on and off like a lamp, Janet conducted herself unbecomingly in the seat next to him. By the end of the second act she had become so obstreperous that Shaw ordered her to go home. Wouldn't he come with her, she pleaded. He knew he wanted to, and they would be cozy together, and she wouldn't touch another drop for days, she swore it. But nothing interfered with Shaw's work, and with a mixture of pity and contempt, he thrust cab fare into her hand. At this, Janet rose to her full height. Did he suppose that she planned to cheat the cab man? Shaw managed to decant her into a hansom and get back to his stall for the last act; then was forced to defend himself against an injured note from Janet the next day. "The matter is simple enough, wretch that you are," he replied. "Whisky and soda is intoxicating: light wine is not. Consequently, you abstained on Tuesday from whisky and soda, and only took four bottles of the wine that Mrs. Henderson (the idiot!) gave you. When you came to the theatre, you were reckless and invertebrate, out of sorts, sloppy, abandoned in your carriage . . . ."[11] To this frankness, Janet replied that he had hurt her deeply, and that if he wished to keep her respect, he had better avoid vulgar abuse in the future. Shaw always feared that his lectures would alienate her; yet he retorted with a temperance sermon:

I really meant that letter to hurt you, Heaven forgive me. I am not afraid of all the lions in your path; but I am mortally afraid of this one pitfall. Your illness is an excuse for it; your inaction is an excuse for it; and when you get an engagement then comes in Charrington's fatal theory that it is a necessary condition of acting, so that health and good fortune are made a better excuse than ever. If I seem to make light of your present hard luck and a great deal of the pitfall, it is because I have had some experience of hard luck myself. I came to London in 1876—in April, I think. I began to make money as a journalist in May 1885. Those nine years were years of unbroken failure and rebuff, with crises of broken boots and desperate clothes, and an attack of smallpox at the worst of it. But I weathered it all safely and boldly and happily enough, penniless, loveless, and hard as nails. I drank the cup and came to like it. I never shut my window on frosty nights, or put hot water into my tub to take the chill off, morally any more than physically. Above all, I never touched a stimulant, not even tea. In 1881 I gave up meat, and have not eaten it since. It was probably just as much the weakness as the strength of my character that enabled me to do these things; but that is not the point, which is, that I am quite certain that if I had drunk as much as a single glass of beer a day (I loathe beer) my powers of endurance would have been enormously diminished. . . . [T]o the routine worker—that is, to the immense majority, a little alcohol makes no difference, since there are no particularly fine issues involved either in their work or their life. But all we who are artists are rallied on a narrow ledge about the millionth of an inch broad, which yet makes all the difference between us and the others. A single drop of alcohol will dissolve this ledge away; and once you are past thirty, it will not have grow[n] again before the next drop comes. I want you to swear off altogether, absolutely and unconditionally. You promised to do it; the doctor told you to do it; you know yourself you ought to do it; you will lose the child's respect if you don't do it; you will go downhill all the rest of your life if you don't do it; and worst of all, you will reduce me to your mere private temperance lecturer if you don't do it. . . .

You know my favorite Hegel epigram: "We learn from history that men never learn anything from history." In the same way, you will never learn anything from me. In future you may drink and do just as you like: I shall say nothing. . . . I will call some evening this week; but I will not tell you what evening, because you would only keep sober on that particular evening, whereas if you don't know, you will be a teetotaller until I come. Forgive this last echo of the for-ever-ended sermon.[12]

His business, always paramount, stimulated him and helped drive Janet's predicament to the back of his mind. He had doubted the ethics of being both a dramatist and a dramatic critic: how easy to exchange a play for a good review or two, or be suspected of the exchange. He forgot his doubts with the realization that the theatre gave him even more scope for reform than music. "I am extremely glad now that I am a dramatic critic," he told Janet. "I shall do the work with a zest." He went to the attack vigorously: a fresh breeze swept through musty, gilded theatreland. The opening of Oscar Wilde's *An Ideal Husband* on 3 January at the Haymarket put his polemical skills immediately to work. Shaw argued Wilde as "an arch-artist" and "our only thorough playwright" because he played with everything—"with wit, with philosophy, with drama, with actors and audience, with the whole theatre." A mild comment, except that it came from a socialist who considered Ibsen superior to Shakespeare for his moral seriousness. Having condemned Wilde, Shaw then put to rout in his fair way the common critical notion that anybody could turn out witty, epigrammatic Wildean plays, remarking dryly: "As far as I can ascertain, I am the only person in London who cannot sit down and write an Oscar Wilde play at will."[13]

In the following weeks he went to battle for two favorite causes, the New Woman and the New Drama, which was largely the drama of the New Woman. The sight of a remorseful Guinevere groveling at the feet of King Arthur at the Lyceum might still be popular among the men whose vanity it flattered; but for the enlightened in the audience, the scene plunged Henry Irving's King Arthur into offensive absurdity. "As to Miss Ellen Terry," continued Shaw, reviving the theme of his July 1892 letter to the actress, "it was the old story, a born actress of real women's parts condemned to figure as a mere artist's model in costume plays which, from the woman's point of view, are foolish flatteries written by gentlemen for gentlemen. . . . I should prove myself void of the true critic's passion if I could pass with polite commonplaces over what seems to me a heartless waste of an exquisite talent. What a theatre for a woman of genius to be attached to! Obsolete tomfooleries like Robert Macaire, schoolgirl charades like Nance Oldfield, blank verse by Wills, Comyns Carr, and Clamour, with intervals of hashed Shakespear; and all the time a stream of splendid women's parts pouring from the Ibsen volcano and minor craters, and being snapped up by the rising generation. Strange, under these circumstances, that it is Mr. Irving and not Miss Terry who feels the want of a municipal theatre. He has certainly done his best to make everyone else feel it."[14]

In his next review, Shaw turned to the Independent Theatre's production of Dorothy Leighton's *Thyrza Fleming*. He could not make any claims for it as a good play, but the production gave him excuse to champion the Cause. "The real history of the drama for the last ten years," he wrote, "is not the history of the prosperous enterprises of Mr. Hare, Mr. Irving, and the established West-end theatres, but of the forlorn hopes led by Mr. Vernon, Mr. Charrington, Mr. Grein, Messrs

Henley and Stevenson, Miss Achurch, Miss Robins and Miss Lea, Miss Farr, and the rest of the Impossibilists. Their commercial defeat has been slaughterous: each scaling party has gained the rampart only to be hurled back into the moat with empty pockets, amid plentiful jeering from the baser sort . . . . For my part, I take off my hat to them. Besides, that is the way things get done in England; so, as a prudent man, I always make friends with able desperados, knowing that they will seize the citadel when the present garrison retires."[15]

The statements were as provocatively bold as ever, but there was a note of detachment, of prudence sounded. Underfinanced productions, shoddy management, amateur casts caused Shaw to grind his teeth in fury. He wanted handsome sets, the ablest direction, the best performers for his plays. He had already established his scrupulously fair but shrewd method for doing theatrical business. He was adept at self-advertisement, at diplomacy, at smoothing the way. His hat was off to the Impossibilists, but surely he himself could scale the ramparts—and take them.

He continued to press *Candida* upon actor-managers, reading it to Lewis Waller, who had just taken the Haymarket to produce Wilde; but he was "not sanguine," as he warned Janet. He would try *The Philanderer* on Waller next if Waller didn't bite at *Candida;* and why, incidentally, didn't Janet think meanwhile of playing Julia Craven? The part would push her to the height of her technical skill and cleverness. No one had ever seen her do a really sharp comedy role, "finished up to the fingernails." If they did, she would have no more trouble getting parts from Pinero, who only needed some fine "filigree work" on her part to convert him from the belief that she could only rant as a tragédienne.

But all the talk about Janet playing Julia was futile, since nobody wanted *The Philanderer*. Meanwhile she had finished *Mrs. Daintree's Daughter*[16] and sent it to Waller, who rejected it. Shaw declared himself not surprised. Her version of their plot was not good drama, only good acting. She had cut her one really original point, the mother's discovery of her daughter's worthlessness, contriving instead to have the mother commit suicide with morphia. Ho hum, yawned Shaw: the first hint of morphia brushed away the last shred of curiosity about the play; and smart West End audiences, thank god, were beginning to look upon stage poisonings with the same weariness as upon broadsword combats. Neither parts nor plays had thus worked for Janet; and privately to Charrington Shaw dashed her recently raised hopes of playing for Pinero:

He wanted her to play *Ellean* in The Second Mrs. Tanqueray, seduced, no doubt, by the thought of how she would look. Alexander, not unnaturally, thought he meant her to play Paula; and Pinero nearly dropped senseless when he heard of the awful mistake. Poor Alexander had to get out of it as best he could by raising some unreal difficulty or another. That's the true story of that business, which was communicated to me under awful pledges of secrecy; so don't tell anybody that you know. The fact is, Pinero has a very fine sense of the people he wants for his particular style of work; and Janet has not adequate idea of how completely she belongs to another epoch. Mrs. Pat is exactly the woman for him. He is in the position to have exactly what he likes; and naturally he is not content with mere acting, which is all that Janet could bring to a Pinero part: he wants *being;* and she *isn't.*[17]

This was not so much treachery, as fact. Janet belonged to the large, emotive school: the school of the tragic cadence and the struck brow. Shaw relished that school when intelligently done, and had seen Janet act magnificently. But morphia and alcohol were blunting the edge such acting demanded if it was to be kept under control. Pinero's elegant, psychological drawing-room melodrama was unthinkable.

Was even the "fine counterpoint" of *Candida* unthinkable for Janet? On 7 January Shaw sent a note to Elizabeth Robins, asking her to listen to a reading of his play. Having either learned nothing from history (as Hegel promised) or by now deliberately needling her "purity," Shaw addressed her again as "Holy Elizabeth" or some such nonsense. Elizabeth replied that she could not hear the play, but would read it with interest if sent. "I must ask you, however, if you should wish to write me about it or about anything else," she added, rising to the bait, "to use the customary forms of address. My name for you is Miss Robins; and I do not see that the fact of my being an actress entitles anyone to call me by any other name. Please do not waste time discussing this. It is simply a question of taste and it is my taste that must be considered in the matter. I cannot prevent your speaking of me in a misleading fashion behind my back and putting your own interpretation upon my motives and conduct, but if the future should by chance bring us into relation again, either by letter or word of mouth, it is as well you should know the terms upon which I am accessible."[18] Nothing daunted, Shaw made an appointment to call on her on 20 January upon her return from an Ibsen tour to Manchester. But Elizabeth canceled; and at last realizing perhaps that this difficult woman's taste in the matter was sound, Shaw prudently addressed her in the future as "Miss Robins."

Balked in London, Shaw turned toward America and Richard Mansfield, who had liked *Arms and the Man* well enough to keep it in his repertory after its brief run ended. "Now let me ask you whether you can play a boy of eighteen—a strange creature—a poet—a bundle of nerves—a genius—and a rattling good part," he wrote in February. "The actor-managers here can't get down to the age. The play, which is called *Candida,* is the most fascinating work in the world—my latest—in three acts, one cheap scene, and with six characters. The woman's part divides the interest and the necessary genius with the poet's. There are only two people in the world possible for it: Janet Achurch, for whom it was written, and Mrs. Kendal. If Janet creates it here, will you pay her fare out and back and give her 300 dollars a week or so for the sake of covering yourself with new and strange fascinations as the poet? By the way, there's probably money in the piece; but it's a charming work of art; and the money would fly somehow."[19]

Besides peddling *Candida*, touring the theatres nightly, writing his reviews into the late hours, lecturing to socialist groups, and pumping for the local elections—working until he became literally sick—he found time to brace Charrington when their furniture went into pawn again: "Surely their hypothecation has been a relief to you and an infernal nuisance to the pawnbroker . . . you will be freed for ever the intolerable burden of useless property." He himself sought solace by having a tooth pulled: sitting back in a chair with his eyes closed, lulled by the buzz of the drill in a tooth while someone else did the work was an extraordinarily restful experience.

He continued to spend frequent evenings at the Charringtons (a sure sign they were not working), and found time too to argue with Charrington, who read his letters to Janet, and used his criticisms of her writing to attack Shaw upon his own. Replying, Shaw set forth his artistic manifesto:

I have my feeling for the exquisitely cultivated sense of beauty—an almost devotional sense—and the great pains and skill of execution which produces work of one kind, and for the bold ideas, the daring unscrupulous handling, the imaginative illusions that produce another kind. And I have a leaning towards the former that you dont sympathise with . . . . I prefer a woman knitting to Ajax fighting the sheep, because I know that although very little will come of the knitting, nothing will come of the fighting. . . . when you see a man like me, trying to do fine counterpoint in even so few as three real parts, as in Candida, or in seven, as in the finale of The Philanderer, never tell him he ought to go and write choruses instead. I grant you the work is not so skilful as if I had been more years at it; but there is no more worthy sort of work to try for.

And this is why he strove so hard to bring Janet under discipline, for if she was to act in his plays, she must believe in his creed: beautiful acting, achieved by "tremendous practice and constant aiming at beauty of execution" through a "cultivation of delicate feeling, and absolute renunciation of all the coarser elements of popularity." "You may depend on it, I will get my plays performed all I can," he concluded. ". . . Also, I will let emotion and passion have all the play I can in my characters. But you must recollect that there is distinction even in emotion and passion; and that the finer kinds will not run through the wellworn channels of speech. They make new intellectual speech channels; and for some time these will necessarily appear so strange and artificial that it will be supposed that they are incapable of conveying emotion. They said for many years, remember, that Wagner's endless melody was nothing but discord."[20]

Responding to telegrams from an enthusiastic Richard Mansfield, Shaw had sent *The Philanderer* to New York. "It is an extraordinary thing," Mansfield told drama critic William Winter; "it turns Ibsen inside out, and the spectacle, as a result, is not a pleasant or agreeable one"—and he suppressed a temptation to produce. Meanwhile in London, Mansfield's brother Felix had urged *Candida*, with the result that Richard asked Shaw for a copy. "I still play youths of 18," he assured him. "The only trouble is I look too young for the part." The manuscript was duly posted. Despite Shaw's claim that only Janet Achurch or Mrs. Kendal could play Candida, Mansfield would of course have given the role to his wife, actress Beatrice Cameron, who had played Raina to his Bluntschli. Then Mrs. Mansfield fell on stage, injuring herself seriously.

On 6 March the Charringtons opened a message from Fitzroy Square. "On arriving here I find the following mad cablegram waiting for me:

'WILL PLAY CANDIDA WILL ENGAGE JANET WILL COME TO LONDON CONTRACT JANET NOT LESS THAN THREE SEASONS SEE FELIX ALL MUST COME NEW YORK QUICK—MANSFIELD.'

So now," said Shaw, "it is all settled and our fortunes are made. . . ."[21]

CHAPTER ELEVEN

1895

A FLURRY OF CABLEGRAMS flew back and forth across the Atlantic before Felix Mansfield, growing grayer and grayer with each successive message, Shaw reported, and now white as snow, finally secured Janet for *Candida*. Shaw was at her elbow every moment, advising, warning, arranging, and even assuring her grandiosely when Richard Mansfield also expressed an interest in Mrs. Patrick Campbell that he would not at all mind seeing her thrown into competition with Mrs. Pat on one side of the Atlantic and Ada Rehan on the other. "You would have to keep yourself in the most perfect and exquisite physical condition—plain living and high thinking, distilled water, oatmeal bannocks, honey and peaches, no cigarettes, no ignoble preoccupations about the size of the type in which your name is announced, none of your numerous methods of breaking my heart." He then dashed off a letter to Mansfield, assuring him that he had not made a mistake in engaging Janet. The real reason she had been out of work so long was that London actor-managers had an understandable reluctance to being played off their own stages by a leading lady. Mansfield need have no fear, however; and Janet would profit by having to stand up to some real acting at last.[1]

Shaw then perhaps went round to Overstrand Mansions to help Janet draft her acceptance to Felix Mansfield, although the opening "Thanks for your letters" is the breezy Achurch style, not Shaw's.

I understand my engagement with Mr. Richard Mansfield as follows [wrote Janet]: I am to play with him three seasons—Candida and other leading parts—at a weekly salary of £50 in America—and £40 when playing in England. My salary to begin from the day on which I arrive in America.

About "starring," it is understood that Mr. Mansfield will distinguish my name from the rest of his company (the manner of doing this can be easily settled, as you said—between him and myself.)

I beg to acknowledge a cheque for one hundred pounds, being an advance on my salary to be repaid at the rate of £25 a week. I suppose matinées to be paid for at the rate of a full night's salary—and costumes for costume-plays to be found by the management.

I think that is all the business. I look forward to the engagement with much pleasure.

I should like to meet you in town early next week to ask a few questions as to luggage, etc. What about the Solferino—Monday—at two o'clock?

Yours sincerely,
Janet Achurch.[2]

Janet was to leave the following Saturday, 16 March. Shaw took the play to Miss Ethel Dickens, granddaughter of the novelist, who ran a typing service in Tavistock Street. When he returned for the prompt copies, he found that they needed careful correction. In despair on 12 March with a political article to be written, the Strand and Garrick theatres requiring his attention, the *Saturday Review* article to write, and the Fabian Executive to attend (among other matters), he nevertheless promised Janet that he would "leave tomorrow with nothing to be done but overhaul the prompt copy for you thoroughly, go down to Miss Dickens's to fetch the other copies & the parts, and go to the Garrick in the evening. . . . I detail my woes because I am in extreme need of being petted. I am the most frightened, discouraged, impotent creature at present in England. But I shall get into bed before half past twelve for once; and in the morning I shall be on my way back to the most insolent self sufficiency."[3]

The next night Shaw went to the Garrick to see Mrs. Patrick Campbell in the much-awaited successor to her *Tanqueray:* all London was eager to see the glamorous star make another sensation in *The Notorious Mrs. Ebbsmith.* As he predicted, he had been restored to the most insolent self-sufficiency, beginning his review, "I disliked the play so much that nothing would induce me to say anything good of it," but allowing that his reader might discount his opinion since he himself wrote plays that were in violent reaction against Pinero's. He objected to the artificiality of this daughter of a secularist agitator who, upon being widowed, takes to the platform and makes a career for herself. Pinero had not the faintest idea of what such a woman's life was really like;

Shaw, who had known Annie Besant and Beatrice Webb and had been on the platform himself for fifteen years, did. He disliked equally Mrs. Ebbsmith's putting on an indecent dress when she finds that a male friend only cares about her sexually, and abandoning herself to him for the one great hour in a woman's life. He objected in print that the action reduced woman still again to a sexual object; he objected in private because he now found physical love "hopelessly vulgar." But none of these crimes was as severe as Pinero's having his notorious lady finally repent by snatching the Bible she has hurled into the flames out again: that was sentimental, artificial cowardice: the gentleman's way of luxuriating in a woman's sensuality and then humbling her for it.

The critic resisted the play; the man, however, appreciated Mrs. Campbell. After all, the unreality of Mrs. Ebbsmith left Mrs. Campbell free to do what she liked with the part, "the result being an irresistible projection of that lady's personal genius, a projection which sweeps the play aside and imperiously becomes the play itself. . . . She creates all sorts of illusions, and gives one all sorts of searching sensations. It is impossible not to feel that those haunting eyes are brooding on a momentous past, and the parted lips anticipating a thrilling imminent future, whilst some enigmatic present must no less surely be working underneath all that subtle play of limb and stealthy intensity of tone. Clearly there must be a great tragedy somewhere in the immediate neighborhood; and most of my colleagues will no doubt tell us that this imaginary masterpiece is Mr. Pinero's Notorious Mrs. Ebbsmith. But Mr. Pinero has hardly anything to do with it. When the curtain comes down, you are compelled to admit that, after all, nothing has come of it except your conviction that Mrs. Patrick Campbell is a wonderful woman."⁴

If only he could be as sure of Janet's success in his *Candida*. *Mrs. Ebbsmith* had proved again that a star could make an artificial play vital. Could Janet make a vital play appealing? More to the point: could she be counted on to be sober when the curtain went up?

On the sixteenth Shaw appeared at the station to see her off, having worked himself into a state of near collapse getting all the parts, the full music score, and a minutely detailed plan of the stage action corrected to send with her on the boat. They were all there: Janet with her brazen hair, Charrington, a young Scandinavian actor named Albert Gran whom Felix had discovered, Felix himself, Mansfield's nephew Alfred, and four-year-old Nora. Everybody was sniveling. "Janet was so affected that she did not know what she was doing, and took an affectionate farewell of Felix under the impression that he was Charrington, who, on his part, lifted Gran in his arms and kissed him in the full persuasion that he was little Nora. She, poor infant, was with great difficulty coaxed up to crying point, Felix having inconsiderately given her emotions the wrong turn by presenting her with a colossal box of Bluntschli's specialty." Exhausted from overwork, his own emotions quenched by the demonstrations all around him, Shaw reveled in the callousness with which he was able to wave off his play and his actress until the train vanished down the track. On his return home, he tumbled onto his bed and "slept like an exhausted dog for an hour"; then roused himself and, still shaky, sat down to write to Mansfield, "If you find at rehearsal that any of the lines cannot be made to go, sack the whole company at once and get in others. I have tested every line of it in my readings of the play; and there is a way of making every bit of it worth doing. There are no points: the entire work is one sustained point from beginning to end. . . . If the play is not successful, fatten Janet, engage a Living Skeleton, buy a drum, and take to the road."[5]

The months of creative passion, the months of lavishing his time, companionship, advice, anger, exaltation, and love upon Janet were now over; and his hopes riding somewhere out on the Atlantic. He could not keep his hands off, however. His parents might have been no parents to him, but he hovered over Janet with the anxiety of a mother for a willful child, on 20 March interrupting his *Saturday Review* work to send her a hasty word about one or two things he had been too timid to mention at the station:

First, and most important, you are, immediately upon receipt of this letter, to send for a barber, and have your head shaved absolutely bald. Then get a brown wig, of the natural color of your own hair. Candida with gold hair is improbable; but Candida with artificially gold hair is impossible. Further, you must not be fringy or fluffy. Send to a photographer shop for a picture of some Roman bust—say that of Julia, daughter of Augustus and wife of Agrippa, from the Uffizi in Florence—and take that as your model, or rather as your point of departure. You must part your hair in the middle, and be sweet, sensible, comely, dignified, and Madonna like. If you condescend to the vulgarity of being a pretty woman, much less a flashy one (as in that fatal supper scene in Clever Alice which was the true cause of the divine wrath that extinguished you for so long afterwards) you are lost. There are ten indispensable qualities which must underlie all your play: to wit, 1, Dignity, 2, Dignity, 3, Dignity, 4, Dignity, 5, Dignity, 6, Dignity, 7, Dignity, 8, Dignity, 9, Dignity, and 10, Dignity. And the least attempt on your part to be dignified will be utterly fatal. . . .

On any point you are more likely to be right than anyone else once you have considered it. I urge you to go to church once a day at least to tranquillise your nerves. If you feel inclined to cry, go and meditate and *pray*. The religious life is the only one possible for you. Read the gospel of St. John and the lives of the saints; they will do everything for you that morphia only pretends to do. Watch and pray and fast and be humbly proud; and all the rest shall be added to you. . . .

Remember—the religious life. No ambition, and no golden hair. I know that you will understand my advice, and take it—for ten minutes or so.[6]

It could not have been reassuring when, just in the midst of his sermon on dignity and renunciation, footsteps thudded on the stairs and Charrington burst in, fitted out in "an exceeding splendor of raiment, like a bridegroom"—having put Janet's £100 advance to immediate and unrenunciatory use.

Given Shaw's magnetism, the vacuum left by Janet Achurch could not but be immediately filled. After a three-year silence, enter Ellen Terry on cue. She was apparently summoned by Shaw, who sent her an invitation to hear him speak to the Women's Progressive Society on the topic "Feminine Meanness" and a newspaper clipping predicting that "even the courage of Mr. Shaw will be pretty thoroughly tested during the course of the afternoon." Ellen replied, stressing feminine *generosity:*

How splendid! What fun. I wish I could be there. But for my wretched bit of work o' nights, I am obliged to shut myself up. My Sundays are the only days in which I dare allow myself to be either interested or amused ('cos it delights and tires me so). And this note is to beg you to let me know if on any Sunday you discourse in public. Don't trouble to answer me now (woman's generosity!) but one line at the time, please, if you can remember it. I wrote you the other day and tore up the scribble. Woman's generosity again![7]

As a result of renewing his letter acquaintance with the leading lady of the Lyceum, Shaw began to cogitate a play for Ellen Terry and Henry Irving.

Another woman reappeared to be looked upon with his newly washed eyes. In February Florence's divorce from Edward Emery had become final. Had she expected Shaw to step forward with a ring, she was disappointed, for it was now that he discovered that she would not do for him at all—a revelation that her freedom probably spurred. They had seen little of each other, but on the first day of spring Shaw went to Richmond to meet Florence at her request, since she had spoken "rather bitterly" about his apparent avoidance. Theatre gossip had kept her in his mind, however: rumor had it that the mysterious backer of the Avenue season was promising a quarter of a million for another venture in four years; as Shaw told Charrington, they had all better spend the interim writing plays with star parts for Florence. "We strolled about the park all the afternoon," Shaw reported to Janet, "from seat to seat (she being rather weak with influenza); and I chatted and chatted and she laughed and laughed in her obliging way and we had something to eat at the Swiss café and went to her sister's in Bedford Park by tramtop and I told her all the news and she told me all the news, about her bicycling, and her literary doings, and the quarter million, which she confirmed with aggravating unconcern, as if she were mentioning that her nephew would be ten years old in four years; and she had nothing in the world to say to me, and I had nothing in the world to say to her."

Of her deeper concerns Florence did not speak: her promotion to Praemonstratrix in the Golden Dawn, her researches into Egyptian magic, alchemy, and hermetic art at the British Museum. Strangely enough, her studies alienated not only Shaw but her partner in magic and the Golden Dawn, W. B. Yeats. For him, her voracious reading was allied to her destructive taste for wit and paradox and skepticism: her erudition in so many heterogenous studies, thought Yeats, was moved by "an insatiable, destroying curiosity." She did not feel her religion; she put it under the microscope. "I used in my rage to compare her thoughts, when her worst mood was upon her, to a game called Spillikens which I had seen played in my childhood with little pieces of bone that you had to draw out with a hook from a bundle of like pieces. A bundle of bones instead of Demeter's golden sheaf!"[8]

That day at Richmond Shaw also felt a brittleness in Florence's mind and soul. "Pleasanter company one could not desire—good humored, adaptable, no trouble, easily amused (frightfully easily), beautiful grey eyes and so on," he continued to Janet. "But what is there lacking in her, and in all the other women of her class one meets? Not brains: she is a clever woman. Not knowledge: it is impossible to mention anything she does not know. Not affection: she would respond gratefully enough to any tenderness shewn her. Why, then, the frightful vacuity, the levity, the shallowness, the vulgarity, the pointlessness that makes me wish, in Richmond Park, that I could have half an hour with the trees and the earth and the sky over the Thames Valley, half an hour of comparatively deep communion? It must be that she has no religion."

Shaw's judgment was not merely the disillusion of the ex-lover for whom all the old charms are now simply irritations, nor the wounded pride of the male who has seen his protégée slip beyond his influence (though both feelings were involved): it was the judgment of the man who had gone through the Candida experience. This experience had not only convinced him that physical passion was ignoble, it had also convinced him that he could be a dramatic poet. His play pitted two men against each other for the love of Candida: Morell, the crusading minister, and Marchbanks, the poet genius. Although the portrait of Morell was very much Charrington, Shaw had not been unlike the minister himself, a man who dazzled his public as an orator and socialist, yet in private depended heavily on the emotional comforts a woman could provide. With the writing of his first poetic, rather than socially realistic play, however, Shaw had begun to think of himself as a Marchbanks rather than a Morell. He had the discipline to be a great writer—that he knew. Did he have the "religious" power? All his life he had opened his windows to the night air, abstained from flesh-eating and stimulants, forced himself to work until dropping with exhaustion. He believed himself better for these disciplines, yet there was a last discipline —the discipline of the priest and the saint—he had not yet embraced. He had always separated romance and passion from his public activity, of course, just as he had remorselessly prevented them from impinging upon his work, believing (as did many) that sexual activity vitiated other energies. Now, perhaps, a final renunciation was necessary before he could achieve real genius, for "ability does not become genius," he believed, "until it has risen to the point at which its keenest states of perception touch on ecstasy, on healthy, self-possessed ecstasy, untainted by mere epileptic or drunken incontinence, or sexual incontinence."[9] It was this ecstasy that had filled him when he renounced his sensual feeling for Janet, and this ecstasy he felt he must now preserve if he were to become a true artist. Great art and sensuality were incompatible.

It was this dedicatory ecstasy he found so conspicuously lacking in Florence that day at Richmond, and to which he was trying to spur Janet, for he criticized Florence to inspire the actress upon whom much of his own success now depended. "Now you have my theory brought home to yourself," he concluded this long letter inspired by an urgent need to communicate seriously with her. "Now you know what I conceive as wanting for Candida, and what Eugene means when he says, 'I no longer desire happiness: life is nobler than that.'" He would not lecture her about her acting: if she occupied herself every moment mentally and soulfully with what he intended Candida to be, she would be Candida. "In short, dearest Janet, be entirely magnanimous and beautiful in your thoughts and never mind the success of the play or of yourself. Believe me, it is not success that lies in our hands—yours or mine. . . . There is a great deal for you to forgive in this letter."[10]

But in New York there was a great deal going on for Shaw to forgive. Janet had not shaved her head and bought a brown wig. The man from the New York *Dramatic Mirror* interviewed a "young woman barely thirty, of more than average height, with a svelte and well-proportioned figure, a frank, open English face, features rather irregular, laughing grey eyes, a sensitive, mobile mouth, a determined chin, golden hair, bordering on the Titian, a well-modulated, musical voice, an ease of grace and carriage, and a charm of manner that at once puts the visitor at his ease . . . ."[11] Janet was less charming with Richard Mansfield, immediately quarreling about billing, pay, costumes, parts, contracts—but especially billing. Cables flew back and forth across the Atlantic; letters followed: Shaw found himself a referee between the impulsive egocentric actor and the impetuous egocentric actress. Having told Janet to be content with a line in diamond type in the bill, he then threw up his hands: "For Heaven's sake star everybody who wants to be starred," he beseeched Mansfield. "Star the callboy . . . polish Janet's boots and cast Mrs. Mansfield for old women exclusively. . . . Star her until she begs you for God's sake not to raise any more expectations. . . . have a new fount of type cast for her, six feet high, and paint the town hell color with her name. These follies drive me stark mad: I hereby authorise you to announce her as the authoress of the play, if that will please her."[12]

At the same time Shaw feared that in advising Mansfield to give Janet her own way he ran the risk of his complying—and that Janet's way would be the old ruinous way. He knew it too well: the grandiose schemes, the extorting of empty promises, the borrowing on vain hopes, the raiding of friends' pockets, the large spending, the crash and bankruptcy. Janet now had a steady job for three years at $250 a week; and although three weeks ago she had not had a penny to bless herself with, her new position had made her exaltedly confident. She began to imagine New York at her feet, to chafe at the parts Mansfield intended for her, to feel sure that she could do better in New York in a theatre of her own, to consider herself above working steadily for a mere salary.

And for every prudent word of advice Shaw sent flying across the Atlantic, Charrington countered by encouraging Janet's discontent, by backing her fiercely against anyone who stood in her way. It was a kind of loyalty that Shaw half envied: he half wished he could be a fool, ruining Janet and himself and everybody, but making her happy and making her like him. He, alas, was always "playing Candida, the scolding mother," making himself hateful, refusing money, offering cold advice. "Charrington is right because he *is* a fool, Parsifal the incorrigible, hating what he doesn't like and loving what he likes, fighting the one and grudging it its crust, backing up the other in the teeth of all justice."[13] And Shaw the fair, the balanced, the reasonable—a man who could neither love nor hate—was left to manage the two unreasonable children: an ungrateful and lonely job.

Charrington was so fiercely partial that he objected to Shaw's praising Elizabeth Robins at such lengths in his latest *Saturday Review* article. Comparing the performances of *Rosmersholm* and *The Master Builder* by Lugné-Poë's Théâtre de L'Oeuvre de Paris with English productions, Shaw had come out heavily for the English. Admitting that Rebecca West still remained to be created in England, he credited Florence Farr with having given an impression of Rebecca's unscrupulousness—one side of her character—still unmatched by subsequent performances. His praise for Elizabeth Robins was higher: Mademoiselle Despres of L'Oeuvre de Paris "could not touch Miss Robins as Hilda

Wangel. . . . Miss Robins *was* Hilda."[14] Charrington fretted: why was not Janet mentioned? "Cannot make him understand Fabian politics," Shaw told Janet; "he wants you to advance as an individual; I want to create the impression that an army is on the march."

To this end Shaw had contrived a newspaper boom for *Candida* and the New Drama: two interviews in the past week, innumerable paragraphs, quotations from his Preface to Archer's *Theatrical "World" of 1894*. In the Preface Shaw had indeed tried to create the impression that an army was on the march. London theatres were held in the grip of the actor-managers, he argued, but the New Drama was creating the New Woman; and the actor-manager in refusing to play the new non-heroic man to the New Woman had relegated the theatres of London to plays as out-of-date as the crinoline. The challenge to the actress, now simply an appendage to the actor-manager as his leading lady, was clear:

> A glance at our theatres will show that the higher artistic career is practically closed to the leading lady. Miss Ellen Terry's position at the Lyceum Theatre may appear an enviable one; but when I recall the parts to which she has been condemned by her task of "supporting" Mr. Irving, I have to admit that Miss Janet Achurch, for instance, who made for herself the opportunity of "creating" Nora Helmer in England by placing herself in the position virtually of actress-manageress, is far more to be envied. Again, if we compare Miss Elizabeth Robins, the creator of Hedda Gabler and Hilda Wangel, with Miss Kate Rorke at the Garrick Theatre, or the records of Miss Florence Farr and Miss Marion Lea with that of Miss Mary Moore at the Criterion, we cannot but see that the time is ripe for the advent of the actress-manageress, and that we are on the verge of something like a struggle between the sexes for the dominion of the London theatres, a struggle which, failing an honorable treaty, or the break-up of the actor-manager system by the competition of new forms of theatrical enterprise, must in the long run end disastrously for the side which is furthest behind the times. And that side is at present the men's side.[15]

And then came Charrington with the news that *Candida* had been withdrawn.

Hard now for Shaw to be on the woman's side, even though Charrington—his countenance swelling alarmingly as it always did in excitement —cried out that Janet was wronged and announced his intention of boarding the next boat to New York so he could throttle Mansfield and comfort his wife. "Oh, million million million millions, how I should like to get one good grip of you and throw you over the next house, across the Atlantic, away irrecoverably into space," Shaw raged to Janet. "For it is you, wretch, you are making all these difficulties, who else can it be?" A letter from Mansfield, however, put the blame elsewhere:

> If we,—by we I mean Beatrice and I,—had lost a very near and dear friend we could not have sorrowed more than when we discovered "Candida" to be of the impossible.
>
> It has been read—read—read—read,—and reading it would revive our courage,—*rehearsed* and hope, faith & even charity dropped below zero. . . . Shaw—my light is perhaps very small and very dim—a mere farthing rush or a tallow dip—but viewed by it, and I have no other to view it by,—your play of Candida is lacking in all the essential qualities.
>
> The stage is not for sermons—*Not my stage*—no matter how charming —how bright—how clever—how trenchant those sermons may be—
>
> *Candida* is charming . . . but—pardon me—it is *not* a play . . . . Here are three long acts of talk—talk—talk—no matter how clever that talk is —it is talk—talk—talk.[16]

Shaw thus found himself confronted by the very actor-manager mentality he had been attacking in his dramatic criticism. Mansfield, it turned out, wanted a hero's play. He wanted to act—not to sit and hug his ankles for three mortal hours and *talk*. Talk was womanish, not heroic. Fine-spun arguments about love and renunciation and the search for nobility were unmanly and would not be tolerated by the hustling, striving, pushing American public. The heroine was clearly the strong part, and he would be damned if he would play the "young, delicate, morbid and altogether exceptional young man who falls in love with a massive middleaged lady who peels onions." The argument was terribly familiar to Shaw: he knew all too well how no manager in England had been willing to touch Torvald Helmer, a husband deserted by his wife, or Lövborg, played off the stage by Hedda Gabler, or his own Sergius, whose heroics are ruthlessly stripped away. Mansfield's "You'll have to write a play that a *man* can play and about a woman that heroes fought for" could have come from any actor-manager's office in London.

And, as the cablegrams and letters continued to pour in, it seemed that Janet had made the best of a bad situation. The business portions of her letters were sensible; and Shaw's faith surged back: "when you shew yourself a capable woman (especially in a matter which I have bungled) the ocean in my heart is moved by a delightful tidal wave."[17] Thus when Mansfield cabled that he was opening at the Garrick with *Arms and the Man* and would produce *Candida* if he need not appear, Shaw concluded mistrustfully that Mansfield wanted to produce the play with a bad cast and, by causing it to fail, prevent any other manager's getting it and keep Janet from making a success in New York. He wrote Mansfield strongly, accusing him of unfair dealing, of being unwilling to do an artistic play, of never having wanted to produce it at all, and of being an abject domestic slave to his wife, who must be jealous of Janet and out to ruin her.[18]

This drew a reply from Beatrice Cameron. Protesting that she had been a friend of Shaw's from the first time she had met him in Archer's box at *A Doll's House*, and that his letter had deeply hurt her, she defended herself and her husband:

I thought Miss Achurch as "Nora" one of the greatest actresses I had ever seen. When Dick showed me your letter saying Miss Achurch was the only woman who could play "Candida" (or Mrs. Kendal) and asked me if I remembered her, these were my words "Oh yes—she is a great actress"—Does that look like petty jealousy? I could not play "Candida" —I know it as well as you do . . . .

Did Dick ever tell you what he lost on Richard III trying to do things artistically— Over 3000 pounds. . . . He *wished* to do "Candida"—would he otherwise have gone to the great expense he did? Would he have sent for Miss Achurch, do you think that cost him nothing? . . .

The people here are not ready for "Candida"—they would not have understood it. . . . You do not know him, you do not know me—how can you? But you might have felt that petty jealousy, and such low motives as you attribute to him were not possible in the man whom you had liked and who liked you.

Has Miss Achurch told you that Mr. Mansfield wishes her to do Camille or anything else that she wishes—so as to give her a chance in New York this season? We want her to succeed . . . . it hurt me that the man whom I have admired and liked, think of me so unjustly and so meanly of my husband.[19]

And apparently Mansfield was willing to have Janet succeed—as long as he did not have to appear on the stage with her. His taste in women was not Shaw's. "I couldn't have made love to your Candida . . . if I had taken ether," he informed Shaw. "I never fall in love with fuzzy-haired persons who purr and are business-like and take a drop when they feel disposed and have weak feminine voices. My ideal is something quite different. I detest an aroma of stale tobacco and gin. I detest intrigue and slyness and sham ambitions. I don't like women who sit on the floor—or kneel by your side and have designs on your shirt-bosom—I don't like women who comb their tawny locks with their fingers, and claw their necks and scratch the air with their chins."[20] Personal preferences aside, Mansfield's dislike obviously boiled down to the "manly man's" fear of the "unwomanly woman"; the idealist hero's hatred of the real. "You're a new woman," Mansfield was saying. "You play Ibsen. I detest new women who play Ibsen." Shaw himself shuddered over the aroma of gin and stale tobacco (Janet had not, evidently, been leading the heavenly life); but he called Mansfield's letter "childishly indiscreet," and refrained from showing it to Charrington lest he rush over to New York by the next Cunard and have Richard's blood.

To Janet Shaw poured out his frustration. "I have done what I could; I have scamped none of the work, stinted none of the minutes or sixpences; I have worked the press; I have privately flattered Mansfield and abused you; I have concentrated every force that I could bring to bear to secure you a good show with Candida. Can I do anything more? And how long must I keep my temper with these rotten levers that break in my hands the moment the dead lift comes?"[21] To Mansfield he wrote a letter designed to wound, though not kill. He had contemplated, he told him, a vengeful answer to his treachery; yet now that the hour had come, he could only laugh. Suffice it to say that he had not an ounce of respect left for him and that his future acquaintance with Shaw plays would have to be made in visits to other managers' theatres. His personal liking, however, remained what it was.[22]

Janet was left with the task of salvaging something out of her trip to New York.[23] She gave out interviews, well salted with the names of the great. After her great triumph as Mercy Merrick in *The New Magdalen* back in 1886, for example, Ellen Terry had written a letter she still kept: "Some day people shall talk of the wonders of your acting," the great actress had promised. "All hail to Janet Achurch!" Many famous people too had come to see *A Doll's House* in 1889, among them Mr. Gladstone, and afterward she had received a letter from Mr. Ibsen, thanking her for her wonderful interpretation of his Nora and enclosing his autographed photograph. Shaw was not omitted. "It was during the first week of The Doll's House that I first made the acquaintance of George Bernard Shaw, the brilliant critic and dramatist," Janet told the New York *Dramatic Mirror*. "He was sitting in the pit on the second night (he prefers to sit in the pit to any other part of the theatre) when I committed what seemed to him an artistic sin. On making my entrance and laying my parcels on the table I bowed slightly to the applause that greeted my appearance. This Mr. Shaw considers a heinous crime, and he said so in a note he at once sent round to me. That is how our acquaintance began, and ever since I have considered his friendship to me as an honor and a privilege. I certainly consider Shaw to be, without exception, the most perfectly equipped man now writing for the press and the stage." She concluded the interview with the statement that her play, *Candida*, would probably be done in London in September.

On 1 June she was able to announce a week's engagement at Hoyt's Theatre beginning Monday next. In this, her New York debut, she would open in *Forget-Me-Not*, followed by *A Doll's House*. The following season she expected to make an American tour under the management of Frederick C. Whitney. But although the *Dramatic Mirror* reported that Miss Achurch possessed "a commanding presence," won enthusiastic applause for her work in the stronger scenes of the drama, and was "unquestionably an actress of striking ability" who would be an acquisition to any company "requiring something more than a merely conventional leading woman," Janet's engagement at Hoyt's Theatre closed after a week. On 15 June the press reported her as possibly playing a week's engagement in *A Doll's House* before returning to England, and assured the public that a well-known Boston manager had made her an offer that she might accept. If the actress did not go to Boston, she would sail the following Saturday. The *Dramatic Mirror* of that following Saturday reported, however, that Janet Achurch had sailed for London a week before on the *Obdam*, having completed arrangements prior to sailing for her return to America next season with her husband, Charles Charrington.[24]

The great *Candida* adventure thus came to a close. But Shaw's temper was amazingly elastic. He had spent Easter week at Beachy Head; he was learning the bicycle and assured Janet that she would be proud of his ability "to sit gracefully on a wheel." "Oh, the spring, the spring, and Janet miles and miles away," he mourned insincerely. When her replies stopped coming, he chaffed: "There will be a mail in tomorrow, I suppose: and if I hear nothing then, F. F. shall be Mrs. Bernard Shaw at the earliest date thereafter permitted by statute."[25]

And on 10 May he had sat down on a bench in Regent's Park, taken out the omnipresent pencil and notebook, and begun sketching a play that might be just the thing for Irving and Terry at the Lyceum.

CHAPTER TWELVE

1895 - 1896

IN DECEMBER OF 1894 Ellen Terry had begun to keep a private record of her increasingly troubled thoughts about Henry Irving. Once she and the subtle actor-manager of the Lyceum had been on the closest of terms. They were days when she was at the height of her career: when she played Portia to his Shylock, Beatrice to his Benedick, Ophelia to his Hamlet, Olivia to his Vicar, Lady Macbeth to his Macbeth. They were days when she would tear open little notes to read "No rehearsal this morning for you, my darling" or "You were very lovely my darling" or "Soon—soon! I shall be near you on Sunday. God bless you my only though Your own till Death" or even "My own dear wife, as long as I live."[1]

A young girl named Blanche Patch in those days remembered hearing voices beyond the garden of the rectory where she lived in Winchelsea and, peering over the wall, seeing two elegant figures declaiming and gesturing as they strolled in the meadow.[2] Of course she knew who they were. The whole village knew. It was that queer-looking London actor come down to stay the weekend again with Miss Terry at Tower Cottage. Well, one knew, after all, what actors were. Hadn't Miss Terry been seen dancing outside her cottage in the grass early mornings, clad in only the thinnest of white gowns! How glad one was that one had decided not to pay a call.

Although any suggestion of indelicacy in her treatment of a part quite blighted her, offstage Ellen indulged in a certain Bohemianism. The world knew of her marriage in 1864, a week short of her seventeenth birthday, to the painter George Frederic Watts, three days short of forty-seven, and of their mysterious estrangement ten months later. The world knew too about her Harpenden idyll with the architect Edward Godwin, and about the fruit of that idyll, her son Teddy and daughter Edy. There had been a second impulsive marriage to actor Charles Wardell in 1877 soon after Watts had finally granted her a divorce. It was a concession to respectability, a name for her children, but an impossible situation for herself. ". . . I should have died had I lived one more month with him," Ellen later told Shaw. "I gave him three-quarters of all the money I made weekly, and prayed him to go."[3] And then there was Irving, whose growing intimacy with Ellen after she joined him at the Lyceum in 1878 had angered Wardell. Soon Ellen and Irving had been hand in glove. Distinguished guests repairing to the Beefsteak Room for one of Irving's famous celebratory banquets were met by the radiant Ellen as his hostess. They toured together, rehearsed together, and often left the theatre after rehearsal together. When Irving's feet were numb with cold, Ellen warmed them under her dress against her stomach. At one point Irving even purchased a house and furnished it, perhaps with the idea that Ellen would come there as his wife. But she did not come; the rooms remained unfinished, weeds grew up in the garden, and finally the Grange was sold. Yet Ellen was a wife in other ways. Like a mother interceding between children and a severe father, she acted as a buffer between the cast and Irving, who was exacting, sardonic, despotic, and sometimes cruel. Like a wife, she depended upon him economically, for he controlled the purse strings. He also determined how she would appear to the public. Of course he wished to star her because of her tremendous popularity; finally, however, it was the roles he wished to play that decided the bill at the Lyceum. "I feel that I have been useful to him," said the wifely Ellen.

Was she Irving's wife in all but law? "Of course I was," Ellen Terry told Marguerite Steen, her companion in later years. "We were terribly in love for a while. Then, later on, when it didn't matter so much to me, he wanted us to go on, and so I did, because I was very, very fond of him and he said he needed me."[4] This seemed definitive, yet Ellen's vocabulary bubbled with darlings, dearests, sweethearts, and assurances of "Oh, I am very much yours"—and the terms "mistress" and "terribly in love" might have been used with equal generosity. In Victorian times the merest wisp of smoke usually meant fire. Here where the clouds were positively dense, it was difficult to find the flame. Of course both Irving and Ellen would count the cost of a scandal to the Lyceum, and for Ellen the mere thought of pregnancy was unspeakable. Still prudence seldom interferes where desire is strong. If Ellen and Irving remained only tender friends, it was chiefly due to their temperaments.

Irving's marriage to Florence O'Callaghan, for example, had ended in less than a year when, riding home in a brougham after his first-night sensation in *The Bells*, she said, "Are you going to go on making a fool of yourself like this all your life?" Irving ordered the driver to stop: without a word he jumped from the carriage: he never returned to his home, and he never spoke to her again.[5] It was the act of a devastatingly insecure yet egocentric man who had already decided that his work was more important than any personal relationship. Friends noted too that Irving was always more at ease with men than with women. He did not rehearse the women in his casts much, for example, and in the presence of the sex was notably shy, polite, and reticent, although this behavior did not apply to older women, whose advice and affection he could warm to like a son. Ellen was nine years younger than Irving, yet her affection for him often displayed a maternal solicitude. His sexual desire for her he could act out on stage. When he did, playing Synorix to her Camma in Tennyson's *The Cup*, Ellen was outraged. Nothing was more unlike the austere actor's appearance than the thick lips and gross voluptuousness of a Roman emperor; yet "he so clearly indicated the ―― of Synorix," cried Ellen, "that I flamed with outraged modesty and felt one night . . . I could strike him—he licked his lips at me—as if I were a bone and he a beast . . . ."

He had gone too far on stage for Ellen's taste, and perhaps would have in private too. Ellen was certainly a rebel; but her rebelliousness had as its object the creation of a free and aesthetically beautiful life for herself. She had always worked, always been independent (except for the two years at Harpenden), and despite her affection for children and lovers, had always finally put her career first. The dominating Irving was a threat to that independence. She had never really understood him, had always been in awe of him. His King Lear in 1892, for instance, had been three hours of inaudibility. After someone in the audience at curtain call had challenged him, Irving sought out Ellen: had he indeed been inaudible? Greatly distressed, she admitted that she had not caught a word he said from start to finish, but had been afraid to tell him so because of his intolerance of criticism in the past. Ellen could not have risked marriage to this high-strung autocrat whose egotism she witnessed at every Lyceum rehearsal. She preferred to retreat after the theatre to her own home, populated by worshiping females and one small male child with almost effeminate good looks whom she coddled to the point of helplessness—a house which ran to her tempo and in which she was queen.

Yet she was hurt and puzzled when, in the mid-nineties, Irving's dependence upon her lessened. Their cooling intimacy coincided with something even more crucial to Ellen: the decline of her importance on the Lyceum stage. As early as 1889 with Ellen's performance in the mediocre *Dead Heart*, there were dissatisfied murmurs at her lack of opportunity. Why was she not given vehicles in which she could display her delicious sense of comedy? In the early nineties her position worsened. Though nine years older and now in his fifties, Irving was just ripe for such great acting parts as Henry VIII, Becket, and King Arthur. To Ellen's lot fell minor parts played in Irving's great shadow. "I don't know what to do with her," she complained to Graham Robertson of Rosamund in *Becket*. "She is not there. She does not exist. I don't think that Tennyson ever knew very much about women, and now he is old and has forgotten the little that he knew. She is not a woman at all."[6]

Her plight was not entirely Irving's fault. Ellen in her mid-forties could not play ingenues; nor could Irving play young lovers. But whereas starring roles for older men existed plentifully in the repertoire, there were few starring roles for mature women. Irving tried from time to time to give Ellen something to do: the 1891 revival of *Nance Oldfield* that Shaw called a silly charade was for her sake. If his conscience troubled him, however, he could always tell himself that with Ellen's failing memory minor parts were perhaps a blessing. She already acted from couch to lamp to table where scraps of paper containing her key lines were fastened. (Never mind that Sir Herbert Tree over at the Haymarket was even more notorious for lapses of memory.) After all, it was the fate of every actress that her days were numbered.

It was with a sense then of trying to fathom the man that in her heyday she had taken for granted—as one takes the sun for granted until it goes behind a cloud—that Ellen began to jot down her observations about "H. I.":

DECEMBER 1894. He is the first to be perfect in his words at rehearsal of any new play. . . .

He sees things at a flash, *after* pondering upon them for weeks! He studies, and studies, and then *has inspiration*.

He is always punctual and never in a hurry. Will not read his parts, nor think of it last thing at night. *Clever.*

He believes in "2 or 3 dress-rehearsals." *Clever.*

1895. . . . He is so careful and cautious. I wish he were more ingenuous and more direct.

A thousand little things prove he has no idea of his own beauty—personal beauty. . . . I grant his intellectuality dominates his other powers and gifts, but I have never seen in living man, or picture, such distinction of bearing. A splendid figure, and his face very noble. A superb brow; rather small dark eyes which can at moments become immense, and hang like a bowl of dark liquid with light shining through; a most refined curving Roman nose, strong and delicate in line, and *cut clean* (as all his features); a smallish mouth, and full of the most wonderful teeth, even at 55; lips most delicate and refined—firm, firm, firm—and with a rare smile of the most exquisite beauty, and quite-not-to-be described kind. (He seems always ashamed of his smile, even in very private life, and will withdraw it at once in public.) His chin, and the line from the ear to chin is firm, extremely delicate, and very strong and clean defined. He has an ugly ear! Large, flabby, ill-cut, and pasty-looking, pale and lumpy. His hair is superb; beautiful in 1867, when I first met him, when it was blue-black like a raven's wing, it is even more splendid now (1895) when it is liberally streaked with white. It is rather long and hangs in lumps on his neck, which is now like the neck of a youth of 20! His skin is very pale, delicate, refined, and stretched tightly over his features. Under the influence of strong emotion, it contracts more, and turning somewhat paler, a grey look comes into his face, and the hollows of his cheeks and eyes show up clearly. . . .

MAY, 1895. The Queen has made him a Knight, the first actor who has ever received that honour. Better late than never. The dear fellow deserves any honour, all honours. He is just as pleased about it as he should be, and I'm much pleased too. . . .

SEPTEMBER 12, 1895. . . . H. I. is odd when he says he hates meeting the company, and "shaking their greasy paws." I think it is not quite right in him that he does not care for anybody much. (I think he has always cared for me a little, very little, and has had passing fancies, but he really *cares* for scarcely any one.)

Quiet, patient, tolerant, impersonal, gentle, *close*, crafty! Crafty sounds unkind, but it is H. I. "Crafty" fits him.[7]

The quickly memorized lines, the still youthful features, the knighthood, the aloofness—all explained Ellen's acute consciousness of the widening gap between herself and Irving; and explained too why in 1895 and increasingly in 1896, she was more than ordinarily vulnerable to a new voice—the vigorous, persuasive siren song of Bernard Shaw.

"This lonely critic's den, on which you have shed a ray from a newspaper wrapper, is wonderfully warmed up by it," wrote Shaw the first day of November 1895 to Ellen in the United States, where she and Irving were making their fifth tour. "It came just when it was wanted. I had just finished a magnificent article, not on the theatre, but on 'Churchgoing' (of all subjects!) for a new quarterly; and the effort, complicated by the inexorable swing round of The Saturday Review weekly criticism, had left me *sore* with labor. At that exact moment your impulse to pet me for a moment came to hand, with heavenly effect. . . . To my great exasperation I hear that you are going to play Madame Sans Gene. And I have just finished a beautiful little one act play for Napoleon and a strange lady—a strange lady who will be murdered by someone else whilst you are nonsensically pretending to play a washerwoman. It is too bad—I tell you you can't play a washerwoman. . . . Will your tomb in Westminster Abbey have nothing but reproaches for an epitaph?"[8]

Having cast this tempting bait, Shaw waited. He did not have long. "If you give Napoleon and that Strange Lady (Lord, how attractively tingling it sounds!) to anyone but me I'll—write to you every day! (I always feel inclined that way)," replied Ellen on 18 November. "Ah, but be kind, and let me know that 'lady.' "[9]

Shaw sent the typescript of *The Man of Destiny*, knowing that Ellen would recognize herself immediately as his Strange Lady. "She is tall and extraordinarily graceful," went his description, "with a delicately intelligent, apprehensive, questioning face: perception in the brow, sensitiveness in the nostrils, character in the chin: all keen, refined, and original. She is very feminine, but by no means weak: the lithe tender figure is hung on a strong frame. . . . Only, her elegance and radiant charm keep the secret of her size and strength. . . . She is fair, with golden brown hair and grey eyes."[10] Yet he warned her that his little play was just a display of stage tricks, "a commercial traveller's sample," and no use now that it was written because nobody could act it.

Naturally gracious, Ellen seemed genuinely to like *The Man of Destiny*, however, telegraphing "Just read your play. Delicious." She put it into Irving's hands, and by the end of February sent Shaw a scribbled note: "H. I. quite loves it, and will do it finely." Shaw was understandably excited, requesting Ellen on 9 March to "befriend me to the extent of letting me know seriously whether H. I. wishes me to hold the play for him, as its production by him would of course be quite the best thing that could happen to it." Yet he was wary: he knew Irving's "princely manner of buying literary courtiers"; he knew—or thought he knew —that Irving would give something to silence the incessantly needling critic of the *Saturday Review*. "He would buy me in the market like a rabbit, wrap me up in brown paper and put me by on his shelf if I offered myself for sale," he told Ellen; therefore he would neither sell his play nor accept an advance, but depend on royalties and percentages from actual performances. "But it is all nonsense," he concluded, mindful that after all he had nothing more solid to go on than a note: "you are only playing with me. I will go to that beautiful Mrs. Patrick Campbell, who won my heart long ago by her pianoforte playing as Mrs. Tanqueray, and make her head twirl like a chimney cowl with my blarney. *She* shall play the Strange Lady—she and the passion worn Forbes [Robertson]. Yes, it shall be so. Farewell, faithless Ellen!"[11]

Over parts of Shaw's letter Ellen must have smiled, particularly over his objection to *The Man of Destiny*'s being produced in New York, because then he should not be able to rehearse it and teach her and Irving how to act—a sentiment that would have caused Irving's face to grow quite gray and hollow. But she took up Shaw's carefully planted reference to Mrs. Campbell with as much alacrity as he could have hoped:

Your letter!
Very well—
Pat-Cat!!!
I open this again to put in a *P.S.*!!!!
I don't know *for certain sure* by yr letter whether or no you regret having said I might have the play— (*we* H. I.—& I—might have the play)

I am sure Mrs Pat wd look much nicer but I think I could play it better—Of one thing I am *quite* sure—H. I. could "look" *&* "play" your Napoleon better than any one in the world—it wd be the *cleverest* thing the work of *you two*—I wish you were friends—that *you knew each other*—I don't want you to know me, for I'm such a fool you'd be sick of me in a week—& that wd be hateful—but he—that's different. You'd love him. I think everything of him (is that "love"?) He can do everything—except be fond of *people*— (I don't mean me) but that's his great misfortune. (Will you put this in the fire if you please) & I wish you knew him to admire him & love him—Love him & be sorry for him.

I'll speak with him about it [*The Man of Destiny*] today when we are driving out.[12]

Shaw must have laughed outright at Ellen's notion of the red fox of the *Saturday Review* and the gray wolf of the Lyceum loving each other. Yet in many ways Ellen was turning for comfort from Irving to a man much like him. "I have lost my father and my sister, with whom I was on excellent terms," Shaw had told Robert Buchanan some months before; "and I assure you their deaths disturbed me less than a misprint in an article. . . . The inevitable does not touch me; it is the non-avoidance of the evitable, the neglect of the possible, the falling short of attainable efficiency, clearness, accuracy, and beauty, that set me raging. I really care deeply for nothing but *fine work* . . . ."[13] About Irving Ellen would write: "His work, his work! He has always held his life, and his death, second to his work." She had said of Irving, "He can do everything—except be fond of people"; she might have said the same of Shaw, for his undoubted helpfulness usually had the disinterested end of encouraging people to finer work. Ellen seemed the opposite: she loved everybody: her radiance poured over the world like sunshine. The acute Shaw, however, had already gauged a certain inviolability in her nature. "Wretch!" he teased her, "perverse, *aluminium*-hearted wretch! I do not know any other way of expressing the lightness, the hardness, the radiance of that centre of your being."[14] If Ellen could radiate charm and affability, it was because life had been rather easy for her. She was one of nature's darlings. She did not have to strive: she played herself on the stage, and was beloved for her own ineffable charm. Both Shaw and Irving, on the other hand, had been scrubs. Unattractive and unlovable, they had fought their way to success by dint of the most arduous self-discipline and hard work. Both had been forced to play roles to mask their natural diffidence, Shaw creating the paradoxial G.B.S., Irving the Machiavellian wizard of the Lyceum. Both were ascetic, both shy with women, both attracted to older women. Both had missions. But they had ended in opposite camps; and now Ellen wanted them to be friends.

Shaw respected Irving, but was sure he thought he was buying a bribe. He could not have been surprised, therefore, when Ellen telegraphed in late March offering payment of three pounds a night, but advising that *The Man of Destiny* could not possibly be performed until 31 December 1897. Irving did indeed want to buy him in the market like a rabbit and put him by on his shelf; and Shaw responded with a cry of rage: "Do you suppose I will let you treat me as you treat Shakspere—play me centuries after I am dead? . . . Million millions! is H. I. blind, is he deaf . . . that he passes by the great chances of his life as if they were pieces of orange peel laid in his path expressly to capsize him?" This burst over, he retreated to open flattery: he would not accept three pounds sterling gold, but would accept three pounds of her "fair flesh" to accumulate to his credit until he could take her "all in a lump"; yet more than her body he wanted her "inner lamp" to shine on him, and for that one ray she could have all the plays in the world.[15] "My correspondence with Ellen Terry," he wrote Bertha Newcombe a few days later, "the blarneying audacities of which would fill you with envy could you read them, has ended in an offer from Irving to buy the Napoleon play. . . . I stipulated for production this year; this was declared impossible and next year proposed, upon which I suddenly and elusively slipped away from business into a thousand wild stories and extravagances and adorations (I really do love Ellen), which are at the present on their way to her."[16]

Bertha Newcombe was filled with envy, if not despair. She was very much in love with Shaw and wanted to marry him. Beatrice Webb was all for the marriage, other Fabians seemed to think it a good idea, and even Janet—back now from New York—liked Bertha. At least she called on her often in her Chelsea studio. "I suppose I must have been anxious to meet Janet Achurch," Bertha recalled years later, "—the siren—the wonderful woman who absorbed Shaw's leisure to an extent of which I was only half-conscious. . . . I immediately succumbed to the charm. She was so accessible, generous & responsive. She was largely made though not tall. There was no prettiness, but loveliness and beauty—especially I always noticed the modelling of her eye-lids & brow." Persuaded by Shaw, Bertha had done the drawing of Janet during the disastrous season at the Royalty; but it was a bad likeness, and foolishly she had never done another. "After that Janet was often at my studio. Some memories I have that are clear—notably when she suddenly stretched out her hands towards me theatrically and said 'Let us be friends.' I expect my response was very prim. I was not accustomed to expansive advances and this I merely appreciated with amusement as being so appropriately played before me as an audience. We did become friends in a fashion though with warmness on both sides."[17]

Could Janet be trusted, however, to promote the Shaw-Newcombe romance? "What I heard was such a revelation to me that the world seems suddenly to have come to an end," cried Bertha to Shaw after one of the actress's visits. "I feel dazed and must rearrange my ideas and take you away from the position you have occupied in my life. . . . knowing that you really admire and wish to do just & honorable things, that you choose a lower way of life, *that* I do not understand. . . . You say all this: you *preach* it really and then I hear all that I have heard from Janet. What can I think?"[18] Shaw appealed to Janet from Monmouth, where he was again staying with the Webbs. Letters were flying from Bertha to Beatrice, from Beatrice to Bertha, from Bertha to him. What in heaven's name had she told Bertha that Bertha did not know perfectly well already? Everyone seemed bent on promoting Bertha as a wife. This alone was fatal to her hopes, if indeed she had hopes. "She is only wasting her affections on me," he assured Janet. "I give her nothing; and I do not even take everything—in fact I don't take anything, which makes her most miserable. She has no idea with regard to me except that she would like to tie me like a pet dog to the leg of her easel & have me always to make love to her when she is tired of painting. And she might just as well feel that way to Cleopatra's needle. When I tell her so, it only mortifies & tantalises & attracts her & makes her worse. If you told her so, it would be intolerable. So I wish somebody would come along & marry her before she worries herself into a state of brokenheartedness."[19]

Shaw launched a campaign to discourage Bertha, refusing to allow Beatrice to invite her on holiday, filling his letters with descriptions of meetings with Mabel Collier and Nellie Erichsen, telling her he must get Nellie to take him to the Grafton Gallery since her departure for France had left him without a picture-viewing companion, beginning a letter "Heavens! I had forgotten you—totally forgotten you." Yet the effect was rather to tantalize than discourage. Had the marriage issue not been forced, he would have continued amiably with her for years; but an eligible single woman who expected marriage was the most disturbing object in the world. And then, too, the Candida experience was still potent.

Thirty-three years later, Bertha remembered their struggle. "Shaw was, I should imagine, by preference a passionless man. He had passed through experiences and he seemed to have no wish for and even to fear passion though he admitted its power & pleasure. The sight of a woman deeply in love with him annoyed him. He was not in love with me, in the usual sense, or at any rate as he said only for a very short time, and he found I think those times the pleasantest when I was the appreciative listener. Unfortunately on my side there was a deep feeling most injudiciously displayed & from this distance I realise how exasperating it must have been to him. He had decided I think on a line of honourable conduct—honourable to his thinking. He kept strictly to the letter of it while allowing himself every opportunity of transgressing the spirit. Frequent talking, talking, talking of the pros & cons of marriage, even to my prospects of money or the want of it, his dislike of the sexual relation & so on, would create an atmosphere of love-making without any need for caresses or endearments."[20]

But Bertha at the time lacked this perspective, and felt only hurt. Her chief rival, she believed, was Janet Achurch. Her uncertainty about Shaw and Janet's sympathy created a temporary bond between them: as she told Shaw, Janet was a good woman, and she liked and respected her. But she finally doubted her sincerity, and distrusted her as a go-between.

After the New York debacle, Janet had finally found employment at the end of October 1895 in a revival of *The New Magdalen* at the Metropole in Camberwall. A few days after the opening she fell ill, and diagnosed the symptoms herself as pleurisy. Shaw plunged immediately into the affair. "I snatch a moment to implore you to go easy with that accursed anti pyrine," he urged Charrington from the *Daily Chronicle* office where he was correcting proofs. ". . . People recover from pleurisy: they dont recover from poison. I am in despair at the discovery of your medical mania. That is always the way: you have only to search an emancipated man's mind long enough to come upon an abyss of superstition somewhere—nowadays generally 'scientific.' " Shaw had no abysses of superstition himself, of course, only insisting that Janet be wrapped immediately in wool sheets which he himself would purchase at Jaeger's. He was wretched that he could not help more with money, but everything at home was going to hell: his uncle drunk, paralytic, and collapsing, his sister declared by his mother to be going mad, Kate Gurly a drunken wreck—all of them damnably robbing Janet just when she needed him. He could at least recommend a doctor: his old friend J. Kingston Barton had become a swell with more patients than he could handle, but at least was not a bloody fool. He felt too savage to ask how Janet felt at the moment, but Charrington might volunteer a card if he had time.[21]

"Sunday," Shaw recorded in his diary for 10 November. "Miserable wet day. Barton, called in to consult about Janet, declares that she has typhoid fever." The next six days in the diary were blanks, as Shaw bicycled to and from Onslow Square, nursing Janet and encouraging Charrington, who had completely broken down. Shaw himself was under great strain, a condition not helped when his cat, purring and stamping cozily on his shoulder, suddenly sprang to the windowsill, overshot her mark, and landed with a "terrific slap" on the pavement below. When he dared to look, she had disappeared. "My nerves are now finished," he moaned to Charrington, but went on to admonish: "Do not let that fool do anything, but insist on the careful straining of all solids out of Janet's food & the keeping of her quiet until all danger of perforation is over. Let me know if I can be of any use, or ought to call. Now that the thing is ascertained & delivered over to the nurses & doctors I abide the issue like a stone."[22]

He could not be entirely stoical, however—fretting over Janet's diet of boiled animals and birds, milk and brandy; worrying that Charrington might resort to ministering the old "stimulants"; taking refuge at Bertha's studio, where, she remembered, "I had the doubtful pleasure of being a witness of Shaw's devotion & anxiety, as he would come and report her condition & his friendly actions for her comfort . . . . He would tell me of the wretchedness of the household, the want of proper nursing and how he himself sat for hours holding Janet up in his arms on her pillow, until I believe at last Charrington jibbed & a nurse was installed."

But Janet grew steadily worse. "Then came a day," said Bertha, "when he came to tell me that he had been forbidden her room & that her death was possible. He had told me long before how he felt towards death. Anxiety, sorrow, and all efforts at prevention would naturally be undertaken, but after the inevitable end he would, as David did, rise, wash & anoint himself and putting death behind him, grasp Life again. He said to me, 'Should Janet die, I should *never* forget her.' He then characteristically spent a quite cheerful evening with me & even told me that he had had a delightful time and enjoyed himself."[23]

Janet did not die; and although Shaw might be able to enjoy himself forgetfully while she hovered between life and death, he continued his solicitude for the Charringtons. It might be a tenner or two, sent in haste after the discovery that the furniture was again in hock. Or a recommendation that Charrington be taken on as co-director of the Independent Theatre at J. T. Grein's resignation, a job Charrington got, although Shaw had also recommended Florence Farr and Elizabeth Robins. Or a promise to Janet that she could play Gloria Clandon in the new play he was still struggling to finish. She might even play his Strange Lady (though he had higher hopes for that part). He still thought of their stage fortunes as linked, speaking of his plays as "our repertoire." Or it might be advice: the old advice, about the old problem. Shaw's hopes had soared during Janet's convalescence: her eyes were clear, her manner quiet, her spirit chastened. Then on a visit to Onslow Square in December, he saw his hopes once more come crashing down. Bright-eyed and drinking brandy out of a tumbler, Janet had treated him to new schemes for getting money for the Independent Theatre, which were only the old schemes. Surely Lady Carlisle could be touched for £150 for Gilbert Murray's play, or for Ibsen, or even for *Candida*. Shaw went home in an exceedingly grim frame of mind, and sat down to write to Janet:

> . . . Do you remember the scene in "Our Mutual Friend," where Rogue Riderhood is run down by a river steamer, pulled out, and laid, apparently drowned, on the bed in the Three Jolly Porters—how his daughter sits by his bed, and sees, for once, everybody kind to him and helpful about him—also how, as he comes to, all his villainy comes to also, and the people fall off from him and the daughter sees that he is coming back to his old brutal self. Now don't jump to the conclusion that the comparison is between his drowning and your illness: it's worse than that: it's between his drowning and your whole period of your being under water since the collapse at Terry's. It seems to me that as this I. T. scheme develops, and your hopes rise, all the innocence of the Battersea [*Candida*] period is vanishing, and you are coming back to your weak wicked old self, your brandy and soda self, your fabling, pretending, promising, company promoting, heavy eyelidded, morphia injecting self. . . .
>
> I cannot lock up the brandy—but I can poison it. You *must* stop now: the change in your appearance shews that you are just at the point where that accursed stimulating diet must be dropped at all hazards. All through your illness you were beautiful and young; now you are beginning to look, not nourished but—steel yourself for another savage word—bloated. Do, for heaven's sake, go back to the innocent diet of the invalid. . . . Anyhow, save your soul and body alive, and don't turn me into granite.[24]

Janet did not want dietary advice from Shaw, however: she wanted *Candida*. Now that Charlie was managing director of the I.T., what was the obstacle? The obstacle was Shaw. There was no conclusive evidence that *Candida* was impossible for the commercial theatre, and meanwhile he ruled out the usual shabby I.T. production. If the I.T. could get a thousand pounds he would hand over his play. All right: Janet would get the money somehow. But Shaw put his foot down again. If a penny of the money had to be "touted for"—an ugly word, but descriptive of her methods—then he swore there would be no *Candida* at the Independent Theatre. Janet replied with "gusts of ice and sulphur," with accusations of cruelty, sacrilege, blasphemy, insult, meanness, and Satanism: she had thought his soul above money. Yes, reflected Shaw, women liked him "like children like a wedding cake, for the sake of the sugar on top"; if they accidentally tasted a bit of citron, it was all over and he was a fiend. So be it.

He felt distinctly fiendish when he contemplated the Charringtons destroying each other. He was convinced that fundamentally they were mismatched. Of course, Janet was fond of Charlie—"bless his heart." "He has so much in him: depths unfathomable," she would tell Shaw. Shaw snorted impatiently. Everyone had "depths unfathomable" in them, since it had taken millions of ages to evolve even a human idiot! The trouble was that Janet did not understand what these depths unfathomable in Charlie were. She wanted him to make a big success as an actor-manager like George Alexander or Charles Wyndham. And since he hadn't, her impatience for his success implicitly branded him a failure. Why, demanded Shaw, must each torture the other with what the other was not? All Charlie wanted was "a pipe, a glass of whisky, and a caress from a respectable woman." He was a born preacher, a critic, a man of ideas. Janet, on the other hand, was contemptuous of talk. She wanted action, results, excitement, luxury, plenty of money. Of course that was why Charlie admired her; it was why he, also a preacher, a critic, and a man of ideas, admired her. But the strain of each trying to drag the other in the opposite way was killing. Always creator "of an atmosphere subtly disintegrative of households," Shaw now openly agitated for separation: "The moral of it all is, leave him free and be free yourself."[25] Unstated, but surely underlying Shaw's insistence, was his notion that both Charringtons would thrive, freed from the incontinence of the marriage bed.

But Charrington could not untangle his life from Janet's, with the result that he distrusted everyone who seemed more successful than she. Archer, said Charrington, was a knave, Elizabeth Robins ugly and no actress, William Heinemann a Jew, Florence Farr a whore, and Shaw an ass. Shaw groaned: what did that make him, and Janet? And the immediate result of this quarrel with the world, according to Shaw, was the loss of Ibsen's *Little Eyolf* for the I.T., and with it the part of Rita Allmers for Janet. Yet if blame could be assigned for this fiasco, surely Shaw was more culpable than Charrington.

As far back as December 1894, Shaw and Elizabeth Robins had quarreled over *Little Eyolf*, each accusing the other of indiscretions in revealing particulars of the latest Ibsen play just come from Norway without the consent of Archer, the translator. Elizabeth had replied high-handedly to Shaw's explanations; he had in turn needled her: "Do you understand 'Little Eyolf'? I doubt it: I see no signs of it in your handwriting. If not, I will explain it to you. But do not fear: the explanation will be in print." He would not, he assured her, make the arduous climb up to her rooms: "the ant will not leave the valley to crawl up those stairs & warm itself at your fire."[26] For Shaw the contretemps was another case of Robins playing the disagreeable lady; for Elizabeth another case of Shaw meddling, and then baiting her with a mixture of flattery and insult.

Elizabeth, who had the rights to *Hedda Gabler* and *The Master Builder*, had secured the rights to *Little Eyolf* from Heinemann as well. Having tried without success to place it with a regular manager, she had finally turned it over to Charrington and the I.T.—"noble conduct," said Shaw. Janet was immediately slated for the part of Rita, but who would play the second female lead, Asta? Charrington, Archer, Grein, and Heinemann were in favor of a beautiful actress named Rhoda Halkett. Shaw screamed in agony at the very thought. He had seen her: she was gorgeous enough to knock them all endways, and that was just why she was totally out of the question for Asta. He appealed to Heinemann. There was only one actress for Asta: Elizabeth Robins of "the beautiful Puritan charm, the 'St. Elizabeth' sanctity, the pure toned voice, the unstagey beauty of movement" that she had displayed in *Karin* and *The Pillars of Society*. Couldn't Heinemann "by some unheard of extremity of flattery" (poor Shaw could think of no other approach) persuade Elizabeth to do the part? *He* could do nothing: his intervention would only anger her. Or was Heinemann himself so infatuated by a pretty face and figure that he would throw up the part to Miss Halkett?

Making these blunders, Shaw yet urged Charrington to be tactful with Heinemann and cautioned Janet to use tact in handling Elizabeth, since Janet did not like her well enough to deal safely and could do considerable harm. But it was Shaw's meddling that apparently capsized this production of *Little Eyolf*. Retorting that only Charrington had the right to administer I.T. affairs, that all too clearly Shaw wanted *Little Eyolf* out of the way so a play of his own could be performed, and that he resented being accused of improper favoritism to Miss Halkett, Heinemann announced himself "free to cancel the whole thing." "I hope I am thereby making way for your play," he told Shaw coldly, "and thus doing you a service." But even this slap failed to daunt Shaw, who continued to instruct Charrington to handle Heinemann carefully with an eye to salvaging *Little Eyolf*, or to the next Ibsen play, or even to Elizabeth Robins's marriage and retirement.[27] Yet he shortly had to report that Elizabeth had "snatched back" *Little Eyolf* from the Independent Theatre.

Shaw seemed to be undergoing in this first half of 1896 an unusual kind of strain. The failure to obtain a production of *Candida* in New York, his deep involvement with the unlucky Charringtons, the struggle to have his plays produced and the frustration when they were not, the knowledge that he was "growing out of journalism," yet needed it for his daily bread, the comedown from *Candida* to *The Man of Destiny* and the knowledge that *You Never Can Tell* ignored the social problems that had characterized his first plays for a certain commercialism, the difficulties he was having writing this latest play—all seemed to be telling upon his nerves. With this there was the sense that time was passing, that the approach of his fortieth birthday meant he was no longer an up and coming young man. A visit to a barbershop in January had proved "a most fearful tragedy." Producing an instrument like a lawnmower, the rapacious barber had sheared his auburn tresses to the bone, revealing— "the climax of the horror"—a white undergrowth that was now the overgrowth. "It is impossible that I should see you for a month at least," he told Janet. ". . . There must be some frightful mistake about my age: I am not in my fortieth year, but in my sixtieth. For God's sake tell me that you believe that it will grow red again—at least that you hope so." To a woman who challenged him to a debate in these months he replied: "I used to do things of that sort myself, but now I am timid, middle-aged, stale, and serious; and the provocative, the mischievous, the risky, the dramatic, have no charms for me; they only frighten me."[28]

Underlying these tensions, there seemed to be also a revulsion against the celibate role he had chosen for himself during the renunciatory mood of writing *Candida*. He still appeared divided. Writing to a London bookseller, for example, he expressed the desire to write two books: one a religious work, "a gospel of Shawianity"; the other erotic. Writing to Janet, who had gone to St. Leonards on the Sussex coast to regain strength, he showed himself acutely conscious of his recent vows. He had seen Florence before she left for France and Florence, now usually cool, had melted in his spiritualized presence and positively cried over him. His heart seemed to be sending out invisible rays: the saintly rays of a man who had renounced passion. "Do you know anyone who will buy for twopence a body for which I have no longer any use?" he asked her. "I have made tolerable love with it in my time; but now I have found nobler instruments—the imagination of a poet, the heart of a child, all discovered through the necessity—the not-to-be-denied inmost necessity —of making my way to an innocent love for Janet. Had there been no river between us, what wretched makeshift might I not have thought-lessly accepted? Now set up a thousand other obstacles, a million other impossibilities, and I will get over them all by discovering a plane on which they do not exist. In the old days saints and abbesses used to say 'Wait until we die: we shall meet in heaven.' Stupid of them, when it is so simple to become an angel on earth."

Simple; yet was it not also rather disturbingly abnormal? "Here am I, the god who *has* been happy, among people who say 'I want to be happy just once,'" said Shaw, adding: "The result, though, is alarming—desir-ing nothing further, I have become a sort of sublime monster, to whose disembodied heart the consummation of ordinary lives is a mere anti-climax."[29]

His heart was disembodied, yet not proof against the supposed fleshly failings of others. Shaw's reaction to the choice of "the voluptuous Rhoda Halkett" for the part of Asta was shrill, obsessive. "Ha! Ha! ha!

ha! ha! ha! ha! ha! ha! ha! ha! ha! ha! HA-AH!" he cried to Charrington, reporting a letter from Archer defending Rhoda. "Well done, Rhoda. . . . Great Bayreuth Festival in the early days of spring" (the Wagnerian flesh and spirit conflict still fascinating him). "Venus—Miss Rhoda Halkett. Tannhäuser: Mr. William Archer. Parsifal—Mr. Charles Charrington. Holy Elizabeth: he is in the Venusberg. He is, as Parsifal has acutely observed, but a boy, and her rounded figure has caught him. . . . I kiss her rounded figure, and recommend to him another quotation from 'Parsifal,' as follows: —Kundry (laughing harshly) Ha! ha! Bist du Keusch?"[30] But it was Shaw's chastity, rather than Archer's, that seemed to be at issue here.

Work continued to run him at a terrific pace. He could not come to Janet because, he told her 19 March, he had to take in the theatre, and after that collect his proofs from the *Saturday Review* office, and after that "go out across Covent Garden in the small hours" and "die peacefully among the cabbage stalks." But peace was illusive. He played duets with Kate Salt, who accused him of being in such a destructive electrical condition that sparks would fly out of him if he undressed in the dark. She made him conscious of "a grinding, destroying energy, and a heart transmuted to adamant." It was in this condition that he submitted to sessions for nerve relaxation with Frances Archer, who had studied the method of Annie Payson Call, the American nerve specialist, and was an enthusiastic disciple. But Power through Repose seemed to elude Shaw, who advised Janet that he was still "hardly safe without a chain and muzzle."

On 18 May 1896 he finished his seventh play. Even though Alexander, Wyndham, and Mansfield had rejected *Candida,* Shaw still thought it possible in an ordinary theatre. The one-act *Man of Destiny* had been a more obvious try for a popular drama. *You Never Can Tell,* however, was Shaw's first open bid for the West End. He chose farce and all its accoutrements: lost parents, harlequins and columbines, false disguises, mysterious lawyers, Box and Cox twins, and a comic waiter. *You Never Can Tell* nevertheless lacked the main ingredient of the kind of farce made popular by Charles Wyndham at the Criterion: salacious sexual misadventure. In its place, Shaw offered his anti-romantic philosophy of sex that had been evolving since the days of *Cashel Byron's Profession* and *An Unsocial Socialist:* he showed how Nature seizes two vital but unwilling people and hurls them helplessly into each other's arms to fulfill her plans for the evolution of the race.

You Never Can Tell is a play of sexual extremes, pitting Gloria Clandon, the new "scientific" woman raised by a rationalist, feminist mother who has never been in love, against Valentine, the very principle of love. Gloria's shock, when she finds that she is not proof against the opposite sex, is cruel: "Oh, you taught me nothing," she accuses her mother:

Ellen Terry.

Ellen Terry. Photograph in Shaw's collection, Ayot St. Lawrence.

Shaw recuperating from a severe foot infection, shortly after his marriage 1 June 1898.

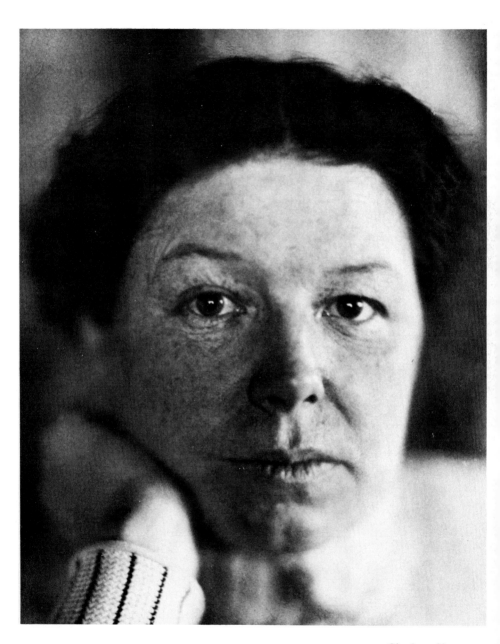

Charlotte Shaw.

Shaw with Fanny Brough (Mrs. Warren) and Madge McIntosh (Vivie Warren) during rehearsals of MRS. WARREN'S PROFESSION *at the New Lyric Club, 1902.*

Madge McIntosh and Harley Granville-Barker as Frank Gardner in MRS. WARREN'S PROFESSION.

Janet Achurch (date unknown).

"nothing." Valentine too is horrified at the depths to which he is stirred. He is not in love: "Nonsense: it's something far above and beyond that. It's life, it's faith, it's strength, certainty, paradise—" Having begun the pursuit mainly to test whether he can bring the "new woman" to her knees, however, Valentine recoils when Gloria herself becomes in earnest. He tries to plead off: he knows nothing about women after all; but before Gloria's new power he reels "like a leaf before the wind." He began in jest with Nature, only to find that Nature was in deadly earnest with him.

You Never Can Tell was thus that strange animal, a religious farce. For the traditional knockabout violence of the genre, Shaw substituted violent extremes: a choice between total renunciation of love and sex and total capitulation to biological fate. Social problems are recognized ("I do not think the conditions of marriage at present are such as any self-respecting woman can accept," says Gloria), but swept away by the imperatives of Nature, and the Waiter's concluding "You never can tell, sir, you never can tell" hardly mitigates the violence of Shaw's duel of sex.

The play seemed to reflect Shaw's own contradictions: his simultaneous dislike of passion and his reluctant fascination with it; his envy, perhaps, of those who can be swept away, escaping for once the ceaseless monitoring of conscience and egotism that preserved him. He offers no mean between sexual bondage and sexual freedom,[31] just as *The Philanderer* had offered no mean between Charteris's unsatisfactory philandering and the bondage of marriage—and his own life offered no mean between philandering and denial. Although the new feminism might have provided some support for Gloria in her predicament, Shaw ridicules the rationalist principles of the New Woman as flimsy matchsticks: Valentine has learned how "to circumvent the Women's Rights woman" before he was twenty-three. So much for the Married Woman's Property Act, divorce reform, women's education, careers for women, the question of the vote. Gloria must submit to being mated; both are as helpless, says Valentine, "as if Nature, after letting us belong to ourselves and do what we judged right and reasonable for all these years, were suddenly lifting her great hand to take us—her two little children—by the scruffs of our little necks, and use us, in spite of ourselves, for her own purposes, in her own way." While it is true that love conquers all (temporarily), and that human beings behave irrationally in the grip of sexual attraction, it was strange to find a socialist laughing at the futility of social reforms when confronted by the Life Force.

The writing of *You Never Can Tell* gave Shaw more trouble than had any other play. He had begun it in July 1895, dropped it, and returned to it in December of that year. On 14 April 1896, as he told Janet, he had finished the second act triumphantly and could be very happy, had he the faintest idea of what was coming next.[32] Again he put the farce aside, and turned to mapping out a scenario for a melodrama he had long been contemplating for the dashing William Terriss at the Adelphi. This he did quickly and effectively. Each act was a drama in itself, ending with a tremendous catastrophe. Shaw felt reassured: "I have no longer any doubt of my being able to carry out that project with considerable force."

For he had been uneasy since *Candida*. Mingled with his growing certainty that he could yet be a dramatic poet was the fear that somehow (as he expressed it to Janet) *Candida* and his subsequent renunciation had been the beginning of "weakness and mollycoddledom." To test his virility, he had, "in a later experiment," thrown away the ecstasy he had achieved through her with "reckless, prodigal, irresistible completeness." Shaw was always oblique about sexual experience: perhaps this was his way of saying that he had gone back to Florence while Janet was in New York. Whatever the experiment, it had utterly drained him of that rapture when he had walked, through Janet, "in the rose valleys" and "on the plains of heaven." Yet he had no regrets: the experiment had proved that "the naked skeleton" of his force was still diabolically strong and resolute. The question now was one of time, life, and health. If these were granted him, he was certain he could realize his genius as a dramatic poet.[33] With this new assurance, he returned to *You Never Can Tell* to embed in farce his first dramatic statement of his religion of the Life Force, completing the play a month later.

His new vision of himself as a dramatic genius left him with an altered view of Janet Achurch, however. He had believed in her since the first night of *A Doll's House*. He had adored, and encouraged, and worked for her. He had taken her side against the world, blaming the world for not appreciating her greatness. Now he looked at her carefully. He saw a woman who counted on fast-fading personal charm to win an audience instead of on the refining of her acting skills; a woman who resorted to golden hair dye and satins to fake an impression of beauty instead of cultivating beauty from the inside through healthy diet and exercise. He had accepted Janet's enthusiasm for Ibsen, languages, writing, metaphysics, and music as proof of a religious spirit; now he began to doubt that she had any real appreciation of the arts or of the exquisitely painful discipline they required. He realized the great difficulties that stood in her way: chief among them was a heartbreaking lack of confidence in herself, a diffidence which had long puzzled him. Yet if she had failed—and she had—the fault was hers. No brandy-drinking actress was going to play his beautiful, sober, and spiritually noble heroines.

A letter of 14 April 1896 contained the first clear warning:

The step up to the plains of heaven was made on your bosom, I know; and it was a higher step than those I had previously taken on other bosoms. But he who mounts does not take the stairs with him, even though he may dream for the moment that each stair, as he touches it, is a plank on which he will float to the end of his journey. . . . I have left the lower stairs behind me and must in turn leave you unless you too mount along with me. I cannot change my pace (if I could I would quicken it) or alter my orbit; and if they take me away from you, I must accept the fact . . . . I know myself so fatally well-prone to overrate the powers of the people I like, but, when I once find them out, turning like a shot and accommodating myself to the new estimate of them with appalling and merciless suddenness.

And if he did find her out? If he discovered, after all these years, that she had no soul? "I know I should drop you instantaneously out of my reckoning, and that your career thenceforth would lie in other men's plays."³⁴

Unstated, but surely present in Shaw's mind, was the knowledge that if Janet was impossible for the Shavian drama, the Shavian drama was equally impossible for her. He called her a tragédienne; and *You Never Can Tell* was certainly not in a tragédienne's line, nor was *Candida*. But the burden of proof rested with her. Had Janet any sense of the value of Shaw's friendship, she must have found it a disturbing letter, despite his kind "I hope these complaints and disparagements will not make you unhappy," and his command "Answer this." Socially as well as professionally he was finding the whole Charrington menage less and less satisfactory. In May, for instance, he rejected an invitation to an excursion into Bucks for Nora's sixth birthday. "Janet Achurch: NO. . . . I foresee it all—the smiling party setting out—the bag of provisions—Mimie—the railway journey—Burnham Beeches—the disillusion & Dead Sea dust between the teeth of three in the afternoon—the seeds of hatred and cynicism—Nora tired and fractious—the thanksgiving that birthdays come only once a year. No, Janet: I shall not be there, I shall not be there."³⁵

Needing a new ideal, a new bosom to mount on, Shaw had turned in his imagination to another woman, a new Candida: Ellen Terry. Ellen had expressed the fear that if he knew her he would be sick of her in a week. Shaw dismissed this boast: was she implying that she could actually entertain him for a week? With what! Art? Politics? Philosophy? He wrote more about them in one year than she had thought about them in her lifetime. (Valentine does not respect Gloria's intellect either: "Ive a better one myself," he tells her; "it's a masculine specialty.") On an intellectual plane they would exhaust and bore each other to death in two hours; but "one does not get tired of adoring the Virgin Mother." If this sounded like Roman Catholicism, he hastened to assure her, it was not: it was the religion of the man who had written *Candida*, for Candida "is the Virgin Mother and nobody else." "And my present difficulty is that I want to reincarnate her—to write another Candida play *for* YOU. Only, it won't come. Candida came easily enough; but after her came that atrocious 'Man of Destiny,' a mere stage brutality, and my present play brings life and art together and strikes showers of sparks from them as if they were a knife and a grindstone. Heaven knows how many plays I shall have to write before I earn one that belongs of divine right to you."

Till now, Shaw's letters to Ellen had been comparatively restrained, the flattery forced, the self-consciousness obvious. Now, however, he found his range with her, and the words poured out. "The weather has frowned; but Fortune has smiled," he wrote at Eastertime from Hert-fordshire. "Ten splendid things have happened: to wit, 1. a letter from Ellen Terry; 2, a cheque for my Chicago royalties, swollen by the dollars of the thousands of people who were turned away from the doors where Ellen was acting and had to go to 'Arms & The Man' *faute de mieux;* 3, a letter from Ellen Terry; 4, the rolling away of the clouds from the difficult second act of my new play, leaving the view clear and trium-phant right on to the curtain; 5, a letter from Ellen Terry; 6, a beautiful sunset ride over the hills and far away, thinking of Ellen Terry; 7, a let-ter from Ellen Terry; 8, a letter from Ellen Terry; 9, a letter from Ellen Terry; 10, a letter from Ellen Ellen Ellen Ellen Ellen Ellen Ellen Ellen Ellen Eleanor Ellenest Terry."[36]

CHAPTER THIRTEEN

1896

"YOUR LOVELY LETTERS!" cried Ellen, and quite naturally began to think of a meeting, despite Shaw's warning that she would find him "a disagreeably cruel-looking, middle-aged Irishman with a red beard." Back in London, struggling with Imogen's lines in the heat of July for a September opening of *Cymbeline,* and now hearing from Shaw that he wanted to kiss her hands, she was tempted. "All the morning yesterday in the scene-painting room up-aloft at the Lyceum," she wrote, "or I should have been sitting on your doorstep at No. 29 F. It was my intention to try and find you in the cool of the evening."[1]

She did not go sit on his doorstep, and was half teasing; yet her desire to see him became her most insistent theme. He was going to Bayreuth: she would like to go too, but was going instead to Winchelsea where she would recover from treatment for her "plague-y eyes." Could he bicycle down to Sevenoaks and come to Winchelsea the next day before leaving for Bayreuth? It would do him so much good. Then her vacation was postponed, again because of her eyes. Well, she would meet him yet, like Iseult, "in Brittany or Heaven." He need not worry about her eyes; they would be "sent to sleep for awhile": she would awake someday to see him in his Jaeger clothing standing beside her.[2]

Ellen's troublesome eyes healed: her fears of blindness were allayed; but she still did not see Shaw. He had won her interest with *The Man of Destiny;* he tempted her now with talk of *Candida,* his mother play—*the* mother play. Now forty-nine, Ellen was perforce interested in "mother plays"; and although Shaw insisted, even while tempting her, that he could not take Janet's "one ewe lamb" away from her, nor repeat a masterpiece even for her sake, Ellen's curiosity was keen. But she could not separate her interest in *Candida* from her interest in meeting Shaw. "You ought to have come down here long ago and read Candida," she wrote from Winchelsea in late August. ". . . Drive down to Hampton Court some Saturday or Sunday and read it to me. Of course you are busy, but never mind. Let things slide and come before the fine warm days are fled. You'll like reading me your own work and I shall like hearing it."³

But the warm days fled, and Shaw did not come. Ellen's time was now taken up with *Cymbeline*. She panicked over lines that would *not* come. Shaw responded at length with acute suggestions for cutting and interpreting the play, without being able to resist the exclamation, "Oh what a DAMNED fool Shakespeare was!" Ellen discovered that she had already cut out nearly everything he suggested. The coincidence stirred her interest and gratitude. "Gods! How you seem to feel with one!" she exclaimed. Encouraged, Shaw posted back two more lengthy letters, letters that Ellen appreciated, but which also demanded answers during this most harassing time. Four days before opening she confessed, "I'm nearly dead. Pray for me, 'wish' for me. My head, and heart, and body all ache. I think I'm just *frightened*."⁴

There was the added strain of performing for the ferocious critic of the *Saturday Review*, for now that they had "met," Ellen would be very conscious of his presence in the darkened stalls. Shaw did not exactly ease the pressure, ending another letter of 21 September, "A thousand successes!—you will break my heart if you are anything less than P E R - F E C T." The morning of the performance, Ellen scribbled an apology: "No inspiration, no softness, no sadness even. Tight, mechanical, *hide-bound*. I feel nothing. . . . Only dull mud. I can't help it, dear fellow. . . ." Shaw received and answered the letter before lunch, assuring her that inspiration would come, but whether it did or not, "tonight or never Imogen must be created." No good comforting herself with the thought that next week she would play better: a week later, after all, Napoleon might have won the Battle of Waterloo. No, tonight would never come again: the red-bearded critic would be out in front—and woe betide the Lyceum and its reputation if she ruined *Cymbeline* as Irving had ruined *Lear*. "Hitherto, you have only *coaxed* me," he concluded. "Tonight you must CONQUER me. I shall fight to the last, as if you were my mortal foe, but oh, with such a longing to be conquered."⁵ A love-death as devoutly wished as feared. Ellen had her own weapons against this foe, one of them a gentle sense of irony: she could tell Shaw she took his letters each morning before breakfast "like a dear pill!" After a first night that impressed both critics and audience (when, as Imogen, she stepped into the king's garden, the audience had erupted with a roar of adoration), she sent a brief note to Shaw, enclosing a few rose petals suggestive of critical bouquets. "You were a great dear to send me that last letter," she told him. ". . . I'm glad they were kind. They love me, you know! Not for what I am, but for what they imagine I am. Oh you kind one, good-night."[6] There was the faintest hint that Shaw had failed to be as kind as the audiences and critics who loved her.

Ellen awaited Shaw's review with interest, but no apparent uneasiness, although he had warned, "The article is finished & gone irrevocably to press. A mass of pounded, smashed, lacerated fragments, with here and there a button or a splinter of bone, is all that is left of your unhappy son, of H. I., of Shakspere, of Webster, and of the Lyceum stage management."[7] Indeed, she thought it might be rather fun to be attacked by Shaw in print, making the public believe that he disliked her while secretly he was her intimate friend. She would consider it quite a favor to be criticized, for Irving, who rehearsed the rest of his cast until they were ready to drop, merely murmured, "Oh, we'll skip these scenes" when his and Ellen's turn came. She was the one person at the Lyceum never advised, never found fault with. She said her lines to herself up in the scene dock or to any stray understudy that turned up. "It is *frightful* not to be found fault with," said Ellen.

She must have been disappointed then when she picked up her copy of the *Saturday Review* on 26 September.[8] Shaw was provocative on Shakespeare: "With the single exception of Homer, there is no eminent writer, not even Sir Walter Scott, whom I can despise so entirely as I despise Shakespeare when I measure my mind against his." He was ruthless with Irving: "In a true republic of art Sir Henry Irving would ere this have expiated his acting versions on the scaffold. He does not merely cut plays: he disembowels them." He was ironic with Ellen's son Teddy: young Craig made a charming Bedford Park Bohemian, but was hardly Shakespeare's noble savage. But Ellen? True, he criticized the difficult scene in the fourth act when Imogen wakes to find a headless body dressed in her husband's clothes in her arms. But the set was at fault, not Miss Terry. To wake up amid the gloomy wolf- and robber-haunted Welsh mountains of Shakespeare's imagination was one thing; to wake up in the sunny afternoon of a nice bank holiday in the Wye Valley was another. The scene had only wanted a trellised porch, a bicycle, and a nice little bed of roses to be completely absurd, said Shaw. But as for criticizing Ellen's acting, Shaw outdid Irving's gallantries. Miss Terry fascinated him so much, demurred the fierce critic, that he had not the smallest confidence in his judgment of her acting. This chivalry was a distinct cowardice; or so Ellen felt. "You know perfectly well that in the acting of this 'Womanly woman' I'm pretty bad, and you might have said so in The Saturday plain and straight," she rebuked him.

Both were conscious that their status had changed. Ellen was no longer just an actress playing to a critic, but "the divine quintessential Ellen" playing to a courtier who longed to kiss her hands. He reacted accordingly. Her entrance had shocked him: she must have spent hours before the glass: she looked extraordinarily young and charming. Was she trying to *écraser* Mrs. Pat?—or—terrible thought—was it all tricks? He had been put five rows farther back than usual. Heavens! Was he the victim of a conspiracy? "I'm glad you think I looked well," Ellen answered simply. His flatteries were often tinged with—what? "I wish I could pick out the sting," said Ellen.

She had begun to express doubts about a meeting. "I think I'd rather never meet you—in the flesh," she wrote late at night, 23 September, from the Savoy Hotel, where she had taken refuge after the exhaustion of *Cymbeline* and the huge reception afterward. "You are such a Great Dear as you are!" Shaw took her up quickly:

Very well, you shan't meet me in the flesh if you'd rather not. There is something deeply touching in that—did you *never* meet a man who could bear meeting and knowing? Perhaps you're right: Oscar Wilde said of me "An excellent man: he has no enemies; and none of his friends like him." And that's quite true: they don't like me; but they are my friends, and some of them love me. If you value a man's regard, *strive* with him. As to *liking*, you like your newspaper—and despise it. I had rather you remembered one thing I said for three days than *liked* me (only) for 300,000,000,000,000,000 years. How would you like to be an *amiable* woman, with semi-circular eyebrows?[9]

Ellen interpreted Shaw's reply as pity for her, a disillusioned woman eternally disappointed in love. "That's not so," she countered. "I've only ever met fine fellows and found they were *all* worth knowing, and have loved them all (don't misunderstand me) and I'm all tired out with caring and caring, and I never leave off (which is so absurd). But I must hear your plays. Mayn't I have Candida? Do you think I'll run away with her?"[10]

They were both working themselves up to an extremely self-conscious state. She could not have *Candida*, Shaw told her: the first scene would bore her to death and she would put it down forever. She must let him read it to her. The reading could be arranged without loss of illusion. She could be blindfolded and placed behind a screen; he would read from the other side, promising not to utter a word that was not *Candida*, swearing not to peep behind the screen. Or perhaps he could read to her through a keyhole. No wonder that Ellen, informed by Irving that he had invited the author of *The Man of Destiny* to his Lyceum office at twelve-thirty on 26 September, was sorely tempted to be there too.

The summons was due to Ellen's good word, for the merits of Shaw's play had been more than canceled by his critical attacks on the Lyceum, and by his sometimes outrageous bargaining for a production. Irving could not have been amused, for example, at Shaw's offering to make him a present of *The Man of Destiny* on condition of his instantly producing works by Ibsen. The play had now sat on Irving's shelf for almost a year: the enigmatic manager would neither make a commitment nor return it, even though he had announced the production of Sardou's *Madame Sans-Gêne*, another Napoleon play. But now a summons to the fortress of the enemy. Shaw approached the Lyceum with some apprehension, expecting to find Irving with the *Cymbeline* review buried "up to the hilt in his heart," fearing that face to face the actor's magnetic personality would annihilate the advantage he had in print.

Ellen drove to the Lyceum that day in the "shay" drawn by the black horse "Nigger" that she regularly hired from a mews. She marched up to Irving's office door fully intending to go straight in, heard voices inside, strained her ears to catch Shaw's, froze on the doormat, picked up her skirts, and "skedaddled home again full tilt," laughing at her self-consciousness. "I *couldn't* come in," she explained. "All of a sudden it came to me that under the funny circumstances I should not be responsible for my impulses. When I saw you, I *might* have thrown my arms round your neck and hugged you! I *might* have been struck shy. The Lord knows what I might or might not have done, and I think H. I. might not have seen the joke!"

The interview went fairly well; and Shaw found himself in the amusing position of having a play firmly accepted by the manager he had just accused in the *Saturday Review* of having no literary judgment. It had also been well that Ellen fled. ". . . I, too, fear to break the spell: remorses, presentiments, all sorts of tendernesses wring my heart at the thought of materialising this beautiful friendship of ours by a meeting. You were quite right not to come in on Saturday: all would have been lost. In some lonely place, by starlight—stop: I am getting idiotic."[11]

In support of this Ellen sent Shaw a clipping from *The Sphinx*. "Poor Ellen Terry!" the paragraphist had begun; and continued to describe the woman he had seen by chance at Charing Cross Station as suffering from a nervous tic, weak-eyed, and just as artificial offstage as on, although she looked wonderfully young. How he wished he had not seen her close up, for then he might have kept his illusions. "You must keep yours!" Ellen told Shaw. Yet she could not give up the idea of a meeting: "Oh, mayn't I throw my arms round you *when* (!) we meet?" she cried. The first night of *Cymbeline*, she had very nearly "trotted round" to him, but had stuck to her post and helped H.I. with the guests that crowded the stage after the performance—and then was glad she had because of something he had said in one of his "blessed letters." She wished she might be invisible so she could watch him at work. Passing Fitzroy Square she looked up at his windows. She was on her way to visit a poor former servant of hers who was dying. "She liked to see me," said Ellen significantly. The very streets of London took on a new glamour because at any moment she might catch sight of a tall, ginger-bearded figure. It was unfair: he had seen her and Irving driving on Richmond Terrace "like two children in a gigantic perambulator." Was she never to have a glimpse of him? He was sitting occasionally to a young woman for his portrait in a little hole of a room off Euston Road. Acutely conscious of his whereabouts, Ellen passed down that road, feeling in her bones that he was quite near. On 26 October she passed his house again on her way from St. Pancras to Kensington—"on purpose, I confess it." "I'd like to go in when you are there!" she wrote him. "But no, all's of no use. I can't compete 'cos I'm not pretty."

They played tantalizing little games, tantalizing at least to Ellen. She sent him pictures of Ted and Edy, pictures he politely returned. He also refused a little gift of a snuffbox with Napoleon's portrait on the cover and "a strange lady"—Ellen—inside. He sent her photographs in which—provokingly enough—his face was averted. She pored over them with the same attention she gave to Irving's appearance. He had a jolly chin, a lively nostril, a lovely forehead and top altogether. But she did not like his ear, the eyes were averted, and the mouth (which told all) was frustratingly hidden. The eyes, replied Shaw, were purposely averted. Supposing her daughter Edy had picked up the photograph by chance. "The fatal spell would operate at once: I should have her here by the next underground train, insisting on my flying with her to the ends of the earth, and utterly disregarding my feeble protests that I adore her mother."

With a kind of mischievous perversity, Shaw began seeing a great deal of tall, dark, and handsome Edy (now almost twenty-seven) and also of Sally (Satty) Fairchild, a young American intimate of the household at Barkston Gardens. Ellen was at once titivated and frustrated by these vicarious meetings. It was detestable that Satty should be with him, and then come all fresh from his presence to her. Shaw kept up the game. He would come to Barkston Gardens and read *You Never Can Tell*—on a Saturday night when Ellen would be onstage at the Lyceum. She teased him back: she would pay a visit that same night to Fitzroy Square and see his mother and poor Kate Gurly. He had written her a devastating description of the household: his embittered sister, his mother, a devotee of the ouija board, his disreputable uncle, his hunchbacked and never quite sober aunt Kate. Ellen understood: "*I've* Kates at home I tell you— sort of different but my house is always full of specimens."[12] She did not go to the Square, however, but spread out her good blue china in the dining room at Barkston Gardens to delight his eye, and promised that she would be thinking of the three of them while she was acting. Shaw came; ignored the lovely blue china; read his play to an attentive Satty and to Edy, who absorbed herself so thoroughly in her embroidery and paid the author so few compliments that, complained Shaw, she might have been married to him for twenty years. He repeated the playreading session on 5 November, but looking for "his gold," found "withered leaves"—his seventh play seemed worthless. Satty saw his terrible fatigue; when Edy was out of the room, she stretched him out on the hearthrug on his back and relaxed him with the Annie Payson Call method, which meant, said Shaw, simply petting a tired man. Both Edy and Satty found Shaw "just the vainest flirt." "He'd coquet with a piece of string," said Satty.

Shaw did stop playing one of the games: he sent her *Candida*, Ellen having pleaded for it finally on the grounds that she was ill and that women get anything if they're sick enough. She found it, like Shaw himself, both horrid and heavenly. She'd wept her eyes out, and had to go out to dinner in blue spectacles. "Janet would look, and be, that Candida beautifully, but I could help her I know, to a lot of bottom in it," she told him. "I could do some of it much better than she. She could do most of it better than I. Oh dear me, I love you more every minute. I can't help it, and I guessed it would be like that!" She read Marchbanks' rejection of a love affair quite personally: "And so we wont meet." Shaw agreed. ". . . I vow that I will try hard not to spoil my high regard, my worthy respect, my deep tenderness, by any of those philandering follies which make me so ridiculous, so troublesome, so vulgar with women. I swear it. Only, do as you have hitherto done with so wise an instinct: keep out of my reach."[13]

But Shaw's references to a meeting were far fewer than Ellen's. His willingness to avoid a confrontation except in the celestial fields on the plains of Heaven was based on something more than diffidence and idealism: it was based on the fact that his romantic life—unlike Ellen's—was at present full. During August and September, when his intimacy with Ellen was growing rapidly, he had holidayed again with the Webbs, this time at a St. Andrew's Rectory leased at Saxmundham, Suffolk. These holidays were not always free from strain. The previous summer at Monmouth, for example, had taxed his balancing skills severely. Used to flirting simply and openly, he found himself in trouble with Beatrice, whose reaction was so strong that it was only by holding his edge "steadily at the most delicately felt angle to her grindstone" that he could avert her hostility. Then he had longed for Janet and the complete freedom of their relationship. Yet he had signed on for another six-week holiday with the Webbs, although this time Beatrice had provided other female diversion. And this time Shaw's letters to Janet took quite a different tone:

> . . . I am up to the neck in infidelities and villainies of all kinds. If the walls of this simpleminded rectory could only describe the games they have witnessed, the parson would move, horrorstricken, to another house.

The nucleus of the party is Webb, Beatrice, myself and Miss Payne Townshend, an Irishwoman with an income of about £5000 a year (as I guess), who has been, so far, able to take care of it and herself, to see the world, to shun matrimony, and finally to get herself attached, as munificent patroness, to the London School of Economics, on the upper floors of which she will reside when she returns to London. We have visitors from time to time. Wallas was here, of course; but we got on his nerves, and he fled from the irksome position of fifth man hovering round a parti carré. . . . Life here is a perfect routine. Breakfast at half past eight; work until half past one (lunch); repair punctures or chat or smoke cigarettes—I wish they wouldn't—until afternoon tea; bicycle until half past seven (dinner); sit round the fire talking or reading plays (as long as my works lasted) until ten; and then to bed. The only variations are that Miss P.T. and I are impatient of wasting the early afternoon, and dont care about tea; so we have made many bicycling expeditions together *à deux*. Also, instead of going to bed at ten, we go out and stroll about among the trees for a while. She, being also Irish, does not succumb to my arts as the unsuspecting and literal Englishwoman does; but we get on together all the better, repairing bicycles, talking philosophy and religion or Shaw table talk, or, when we are in a mischievous or sentimental humor, philandering shamelessly and outrageously. Such is life at Stratford St. Andrew.[14]

Having fastened on Bertha Newcombe for Shaw and concluded that Charlotte Payne-Townshend "would do very well" for Graham Wallas, Beatrice was forced to reappraise Charlotte. "In person she is attractive," Beatrice confided to her diary 16 September, "a large graceful woman with masses of chocolate-brown hair, pleasant grey eyes ['They are green,' she observed on rereading her entry], *matte* complexion which sometimes looks muddy, at other times forms a picturesquely pale background to her brilliant hair and bright eyes. She dresses well; in flowing white evening robes she approaches beauty. At moments she is plain. By temperament she is an anarchist, feeling any regulation or rule intolerable, a tendency which has been exaggerated by her irresponsible wealth. She is romantic but thinks herself cynical. She is a Socialist and a Radical, not because she understands the collectivist standpoint, but because she is by nature a rebel. She has no snobbishness and no convention; she has 'swallowed all formulas' but has not worked out principles of her own. She is fond of men and impatient of most women; bitterly resents her enforced celibacy but thinks she could not tolerate the matter-of-fact side of marriage. Sweet-tempered, sympathetic and genuinely anxious to increase the world's enjoyment and diminish the world's pain."[15]

There was much in Miss Townshend to attract Shaw: intelligence, anarchism, a longing to be useful, romanticism, and, as Beatrice also noted, "certain volcanic tendencies." He had read her *The Philanderer;* she had thought it farce and filth; yet her squeamishness about sex did not particularly disturb the new saint. She had not told him her age. Privately he calculated "not less than 37 and looks 40." She was in fact thirty-nine, six months younger than he. Perhaps her most fascinating quality was the fact that she did not fall immediately into his arms.

The foursome left Saxmundham on 17 September, Shaw on a new cycle (his old having been demolished in a head-on confrontation with a horse and van last July on his way to meet Florence) and Charlotte on her new American Cleveland. Peddling through Felixstowe, where they spent a night and day, Harwich, Colchester, Braintree, Hertford, and St. Albans, they arrived in London on the twenty-first. That night, after finishing a long letter to Ellen, Shaw wrote two lines to Miss Payne-Townshend: "The enclosed belongs to your [bicycle] pump. I forgot to give it to you. What a lonely evening, and a cold going to bed!" The note was exceptional for its brevity and its direct sexual reference. Was he at last, perhaps, confronted by the Real Thing? "Words are the counters of thinking, not of feeling," he had once written; now he had met a woman he had rather be with than write to. "I want to tell you lies face to face—close."[16]

Not knowing Shaw well, Ellen could not distinguish between his various romances; she only knew she was rather tired of hearing about them. "Darling," she rebuked, having scanned and thrown down a "horrid" typewritten communication, "I've not read your letter, but I must tell you I dislike folk who are not reserved, and will tell me of your *Janets* and things and make me mad, when I *only* want to know whether they think you would, if we met, have a horrible dislike of me when you found me such an old thing, and so different to the Ellen you've seen on the stage. I'm so pale when I'm off the stage, and rouge becomes me, and I know I shall have to take to it if I consent to let you see me. And it would be so pathetic, for not even the rouge would make you admire me away from the stage. Oh what a curse it is to be an actress!" Despite an unsympathetic answer, she still hoped for a meeting; three days later she had her little chaise stop at Nellie Heath's studio off the Euston Road where Shaw was sitting again for his portrait. Feeling a terrible fool and very queasy, she climbed three flights of stairs, raised her hand to knock, had a sudden attack of shyness, and ran back to her shay. "Oh I'm ill," she rebuked him. "I'll just go back to bed, and if you ever dare write me another unkind letter I promise you it shall not draw me out again into the cold and the hateful fog."[17] Shaw's "unkind" letters from these days are missing, probably destroyed by Ellen. In contrast he was writing to Charlotte, who had the wisdom to leave for Ireland just when their romance was quickening, "I'm unspeakably hurried and worried—oh for ten minutes peace in the moonlight at Stratford! Keep me advised of your address; keep me deep in your heart; write me two lines whenever you love me; and be happy and blessed and out of pain for my sake. . . . I had rather you were well a thousand miles away than ill in my wretched arms."[18]

If ever Ellen was in danger of taking Shaw seriously, it had been in these fall months of 1896. By November, however, she was made to realize that Charlotte Payne-Townshend was not just one of his "*Janets* and things." She reacted as Shaw counted on her to react: sympathetically, generously, like the good heart-wise Ellen she was. And heart-wise meant that although Ellen looked back on her romantic, erotic past with some longing, and felt the charm of a possible repetition with Shaw, another past claimed her emotions even more strongly. Indeed, Ellen had not much of an erotic past to yearn for. Her child marriage to Watts had perhaps not even been consummated. Her life with Godwin, during which Edy and Ted had been born in December 1869 and January 1872, had lasted only four or five years. There is reason to believe that she was unwilling to consummate her marriage of convenience to Wardell. Her relation with Irving was intensely emotional, perhaps not physical. But her children had been constants, and she was able now to sublimate sexual longing in maternal feeling. She had not always been a wise mother; not sure how to deal with males, she had spoiled her son until he was self-confessedly "as helpless as a penny toy in a shop window." With Edy, on the other hand, there was the most intense identification. She wished Shaw would marry her: then he'd belong to Ellen and, if he didn't like Edy, she could have her back. Teddy was a donkey, she told Shaw: Edy was the clever party. The mother clung to the daughter; the daughter in turn (according to Ellen) adored her with the fiercest protectiveness—"let anyone try to hurt me!" Yet in reality Ellen dominated Edy. She had already rejected one of her daughter's suitors, an American painter Edy had fallen in love with in 1890 on one of the Lyceum tours; she would as firmly reject another. Teddy had fled home in 1893, married May Gibson in 1894; and although Ellen was not pleased, she took no steps to thwart the marriage, and accepted her grandchildren enthusiastically, since they proffered the charm of mothering without its burdens. "Oh, I'd love to have a baby every year!" she cried to Shaw. Shaw magnified the mother in her, both as a safeguard and an ideal: if he could only get away from his wretched work to some corner of heaven, and be rocked to sleep by Ellen.

The mother role now enabled Ellen to be "sensible"; and she was severely tried, for Shaw was quite shaken by Charlotte's departure and her professed reluctance to forfeit freedom for marriage. "She doesnt come back until Tuesday," he wrote Ellen forlornly. "And she doesnt really *love* me." Should he marry her? He could have ever so many hundreds a month for nothing. And he was fond of her, and believed he could prevail. What did Ellen's loving wisdom say to it?[19]

Unaware that she was being half baited, Ellen responded seriously and like an angel:

> *You* wd not be afraid my dear dear Heart of yr Irish girl *because* of her money. I'm sure you *must* have courage amongst your other admirables—but if you were weak for the moment from pressure (say thinking of what you might be able to do for—your Mother in gratitude—"The Cause"!—or any other), then—good Lord good Lord how you wd be punished afterwards—beyond the fault & I could not bear it for you.
>
> *Your dearest letter*—how sad you are sometimes. I suppose people *must* marry!? I give it up—ask me an easy one. I cannot think good work can be done, or good thought diffused without the warmth & *peace* of Home. . . .
>
> So, she comes back on Sunday! & she "doesn't believe in marriage." I don't quite believe she believes that. You try!—but only *if*—oh, you know—for in the great heart of you you know everything—the wisdom we learn in the world—what poor powder-y little stuff it comes to. You know too I cd not forgive you if you married just because—but you won't. So if you marry that girl *I'll know you love her*. And I'll love her too— (& she need not perk up her pretty nose at that: by the way I hope her nose *is* pretty?), because it's a little bit of a thing worth-er than all her gold I offer her. I mean my *love*, not my nose! Good bye the other woman's sweetheart. I wish you were mine—no I don't. What does this mean I wonder—tell me someday. *All my sweethearts have become my friends*—& most of my friends have become *my sweethearts*. I'm speaking of *not now*. Peace in your heart.[20]

Taken seriously, Shaw unleashed a pack of letters in the days following that hurt and disillusioned Ellen. She felt tricked, as though he were deliberately trying to draw her. She found it "a little naughty" of him to send her one of Miss Payne-Townshend's letters. She put it in the fire, but only after reading it "about 18 times" and having her cousin analyze Charlotte's handwriting, which Ellen thought exactly like her sister Kate's. "I could find out nothing about her feeling towards *you* in it," she told Shaw. "I wouldn't marry her in a hurry if I were you. *I don't believe you love her*. How COULD you kiss her! Of course tho' there's kissing & kissing. . . ."[21]

Shaw was probably surprised and genuinely excited at the new emotions Charlotte and her absence aroused; he was, however, callous in displaying them for Ellen and luxuriating in her angelic consolation. Having secured her sympathy, he tormented her with threats to marry even though he did not love. Such statements were a deliberate retaliation for people like the Webbs, who regarded Charlotte as an "excellent settlement" for him; yet they were pointless with Ellen, who had never taken a mercenary view. Poor Ellen took it all seriously. "I've stormed at you—reviled you—implored you," she wrote him Tuesday, 10 November, the day of Charlotte's return. "It all means *don't marry YET*—for *her* sake." She wished more than ever she could come to him, talk to him, rather than writing "enough words to fill a cart." Balked in this, she spent Tuesday evening writing:

Perhaps I'll never write to you again, so read me now quietly & carefully twice through before she comes.

Yes—I *do* "feel tragedy ahead." I WISH she were not coming back for a fortnight, & that with only your own thoughts you'd be quiet for a few days & talk to no one—not to Webb—not to me—nor Lancelot[?] nor another. Certainly not to little Painter Girls [Nellie Heath]. Do you *want* to get into another mess my dear stupid? These young people grab at you & it's really your own fault— (Sweet old Dear) it is.

I wish now I *had* sent off the first-long-letter I wrote you last night. I had been struck by your—coarseness, & affronted somewhat, & torn up into *mince* one of the sheets of your letter, told you not to do it again— but thinking for 2 minutes I *knew* it was not "my Shaw." Besides I wanted to try to avert the tragedy—& I still Hope and trust you. You will not read *anything* I have sent you to *her*. Please—I *ask* you this. It wd be very unwise—for it is probable she wd read me all wrong, & I could not stand that with patience. How absurd I am—*as if it signified* . . . . And now my Sweet my friend my dear dear Son (I go a little way back to that—it's such a good helpful love to give you—"I've tried it on the Dog" —Ted!) I ask you to gather your fine wits together & *think* for a while. There's much truth in this "IN SILENCE & Quiet the devout Soul goes forward & Learns the Secret of the Scriptures"—& the Secret of all other things. *In Quiet.*

"Respect" you say! why how odd you are. It never crossed my mind that you did not respect me. I *expect* to be respected by a man who isn't a fool. Fools never respect anything. Now don't write any more sweetheart love, but if you *really* need my help after this week (meantime think & be quiet) tell me & I'll send for you—or go to you.

Your Sweetheart—Mother[22]

But the evening Ellen spent frantically writing, Shaw spent with Charlotte at Adelphi Terrace, an evening so happy that he felt selfish in his blessedness. He had warned her during her absence that the moment she felt she could not do without him she was, like Bertha Newcombe, lost. She must keep a tight hold of herself, and remain to herself the center of her universe—as he was to his. And yet he had wanted to see her desperately. The need terrified him: if he could, he would run. He could not.

The next morning Ellen marked her letter *"Immediate"* and sent it, reply paid, by cab at ten o'clock. But Shaw had already left for Paris to see a production of *Peer Gynt*, staying at the boardinghouse where Bertha Newcombe had been living since the previous spring. He found the letter when he returned; but Ellen's warnings had quite the opposite effect:

> The moment I read that exhortation in your beautiful large print to sit in devout silence and feel beautiful and *do nothing* [he wrote her], I was up like a lion. Aha! were you made what you are, oh heartwise Ellen, with unshrivelled arms and fulfilled experience, by men who *spared* you, and sat in corners seraphically renunciating? And must a woman who is nervous, and sensitive, and sleeps badly, and longs for healthy rest, be *honorably* charged for a very simple remedy the modest price of £5000 a year & her hand in marriage? What kind of a swindler and fortune hunter do you take me for? I swooped on Paris, and swooped back like a whirlwind; and now, dear Ellen, she sleeps like a child, and her arms will be plump, and she is a free woman, and it has not cost her half a farthing, and she has fancied herself in love, and known secretly that she was only taking a prescription, and been relieved to find the lover at last laughing at her & reading her thoughts and confessing himself a mere bottle of nerve medicine, and riding gaily off.[23]

Shaw never spoke directly about sexual matters and did not do so now; yet the meaning of his letter seemed unmistakable. Charlotte had confessed that she lacked "physical experience"; Shaw had diagnosed her nervous malaise as sexual frustration. Must she really have him as a husband to achieve a "healthy rest"? No, there was "a simple remedy." He had provided it on his return from Paris: Charlotte was now at ease. Shaw was desolated. He had at last come to the point of merging love, desire, and emotion; the vows of chastity could at last be broken. He had not intended just a simple remedy—that was bravado. And now he had discovered—or believed he had discovered—that what Charlotte had imagined to be love was not love at all. He had found himself used like a bottle of nerve medicine. "What else can I be to any woman," he despaired to his confidante, "except to a wise Ellen, who can cope with me in insight, and who knows how to clothe herself in that most blessed of all things—unsatisfied desire." Of course, he pretended invulnerability, writing to Charlotte that although he was "in the blackest depths, waiting grimly for a ray of heavenly light," he was also "quite hard & happy, ironically, sardonically, gimleteyedly happy." He had squandered all his illusions upon her, yet had not made her feel anything, "except nervously." She did not love him "the least bit in the world." Pah! He was "all the more grateful."[24]

But Shaw had been reading his own fear into Charlotte. Unable himself to merge love and sex, he now believed her disillusioned by the sexual experience, when it was only himself. Physical gratification *must* destroy the higher love. There was no mean between Venus and holy St. Elisabeth. Hell had driven out heaven, and in a burst of reaction he had run to Ellen, who knew how "to clothe herself in that most blessed of all things—unsatisfied desire."

But sexual experience did not destroy their feeling for each other, as Shaw the idealist feared. The ray of heavenly light beamed forth again. They went everywhere together. He found himself arranging his time to accommodate her; he found himself falling in with her plans—any plans —just to have an excuse for going somewhere with her. "What an exacting woman you are!" he complained happily, a few days after he feared that satisfaction had ended his business with her. "Is this freedom?" Of course he informed Ellen of this turn of events, recounting a particularly blissful walk in St. James's Park with Charlotte and at the same time asking Ellen to marry him.

With the proof that contact did not dispel romance, it was perhaps a little hard that he still insisted that his mere materialization before Ellen's eyes would shatter their friendship. He had a thumping new melodrama written for Terriss down in his notebook. He wanted to read it to her; he was reading it to everyone else, "but not to—well, no matter." The fact that Ellen had at last seen *him* only firmed his determination never to meet. She had sent him a ticket to the Lyceum: he had used it to see her in Mrs. Craigie's *Journeys End in Lovers' Meetings*. Ellen had applied herself to the peephole of the Lyceum curtain, and there indeed was Shaw, just where she knew his ticket would place him. "I've seen you at last!" she cried. "You *are* a boy! And a Duck! (I must not call you names now, but always remember St. James Park, & that your spare time is wanted)." If Ellen thought that the way was now clear to a meeting, she was mistaken. He pleaded that he was more than ever terrified "to come stumping in my thickbooted, coarse, discordant reality, into that realm where a magic Shaw, a phantasm, a thing who looks delicate and a boy (twelve stalls and a bittock off) poses fantastically before a *really* lovely Ellen . . . ."[25] To encounter the goddess would be a kind of rape, and: "I dont ask that the veil of the temple shall be rent."

But Ellen had at last given up talking about meetings. She bowed to the situation, outwardly at least, and accepted her role as confidante. As she had projected herself into an imagined affair between Shaw and Edy, she managed now to project herself into the new affair of Shaw and Charlotte:

Oh I see you, you two, walking in the damp and lovely mist, a trail of light from your footsteps, and—I don't think it's envy, but I know my eyes are quite wet, and I long to be one of you, and I don't care which.

The common usual things appearing so beautiful as you tell me. Yes—I know. It's a long time ago, but "praise be blessed" I'll never forget! Why you dear precious thing, if you are not as happy as she, you *are* wasting precious time. But you are happy, aren't you? Tell me.[26]

CHAPTER FOURTEEN

1896

ELLEN WAS GRACIOUS; but how did the woman who had occupied Shaw's emotions for seven years react to his defection? Since Shaw evidently destroyed Janet's letters, her voice is silent, though much can be deduced from his letters. It was perhaps the earlier defection that came hardest: his warning that if she could not climb with him, he would ruthlessly leave her behind. An intelligent as well as a hopelessly undisciplined woman, she must have known he would soon be out of reach.

A month after that April letter she was pregnant. She was a motherly woman, or at least enchanted with the idea of motherhood, giving Nora birthday parties and jollying Charlie with "dear boy" and "bless his heart" and generally discussing him with Shaw as if he were a child. She had become inconveniently pregnant the first time in late August of 1889 just as they were beginning the Australian tour; she might have become accidentally pregnant again. On the other hand, motherhood might now appeal to her as an antidote to professional failure, or even as a way to recapture Shaw's admiration. For he had written *Candida, the* mother play, for her. And she knew how he preferred mothering to love.

From the rectory at Saxmundham in August, however, Janet did not receive tributes to motherhood, but a long letter from Shaw describing his flirtation with a Miss Payne-Townshend. Upon his returning to London and visiting their rooms, she therefore demanded of him in Charrington's presence whether he still loved her; and then on being reassured, relented and informed him that she had been faithless to him with Charrington "to the extent of making 'Candida' impossible until after next February when she expected once more to become a mother." She reveled in her pregnancy for Shaw, who in turn told Ellen that she and

Janet were the only two women he had ever met whose idea of voluptuous delight was that life should be one long confinement from the cradle to the grave. "It must be a curious thing to be a mother," he mused: to watch the creature that had been a part of oneself evolve into an independent human being that one might never dream of caring for had the accidental service of birthing been performed by someone else. "Of the two lots, the woman's lot of perpetual motherhood, and the man's lot of perpetual babyhood," he concluded, "I prefer the man's, I think."[1]

His encounters with Janet were rarer now, their letters rarer still. When he did call at the end of October, he found the kind of scene he dreaded most: Charrington in the martyrdom stage and Janet unusually beautiful: her eyes like moons in a wet fog, her moral nature totally submerged, her wits rapaciously alert. Was it motherhood—or morphia. She seemed distraught: she accused him of rowing strokes in someone else's boat. The idea of her helping herself out pharmaceutically with her pregnancy appalled Shaw; he lashed out brutally. Her mood turned out to be motherhood this time, and Shaw apologized without regretting his outburst: if it wasn't morphia this time it would be the next. "Besides, dear Janet," he evaded, blasting any hopes she might have had that motherhood might win him back, "I *daren't* be devoted now. The appeal of your present experience to my sympathy is too strong to be indulged. So don't be angry with—Shaw, Limited."[2]

From Charlotte, Shaw was learning a different version of motherhood. Charlotte had endured "a perfectly hellish childhood and youth" with an unhappy mother who tyrannized a passive father—a childhood much like Shaw's, except that Mrs. Shaw had tyrannized by superiority to anger, not temper. Like Shaw, Charlotte had learned from her ill-matched parents that marriage was "unnatural and disastrous." She had extended her horror of marriage to the conception, bearing, and rearing of children: she found the idea physically repulsive to the highest degree.[3] Now Shaw began to look at Janet through Charlotte's eyes. "Janet carries out your worst theories of maternity," he reported: "all her animal forces are thrown into a sort of liquid suffusion & eruption, & she's stark mad." Hurt at Shaw's disloyalty, Janet took out her feelings on the nearest victim, Bertha Newcombe, torturing her with tales of Shaw's engagement, insisting she would rather see Shaw married to Charlotte than to anyone else. Bertha recoiled and accused Shaw of fortune-hunting. Exasperated, Shaw baited her: yes, he and Miss Payne-Townshend were engaged. The date was set, his fiancée had already settled huge sums of money on him, they had taken an elegant house, he would live in luxury the rest of his life. Shaw's annoyance was understandable: suspicions of fortune-hunting threw all his socialist principles into doubt, besides being patently untrue. Perhaps his anger also masked a yielding to the idea of marriage. He had talked it since his youthful correspondence with Elinor Huddart:

"Marry, marry!" she had complained. "It is always your cry." Bertha and Ellen had also suffered through Shaw's indecisions over marriage, and had spent long hours relaying advice. Outwardly objecting to the terms of marriage under law, flinching from its intimacies, yet always considering it, Shaw perhaps expressed in his letter to Bertha his deepest wish.

Shaw suspected that Janet would help herself out pharmaceutically not only with pregnancy, but with her new role; for at last Elizabeth Robins was to produce Archer's translation of *Little Eyolf* at the Avenue Theatre for a series of matinees beginning 23 November, with Janet as Rita Allmers, the mate-devouring wife. The part was terrifically emotional; Shaw therefore went out of his way to assure her that she could do it on her head, fearing that if Janet, now six months pregnant, worried over it, she would resort to brandy and morphia rather than rest, exercise, and diet.

He hardly dared interfere with Elizabeth Robins after the fiasco over *Little Eyolf* with the Independent Theatre. Their relationship had not improved: she was still torn between acknowledging his usefulness as a critic and one-man publicity band and distrusting him. In July, however, she had intimated that she needed his advice about the fall production. Shaw replied in some exasperation: she knew perfectly well that if he made an appointment, she would counter the same day with a letter forbidding his approach and refusing his acquaintance. Perhaps they could meet at the Haymarket, where, in the midst of the crowd, she surely need not fear molesting?[4] Now he suggested only that *Little Eyolf* be postponed until March for Janet's sake, and also ventured to deplore Miss Robins's inattention to publicity. He had come across one of her circulars by merest accident. Might he suggest that the same accident happen to every theatre critic in London as soon as possible? Beyond this, he scarcely dared, although he immediately began advertising the production in his column, announcing provocatively that although playgoers had put off the torture of *Little Eyolf* as one would put off a visit to the dentist, they now seemed not only prepared to be tortured, but had actually subscribed to help Miss Robins pay for the rack. Yes, there were rare afternoons ahead at the Avenue Theatre: if the public did not get its eight shillings' worth of agony, it would not be Ibsen's fault.

The cast was a strong one, though predictably no eminent actor had volunteered his services. What leading man, after all, wished to be slowly and remorselessly stripped of all masculine pretensions before an audience, instead of dazzling it with heroics? "Women do not mind ill usage so much, because the strongest position for a woman is that of a victim," said Shaw with, one hopes, irony; besides, since Ibsen was evidently highly susceptible to women, actresses forgave him anything. Therefore audiences could look forward to the strongest female cast ever assembled for an Ibsen production in London: Elizabeth Robins playing the sympathetic Asta Allmers, Janet Achurch as the harrowing Rita, and Mrs. Patrick Campbell herself appearing as the Rat Wife, the smallest but most fascinating part in the play.

The appearance of Beatrice Stella Campbell in a series of low-budget Ibsen matinees was something of a mystery. Since her West End triumph in *The Second Mrs. Tanqueray*, she had played standard parts: Princess Fedora Romanoff, Juliet, the slave girl Militza, Magda, Lady Teazle.[5] Shaw had followed her in print since joining the *Saturday Review* in January 1895, chopping away at her acting ability while succumbing more and more to her fascination. She was Circe, and all he could do was struggle to play Odysseus. When Mrs. Campbell finally walked onstage as Militza in *For the Crown*, Shaw's bark crashed upon the siren's shore. "You will tell me, no doubt, that Mrs. Patrick Campbell cannot act," he raved in his column of 7 March 1896. "Who said she could?—who wants her to act?—who cares twopence whether she possesses that or any other second-rate accomplishment? On the highest plane one does not act, one *is*. Go and see her move, stand, speak, look, kneel—go and breathe the magic atmosphere that is created by the grace of all these deeds; and then talk to me about acting, forsooth!" Then Shaw went to *Magda* and found his "Who wants her to act?" embarrassingly answered. He did; but the bewitching actress made a childish failure. If readers thought him too harsh, they could go to the Lyceum and see for themselves—but they had better hurry, for *Magda* would not run long. "This is not the fault of the play," said Shaw with deadly honesty, "which does not fail until she kills it."[6]

Stella Campbell read the harsh notices, and found that of the terrible trio—Walkley, Shaw, and Archer—Shaw was by far her severest critic. But then Shaw was not only the most demanding critic in London, he was the critic she had most enchanted, and would blame most where he had praised. And adroit as Mrs. Campbell was at finding excuses for the failure—the cavernous and unfriendly depths of the Lyceum, the play's opening on Derby Day, the popular Forbes-Robertson relegated to a minor role, the unfamiliarity of Lyceum audiences with psychological drama, the monotony of one set for all three acts—she admitted to bitter disappointment over *Magda*.[7] Shaw was right about its run: the play opened 3 June, and on 20 June the Lyceum curtain rose on *The School for Scandal*, Forbes-Robertson's desperate bid to save the season from ruin. On Stella's Lady Teazle Shaw and Walkley shifted ground, Archer remaining stoically unfavorable. Writing his review in the train bound south for the coast, Walkley was bored: "Mrs. Patrick Campbell looked very charming in pale green and silver last night, and the Kentish hops are looking very healthy this morning. . . ." Shaw, finding a moral in every production and as usual, giving his readers ten times the content they expected or even deserved, found that *The School for Scandal* had dated on the Woman Question as badly as *The Taming of the Shrew*, but declared Mrs. Campbell "exactly right."

These then were the professional experiences that preceded and perhaps explained Stella Campbell's condescending to the Rat Wife, a part with only a dozen or so lines, at the unfashionable Avenue, the whole venture a forlorn artistic hope led by Elizabeth Robins. Demoralized, tired, the collapse that would fell her in the near future well on its way, she felt it a good moment to propitiate the gods by repaying the actress whose generosity had made her career. She had been interested in Ibsen before, of course, and although too conventional to play the lover of an erotic clergyman in *Michael and His Lost Angel*, written by Henry Arthur Jones especially for her and Forbes-Robertson, she was acute enough to see that the Pied Piper-like Rat Wife was just the part to which she could bring her poetically morbid charm. "Clever Mrs. Pat," congratulated Shaw.

How much did Mrs. Campbell heed the critic of the *Saturday Review?* Always able to dismiss him as an unfashionable socialist fanatic, she could scarcely be indifferent to the fact that his reviews were a struggle to maintain his critical judgment against her sheer personal force —a struggle he too often won. Perhaps the most insulting part of his *Magda* review had been his hope that she would not lock up the part after her failure lest another actress demonstrate how it should be done. He could name two actresses at least who could do it twenty times better than she: Elizabeth Robins and Janet Achurch, "able and energetic women" who had had "little to repay them except unlimited opportunities of looking on at fashionable dramas, in which placidly pretty and pleasant actresses enjoy a heyday of popular success by exhibiting themselves in expensive frocks, and going amiably through half a dozen tricks which they probably amuse themselves by teaching to their poodles . . . ." Was this Shaw creature calling her placid, pretty, and pleasant? She did not have a poodle, but was notoriously infatuated with "Buttons," the current griffon. Fortuitously, therefore, the Rat Wife gave Stella the chance to prove she could hold her own against, if not outact, the two actresses that Shaw was always dragging into his reviews by hook or crook to shame the popular favorites. Publicly Stella Campbell confined herself to the explanation that she was thankful for the chance of being able to do something for Elizabeth Robins at last.

Now that the Farr-Shaw contingent was no longer competing for Ibsen with the Robins-Archer band, Archer liked Florence better, and she sat next to him at rehearsals. Unable finally to keep out of the event, Shaw had recommended her to Robins as a possible business manager: although she couldn't act, she was "an intelligent woman of business, and honorable in money matters." Florence was there, however, being paid ten pounds to understudy Janet, for as Shaw told Elizabeth, "it is useless to blink the fact that the risk is greater than usual in her case." He suggested, however, in case of Janet's incapacity, that Florence do the Rat Wife and Mrs. Pat be got to do the part of Rita Allmers: the audience would consider it quite an event.

Shaw had also suggested to Elizabeth that Charlotte Payne-Townshend could be expected to subscribe handsomely to stalls. His note carried a rather proprietary tone, almost as if Charlotte's support was already his to dispose of. They both attended the opening matinee on Monday, 23 November. Thanks to the presence of Mrs. Campbell in the cast, the audience rose above the usual assortment of Ibsenites, Bohemians, anarchists, and Fabians. Pinero and Lady Burne-Jones were there, and Forbes-Robertson, in love with Mrs. Campbell but terribly glad that some other manager had the handling of her willfulness for a change. Everyone was waiting to see what Mrs. Pat would make of a part that called for rags, a bent back, and a lot of aging charcoal about the mouth and eyes. "She played supernaturally, beautifully," said the captivated Shaw: "the first notes of her voice came as from the spheres into all that suburban prose: she played to the child with a witchery that might have drawn him not only into the sea, but into her very bosom." Her part over after the first act, Mrs. Campbell then appeared in the audience—ravishingly beautiful, completely conspicuous, and totally damaging the illusion. She offered her opinion of the remaining acts in sibilant whispers, having done her bit for charity.

During the second interval Shaw tried to get to Charlotte in the dress circle, but was waylaid by Nellie Erichsen and H. W. Massingham, editor of the *Daily Chronicle*. The lovers were both disappointed, and Shaw proposed that they see it again someday when they could sit together. Meanwhile, if Charlotte had extra stalls at her disposal, would she please give them to him for his mother. Again, there was a subtle note of claim.

Charlotte saw Janet Achurch act that afternoon for the first time. Given Shaw's inability to keep quiet about his romantic interests, Charlotte was certain to be vicariously acquainted with Mrs. Charrington and, in her controlled, well-bred way, hostile too. Shaw perhaps deprecated Janet's performance to Charlotte; certainly he did to Ellen, who replied the day after the opening, "That *poor* Janet. In *such* a part! how unfortunate. I've seen no account of it as yet."[8] Shaw went home to write his review, and it confirmed Janet's fall from grace during the past year. It was perhaps significant that his first real disloyalty to Janet in print came now, at a performance attended by Charlotte and certainly discussed with her. As Beatrice Webb had observed, Charlotte was impatient with women; and there was excellent reason for her to be more impatient of this woman than others. This did not mean that Janet was innocent of the crimes with which Shaw charged her, only that Shaw had never seen them so clearly before.

A year ago, indeed, he had trumpeted her in his column as "the only great tragic actress of genius we now possess."⁹ In that production of *The New Magdalen*, Janet had passed the supreme test of tragic acting: she left the spectator in that "indescribable disturbance of soul" that the reviewer felt perfectly safe from experiencing in London theatres except when Eleonora Duse was in town. Now her Rita Allmers had disturbed him, it was true, but not so much his soul as his nerves. She played with all her old power and more—far too much more.

> For the first time one clearly saw the superfluity of power and the vehemence of intelligence which make her often so reckless as to the beauty of her methods of expression [wrote Shaw]. As Rita she produced almost every sound that a big human voice can, from a creak like the opening of a rusty canal lock to a melodious tenor note that the most robust Siegfried might have envied. She looked at one moment like a young well-dressed, very pretty woman: at another she was like a desperate creature just fished dripping out of the river by the Thames Police. Yet another moment, and she was the incarnation of impetuous, ungovernable strength. Her face was sometimes winsome, sometimes listlessly wretched, sometimes like the head of a statue of Victory, sometimes suffused, horrible, threatening, like Bellona or Medusa. She would cross from left to right like a queen, and from right to left with, so to speak, her toes turned in, her hair coming down, and her slippers coming off. A more utter recklessness, not only of fashion, but of beauty, could hardly be imagined: beauty to Miss Achurch is only one effect among others to be produced, not a condition of all effects.¹⁰

What, dear god, Janet might well have asked, does the man want? Scornful of pretty doll actresses who think first of their frocks and faces; critical of actresses who neglect them. Yet she might have understood by now that for Shaw the words "untamed genius" were a contradiction in terms. Genius for him could not be untamed, just as life could not be lived except under strict rein. Discipline over voice, costume, movement —over every lift of the hand and syllable of a phrase—were fundamental skills without which no power of interpretation could rise to genius. His own prose had that discipline: it never rose to tempestuous heights, it never foundered: it flowed forth under control: elastic, lucid, precise. Of course, Shaw did not totally annihilate Janet. Telling her she could play Rita on her head in private, in print he called Rita Allmers one of the heaviest parts ever written, a single act of which would exhaust an ordinary person. It had not, he observed ambivalently, exhausted Miss Achurch. In conclusion, he must classify her as a heroic actress who needed a repertoire as specialized as that of Duse or Irving: tragically enough, this kind of repertoire was no longer fashionable. Yet in Shaw's admission that he preferred the beauty of Mrs. Campbell's acting to Janet's power, she might realize that he had discovered her missing qualification at last: the beauty of self-discipline in art that comes from self-discipline in life.

Another cast member did not care what he said, and told him so. Elizabeth Robins acted best, according to Shaw, when she could portray a nervous, restless, intensely self-conscious, and eagerly energetic type. When a role did not call upon these qualities, she played weakly, with the vestiges of American ladylikeness. The part of Asta gave her little chance to express herself; consequently "Asta was only a picture, and, like a picture, did not develop." Elizabeth informed him that she had not read his strictures, a typical snub which provoked Shaw to retort with ill-concealed impatience: "*Never* tell a critic that you haven't read his notice. First, because every actor tells him that, and he doesn't believe it. Second, because it annoys him. Third, because it is the stupidest thing you could possibly say to him. Fourth, because (in my case) you *ought* to have read it. Fifth (also in my case) because such remarks are lost on my insufferable self sufficiency."[11]

Charrington and Shaw had worried that Janet's health might drive her prematurely from the cast of *Little Eyolf,* or even that the strenuous role might harm the baby. Quite a different development ended her career as Rita Allmers, however. The good business done on account of Mrs. Campbell had brought the production to the attention of a theatrical syndicate who proposed taking the play financially off Elizabeth Robins's hands. Getting wind of the matter, Janet approached the syndicate independently and negotiated her own terms: £25 a week and 3 per cent on receipts over £500. Outraged that Janet had acted privately, and never a particular friend of hers, Elizabeth encouraged Mrs. Campbell to underbid Janet for the lead. On Friday, 4 December, having played less than two weeks, Janet learned just before the curtain went up that the part of Rita was no longer hers.

Shaw first thought of the effect of the news on her "condition." He found her distraught and angry, but bullied her into accepting the situation: for her health's sake it was the best thing that could have happened, and in any case, she would have to leave the cast soon. With his support, she managed to carry herself "with sufficient gallantry in the face of the enemy." She was to leave the cast on 6 December, being allowed to play out a full two weeks. On the fifth Shaw asked Charlotte to make a friendly gesture to the unfortunate Janet. She had to play both a matinee and an evening performance that day; she did not have time to return to Chelsea in the interim; she was planning to sit out the time at the Solferino, a cafe in Rupert Street (and the same cafe where, in happier times, she had met Felix Mansfield to arrange the *Candida* details). The Solferino was the worst place in the world for Janet to try and rest: she would only "fidgit & talk & calculate the prices of the things in the bill & drink brandy and soda & generally worry herself into the worst condition for the second performance." Could not Charlotte send "an angel's message" around to the Avenue, and invite Janet to Adelphi Terrace to rest? Assured that Shaw had only thought of the mercy mission as an excuse to call on her, Charlotte complied like the polite lady she was, going to the Solferino herself, yanking Janet, half dead, away from her brandy and soda (according to the ever exaggerative Shaw), putting her to bed at Adelphi Terrace, and delivering her restored for the evening performance.

Shaw went to the Avenue on Tuesday, 8 December, to see the new Rita, as did Janet. Stella Campbell had had about four days to learn the new part, but they were not enough: she got through two acts, but in the third entered with the playbook hanging from a ribbon tied around her waist. "You were divine and the book was scarcely noticed," William Heinemann assured her afterward. "In the third act, the smoothness of the proceedings was somewhat marred by the fact that Mrs. Campbell, not knowing her words, had to stop acting and frankly bring the book on stage and read from it," noted the less tactful Shaw. He presumed that in the audience Janet was enjoying Mrs. Campbell's incompetence immensely—not the playbook incompetence, for that was little, but the incompetence that was making Mrs. Campbell turn one of Ibsen's most anguishing heroines into a well-bred housewife. The syndicate had transformed *Little Eyolf* into "a full-blown fashionable theatrical speculation"; and the star was thoroughly entering into the spirit of the new production. "She has seen how unladylike, how disturbing, how full of horror even, the part of Rita Allmers is, acted as Miss Achurch acted it," Shaw wrote in a devastating notice titled "Ibsen Without Tears." "And she has remedied this with a completeness that leaves nothing to be desired. . . . She looked charming; and her dresses were beyond reproach . . . . Her performance was infinitely reassuring and pretty . . . . Goodness gracious, I thought, what things that evil-minded Miss Achurch did read into this harmless play!" Shaw had declared before that he enjoyed being fascinated by Mrs. Campbell more than being harrowed by Miss Achurch; now, however, he reversed himself: he would choose the flogging.

Stella Campbell remembered playing Rita at the Avenue as an "alarming ordeal." She also remembered she had only taken the lead because Miss Achurch had suddenly fallen ill. Shaw, however, offered a better reason for her having accepted the part: commercialization, before which all artistic criteria fall. The syndicate had no intention of wasting an expensive star on a minor part that could be filled for a few pounds

(Florence's fate) when the star could be transferred to the leading role, and Miss Achurch's salary saved, he pointed out, evidently forgetting that he had suggested the same casting. They would have tossed out Elizabeth Robins too, thought Shaw, relying on Mrs. Pat to draw; but Miss Robins had power over the stage rights.[12] The result was prettified Ibsen. The play finally closed on 19 December. For her part in encouraging Stella Campbell to underbid Janet, Elizabeth had the satisfaction of seeing her Asta critically overshadowed by the blaze of publicity attending Mrs. Pat. In the spring of the following year, the Avenue's bankruptcy disclosed a loss of £200 on *Little Eyolf*, bearing out Ellen Terry's prediction that there would be "no money from that Eyolf for *anybody*."

Shaw had kept Ellen abreast of developments. She would have liked to see "Little Eye-opener," she told him; but plays made her so fatigued, and if she couldn't play at night, what would H.I. say? Edy had told her that Janet was the only one of the three women who could act. Ellen had not seen her recently: there was no discipline in her acting or she would have gone—who knows how far. "But I know her future I think pretty exactly & it's not a bad lookout," said Ellen: ". . . tell her to wait. One gets everything if you will only wait, and she can. She's young and clever."[13] In a sense, Ellen's isolation from the minute-to-minute crises of Shaw's engaged existence made her all the more appealing. She was his rest, his peace, his refuge: his wise and eternal Ellen to whom he could turn when harried by the thousand pressures upon a man of affairs. And now she was to participate in a very special event, an event which raised again the old question: to meet or not to meet? Ellen had added a postscript on 1 December: "Won't you bring her to see Cymbeline before Imogen goes away? If you do, let it be on Thursday Friday or Saturday —& *tell me first*." The postscript is supposedly the most important part of a woman's letter; and Shaw forwarded it to Charlotte with a brief "What do you say?" The apparently simple invitation ruffled Charlotte considerably. She was extremely reluctant, Shaw told Ellen, to be put on view for Miss Terry's pleasure. Innocently, Ellen replied: "Oh I hope Miss T. will come. I should like to see her, but I promise not to look at her, if she doesn't like it, only at you! Why don't you both come round after the play up to my room? Mayhap she doesn't like playacting folk? I don't like some of 'em myself, but most of 'em I love."

Worse and worse. They could come on Thursday but, "She is not cheap enough to be brought round to your room and *shewn* to you," Shaw replied severely; "she isn't an appendage, this green eyed one, but an individual. No prejudices—has too much respect *for* you to put up with anything less *from* you. In a dressing room interview you can do nothing effective except by playing the charming woman of experience & talent receiving with affectionate interest, condescension, and a lovably artless childishness of delight, a young creature just venturing into the life you are queen of. You'd feel instantly with her that such a line would be actressy and that the dressing room was the wrong *scene* for the right line. No: I wont go round to your room; and you know that perfectly well, you tantalising fiend, or else you wouldn't have suggested it."

With infinite good grace, Ellen admitted that she had been "pretending a little" in inviting them to visit her room. She had really only wanted to hear the voice of her dear friend's beloved. Shaw did not understand, perhaps, how she felt about Miss T: it was the way she felt about her children's friends: her heart was on its knees to them; and what was Shaw but her child, her dear boy, her Bernie? But Shaw was not to be beguiled: he would not exhibit Miss Payne-Townshend as his latest fancy. "Will you never understand what I mean when I say that I can respect people's humanity as well as love their individuality. I should feel nice standing there between you. Of course she is greatly interested in you, as everybody else is; and she is quite capable of understanding your feeling. But you must manage it for yourself if you want to see her." Ellen gave up. They could come to *Cymbeline* feeling perfectly safe that she would not so much as even peek through the curtain at stall F.18. Was Shaw satisfied at last? No. "If you don't look at her I will never forgive you. Oh, I can't explain; and you understand perfectly well. I want you to meet one another without any reference to me: I hate these contrived occasions. . . . Only, *do* look at her; and yet how can you? F18 and 19 is six rows off." "I love you," concluded this hypersensitive romantic rather lamely. ". . . Of course I will love you after Thursday; but the point is that I love you *now*."[14]

The event was typical Shavian dramatics, followed by anti-climax. On the evening of 10 December, Shaw and Charlotte took their seats at the Lyceum; Ellen Terry looked at them through the peephole; all three survived, their sensibilities intact.

Shaw's militant concern for Charlotte's feelings indicated (besides a projection of his own delicacies) the depth of his involvement. Indeed, he was at her beck and call and constantly struggled to fit his schedule to hers. Every free evening was hers; if not free, he did his best to secure tickets for the both of them, or contrive late or early meetings. When Charlotte's younger sister Mary Cholmondeley visited from Keyham Hall, Leicester, he found the intrusion unbearable and suggested the Caledonian Hotel across the street. When Charlotte visited Keyham Hall, he urged her to make haste back again. To Janet he was now curt. "No, totally impossible," he replied to an invitation to read his play: "I have to go to the theatre on all three evenings, & to work too much in the day to admit of reading in the afternoon. All I can do is to read it on Sunday (afternoon or evening) provided I may bring Miss P. T. . . ."[15]

He had dismissed another old love from his life that autumn of 1896: the amiable lady with the crescent eyebrows. Shaw was amiable himself, and sometimes curiously passive: he often claimed he would not do anything unless pushed. He had lingered through six years with Florence; and although the *Candida* business had put an end to their sexual intimacy, he had told Ellen as late as October that their affair was "just perishing." That month the sense of the futility of love was strong. His love, his friendship meant nothing, he warned Ellen: he must be *used:* built into the solid fabric of her life as far as he was usable brick, and thrown aside when he was used up. "It is only when I am being used that I can feel my own existence, enjoy my own life. All my love affairs end tragically because the women *can't* use me. They lie low and let me imagine things about them; but in the end a frightful unhappiness, an unspeakable weariness comes; and the Wandering Jew must go on in search of someone who can use him to the utmost of his capacity."[16]

The same day (12 October) he pleaded utility to Ellen, he officially said goodbye to Florence. For years her adventures in the occult had alienated him, but publication of S.S.D.D.'s *A Commentary on Euphrates* or *The Waters of the East* and *Egyptian Magic* in 1896 thoroughly disillusioned him. She was a lost soul, working feverishly at her unreality, her "shilling's work of exoteric Egyptology." She had not heeded his call to work. She had preferred freedom, happiness, and irresponsibility to care, suffering, and labor. She had lived for herself instead of for the world. She had rejected the deep universal material of human ties and luxuriated in love and amusing friendships. She had rejected, in short, all the ideals Shaw lived by, and was in consequence a desperate and irreclaimable fool.

He said as much of her performance of the Rat Wife. While she deserved more public sympathy than any other Ibsen actress since she had dared not only Ibsen but Shaw, Florence's interpretation of the part was weak, unsustained, skin deep. And why? Because she neither devoted herself to acting nor let it alone: she had strayed into writing clever novels and arcane treatises instead of pursuing one art with sufficient constancy to attain authority over it. She was weak, weak—the large eyes, the crescent brows, the gypsy charm, the approachability on any level at all—how they palled on one. She now approached him, demanding to know the status of their relationship. Behind the veil of metaphor, the dismissal was absolute:

> . . . I can wait no longer for you: onward must I go; for the evening approaches. To all your flowermaidens I have given more than you gave me, and offered more than any of you would take. My road is the highroad; your bypaths and shortcuts only lead backwards. I have often looked down them & sometimes laughed, sometimes warned you vainly.

Now a great horror & weariness comes on me. I cannot help anyone except by taking help from them; and you cannot help me. You have brains & imagination—the means of deceiving yourself, without faith, honor, heart, holiness—the means of saving yourself. I have the greatest regard for you; but now to be with you is to be in hell: you make me frightfully unhappy. What *is* "the true relation" between us? The relation of the North Pole to the South. Forgive me; but you have driven me to utter desperation: I can no longer be satisfied to suffer & shake my fist at the stars.[17]

With freedom, connections, and money at her disposal, this was still not a happy period in Florence's life. She had the highest aspirations, but could succeed at nothing. She had hung on the fringes of the *Little Eyolf* venture, and acted indifferently for a meager salary in twelve performances. She tried a little painting, representations of Egyptian figures commissioned by a fellow mystic. She tried a little embroidery, picked up in her Morris days, yet did not persist. The Golden Dawn was far from solving all her problems. Although she believed in the occult, she did not believe in or follow all the Society's rules, and was, in fact, thinking of chucking the whole thing that very year. Instead, she willed herself to continue. "When things are bad," she declared with a determination Shaw must have admired had he known it, "it is the moment for work not the moment for sitting idle."[18] And now Shaw's farewell. But Florence would have been naive had she believed that Egyptology finally cut the bond.

Charlotte was rather Shaw's reason for now sweeping the boards. Her character had finally thrown all of Florence's shortcomings into sharp relief. Shaw had utilized but rather despised Florence's cynicism about sex. On the other hand, Charlotte's puritanism was an attitude he could understand and respect. Emotionally deprived, as he was himself, fearful of emotion and sex and therefore idealizing love, she was inhibited, vulnerable, demanding. She was enjoying her freedom since the death of her mother and her sister's marriage, yet did not count it as freedom from responsibility: on the contrary, she was oppressed with the need to right social wrongs. Although Florence as New Woman had inspired much of *The Quintessence of Ibsenism*, it was Charlotte, suffering from a broken heart over Dr. Axel Munthe, who picked up his book to find therein "gospel, salvation, freedom, emancipation and self-respect." It was exhilarating to find himself used, not only intellectually but emotionally, for Charlotte feared that without "experience" she would soon be an old maid. And then Florence's Bohemianism had been charming, but he had never had any real sympathy with her gypsyish tendency to pitch her tent in any field. Charlotte, on the other hand, was a "perfectly placid and proper and pleasant" person, so impeccably right that her presence was scarcely noticeable, unless she chose you for intimacy. And her intimacy had a high price. No batting about London with Charlotte, meeting her in the park or in cheap cafes, picking her up at a tube station and dropping her there to make her own way home. Shaw now made arrangements to call, asked nicely whether she would care to go to the picture galleries or the theatre, informed her punctiliously of his whereabouts, tailored his timetable to hers. Charlotte was ruthless, a quality Florence did not know the meaning of. She did not coquet: at Saxmundham she had made no secret of the fact that she liked Shaw a great deal. Her forthrightness set Shaw the coquet back on his heels. All that proper breeding—"she takes it off like a mask when she selects you for that intimacy," Shaw marveled to Ellen, "which she does in the most coldblooded way." Charlotte had will and dignity. They deservedly captivated Shaw.

Three days after he told Florence, "I renounce spiritual intercourse with you," he wired Charlotte: ALL CLEAR NOW   YES A THOUSAND TIMES.

CHAPTER FIFTEEN

1896-1897

Paradoxically, Shaw had finished the first of his *Plays for Puritans* while falling in love with Charlotte. *The Devil's Disciple*, as the Preface four years later claimed, retaliated against the romantic plays that drove him to despair as a critic: plays in which the hero never lifts a finger except for the sake of the heroine because sensuality, though never courageously spelled out, motivates all action. For the theatre to make sex, that "most capricious, most transient, most easily baffled of all instincts," the basis of its appeal was not only an "intolerable perversion of human conduct," but a terrible bore. Were great deeds ever done for love? Never. For deeds done for love one could turn to the murder column in one's newspaper; it seldom disappointed. Shaw's answer was Dick Dudgeon, a hero who goes to the gallows in another man's place with no more motive than Parsifal's *Mitleid*, but pointedly not for love, a word that "comes from him with true Puritan scorn." Shaw had created the type before in Vivie Warren and Marchbanks. The trio of *The Devil's Disciple* was, in fact, very much the trio of *Candida;* the message of the plays the same: while Marchbanks discovers in time that the gate to heaven—possessing Candida—is really the gate to hell, Dudgeon proves there is a way to heaven even from the gates of hell, for the reprobate who champions the devil against a corrupted Puritanism is, like Marchbanks, a religious hero.[1]

Shaw had been eager to write this play, and was reassured by its vigor that *Candida* had not been the beginning of weakness and "mollycoddledom." He looked back at his three unpleasant plays with some apprehension for a tough social realism lost. He would substitute a sexual realism, showing that men have died and worms eaten them, but not for love. The denial of love was a deliberate reversal and, as such, as challengeable as the false romanticism of the commercial stage that never denied it. But the denial seemed associated in Shaw's mind with strength and energy and purpose. Ever since the days of Alice Lockett he had insisted upon dividing work and love into airtight compartments, and had worried about the infringement of the latter. He saw himself as two George Shaws, one a sympathetic lover, the other a devil who whispered that love wasted energies better devoted to work. It was a short leap to the fear that the sexual act itself debilitated, spent the precious powers. In a telling simile, he admitted to Ellen that he dreaded success, because to have succeeded was to have finished one's business on earth, like the male spider who is killed by the female the moment he has impregnated her. He wanted "be coming"—never "have come." He had kept count in his diary of the number of sexual encounters with Jenny, subconsciously hoping, perhaps, that in recording like a clerk what he had "spent" he did not entirely suffer a loss. The fear worked itself into his plays: into Vivie Warren, who cannot combine work and love; into Marchbanks, who, on the verge of passion, has a sudden vision of a castrating sword that bars the way to his heaven—"a flaming sword that turned every way so that I couldn't go in; for I saw that that gate was really the gate of Hell." Now in his *Devil's Disciple* he had given full heed to that other "diabolical" Shaw: the force of the play lay not only in its rousing melodramatic catastrophes, but in its hero's reassuring rejection of romantic temptation.

Shaw needed reassuring on another count. Five unsuccessful novels had taught him that he might serve an equally discouraging apprenticeship as a playwright. There were obvious and honorable reasons why *Widowers' Houses, The Philanderer,* and *Mrs. Warren's Profession* had won two performances among them. It was less easy to accept the fact that of the four plays that followed only one had seen the light of day, and might not have, had an actress who loved him not come into some money. And this despite the fact that he had propitiated, creating *The Man of Destiny* for bravura star work, keeping the production expenses of *Candida* minimal in hopes some enlightened commercial manager might be tempted into a series of matinees, tailoring *You Never Can Tell* specifically to the requirements of managers wanting fashionable comedies for the West End. But the Napoleon play languished on Irving's shelf, no manager had seen the light with *Candida,* and although Shaw reported in September 1896 to Ellen that the Haymarket people appeared "to be making up their minds to ruin themselves" with *You Never Can Tell,* the negotiations dragged.

One of Ellen's uses, therefore, since their paper courtship had become intimate, was as a professional judge of his plays. He declared himself pessimistic. *The Man of Destiny* was a mere bagatelle, a "baby come-dietta." As Janet declined in favor, Shaw began to think he had overrated her play as well; Beatrice Webb's calling Candida "a sentimental prosti-tute"—his Candida, his Virgin Mother—had not bolstered confidence. Ellen did, however, crying over *Candida* and enthusing, "Write more plays, my *Dear*, and let me read them. It has touched me more than I could tell of." Encouraged, Shaw tried out *You Never Can Tell* in early November, not on Ellen but on Edy and Satty—and found that his words had turned to dust and ashes. "I always said I should have to write twenty bad plays before I could write one good one," he lamented; "and yet I am taken aback to find that number seven is a phantom." A few weeks later he handed the play to Edy to take to Ellen. "Why my dear blessed friend," cried that sympathetic woman, "it is tremendous. Fright-fully funny. Interesting, Interesting, INTERESTING. . . . You never can tell, but I should say it would be a tremendous go with the B. P."

Four days later, on 30 November, Shaw finished *The Devil's Disciple*. He wanted her *dry* opinion. He had not tried outright melodrama be-fore: perhaps the sobbing, declamations, courts-martial, and hanging were more farce than heroics. But it was only a scrawl in his notebook at present, and in the meantime he would send her *The Philanderer*. He could not make up his mind about it. Janet and Archer called it dull, vul-gar, bestial, and worthless; half the time he was inclined to agree. She must tell him something serious about it; and would she like to play Julia? Ellen came through again: the play was perfectly wonderful, "with a swing in it from beginning to end." But play Julia? "Heavens no! I couldn't. Comedy is my 'line,' and Julia is a very tragedy. . . . A fine part. I could play it from the life, if I played it. For three years I lived with a *male* Julia. He was my husband, Mr. Wardell ('Charles Kelly') and I'm alive!"[2] And yet 1896 slipped away with Shaw noticea-bly unperformed. Although Charlotte had as much money to contribute to a Shaw venture as Annie Horniman gave to Florence, there clearly was to be no question of her underwriting his plays as she had supported the London School of Economics.

In January of 1897, however, he reported to Beatrice Mansfield that Irving was to produce his Napoleon play sometime that year, that *You Never Can Tell* would follow *The Red Robe* at Cyril Maude's Haymar-ket, and that he had completed *The Devil's Disciple*, a War of Inde-pendence play set in New Hampshire and just the play for America. Useless, of course, to offer it to Mansfield, said the wily Shaw, employ-ing the one tactic sure to arouse the actor's interest. He did not let the matter rest there, but went to Mrs. Patrick Campbell's house at 10 Man-deville Place on the afternoon of 18 February to read the play to her and Forbes-Robertson. It was his first meeting with the actress, who, how-ever, was quite wrong for Judith Anderson; and he immediately forwarded to Ellen the news that he loved Mrs. P.C. Not quite heart-wise at the beginning of their correspondence, Ellen knew better now how to take such news. He had taunted her with Mrs. Pat from the beginning; she had, in fact, "smiled all over" at his claim to have "smashed up Mrs. P. C." in print for her Rita Allmers performance, believing quite the reverse. Now she acquiesced: "Well, she's a very lovely lady, and clever and amusing. I've always liked her, tho' I scarcely know her." On the other hand: "If Mrs. Pat were less vain, she'd do much more on the stage."[3]

Forbes-Robertson did not snap up *The Devil's Disciple*, but the day after the reading Shaw went to the Haymarket to settle the agreement for *You Never Can Tell*, and in early March was telling Ellen that Cyril Maude for the Waiter and his wife Winifred Emery for Dolly were "all werry capital," though he felt at present that nothing could bring him to witness a performance. The remark suggested that although Shaw understood the Haymarket very well, the Haymarket did not yet understand Shaw.

On 16 March, Shaw traveled to Manchester to witness a different sort of production. Less than a month after Janet had left the cast of *Little Eyolf*, she had an offer from the actor Louis Calvert to play Cleopatra to his Antony in Manchester, £20 a week and dresses. Shaw advised her to take it; it was handsome, and if Manchester seemed a comedown she could always pose as a patriotic Manchester woman full of enthusiasm for her cradle. And what of that other cradle that Janet was by now supposed to be rocking? Silence surrounds the fate of that pregnancy. Given drug addiction, alcoholism, and the fatigue of playing Rita Allmers, it is probable that Janet miscarried; remotely possible that the pregnancy was a hysterical one. In seemingly good spirits now, she wrote Hubert Bland from shabby lodgings at 8 Ackers Street that they were doing wonderful business and that she loved her part. Thanking him on 15 March after he had reviewed her favorably and sent tulips, her favorite flower because their scent was "unspeakably delicious," she noted that "Bernard the Erratic" might come that day, though she had no idea whether he would turn up or not.[4]

Shaw was being particularly erratic because the trip sparked a disagreement with Charlotte, who wanted to go with him. The chief difficulty seemed to be the question of spending the night together. "Of course you solve the difficulty by the usual proposal to part at the church door, so to speak," he fumed. "The exasperation of having *that* offered is all that is needed to whiten my hair. The devil take Manchester and Antony and Shakespere and the whole institution of sex!"[5] Ready to give up sainthood himself, Shaw now seemed to find the reluctance coming from the other party. It was the last straw, he declared: he would not go. The courtship was not running altogether smoothly, although on

Shaw's part, if he could not see her regularly, he would "go straight down to the Embankment and plunge into the flood." Conversely, his open willingness to be used by other women, to admit that there were castles in his life which she left empty—"This philosophy rather appalls the Green Eyed One with a sense of having no hold on me," he told Ellen.

Shaw went north alone, viewed Janet at the Queen's Theatre as Cleopatra, had supper with her and Calvert, watched her feed him three or four pounds of sausage in horror, but concluded that the "fat comedian" seemed "to have a feelin' 'art smothered up in his tripesack somewhere." Calvert was, in fact, a charming Antony, his tremendous gut only disconcerting when at the end he set about "the Happy Despatch," causing the pit to shriek with horror at the imagined consequences. Janet was something else; and he seized pen to "prepare Charrington for the worst." "It is a glorious rampage for Janet," he reported: "she enjoys herself to her heart's content; and makes such faces and tries such vocal effects as were never before conceived by a human being. . . . She has devised a lot of wailing effects, and—oh my gracious heavenly GOD, you should hear them. They sawed my vitals in two." In the *Saturday Review* he turned on Janet in his best "tomahawking style." Coldly he opined that she ought now to have a great London vogue, since she had at last done something thoroughly wrong from beginning to end.[6]

He had exaggerated her failure in still another attempt to jolt her to a sense of danger. His waning intimacy with the Charringtons was spoiled that spring and summer by quarrels, accusations, and counteraccusations. Janet was up to her ears in theatrical promises and maneuverings. And now she wanted *Candida* again, having withdrawn *The Lady from the Sea* after announcing it, because she found she couldn't stage it "with fifteen & sixpence worth of Independent Theatre scenery after all." Shaw refused to help. "If you gave Janet the Koh i noor she would pawn it for half a crown the first time she forgot her purse and wanted to take a cab home," he complained to Ellen. "I have refused with iron brutality, with insanely reproachful results."[7]

But that summer the Charringtons went on tour with *Candida*. Undoubtedly the fiasco at the Haymarket that spring was one reason for Shaw's relenting. There had been trouble from the beginning. On 9 April Shaw had arrived to read the play to the cast in a suit of clothes "which the least self-respecting carpenter would have discarded months before," inspiring distrust before he ever opened his mouth. At the end of the first act, Jack Barnes withdrew. Two hours and forty minutes later it had become apparent that the play was far too long and would cut into the fashionable dinner hour. Meanwhile during the reading Winifred Emery had begun to prick up her ears. She had wanted the part of Dolly; now however she passed a note to her husband: "I shall play Gloria." Who was to play Dolly? Shaw staggered home that night, dead tired, to pare down *You Never Can Tell* to a fashionable length. Three days later they went through the first act, Shaw silently watching, but wondering how soon his patient attention would begin to fray their nerves. There was not long to wait. Fanny Coleman soon threw over Mrs. Clandon in disgust at a part with "no laughs and no exits." Then it became apparent that Alan Aynesworth as Valentine could never carry off the very scenes with Gloria that carried the point of the play. As Shaw prowled about the theater, ever more patient, more helpful, more quietly insistent, the company grew unhappier and unhappier. Beaten by the part and driven to distraction by the author, Aynesworth walked out because "he couldn't stand Shaw."[8] Eventually Maude himself decided that the Valentine-Gloria scenes would fail as they now stood. He put it very nicely: what a pity for a young and brilliant playwright to lose the opportunity for a first-rate production in a first-rate theatre and in Jubilee season—a chance in a lifetime. Now, if Shaw would only "deshawize" by cutting out all that irresistible force stuff, and tailor Gloria into a recognizable heroine . . .

Instead, Shaw went to manager Frederick Harrison and suggested dropping the whole business quietly. It is difficult to believe that besides Shaw's unwillingness to compromise, the same diffidence that had made him warn prospective publishers even as he submitted his manuscripts was not operating here. For according to Shaw, Maude gave up the production reluctantly: the scenery was ready, "nine-tenths of the play shaping up very cheerfully," and only one actor out of his depth.[9] Ellen too urged him not to give up: "I'm your loving old friend and I KNOW it will hurt your success." Yet for one actor and one tenth, Shaw forfeited a West End production. Hating the Jubilee fuss and convinced he was not made for the contemporary stage, he decided to give his plays to the public in print: if he could not be played, perhaps he could be read. Coolly as Shaw took the Haymarket failure, however, it must have made the production of *Candida*—even in the provinces and even with a fallen Janet—considerably more attractive. And, of course, the play was her "ewe lamb."

Then, in the midst of the Haymarket rehearsals, trouble with *The Man of Destiny*. On 16 April Shaw warned Ellen they were soon to meet at rehearsals, for the Napoleon play was due that year. The next day he received from Bram Stoker, Irving's business manager, "a cool official intimation" that the actor had changed his mind about producing the play. Having dispatched the message, Irving knocked at Ellen's dressing room shortly before curtain time. He appeared furtive and embarrassed, but announced he was going to send her friend's play back to him. In response to Ellen's dismayed questioning, he was vague. He had been much vexed by Shaw's attacks in the *Saturday Review:* the *Olivia* notice last

February had particularly annoyed him. He murmured other excuses: *Madame Sans-Gêne* was in for a long run and the two plays could not coincide. "I believe you have another reason," challenged Ellen; but she did not bother him further. He looked ashamed; and she could not bear that he should be ashamed—her pale, secretive, black-winged Irving: she felt instead "strangely powerfully sorry for him." So she let him go, and picked up Shaw's letter, sent after Stoker's communication and come only fifteen minutes earlier. "Look out for squalls," she read. ". . . I am in ecstasies: I have been spoiling for a row. . . . Hooray!" Ellen did not feel ecstatic. She felt, for the first time in her life, frightfully dispirited. The past week had required real courage just to consent to live. Nobody saw her depression and she could talk about it to no one. But, oh God, how frightful life was. And now, her two friends to quarrel.[10]

The next day, Sunday, Ellen and Irving took their usual long carriage drive (like two babies in a giant perambulator), and Irving was rather more specific. Shaw had implied in a review that his "emotion on the stage was stimulated artificially." Ellen hunted out the *Olivia* review as soon as she got home, but although she knew Shaw might be right—she could recall days when Irving, corpse-like from overwork, took wine to get him through a double performance—she found nothing. But for Shaw the murder was out: the culprit was his notice of *Richard III* the previous December. Irving or his Lyceum henchmen had taken statements such as "not answering his helm satisfactorily," "odd slips in the text," "exhaustion too genuine," and above all a reference to Edmund Kean's playing Richard too drunk to keep his feet, as an accusation that Irving had been drunk on opening night. Nothing Shaw had written since had reconciled the Lyceum. Shaw received Bram Stoker's "intimation" the same day his notice of *Madame Sans-Gêne* appeared; the connection seems likely. Irving had done the play for Ellen's sake, recognizing that she had been lately given too little to do. Encouraged by Shaw, Ellen had only become more and more dissatisfied with her part, however; and by opening night the feeling at the Lyceum was strong enough for Irving to order that Shaw be kept out. Shaw got in. Since it was Ellen's play, Irving could not have been annoyed that Shaw devoted seven paragraphs of his review to Ellen and one to him. Rather, Shaw's obvious contempt for the play may have been the last straw. For Irving's enterprises had not been running smoothly of late.

He had long counted on his American tours to make up for his lavish spending on scenery, decoration, staff, and the Beefsteak Room entertainments. The last American tour, however, had been disappointing: expenses staggering—nearly £70,000—profits barely £6,000 after seven months' hard work.[11] To get back on his feet, Irving revived the ever popular *Richard III* in December 1896. Ellen left for Monte Carlo to rest. She quite understood Shaw's observation in the *Saturday Review* that Irving "was occasionally a little out of temper with his own nervous condition": H.I. was always out of temper when she didn't act with him because no one else knew so exactly what he wanted onstage and did it so readily. But H.I. was more than out of temper. On 19 December, after an acclaimed first night—five hundred onstage afterward, the Garrick Club for a late supper, more conviviality after that at Dewar's Rooms—Irving slipped as he went up the dark narrow stairs of his lodging house in the early morning hours, struck his knee against a chest on the landing, and ruptured the ligatures of his kneecap. The accident did not make Shaw's suggestions in the *Saturday Review* more endearing. In January Ellen reported that Irving was resting on her sofa and about to be transported to Sevenoaks for some fresh air. *She* would hurry back to London to begin rehearsing for *Olivia*, for Irving was losing over £1,000 a week, "and *that* must not go on." But by the end of February, the Lyceum showed a loss of £10,000.

Although Irving had drifted away from Ellen, he did not appreciate her relationship with Shaw. He had taken the man's play on her recommendation, but did not imagine he would trip over the red-bearded critic every time he turned around. When in March Irving got away from London and went down to Ellen's cottage at Winchelsea as was his custom, for example, he found Shaw there before him. Though quite ill, Ellen had just finished the second act of *The Devil's Disciple*, and found it so tremendously exciting that she had to catch her breath by lying out flat on the dining room table. She bubbled with its praises; she was certain that Terriss could play Dick Dudgeon to the hilt. "There has never been anything the least like it!" she raved. Irving's sardonic eye took it all in: she was in love with Shaw. But they had never even met, protested Ellen. Had they not? Irving refused to believe it, a sentiment that touched Shaw—what "man of feeling *could* believe such heartlessness"! Financial disaster at the Lyceum, Ellen's intimacy with Shaw and dissatisfaction with her career and Irving, Shaw's constant needling, Irving's genuine belief in his theatrical mission and Shaw's implacable contempt for that mission—all explained his refusal to deal "fairly" now with Shaw on the critic's terms.

Shaw ignored these explanations, however. No: Irving had rejected *The Man of Destiny* because its author had not delivered the favorable notices tacitly purchased along with the play. Yet it is hard to believe that Shaw believed Irving capable of such blatant critic-buying. Rather, with all theatrical London aware that Irving had accepted his play, he was perhaps overeager to display his integrity. Irving could not have expected praise from the Saturday reviewer, but perhaps he did not expect to be told either that "my regard for Sir Henry Irving cannot blind me to the fact that it would have been better for us twenty-five years ago to have tied him up in a sack with every existing copy of the works of

Shakespeare, and dropped him into the crater of the nearest volcano." Yet the key word was *regard*, for as Shaw often told Ellen, he respected Irving, even liked him. Shaw seemed to expect this regard to sweeten every bitter drop he forced down the actor's throat. If he handled him rigorously, he after all handled him professionally, mindful that Irving stood for a tradition, even as he stood for demolishing it. Trusting Irving to recognize that regard, Shaw went to all lengths, rather like a child testing its parents' fundamental tolerance. But Irving had no regard for Shaw; and it was the wounding realization of this fact that helped provoke him to loud protest.

Shaw now requested that Irving transfer *The Man of Destiny* with Shaw's "reluctant consent" to Forbes-Robertson as a gesture of goodwill to a younger colleague. Irving smiled grimly at this demand from a man whose habit, he felt, was "to worry the helpless"; and got his secretary to draft a cold reply. When he read it to Ellen on the evening of 10 May, she "screamed with laughter when he came to 'callous to the feelings of others' and 'lost consciousness of vulgarity.'" Her reaction did not endear her to Irving. They were already "out," though Shaw had prudently advised her to be entirely sympathetic since the actor, he believed, was heavily outmatched in the contest, and making one blunder after another in his attempts to extricate himself from a tight corner. Yet on 12 May Shaw found his manuscript at his door. A letter from Irving followed, a sincere document which said in essence, "For God's sake, leave me alone." "Oh my dear, dear, dearest Ellen," Shaw wrote immediately, "I'm beaten." And certainly between the actor who lost the play and the playwright who had lost his actor, Shaw's was the greater loss, for a Terry-Irving production at the Lyceum was not to be scoffed at. Yet Irving too lost something. "Forgive me; but your Henry is not a hero off the stage," concluded Shaw. ". . . I am sorry to have lost my regard for him."[12]

The contretemps underlined Ellen's weak position in the patriarchal Lyceum system: all her enthusiasm for the play had not changed Irving's mind. She had always been both indulged and ignored there, the first a chivalrous compensation for the last. Irving tolerated her breathless last-minute arrivals, her lapses into giggling onstage, her worse lapses of memory, her popularity. But he in no sense shared his theatre's operations with her. He was chief to a loyal group of henchmen; she was expected to fall in gracefully with his orders. Ellen became intensely aware of her position during *The Man of Destiny* controversy, and complained of it in her gently wry way to Shaw, who, having pointed out her subservient role from the beginning, was sure to sympathize. Why did Irving value her as a partner, Ellen now asked herself. Because she saved him trouble: "every little miss" at the Lyceum gave him more trouble than she did. And what was her reward? He would tell her nothing. He had remained severely silent about that first meeting with Shaw in his office; he would only hint at his plans for her friend's play. From his own instruction, she had learned to let him talk and hold her own tongue: "I never *ask* him things." Nor did she express disagreement, "because he's vexed always with people who won't agree always and entirely with everything he says." During *The Man of Destiny* conflict she had let him guess her disapproval from subtler signs. With Shaw she need not be subtle, and her exasperation at last flared: " 'Be gentle' you say 'with H.' I am *always* gentle with him. Better for him if all these years I had acted being something else. . . . I've spoiled him! I was born meek. (Ugh.) . . . 'Gentle!' He wants a good slapping. . . ."[13]

Finally her anger burst out at Shaw himself. He had found his own behavior irreproachable in the matter, particularly a public interview he had drafted calculated to allow both Irving and himself come out with "halos of glory" round their heads. To her, however, he poured out his real opinion. Her career had been sacrificed to "the egotism of a fool." "Oh Ellen, Ellen, this infinitesimal actor-nothingness whimpers over the things I have said of him. But if he knew the things I have *not* said, he would shudder and die."

Ellen replied, incorrectly rebuking him for not having let Irving keep the play, but objecting with some justice that he egotistically overestimated his impact on London's leading actor-manager. She believed that Shaw did not understand practical matters: "Sometimes in the Saturday you speak just like an amateur on the subject of conduction of a theatre (Forgive me darling)." The quarrel had disillusioned her. "I'd like to say 'I hate you and detest you'—but then I'd 'remember' THAT *too*. Well, you are quite stupid after all and *not* so unlike other people. . . . Don't pity H. He thinks he has quite got the best of it in the recent altercation. The fact is he don't think the whole thing matters much. I do, and I'm angry with you. I keep out of the affair as you tell me to.—What I cared for more than for you or H.—or the parts, was the PLAY—and NOW— well go your ways—Oh my darling you are the horridest old—"[14]

But Irving was not quite so oblivious of Shaw as he pretended. To his son Laurence he confided that he would cheerfully pay Shaw's funeral expenses at any time. Nor was Ellen indifferent to the part, replying to Shaw's weary declaration that he might as well try Forbes-Robertson and Mrs. Campbell as shelve *The Man of Destiny*, "Mrs. P. is young and lovely and would do the Lady *well enough* . . . but Mrs. P is not a reliable person at present, & on the whole I'm your best card."[15] Shaw went to talk to Forbes-Robertson, and found him surrounded by Mrs. Campbell on easel, mantelshelf, and wall, but bearing out Ellen's words, no Mrs. Campbell to play the Strange Lady. Ever discreet, since a Mr. Campbell hovered vaguely in the background, the handsome actor said only that his leading lady was ill. Shaw also guessed nerves, disappointment, "alarm at engagements not coming and money going." He was right about the nerves. That spring the fatigue and tension that had plagued her even before *Little Eyolf* overwhelmed Stella Campbell: she could not work any more, and was borne away to a nursing home, where, laughing as tears streamed down her cheeks, she felt a doctor's fingers at her pulse and heard a grave voice say, "All the acting has done this."[16]

With two more plays rejected, Shaw continued to prepare his works for the printer, revising and filling in the stage business for *Mrs. Warren's Profession* during the last days of May. The play gave him pause: he could not help comparing it with his later work. "It's much my best play; but makes my blood run cold," he told Ellen, who had read every other play but this: "I can hardly bear the most appalling bits of it. Ah, when I wrote that, I *had* some nerve."[17] What, if anything, had happened to Shaw's nerve? Several explanations offered. *Plays Unpleasant* had proved unpalatable for their realism; with all his incorruptibility, Shaw needed public exposure as he needed air to breathe. *Arms and the Man* supplied it; the taste of success was irresistible; the playability of witty anti-romanticism against the unplayability of anti-capitalism inevitably forced itself upon him. And although he still professed Fabian Socialism, socialism had by this time disappointed him. His hundreds of socialist harangues, from Hyde Park soapboxes to East End docks and cellars, from Oxford to Bradford and back again, seemed to make little impact on the working classes. Where were those hordes of laborers driven to embrace the cause by subsistence wages that socialist theory had promised? Where, even, were signs of inevitable gradualism?

Yet even had socialism triumphed, Shaw the maverick would have dissented. He could not help seeing the ridiculous and the sham in any creed. In *The Philanderer*, seeing that Ibsen could be idealized as much as anything else, he had ridiculed the Ibsenites rather than supported them. Instead of making the servant Louka in *Arms and the Man* a working-class heroine, he portrayed her as a materialist with ultimately romantic notions about womanhood: little wonder she emerged as "enigmatic." The powers of the socialist clergyman Morell turned out to be hollow. Bluntschli, his realist hero, possessed nevertheless two hundred horses and seventy carriages—a Swiss capitalist. Marchbanks was a poet, but also the son of an earl. He intended Candida as the master of her doll's house; she emerged in some people's opinion a clever slave. Mrs. Clandon's feminism he treated as outmoded; Gloria's lessons in emancipation as worthless. Thus Shaw seemed to mock the very principles he believed in. Since his plays were still too unconventional to be performed, he perhaps believed mockery the only way to air social questions on the London stage at all. Or else his fundamental puritanism was proving far stronger as a creative force than his acquired socialism. *The Devil's Disciple* had glorified a different kind of toughness. Dick Dudgeon did not want to die for social reform, but from a sense of spiritual necessity. Shaw had traveled some distance since creating Sidney Trefusis, who rejected love to live as a socialist. Perhaps Charlotte had helped a little on the way—Charlotte with her wealth, her distrust of dogma, and her own well-developed puritanism. For all or any of these reasons, Shaw's early radicalism now made his blood run cold.

His reacquaintance with *Mrs. Warren's Profession* may well have decided him to agree to a draft for municipal service. On 18 May 1897 Shaw was elected a member of the Vestry of the Parish of St. Pancras, a municipal group administering the local affairs of a quarter million Londoners.[18] The Vestry took him out into the daylight after the artificial lighting of the fantastic world he haunted as theatre critic, and reaffirmed his ties to the people. ". . . I love the reality of the Vestry and its dustcarts and H'less orators after the silly visionary fashion-ridden theatres," he enthused to Ellen. He was as usual being worked to death, forced to do any reading while dressing and undressing, piling open book upon open book until a mountain accumulated, all half read and all smudged with the dust and soot that blew through his ever open window. When he could tear himself away, he retreated to Dorking in Surrey, where on Tower Hill in a cottage called "Lotus" he joined Beatrice, Sidney, and Charlotte. The Lotus, however, had failed to lull its inhabitants into indolence. "I wonder what you would think of our life," said Shaw to Ellen, whom he teased with invitations to join them: "—our eternal political shop; our mornings of dogged writing, all in separate rooms; our ravenous plain meals; our bicycling; the Webbs' incorrigible spooning over their industrial & political science; Miss P. T., Irish, shrewd & green eyed, finding everything 'very interesting'; myself always tired and careworn, and always supposed to be 'writing to Ellen.' You'd die of it all in three hours, I'm afraid. Oh, I wish, I wish—"[19] He did write to Ellen—two dozen or so letters in April and May, hastily scrawling them in the midnight train to Dorking, blazing away at the correspondence in front of Charlotte and the Webbs, asking for her letters when he came striding in. Ellen was a feather in his cap: he displayed it.

She was more—a release for emotions and desires the green-eyed one was perhaps too rigid to appreciate. Of course, his frenzied activities usually kept his hankerings at bay; yet one day in June, wandering down a London street, his mind full of the school board election, the Fabian Executive, and revisions of the Webbs' *Industrial Democracy*, he was brought up short by the sight of Ellen's photograph in a shop window—Ellen in her *Sans-Gêne* dress, her bosom swelling tenderly above the low Empire bodice; Ellen, laughing at him wickedly and saying: "'Look here: restless one, at your pillow, at what you are really thinking about.'" Yes, he *was* restless, full of longing; he told her so, scribbling rapidly in the midnight train to Dorking, looking out at "the ghostly country and the beautiful night," unable to concentrate on his book, overwhelmed by the urgent need to talk to her—for it was only now, in this suspended dark rush between London and Lotus, that they could be "so perfectly alone." She had listened to this kind of nonsense from men all her life, he knew; he knew she despised him for it: and yet his longing stirred up great waves of tenderness in him, and in this tenderness there was no guile. She had not written lately; he was terrified that she found him flat and stale, and that the end had come. All these words, words, words—and he only wanted to sleep with her. And did she know what would happen if he did? "Well, about tomorrow at noon when the sun would be warm & the birds in full song, you would feel an irresistible impulse to fly into the woods. And there, to your great astonishment & scandal, you would be *confined* of a baby that would immediately spread a pair of wings and fly, and before you could rise to catch it it would be followed by another & another & another—hundreds of them, and they would finally catch you up & fly away with you to some heavenly country where they would grow into strong sweetheart sons with whom, in defiance of the prayerbook, you would found a divine race. Would you not like to be the mother of your own grandchildren?"[20] The notion seemed tantalizing to Shaw, the sweetheart-son of Ellen, the mother-lover with whom he wished to lie.

Did Miss P.T. find the Ellen affair "very interesting" along with everything else? One could hardly murmur at an innocent enthusiasm for a great actress, unless one understood how much Shaw liked to "feel his heart in his pen." To combat Ellen, she cultivated Shaw's doctrine of usefulness: she had learned how to operate the typewriter and was now readying his manuscripts for final revision. The Webbs were always before her eyes, an example of the kind of intellectual partnership possible between a man and woman. She could not offer Shaw artistic collaboration, but she could offer order, security, and what Shaw called an "appalling" sense of responsibility to a life that impressed her as frenetic, nerve-tearing, and financially perilous. With this end in mind, she determined to propose marriage to Shaw. Certainly he was not going to propose marriage to her. Her considerable pride was at stake; she would risk it.

To Ellen Shaw reported that he received "the golden moment with shuddering horror & wildly asked the fare to Australia." In actuality he rejected Charlotte's offer on the grounds that he could not sell himself. Having proclaimed for years that marriage for property was prostitution, he balked at the thought of becoming the prostitute in the relationship. Ellen disagreed; but Shaw urged his case again: it would be, he told her, an irreparable wrong to marry Charlotte in his present circumstances. Ellen replied patiently. "I *never* assumed you were going 'to sell yourself'—Stupid. But I was not thinking of *you* (for once) I was thinking of *her*—& if I were a man & she wished me to do her the *irreparable wrong* of marrying her under *some* circumstances I shd give her her way. But there—I know you are wise—and *kind*." But Shaw was perhaps more blunt than kind. His refusal occasioned "a sort of earthquake": Charlotte was considerably taken aback, and her pride much startled. Ellen however had already decided: "Well, you two will marry."[21]

Charlotte might have taken some comfort from the fact that an old rival was being thoroughly routed that year. Shaw viewed the Independent Theatre's offering of *A Doll's House* and *The Wild Duck* at the Globe that spring, but he was not the same man who had been bowled over by Ibsen and Janet Achurch in the summer of 1889. Granting that her performance still placed her far ahead of any living English actress in "thinking women's roles," granting that she still created the impression of youth, still danced blithely, sang unmercifully, dressed herself recklessly, he found the freshness gone.

No, this time around his sympathy had not been with Nora. The slam of the door no longer shook him to the bone. And why should it? "The play," said Shaw, "solves that problem just as it is being solved in real life. The woman's eyes are opened; and instantly her doll's dress is thrown off and her husband left staring at her, helpless, bound thenceforth either to do without her (an alternative which makes short work of his fancied independence) or else treat her as a human being like himself, fully recognizing that he is not a creature of one superior species, Man, living with a creature of another and inferior species, Woman, but that Mankind is male and female, like other kinds, and that the inequality of the sexes is literally a cock and bull story . . . ." Woman's destiny was all but solved; but what about the Helmers, the Ranks, the Krogstads? This time the plight of Helmer, the real doll in the doll's house, overwhelmed him. The opening sentence of his review announced his reversal: "At last I am beginning to understand anti-Ibsenism. It must be that I am growing old and weak and sentimental and foolish; for I cannot stand up to reality as I did once."[22]

In one sense, Shaw's change of mind testified to a broader social sympathy. Yet for all his official support for the New Woman, his sympathies in fiction gravitated toward the man trapped in the love nest: the theme had run through all his novels, emerging in spite of himself in *Candida* and deliberately in *The Devil's Disciple*. But this identification with the trapped man was less important than Shaw's glib assertion that patriarchy had received its deathblow with the slam of the Helmers' door, and that the problem of women's equality was being solved so rapidly that it hardly needed attention any longer. For how many English housewives had actually slammed their own doors? Of those who did, how many had crawled back again, unable to earn a subsistence wage or face social ostracism? Shaw's vision was long: he saw that the decades of the eighties and nineties had marked a decisive step forward for women's rights. His vision in this review seemed short, influenced in part, perhaps, by the fact that the Ellen Terrys, Beatrice Webbs, and Charlottes that he knew were exceptionally emancipated.

A new sympathy for Charrington accompanied this new sympathy for Torvald Helmer. Looking back now at the whole movement of the uncommercial drama, Shaw declared, one pioneering figure stood out: Mr. Charles Charrington. When he began, his experiments had seemed reckless, ruinous, inexcusable; today everyone was doing what he did, but nobody had foreseen so clearly nor suffered so much as Mr. Charrington. When *The Wild Duck* without Janet replaced *A Doll's House* at the Globe on 17 May, Shaw this time sat "without a murmur in a stuffy theatre on a summer afternoon from three to nearly half-past six, spellbound by Ibsen." Charrington had always been overshadowed by his wife, he went home to announce in his notice: her acting had cast his triumphs of stage management into the shade. But for his wife, Charrington's production of *Alexandra* would have established his reputation as "the best stage manager of true modern drama in London." Similarly, her acting had always stolen the spotlight from his. "Now, however, we have him at last with Miss Janet Achurch out of the bill," rejoiced Shaw. "The result is conclusive."[23]

Shaw's disgust when he found that Janet in *Antony and Cleopatra* would replace *The Wild Duck* as the third Independent Theatre enterprise knew no bounds. He had put down his money as shareholder for the express purpose of being protected from such exhibitions. He was not soothed to find at Dorking a letter from Janet admitting that *The Wild Duck* had been wonderful for Charlie's morale. "Do you suppose I did not know that 'The Wild Duck' was his chance?" Shaw hurled back. "And you—*you*—YOU did your best to spoil it for the sake of flaunting as Cleopatra in that absurd provincial entertainment. You are a monster, a moral monster." Time was when he had egged on Janet endlessly to leave Charrington. Now he saw that household, as he had seen the Helmers, in a different light. "Yes: I note that you never will desert Mr. Micawber," he told her brutally. "Oh, if only he could be induced to desert you!"[24]

Of course Charrington was not exempt from the accusations and disillusionments that were corroding the friendship. As one of three Independent Theatre directors, Charrington was using I.T. capital to back this decidedly non-experimental production of Shakespeare. Subscribers were murmuring: Grant Richards had asked for his money back; so had Bertha Newcombe. "*Youve no right to use the money for that purpose*," exploded Shaw: "Janet being your wife gives you a corrupt interest. Don't you *see* it, confound it all!"[25] But his chief target was Janet. Clearly she was not going to act any more—no more brains, no more pains: just let everything rip and give it to 'em "hot and strong." The bite of Shaw's review of *Antony and Cleopatra* was this time as good as his bark; and his bite was even sharper in the mail. "I ask myself how I have ever consented to know a moral void—a vacuum. . . . It's no use: you're going to have your way at last, to tear and rage and be a success. Thank Heaven, I am going to publish—to renounce the theatre and all its works. Janet was an illusion; the reality is Mrs. Crummles."[26]

When he finally consented to *Candida* that summer, therefore, he turned it over not so much to the woman for whom it was written, but to her husband, announcing to Ellen, "Charrington is taking out a Doll's House tour; and he's going to try 'Candida' on the provincial dog." He suggested Edy for Prossy. Since the tour was a Charrington enterprise, his recommendation had weight; and the Charringtons signed Edith Craig not only for Prossy but for Mrs. Linden at a salary of £20 a week.

The relief to Ellen was enormous, for Edy of the dark eyes and melodious voice, at once passionate and cold, jealous of Ellen's love and evasive of it, troubled her. As for Ted, he no longer drove with her to the Lyceum, played scenes with her onstage, and drove home with her again in the shay through the dark wet streets, but had moved to a small cottage at Thames Ditton and was taking a few minor roles with other managers. Upon Ellen had devolved the business of sending money to Ted's wife May with whom he no longer lived and—happier duty—of playing with the babies when May brought them to her. Upon them she lavished her love. She had no lovers, she told Shaw, only loves—he had no rivals. The grandchildren compensated for her often tiresome children; indeed the younger generation quite disillusioned her at times. Responding to Shaw's suggestion that Irving might have been drunk in *Richard III* since his own son was saying so, she sighed, "I never thought *much* of Henry's sons (Laurence is very clever) but ALL young people nowadays speak idly—with no thought, with no kindness." She had brooded rather much on that theme the past months, complaining to Shaw again, "Oh, my Dear, my Dear—children are tormenting comforts. When they begin to love one of the opposite sex *then* & not until then do they begin to *understand* & be a little tolerant. Most of the present day girls will die before they are worth anything to themselves or to any other—for they are so *careful* that they *refuse to suffer* & are absorbed in themselves. I find them so lovable but not loving!"[27]

Of what were Ellen's children being intolerant? Of her flirtation with Lyceum actor Frank Cooper, which annoyed Irving and even provoked teasingly jealous references from Shaw to "that stupid Cooper." Of dear "Bernie" himself, as Edy and Satty laughingly called him. Or had her son already expressed his dislike of Shaw, a dislike that would burst forth years later over the publication of their letters? Writing from Genoa in 1929, Gordon Craig reminded Shaw coldly of his intrusion, as he saw it, into their lives. He had poked his eagerness into the affairs of Irving: he had bombarded his poor mother with letters ("I remember how every night they used to arrive—I was there, she used to talk to me about them"): he had concerned himself with all of them, without ever risking a hair of his own head.[28] Reverent of Irving, Craig chose his side in the conflict early and, in Ellen's eyes, intolerantly.

On 1 July *The Man of Destiny* played at the Grand Theatre, Croydon, with Shaw torn between wanting it to fail hideously and wishing Murray Carson to succeed so brilliantly that he would be created a Jubilee baronet. For Ellen the comedown to the Grand was tragic: if he did not think his play thrown away at Croydon, she did. She need not trouble herself, said Shaw: *all* his plays were thrown away on the stage: if *The Man of Destiny* had run for a thousand nights at the Lyceum its meaning would still be a secret between the two of them. He himself felt so indifferent that had he not wished to slight the company, he would have stayed away. He attended; and claimed that the accidental entrance of a disreputable-looking kitten that stared at Carson's Napoleonics as if it thought him demented was the highlight. The blundering and incompetence were fearful: the actors could no more grasp his melody than the Italian opera companies had been able to grasp Wagner's twenty years ago. The applause had been a groan, testimony to the audience's bafflement; the experience agonizing for the author.

The Charringtons left for Aberdeen on 27 July. Shaw had supervised rehearsals of *Candida* before they left, getting on everyone's nerves by his habit of sitting in intent and apparently suffering silence. Janet had been good in the second-act scenes with Morell; not good in the big third-act speech. He had coached her in it, and Charrington reported the results from Aberdeen after opening night on the twenty-ninth. Janet played the second act very well again but, cowed by Shaw's instructions, had ruined the final speech by religiously imitating his staccato way of doing it. Edith Craig had been too sympathetic as Prossy, and Courtenay Thorpe totally misunderstood as Marchbanks. But Lionel Belmore's Burgess had gone over well and his third-act drunk scene was applauded uproariously. Critics were rather less sanguine. The *Northern Figaro* noted that the baffled audience did not know when to laugh or keep silent, and lavished much sympathy on Miss Achurch for her trials in an uncongenial part, concluding darkly that Shaw's *Candida* would not be around long. So tired that he could scarcely crawl out of bed mornings, and so dizzy when he stood up suddenly that he had to catch hold of the nearest object to keep from falling, Shaw left theatrical cares behind for a six weeks holiday at the Argoed in Wales. There he let the fresh air and the views from 800 feet above the Wye Valley looking across over the Forest of Dean restore him.

It was a year almost to the day since the long vacation with the Webbs and Charlotte at Stratford St. Andrew. The relationship with Charlotte had progressed from instant attraction to deep affection to the quarrel over marriage at Dorking to a deeper understanding. Appalled by her discovery of his "self-centeredness as a mere artistic machine," Charlotte had managed to regain her poise. She endeavored to take him more casually, responding to apparent callousnesses with "What a curious person you are!" or "What an utter brute you are!" She was beginning, Shaw thought, to understand him at last.

But theatrical cares had not been left behind. He recovered there enough to make a terrible row over Janet's latest crime: a telegram from Aberdeen asking Charlotte for the loan of fifty pounds. "Can you imagine a more morally *thriftless* thing to do than to take advantage of a rich woman being fond of me and of a play of mine being in the repertory to extract money," Shaw cried to Ellen, "knowing all the time what she must think of the transaction and what I must feel about it." Both Webb and Charlotte calmed his fury, Webb remarking sensibly that it was bound to cost Charlotte something if she wished to be thought friendly, and Charlotte claiming that she had known all along that Janet would dun her someday, and already decided to go fifty pounds. She would send the money: the tour might be stuck, and she was genuinely anxious for Ibsen in the provinces. Shaw made her promise to accept repayment out of the profits, if any; he would otherwise withdraw *Candida* from the repertoire. "You've done it at last," he fumed to Janet: "I knew you would." Janet retaliated with abuse, reminding him of the disgraceful circumstances under which he had made use of Florence Farr to get *Arms and the Man* produced, and calling him consistently treacherous over *Candida*. Shaw replied ruthlessly that with fifty pounds owed on *Candida*, he considered that she had sold her monopoly of the play, and would not now refuse any good offer—with or without her. This ploy would, he knew, drive her into fits of weeping, threats of suicide, and flurries of abusive letters—after which she would ask for ten more pounds. Amazing how a woman who had the most exalted appreciation of heroism and nobility could no more resist a five-pound note than a cat resist a penn'orth of fried fish.[29] But Shaw's reaction here seemed to exceed principle, a response due more to the delicacy of his feeling toward Charlotte than to Janet's familiar depravities. Five days later Janet returned twenty-five pounds of the money to Charlotte: the tour was not doing badly, she did not want to lose her monopoly. She seemed to sense she had at last gone too far.

The question was whether *Candida* would draw enough on the road to risk it in London. Although he did not pay the tour the compliment of a visit himself, Shaw urged Ellen, resting at Winchelsea between the closing of *Madame Sans-Gêne* and the start of the Lyceum autumn tour, to go see it at Eastbourne. Ellen went, put up at the Albion Hotel, and saw *A Doll's House* on the evening of 26 August. Edy was of course too young for Mrs. Linden, but Ellen decided that her repose on stage contrasted well with the impetuosity of the others. "Janet played splendidly. They *all* played very cleverly," she told Shaw the next day. ". . . I was just wrapped up in the play from beginning to end, and I think the audience was also. Janet's voice was admirable . . . . What a nice fellow Charles Charrington appears to be. . . . I love you, and I'm going to see Candida to-night. Don't you envy me?"[30]

She went for an afternoon drive with the Charringtons the same day, and liked Mr. Charrington. Janet she thought a dear thing, but found the "borrowing business" nearly unpardonable, especially since Edy had also been touched for a loan. "All very well to *you* or to *me*," she wrote Shaw, "but to friends of yours or friends of mine—ah, it is so vexing. It's very strange how she can endure it." That evening she saw *Candida*, and with her usual buoyance saw only good in the performance. Well, perhaps there were one or two objections. Thorpe as Marchbanks—"that impossible person, that mass of horrid affectation, that work of art"— *haunted* her: ugh, how offensive he was. And then another little matter. Toward the very end, when Candida says to Morell and Marchbanks, "Now let's sit down and talk the matter over," several people had pulled out their watches and some had abruptly reached for their overcoats. It interrupted the attention of all who stayed: shouldn't the line be omitted? And then she intended to write Janet about one or two trifling points. . . . Aside from this, *Candida* had been utterly absorbing, and she longed to see it done in London.[31]

Shaw too had longed. But Janet had not been able to control her "congenital mendacity," telling the press that *Candida* was shortly to be played in London with the result that everybody concluded the market closed. Worse, her diction had evolved into "such an unholy abyss of mannerism" that London would not tolerate her unless she dropped it. His actress had made his play impossible. On 17 September from Moorcroft, where the party had shifted from the Argoed, Shaw told Charrington, "We must banish the notion that Candida can be played as a London success."[32] With his usual resilience, he followed that death knell with the news that he and Miss P.T. had taken to renting a tandem at thirty-five shillings a week—good fun. He had not finished revising his plays, but had come to certain conclusions. *You Never Can Tell* was an awful play, a "frightful example of trying to write for the popular theatre"; *Widowers' Houses* was the best of them, next to *Mrs. Warren*.

Yet success, which had eluded him thus far with breathtaking agility, was at hand. Richard Mansfield had balked at sitting for three hours, hugging his ankles and talking; Dick Dudgeon's heroics were another matter. Despite Mansfield's conviction that all fine and intelligent people would like the play and thus it would play to empty houses, *The Devil's Disciple* went into rehearsal in September. By mid-October Mansfield discovered he had a success on his hands; by 18 October rumors of success had reached Shaw from New York; by 1 November he was telling Janet that *The Devil's Disciple* had "swept the boards in New York" with average receipts the first week over £250; on 4 November the triumph was final: " 'The Devil's Disciple' has really been a sensational success: the royalties for the first week have come, and I am richer than ever I was in my life before—actually £314 in the bank to my credit."[33] An added financial shock was Charrington's repayment of the money he had borrowed for the *Candida* tour. Although Shaw had championed Ibsen as a woman's dramatist, had urged the need for women managers, and written plays for women, his only two successful plays had now been hero plays: *The Devil's Disciple* and *Arms and the Man*.

Charlotte was not on hand to share his triumph. Strangely restless, she had left London for Leicester to visit "the infant," Mary Cholmondeley, had returned 14 October, left again for another visit, returned, and finally at the end of October left for Paris to visit friends. When she was in London that October, she contrived to be unavailable. The effect upon Shaw was magnetic. On his way to meet old friends at the Metropole, Shaw hesitated under the Turkish Bath clock in Northumberland Avenue, willed his feet to cross the street to the Metropole, but found himself to his astonishment walking off through the railroad arches to Adelphi Terrace instead. He found the big staircase light "blazing Eddystonianly through the night," but the rooms all dark, except two at the top, one of them (he knew) her bedroom. When he failed to see her at the New Century production of Henley and Stevenson's *Admiral Guinea*, he fretted that the sharp cold had given her neuralgia; calling at the Terrace, however, he was told by Martha that Miss Townshend had been out all afternoon, not the first time he had received that message.

Shaw claimed, of course, that he only needed her between working hours to keep his brains quiet and waste his time until he rushed off on some other business; but the loss was serious: "I do not know where the devil to go—what the devil to do!" He was glad she was escaping some hideously cold London weather in Paris; yet he must tease her, with a kind of childish insecurity, with the names of other women. Kate Salt had taken her place as his secretary: they were having "a rare time of it playing duets." He had fascinated an Italian woman at the Metropole who had "shivered like a steel filing confronted with a powerful magnet." They had been chaperoned, however, by the brother of his old flame (he had to mention her) Katie Samuel. Still, it was "damnably inconvenient" to have her out of his reach.

Charlotte returned from Paris, and without a qualm about being damnably inconvenient, left again immediately to visit her friends the Phillimores in Hertfordshire. Shaw paid them a visit at Radlett, and on the way home had another of his near-disastrous bicycle accidents. This time a woman had gotten inconveniently in his way as he was hurtling down a steep hill; he veered, missed her, toppled, and wiped the road with his face. It was one way of getting Charlotte's attention, and he rejoiced that he had gotten hurt just enough to make her tender. To Ellen in Charlotte's absence he wrote plaintively that he wanted a mistress: did she have a twin? Lonely, weary, Ellen replied from the tour at Bradford with Shavian contempt. "What rubbish! . . . We must do without these luxuries. There's so much work, so little time."[34]

Relentlessly, Charlotte then decided to go to Dieppe with Lion Phillimore, who was ailing. She paid Shaw the dubious compliment of asking him to go along. He emphatically declined: he had no desire to embark in the bitter depths of winter for a watering place where there would be nothing to do and nowhere to go, and in company with two women, "each determined that the other shall seduce me and each determined that I shall not seduce her." Feeling that he had scotched that notion successfully, he sent off one curt line to Adelphi Terrace on 6 December: "Secretary required tomorrow, not later than eleven." The next morning he bounded out of bed, stoked the fire, swept the hearth, and, while the servant smiled broadly at his pains, set out Charlotte's shawl and footwarmer in readiness. She was late, he noted, but with perfect confidence in her reliability, put off starting work and waited for her step on the stair. But Charlotte did not come. His vexation upon discovering that she had left for Dieppe without a word was considerable:

What do you mean by this inconceivable conduct? Do you forsake *all* your duties—even those of secretary? . . . Are there no stamps? has the post been abolished? have all the channel steamers foundered?

Go, then, ungrateful wretch: have your heart's desire: find a Master— one who will spend your money, and rule in your house, and order your servants about, and forbid you to ride in hansoms because it's unladylike, and remind you that the honor of his name is in your keeping, and decline in your name any further acquaintance with me, and consummate his marriage in the church lest the housemaid should regard his proceedings as clandestine. Protect yourself forever from freedom, independence, love, unfettered communion with the choice spirits of your day, a lofty path on which to go your own way and keep your own counsel, and all the other blessings which 999 women cry for and the thousandth cries to get away from. But at least tell me when youre *not* coming; and say whether I am to get a new secretary or not.[35]

For comfort he went round to the Charringtons the next evening. Although Janet tore his affection out by the roots with every syllable she uttered onstage these days, Shaw still did not have the heart to take back *Candida;* still hoped—now that the prospectus was out announcing the publication of his plays next February—that enough interest might be generated to finance her in a series of London matinees. When Janet came into the room to greet him, she was his Janet, "desirable and adorable." Then during dinner the inevitable metamorphosis began. Shaw watched in agony as nearly a tumbler of brandy loosened her tongue, until she rose from the table, loud, disheveled, unsteady. He protested angrily: was Charrington to be ruined by her debaucheries? Was Nora to watch her mother turn into a clinical case? At his accusations Janet grew maudlin: she wept: she moaned about women's suffering: she turned inarticulate. Nothing could distress the master of articulation more. Shaw fled. There was no use remonstrating any more. Presently he might learn to laugh at her, as he had learned to laugh at his drunken father; now, however, he suffered too much. No punishment, no revenge— only no luxury of forgiveness either. He must at last renounce all "spiritual intercourse" with her. Back in his study, he took down her picture from the wall, the face that had once seemed like a beacon shining to him over the stormy sea, and sat down to write:

No use, dear Janet: I can't be your taskmaster and schoolmaster any longer. . . . I can only make myself uselessly disagreeable and load my heart with a crown of swordpoints. Let us drop the subject and say goodbye whilst there is still some Janet left to say goodbye to. The only service a friend can really render is to keep up your courage by holding up to you a mirror in which you can see a noble image of yourself. The moment the image loses its elevation, then away with that friend: however remorseful he may be, he has become a malignant influence on your life. I held up the mirror in which Janet was beautiful as long as I could, in private and in print: now I've held it up with Janet inarticulate and rowdy. Avoid me now as you would the devil; for this time I will destroy your self respect if you let me near you. Restore the image, and look at it in a new, clean mirror—the archangel's with the purple wings, perhaps: mine is spoiled and done for. I am growing old and cowardly and selfish: it's sufficient that I loved you when I was young. Now I can do nothing but harm unless I say farewell, farewell, farewell, farewell, farewell, farewell, farewell, farewell.[36]

CHAPTER SIXTEEN

1897-1898

THE SUCCESS OF *The Devil's Disciple* aroused interest in London. Shaw had written Dick Dudgeon for the handsome, dashing William Terriss, "a play in himself," and Terriss was first in his calculations.[1] These were upset when, on the evening of 16 December, a bit-part actor with an imagined grievance accosted Terriss as he was entering the stage door with his leading lady and mistress, Jessie Millward, and stabbed him. He died in Jessie Millward's arms, like a hero from one of his own melodramas. The lurid stage door murder (it was still a brothel door in many people's minds) brought Henry Irving back from Bradford, and prompted one of the most masterful of his gestures. Sure that Terriss's murderer would get off because Terriss was only an actor (he was right), and anxious to assert the dignity of his profession, Irving first obtained a message of condolence for Terriss's widow from Queen Victoria. On the morning of the funeral, however, he appeared at Jessie Millward's door, presenting her with a knot of his favorite violets and a message of condolence from that more tolerant member of the royal household, the Prince of Wales. He then offered his arm as escort to the funeral. Barred from attending as the actor's mistress, Jessie dared to appear under Sir Henry's protection; and Irving, looking strained, pale, and austere, won the renewed respect of the theatre world for his display of sensibility.[2] "H. I. scored nobly by standing by her at the funeral," wrote Shaw to Ellen, who had also called on Jessie. Supposing Irving had been assassinated, he could not help thinking. Then Lady Irving, like Mrs. Terriss, would have received the Queen's condolences, and Ellen?— would have been taking a pleasant carriage ride through Richmond Park with him!

The implication that he thought of her as Irving's mistress was plain, and indeed Shaw continued to think of her in sexual terms. He suffered from Ellen hunger. If she would take that new house she'd been talking about, and see to it there was a gamekeeper's cottage with a secret passage to the best bedroom, he would see to it that the cottage had a tenant. Ellen too loved Shaw physically, as long as there was no chance of requital—threatening to press him to a jelly unless, of course, he made her so angry that she would rather pinch him hard or *lard* him all over with pins. Aching and lonely, sick of hotel rooms and ugly cities on that fall tour, she complained to Shaw. If only she could be in love. It was horrid: she was "cold as a vegetable marrow"; she felt like frozen leather. Sometimes, when Edy was away and Ted all taken up with his women, and Henry full of his work (and Shaw full of Miss P.T.), she wanted so much to find someone who could be full of *her*, if only for five minutes. Sometimes, she'd just like to stop work: to marry a man, rich and old. "Then I butter the stairs, and wear a widow's cap next day!" But when a suitor actually materialized in Edinburgh, she shuddered. ". . . I admire and respect him from top to bottom, in and out, and all over," she told Shaw. "Only if he touched me I'd die." She felt differently about Shaw. "Kiss me my sweet & thank you," she teased. All her longings and loneliness, however, always evaporated immediately whenever Edy turned up. Dear cool, provoking, charming Edy. People said Edy cared for her, but Ellen didn't believe it. Edy cut her heart to ribbons sometimes.[3]

She and Irving were drifting further apart. "Very odd," she recorded in her diary for 1897. "He is not improving with age." She did not realize at first that he had finally replaced her with another woman. Vacationing at Cromer before the autumn tour, he had accepted an invitation to tea from Eliza Aria, a woman he remembered as a former dinner partner, a London journalist, and a Jew who had thanked him in the name of her race for his Shylock. Sophisticated, witty, clever enough to act as a foil rather than compete with men, she attracted Irving most perhaps because she made no demands upon the secretive actor. Like Irving, she had suffered marital disillusionment in a carriage: driving away from the synagogue, her new husband had exclaimed enthusiastically, "I wonder what has won the Lincoln handicap!" She had not immediately jumped out, but after five years concluded that nothing became her husband so much as his deserting her for South Africa.[4] By February 1898 Ellen was asking Shaw, "But who is Mrs. A.?" Being a heart-wise Ellen, she could not complain; yet could not help longing either for someone who would put her first.

Was she even first in Shaw's dreams? There had been little talk since *The Man of Destiny* fiasco about Ellen plays. The spectacle of the ranting Janet's lovesick folly in *Antony and Cleopatra* had so set Shaw's teeth on edge that he had then and there begun to plot a counterdrama.

No love-death this time, but Caesar spurning a mere kitten of a Cleopatra: and it was Mrs. Campbell and Forbes-Robertson, an infinitely more intelligent actor than Irving, he believed, that he saw in the parts. Then, vacationing at the Argoed in September, another inspiration had struck him. That "rapscallionly flower girl" of Forbes-Robertson's, that beautiful Mrs. Campbell with the vulgar tongue, had suddenly driven *Caesar and Cleopatra* clean out of his head with the idea of another play with Forbes-Robertson as a West End gentleman and she an East End "dona in an apron and three orange and red ostrich feathers." Ellen received the news and, as a sop, the suggestion that she might do a matinee with Forbes-Robertson of *The Devil's Disciple*.

Shaw took his new enthusiasm along with him to Forbes-Robertson's fall production of *Hamlet* at the Lyceum. Not surprisingly, he found that Irving's absence had improved Shakespeare considerably. Instead of "the craft, the skill double-distilled by constant peril, the subtlety, the dark rays of heat generated by intense friction, the relentless parental tenacity and cunning with which Sir Henry nurses his own pet creations on Shakespearian food like a fox rearing its litter in the den of a lioness," the audience got naturalness, credibility, and Shakespeare. Forbes-Robertson was a classic actor; classic because he could "present a dramatic hero as a man whose passions are those which have produced the philosophy, the poetry, the art, and the statescraft of the world," not merely its "weddings, coroners' inquests, and executions."[5] London agreed with Shaw that Forbes-Robertson's Hamlet ranked among the greatest Hamlets of all time; it disagreed with him about Stella Campbell's Ophelia.

Forbes-Robertson had proposed Ophelia during that summer in which Mrs. Campbell had progressed from endless, wakeful nights drenched by everlasting tears to gradual recovery and long solitary bicycle rides at Salisbury where Lady Sybil Queensberry had lent her lovely Hatch House with its postern gate and rose garden where Queen Elizabeth had walked as a girl. She received the offer with alarm. She appealed to Uncle Henry Tanner, who urged her to fight and come out conquering; she appealed to Pat, working somewhere in the City and trying his best, who suggested rejoining Forbes-Robertson but not with Shakespeare. Nevertheless, Stella decided to attempt Ophelia. The harrowing nervous breakdown just behind her, she chose to make her Ophelia genuinely mad. Shaw was surprised and enthusiastic. The part had seemed incapable of progress; but this stark mad Ophelia, her dark hair twisted with purple woodbine and anemone, chilled his blood with real tragic power and significance.

Ellen objected. "I *am* so sorry we don't like the same things," she apologized smoothly. "Quite honestly I'd love to like all you like, but Mrs. Campbell as Ophelia I know I could not like. Don't be that kind of donkey to say, 'Ah, yes, jealousy!' I admire Mrs. P. C. as much as most people but I cannot like her Ophelia. If she plays that rightly then she played Mrs. Ebbsmith wrongly, and Mrs. E. was just splendid. . . . I guess you had a 'headache' when you were seeing Ophelia!"[6] Stella had been quite conscious of Miss Terry's presence in the audience one night, and responded by playing half her scenes in a blond Ellen wig. Ellen was not amused at this typical Campbellian escapade, perhaps because it reminded her of her own little show-stopping ways such as sighing, giggling, and not paying attention. She cleverly did not react at all; and on the whole Stella was left with unfortunate memories of that record run, even though the great Irving had appeared onstage after one performance to put his arm around her and murmur, "Beautiful, my child, beautiful." She excused her failure—she thought it one—on the grounds that Ellen Terry's lovely Ophelia was still so fresh in memory that there was no room for hers. But Ellen Terry's Ophelia had been played nineteen years before.

On 18 December Shaw visited the Lyceum again for a record-breaking hundredth performance. He found that while the minor players were just beginning to enjoy themselves, the stars were sleepwalking through a blank-verse dream. The fact that Ophelia's madness had blurred into placid idiocy did not banish Mrs. Campbell from his plans, nor Forbes-Robertson from his consciousness. To Ellen on New Year's Eve he reported a strange dream of the night before. "When I went to bed I dreamt that I had to play an important part with Forbes Robertson in a drama which I didnt know. It was necessary—I dont know why—that I should bluff it out at all hazards, and improvise my part. Whilst I was remonstrating about it, F. R.'s call came, and he bounded on the stage (a street, with a great tower & a harbor at the end—all real, not scenery) and I had to follow & begin. My first utterance, delivered from the top of the tower to him as he stood below on the quay, made him shriek with laughter; and I was anticipating utter disaster when I noticed that nobody was listening to us, and then the dream changed."[7] Was the play the yet visionary *Caesar and Cleopatra*, and Shaw's anxiety the anxiety of creation? Consciously or unconsciously, he would use the dream landscape as setting for the third act of that play: "The edge of the quay in front of the palace, looking out west over the east harbour of Alexandria to Pharos Island, just off the end of which, and connected with it by a narrow mole [street], is the famous lighthouse, a gigantic square tower of white marble . . . ."

The next day Shaw forfeited his holiday with the Webbs to come up to London for the opening of Laurence Irving's *Peter the Great*; found he had been struck from Irving's critics list; spent the evening of New Year's Day writing letters until 2 A.M. instead. The next morning he rose and rushed to Charlotte at Adelphi Terrace, where he dictated his review of *Peter the Great*—a much better notice, he felt, than any written by critics who had seen it. A thundering headache grew as he dictated; disregarding it, he went to a supper at Clement Shorter's; grew nauseated at steaming turkey and mince pies, could not eat, and came away to collapse into bed fully clothed. The next day he showed up at Adelphi Terrace for more work, but by four "lay like a log," while Charlotte soothed and petted him and rubbed vaseline into the still visible bicycle gash on his cheek. The scene was prophetic of the events 1898 would bring.

The year was to bring considerable change to many. After a year playing *Madame Sans-Gêne*, Ellen again found herself relegated to insignificant parts. As Catherine in *Peter the Great* she had little to do except sport in breeches, hoist her heels up on the table, and watch the young American actress Ethel Barrymore be enchanting as Euphrosyne. Unengaged by her work, Ellen dreamed more and more of the country. She had always loved it, and had often fled in her pony trap through the empty London streets after a Lyceum performance to see the dawn rise as she neared Winchelsea. Now a place of her own within reach of London but out of its dirt and smoke seemed urgent. She would be fifty in February. In London she seemed only to exist. "I've rheumatism in my knee!" she cried to Shaw. "And my heart is cold, and 'I wish I was dead!' No I don't! I love you a little and no one else (except Edy) even a little!"[8]

Shaw himself sometimes had "flashes of anxiety" about her. Irving was so drastically behind the times, falling back now that audiences at *Peter* were thinning (so he heard) upon his first triumph *The Bells*, just as if this were still 1871 instead of 1898. The younger generation were knocking on the door, and Irving was stone deaf. Theatres could lose money so fast, and with all his craft and subtlety, Irving had no brains—her money would go after his. Ellen defended the Lyceum's soundness, but admitted that Henry's plans were far worse than *The Bells*. Having turned down Conan Doyle's offer to write him a play about the detective Sherlock Holmes, a part seemingly made for him, Irving had got hold of a new play called *The Medicine Man:* a coat-and-trouser melodrama about a Jekyll-Hyde human vivisectionist. "My new part in it is just drivel," despaired Ellen. Surely it was bad policy for Irving to cut her out like this. She was not vain, but she knew she played a big part in Lyceum plays with the audiences, and it was so silly of H.I. not to see this. Could she have his advice? But Shaw had no ready advice. Ellen was an inevitable sacrifice to Irving's methods. Of course, he had been generous about her triumphs in *Nance Oldfield* and *Madame Sans-Gêne:* since he was not onstage, her acting did not interfere with his. But when he was onstage, he *would* work out his "slow, labored, self-absorbed" conceptions no matter what his leading lady's temperament or tempo. And of course her temperament and tempo were not his.

He had no help for Ellen; he did have ten pounds to advance to Janet, but only with the firm understanding that this time he was to get his money back. Both Charringtons had migrated to Manchester, where Janet was appearing as Lady Macbeth; yet even with an engagement, Janet managed to be broke. Shaw was not amused. He had donated to *Candida* and to *Cleopatra*, but all his money had ever done was to stimulate her creditors to worry her with increased vigor because they'd drawn blood. "Janet's view is that as I have no debts of my own I can pay hers," he told Charrington (it was usually Charrington to whom he wrote now): "—an unspeakably exasperating one to me. . . . I am now determined to make myself so hideously disagreeable that she will dread me more than all the rest of [her creditors] put together. Tell her that I must have my pound of flesh next week."[9]

In reply Charrington brought into the open an issue both he and Janet had brooded on for some time. Shaw had changed toward Janet, and it was all because Charlotte Payne-Townshend had appeared on the scene as a rival. Would he admit it? Shaw would not. Janet had cut her own throat by asking Charlotte for that fifty pounds—foolishly, destructively throwing away the good will of a woman who would have lent her thirty or forty times the sum at the right moment had she been "thriftily dealt with." His new hardness of heart had nothing to do with Charlotte: Charrington was "cynically wrong—as usual."[10] But Janet had little doubt about the force that had turned the tide of Shaw's affections at last.

A pity that the Charringtons could not now take hold; a pity that Charrington had managed to convert the shareholders' capital into thin air, so that the I.T. was in deeper difficulties than ever. For one longtime rival was deciding to quit the theatre forever. Ever since her realization in 1891 that her destiny lay in plays like *Hedda Gabler* and *The Master Builder*, Elizabeth Robins had worked courageously to make her dream of a progressive theatre come true. She had from the first displayed an extraordinary ability to inspire confidence in herself and her projects, winning as allies Ibsen's translators and publisher and acquiring virtually a monopoly. She had made no more money with her pioneering than the Charringtons; she had not, however, acquired their debts and consequent reputation for unreliability.

She had most recently established the New Century Theatre, an organization growing out of her ventures with *Little Eyolf* and José Echegaray's *Mariana*. Shaw had noticed its existence in the *Saturday Review* of 10 April 1897. The group was "the latest combination of enthusiasts for the regeneration of the drama," he remarked with some boredom, an organization so like the Independent Theatre that the public would have little more to choose between them than between George Alexander and Beerbohm Tree. What discouraged him most was the conflicting scope of the new society's aims and the tediously familiar way in which it intended to realize them. He had complained in the past of "this folly of collecting money for our Janets and Elizabeths to give matinees with and calling that the new drama." A considerable sum of money was what they really needed so that they could march armed to Tree or Irving and demand a series of classical matinees. The New Century Theatre, in short, should be able to announce its new season from the Lyceum, and follow it with a demand for a government grant like those to the National Gallery or British Museum. Apart from that hope, the New Century Theatre was regrettably old and advanced the English drama not one step nearer to the ultimate goal: the foundation of a standard theatre.

Although Elizabeth retrospectively wished that Shaw's sober sense had tempered the committee, at the time Shaw and the Charringtons with their rival Independent Theatre were distinctly shut out from the New Century clique, as Shaw came to call it. The misunderstanding between them had not dissolved. She thought him a crass flatterer and no gentleman; he recoiled from the "cold stupidity" of her personality: both thought they had a corner on morality. As an intelligent actress Elizabeth was of course experiencing the same frustrations Shaw was experiencing as a playwright, frustrations which could have, but did not, unite them. And now even the New Century Theatre venture seemed stale. She had been in the business longer than the rest, and had begun to ask herself more insistently: What did it all come to? Wasn't it coming to be just one more of those efforts, effectual at the moment, but doomed to ineffectualness and the little day? If so, it was because the society remained in isolation: it did not hitch on to anything. She looked about her, and asked what there was to hitch on to.[11] Her sense of the futility of the New Century Theatre began to match Shaw's, and was undoubtedly helped along by his comments in the *Saturday Review*.

But Elizabeth had other resources to fall back upon. Under the name C. E. Raimond, she had for years been "sipping in secret at Henry James' divine cup": she had been writing fiction. It had struck her in the early nineties that she had another talent, that writing would give her more independence than the theatre, and that after all, she would still be playing a part. She chose a pseudonym, she told herself, from the conviction that an actress would never be given a fair hearing. Probable enough, another reason lay in her secretiveness, her compulsion to mask her identity behind another's, in this case her intensely loved brother Raymond's. *George Mandeville's Husband* (1894), *The New Moon* (1895), and *Below the Salt* (1896) had all excited interest, particularly *George Mandeville's Husband*, a bitter satire against women novelists. "George" is the unsexed, slovenly female artist who dashes down her emotions on paper without a thought for artistry, lowering both artistic standards and the reputation of women. Archer had murmured against the "implacable ferocity" of C. E. Raimond's attack, and Elizabeth had enjoyed it all immensely. How much fun to sit at a dinner party and hear C. E. Raimond's works introduced. If her partner praised, she was sure to find fault; if the lady across the table condemned, she rose spiritedly to Raimond's defense.

She had last acted Ella Rentheim for the N.C.T.'s production of *John Gabriel Borkman* in the usual series of matinees beginning 3 May 1897 at the Strand. The production, noted Shaw, took place under the usual shabby circumstances: the next time he hoped the N.C.T. would apply to him when it came to mounting—if he could not come up with a tenner at least he could lend them a couple of decent chairs. As for the acting, it was fairly good when the performers were more or less in their depth, lugubriously well intentioned when they were out of it. Unfortunately they were usually out of it. As for Elizabeth, she proved herself an Ibsenite, not an Ibsenist. She could be brilliant, that is, as long as she was playing the New Woman in revolt against the intolerably unjust feminine ideal or against the male treating her merely as sexual prey—not by understanding the character, but by being it. But in parts demanding "wisdom of the heart and a sense of identity and common cause with others"—religious parts—Elizabeth Robins was sympathetic as a flute is sympathetic: "she has a pretty tone, and can be played on with an affectation of sentiment; but there is no reality, no sincerity in it."[12]

This was probably not a fair appraisal of Elizabeth and the production. Shaw was the first to admit that he distorted ruthlessly for a cause, and his current cause was backing the Independent Theatre against the New Century. Difficult to believe, too, that Shaw's personal experience with Robins's feminism—a feminism that took the form of objecting to his flattering her as a woman rather than respecting her as a colleague—had not influenced his opinion of her performance, the last he was to review and the last Ibsen role she would create. On 2 February 1898, Elizabeth sailed for the United States, private business coinciding with an engagement to play Hedda Gabler, sent off with one of Henry James's sympathetic little notes that hailed her as a "mighty spirit" and hoped that wishes for a prosperous journey were "not too *banal.*" But *Hedda Gabler* met with such hostility when it opened at the 5th Avenue Theatre in New York that it was withdrawn the next day, a reaction explaining why Elizabeth had left America, where Irving had triumphed and even Shaw had been played.

The days of Irving's triumphs were numbered, however. In love with his theatre rather than its profits, Irving had poured his takings back into costumes, lavish theatre decor, generous salaries to the trusted band of retainers who shielded him from the public, a generous salary of £200 a week to Ellen Terry that probably made her, with the exception of the Queen, England's highest-paid woman, sumptuous entertainments for hundreds in the Beefsteak Room. Unnoticed in the glare of these huge bills, money trickled quietly away down dozens of small drains. Soon not even American tours were enough to stabilize Lyceum finances. One of Irving's most lavish expenditures had been upon stage sets and properties: the delicate splendor of fifteenth-century Italian dresses and armor, the halls and colonnades of King Arthurland, woodland springs and forest sunsets, castles, temples, battlements painted on cloths thirty feet high rolled on forty-two-foot battens, or constructed into framed scenes of gigantic proportions. This treasure trove, representing years of work by the best stage artists of the day and an investment upward of £50,000, Irving had stored for safety in two arches under the Chatham and Dover railway at a point on the line in Southwark where the tracks soared high over the streets. Sometime during the night of 18 February 1898 Irving's cache began to burn. By the time a message from the Bow Street police brought Stoker to the scene the arches were glowing like furnaces; by the time Irving got the news the next morning, the contents of the arches lay in ashes. Guarded as always, he commented only that perhaps the indignation of those avant-gardists who believed in producing plays without scenery had struck the spark. The accident to his leg that had forced him to withdraw *Richard III* had cost him dearly; the arches were a second and more serious misfortune. A superstitious man might have felt some apprehension for the future.

And in fact, the Lyceum institution Shaw had attacked so unremittingly since joining the *Saturday Review* in January 1895 was already a dying animal. Institutions outwardly flourish long after the impetus which gives them birth has lost its vitality. Irving's knighthood in 1895 signaled ends, not beginnings, ends in no way caused by Irving, who continued to do brilliantly what he had always done, but by the inevitable changes time brings. Baffled and contemptuous of Shaw's attacks because he felt he knew his art and his public, Irving closed his eyes to change with the rigidity of an autocrat. Shaw mercilessly attacked this paternal autocracy. Everything, he claimed, was sacrificed to Irving's ego: the text of the play, the roles of the rest of the cast, the repertoire, the leading lady. Shaw had the socialist's hatred of a monarchy and the rebel's hatred of authority; as a playwright, he favored the autocracy of the play. Privately, Irving's indifference to his criticisms exasperated him. But in fact, Shaw's own days as a critic were numbered.

An indirect cause of his giving up theatre criticism seemed to be Charlotte Payne-Townshend. The few notes that survive the late winter of 1898 hint of strain in their relationship. Shaw had come to rely upon her heavily for secretarial duties, yet inevitably his other affairs interrupted their sessions. When that happened, Shaw would dispatch a brief note informing her she would not be needed. Understandably these curt dismissals annoyed Charlotte, who felt in any case ambivalent about functioning as his secretary. "We must adopt some less heart-lacerating way of getting rid of one another than 'Good afternoon: shant want you till tomorrow,'" Shaw was forced to admit after some unexpected Vestry business caused Charlotte to explode. "Besides you dont play fair: you make a scene of it—as if *I* could help it!" On 4 March play copies printed up for copyright performances arrived, requiring "endless cutting & folding and stapling into brown paper covers." Could she spare a little time? he asked cautiously, for his nerves were shattered by recent scenes that made him feel that he had allied himself "to a fountain of tears."[13]

On 12 March Charlotte left for Rome with Lion Phillimore. It is tedious to assume, as it always is assumed, that women's actions are reactions to men; yet Charlotte's departure seemed a clear announcement that she did not intend to be taken for granted. And by being elusive, she hit upon the best way to manage the elusive Shaw.

"Charlotte deserts me at 11.

"Divide the rest of the day between tears and answering letters.

"Digestion wholly ceases.

"Try to sing 'Egypt was glad when they departed,' by Handel. Failure.

"No exercise today."[14] He announced his new availability to Ellen, who replied with notable unenthusiasm, "I can't write to you, can't feel, can't think. I work and work but am ill and hate it all. . . . Henry . . . is naughty all along the road lately, and I shall have to propose we give each other up. . . . Can't see. My head is so full of ache. The Merchant of Venice last night drew one of the biggest houses we have ever played to! . . . But oh, I'm tired out. You, half dead, will spring up again, but I shall go whole dead very soon." The scenery loss had touched Ellen as well as Irving: she had offered to take £100 a week on tour instead of her usual £200, and to draw no salary unless actually working. But her work discouraged her: her repertoire had dwindled to two parts: Portia and Henrietta Maria in *Charles I*. Immediate assurances from Shaw of his longing for her brought no comfort. "Stupid!" she wrote back. "I wish you would not write to me as if you thought me as big a donkey as all that! This 'Ellen hunger' stuff I've laughed at long enough."[15]

Abandoned, Shaw resorted to keeping an almanack for Charlotte, jotting down his activities on the leaves of his desk calendar and posting them with cover letters. He felt like the world's workhorse as usual: rushing to Vestry meetings to listen to widows begging to be let off their taxes, expurgating *Mrs. Warren* for the censor, who had refused to license a copyright performance, dashing to Ratepayers' Association meetings in the evening, pegging away at the *Saturday Review* articles, biking twenty-five miles to Hampstead and Hendon, sixteen miles of it uphill, racing in from the Ratepayers' meeting to come face to face with Jenny Patterson "audaciously" sitting in the parlor with his mother, so that he was forced to dive into the study like a rabbit and cower there until she went away. The morning after that "fearful contretemps" Kate Salt turned up at breakfast ready for secretarial duties. Unspeakably cross at having to adapt to a new secretary, Shaw sat her down to finish an article from his dictation. "For three sentences, I feel resentful, uncomfortable, and quite put out," he comforted Charlotte. "At the fourth the switch operates and I am on to the new line as if I had never dictated to anybody else. Such is manly fidelity." This was cruelty to be kind. She must get on with her own project of studying the Roman municipal system while abroad (a rather dismal attempt at imitating Beatrice Webb). There was clearly no future for her as his secretary: "You must get your own work, your own, own, own work," he commanded. "Do you hear?" Kate, he assured her as the days went by, was tearing through the work at a terrific pace. *She* did not halt her work to go to lunch with him, but ate her bananas between sentences; moreover there were no "sentimental interruptions." He was getting along famously.

By 30 March he was positively rejoicing. "After all, it is magnificent to be alone, with the ivy stripped off. As I walk round the park at night, looking at the other stars, I no longer feel 42. The hopples are off; my soul is disentangled from Martha's parlormaid's uniform; I am natural once more. You count that I have lost only one Charlotte; but I have lost two; and one of the losses is a prodigious relief. I may miss 'die schöne grünen Augen' occasionally, though the very privation throws me back, brutally great, to my natural dreamland; but then think of the other Charlotte, the terrible Charlotte, the lier-in-wait, the soul hypochondriac, always watching and dragging me into bondage, always planning nice sensible, comfortable, selfish destruction for me, wincing at every accent of freedom in my voice, so that at last I get the trick of hiding myself from her, hating me & longing for me with the absorbing passion of the spider for the fly. Now that she is gone, I realize for the first time the infernal tyranny of the past year, which left me the license of the rebel, not the freedom of the man who stands alone. I will have no more of it: if you hate women who pull flowers, what do you think of women who cut down trees? *That's* the Charlotte I want to see married."[16]

With nothing to embrace but freedom, however, Shaw began to fret. He dictated his *Saturday Review* article of 26 March to Kate for three hours straight: a stupendous effort, and a terrible strain not to be able to kiss the secretary. And why did Kate have to start every session by "producing a comb & titivating herself at the glass at the sideboard"? He did not mind playing the *Pastoral Symphony* with her four-handed, but when he tried to teach her the typewriter she exasperated him fright-fully. She was "a dense divil," as his mother would say. He was growing more and more irritable, and Kate was complaining of his savagery.

The weather, moreover, was fearful: blizzard, hurricane, and tempest: London almost torn up by the roots. He was getting no exercise; his digestion had ceased. Work drove him mercilessly. He was scrambling to put together a lecture on "Flagellomania" for the Humanitarian League. Henry Salt had lent him *History of the Rod* for inspiration: he found it perfectly disgusting and dashed out to bike around Regent's Park in the clear cold night air to purge his soul after the desecration. On the evening of 24 March, after a frightful afternoon repulsing a determined and emotional actress who wanted to play Judith in *The Devil's Disciple*,[17] he rose to speak on flagellomania, "a frantic, muddled wreck," and for a blessed one hundred minutes "riveted the wretched audience to their chairs" before staggering home to fall in bed "like a stamped-on beetle." Charrington assured him it had been one of his best performances, yet wondered why a fearful scowl had scored his brow the whole time. Per-haps it was the headache: they were getting chronic now, although his energy surged rather than flagged under the pain. Although he continued to walk in the park before bed to embrace his true mistress, the Night, her embrace was becoming increasingly cold. The day after the lecture he had run into Bertha Newcombe at the Fabian; escorting her to Tem-ple Station afterward, he had been told for his pains that she had found it strange to hear him discoursing against flogging. "Because you are so horribly cruel." *Was* he? He was bullying Kate Salt mercilessly; his irri-tability had reached high pitch. The Webbs had sailed for New York on an extended journey: there was no Beatrice to mother him. Worse, there was no letter from Rome.

The first day of April he found a letter waiting on his return from the Fabian Executive. He melted: he wanted to hug her now, not batter her "and stalk off to commune proudly with the stars." The letter and a lot of country cycling and fresh air revived his "brute strength," however, and brought unrest: "I want a woman & a sound sleep." He was never happy now except when worked to desperation and eating little. Yet he was never unhappy. It was a condition, he assured her continually, that he simply did not know. Nor was he lonely—"no, by God, never—*not* lonely"; but he *was* "detestably deserted." Then seven days passed with-out another letter. He continued to jot down his days for her. It had been a lovely night "with a moon bigger than Big Ben's dial"; yet he was too done up to enjoy it. No letter. Some Italian doctor, no doubt, was the reason for the silence. The tactless reference to Dr. Axel Munthe, for whom Charlotte had conceived an unrequited passion in Rome four years before, indicated the depth of his insecurity. But he rallied: "Well, I shall not be for ever snivelling to be petted," he assured her. "In this grim solitude I shall recuperate: the steel armor will harden again, with a fresh deposit of adamant all over it." Only Ellen remained faithful—Ellen, to whom he sent his "first kiss of spring." He made sure Charlotte heard about it.[18] To Sidney Webb he wrote that he was living the life of a dog.

Superior in culture, wealth, and position, Charlotte still affected Shaw much like Alice Lockett. Both were private, "respectable" women with whom he could not trifle—either by philandering or by regaling them with fantasies from his "natural dreamland." With Florence and Jenny he had indulged his passion without feeling he must repay them with marriage: it had been their great attraction. With Janet and Ellen he could indulge his fantasies without having to repay them with sex: it was theirs. Alice and Charlotte were women with whom he felt a sense of responsibility. He squirmed under that sense, torn between attraction and flight. He projected his ambivalence, as he had with Alice, upon Charlotte. Alice had been Miss Lockett the prude and Alice the adorable; Charlotte was the spider poised for her victim and the warm friend of Saxmundham. Sometimes he could hardly believe they were one and the same. Again, he did not seem to consider the effect of his own ambiguity upon her: he could be Shaw the tender lover and Shaw the inhuman machine. He only knew that he veered violently between wanting to crush her in his arms and wanting to arm himself against her. It was a miserable dilemma (when he took the time to think about it); and the headaches continued in full force.

His spirits were not lifted by the tragedy of Eleanor Marx. On the last day of March she had sent her maid to the chemist at the end of Jew's Walk with a note, "Please give bearer chloroform and small quantity of prussic acid for dog." The previous summer her common-law husband Edward Aveling under the alias Alec Nelson had married a twenty-two-year-old woman named Eva Frye. Sometime during that year Eleanor, now forty-three, had discovered the fact. She was unable to endure this last betrayal. In Aveling's presence she signed the poison book sent by the chemist, went upstairs to her bedroom, undressed, got into bed, and swallowed the prussic acid, upon which Aveling evidently left the house. Toward eleven her maid entered her bedroom and found her scarcely breathing; by the time the doctor tardily arrived, she was dead.[19]

Ellen heard the news with some shock. Back in January, Aveling, under the name Alec Nelson, had actually asked her for money. She in turn had asked Shaw whether the man was "fairly decent": should she lend him a small sum? Shaw's reply was vehement. "Just walk into a room where we are all assembled, and say, in a cautious tentative way, 'What sort of fellow is Dr. Aveling?', and you will bring down the house with a shriek of laughter, and a shout of 'How much have you lent him?'" If Ellen couldn't shut her purse tight against such swindlers, she had better send her money immediately to Shaw for safekeeping. Now, however, she thought she should have lent that money to Aveling when he asked. "Poor Eleanor Marx!" she sighed with that sympathy of hers that could be quite perfunctory at times.[20] Shaw was more deeply affected. Eleanor's death brought back the old days of socialist struggle: Bloody Sunday, police cordons, crowded meeting halls, Sundays at East End rallies and Hammersmith: the old excitement for the cause. Eleanor had fought to the end, privately disillusioned from time to time, but never renouncing her radicalism and never losing faith in the potential of the working classes for social revolution. Shaw's note to Charlotte for 5 April, the day of Eleanor's cremation, exuded weariness, hypochondria, loneliness: perhaps it expressed his sense that his strongest personal link with Marx had snapped.

On Tuesday, 19 April, an event of quite a different kind: the publication of *Plays Pleasant and Unpleasant.* His work, ephemeral to this point, was at last a solid fact. He sent the first copy

> From the Author to Ellen Ellen
> Ellen Ellen Ellen Ellen Ellen Ellen
> Ellen Terry. *Easter 1898.*

"Your fun comes spouting out, 'all alive oh,'" she cried, reading through the plays once again. "All sparkle. Young, strong. It catches hold of one, shakes one, wakes one! And however devilish you may choose to try to appear, in the end you are all heavenly! I knew of all your pains before your big book came out, but as I read (each night) the result appears to me MIGHTY, and effortless."[21] It was an acute judgment.

William Archer also read and, unlike Ellen, reacted with violent ambivalence. *Plays Pleasant and Unpleasant* aroused "a tangle of emotions" that made comment the most difficult task he ever faced. How to describe the heights to which Shaw rose in *Candida* and the depths to which he sank in *The Philanderer;* how to take with patience the author's setting that "crude 'prentice-work" *Widowers' Houses* next to *Mrs. Warren's Profession,* an undoubted masterpiece. Particularly Archer disliked the Shavian hero, always Shaw whether Charteris, Bluntschli, or Valentine—always quick-witted, unillusioned, cool, blarneying, fascinating, intellectual, and maddeningly imperturbable; always engaged in the same "agreeable task—that of disillusioning and dominating a beautiful and headstrong young lady." The ladies were for the most part disagreeable themselves; and why? "It is exceedingly difficult for a man to see a woman objectively," said Archer, "because a woman, even in the most superficial and conventional relations, is very largely what a man makes her. The converse, of course, holds good to some, but not to the same, extent. Mr. Shaw has gone through life seeing Shaw women, because women who were probably quite different both before and after, became Shaw women the moment they entered his sphere of magnetism, his 'aura.' . . . It was Mr. Shaw's misfortune (so I conjecture from the female characterisation of his earlier plays) at one stage of his development to bring out the worser elements in the nature of women he came in contact with."

Archer did not totally conjecture from the plays, of course: he had witnessed the Shaw-Robins and Shaw-Mrs. Archer fireworks. That phase, however, Archer now hoped was past, for the beauty, humor, and tenderness of *Candida* seemed to signal that Shaw had at last risen above mere anger, violence, and nastiness in his treatment of men-women relationships. Candida herself more than made amends for his Julias and Blanches, Vivies and Rainas. If only, Archer concluded, Shaw would cast out four or five of his six natures (Charteris first), "thus leaving room for the development of the poet-humorist-technician Shaw who wrote *Candida,* he might have the future of the English theatre in his hands. When I say and reiterate that *Candida* is a work of rare genius, it is in the desperate hope of begetting in its author a little—humility. That would be the saving of him."[22] But Shaw had no intention of repeating the tender domesticities of *Candida.*

The evening of that momentous publication day, Shaw got on his bicycle to ride out to Ealing to visit his old friends, the Pakenham Beattys. On arrival he found his foot unaccountably sore, and was forced to pull off his shoe for relief. He could barely get it on again when it came time to leave, and when he pried the shoe off later at Fitzroy Square, the foot swelled alarmingly "to the size of a leg of mutton." He could find no explanation for the disaster except that a week or so previously he had laced his shoe too tight and pinched a nerve. Two days later it had become excruciating to get about: the foot looked terrible: could a vegetarian have the gout? "Am a fearful wreck," he moaned to Charlotte, who was not helping matters by refusing to give him the faintest clue as to her movements in Rome. The next day he solved his transportation problems by simply hopping down stairs and up streets and into the Fabian Executive, to which council, incidentally, he told Charlotte she had been elected by a handsome two hundred votes.

His secretary having collapsed with a sick headache, but deterred by nothing himself, Shaw picked up his notebook the next day and started jotting down the play about Caesar and Cleopatra that had been gestating for more than a year: invalidism, he decided, was going to save his playwriting career. The doctor arrived after post hour, Alice Lockett's husband, William Salisbury Sharpe. While Sharpe shook his head over the foot and ordered three hours hot water bath in the morning and one and a half at night ("Amputation sooner," snorted Shaw), Alice waited in the other room without making her presence known. It was rather a coincidence that the one woman he had thought of marrying should reappear on the eve of his marriage.

Four days later on 26 April Shaw was still housebound and polishing off "the whole scene of Cleopatra—Sc. 2 of the 1st act—quintessence of everything that has most revolted the chivalrous critics. Ha! ha! Julius Caesar as the psychological woman tamer. Ho! ho!" The next day, Wednesday, he jotted down the last leaf for Rome since Charlotte was to start for England on Friday. "I will try to find out when your train is due on Sunday night," he told her eagerly; "and if the hour is not absolutely scandalous I shall present myself at the Terrace & crush in all your ribs with an embrace that has been accumulating for 2 months."

"At last. Charlotte due at 19½ Victoria," he rejoiced on Sunday, 1 May. That morning he worked at the essay on Wagner he had started; then, too restless to concentrate, struck work and leafed aimlessly through the Sunday papers and a novel. At eight, he hobbled down the stairs from his study, made it to Tottenham Court Road, caught a bus, got off at Charing Cross, and limped "slowly, slowly, slowly" to Adelphi Terrace, all his troubles over at last. With a long sigh of relief, he laid his two-month burden of loneliness and frustration down, and rang the bell below the lighted globe inscribed "London School of Economics." Footsteps descended the stairs, Martha opened the door. Expecting to be led straight up, he was informed that her mistress had not returned by the seven-thirty train. Would Mr. Shaw care to wait?

"Wretch, devil, fiend!" fumed Shaw. The train had arrived, she had not been on it. Stopped over in Paris to see a play, had she? "No: Satan's own daughter would have telegraphed." He could *not* wait; and instead hobbled back to catch a bus, cursing her heartily.

The next morning a letter from Charlotte, smooth as silk. "Well, here I am anyway now! Yes: I *might* have telegraphed: it was horrid of me. I am a wreck, mental & physical. Such a journey as it was! . . . My dear— & your foot? Shall I go up to you, or will you come here, & when? Only tell me what you would prefer. Of course I am quite free—Charlotte."[23] Shaw had met his match.

She found him in his study, foot propped and swathed in cotton wool, buried in a litter of papers, plates, cups, books, manuscripts, and, as she concluded, totally neglected. Maternal feelings rose in her: it was outrageous: why was he not better looked after: what was the doctor thinking of. Events moved swiftly after that. The evening of 9 May the surgeon and chloroformer appeared at Fitzroy Square: the foot must be drilled to let the infectious matter out. Ten minutes before the operation Shaw was scribbling a note to Janet to let her know she would find him at home on Wednesday; an hour later the doctor threw Charlotte into consternation with the announcement that the bone was carious and that

Shaw was in critically weak condition—probably because of his damned vegetarianism. Shaw protested. He was exhausted, not undernourished: the theatre reviewing had sapped the last ounce of energy he possessed. He was, he finally admitted, at the limits of his physical stamina.

He was ordered to rest and, according to Shaw, the Square soon filled with "pretty bonnets, tears, flowers, and fruit." Janet came and was repulsed. "They didn't tell me not to see you," Shaw apologized: "they knew better. They stopped you off their own bat. . . ." There were other restrictions. "So you are forbidden to write to your Ellen!" protested his old sweetheart, who sent him a soft little kiss in the middle of his cheek. "You don't write with your little *Hoof!!*"[24]

Shaw had already decided in early April that he had had enough of theatre criticism, writing to Frank Harris that he must hand over his column at the end of the season. He had been hopping around to the St. James's, the Globe, the Comedy, and the Avenue as usual; however, it was clear that he must give up the *Saturday Review* business at once. *The Devil's Disciple* had put enough money in his pocket to free him from the journalistic treadmill; his health now demanded it.

His last assignment took him by strange chance to the theatre he had made the target of his criticism ever since taking up pen for the *Saturday Review*. "Personally I have only one desire concerning the theatres of this accursed metropolis," he told Bram Stoker, who had invited him privately since he was off Irving's critics list, "and that is to see them, with their actors, managers, critics, and all complete, plunged into the blinding white hot heat of hell until everything theatrical is consumed out of them & nothing remains but a virgin art and a small heap of clinker representing the press."[25] So had the puritan hero of his first novel *Immaturity* revolted against the theatrical artificiality that had once attracted him. Since he had to review *The Medicine Man*, however, his task might prove less dull if he actually saw it. Accordingly, on the evening of 4 May, he passed under the great portico supported by the six soaring Corinthian columns and through the Lyceum doors for the last time as a critic.

Shaw had attacked Irving again and again for refusing to play modern authors. Tonight, almost as if to appease his enemy, Irving had abandoned the classics for a contemporary play. Did Shaw congratulate Irving for coming to his senses at last? Alas, he could not. *The Medicine Man* might have been written last week, but it was written in the stale Macaulayese that the New Journalism had overthrown in the eighties. The plot itself was utter nonsense, consisting chiefly of Irving gliding across the stage, rubbing his hands, and fixing his cast with a hypnotic eye. "There was infinite comedy in the first night of the play at the Lyceum," Shaw reported, unyielding to the end. "It lasted from eight to past eleven, and contained just matter enough for a half-hour pantomimic sketch by Mr. Martinetti. Sir Henry Irving, pleased by the lion-taming notion, was perfectly delighted with his part, and would evidently have willingly gone on impressing and mesmerizing his devoted company for three hours longer. Miss Ellen Terry, on the other hand, was quite aware of the appalling gratuitousness of his satisfaction. To save the situation she put forth all her enchantments, and so beglamored the play act by act that she forced the audience to accept Sylvia as a witching and pathetically lovely creation of high literary drama. The very anguish the effort caused her heightened the effect. . . . Hand-in-hand with the innocently happy Sir Henry, she endured the curtain calls with a proud reticence which said to us plainly enough, 'I will play this part for you unworthy people, since you have no better use to make of me; but I will not pretend to like it' . . . ."[26]

Choose your side, Shaw had once told Ellen, and stick to it. As a theatre critic he had taken his own advice. Admitting that he was often flagrantly unfair, he had viewed his job as "a siege laid to the theatre of the XIXth Century by an author who had to cut his own way into it at the point of the pen, and throw some of its defenders into the moat." As Marx had made a man of him, so did this purpose give muscle to his criticism. Other reviewers temporized, liking one play for its enchanting leading lady, another for its scenery, disliking another because the lead was inaudible: they lacked a point of view. Shaw brought the theatre to one test. No matter that actor-managers were succeeding brilliantly in what *they* were trying to do; were they coming his way, asked Shaw, or staying in the old grooves? If the latter, he bent all his formidable powers to making them look as ridiculously old-fashioned as possible.

To this end he had quite shamelessly plugged his own side. Although Janet Achurch, for example, had appeared in only four minor productions during his tenure on the *Saturday Review*, he managed to bring her name into his reviews on twenty-one occasions, Charrington's fourteen, *A Doll's House* eleven, and Ibsen's over a hundred times. Elizabeth Robins, struggling with matinees, had received more attention than the leading lady of the Lyceum and the immensely popular Mrs. Patrick Campbell. Above all, actresses had received his attention, both because temperamentally he took more interest in a woman knitting than Ajax fighting, and because he had viewed the battle of the new theatre against the old chiefly as a battle of the sexes. Privately he did not particularly believe in the woman's side. "I don't think the actress-manageress is going to do much good," he had written R. Golding Bright in April 1895, "because, obviously, she will want plays with good parts for the woman and bad parts for the men; and so, though we shall have two sorts of bad plays instead of one—the actress manageress's play at half the theatres and the actor-manager's play at the other half, we shall be as far as ever from the genuine drama."[27] His Preface to *The Theatrical "World" of*

1894 had not advocated the changes he saw coming, he claimed, but simply stated them. The public had certainly interpreted his criticism as advocacy, however; and Shaw himself must have admitted that woman's emancipation had been an effective symbol for the broader class struggle to which he as a Marxist had pledged himself. From his first attack on Irving's *King Arthur* in January 1895 to his ridicule of *The Medicine Man* in May 1898, he had pounded home the doctrine that women on the stage (and in society) must be "something more than a piece of sweet-stuff to fatten a man's emotions"; that the London actress was constantly and monstrously misused in sentimental, reactionary plays written as foolish flatteries for the male sex by the male sex. That much of his antipathy to these plays stemmed from his distaste for romance and passion, and that some of this distaste inevitably rubbed off on their objects, women, did not weigh heavily in the outcome. He had almost consistently urged that women must be treated as more than sexual objects: his criticism was indirectly socialist, overtly feminist.

He was turning it over to a successor who was neither, yet his "Valedictory" of 21 May in the *Saturday Review* sounded an optimistic note. The younger generation was knocking at the door, and as he opened it, there stepped sprightly in Max Beerbohm—"the incomparable Max." "For the rest," he concluded, "let Max speak for himself. I am off duty for ever, and am going to sleep." The battleship had been replaced by a bright-sailed little yacht.

Shaw was not asleep, however, but wide awake and up to his ears in marriage plans. As he was unable to resist leaving one woman's love notes around for her rival to read or reciting his enthusiasm for one conquest into the unwilling ear of another, so now he could not resist dropping hints everywhere that marriage was imminent, at the same time enjoining the strictest secrecy. He hated presents; he railed against the "votive pigskin" case Graham Wallas dropped off at the Square; he was determined to put up as much resistance to the ceremony as to a hanging. And actually the proceedings were conducted in a thoroughly iconoclastic way. Turned down by the official next door because he only did births and deaths, Shaw sent Charlotte out in search of a registrar, which she finally found in Henrietta Street, where her statement that she wanted to get married was relayed up a tube from office boy to official with shrieks of laughter. She then had to hunt up a West End jeweler's which she had not patronized before, and "suffer the final humiliation" of buying her own ring.

Life was too serious not to laugh at. The decision to marry had actually accompanied a change in his own nature. Always fearful of the love-death, he had looked death in the face, and found not only that he was unafraid to die but that his objection to his marriage ended with his objection to his own death.[28] But he dealt with the events surrounding this psychic change with the greatest levity. At eleven-thirty on 1 June, he recounted, he and Charlotte met witnesses Graham Wallas and Henry Salt at the West Strand Registry Office, where the registrar, assuming that the bearded eccentric propped on crutches that had worn his old jacket to rags was the "inevitable beggar who completes all wedding processions," was proceeding to marry Charlotte to the imposingly handsome and impeccably dressed Wallas, until Wallas, alarmed at the seriousness of the formula, hesitated at the last minute and left the bride to Shaw. As he had always written his own best interviews, he now scooped his marriage for the *Star:* "As a lady and gentleman were out driving in Henrietta-st., Covent-garden, yesterday, a heavy shower drove them to take shelter in the office of the Superintendent Registrar there, and in the confusion of the moment he married them. The lady was an Irish lady named Miss Payne-Townshend, and the gentleman was George Bernard Shaw. . . ."

He had announced his marriage on its eve to his old sweetheart Ellen. She sent a wedding day reply: "How splendid! What intrepidity to make such a courageous bid for happiness. Into it you both go! Eyes wide open! An example to the world, and may all the gods have you in their keeping." Heart-wise to the end, she outwardly rejoiced. Inwardly, however, there must have been regrets. Accustomed to destroying letters from Shaw she did not like, she did so now with a vengeance: of the dozens of messages he sent in that decisive year, she preserved only seven. She was a little weary of his vanities, his teasing, his trick of repudiating love even while enjoying it. He was a "dearest silly-billy," but often a silly-billy after all. She had not been so worried about his illness at heart. It may have been enough to kill any man, "but of course," she told him, "*you* survive for, as I knew all along, you never were a man."[29] Her son had seized on the same elusiveness in Shaw's nature, but despised him for it. Protective of his mother at the same time he lived off her, he resented the fact that Shaw had not come forward to claim her. As for the man's genius, he disliked it as much as he reverenced Irving's. Shaw's marriage to a wealthy woman: "*That* is genius if you like," sneered Craig. But Ellen Terry was left with the vexing knowledge that the very qualities that most appealed to her in Shaw's nature had made him at last inaccessible.

CHAPTER SEVENTEEN

1898 - 1900

INSTEAD OF THE CUMBERSOME ring she had bought, Charlotte wore Shaw's grandmother's wedding band. Shaw's mother presented it to her, the surviving token of interest in the woman she called, to mock her regality, "Carlotta." As part of the business of marriage, Shaw settled an annuity upon his sixty-eight-year-old mother for life; if he could not make the payments, Charlotte would, without appearing to be the source. More delicate were the financial arrangements between Shaw and Charlotte. He did not want a lady bountiful (Charlotte liked playing one); nor did he wish to pay for her decidedly luxurious tastes in clothes, food, whisky, and travel. He could not, had he wanted to: although royalties from *The Devil's Disciple* were now well into their third thousand, his still uncertain earnings could not support a woman accustomed to living on a £4,000 yearly income from 100,000 well-invested pounds. They decided to share basic expenses, but not to pool their incomes. The arrangement was sensible, honorable.

Another reason for his capitulation to marriage, Shaw told Beatrice Webb, was the fact that with his serious illness, Charlotte had at last got beyond "a corrupt personal interest" to care for him in a less selfish way. She had emerged as a mother, as well as lover. Thus after twenty-two years Shaw, now almost forty-two, transferred from the house of the mother who had failed to a new wife-mother who would not. Horrified at Mrs. Shaw's neglect (the Mar had not seemed to notice the foot), Charlotte immediately transported her new husband to Pitfold, a rented house at Haslemere, Surrey, where air and care were to restore him to health. Shaw found himself fed promptly and well, doctored carefully, sheltered from stress. There would be no more hasty meals of porridge stirred up with one hand while he jotted down an article with the other. There would be no more squalor: no more littered study, soot-grimed desk and papers, unswept hearths. No more macaroni and eggs grabbed on the run at the Orange Grove or Gatti's. No more ramblings either through London: no more dashing off to the Charringtons in Chelsea, argumentative strolls with Archer along the Embankment, cycling in Battersea Park, strolls on frosty nights through Regent's Park or solitary stargazing atop Primrose Hill. No more scribbling on park benches, under lampposts, on racketing underground trains. No more appearances of the "terrible trio" in the stalls on opening night. No more stumping for socialism from London docks to Yorkshire meeting halls. Shaw had made a decisive break with the past.

He had married a woman accustomed to getting her way in most things. She was less easy with her role as wife and surrogate mother. For experience in love she could claim only a broken heart in Rome. She objected violently to the ordinary man-woman relationship: she thought it degrading, vulgar. She wanted a spiritual and intellectual union, yet doubted, perhaps, her ability to achieve it with the ever self-sufficient Shaw. She disliked women: it was an emotion founded in resentment of her mother, and her own self-doubt, for thinking meanly of her own sex gave her superiority. This insecurity combined with a proud reserve to make her prickly over things that bounced off the more hardened and tolerant Shaw. He had experienced her hypersensitivity over the proposed meeting with Ellen Terry. He found himself having to warn friends to be tactful, reminding Archer, for example, that he had been introduced to Charlotte at the Comedy Theatre, so "when you meet her remember that you know her already." The issue of his friends was a touchy one. She feared his past, which never *was* past for him. Often uneasy with Charlotte's "wincing at every accent of freedom" in his voice, Shaw now found that in exchange for love, care, and comfort, she was to regulate his life in other ways as well. Clearly there was going to be trouble with the Charringtons.

> I should like to see you down here [Shaw cautiously informed Charrington after they had been settled in the pleasant house on the south slope of Hindhead for more than a week]; BUT I rather suspect the thing will require some stage management; for Mrs. S. has a way of admitting that Mrs. C. has "genius" which does not absolutely convince me of her intention of joining our confederacy, which, after all, is a confederacy of three geniuses of a sort not largely represented in my wife's previous state of existence. . . . for the moment my instinct warns me to avoid any appearance of being unable to exist without seeing Janet. Not, observe, that she

is jealous of Janet, but that she sees herself on the verge of being hooked on to this confounded confederacy in which she has naturally neither part nor lot, and being compelled to *act* a theatrically effusive friendship with Janet, she acting badly and with scruple, & Janet acting floridly and with the greatest relish, the whole situation being quite revolting to her reserved habit.

I am not equal in my present condition to working this out to an exact manual of conduct for all parties; but for the moment I shall go slow in arranging a joyful meeting. I *must* coach Janet not to be magnanimous, not to be soulful, not to magnify the duty of being civil to Shaw's wife into an obligation to take that wife to her bosom like a radiant modern Mrs. Crummles. If she does, there will be hell, Charles Charrington—HELL.[1]

Shaw's new scruples did not prevent Charrington from requesting a loan of fifty pounds by return post. Shaw replied from a martyr's couch. The honeymoon had turned into a disaster. Barely restored from the operation, he had plunged into work again on his Wagner essay. On 17 June, dictating to Charlotte, he suddenly felt overcome by gloom and an intolerable sense of pressure. Calling a halt, he maneuvered upstairs to his bedroom on crutches to fetch some materials; coming down, however, "the crutches got planted behind my centre of gravity & shot me into the air. I snatched at a bannister on the landing above, and caught it in my right hand; but it snapped like an Argoed tree; and I was precipitated fifty fathom or thereabout into the hall, with my left arm doubled up in ruin under me . . . . Imagine poor Charlotte's feelings."[2] Worse than the splinted arm and bandaged foot, he had contracted nettle rash—frightful! —he was scratching in torment all night, ready to tear off the splints. No, Charrington could not have fifty pounds. Contrary to appearances, he had married without a settlement and had no more money than before. And it was no good either to assure Charlotte that Janet was just an impetuous child who meant no harm: Charlotte was far more impressed with Janet's cleverness than with her innocence. The two women would have to find each other's measure in time, without pressure from third parties. Since Shaw had offered Arnold Dolmetsch fifty pounds that July, assuring the musician he had more money "lying unused in the bank" than he needed, he had money to lend. The message was clear: there would be no money going out and no Janet coming in. Charlotte was not going to adopt Mr. and Mrs. Crummles along with Shaw.

The fortunes of the couple were at lower ebb, if possible, than ever before. The Independent Theatre had floundered, and after the Manchester *Macbeth*, Janet had few prospects. She was contemplating a tour of the Continent, particularly Germany, since she could play in German. Charrington was contemplating starting management again in London in the winter. Alternatively he was thinking about writing a history of the drama as a social force. What did Shaw think about it all—and could he, by the way (this in October)—possibly spare a hundred pounds for an old friend who had sacrificed himself to educate the British public in art?

"Your proposal to start management in London in the winter is just possible enough to fill me with terror," groaned Shaw. Charrington would want a drawing play, and where was he to get it? He could not count on Shaw. Besides, who would trust Charrington with a municipal theatre when everyone knew that he only wanted it as a pedestal for his Galatea? If he did write a history of the drama, he should write it alone, keeping Janet firmly out of it. "Only, that requires application & perseverance," lectured Shaw; "and you are a lazy old Alnaschar, always dreaming of vast enterprises between each smash of your basket of glass." As for Janet, the German notion was not at all bad. Let her go, let Charrington settle down to writing, and if Janet ran off with a German prince in the meantime—"so much the better." And in the meantime (he had apparently not made himself clear), he could not come up with one hundred pounds. Having decided that the Charringtons had shamelessly exploited her husband's meager income in the past, Charlotte had hardened her heart against them. Should he hand over £100 now, she would seriously set herself to counter the Charringtons' "malignant influence" over him. Did Charrington really want to stir up an infernal row? After all, he should console himself. Far better "to be on the hill of Difficulty than in the Valley of the Shadow of Death" like Shaw.[3]

It was a valley into which Shaw had gazed more than once that year since that first glimpse of those dark reaches which had reconciled him both to death and to marriage. In late September Charlotte had written jubilantly to Lucy that the foot had all but healed; a few days later she was in despair: the wound had burst; no healing process had been going on after all.[4] Reckless at the discovery that he was no better, Shaw revolted against his invalid chair and had his new bicycle brought out. Disregarding Charlotte's terror, he attempted to mount, felt his long disused foot turn under him, and pitched headlong to the ground. The sprained ankle proved more anguishing than either the foot or arm. Worse, another operation awaited him, and until then, the endless warnings of the doctors who threatened him with death unless he relented and ate meat. But he had no faith in doctors, in medicine, or in the success of another operation, although he would submit to it. Satisfied he had not shirked life, he did not much care now about the outcome, except that, inconveniently, Charlotte had set up an interest in his life.[5] This was not stoicism, which Charlotte could understand, but indifference; and as Shaw knew, it disturbed and frustrated her. She was a prime worrier anyway. She had longed for a cause to engage her mind and heart, and thought she found it in nurturing genius. How unflattering really that

Shaw had responded first by falling down the stairs and now off his bicycle: it appeared he was not taking her cause seriously. She seethed with misgivings, with a solicitude for his welfare that she could not make him feel. There was, she had discovered, a "certain way" in which her husband did not care for himself: he did not seek happiness, nor care whether he lost it. And again, this indifference was not flattering: a new husband should cling to life for the happiness of sharing it with his new bride. She could perhaps take a little comfort in the fact that his invalidism had postponed the troublesome question of sex indefinitely.

Charlotte struggled to cope, and succeeded in most things admirably. Their visitors were limited to Shaw's male friends, whom she liked. The nurse, a good-looking woman, displayed under attentive eye a properly professional devotion to her patient. She duly found and rented a new house, Blen-Cathra, when the pending operation made it clear they could not return as planned to London. But life with a sprite who dreamed now instead of slept and found consolation in the Book of Job tested her self-possession to the utmost. "I shall be *very* glad to have you back for every reason," she confessed to Beatrice Webb in November; "but, among others, for the selfish one that I long for a little advice and help from someone whose judgement and good sense I really feel that I can depend upon."[6]

The only power a god can teach, Shaw had written in *The Perfect Wagnerite* that long summer of marriage and illness, is "the power of doing without happiness." Besides being "jam full of socialism in the manner of Ruskin," this explication of *The Ring* tackled another facet of Wagner that had disturbed Shaw since the days Archer had observed him in the Reading Room turning over the score of that "poem of destruction and death" *Tristan und Isolde:* the composer's decadent fascination with love and death—not "*leuchtende Liebe, lachender Tod*": "Love that illumines, laughing at death," but love and death "involving each other so closely as to be virtually one and the same thing." Shaw found *The Ring* still tainted with that decadence, but only when philosophy failed Wagner and he was driven back to the love panacea: the "prescription of a romantic nostrum for all ills." Now Shelley had prescribed love as a cure for all personal and social ills, but in Wagner "a certain shadow of night and death" had fallen over love, the degenerate notion that "the supreme good of love is that it so completely satisfies the desire for life that after it the Will to Live ceases to trouble us and we are at last content to achieve the highest happiness of death." Shaw fought the concept vigorously. The love duet in the first act of *Die Walküre*, the ecstatic love duet of Siegfried and Brynhild—these were experiences of passion which it was much better, like the vast majority, never to have passed through except, perhaps, as brief moments of holiday recreation. They did not play a large part in Wagner's life, surely, nor even his works. Finally, argued Shaw, the "only faith which any reasonable disciple can gain from The Ring is not in love, but in life itself as a tireless power which is continually driving onward and upward—not, please observe, being beckoned or drawn by *Das Ewig Weibliche* or any other external sentimentality, but growing from within, by its own inexplicable energy, into ever higher and higher forms of organization, the strengths and the needs of which are continually superseding the institutions which were made to fit our former requirements."[7] It was interesting that he pointedly affirmed Life and Will over Love and Death just when he had surrendered, in effect, to the latter.

During that summer and fall of chair-bound invalidism, Shaw had not entirely forgotten Ellen. She had begun rehearsals for a spring tour of her own that offered an alternative to minor parts with Irving; and although Shaw naturally jumped on her choice of *Othello* and *The Lady of Lyons*, Ellen's reply was irrefutable: she had nothing else of interest. The same letter thanked him for his concern over other "difficulties": that summer her twenty-six-year-old son, sick of a rabbit-cozy marriage, abandoned his wife to rendezvous by the sea at Dunwich with a young actress. They had spent the night in the same bed only to be greeted unpleasantly in the morning by "two legal persons writing down in their notebooks the answers to questions put on behalf of the wife."[8] No, Ellen assured Shaw: nothing serious had happened. Ted was a fool—a clever one—but not a rascal; she was not in trouble. *She* had been worried about Shaw, writing Charlotte at news of the accident on the stairs, "Oh you poor poor darling woman—it makes me shrill all over to read your news—I can see him! . . . Poor 'Gill'! Poor 'Jack'!"[9] But now, besides a dimming career, she felt the fate of Ted's wife May and their four children rest heavily upon her shoulders.

The fate of Henry Irving that fall did not seem to touch her as it once would have. Attempting to make up a loss of £6,000 on the past season, Irving had set out for the provinces with cast and crew. In Edinburgh, making his way in the dark to a railway station still under construction, he found himself mired in mud and puddles. He rode to Glasgow in an unheated car, his elegant thin shoes wet. He struggled through *Madame Sans-Gêne* on 6 October although every breath was a swordstab; a doctor summoned by Stoker hurried him back to his hotel after the last curtain and there diagnosed pneumonia and pleurisy: Irving was dangerously ill. The third catastrophe was upon him. For Ellen it meant playing to thin and disappointed houses. She was desperate enough to turn to Shaw the unplayable. As luck would have it, none of the plays they were equipped to present on tour had any good parts for her, now the star. What about *You Never Can Tell*, the play that had so nearly opened in the West End? And where was the Cleopatra play?[10]

But Shaw had settled upon Forbes-Robertson and Mrs. Campbell, Irving and Terry's "heirs apparent," for his *Caesar and Cleopatra*, finally completed 9 December. His opinion of the play had fluctuated with his health. Writing to Charrington from the Valley of the Shadow of Death, he called it "no use," "the same silly stuff," "no drama in it." By 30 December, however (the foot was healing after all), he liked it well enough. "Caesar is a fine part and Cleopatra will pass," he told Ellen, whom, with his returning health, he now loved again in "the ungentlemanliest, ungodliest manner." To Charrington he announced that he had at last "gotten up behind the carriage." He had felt some scruple about *You Never Can Tell;* that was over. His new play was "an unashamed prostitution of [his] talent to the sole purpose of pleasing people."[11] On Friday, 13 January 1899, reported Lucy, her brother and his bride appeared at Fitzroy Square, Shaw "looking splendid but still going on crutches and not able to put his foot to the ground." They were going after lunch to tea at Forbes-Robertson's to talk about *Caesar and Cleopatra*. Stella Campbell had once more proved she could not play Shakespeare: her Lady Macbeth that fall had been roundly condemned, and by no one more than herself. If she could not play Shakespeare, perhaps she could play Shaw. If she could not, Caesar played by the classically handsome Forbes was after all the fine part. It appeared that at last Shaw had another prospect of a West End production at his fingertips.

In early December, after two months convalescing in dreary Glasgow, Irving had been well enough to be moved. "Poor old King H. is at his downest," Ellen noted in her diary for January, "and I'm amazed at the few in number of his useful friends." The actor-manager was now at Bournemouth: "No word from him, however! Is it shyness? Indifference? Anger? *What?* I rather think self-consciousness by indifference out of conceit! . . . I wonder how his other friends and lovers feel to him. I have contempt and affection and admiration. What a mixture!" Eventually she received a letter, asking her to come to Bournemouth. She went and found him "stouter, very grey, sly-looking, and more cautious than ever. Bother!" He had summoned her, he solemnly announced, not only to inform her that he was broken in health, but that he was what was commonly called *ruined.*

Ellen refused to shed tears. As long as they could act, she argued, they could trot around the world and pick up money, with only "the magic book of Shakespeare" in their suitcase. But Irving had other plans, and had summoned her to Bournemouth to impart them. He intended to go around the English provinces with a very small company playing *The Bells, Louis XI,* and *Waterloo.* A stunned Ellen could hardly believe her ears. Where did *she* come in? "Oh, well, for the present, at all events, there's no chance of acting at the Lyceum," said Irving, looking exceedingly silly. "For the present, you can, of course, er, *do as you like!*"[12] Ellen stormed back to London the next day, immediately asked for a tour, and within a week had dates penciled in till the following Christmas. She vented some of her feelings upon Shaw: Henry was "a dear Silly Billy—just an *H-ass!*" even "a silly Ass," even "silly fool-assical."[13] She was only mildly comforted when told that plans had changed, that a syndicate would take over the Lyceum, and that a play would be produced that spring after all. *She* had already suggested a syndicate to H.I. at Bournemouth, had even recommended the half-written *Robespierre—* and Sardou's play it was to be with no acknowledgment, of course, that they had acted on her suggestions. No: only the assumption that she would immediately cancel her tour and trot back to them; not a word of thanks; all taken as a matter of course. And even though she had suggested *Robespierre*, she knew it was a one-man play with her part a nothing that any beginner could walk through. "If H. were not in the dumps just now," she told Shaw, "I'd 'see him further' before I'd do it!"[14]

Robespierre opened 15 April, and a captivated audience realized that once more Irving had seized upon a character and made it triumphantly his own. Exhausted from her tour, dulled by work, Ellen stumbled over her lines noticeably but, though Archer winced in his review, was forgiven again by an indulgent public. The emotion, the showy production, the glittering audiences—the Lyceum seemed reassuringly what it had been. Yet behind the scenes, Irving, no businessman, and baffled by a poor contract with the new Lyceum company, still saw his receipts fall below his gigantic expenses; and Ellen brooded on the withering of her career.

She turned more and more to Shaw. She had encouraged *The Man of Destiny*, but not with the sense of urgency that marked her pleas to see his *Caesar and Cleopatra*. Was it really, firmly in the hands of Mrs. Pat? It had been, and was not any longer. Charlotte herself had suggested that Stella Campbell might do a copyright performance; surprisingly the lady agreed. Having temporarily separated with Forbes-Robertson, Stella went on tour with a company of her own. At the Theatre Royal in Newcastle-on-Tyne on 15 March 1899, Mrs. Pat successfully turned Shaw's anti-romance back to romance, playing his young kitten of the Sphinx as an experienced pantheress.[15] Despite that disappointment, Shaw tried to lure "the Pat-Cat" down to Blen-Cathra to talk about playing the first act as a curtain raiser, but Mrs. Campbell did not come—a good thing, perhaps, since, typically, Charlotte resented her performance far more than Shaw. Nor did she commit herself further to Shaw's great play. As for Forbes-Robertson, *Macbeth* had cleaned him out: he had no theatre and no money, he told Shaw, and could not risk the elaborate production. Even Mansfield betrayed him. "Oh, oh, oh!!!" taunted Shaw, swallowing his disappointment. "*Can't* play Julius Caesar, and want an-

other twopenny melodrama. . . . Caesar will await you at Philippi."[16]
Apparently he had gotten up behind the carriage in vain.

Mrs. Campbell having disappointed him, Shaw turned his thoughts
again to Ellen. He had been frankly unchivalrous over Cleopatra, sending
her the play to read, but telling her that she was too old for the part—an
opinion which Ellen said she "took unquestioningly," although she could
not believe the public would agree with him. On 3 May he began Ellen's
play in compensation. "My conscience was so burdened with the infamy
of having written plays for Pat-Cats and other people about whom I
dont care a straw . . . and made no play for you, that it had to be
done."[17]

"Made" was an apt word, for Shaw conscientiously tried to compensate Ellen for all Irving's one-man shows by creating a one-woman show
of her own. He had written an anti-siren part for Mrs. Pat, who played
sirens; now he created an anti-romantic part for Ellen, who played romantic heroines—and evidently expected appreciation from both. On
7 July he polished off Lady Cicely's dismissal of Brassbound ("I have
never been in love with any real person; and I never shall. How could I
manage people if I had that mad little bit of self left in me?"), and notified Ellen that her playwright had finished her play—"a shocking leading
lady business" with all the other characters merest doormats. "Two
months work, with some £60 worth of journalism stolen out of the
middle of it. And yet you think I do not love you: you do *not* believe
each word I say."[18] He could not put the play in her hands yet: Charlotte
had to decipher his notebook scrawl and make a typed copy for Miss
Dickens in London; but the play existed, though he died tomorrow.

His reward came quickly. "I don't think that Play of yours will do for
me at all! You suggest it is a *one part play!* I loathe that sort of thing."
Two days later she was equally unenthusiastic: "I don't like the play one
bit. Only *one* woman in it? How *ugly* it will look, and there will not be
a penny in it." Undeterred by these incivilities, Shaw posted the play at
the end of July. It was done: the only thing on earth in his power to do
for her.

Her reply was long enough in coming to make him fear she had tossed
the script into the wastebasket:

No one but Shaw could have written the last Play Cap. B's Conversion
(?) but it's not the sort of play for me in the least. The three I think
finest are Arms and the Man, Mrs. Warren's Profession, and the Cleopatra thing.

I couldn't do this one, and I believe it would never do for the stage.
The two parts, the man and woman, are right; but that *bore* Drinkwater!
Mrs. Pat for Lady C again! I couldn't do it . . . it is surely for Mrs. Pat.
Not for me. . . .[19]

How was it that Ellen dismissed a play with a heroine "between thirty and forty, tall, very good-looking, sympathetic, intelligent, tender and humorous . . . of great vitality and humanity" as not her kind of play? For one thing, she had been corrupted by Lyceum spectacle, and had difficulty believing that a play without splendid scenic and atmospheric effects, choreographed crowd scenes, and gorgeous costuming was really a play. Much of her stunning effect on the Lyceum stage had been pictorial. She could see no pictorial effects in *Brassbound*, and concluded that it was "more fitted for the closet than the stage," and would not act well. The atmosphere of the play also distressed her. Shaw had pitted the civilizing impact of a humane, well-bred woman against male barbarism, yet the whole impressed her as altogether too masculine and barbarous. And then to play a woman who has never loved, who dismisses the hero with "And what an escape!" It might be Shaw, but it was not Ellen Terry. But at the heart of her protest lay perhaps the fact that Shaw had understood her too well. For the truth was that she was very strong, and the result had been that men very much let her stand on her own two feet and even, occasionally, prop them. And here was Shaw, seeing through and through her; recognizing how much she cherished that "mad bit of self"; revealing that much as she wanted to see herself as a romantically weak woman, she would feed any number of lovers to the sharks in order to maintain her independence. Oh, he had not understood her at all!

"Alas! dear Ellen, is it really so?" replied Shaw. "Then I can do nothing for you." It was a bitter moment, for, as he had told her from the start, love for him was based on usefulness. He could not take unless he could give, and she had refused his play, the only important thing he had to give her. She had also refused him an Ellen Terry success, the only important thing she had to give him. The moment was equally bitter for Ellen. She needed a play very badly, yet was convinced now that Shaw had meant her play either for Mrs. Pat or to be published along with the other two Plays for Puritans. "Of course you never really meant Lady Cicely for me," she goaded.

Recovered from his disappointment, Shaw launched an attack, using the same weapon he had hurled at Alice, at Florence, at Elizabeth, and at Janet. He had not failed Ellen; Ellen had failed him:

Listen to me, woman with no religion. . . . Think of all that has been rising up under your eyes in Europe for years past, Bismarck worship, Stanley worship, Dr. Jim worship, and now at last Kitchener worship with dead enemies dug up and mutilated. Think also on the law—the gallows, penal servitude, hysterical clamoring for the lash, mere cowardice masquerading as "resolute government," "law and order" and the like. Well, how have you felt about these things? Have you had any real belief in the heroism of the filibuster? Have you had any sympathy with the punishments of the judge? Have you found in your own life and your own small affairs no better way, no more instructive heart wisdom, no warrant for trusting to the good side of people instead of terrorizing the bad side of them. I—poor idiot!—thought the distinction of Ellen Terry was that she had this heart wisdom, and managed her own little world as Tolstoy would have our Chamberlains & Balfours & German Emperors & Kitcheners & Lord Chief Justices and other slaves of false ideas & imaginary fears manage Europe. I accordingly give you a play in which you stand in the very place where Imperialism is most believed to be necessary. . . . I try to shew you fearing nobody and managing them all as Daniel managed the lions, not by cunning—above all, not by even a momentary appeal to Cleopatra's stand-by, their passions, but by simple moral superiority. . . . In every other play I have ever written—even in Candida—I have prostituted the actress more or less by making the interest in her partly a sexual interest: only the *man* in the Devil's Disciple draws clear of it. In Lady Cicely I have done without this, and gained a greater fascination by it. And you are disappointed. . . . Oh Ellen, Ellen, Ellen, Ellen, Ellen. This is the end of everything.[20]

A woman who has faced the loss of youthful sex appeal and with it her career perhaps could not be expected to enjoy having this loss confirmed with a heroine who excites no sexual interest. Besides, it was only Shaw the puritan who found such sexual interest degrading. Nor did Ellen Terry particularly care whether onstage she stood "in the very place where Imperialism is most believed to be necessary." But Shaw's attack stung her. She replied that he had mistaken her objections: Lady Cicely was so much herself that the public would not think she was acting and would not come in great numbers—and she wanted them to come in great numbers. And how could he hurt her so cruelly!

If you wanted to make me weep on a nice morning and feel quite miserable you have done it. . . . And why do you pitch into me so and make me feel quite ill just as I'm going for a ride. . . . Half an hour ago I was so quiet and merry and then comes your letter and you talk to me of the brute donkey STANLEY! And as if that were not enough to upset any calm and quiet peacefullness in a woman, you also are unkind between every line of your dear blessed letter.

I hate it.

I was getting well, and now I shall be ill again—and all you![21]

Ellen did manage to come down with a sharp attack of flu, during which her maid read her *Captain Brassbound's Conversion* several times through, exclaiming loyally that she would never *dream* Lady Cicely could be her mistress. Paying a charity visit to the poor after her recovery, however, Ellen noticed a flash of recognition light her maid's face; mixing with high society a week later, Ellen caught the same ripple of amusement. She tackled the maid the next morning. Suppressing laughter, the servant stammered, "Oh, I'm very sorry. Excuse me, but Lady Cicely is *so* like you! She gets her way in *everything—just like you!*" "I can't understand it," protested Ellen; but by mid-September she had come to love the play more and more. Could she show it to Irving?

"With pleasure," Irving replied gravely when Ellen proposed his reading the play. Oh, how she knew that "with pleasure"! It struck terror into her heart. Perhaps she should not let him see the play after all. And then he absolutely rejected her timid proposal that *Brassbound* might do for their American tour in October, and as for the Lyceum opening the following March, he had already chosen *Charles IX*. Ellen knew that play—it was "simply *frightful*." She had submitted to *The Medicine Man,* but if *Charles IX* could not be rewritten into something decent she would be obliged to leave the Lyceum. And then she would do *Brassbound* herself in a first-class London theatre like the Garrick and afterward take it herself to America. Could she have the play for her own, she asked Shaw, even though she could not play it at once? Lady Cicely in her hands was worth a great deal more to him than Lady Cicely in anybody else's.

Shaw replied from Ruan Minor, Cornwall, where Charlotte had taken him to bathe the still weak ankle he had managed to sprain a third time alighting from a high-frame bicycle on the bad foot. Co-operative enough to quote her pages of terms should Irving want the play, he had little faith this time in either a Lyceum or a Terry production. Ellen must search her conscience. Did she really intend to leave the Lyceum? If not, did she seriously think she could elope with his play and remain Irving's leading lady at the same time? Was there actually a ghost of a chance that she would venture America on her own? If, as he strongly suspected, the answer to these questions was no, then could she, in all fairness, expect to monopolize a play she could not perform? Charlotte was spiriting him off on a southern cruise on 21 September to restore his health completely: he could do nothing for six weeks about anything. Besides her letters were incorrigibly vague.

Shaw must have known that Irving would never produce a play of his. "Good Lord!" the actor had exploded when Ellen mentioned Shaw's scale of rising percentages. "Simply absurd! *No* one has such terms. The utmost should be £60 per week. That's what I gave Tennyson."[22] "He was quite excited," Ellen reported to Shaw. But Irving did agree to allow Ellen to copyright the play. The Lyceum Company with the three sets spared in the fire set out for the provinces in September prior to sailing to America. In Liverpool on 10 October, having gone through the motions of posters, programs, and the token guinea at the box office, Ellen read Lady Cicely against Laurence Irving's Brassbound. The play had grown on her during the past weeks: she had studied Lady Cicely and been *transported*. The ending—Shaw's comic, triumphant ending—had seemed to her more and more tragic: she could just *see* it: it would be a triumph for them both. But the copyright performance blasted her hopes. "They all loathe Lady Cicely," she told Shaw, now sailing through the Grecian archipelago on the SS *Lusitania*. "A 'tremendous humbug.' 'Arch' (!). 'Detestable woman,' etc. etc. I said 'It's because I read it wrong,' but Edy who was in front, absorbed, and loving the play, says I could not read the lines other than I did, but that it seemed to her you *thought* your Lady C. *one* sort of woman and have *written* another. Conveyed another idea. She doesn't think Lady C. is shown to be either very clever or humorous, or vital, and certainly not 'of great humanity.'" If nobody had loved Lady Cicely, however, everybody had loved the play—or almost everybody. Henry Irving had not come near the place. "Horrid of him," said Ellen.[23]

As Ellen sailed for America, another actress returned to England. War had been declared in the Transvaal, and Janet Achurch, playing Ibsen in Vienna, had found her contract canceled and nothing to do but return to Mr. Micawber's bosom again. She found Charlie in fine fettle: elected to the Fabian Executive, lecturing on imperialism, full of a new theatrical experiment, the Stage Society and, ever loyal, of schemes for starring Janet in all the Society's productions.

The Shaws returned on 30 October, the cruise having taught them much about each other. Shaw had discovered that in moving about from port to port, from cathedral to mosque, from hotel to inn, Charlotte was in her element. Seasickness, wretched weather, uncivil waiters, bad food, sight-seeing fatigue, late trains, bumpy roads, missed connections, bedbugs, indigestion, filth—all wrought her talents for coping and subduing to the highest pitch, talents which, in the quiet luxury of everyday living, were quite wasted. A real Lady Cicely, she demanded, coaxed, charmed, and paid; and Shaw found himself organized, waited on, and provided for as he had never been in his life. Charlotte found, on the other hand, that her husband heartily disliked the "guzzling, lounging, gambling, dog's life" on board ship as well as the peripatetic roving from hotel to hotel; that he never forgot work for a moment, even if he abstained from pencil and notebook; but that he was remarkably good-tempered and obliging about pleasing her, and thus a good companion.

Of course, he *would* let himself fall into the arms of other women. She had been furious (or so Shaw hopefully reported to Beatrice Webb) to find Beatrice's sister Maggie, who sailed with them, nursing her seasick bridegroom on arrowroot tea when she came up on deck from her cabin.

Nor was she pleased to go back to her hotel alone one evening in Granada, leaving Shaw and Maggie prowling happily about the shops. "The strain on Charlotte's good sense is fearful," Shaw told Beatrice, "—all the worse because I am by no means a reluctant victim, there being between Maggie & myself a sort of rapscallionly freemasonry, as between a couple of tramps, of which Charlotte intensely disapproves."[24] It was that freemasonry Charlotte had dreaded with Janet and with anyone else from Shaw's past; she had hoped to leave the past behind by abducting her husband abroad. She had not succeeded; and the conflict between Charlotte's proud reserve and Shaw's irrepressible flirtatiousness could be severe.

On returning, Shaw moved some of his belongings from Fitzroy Square to a third-floor converted boxroom off Charlotte's bedroom at 10 Adelphi Terrace. The year drew to a close with irresistible predictability. There was a preface to write for his *Three Plays for Puritans;* there was a single performance of *You Never Can Tell* at the Royalty on 26 November which was largely ignored by the press[25]; and there was a letter from Janet asking for thirty-five pounds. Still patient, but adamant, Shaw offered Janet a list of his expenses. Out of the £750 a year Charlotte had finally settled on him, £300 went to his mother, £400 must go for repairs at Fitzroy Square and £150 for the rent, £100 for the education of one of Pakenham Beatty's daughters, and the rest for half the expenses at Adelphi Terrace—which of course he could not pay. He would not lend her money again, not "whilst grass grows or water runs." And again, it was with irresistible predictability that he then heard that the Charringtons were taking rooms opposite the British Museum. "If I mistake not," Shaw answered dryly, "Charlotte once thought of taking a flat there, but found it too expensive. That would be so jolly like you."[26]

With the arrival of the twentieth century, Shaw looked back at what the nineteenth had taught him as a playwright. His plays, even when written for the Forbes-Robertsons, Irvings, Terrys, and Campbells, were still not commercially practicable in London. "But it doesnt matter," he told Beatrice Mansfield: "I shall write no more practicable plays—no more Devil's Disciples & Caesars & Captain Brassbounds. The contemporary playgoer doesnt want me, and I dont want him (or her); and there are terrible things still to be said. My next play will be a horror—and a masterpiece."[27]

Whatever hopes he still may have entertained for Ellen doing *Brassbound* independently in the near future were canceled by a letter of 28 January from Toledo, Ohio—a letter at once penitent and firm. Until this very moment, she assured Shaw, she had virtually made up her mind that she would never act with Irving again. And then Irving, impressed with the crowds for *Robespierre*, had proposed another American tour in the autumn of 1900. What could she say? Her wheat-pale hair was getting quite gray. Frequent headaches terrified her with the thought of breaking up under anxiety and pressure. Would even a farewell tour provide enough harvest against old age? She rather dreaded poverty. Her needs were few, but if she could not help others she would take it very hard indeed. Most of all, Irving had touched her deeply by wanting her. "I appear to be of strange *use* to H.," she told her "old sweetheart" who seemed to need no one, "and I have always thought to be *useful, really* useful to any one person *is* rather fine and satisfactory." If he only knew how hard it was for her to agree to another tour, he would think her angelic: she loathed the very idea. But did this mean that she must give up Lady Cicely since there was no chance now of playing her until the autumn of 1901?[28]

"Very well, dear Ellen: we cry off Brassbound," replied Shaw, who could not well argue his own doctrine of use. He had always known and said that when it came to the test, she would not leave Irving and the Lyceum. The next words from the man who had urged her defection for years must have amazed her. "And apart from business reasons, the breaking up of an old partnership like yours and H.I.'s is not a thing to be done except on extreme occasions." She was quite right in signing for another tour: to throw away a certain £2,400 for uncertainty was madness. However:

> . . . I want you to face the fact that this means that you are not going to do Brassbound at all—never, world without end. . . . So now for one of my celebrated *volte faces*. I hold on pretty hard until the stars declare themselves against me, and then I always give up and try something else with a promptitude which seems cynical and unfeeling to the slow witted Englishman who only tells himself his misfortunes by degrees. And now I recognize that you and I can never be associated as author and player—that you will remain Olivia, and that Lady Cicely is some young creature in short skirts at a High School at this moment. I have pitched so many dreams out of the window that one more or less makes little difference—in fact, by this time I take a certain Satanic delight in doing it and noting how little it hurts me. So out of the window you go, my dear Ellen; and off goes the play to my agents as in the market for the highest bidder.[29]

The loss of Ellen was somewhat tempered by the fact that both the New Century Theatre and the Stage Society were clamoring for his plays. Archer had approached him in January in the name of the N.C.T.: why shouldn't their fourth production be Shaw? His only stipulation was that whether they tried *Brassbound* or *Candida*, Elizabeth Robins must have the lead.

Time had not mellowed the relationship between Shaw and Elizabeth Robins. It was true that upon discovering back in December 1898 that she and the novelist C. E. Raimond were one and the same, he had gotten hold of *An Open Question*, her latest, read it, and announced to Janet: "The egotism turns out to be genius after all." To Robins he had written that he was glad to see his original estimate of her vindicated: to discover that Miss Robins, the American snob, was a lie, and St. Elizabeth the truth. Yet he could not forget her chilling dislike. "Don't answer this letter," he cautioned. "You write novels & plays very well; but the thing you can't write well is a letter to me. I am very sorry for it, and do not deny that it is my own fault."[30] On second thought, however, he found her only another George Eliot, burdened with the same outmoded ethical system he had rejected back in the eighties for Marx. Archer's judgment with its "Sir Walter Scottish social consciousness" was similarly disabled. He expected any day, in fact, to meet Archer in an overcoat with an Astrakhan collar and his hair dyed purple, talking literature from a world of outworn shadows. No, the N.C.T. might have had Shaw for the asking—and had never asked. Best now for it to specialize in the George Eliot direction: that was his serious advice to the Astrakhan collar and Miss Elizabeth.[31]

To Charrington's Stage Society, a sort of Sunday night Independent Theatre that had culled a surprising three hundred members at two guineas each, Shaw had bequeathed *You Never Can Tell* and *Candida*. He watched the single performance of the former in November and concluded that although he was ashamed of its "tricks and laughs and popularities," he would hear no more nonsense about its being a bad stage play. By May Shaw's old hopes of Ellen as Lady Cicely had revived; if he could possibly induce Forbes-Robertson and Terry to do a performance for the Stage Society, he asked Charrington, could funds and room be found for it? Ellen loved the part so much (or pretended to); and he could see no other possibility of her playing it, tied firmly again to the Lyceum as she was. But dreams of a Terry-Forbes-Robertson *Brassbound* evaporated in the more tangible realities of a performance of *Candida* by the Stage Society and Janet in July. Not that he did not try to lure Ellen with *Candida* under Janet's very nose. But: "Bernard I *am* back," wrote Ellen. "But I can't act on the first of July. . . . I say No—I also say D— no."[32] She was rehearsing in fact for still another revival of *Olivia*—Olivia at her time of life, she moaned, angry at having to do the revival. It was the audience she pitied, for though she felt quite young, even playing with actors half her age, her public would not know how young she felt if she could not look young.

Shaw turned rather testily to the matter of casting Eugene Marchbanks who should be able (so much for *Candida* as a woman's play) to play both Candida and Morell right off the stage. Charrington was urging a young man named Harley Granville-Barker; Shaw wanted Henry V. Esmond: he had seen both act, and since he couldn't remember Barker at all, concluded that Esmond was the man. "I am prepared for a struggle on your part and Janet's to induce me to consent to everything most ruinous to both of us," protested Shaw. "But I WONT. Unless I can get a Eugene of Esmond's standing, the play shall not be done." He thought he knew very well why the jealous Charrington wanted Barker: Esmond would outclass Janet.[33] Then Shaw went to a Stage Society production of Hauptmann's *Friedensfest* on 10 June, translated by Janet and a Dr. Wheeler, and starring Janet, Charrington, and the despised Barker. Despite a terrible headache, Shaw underwent an immediate conversion, notifying Charrington the next day that he withdrew his objections to the elegant and high-strung, twenty-three-year-old actor. If Esmond could not be had, Barker would make "an excellent and rather more interesting substitute."

In the event, Harley Granville-Barker did play the poet. One Sunday evening private performance at the theatrical dead of the year was not what Shaw had hoped for *Candida*, yet the cast did not utterly disgrace her. Charrington as Morell began well, but affected more and more by the pathos of the part, became almost inarticulate with emotion: how fortunate the play had not gone five acts, thought Shaw, as he surely would have been speechless in the fourth and petrified in the fifth. Yet although Edith Craig had not been able to muster a trace of expression during rehearsals, she managed to bloom that night as Proserpine Garnett. And Janet—well, he had held the part for her for six and a half years simply because she once said that for two hours she could *be* Candida, but since then Janet had lost the power to express anything onstage but Janet. Shaw despaired; then decided that her genius finally kindled and "she won at the post." But it was Barker who was the success of the piece. "It was an astonishing piece of luck to hit on him," said Shaw to Archer, forgetting Charrington's acute talent-scouting.

Candida was scarcely performed when Shaw began to worry about a cast for *Captain Brassbound's Conversion*, the next Stage Society undertaking planned for December. By the end of October the question of a Lady Cicely had become pressing enough for him to cast out one last bait to Ellen. "A play of mine entitled Captain Brassbound's Conversion is to be performed privately by the Stage Society, probably under the new title 'Ellen Brassheart's Obduracy,'" wrote Shaw, attempting to sweep up the pieces of the actress he had thrown out the window. "It was written for a deserving actress employed in a subordinate capacity by an Ogre at one of our leading theatres. Neither my personal advances nor my play, however, made any impression on this insensible female; and now the question is, who is to play the part? The matter is urgent;

and I shall have to appeal in desperation to Mrs. Kendal . . . unless you will be good enough to suggest another way out of the difficulty."[34]

A sick Ellen answered from uncomfortable lodgings in Manchester, where she had been stuck for two weeks. Although the tour had been thus far successful, both the stars were ailing. Irving terrified her sometimes by his exhaustion and weakness, although it was only then that he permitted himself to express some gratitude toward her and the company. When he was well, "anything so icy, indifferent, and almost contemptuous" she had never seen. She might (she told Shaw, scribbling between visitors who kept streaming in and out) approach Irving once more about Brassbound; he might consent if she were to act one Saturday matinee a week and he were clear of it, for he emphatically did not like Shaw's Comic Opera, as he called it.[35] "Oh let us have done with it," replied Shaw by return post, "and never mention it again." His reply was an admission of respect for Irving. If his play went to the Lyceum, Shaw wanted Irving to bind himself to produce it in London, to nurse it as tenderly and as lavishly as he nursed his other plays, and above all, to play in it himself.

From Liverpool Ellen admitted defeat. Had these been the old days, she might have persuaded Henry—but now, "farewell Lady C." "Ah, I feel so certain Henry just hates me!" she cried to Shaw. "I can only *guess* at it, for he is exactly the same sweet-mannered person he was when 'I felt so certain' Henry loved me! We have not met for years now, except before other people, where my conduct exactly matches his of course. All my own fault. It is *I* am changed—not he. The last four or five years, grain by grain, my respect for him has filtered out, & now I can only *care* for him, & think not highly at all of him. It's all right, but it has squeezed me up dreadfully. . . . So on I go—oblige me by burning this at once my dear friend."[36] Shaw instantly took the credit: "Of course he hates you when you talk to him about me."

Despite Janet's post win in *Candida*, Shaw shuddered at the thought of Ellen's part in her hands.[37] He wanted Lena Ashwell, who had impressed him at the Lyceum, he wanted Irene Vanbrugh or Mrs. Kendal or even May Harvey—he wanted anyone but Janet. On 7 November he confronted the Charringtons, whom he had not seen since the *Candida* performance. The issue was not Lady Cicely, however, but *Candida* again, which they wanted to produce at the Comedy as a matinee. Shaw refused point-blank. The truth was finally out: Janet had only pulled through *Candida* by a miracle and wasn't the right woman for the part at all; Charrington had been "grotesquely damnable" as Morell; he would be damned before he let them touch his play again. Rage. Fury. Janet hissed "everything she could lay tongue to"; Charrington was "cut to the soul": loud were the lamentations and accusations. "It was the more cruel," Shaw reported to Ellen, "because my marriage has cut me off a good deal from them, Charlotte being most rampageously anti-Charringtonian." Shaw stood unmoved as the tempest raged, however, until "the exhausted ocean calmed itself & the sky shone again." The Charringtons eventually drew the tatters of their dignity about them, and renounced all moral rights to Janet's play forever; and Shaw could return to Adelphi Terrace to report that he had successfully withstood the siege.

A month before the scheduled production of 16 December Lady Cicely was still not cast. Marion Terry? Dorothea Baird? Winifred Emery? Alma Murray? Mary Moore? Lena Ashwell? Mrs. Kendal? Ada Rehan? "There's nothing to be done but drop the play & turn on The Lady from the Sea, (or When We Dead Awaken) without any further hesitation," Shaw told Charrington. But Charrington had one last card to play, and played it. On 30 November Shaw went before a frustrated Stage Society committee and announced that Janet Achurch would play Lady Cicely. He, Shaw, had insisted upon it.

In the end a month's rehearsing had to be compressed into a few days. Laurence Irving, with considerable talent but, like Janet, constitutionally incapable of striking less than twelve on stage, took on Captain Brassbound. Barker rehearsed the part of the American naval officer Captain Kearney with such a sprucely British accent that Shaw insisted he immediately seize a real American off the streets and live with him day and night until the curtain went up. The scenery came in piece by piece, scraped together from various theatres and various plays. Laurence Irving seldom could rehearse since he was playing on tour with the Lyceum Company and had to commute by train from Sheffield and Leeds. He could not even be let off on the Saturday before the production, Ellen told Shaw: he had a long, excruciatingly funny part in *The Lyons Mail*, and with the best will in the world (which Irving notably lacked) his father would not let him go. If it would be any help, Laurence could come straight from Leeds to Barkston Gardens with his man on Sunday, where she would feed him and care for him and deliver him to the Stage Society in one piece.

Ellen had heard the news of the production with enthusiasm. The Lyceum tour ended 22 December: she would miss Lady Cicely, or so she thought, until Irving suddenly gave in to the doctors, admitted he was very ill, and cut short the tour. So she would be there after all for her play—what excitement, and could she trouble Shaw to get her a box "by any means, rough or smooth"? If he didn't want her to be conspicuous, she'd sit anywhere—in dress circle, pit, or gallery. "Brassbound!" she cried. ". . . I'm going off my head!" Mixed with the enthusiasm, however, was considerable chagrin. Too, too bad really that she was not to be Lady Cicely. Not a word to Janet, but she was certain Laurence would rather have played with her. Really, Shaw might have let her have the play for a couple of Lyceum performances a week. When she heard that some parts were still to be cast, she burst out indignantly. Did Shaw really accuse *her* of not taking his play seriously? What about *his* seriousness! Twelve careful rehearsals were needed for that play, not one less, and now Shaw was actually proposing to get together a company, rehearse, and produce a play in less than a fortnight. It was madness: *she* would not have treated his play so carelessly. He must put off *Brassbound* and throw *Candida* into the lists. "POSTPONE," she begged. "DO, DO, DO."[38]

But Shaw did not postpone. On the night of 16 December the author watched the performance, the float right under his nose and only half the stage visible, from the back of the worst box in the house. Janet half fulfilled his predictions. Had he taken a poker to her and beat his conception of Lady Cicely into her stubborn hide, she might conceivably have subdued herself to the part. And indeed at first he almost thought she had. She was acting for the first time in her life "in the sense of painting a picture instead of merely looking into a mirror in a volcanic manner, and saying: There! there's your Nora, Candida, etc." But then the excitement of finding the thing coming off began to intoxicate her like brandy and soda. She began to make points and, when the laughs rolled up over the footlights, to make them ten times harder. The result was a rollicking, obstreperous, boisterous Lady Cicely who got her dress caught between her knees when she sat down, and threw her dignity to the winds. A real lady, Shaw knew from observing Charlotte and her sister, would never stoop to show real excitement or temper, would never "lose her distinction and immense self-conceit and habit of patronage." She would be as far removed as possible from the middle-class woman who lived "her whole life under suspicion and shortness of cash." And yet Janet had for the first time, he thought, given sign that she had reached the wisdom of comedy and shown the ability to play the fiddle as well as the trombone and drums. In token of this fact Shaw dispatched a long letter of advice to Janet on Christmas Day, the first since he had renounced spiritual intercourse with her. His ever alert eye, however, had been intent on another member of the cast as well. "Barker was *very* good," he concluded. "We must stick to Barker."[39]

Had he glanced in the box where Ellen sat? Had she dared turn her head to look at him? From the beginning she had wanted to meet him, even though fearing that she would disgrace her years by "plunging into love again." From the beginning Shaw had longed for and feared a meeting: "Dont let us break the spell, *do* let us break the spell, dont, do, dont, do, dont, do, dont . . . ." They had been in the same theatre before, and acutely conscious of the fact. In January 1897 they had both appeared at the Shaftesbury on the same night, and Ellen had almost fallen into his arms, for being alone she had declined the front row and settled herself farther back in the stalls. He had not spied her, but she saw all his "so charmingly disguised yawns" during and between the acts. They had almost met again at the Criterion. "I could not go any nearer to you tonight (even if you had wanted me to—say that you did—oh say, say, say, say that you did)," wrote Shaw to his "Dearest and Everest" back at Fitzroy Square the night of 25 March 1897, "because I could not have looked at you or spoken to you otherwise than as I felt; and you would not have liked that in such a host of imperfectly sanctified eyes and ears. I was on the point, once or twice, of getting up and asking them all to go out for a few moments whilst I touched your hand for the first time." Wanted him to come nearer? Of course she had! And yet she was not sure, for she had his letter, his unread letter that she would not open until she went to bed that night, tucked into her bosom, and she felt *very* close to him indeed. Still, she would have liked to touch him after all: to lay her hand on his arm—no, on his coat sleeve!—and enjoy the performance with him. But she *had* seen him, and he had "the very strangest young, quick expression" she'd ever seen on a two-legged creature. He was a very MINX and a very DUCK too![40] And yet they had never come face to face.

Only recently, Shaw had raised the old issue again. "How could we two be such fools as to avoid meeting each other lest we should rub the bloom off our relations, and then enter into that most accursed of all relations, the professional relation?" he had written in the midst of their dickering over *Brassbound.* "Why did I not rather spring on that foolish Lyceum stage, drag you bodily away, and ravish you a thousand times rather than write a play for you?" Ellen had that to think about as she tried to make up her mind during this performance whether or not to confront Shaw; and she also had his retraction in the very next letter: "You were a thousand times right to keep me out of reach of your petticoats: what people call love is impossible except as a joke (and even then one of the two is sure to turn serious) between two strangers meeting accidentally at an inn or in a forest path. . . . A delusion, Ellen, all this love romance: that way madness lies."[41]

Weighing this incredible mixture of idealism and cynicism (that is, romanticism), Ellen decided to go backstage after the performance to congratulate the author. They met briefly under the stage, then went their separate ways. Soon after that night Ellen was told that Shaw "could not bear her." The carrier of these tidings is unknown. Perhaps it was Edy—cool, jealous, gossiping Edy: one of the few persons privy to both Shaw and Ellen, and one of the few people with a motive for destroying her mother's romance with a man, since her mother had destroyed two of hers.[42] But whether Shaw actually said he could not bear Ellen Terry or not—the idea seems preposterous—Ellen thought he had; and the loving letters of five years now stopped.[43]

Nora Charrington.

Lillah McCarthy (Mrs. Granville-Barker), Charlotte Shaw, and Harley Granville-Barker photographed by Shaw on one of their frequent weekends together.

Lillah McCarthy as Ann Whitefield in MAN AND SUPERMAN *at the Court Theatre, 1905.*

Lillah McCarthy.

Lillah McCarthy.

Lillah McCarthy as Margaret Knox in
FANNY'S FIRST PLAY *at the Little Theatre, 1911.*

Lena Ashwell in Tolstoy's
RESURRECTION.

Lena Ashwell.

Ellen Terry as Lady Cicely in CAPTAIN BRASSBOUND'S CONVERSION *at the Court Theatre, 1906.*

Shaw rehearsing Lillah McCarthy as Lavinia in ANDROCLES AND THE LION *at the St. James's Theatre, 1913.*

CHAPTER EIGHTEEN

1901-1906

SMALL HAD RECOGNIZED almost immediately the importance of Harley Granville-Barker's acting to his drama. He did not foresee that a theatre venture launched by Barker with J. E. Vedrenne at the Court Theatre would make his reputation as a playwright in London at last. Nor could he know that a young actress who was to marry Barker would emerge as the ideal instrument for his dramatic music, although he had begun to realize that the actresses of the eighties and even the nineties were useless for his purposes, and that the women who could play his heroines were still schoolgirls in short skirts.

Convinced more and more that the playgoing public was as unfit for his plays as he was unfit to write popular drama, he had threatened that his next play would be a masterpiece and a horror. He found its source in the suggestion of A. B. Walkley, another pioneer of modern journalism, that he write a Don Juan play. In July 1901 he began to sketch a scenario for such a play.[1] As the drama grew in his mind, he felt overwhelmingly that *Man and Superman* would indeed be a masterpiece. Certainly he had constructed a philosophical framework for this play that in breadth and depth surpassed anything he had attempted before. But although he scoffed now at "nursery plays like Candida," announcing to his new translator Siegfried Trebitsch that he wished the Germans to know him as a philosopher rather than a playwright, *Man and Superman*, like *Candida*, had its sources deep in Shaw's emotional nature, emerging, despite its Nietzschean basis, as the most personal of philosophies.

Its most personal quality was Shaw's ambivalent feelings about the

273

male-female relationship. His *Plays for Puritans* had countered sexuality onstage with three protagonists who rejected variously love, romance, passion, or marriage; yet it was not sexuality on the London stage that maddened him, Shaw claimed, but the fact that the contemporary British drama was "forced to deal almost exclusively with cases of sexual attraction, and yet forbidden to exhibit the incidents of that attraction or even to discuss its nature." Sex was thus disguised as poetic voluptuousness: love was elevated as the sole motive for human conduct: the theatre simmered in an overpowering *odor di femmina*—Julia Neilson falling in love with the man she believes has raped her in a swoon; Ellen Terry sensuously yielding to Forbes-Robertson's Lancelot in the eternally glamorous ritual of the Lyceum; Lily Hanbury, voluptuous as a daughter of Babylon; Mrs. Patrick Campbell, most powerful wafter of the *odor*, baring her white shoulders and in her lover's passion for the naked flesh finding love and life at last.[2] But for Shaw, women and love were "the most tedious subjects on earth."

He seized upon Walkley's challenge, therefore, as a chance to shock the British public with a play which would openly display the primitive attraction of the sexes for one another as the mainspring of the action. Stripping the male-female relationship of all its trappings of romance, love, sentiment, courtship, chastity, and flirtation, he created a heroine who pursued her male prey with the female's instinctive drive to find a father for the child she instinctively desires to bear. The whole world, Shaw wished to show, "is strewn with snares, traps, gins, and pitfalls for the capture of men by women"; the notion that women are passive until wooed is utter farce. Passive they may seem, but only as the spider who waits motionless in the web she has spun for the fly. Compared to this ruthlessness, the male is morally and physically fastidious, ascetic even, in his tastes. Yet woman's indelicacy is necessary, for her cause is selfless: she pursues man only because she needs him to carry on nature's most urgent work. She pursues in the face of humiliation, servitude, danger, and even death—ready to sacrifice herself and her mate for procreation. The future of the race is in her hands. Ann Whitefield was not only Everywoman, she was the Irresistible Natural Force, and the potential mother of the Superman.

It was not unusual that Shaw glorified in art a power that he personally feared: his public statements were usually impeccably just, his private behavior with women often dubious. In *Man and Superman* private fears predominate. Although thoroughly grounded in economics, for example, he did not portray woman's quest for a mate as the very fundamental reliance of unskilled, uneducated, economically dependent women on men for their room and board. Nor, although he and Charlotte had married for companionship, did he see anything companionable in Ann and Tanner's struggle. He forgot, too, all evidence that a powerful sex drive makes the male often the aggressor. For Shaw personally, woman was the aggressor; and his (and Tanner's) fear of that drive is potent, formulated in images of woman as lioness, siren, viper, boa constrictor, and, one of Shaw's favorite nightmares, the spider in her web. Female sexuality threatened his temperament, which, like the coquette's, flourished on romance: the titivation of emotion and passion. He did not want fulfillment. The male spider, Shaw had reminded Ellen, is killed by the female the moment he has succeeded in impregnating her. The thought horrified him. He had made love to Charlotte, and found himself used (so he thought) like a bottle of nerve medicine, his function ignominiously ended with her satisfaction—a curiously female fear. Ejaculation itself seemed to him something shameful, for which he should apologize afterward. Thus he clung to an ideal state of eternal be-coming. He exulted in his power of starving on imaginary feasts. He championed that "most blessed of all things"—the state of unsatisfied desire. The spending of sexual energy was inevitably connected with the waste of genius, and the duel of sex between woman and the man of genius was the most tragic of clashes. Thus Jack Tanner struggles violently to preserve his one and indivisible self. His whole instinct has been to enjoy Ann's femininity and his masculine power over it indefinitely, without committing himself to consequences, to fight against being used as a mere instrument for woman's purpose. It was Shaw's pattern, and he knew it. "What a shocking flirt you are, Jack!" exclaims Ann. How often Shaw had heard that accusation.

His marriage to Charlotte had considerably cleared his character, of course, as a notorious flirt; and in one sense *Man and Superman* was about that courtship and marriage, and could not have been written before it. But it was a highly idealized version. Tanner's final capitulation to the mission of the Life Force was, after all, on the level of heroism; his speech to the spectators closed in to watch the kill, expressive of the puritan Shaw's conviction that personal happiness must be sacrificed to a higher good and that sex must be functional rather than pleasurable. "I solemnly say that I am not a happy man," says Tanner. "Ann looks happy; but she is only triumphant, successful, victorious. That is not happiness, but the price for which the strong sell their happiness. What we have both done this afternoon is to renounce happiness, renounce freedom, renounce tranquillity, above all, renounce the romantic possibilities of an unknown future, for the cares of a household and family." Shaw's reality was less exalted. He had renounced freedom, it was true: for the first time in his life, he found it necessary and even satisfying to put someone else's welfare before his own. Yet Charlotte provided him with financial security, with good food, with servants to care for his needs, with ego reinforcement (he was, to her, "the Genius"), with love, and beyond love, devotion. The household was largely hers to worry about, and there had never been a question of a family. Cares? They were largely imaginary, a sobering thought to a puritan. The price had been minimal; and as for selling his happiness, he could not part with something he had never sought. Tanner's heroic destiny was a destiny Shaw was not fated to know.

"The Revolutionist's Handbook and Pocket Companion," an afterword, argued not for Tanner's marital destiny, therefore, but for his own. He argued that for the breeding of a superior race of human beings —the only course that would save mankind—marriage and conjugation must be separated. Most people now could not separate the idea of marriage from the marriage bed, but viewed marriage as simply a license for unlimited sexual intercourse. Most people were wrong, however: intercourse was "the one purely accidental and incidental condition of marriage" and essential to nothing except the propagation of the species. The minute it was separated from marriage—by government subsidization of childbirth, for example, or by state-funded nurseries—marriage would be seen for what it essentially was: an economical, convenient, and comfortable arrangement for a man and a woman. Tanner's lifelong bondage to Ann Whitefield in the hideous stringency and irrevocability of marriage was not necessary: only his genes were needed by the Life Force, and these he could donate with a minimum of inconvenience. Domesticity, concluded Shaw, was the only function essential to the existence of marriage, "because conjugation without domesticity is not marriage at all, whereas domesticity without conjugation is still marriage: in fact it is necessarily the actual condition of all fertile marriages during a great part of their duration, and of some marriages during the whole of it." His marriage had proved to be one of the latter. "What people call love is impossible except as a joke," he had assured Ellen two and a half years after he had married. ". . . Why, I dare not for my life's happiness make love to my own wife. A delusion, Ellen, all this love romance: that way madness lies." Charlotte had evidently closed the door on sex, a door that Shaw's own fastidiousness and philosophy would not permit him to break down. He knew, of course, that his view was personal and even perverse. The artist could never catch the point of view of the common man, he reminded Walkley in his "Epistle Dedicatory," and anything he wrote on the relationship of the sexes was apt to be misleading.

Finished in June 1902, *Man and Superman* appeared to him a stupendous creation, a colossal effort of mind. He immediately proposed reading it to the Charringtons. The play was still rough, so he would rather they keep the occasion intimate—preferably the two of them alone. "Still, as you know, I am not shy of people who can get on our plane."[3]

"On our plane"? The words enticed Janet, always desperate for work. She had been having a run of luck with Shaw in recent months. There had been his letter to the *Manchester Guardian* in praise of her Lady

Cicely at the Queen's Theatre, Manchester, in May. More encouraging than this press release was his praise after witnessing her Ellida at the Royalty in London. "Janet seems to be having a streak of genius just now," he had told Charrington. "The Lady from the Sea was immense. . . . The lucidity of her acting in difficult plays is extraordinary: I have serious thoughts of refusing to let anybody else touch my plays, although she is too fat for Cleopatra."[4] And Ann Whitefield, Shaw's new heroine, was Candida again, as Janet must have realized as the play unfolded: Candida before the children and the onions and the lamp-filling and an egocentric husband had turned her into mother and housekeeper; Candida, young and supple and on the traces, ruthlessly hunting down the male she had marked for her mate. But Shaw really had no intention of keeping his plays for Janet. As he told her in April 1903, when she was desperately trying to round up plays for another tour, ". . . I have for some time begun to see that I myself am one of your pieces of ill luck—that my plays, tempting as they seem, are not the right vehicles for your genius. . . . You are not Candida and you are not Lady Cicely. You want much more powerful parts . . . . You are getting too old for Nora: the squirrel's jumps make the house shake. . . . The Doll's House is stale & you have outgrown it. . . . try something that will carry your weight. . . . My plays are not heavy enough."[5] The message was hardly subtle: Janet was too "fat" for Shavian drama altogether.

Janet had become one of his pieces of ill luck, for, much as the Charringtons appreciated and wanted his plays, they could not come close to the "Mozartian joyousness" that pervaded his drama. These were years of great frustration for Shaw: he had written twelve plays, the last assuredly a masterpiece: he was translated and performed abroad; yet to the London public he was still virtually unknown as a playwright. Hard to endure Archer's reaction after reading *Man and Superman:* "[I]n no way are you making the mark either upon literature or upon life, that you have it in you to make. The years are slipping away . . . and you have done nothing really big, nothing original, solid, first-rate, enduring. If you were to die tomorrow, what would happen? In the history of literature you would find a three-line mention . . . as an eccentric writer, hard to classify, whose writings a few people still remember with pleasure. . . . You are a great force wasted . . . ."[6] Hard to endure when one considered oneself the greatest playwright since Shakespeare, and was certainly the greatest contemporary British dramatist.

Yet recognition was at hand. While Archer was confessing that *Man and Superman* had "rather dashed" his hopes of something great from Shaw, Harley Granville-Barker was plotting to realize the hopes of the Independent Theatre, the New Century Theatre, and the Stage Society with a season of uncommercial and heavily Shavian drama at a theatre whose intimacy and location far, but not too far, from the West End seemed ideal. Recommended by Archer as a director for J. H. Leigh's series of "Shakespeare Representations" at the Royal Court Theatre in Sloane Square, Barker saw his chance, and bargained his services in exchange for the chance of independently producing a matinee series of *Candida*. Permission granted, and the services of John Eugene Vedrenne, Court lessee Leigh's manager, thrown in to the bargain, Barker did *Candida* for six performances beginning 26 April 1904, playing Eugene Marchbanks to Kate Rorke's Candida. And although Kate Rorke was one of those actresses from the eighties whom Shaw thought no use for his drama, he was able to report, "Result very satisfactory, heaps of press notices, all compliments for the company, and a modest profit for Barker & the theatre, besides some thirty pounds or so fees for the author."[7]

As he had told the Charringtons, "we must stick to Barker." But Barker had no intention of sticking to the Charringtons. "We must begin again," he told Shaw, who, in the softness of his heart, would probably have pulled Janet and Charlie into the new venture along with him: "there must be none of the old people." And Shaw agreed: "I dont want any of the old people: I dont want—and we cant afford—anybody that costs more than £5 a week."[8] The plays would have to make the reputation of the new repertory at the Court, not the players. The policy would prove a sound one, and yet in the excellent critic Desmond MacCarthy's opinion, Kate Rorke was not as effective as Janet had been, and the production no better than Charrington's except for the substitution of Miss Sydney Fairbrother as Prossy.

Inspired by success, Barker negotiated with Vedrenne for a series of matinees at the Court beginning that autumn of 1904. In Scotland on another of the "accursed holidays" which had been his lot since marrying the peripatetic Charlotte, Shaw struggled with a new play although he could find no place to write and felt quite wrecked and put off his stride. He had decided a year ago that his next play was to be an Irish one; he was working now toward an 18 October completion date, since Barker wanted *John Bull's Other Island* to follow Gilbert Murray's translation of the *Hippolytus* of Euripides. As usual casting preoccupied Shaw a great deal: there were twelve in the play and none of them needed to be expensive. For his Irish heroine, Nora Reilly, he had only two suggestions: the Irish-born Ellen O'Malley or a young actress named Lillah McCarthy. "Lillah is a frightful temptation," he told Barker: "my heart cries Yes By All Means; but there will be grave risk of scandal. She is a gorgeous creature: I could almost make another Rehan of her."[9]

Shaw must have remembered the first time he had laid eyes on the gorgeous creature. In May 1895, the month that had seen Irving knighted for pursuing his ruling passion and Oscar Wilde sent to prison for pursuing his, Shaw had turned up at the Shakespeare Reading Society's amateur production of *Macbeth* at St. George's Hall. Halfway through the performance, the producer had come to the nineteen-year-old girl playing Lady Macbeth with the news that the well-known critic from the *Saturday Review* was out in front. The news electrified Lillah McCarthy. "He won't eat you," joked her brother Dan to the suddenly nervous actress: "he's a vegetarian." Back onstage, Lillah dared a glance at the critic's chair, "and saw nothing but two eyes staring out of a white face surrounded by a halo of red hair." Instantly she rallied. She would show Mr. Bernard Shaw how Lillah McCarthy could act Shakespeare: she would "freeze him with horror," she would "melt him with pity," she would cast a spell over his Irish heart.[10] Having given her all, she opened the *Saturday Review* in apprehension. "As to this performance of Macbeth at St. George's Hall," Shaw began, "of course it was, from the ordinary professional standpoint, a very bad one. . . . I desire it to be distinctly understood that I do not recommend any members of the Macbeth cast to go on the stage. . . . Macduff was bad . . . . As to Lady Macbeth, she, too, was bad—"

The spell, alas, had not worked. Petrified with mortification, Lillah dropped the paper; then in a burst of rage, burnt it, crying aloud that she was a much wronged woman. How startling a moment later to have her brother Dan burst in waving the same sheet. Wasn't Shaw's notice splendid! Snatching it from him, she read on: ". . . it is clear to me that unless she at once resolutely marries some rich gentleman who disapproves of the theatre on principle, she will not be able to keep herself off the stage. She is as handsome as Miss Neilson; and she can hold an audience whilst she is doing everything wrongly. . . . I venture on the responsibility of saying that her Lady Macbeth was a highly promising performance, and that some years of hard work would make her a valuable recruit to the London stage."[11] Oh, he was a dear after all. Would she take his advice and go off to learn her trade in the provinces the hard way, her brother wanted to know. "Go? I would go to the end of the world for him!" exclaimed Lillah.

Impressionable, and prone to violent hero worship, Lillah McCarthy took Shaw's advice, touring first with Ben Greet's Comedy Company and then joining Wilson Barrett's touring group, which took her through England to America to the Antipodes. After eight years, Barrett had suggested that she go out with her own company; plans were being made when Barrett fell ill, then died, leaving her, she believed, "without a friend in the theatrical world" and with an outmoded training in the broad, rhetorical style that had suited the romantic dramas Barrett preferred. Desolate and at loose ends, she tramped through Cornwall for two weeks, eating bread and cheese, wearing her shoes thin, pondering her future, and gradually seeing that she must learn her art anew and push on farther—much farther—than she had yet gone. The years of banishment were over; she would return to London. There she wrote

Shaw. She had done his bidding and was back and ready. "All my announced plays are already cast," Shaw replied 7 February 1905; "so I am afraid I can be of no immediate service to you. But come round Friday the 10th & talk." She obeyed, climbed the stairs behind the iron spiked gate in trepidation, and announced herself with a confidence she did not feel. Shaw saw "a gorgeously goodlooking young lady in a green dress and huge picture hat in which any ordinary woman would have looked ridiculous, and in which she looked splendid, with the figure and gait of a Diana." "Why here's Ann Whitefield!" exclaimed Shaw. Thinking he had confused her with someone else, Lillah explained: "Ten years ago, when I was a little girl trying to play Lady Macbeth, you told me to go and spend ten years learning my business. I have learnt it: now give me a part." "Here you are," said Shaw simply, handing her the book of *Man and Superman;* and Lillah took her leave, wondering and hoping. A letter a few days later made it official: would she, if asked by the Stage Society, take on "an exceedingly difficult & possibly shockingly unpopular leading part" for three guineas pay and fifty guineas worry?[12]

Lillah would, and the acute problem of casting Ann was solved. Everybody had said Ann Whitefield must be ultra-modern; Shaw, however, had set his heart on a young Mrs. Siddons or a Ristori: an actress with the executive art of the grand school combined with the free and energetic beauty of the New Woman. Lillah combined both. She was beautiful, thought Shaw: "plastic, statuesque, most handsomely made, and seemed to have come straight from the Italian or eighteenth century stage without a trace of the stuffiness of the London cup-and-saucer theatres." She was imaginative, poetic, with a stunningly rich voice and elastic delivery. She was vital, passionate—sometimes, perhaps, too passionate: as a child she had taken a kitchen knife to a maid who borrowed her blue sash; rehearsing *Romeo and Juliet,* she had driven a dagger into her breast. Most important of all, perhaps: Lillah would let herself be molded by Shaw. It had been the great fault of Florence Farr, Elizabeth Robins, Janet Achurch, Ellen Terry, and Mrs. Campbell that they had read his advice in column and letter, but had stubbornly gone their ways. Lillah McCarthy, however, submitted to male authority and even yearned for it. Her father, for example, had come into her life "like a rushing mighty wind." She was "the seventh of his children and the child of his choice." He ruled her and loved her: a tall, handsome, masterful, wild, and eccentric Irishman who taught her when she could not learn in school and seemed to her like mighty poetry while her mother, burdened with eight children, assorted relatives, housework, and a meager income to make do, was only dull prose.[13] She had already proved her discipleship by taking Shaw's critical advice literally; in looks, training, and temperament, Shaw had found the ideal actress for his kind of plays. "Thus began my association with Shaw and Shaw's plays," she recalled, "and with it a new life began for me; the new life of the Court Theatre and of the new woman—ever certain, ever Shaw."

Before playing Ann, however, Lillah replaced Ellen O'Malley in *John Bull's Other Island*, walking in Hyde Park round and round the Serpentine, memorizing lines and, between performances, fielding notes from Shaw advising her to use violet or purple ribbons instead of blue against Ann's white muslin dress and to attempt "a certain pomegranate splendor lurking somewhere in the effect." The *Superman* was postponed until 21 May, and in the interim Lillah studied Shaw as much as her part, deciding that she now knew what vivid personality meant. During rehearsals they lunched at the little Queen's Restaurant near the Court, Lillah starving on apples, cheese, macaroni, salads, and chilly milk and sodas because Shaw ate them, and because everything he did seemed right. She discovered over these lunches that Shaw was always ill at ease and not a listener at all: his pale shy eyes shifted away with his attention and he was off again chasing his own train. In the theatre itself he was all attention: "serious, painstaking, concentrated, relentless in pursuit of perfection." He did not interrupt the cast in the early stages; only as he sat out front with head cocked, his pencil scribbled mercilessly—and at the end of rehearsal, most of the company had brief, brilliant little notes to take away and ponder. Later he would come up onstage to interrupt, courteous, amiable, his hands eloquently describing the effects he wanted. Lillah watched them, fascinated: "I learned as much from his hands, almost, as from his little notes of correction." Or he could be more precipitous. Seeing her clutch Barker fiercely one day in rehearsal, her muscles tight, he came bounding onto the stage to separate them and remonstrate. She could not play the role gripped in a series of attitudes like a tragedian: she must learn to relax. The next day Frances Archer, devotee of the Power in Repose method, turned up at the theatre. In a month Lillah learned to move and relax any muscle separately and at will, and how to be quiet and do nothing onstage with great effectiveness. "How *can* you do it?" Mrs. Campbell was to marvel. "It would drive me mad."

Man and Superman was played on 21, 22, and 23 May, and then taken into the Court repertory for a series of matinees.[14] The "horror," "masterpiece," and "colossal effort of mind" went brilliantly, playing itself, thanks to Shaw's superb instinct for pace and comedy, the omission of the philosophical "Don Juan in Hell" episode, and a cast that seemed made for their roles. Again it was Barker who dominated: Barker made up with Mephistophelean moustaches and red beard to look like the diabolical Shaw of the nineties; Barker—voluble, witty, nervous, alert, brainy, mischievous, exuberant, and evidently born to play the reluctant Shavian male. Lillah's role was more difficult, carrying as she did the symbolic burden of Ann as Everywoman, instrument of the Life Force, mother of the Superman. This burden oppressed a nature passionate, imaginative, but essentially humorless. Critics noted as a result that while she managed to make Ann Whitefield an agreeable woman, she did not quite make her a real person. Lillah got all of Ann's audacity, and perseverance, and fascination, but if Ann had one redeeming quality from the ordinary playgoer's point of view, it was her sense of fun—and Lillah missed that point completely.[15]

For Lillah playing Ann Whitefield was a personal triumph: the part made a new woman out of her. "The women of the previous day, on or off the stage, had been of the stage, stagey," she wrote in her autobiography. "Ann was of the earth, earthy. What an affront to tradition! A real woman on the stage! No wonder people were scandalised! . . . Women, many of them, have told me that Ann brought them to life and that they remodelled themselves upon Ann's pattern. The men—the conventional men who had made women after their own imagining and according to their predilections—disapproved of Ann: unladylike! She was insistent when she should have been submissive. What is to become of the home? She had a will of her own instead of one of theirs. . . . Ann set the leading lady—and with her all the ladies of the theatre—free, and she set the world of women free. Whenever the slim girl of the present day lights up a cigarette whilst she stands waiting for a train, I feel I must go up and say to her, as Shaw once said to me: 'Why you're Ann Whitefield,' and when Amy Johnson flies across the deserts and the seas from here to Cape Town and back again, I want to tell her 'Ann Whitefield gave you those strong and lovely wings.' Mrs. Pankhurst, who Heaven knows never lacked resolution, herself told me that Ann Whitefield had strengthened her purpose and fortified her courage. Shaw was the Perseus who rescued Andromeda from the talons of the dragon!"

Not all women appreciated Ann Whitefield. Shaw may understand women, "but we do not like our Bernard," one female critic would write; "he sees too much with that chill grey eye of his. He would be good to us in actual life, clothe us and feed us and give us good wages, but what woman can forgive 'Man and Superman'?"[16] Josephine Peabody, American poet and dramatist, greeted Ann's appearance with "How bestial!" Now if this was only ladylike outrage at Shaw's revelation that women's interest in securing a mate is more urgent and therefore aggressive than man's, Shaw would be quite right in calling such false propriety "extremely wicked," as he did. But there was another facet to Miss Peabody's dislike of Ann besides outraged purity. The American writer did not like Shaw's insistence that Ann was representative of all women, since she, for one, was not at all like Ann. Shaw's reply to this was neat. Miss Peabody and her sort were obviously Artist Women, but Ann was the Mother Woman. She must learn to respect the calling of mothers as a job equal to her own, indeed superior to it—for as

Shaw plainly showed, Octavius's poetry and Tanner's politics are mere fluff compared with Ann's mission. This hardly seemed the same Shaw who, in the *Quintessence,* had championed Marie Bashkirtseff as the artist woman, and declared mothering no more natural to women than soldiering to men. "Dont, I beg of you," Shaw concluded to Peabody, "write to me again until you have learnt to respect your sex, and to appreciate that very vital protest of Don Juan against the degradation of the sex relation into a personal & sentimental romance." But for those accustomed to integrating sex and emotion, or accustomed to considering the sex relation degrading without the personal element, Shaw's great play still did not satisfy as philosophy.

Meanwhile, Shaw had not forgotten *Captain Brassbound's Conversion.* He had broken a silence of sixteen months in April 1902 to ask Ellen whether now, since Lillie Langtry had shown interest in Lady Cicely, she might at last be willing to play the part. Ellen's reply measured the wound she had been dealt the night Janet played Lady Cicely, although, as was her habit, she immediately covered a harsh word with a conciliatory one:

> . . . Don't break her heart along with the rest but let her have the play. You write great plays and always ruin them with the first start off. You have no powers of selection. You know everything. You know nothing.
>   You are a great man.
>   You are "a silly Ass."
>   You are a dear.
>   You are a "worry."
>   Poor Charlotte!*
> (*That's envy, isn't it?)
>
> Your ownest Ellen
>
> My love to Charlotte and her husband. . . .[17]

In December 1902 he approached her again, but she still could not commit herself to business. He had told her he could not guarantee a financial success. Bless him! A financial success was all she wanted. Shaw waited another year and a half; then with the Court's successful *Candida* as bait, tempted her again with six matinees and interesting press notices. No salary, of course, and "find her own gowns"; on the other hand, no financial risk in the least, and a promotion from Shakespeare to Shaw.

Much had happened to Ellen, Irving, and the Lyceum in the interim. With the bankruptcy of the Lyceum Company, Irving had reluctantly faced the fact that his reign as first London theatre manager was over. He decided to go out in a blaze of glory. On the night of 3 July 1902, he played *Waterloo* and *The Bells* to a glittering international audience gathered in London to celebrate the coronation of Edward VII; then caused the Lyceum to be transformed in forty minutes by hundreds of hands into a red-carpeted, scarlet-draped, palm-encircled banquet hall lit by blazing chandeliers and dominated by a gigantic Union Jack surmounted by a crown of red, blue, yellow, and violet electric lights. There he greeted rajahs, sultans, potentates, lords, ladies, and an occasional actor—a thousand guests in all—while detectives kept a sharp watch for anarchists and jewel thieves. On 19 July Irving led Ellen forward by the hand to acknowledge the applause for *The Merchant of Venice*. Conscious that their partnership was nearing its end, both struggled to keep back tears. "I shall never be in this theatre again," said Ellen to Irving after the curtain had been rung down for the last time: "I feel it . . . I know it." She never would be: Irving's thirty-one-year management was over. She refused £12,000 to tour with him in *Dante*. They took their last bow together as Shylock and Portia in a benefit performance at Drury Lane on 14 July 1903, and that fall Irving sailed for America to recoup his losses for the first time without Ellen.

Feeling "strange and somewhat sad" without Ellen, Irving worried about her future. Poor Nell—in the last year she had fallen absolutely under the spell of her two children, who had plunged her into ruin. The "ruin" was Ellen's venture into management and production with Ibsen's *The Vikings at Helgeland* at the Imperial Theatre the previous April. It had been a family venture, Edith doing the costumes and Teddy the scenery and lighting; but although Ellen had failed conspicuously as the fierce Hiordis, whom she played benevolently in fluffy white furs, and although the experiment had been a terrible drain on her purse, *The Vikings* had done the job she intended it to do: it had established her son Gordon Craig as the most exciting new designer in the theatre.

Much of this pain and triumph, she felt, Shaw would not appreciate. There had been other changes too. She had left Barkston Gardens at last for a smaller house at 215 King's Road, Chelsea, with "no room to swing a kitten." Her real affections, however, she had transferred to her farm Smallhythe at Tenterden in Kent, a fine old timbered Tudor dwelling she had bought at Michaelmas in 1900. Edy had moved into a cottage of her own on the grounds, and there mother and daughter seemed closer than ever before. "Did I tell you she is my right hand," Ellen asked Shaw, "and still growing to be my left hand, and happy as a sandboy all the while? I fear to be too happy in her—I try to be very quiet with it all." And now Barrie was writing her a play all her own. She therefore continued to send Shaw and Charlotte "a priceless treasure"—her love and friendship ("Keep it warm—don't leave it 'Out in the cold wind, out in the snow'"); yet she rejected *Brassbound* once more: "From the 18th of August to Xmas I am disporting myself in the Provinces. The arrangements are made and there's an end."[18] Had she really only pretended to like the play, as Shaw suspected? Her query—"Where is a fine part for a woman between 50 and 60? Please let me study one"—was not flattering. Or was all her playing with him over the years (he darkly suspected it) her revenge for his marriage to Charlotte!

Two weeks later, therefore, Shaw took different aim. "Have you ever by any chance read a play of mine called Captain Brassbound's Conversion?" he asked Ada Rehan, Irish-born American actress and star for twenty years of Augustin Daly's company. ". . . You were in the author's mind when he wrote the play; and he has often wished to approach you on the subject."[19] Shaw thought of Ada Rehan as Ellen's American counterpart, an infinitely fascinating comedy actress of wonderful technique who at middle age still languished in dated roles that shamefully wasted her talent. He had attacked her manager Augustin Daly as he had attacked Irving: how was one to open poor, benighted Mr. Daly's mind to the fact that he stood "on the brink of the twentieth century in London and not with Mr. Vincent Crummles at Portsmouth in the early Dickens days?" Did not Daly realize that *A Doll's House* had smashed up British theatre so that nothing could ever be the same? "In short," declared Shaw in the *Saturday Review*, having just been staggered by a positively fossilized production of some antique called *Railroad of Love*, "a modern manager need not produce The Wild Duck; but he must be very careful not to produce a play which will seem insipid and old-fashioned to playgoers who have seen The Wild Duck, even though they may have hissed it."[20] Writing to Rehan now, Shaw was forced to admit that the implacable and vindictive malice with which he had pursued her late manager might have impressed her unpleasantly; he had, however, only been trying to slay the dragon which held her in thrall.

At three o'clock on Saturday afternoon, 2 July 1904, Shaw read *Brassbound* to Ada Rehan, who, even though Shaw was not in top reading form, caught fire, and dismayed and excited, "floated and flowed around the room," exclaiming over the play's upsetting ideas. "But alas!" Shaw admitted to Ellen, "this stately Rehan [was] a most fiery, simple, sentimental, loyal, faithful soul" who found out his crimes: first, that he actually wanted her to make terms with the syndicate which almost bankrupted her dead manager and mentor, Augustin Daly, and second, that Shaw's contempt for Daly as a manager for a woman of genius equaled his contempt for Irving. "She is simpler than you and has not your literary genius; so that I am much more disagreeable and bewildering for her."[21] Although Shaw capitulated to Rehan's objections, besieged her with letters, and assured her that she should lead in the negotiations, the actress's departure for America and later her illness finally brought plans for a Rehan Lady Cicely to a halt. The doctor had positively forbidden her to play for a year, Shaw told Vedrenne in July 1905; they had better let *Brassbound* go for the interim. Ellen Terry was the only one equal to the part, and she did not believe in it. A month later, however, Vedrenne had done what Shaw had not been able to accomplish in six years: he had secured Ellen to play Lady Cicely at the Court.[22]

She capitulated for several reasons. That February she had hurried to Wolverhampton at news that Irving had collapsed on tour and was dangerously ill. She came carrying bright daffodils, her favorite flowers and the flowers with which Irving had decked her dressing room after her mother's death, "to make it look like sunshine." She found him gray and exhausted, but indomitable. "Fiddle!" he snapped when she begged him to follow the doctor's orders. "It's not my heart at all! It's my *breath!*" There had been nothing personal between them for many years, and they talked conventionally now about business. But Ellen could not bear to let their last meeting, perhaps, end in formality; she cried at last impulsively, pleadingly, "What a wonderful life you've had, haven't you?"

"Oh, yes," said Irving quietly, "a wonderful life—of work."

"And there's nothing better, after all, is there?"

"Nothing."

"What have you got out of it all? You and I are 'getting on,' as they say. Do you ever think, as I do sometimes, what you have got out of life?"

Irving stroked his chin and smiled faintly. "What have I got out of it? Let me see. . . . Well, a good cigar, a good glass of wine"—he paused, took Ellen's hand, and raised it courteously to his lips—"good friends."

They sat quietly together for several hours, Ellen thinking how like some splendid Doge of Venice he looked, sitting up in bed, his beautiful supple hand stroking his chin; then she left, certain now that she and Irving would never play together again.[23] On her heels came the faithful Mrs. Aria.

And then her play from Barrie was a disappointment. Barrie had come with syndicate producer Charles Frohman to Smallhythe to tell her about it, and she had been enchanted. She opened in *Alice-Sit-by-the-Fire* at the Duke of York's Theatre on 5 April 1905, but Barrie had told the play better than he had written it.[24] "I was never happy in my part," Ellen confessed in her memoirs, "perhaps because although it had been made to measure, it didn't fit me. I sometimes felt that I was bursting at the seams! I was accustomed to broader work in a larger theatre." Like Shaw, Barrie had drawn Ellen as a charming woman who always gets her way. Barrie gave Alice Grey a domestic setting, however, and showed her, until her decision to grow up at the end and sit by the fire, as a mercurial, harum-scarum, flirtatious, cajoling, adored woman who in spirit is much younger than her children, and always gets people to love her by letting them think they are protecting her. Ellen had missed breadth in Shaw's play as well, calling it more fit for the closet than the stage; yet compared with Barrie's pleasant little spoof of stage adultery, Shaw's vitality and the more imposing character of Lady Cicely must have seemed more attractive.

Alice-Sit-by-the-Fire ran for 115 performances, however; and Ellen took it on tour that autumn of 1905. On Friday, 13 October, Irving, now sixty-seven, and also on tour against all medical advice, played a "farewell" performance of *Becket* at the Theatre Royal, Bradford. Dazed after the performance, Irving managed to get back to his hotel in a cab, where he collapsed on a chair in the vestibule and then, losing consciousness, slipped to the floor. The news of his death reached Ellen in Manchester. The next night she ordered the curtain to go up on Barrie's play as usual; she managed to play almost until the end when she came to the lines, "It's summer done, autumn begun. Farewell, summer, we don't know you any more. . . . I had a beautiful husband once, black as the raven was his hair—" Then she broke down in grief for her old love and friend and partner, while stagehands quickly lowered the curtain and the audience filed out of the theatre in respectful silence. It was a scene Irving would have appreciated.

She may now have regretted yielding to Irving's old enemy. Shaw had been approached by the Vienna *Neue Freie Presse* for an obituary notice of Irving; the translator, assuming that Shaw always wrote maliciously, translated his often stern truths about the actor into a sniping attack on Sir Henry's ambition and egotism; retranslating the article back into English, the London papers created a more vituperative version than the German. Public indignation exploded. In self-defense, Shaw sent copies of his original article to all the leading British papers; but scandal was more interesting than truth, and most people persisted in thinking Shaw "a monstrous Yahoo for whom nothing but excommunication" was fitting. Without having read the article, Ellen protested disbelief: "You never wrote the words they say you wrote, except when Henry was well, was at work and *fighting*. Then it was all right enough—fair." Then Shaw sent her a copy of the original text, and after skimming it, she wanted to burn his words. "Well, it was just stupid in you, that's all," she replied—"and that's enough I should say for *you*."[25] Frustrated, Shaw felt he could not make her understand; but it was perhaps his timing she objected to even more than his words; for she had done her own criticizing of Irving in her time.

Ellen's consent to *Brassbound* brought up the old question of their meeting. They had as usual been flirting with the notion since resuming the correspondence in 1902—"Why don't you and Charlotte balloon, or motor down here" and "There is a 1.15 train from King's Cross in time for lunch"—but invitations were now for prosaic meetings *à trois*, rather than for assignations on the plains of heaven. He was, Shaw assured her, looking forward to rehearsals "with malicious glee" when he would have his revenge upon the tiresome woman who wouldn't do his play. In reality, he was worried. "Ellen will fidget and flounce all about the place unless I freeze her with mere terror," he told Lady Barrington, Ada Rehan's friend and protectress; "and then she'll forget every word of her part." Christmas Day evening he came around to the Duke of York's after a performance of *Alice-Sit-by-the-Fire* with Barker in tow as chaperon because, so he said, he *must* accustom himself to meeting her. The first meeting failed to accomplish it: old and unfit as he was for love, he protested gallantly, "something wild happens inside me; and I have to look on gasping for breath whilst an artificial G.B.S. talks to an equally artificial Miss Terry, the two minuetting on the carpet while we stagger at the immensities." Actually his cool eye took in the facts: an actress now fifty-eight, weak-eyed, buxom, jowly, gray streaking the straw-blond hair—a woman poised awkwardly between lost youth and the grace of age: too old, too old, despite the ineffable Terry charm, for his Lady Cicely; an actress ready to celebrate her jubilee the following year: fifty years in the theatre. He had not brought along Barker to keep the Shavian ardor in check but, as co-director of the Court, to see firsthand the difficulties that lay ahead.

Yet Shaw had little to lose, even from a bad performance from Ellen. The situation had changed dramatically since 1899, when, still unplayed, he had hoped that a Terry performance would make his name. *Candida*, *John Bull's Other Island*, *Man and Superman*, *You Never Can Tell*, and, opening the previous month on 28 November 1905, the great *Major Barbara*, had made him the most talked-about, if not the best-paid, dramatist in London. "We have now finished our six matinees," he had written Eleanor Robson, the twenty-six-year-old British-born actress for whom he had written the role of the Salvation Army major, but disappointingly failed to capture. "Every one of them has been crowded to bursting; and hundreds of people have been turned away. Poor Candida is eclipsed—a back number—people write frantic letters to me about Barbara. The audiences suffer horribly; they are pained, puzzled, bored in the last act to madness; but they sit there to the bitter end and come again, & again."[26]

Beatrice Webb noted in her diary this reversal in Shaw's fortunes with mixed feelings:

The smart world is tumbling over one another in the worship of G.B.S., and even we have a sort of reflected glory as his intimate friends. It is interesting to note that the completeness of his self-conceit will save him from the worst kind of deterioration—he is proof against flattery. Where it will injure him is in isolating him from serious intercourse with intimate friends working in other departments of life—whenever he is free there is such a crowd of journalists and literary hangers-on around him that one feels it is kinder to spare him one's company—and that will be the instinct of many of his old friends engaged in administration, investigation or propaganda.

What a transformation scene from those first years I knew him: the scathing bitter opponent of wealth and leisure—and now! the adored one of the smartest and most cynical set of English "society" . . . .

Instead of Ellen's gratifying him by consenting to Lady Cicely, therefore, Shaw was now doing Ellen Terry the favor of letting her play him.

Rehearsals began in February 1906, with a nervous and anxious Ellen struggling to get her lines, and a cast that included Frederick Kerr as Brassbound (Ellen had unfortunately vetoed Louis Calvert, a hit as Andrew Undershaft in *Major Barbara*), Edmund Gwenn as Drinkwater, and a young American actor named James Carew as Captain Kearney. Watching out front, Shaw fired off one of his notes to Barker: "Do not let Ellen repeat any scene. . . . She always goes to pieces the second time & discourages & demoralizes herself more & more every time. . . . Go straight through & dont let them stop for anything."[27] Ideally Shaw wanted to closet the two of them together while he read her her part. If her maids or her everlasting young ladies read, she would get it into her head all wrong; if she read it herself she would wreck her eyes and her nerves; from him, however, she would get it as easily as "a child learns hush-a-bye-baby." Unable to get her alone, he coached her by postcard. "Have you ever thought of the GRANDEUR of wickedness?" he wrote, trying to get the stress of the lines into her head. "Grand! That's the word. Something grandly wicked. Not very wicked, not dreadfully wicked, not shockingly wicked, but GRANDLY WICKED. GRANDIOSO. SOMETHING Grandly WICKED to their enemies. . . ."[28]

But illness plagued her: pain in the eyes and head. She had missed rehearsal, but would come tomorrow if she had to crawl. All gentleness, Shaw told her to let Lady Cicely go hang. He could get the play into shape without her: she must take a week, a fortnight, if she wanted it. Four days before opening on 20 March, Ellen was still fearfully uncertain of her part, and Shaw still angelically patient and sending her suggestions. "The only other point of importance," he concluded one of the famous little notes, "is that you look 25; and I love you. . . . You will be most ausserordentlich good in the part. I never realized how well I did that job until I saw you rehearse."[29]

The morning of opening day, however, Shaw opened a penciled scrawl from his actress marked "Private":

Beloved Patient One [he read] —I shivered & shook from cold until 5 this morning—then fell asleep, to awake later on with a *swamping* cold— worse than I have ever been, in that line— (Oh, that Hall Door at the Theatre—).

Spite of all, however, I'll make a plunge today, & "still retain the Empire of my Soul"—

Don't, *don't* expect anything of me whilst I am so overpowered by this cold, only *hope for me* that I may get through this morning [sic] without disgracing myself, & hampering you & the others.

I *never* take my opportunity! Mr. Vedrenne gave me one to postpone the play until I was well, and *Fool—Fool! Fool!* . . .

I'll play Lady C before I've done with her yet.

Sneeze — Sneeze

Blow — Blow

Bless G.B.S.

Courage E.T.[30]

It was not exactly the kind of merging of the Shaw-Terry genius Shaw had envisioned when he began the play seven years before, and his misgivings were confirmed that afternoon: Ellen played uncertainly, as though she were uncomfortable in the part. Desmond MacCarthy found that the play made the audience think seriously about human relationships and laugh at the same time—a rare merit; yet found the Court performance below standard, and not so good as the Stage Society and Janet Achurch had given back in 1900. The cast, he believed, did not pull well together and, although Ellen Terry blessed Lady Cicely with all her own charm, her lack of sureness spoiled the effect. No one felt worse about her performance than Ellen herself, assuring Shaw that she would "try, try again" until she got Lady Cicely right, crying that he was "a faithful heroic DEAR" to pretend she had done well when he knew very well she had failed. Yet had Ellen really failed? After six matinees, *Captain Brassbound's Conversion* was revived on 16 April for twelve additional weeks, a long run for the Court and certainly due to Ellen rather than the play, which did not rival *Man and Superman*, *Major Barbara*, or even *Candida*. But Shaw complained to Vedrenne that the returns were "not at all satisfactory." The average evening house was running some £57 below the matinees, and that made about £85 for the management, £6.18.0 for the author, £23.11.0 for the leading lady, and £2.10.0 apiece for Barker and Vedrenne to live on and build capital for the future. It was not Ellen's fault, however, he felt bound to say. Drinkwater was not amusing in the first act, nor Brassbound thrilling in the second. "Sometimes I think the play is no good," he admitted. "Sometimes I wonder whether the cast just misses the mark."[31]

On 11 June the Court was dark, for Ellen was gathering her strength for a huge celebration the next day: a star-studded matinee at the Drury Lane to celebrate her fifty years in the theatre. Shaw's poetic tribute, mailed to reach her the day of her gala, betrayed as much consciousness of his own age as of hers: "Oh, Ellen, was it kind of Fate/ To make your youth so thrifty/ That you are young at fifty-eight/ Whilst we are old at fifty? . . ."[32] She adored the demonstrations of affection and homage that showered upon her that year (friends felt they should have included a title); yet took them humbly, conscious that in part they were tributes to Irving, who, had he lived, would also have celebrated fifty years, since both she and Irving had stepped onstage in 1856, the year of Shaw's birth. For Ellen the jubilee fuss reduced the importance to her of *Brassbound*, although she took comfort in the fact that the celebrations did not fete an actress on the retired list. After reveling in tributory performances by Eleonora Duse, Caruso, Sir Arthur Sullivan, Réjane, Coquelin, Lillie Langtry, and Mrs. Patrick Campbell in a dazzling five-hour parade, how gratifying to have to rush away to Sloane Square to act London's most advanced playwright. She was not a has-been: she still served the public; and for that she blessed Shaw.

How even more gratifying to find "Jimmy" backstage when she arrived at the Court, and to fly into his arms. "*Who is that?*" Ellen had exclaimed to Shaw at an early rehearsal, catching sight of a tall, burly young man coming through the door. "That's the American captain," said Shaw, and then watched, fascinated and horrified, as Ellen sailed across the room and simply proceeded to put James Carew in her pocket. "I was awestruck," recalled Shaw: ". . . so swift a decision by a huntress who, far from being promiscuous in her attachments, was highly fastidious, made me marvel and say to myself 'There, but for the grace of God, goes Bernard Shaw.'" Of course he protested at the time, shooting off one of his little notes: ". . . I love you; and I am furiously jealous of Carew, with whom you fell in love at first sight." It was true: Ellen Terry at fifty-nine had fallen in love with an actor in his thirties. Said Carew simply (he was a simple, stolid fellow): "She was mad about me."[33] Shaw's play did not revive Ellen's career, but paradoxically revived her heart, providing her with what she had longed for from Shaw. After *Brassbound* closed in July, she whisked Carew off to Smallhythe, where she rattled him down country lanes in the pony cart, he heard her until she was word-perfect for Hermione with Sir Herbert Tree that fall, and they plotted an American tour for January 1907—together. And the Court had made another match: Harley Granville-Barker and Lillah McCarthy had married on Tuesday 24 April at the same registry office in Henrietta Street where Shaw had hobbled on crutches to marry Charlotte. The Shaws observed the occasion with the gift of a Bechstein piano with a pianola attachment; and Barker became almost as much a devotee of the instrument as Shaw.

The Court had also brought Florence Farr back into Shaw's range. Not that she had ever drifted entirely out of it: she had obliged him with copyright performances of *Man and Superman* and *How He Lied to Her Husband* at the Bijou Theatre, Bayswater, in June 1903 and August

1904.[34] This favor Florence performed more out of friendship than an intense belief in the Shavian drama, however; for her path had led in the opposite direction into the realms of poetry and incantation. Down this path went Yeats: together, in fact, they had plunged into a new art form, the art of speaking poetry to music. For Yeats the poetical revolution was also a mystical revolution, "for the magical word is the chanted word." What better partner in this revolution than S.S.D.D., whose low voice chanting incantations at the rituals of the Golden Dawn had thrilled him in the past? With Florence as his instrument, magic would become incarnate in the chanted word, which in turn would induce in the hearer a state of mystical ecstasy.

Their first attempts, with Florence plucking at the single string of a crude homemade lyre and the tone-deaf Yeats encouraging a circle of devout ladies to chime the beat of the poetry with the twang of the string, were less than successful. Professional help was necessary, and the pair found their way to Arnold Dolmetsch, who designed for Florence's golden voice (so he thought it) the first modern psaltery, thirteen-stringed and pitched to semitones; then instructed both of them in its possibilities. "Within the limits of an octave of semitones," Florence wrote later in her *Music of Speech*, "I set to work to discover and write down the inherent melody of a number of poems. I reduced everything connected with the art to the simplest possible terms, and used letters to indicate the notes of my scale . . . I then spoke the first line of a poem in the most impressive way that occurred to me, and immediately after sang and wrote down the notes I found I had used as starting points for the spoken word . . . I do not chant . . . I simply speak as I would without music, and having discovered the drift of my voice in the phrase, indicate that on the psaltery."[35]

Often annoyed with the inexplicable unevenness of her performances and energies, Yeats thought highly enough of Florence's talent to appoint her stage manager for the Irish Literary Theatre, founded after years of hopes and dreams in 1898, and to give her the role of Aleel in his *The Countess Cathleen*. Rehearsals were held in London at the all-purpose but unfashionable Bijou at Bayswater, then moved to the Strand; and George Moore, called in to take charge of the chaos, satirized the proceedings years later in "Ave." He had never thought much of Florence's acting; and now he laughed at the attempts of W.B. and Florence to instill the cast with the New Art. Swathed in a green cloak, Florence sat on the stage plucking her psaltery and chanting "Cover it up with a lonely tune," while May Whitty, engaged by Moore to play the lead that Yeats wrote for Maud Gonne, paced "like a pantheress" waiting for Florence to summon up a few practical stage directions. They were not forthcoming: pressed, Florence rummaged through a huge reticule for memoranda, but finally locating them, could not interpret her own notes;

and resorted instead to dropping prone upon the stage boards and speaking through the cracks. Although explaining that by this ritual she meant to evoke the powers of hell, she looked for all the world—so thought Moore—as though she were "trying to catch cockroaches."[36] Yeats's play opened 8 May 1899 in Dublin, and won mixed reviews depending on whether Yeats had primed critics for the New Art or not. Curiously, his art was criticized for the very qualities found lacking in Shaw—dramatic action and plot; praised for its poetic content, as Shaw's was praised for its intellectual. *The Countess Cathleen* proved successful enough, however, to encourage Yeats to envision a play that could be half acted, half chanted, merging magic with the music of poetry. His enthusiasm for poetry as a spoken art soared.

Shaw was among the audience gathered at Clifford's Inn in Fleet Street at 5 P.M. 29 May 1902 to hear Yeats discuss "Poetry and the Living Voice." Accompanied by Dorothy Paget and her sister on their psalteries, Florence then chanted Shakespeare, Shelley, Keats, Blake, Rossetti, Whitman, Lionel Johnson, and Stevenson to the vibrations of her lyre. Then, although she should have known better, she sought Shaw's opinion. Shaw replied:

> The fact is, there is no new art in the business at all: Yeats thinks so only because he does not go to church. Half the curates in the kingdom cantilate like mad all the time. Toastmasters cantilate. Public speakers who have nothing to say cantilate. And it is intolerable except in one obvious & complete instance—the street cry. Sarah Bernhardt's abominable "golden voice," which has always made me sick, is cantilation, or, to use the customary word, intoning. It is no use for Yeats to try to make a distinction: there is no distinction, no novelty, no nothing but nonsense.[37]

They would never see eye to eye. She had always, like Yeats, put form before content, sound before meaning, feeling before thought, the unintelligible before the intelligible. For Shaw the nonsense was non sense. He had only the same advice for her: she must first get "an athletic articulation" (Terry had it, so did Janet), and she could only get it by working at the consonants hard (the vowels would take care of themselves). Her articulation perfected, she could then convey her sense of the meaning of the words with emotional and intellectual conviction. Without that conviction, warned Shaw, "cantilation can do nothing except intensify ordinary twaddling into a nerve destroying crooning like the maunderings of an idiot-banshee. . . . Cats do the same thing when they are serenading one another; but the genuineness of their emotion gives them poignancy."

Barker had also listened to Florence at Clifford's Inn; he remembered her when he came to direct Gilbert Murray's translation of the *Hip-*

polytus of Euripides for the Court in October 1904. While the pragmatic Shaw was urging her to go study phonetics and become a dramatic professor of speech, Barker engaged Florence to write the music for the *Hippolytus*, and also to direct the chorus. Attending a rehearsal, Archer found Florence's compositions "strikingly beautiful," but missed "firmness of attack" in her pupils. Others were more severe. Admitting that of several ways to treat Euripides, Barker's playing him as though written for the modern stage was the most difficult, Desmond MacCarthy found Florence's handling of the chorus disastrous. It was "represented by seven or eight ladies, who moved about with slow, elaborate caution, posed like *tableaux vivants*, and uttered the most various sentiments in a monotonous and lugubrious chant, tapering into dismal contralto notes, and conveying no definite emotion beyond suggesting the earnest desire of the performers themselves to do their best. . . ." A *fin de siècle* weariness wilted Florence's effects; and MacCarthy concluded that for the first time Vedrenne and Barker had obviously lapsed: a chorus of men would probably have been more effective.

No one could have agreed more than Barker, who regretted Florence and her psalteries acutely. He would spend considerable energy trying to keep her out of future Greek performances. ". . . I *dread* that she may be writing tin-pot choruses," he wrote Gilbert Murray when *The Trojan Women* was imminent; ". . . I am really worried." Florence led the chorus for this second Euripides, only confirming Barker's opinion that she lowered the standard of the production with music not archaic, but "archaotic." For *Electra* in 1906, he pondered how to appropriate Florence's psalteries without Florence, or at least "to replace her jejune harmonies with something better, and her muddling with a little real training of the chorus"[38]—but this time succeeded in eliminating her altogether.

"I've tried to get people to speak beautifully," Florence confided in her diary, "but not a soul sees the truth any clearer for all I've said and written." Shaw's *John Bull's Other Island* followed Euripides at the Court, a play offered to but rejected by Yeats for the Irish Literary (later the Abbey) Theatre, ostensibly because it was too long, in reality because Yeats found Shaw "fundamentally ugly and shapeless." Torn between the philosophies of these two men, quick to realize the genius of both, yet like many only talented people, skeptical of the deep and unalterable conviction genius has in itself (Shaw and Yeats were both half-baked, thought Florence), she expended her energies on a wide variety of aesthetic ventures during these years without feeling that she accomplished anything tangible. Restless, she left Dalling Road, where Shaw had anchored her, moving from rooms to rooms, searching for a means to express and discipline the thoughts about Truth, Wisdom, Being, Peace, Space, Eternity, and Beauty that filled her. On 17 January 1905 she booked the Albert Hall and presented a program that epitomized the Farr-Yeats-Shaw triangle. Her masque, *The Mystery of Time*, combined the sybilline mysticism of Yeats with Shavian paradoxes like "The supreme desire is to be without desire" and "The smallest of the small is the greatest of the great." She followed the masque with incantations of Yeats's poems and then—she was not without humor—a selection of Shaw's "Maxims for Revolutionists" from *Man and Superman* which she actually cantilated in her golden voice to the psaltery. She began a novel, *Life Among the Supermen*. She had fed the imaginations of both her supermen; why did she herself remain empty?

"I hear a postman now and I think I'll go and see if there is a letter for me," she wrote in her diary in 1904. "I expect nothing—I am rather an elderly woman with no great prospect of anything in the world that could give me more than a momentary gratification." Spiritually atuned to Yeats, she continued to turn to Shaw for advice. Sympathetic and friendly now that he had washed his hands of her spiritual education, Shaw stated her problem more clearly than she had herself: "I dont see why you should not reblossom and have a great period now that you are about forty (*I'm* 50!). In the old days you caught on prematurely to old men and egotists—Ibsen, a grim old rascal; Todhunter, exactly like God in an illustrated family Bible, and me, an unintentional blighter of every purpose but my own. You were eaten up & preyed on: now you can have your turn with the knife and fork whilst we, whitehaired & doddering, look on at you with watering mouths."[39]

Well, she was forty-five, yet her turn might still come. Meanwhile she figured in four Court Theatre productions, sometimes going to sleep (Did she not have a mother, Gilbert Murray asked Shaw, to keep her awake with a big stick?), played Dectora in Yeats's *Shadowy Waters*, produced the first *Salomé* (with some delight, perhaps, in the beheading of the prophet-poet Jokanaan), played Herodias in the Literary Theatre Club's version of Wilde's play, and encouraged by John Quinn, an American lawyer and friend of Yeats, began to plan a lecture tour for America. She approached the tour with much trepidation, not sure whether she should talk or chant or read or recite; not sure about her fees, nor about her welcome. She must make £100 at least, that she knew. She worried about a list of "patrons" for advertisement, not liking to claim favors; reluctantly she drew up eighteen names, among them Lady Gregory, Gilbert Murray, Elizabeth Robins, G. K. Chesterton, Mrs. Patrick Campbell, and, of course, W. B. Yeats and Bernard Shaw. "Mrs. P. C. is a clever and lovely child of about 13," Shaw had told her. "By all means tout with her." Florence had met the actress, of course, in *Little Eyolf* days when she had played the Rat Wife to her Rita, and since then had managed to interest her in her New Art of cantilating to the psaltery. Apparently charmed, and an authority on dressing for

America since her 1904–5 tour, Stella Campbell kindly dispensed advice about wardrobe and itinerary, only adding rather disturbingly that she believed in Florence much more "*without* the psaltery." Florence sailed on 20 January 1907 (Ellen Terry had just left with James Carew on her eighth American tour, her first without Irving), writing hastily to Lady Gregory, "I am hoping to really get something from this . . . which will make me of more use to all my friends."

There were two whom the Court did not draw into its precincts. Shaw was not as firm as Barker about their exile: during the casting throes of *John Bull's Other Island*, for example, he had assured Barker that he did not want to give Charrington a part out of sympathy, but that all else being equal, he saw no reason not to give him anything that fit.[40] But Barker remained adamant. Janet, however, knew her G.B.S. If he would not give her a part, he had other uses. In April 1905, he opened a pathetic missive. She had, she announced tragically, finally been brought to a new and appalling step. Hollow-cheeked and unemployed, Charlie was devoting himself to the education of his little Nora "with cheerful industry, but with the worm gnawing at his heart." He might remain silent, but she herself, her career in ruins, had at last lost all shame. Lawyers, creditors, bailiffs pounded at the door. The new and appalling step was this: could Shaw come up with a hundred pounds? A hundred pounds would clear all their debts, and she could almost guarantee him 15 per cent interest. And if he could not manage one hundred, could Mrs. Webb?

Charlie's gnawing worm and her mantle of shame left him "a man of stone," Shaw informed her; yet he came to the rescue once more. He had some money now (*You Never Can Tell* had captivated New York); he had always evidenced some guilt at excluding the Charringtons from the Court enterprise; he was a generous man on principle. If Janet could put him directly in touch with her solicitor who could convince him that one hundred pounds would *completely* wipe off the debts for which they were being sued, he would risk the money—reserving the right, of course, to be "moral and sarcastic to its full value." Privately, he asked Charrington to draw up a list of debts; its arrival confirmed his darkest suspicions. "By a series of romantic discounts you have succeeded in reducing Janet's £100 to a minimum of £270.11.6½," he groaned. "You might as well have knocked off the halfpenny when your hand was in." It was hopeless: Charrington's appetite for debt was a neurosis. "You can keep out of temptation, but not out of a shop. You would walk to London to save the price of a 3rd class ticket; and on your arrival you would order a Mercedes car as a birthday present for Janet—another form of ordering a bailiff for her. . . . Why were you ever born? Why did you get married?" He sent £30 to retrieve three immediate executions; complied with another sum in July "in an idle moment, as a man might wantonly chuck a sovereign into the sea for want of a stone"; then was electrified by word from Charrington in October: "£300!!! Where the devil did you borrow it?"[41] No matter: he finally saw one thing clearly. The bogus manager—the man who spends his last borrowed penny on production and trusts his company's salaries to the take at the gate—was the actor's worst enemy. Charrington was such a blackguard: his credit as a manager was gone.

The Charringtons, however, did not excel at facing the truth. Exiled to Bourne Cottage, Beenham, near Reading (another exile, Oscar Wilde, had known the territory well), they brooded upon their wrongs, drawing up a list of the "crimes" for which they believed the world had condemned them to this cell of inaction: the Crime of Being Didactic, the Crime of *Not* Being Didactic, the Crime of Being Literary, the Crime of Being Serious, the Crime of Being in a Hurry, the Crime of Being Themselves.[42] More robust than Charrington, and more or less serene on great doses of morphia and now cocaine, Janet took to gardening, while her ever adoring husband decided that after all, working with living soil was the great modern art.

CHAPTER NINETEEN

1906-1912

HAVING PLAYED Nora Reilly, Gloria Clandon ("an exquisite performance"), and been made a new woman by Ann Whitefield, Lillah
McCarthy eagerly awaited the new play called *Jennifer* that Shaw had
promised to write especially for her. Then, however, she opened a letter
from Mevagissey, Cornwall, where he and Charlotte had gone to bathe,
announcing that both Jennifer Dubedat and her artist husband had taken
a back seat, and that moreover, "I am sorry to have to tell you that the
Artist's wife is the sort of woman I hate; and you have your work cut
out for you in making her fascinating." Reading those words of betrayal,
she felt he had nearly broken her heart, and was hardly comforted with
his assurance that the new play was sure to be lucky "as this morning,
coming up from the beach by a special act of Providence (to retrieve a
book Charlotte had lost) I found in my path a most beautiful snake, two
feet long, with an exquisite little head about the size of the tip of your
little finger, and a perfect design in lozenges on its back. . . . It finally
vanished into a bramble; but we parted the best of friends; and I am now
convinced that The Doctor's Dilemma will be a complete success for
you, for me, for the Court & for the universe."[1]

The Court needed a success, for its financial state was bleak, and quarrels between Vedrenne and Mrs. Granville-Barker rose with alarming
frequency. Signing himself "disinterestedly," Shaw attempted to keep
peace. Madame Hayward, it was true, wanted £120 for Jennifer's
dresses, but Vedrenne must consider that there was only one woman to
dress instead of the usual six. "I am deliberately spoiling Lillah to get the
best out of her for this play; for it will depend on her getting as much
enchantment into it as possible. The alternative is Mrs. Patrick Campbell;

and just think what it would cost to dress *her*, not to mention her salary."[2] To Lillah he wrote placatingly that a "salary is not everything." But bad feeling between Lillah, who felt she was understarred and underpaid, and Vedrenne, who felt she was not, continued to disturb the peace.

Jennifer Dubedat was indeed the kind of person Shaw disliked: an idealist and hero worshiper—the kind of romanticist Raina appeared to be before Bluntschli discovered her common sense. Worse, Jennifer was the type of sacrificing idealist who always lands on her feet. After her husband's death, she turns up at a showing of his paintings: she is gorgeously dressed, the author of a hagiography of her late husband (which, one suspects, will sell briskly), and happily remarried. How does she account for her good fortune? It is only the result of her devotion to her husband, who wished her to dress brightly, to remarry, and who inspired the book. Had her husband been heroic, her hero-worshiping might be tolerable; but Shaw partly modeled Louis Dubedat on the unscrupulous Edward Aveling and, in his intimate knowledge of pawn shops, Charles Charrington. True, the artist is a genius; but Shaw's opinion of unscrupulous genius is voiced by Sir Colenso Ridgeon: "The most tragic thing in the world is a man of genius who is not also a man of honor," although unlike Ridgeon, Shaw understood the artist who sacrifices everything and everyone to his own cause. But Jennifer Dubedat can see no wrong in her husband; her moral blindness is equal to his. Having created a woman he disliked, Shaw hastened to reassure Lillah: the public would find Jennifer charmingly sympathetic, no fear.

Lillah did not perhaps realize how much of her own nature Shaw had put into Jennifer—her own intensity, impetuosity, idealism, and propensity to hero worship. She records only that *The Doctor's Dilemma* was a success, and her "name praised in high places." Desmond MacCarthy, however, after expending much print on the doctors, gave her only two lines, and Max Beerbohm in the *Saturday Review* devoted all his space to comparing Dubedat with Henry James's Roderick Hudson. She had, in a sense, been betrayed; and discontent with the Court repertory system festered. There had been the time at one of the rehearsals for *You Can Never Tell*, for example, when Louis Calvert had turned to her and said: "You would be a great dramatic actress—a great tragedienne—away from plays like this." She protested: away from plays like Shaw's, she "would never have developed as a woman."[3] Yet Jennifer's gorgeous costumes did not entirely placate her.

The Court's financial statement for 1906 was depressing. "I am on the economical tack just now," Shaw wrote Vedrenne 22 January 1907; "that balance sheet is hard to swallow. The stars did not pay . . . ." He meant, of course, Ellen Terry. Seven matinees of *The Philanderer* were scheduled to begin 5 February. It was a play Shaw had always defended, always hoped much for. With the right Julia, with the right Charteris . . . But Shaw could not get the cast he wanted. The dark emotional Lillah rehearsed the dark emotional Julia; then was rushed to the hospital during dress rehearsal and replaced with Mary Barton. Ben Webster played Charteris with dignity but no understanding—not surprisingly, thought Desmond MacCarthy, since the person who understood Charteris probably did not exist. Few liked the play. Lillah loathed it "like hell"; Walkley found it one of Shaw's "least happy experiments"; Archer had always thought it a prime example of Shaw's tendency to wallow in filth; the audience missed Lillah. One problem seemed to be the discrepancy between Shaw's notion of a philanderer and the rest of the world's. "A philanderer," Shaw would advise Swedish translator Hugo Vallentin, "is a man who is strongly attracted by women. He flirts with them, falls half in love with them, makes them fall in love with him, but will not commit himself to any permanent relation with them, and often retreats at the last moment if his suit is successful—loves them but loves himself more—is too cautious, too fastidious, ever to give himself away."[4] People, however, seemed to find Charteris more callous than fastidious and, just as May Morris had not been able to smile at Shaw's contempt for Jenny Patterson, could not smile at Charteris's manipulation of the infatuated Julia.

Hedda Gabler followed *The Philanderer* on 5 March; and although "the stars did not pay," Mrs. Patrick Campbell played Hedda, like Shaw's Charteris, a character too fastidious, too cautious, too artistic ever to give herself away. Unlike Ellen Terry, Stella Campbell did not appear at the Court for want of better or to be agreeable to Shaw; she did Hedda because she was accustomed to doing what she liked, and she liked *Hedda Gabler*. Since breaking with Forbes-Robertson and going into management on her own, she had followed very much her own taste: José Echegaray's *Mariana*, Frank Harris's *Mr. and Mrs. Daventry*, Sudermann's *Magda*, Maeterlinck's *Pelléas and Mélisande* with Sarah Bernhardt as Pelléas, Bjørnson's *Beyond Human Power* were not exactly crowd pleasers, although she continued to draw the public. Now she descended upon the humble Court—imperious, malicious, fascinating. She was forty-two and, although past her Tanqueradiance (Shaw's term), still beautiful. Yet she was acutely conscious of encroaching middle age. "I dread seeing my photographs," she had laughed to Shaw; "the days of dewlaps have arrived! God help me and all women!"[5] An absolute terror at rehearsals, she cowed Barker, who attended rehearsals regularly, and Shaw, who came occasionally, and remembered that although their "basso-relievo" methods fidgeted her, they left her alone. Barker, however, had the courage to insist on the terms of the contract. No matter that she had packed the theatre at every performance: the Court was not for stars: the play would be taken off after seven matinees. They had already disagreed over a contract in 1900. Barker, substituting in *Magda* at the Royalty, insisted he be paid for the run of the show, since he had not understood that the original actor would return. Stella took him to court. Appearing cleverly in very shabby clothes and a much worn hat, Barker won a £60 decision and a decidedly cool handshake from Stella. Barker won with *Hedda* too; and Stella Campbell, like Ellen, decided that there was nothing to do but tour America to make some money.

On 22 March, as *Hedda Gabler* was ending its run, Ellen Terry married James Carew in smoky Pittsburgh. Although brushing off her marriage in her *Memoirs* as strictly her own affair, she did admit that the audiences and the press of America married them. "If I was coldly received, in other words plainly told I was too old and ugly to remain upon the stage, I had determined to give up all thoughts of the marriage, to put away 'all foolish fond records,' and leave the stage quietly at the end of the tour. But they opened their arms to me, flattered and spoiled me delightfully to the top of my bent, and I was married . . . ."[6]

She did not announce the marriage until June, when she was on her way back to England. In her cabin, she was taken sharply to task by Christopher St. John, friend of Edy, for her callousness in keeping something so important a secret from her daughter. Ellen Terry resented her resentment, Christopher discovered; and the breach between them was not healed for several years. Of course, Ellen had anticipated Edy's disapproval, and it was forthcoming, not so much against the marriage, thought Chris, as against the unworthy and inappropriate husband. "I give it two years," snapped Edy. Mingled with her disapproval was Edy's natural resentment of her mother's freehanded way of satisfying herself while dominating her daughter. Yet Edy had managed to escape that domination herself, secretly. In the autumn of 1899, while Ellen and Irving were touring America, Edy and her friend had moved into rooms together in Smith Square, Westminster. While Ellen was calling Edy her right hand and her left, Edy was in fact pleasing herself in a lesbian relationship with Christopher St. John.

Trouble started very soon after Ellen and James Carew arrived in England. As they set out to tour the provinces, several facts became clear. The first was, of course, that Ellen Terry was the star and Carew not a very interesting actor, although Ellen had promoted him from Captain Kearney to the role of Brassbound opposite her. His problem, she told Shaw, was monotony; yet he "goes on trying & striving & acts better & better every week. His sincerity *tells* upon the audience." Unfortunately, there was sometimes not much of an audience for it to tell upon. "We return to London tomorrow," Ellen informed Shaw that September, "—very bad business here & at Portsmouth. The Gallery & Pit at both places have stayed away, with the odd result that those who *did* come enjoyed the Play immensely & it *went* splendidly!"[7] A second problem was that both Ellen and Carew were stuck in a play that neither of them really liked, a play which did not draw well, yet one of the few plays that provided a vehicle for them both, so that they could not very well drop it. Carew played Brassbound until, as Shaw quipped, his brain was "visibly half gone"; he hated the part: it put him strangely out of temper.[8] Ellen coped with ceaseless Lady Cicely by throwing out Shaw's character and playing herself. Again Shaw had become the third of a triangle. He was their great hope professionally; the promise of his plays tantalized them both.

Nothing could be worse for a marriage, Shaw had always said, than two people cloistered together without other interests—the wife feeding on her husband's soul, the husband "almost damned in a fair wife." Of the two lots the husband's was the worse. Shakespeare's phrase was not at all obscure, said Shaw: "you have only to look round at the men who have ventured to marry very fascinating women to see that most of them are not merely 'almost damned' but wholly damned. Without occupation, without any other centre for their lives but their wives, such men lose self-respect and their very souls." Virtually unemployable except with Ellen, Carew found himself so damned.

No one knew the problem better than Ellen herself. Once Shaw had petitioned her to get his plays done at the Lyceum. Now she became the petitioner: her husband must have work, at any cost, at any price. "I want him to have a very good engagement—will you give him one—& as for me whether I act or whether I don't [she lied] it matters not the least to me," she wrote Shaw in August 1907. 12 October 1907: "Don't you think Jim (and I too?) could have played in your Devil's Disciple. I should have loved it, for both of us. We *must* work. . . ." 15 October 1907: "I'd like you (for he loves you) to make him an offer. Oh, do be quick and ask him to play a fine part with a fair salary, or a mere good part with an unfair salary! . . . For Goodness' sake if you have anything good to offer Him, offer it him at once . . . ." 1 March 1909: "If you will serve me you can *most mightily* by speaking for James to any & every manager & telling them all to engage him—any part—any salary, only *work* he must. It wd be so good for him & he knows it. We are down here at the Farm enjoying it all well enough, but we feel we oughtn't to—we ought to work! . . . Do do remember to put in a word for him—Jim—or *more* put in a whole recommendation for him, it wd give me so much happiness & I feel you wd try to give *any*body happiness if you were able." 17 January 1910: "Remember James Carew is a very good actor of some parts, & give him one if you can. *It would do me such a good turn.*"[9]

Had James Carew been able to hold his own at home, the situation might have been less strained; but of course he could not. Smallhythe was Ellen's; "the Pony, the kitten, the wee doggie, the roses, the chix, the big ticking clock in the big kitchen"—all Ellen's; the grandchildren Ellen's; the visitors Ellen's; the hostile daughter in the nearby cottage Ellen's. Carew tried his hand at managing at first. "He bosses me nicely," said Ellen. But apart from her young love match with Godwin, during which she had played at housekeeping and mothering in a country cottage, Ellen had always been boss in her own household, father and mother to her children, father to her grandchildren. Smallhythe revolved around her and depended on her. In this household Carew played an uneasy role.

Ellen herself was uneasy, her concern for her young husband's career masking a greater concern for an aging wife's. Sick to death of *Brassbound,* she would have given a lot for a different Shaw play. "*Must* it be Fanny Brough & not me?" she asked 14 March 1908, the very day Shaw finished *Getting Married*. "Am I too old? I *must* act. . . . DO let me read your marriage play." But *Getting Married* opened 12 May at the Haymarket with Fanny Brough, who had created Mrs. Warren in 1902, playing the clairvoyant earth mother, Mrs. George Collins. A year later Ellen was writing wistfully: "Are you writing some more grand things— *great* plays like 'Mrs. Warren's Profession'? I suppose I'll never act you any more? Oh Dear. . . ." By September 1910, she had given up: "Farewell to you & Charlotte. I am about to live (!) day & night in a beastly jolting overheated-by-steam American railway car—for 2 whole months on end—always going going until I shall *be gone*—I feel it. It's enough to kill a horse. Well, I *must* go & so an end— ('unemployed' in London). Oh the filthy heat of an American winter."[10] Despite her complaints, she was still amazingly vital and buoyant. So she struck Lena Ashwell, a former colleague at the Lyceum, when she danced into her dressing room in Toronto that winter. "Almost blind, alone, stripped of all the luxury and care which had for so long been hers," remembered Ashwell; "courageous, undefeated, young, she hugged me and said: 'What do you think of me Lena? Sixty-three, and on one-night stands.'" She came to the dress rehearsal of *Judith Zarane*, which lasted nearly all night; and although she kept urging herself "You must go home, Nelly, you must go home," she stayed on, interested, cheerful, alert.[11]

Carew did not sail with her; the marriage had ended in an unofficial separation two and a half years after it began. "If I had had a place of my own," Carew told Edy after Ellen's death, "I should never have quarrelled with Nell. The only way to get on with her was not to live in the same house." "He is a child," countered Ellen. "A mixture. He is a half-wild thing . . . ." It was a charm which had quickly worn thin.

Eleven Shaw plays had dominated 701 performances out of 988 since the start of the Court Theatre venture in 1904. The experiment had made his reputation, had established Barker as a brilliant director, actor, and playwright, and had changed Lillah McCarthy from a romantic heroine into the modern Shavian woman. On 28 June 1907, the management at the Court closed its doors with Shaw's *Don Juan in Hell* and *The Man of Destiny;* however, the trio had already set their sights on the Savoy Theatre in the West End. Shaw underwrote this new project heavily, putting down £2,000, not as a partner, he told Vedrenne, but simply as a usurer who expected 5 per cent and no profits for the management until he was paid off. In October Barker played Burgoyne at the Savoy in *The Devil's Disciple;* at the end of December, despite Shaw's campaign to get her to do Louka because she would play "very magically" to her husband's Sergius, Lillah played Raina, looking lovely in costumes by the brilliant Charles Ricketts—she would not be shoved into the back seat again. All the ingredients were the same; yet somehow the Savoy collaboration lacked the luster of the Court. Vedrenne was ill; Barker very moody; Shaw constantly trying to save five pounds on necessities while Barker spent a hundred on luxuries; the trouble between Lillah and Vedrenne, alternately fanned and cooled by Shaw, whose position between them was "fearful," did not disappear; and Lillah, when she was not pondering her husband's increasing aloofness, fretted over the roles she was given or not given. One of the latter was the part of "Mrs. George" in *Getting Married*, an "uncommon woman," thought Lillah. There she was wrong, said Shaw. Mrs. George was a part for a "sublime low comedian" and Lillah would have ruined the play.[12]

Shaw's new play, begun in August 1907, had come slowly. Although really "a sermon on Equality," Shaw told Lillah, it was also a discussion of marriage, and the first of Shaw's plays to be frankly labeled "disquisitory." In *Man and Superman*, Shaw had managed to have it both ways: in the comedy proper, Jack Tanner succumbs to mating; in the philosophical dream sequence, Don Juan does not. In *Getting Married* Shaw had it thirteen different ways, from the puritan Reverend Oliver Cromwell Soames who shudders at the very idea of marriage, to Mrs. Bridgenorth who believes that the tie is for life, to Lesbia Grantham who wants a child but no husband, to Mrs. George who takes lovers, but would fry them with onions for her husband's breakfast.

The long Preface began with the thesis that the marriage law as it now stood was inhuman, unreasonable, and abominable, both for individual and social good. The pretense that marriage was founded for bliss or for children was patently false, since neither unhappiness nor childlessness were grounds for divorce. The real basis of the marriage contract was the fact of woman as man's property and slave; that was why any critic of the institution brought down cries of outrage upon his head, for an attack on marriage was an attack on property. But although the British Government shuddered at the least mention of the marriage question, reform could not be put off forever, argued Shaw; and when it came, several issues would clearly have to be tackled. At the heart of the problem lay economics, for "The truth is that family life will never be decent, much less ennobling, until this central horror of the dependence of women on men is done away with," a dependence that reduced "the difference between marriage and prostitution to the difference between Trade Unionism and unorganized casual labor . . . ." Even the question of divorce (which should unequivocally be granted for all improper, inconvenient, or unhappy marriages) ultimately depended on woman's economic independence; for though convinced that a husband or wife should be able to discard each other under unhappy circumstances without difficulty, Shaw could hardly recommend that a dependent woman be cast out into the streets, stripped of the one law that now protected her. Divorce reform could only follow economic reform; and one answer to economic reform was paid housework and motherhood, so that woman's desire for children could be separated from the necessity of enslaving herself to a man. No man would consider working without a wage; no woman should. Until such reforms could be introduced, concluded Shaw, British marriage would remain what it now was: a monstrously unreasonable and degrading institution preserved only by pious lies and the blindness of men and women who do not realize the trap until it springs shut on them.

As Shaw's dislike of sensuousness on the stage rose not only from his conviction that it degraded women and lied about life but also from personal distaste, so his attack on marriage had its source not only in his certain knowledge that it enslaved one half of the human race to the other, but in his abhorrence of sexual promiscuity. Of course, Shaw argued against the almost unlimited opportunity for intercourse that marriage provides on social grounds: promiscuity was no longer recruiting the race, but destroying it. But the shudder at sexuality that ran through the whole argument was subjective and strong, and would prevail (one suspects) even if, for example, birth control removed the dangers of overpopulation. Shaw began by setting up the existence of "very real, very strong, very austere avengers of outraged decency" who were more and more objecting to marital licentiousness; yet it was unclear who these avengers might be. Surely St. Paul, cited for his "instinctive recoil" from marriage as "a slavery to pleasure," was not a happy example, although Shaw went on to insist that today there were "more and more Pauline celibates" who found the idea of marriage as a sanctuary for pleasure an intolerable indignity. He apparently was the only Pauline present, however, at a London conference devoted to the problem of marital relationships. "It was certainly a staggering revelation," relates the appalled puritan. "Peter the Great would have been shocked; Byron would have been horrified; Don Juan would have fled from the conference into a monastery. The respectable men all regarded the marriage ceremony as a rite which absolved them from the laws of health and temperance; inaugurated a life-long honeymoon; and placed their pleasures on exactly the same footing as their prayers. It seemed entirely proper and natural to them that out of every twenty-four hours of their lives they should pass eight shut up in one room with their wives alone, and this, not birdlike, for the mating season, but all the year round and every year. . . . Please remember, too, that there was nothing in their circumstances to check intemperance."

But the real terror for Shaw was this: "If I had adopted [the respectable men's habits], a startling deterioration would have appeared in my writing before the end of a fortnight, and frightened me back to what they would have considered an impossible asceticism." It was the old fear, shared in this instance with austere avenger Beatrice Webb, with whom he apparently thrashed out the problem of unlimited sexual relations. Beatrice's diary entry for 18 October 1906, written while Shaw was in the midst of *Getting Married*, echoes his Preface closely: would unchecked intimacy, she asked, leave one any brain to think with?[13] Beatrice, of course, was referring to the kind of sexual promiscuity outside of marriage that H. G. Wells had glorified in *The Days of the Comet*. Shaw marked marriage as the villain, reiterating to clergyman John Oliver, "There is another objection to marriage—quite the most formidable of all—which has not yet been grasped; and that is its appalling licentiousness."[14]

Of course, there *were* new "austere avengers of outraged decency," though Shaw's rhetoric did not state their case or identity plainly. These were not Pauline ascetics, however, but growing numbers of women who were beginning to see that a husband's "right" to sexual intercourse on demand was still another fact of women's subordinate position, and who were beginning to resist such control over their bodies. Shaw's objections—personal and ideological as they were—thus once again coincided with the immediate problem of women's rights.

There was one other Pauline at least who shared his horror: Charlotte. How much she nourished the already strong antipathy in Shaw for sexual intimacy is difficult to say. From all evidence they avoided sex; and Shaw's consciousness of the unusual nature of their relationship undoubtedly caused him to attack "normal" marriage in self-defense, just as the success of their relationship inspired him to urge sexless marriage for others. Their marriage had by now settled down into a familiar routine. Shaw worked and Charlotte helped him work—feeding him regularly, answering correspondence, typing scripts, arranging luncheons with the famous, fending off intruders. Her diary chiefly recorded the triumphs of G.B.S., her travel diary the wanderings to which she subjected him and which were his chief form of punishment. They seldom stayed more than a few months in one spot, moving from Adelphi Terrace to The Old House at Harmer Green, Hertfordshire, to Edstaston in Shropshire to Derry in Ireland to the Marine Hotel at North Berwick in Sussex to Hafod y Bryn in Wales to Mevagissey in Cornwall to Ayot St. Lawrence, Hertfordshire, and back to Adelphi Terrace—not to mention their travels abroad.

On her part Charlotte suffered from the constant intrusions of admiring women into Shaw's life, women whom his vanity encouraged and his elusiveness drove wild. The strangest of these was Erica Cotterill, a young woman who first adored the plays and then the master, bombarding him with letters and finally announcing in April 1908 that she was violently in love with him. Shaw's answer was tolerant, amused. "It is all very terrible and agonizing and glorious and tragic and unbearable, isnt it?" he teased. "You are certainly enjoying it enormously and rising to it with great literary power." Then Erica began making alarming intrusions upon the Shaws at Adelphi Terrace, and Shaw took a sterner tone: ". . . Now that I have taught you some respect for business and the law, let me assure you that marriage is more sacred than either, and that unless you are prepared to treat my wife with absolute loyalty, you will be hurled into outer darkness for ever. The privilege of pawing me, such as it is, is hers exclusively." A year later all patience had evaporated: ". . . you are a little insane; and insane people, Emerica, are frightful *bores*."[15] This was brutal, but as he had warned her—"if you dare to fall in love with a god, you must be prepared for thunderbolts."

Besides the private woman question from which he had always suffered, Shaw found himself in the years between 1907 and 1910 gradually forced into the public woman question. The problem of women's political emancipation, addressed when the women's suffrage movement was organized in Manchester in 1865 and simmering ever since, had burst forth again in the militant activities of the Women's Social and Political Union (W.S.P.U.), led by the Pankhursts; and it was a movement in which virtually every woman Shaw knew participated. Elizabeth Robins, returned intermittently to the stage (in 1902 Max Beerbohm condemned her violence in *Paolo and Francesca*, praised her power and imagination as the mad woman in Mrs. Humphry Ward's *Eleanor*[16]), and always a feminist, emerged now as a dramatist. Doing so, she joined Florence Bell, Mrs. Oscar Beringer, Constance Fletcher ("George Fleming"), Mrs. W. K. Clifford, Mrs. Craigie ("John Oliver Hobbes"), Mrs. Montague Crackenthorpe, Mrs. E. S. Willard, Lalla Vandervelde, Lady Violet Greville, Lady Colin Campbell, Mrs. de la Pasture, Clo Graves, Florence Warden, Dorothy Leighton, Cicely Hamilton, Madeleine Lucette Ryley, Risden Home, Estelle Burney, Martha Morton, and Mrs. Humphry Ward —the New Drama was not only about women, but often by them. Her *Votes for Women!* opened at the Court Theatre 9 April 1907; of the incredible flood of words that poured forth on the subject, it proved perhaps the most effective piece of feminist propaganda to come out of the suffrage movement, not the least for popularizing the "Votes for Women!" slogan first coined by Christabel Pankhurst and Annie Kenney.[17]

John Masefield, soon to become an ardent personal admirer of Robins, wrote to tell her that he found her play splendid, noble, and full of beauty. Others were more cautious. Desmond MacCarthy admitted the "customary cleverness" of the author, but found *Votes for Women!* chiefly memorable for the brilliant realism of the second act, which staged a suffragist meeting in Trafalgar Square. The crowd scene, thought MacCarthy, was from the life. They were all there: the suffragette on her soapbox, the working woman, the youthful enthusiast, the chauvinist, the socialist, the professional rebel, the moderate—"reality overwhelming enough to be almost inartistic," as Max Beerbohm said. MacCarthy avoided, however, the central theme of the play: the sexual antagonism between a militant suffragette (inspired by the personality of Christabel Pankhurst, whom Elizabeth adored) and her former lover, an antagonism over which, Max confided, he could not suppress a yawn. Vida Levering has undergone an abortion in the past because her ambitious lover was too prudent to marry her. She has her innings when Geoffry Stonor, now an M.P., falls in love with a wealthy young woman. Holding over Stonor's head the threat of raising his fiancée's consciousness and winning her over to the woman's movement, Vida forces the strong man of the Tory party to support the suffrage bill. How unlikely, thought Max, that a prominent politician would turn a somersault over a great national problem; and how fallacious the logic of "I was seduced: I had not the vote: Therefore all women should have the vote." Finding Elizabeth "one of the cleverest of her sex," Max decided that she had originally and treacherously meant *Votes for Women!* as a satire, only passing it off at the last moment as a "tract." Max thus dismissed Elizabeth's feminism as a joke, something his predecessor would not have done. Yet Shaw did not like the play very well, writing Barker, who stage-managed the production, that the stage business went like a quadrille "but the parts simply did not exist." The New York *Times* would have pleased Elizabeth best: *Votes for Women!*, said the critic, "has the tang of Shaw, without his brutality, and that insight into the heart of woman which is Pinero's greatest gift."[18]

Votes for Women! was most interesting for the sexual antagonism that coruscated through the play. Indirect, veiled, tortured—the struggle between man the rapist and woman the victim gave the drama its force. Elizabeth had always seen man as the sexual aggressor, flinching from the attentions of the men in her boardinghouse, shrinking from the touch of a solicitous male anxious to help her across a muddy street, treating Shaw's philandering as a crime. She had not remarried, content to find in her deep attachment to her brother a safe passion. This passion had reached its height when in 1900, hearing that her brother had disappeared into the Klondike, she threw up everything, outfitted herself for an expedition, and set out to find him. "She disappeared into the snows of Alaska," said Leonard Woolf, who admired Elizabeth, "but she found Raymond and stayed with him in the wild mining town until she got ill and had to return to London." A severe case of typhoid fever prostrated Elizabeth for years following that adventure, but it was the lesser tragedy, for in those years her beloved Raymond met Margaret Dreier, a beautiful and intelligent woman as dedicated to progressive causes as he, and married her. Although Elizabeth cabled "Loving congratulations" to her brother in Chicago on 29 May 1905, she would have been devastated had she known that on that very day Raymond sent Margaret the picture of "Bessie" he had carried for thirteen years from the tangled cypress swamps of Florida to the icebound peaks of the North, the picture that had sustained him in all his struggles with the powers of darkness. Bessie had been his "great light," but the light of his own "beloved One" now irradiated him, and he did not need his sister any more. There is evidence that Elizabeth never forgave her brother for his betrayal of the pact of chastity they had sworn to. She herself turned to younger women like Octavia Wilberforce, whom she took into her house and financed through medical school; and they turned to her, sometimes with passion.[19] She fascinated many men—John Masefield poured out his devotion in hundreds of letters—but she chose her male friendships cautiously, preferring married men like Archer or confirmed bachelors like Henry James. "St. Elizabeth," Shaw had taunted her—recognizing in the actress a disturbing reflection of his own "St. George."

She had chosen to act the plays of Ibsen because they offered more scope for the actress than any others.[20] She found an outlet now in the women's suffrage movement, which brought her combined talents of writing and speaking into play. *Votes for Women!* was a commercial success; with the profits she bought Backsettown Farm, Henfield, Sussex: it became a shelter for suffragettes before or after their prison terms, and for women medical students. She served on the board of the W.S.P.U. with the Pankhursts, she helped organize the Actresses' Franchise League, she helped organize and served as president of the Women Writers' Suffrage League. She was very much concerned, now that she had acknowledged C. E. Raimond's identity, about women and literature: besides she had a debt to pay for the insult to women writers of *George Mandeville's Husband.* What were women really like, she challenged. Did men know? "If I were a man, and cared to know the world I lived in," she wrote in a W.S.P.U. tract called "Woman's Secret," "I almost think it would make me a shade uneasy—the weight of that long silence of one-half the world." She tried to lift that weight—persuading, charming, exhorting. Perhaps her great failure was Henry James, who, although *devoted* to and *thrilled* by her "mighty spirit" and "panoramic" character, resisted signing a petition for votes for women, and was rewarded for the omission when a suffragette (or provocateur) slashed his new portrait by Sargent in 1914.

On a train one day in 1900, Elizabeth Robins had met another young actress and feminist named Lena Ashwell, who, she told Robins, had given up the lead in H. V. Esmond's *Grierson's Way* because she was hard up and had no suitable clothing. Suspecting that Lena's reluctance really stemmed from the fact that the censor had refused the play a license, Elizabeth told her she was a fool to pass up the chance of such a fine part. Lena reconsidered, did one private performance, and through it won the part of Mrs. Dane in Henry Arthur Jones's *Mrs. Dane's Defense*, a triumph for Lena and a popular play unfortunately cut short by the death of Queen Victoria. She had already won the attention of Shaw in 1895, although he had omitted to mention her Elaine in the heat of his attack upon the absurdities of *King Arthur* and the waste of Terry's genius at the Lyceum. Irving next cast her as one of the little princes in *Richard III*. Ellen thought she would be "a little picture" and would act very well. Shaw agreed that Lena was "a fascinating squawker," but could Ellen convince her that it was not possible "to stand on her heels & point up to the flies with both big toes simultaneously!" He did not appreciate Lena as a little prince: the moment the pretty actress in tights walked onstage, all serious historical illusion vanished. "Probably Sir Henry Irving cast Miss Ashwell for the part because he has not followed her career since she played Elaine in King Arthur," said Shaw. "She was then weak, timid, subordinate, with an insignificant presence and a voice which, contrasted as it was with Miss Terry's, could only be described—if one had the heart to do it—as a squawl. Since then she has developed precipitously."[21]

The precipitous Lena Pocock had always been something of a heller. Born on a training ship in the mouth of the Tyne, she had immigrated to Canada with her family when Captain Pocock's health broke down. There she learned to bake, scrub floors, fetch water from the river, paddle a canoe, and swim. She was expelled from school because she loved words, particularly the word "illegitimate," which she pronounced with much relish; suffered from her family's move from the wilderness to a slummy neighborhood in Toronto; got more bad marks than any other girl at Bishop Strachan's School for Young Ladies; played male leads in pants for the Dramatic Club; inspired passionate crushes in at least one of the young ladies; and was introduced to tragedy when, on a shopping trip to buy ribbons for her sister's bridal bouquet, her mother was thrown from the carriage by a bolting horse and killed. After graduating from the University of Toronto, she found her way back to London, where she began to think of the stage, an idea that was met with cries of horror from her father's relatives, one of whom locked her in the strong room of his office with advice to reconsider. She did not, but enrolled at the Royal Academy of Music, and after straining her vocal cords impossibly (hence the squawl), took up elocution instead. At the end of the year, as all the students knew, Ellen Terry would come to examine and distribute the medals. "How can one ever express what Ellen Terry meant to us?" Lena exclaimed. The young woman had haunted the gaslit Lyceum, forgetting the hard bench with its uncomfortable iron arm dividers in her rapture at the radiant figure on the stage. She had adored *The Dead Heart.* "I can still see Ellen Terry signing the paper which broke her heart, the tears pouring down her face and mine and the faces of all the audience. Times have changed; very few tears are shed now in a theatre."[22]

But they were shed on that prize day. Ellen Terry was struck immediately by the "queer-looking child, handsome, with a face suggesting all manner of possibilities. When she stood up to read the speech from 'Richard II.' she was nervous, but courageously stood her ground," recalled Ellen. "She began slowly, and with a most 'fetching' voice, to *think* out the words. You saw her think them, heard her speak them. It was so different from the intelligent elocution, the good recitation, but bad impersonation of the others! 'A pathetic face, a passionate voice, a *brain*,' I thought to myself. It must have been at this point that the girl flung away the book and began to act, in an undisciplined way, of course, but with such true emotion, such intensity, that the tears came to my eyes. The tears came to her eyes too. We both wept, and then we embraced, and then we wept again. It was an easy victory for her. She was incomparably better than any one. 'She has to work,' I wrote in my diary that day. 'Her life must be given to it, and then she will—well, she will achieve just as high as she works.' "[23]

Encouraged by the great Terry's demonstration, Lena dared to go round to the Lyceum, thinking to ask for a walk-on; but her reception there was rather different. Miss Terry "came down the stairs in a whirl of collecting all her things for rehearsal, giving directions to all sorts of people, paused for a moment on the landing, heard me for a second, and said: 'Get experience; do anything, go anywhere, but get experience.' " Then she swept out of the theatre where her beautiful blond Teddy stood waiting by a brougham, slipped inside, and disappeared. "I almost hated her at that moment," said Lena, "but later I knew how right she was." She got experience: went on tour, met an actor, found out after marrying him that he was an alcoholic, left him, and returned to the Lyceum, where as Elaine she had a scene with Ellen in the first act of *King Arthur* and came on as a corpse in the third. But "to be allowed to speak to Ellen Terry, to adore Forbes Robertson, to wear beautiful clothes"—it was all very wonderful.

But Lena Ashwell did not make the kind of success that Ellen had envisioned. She was nobody's leading lady—too brainy, too rebellious, too
independent to further her career in ordinary ways. Instead she began to
acquire a reputation for her work in "advanced" plays. Max Beerbohm
shuddered delicately over her performances in Shakespeare, where she
had no romance, no poetry, no graces—begging as Portia, "Tell me your
counsels; I'll not disclose 'em." But in modern plays like *Mrs. Dane's Defense, Leah Kleschna, The Darling of the Gods*, and Tolstoy's *Resurrection*, the intelligence, sincerity, and realism of her acting made a powerful impression. Yet her success was uneven: she toured the provinces
and failed, unknown outside of London.

At Christmastime in 1904, lying in bed and brooding over her troubles
—the failure of the tour, no money in the bank, the rent due, her
crippled sister dependent upon her as well as a cousin's small child (people whispered it was illegitimate and Lena's, and the word did not seem
so fascinating any more)—she was interrupted by a messenger bearing a
parcel tied with red tape. Opening it, she found a jewel case labeled "To
'The Darling of the Gods,' from One of the Gods" and, lifting the lid,
the sum of five hundred pounds. Like Florence Farr's Avenue money,
the gift proved to have come from a woman, ostensibly an American patron of the arts named "Jane Emerson," but actually, as Lena would discover, from a small, attractive, wealthy, and power-hungry woman who
had seen Lena in *Resurrection* and taken an immediate fancy to her.
"Lady Caroline's" intrigues and jealousies; her hatred of Henry Simson,
the Scots doctor Lena sent for when ill, recognized from a dream, fell in
love with, and married in 1908; Lena's discovery that the lovely little
house in Cowley Street presented to her by "Jane" in reality belonged to
"Lady Caroline," who wished to make her a kept woman—all made the
possession of five hundred pounds both bitter and exciting. With the
money she purchased a ninety-nine-year lease on an unlucky theatre, the
old Novelty in Great Queen Street, where Janet had bewitched Shaw as
Nora, since then gone through half a dozen name changes and failures.
She renamed it the Kingsway, redecorated it in Louis XVI style, and
opened on Friday the thirteenth, 1907, with thirteen in the cast of Anthony Wharton's *Irene Wycherly*. After 139 performances, Cicely Hamilton's *Diana of Dobson's* came on for 142; and the Kingsway took on a
decidedly feminist tone, for Lena would become an active member of
the Actresses' Franchise League, and Cicely Hamilton a founder of the
Women Writers' Suffrage League. As the only woman then in management, Lena represented the Actresses' Franchise League in a deputation
to 10 Downing Street, where they were received by a hostile Prime
Minister Asquith like smelly animals just escaped from the zoo. It was
impossible for anyone not living the experience to realize the scorn
heaped on the suffragettes, said Lena, remembering how on another oc-

casion Sir Herbert Tree, seeing her with a book *The Soul of a Suffragette* in her hand, snatched it from her "and with a magnificent gesture of contempt flung it into the far corner of the room." The Kingsway was an unlucky theatre, but its manager's militancy also contributed to her eventual failure.

Charlotte Shaw knew Lena Ashwell as an actress, admired her, and wanted her for Brieux's *La Femme seule*, which she had translated and vowed to see produced. The cause of votes for women drew them together. On 13 June 1908 they were among the thirteen thousand suffragists who gathered on the Embankment for a great procession to the Albert Hall intended to stir enthusiasm for the coming Hyde Park demonstration of 21 June, when the W.S.P.U. hoped to break all records for a public gathering. The purple, white, and green colors of the W.S.P.U. were raised that day among thousands of brilliant silk and velvet banners, the larger ones emblazoned with the symbols of Joan of Arc, Queen Elizabeth, Boadicea, Sarah Siddons, Elizabeth Browning, Fanny Burney, St. Theresa, Lucy Stone, Florence Nightingale, Mary Wollstonecraft, and "Victoria—Queen and Mother." The suffragist leaders were there: Mrs. Despard, Mrs. Israel Zangwill, Lady Frances Balfour, Beatrice Harraden, Cicely Hamilton, Dr. Garrett Anderson, Mrs. Ayrton. A contingent of international suffragists displayed their national flags, the Reverend Dr. Anna Shaw leading the American women under the Stars and Stripes. Scientists marched with women of the medical profession in robes of crimson and black with purple, blue, and red hoods. Bands of women from Newnham and Girton colleges swelled the ranks. Elizabeth Robins marched with the women writers under the Scriveners' banner. Then came the actresses, among them Lillah McCarthy, Gertrude Elliott (Shaw's Cleopatra), and Lena Ashwell; then artists; then nurses in uniform; then crowds of typists, shorthand writers, pharmacists, shop assistants, factory workers, homemakers; and after them the members of political women's organizations, Charlotte Shaw marching with the feminist members of the Fabian. "Altogether the procession was acknowledged to be the most picturesque and effective political pageant that had ever been seen in this country," said Sylvia Pankhurst (whom Shaw called with fondness his "idiot-genius"), "and every newspaper spoke of its impressive dignity and beauty."[24]

Charlotte and Lena became close friends, unusual, since Charlotte, according to Beatrice Webb, did not admire women. But perhaps she merely did not admire women who admired Shaw too well; and Lena Ashwell was to remain curiously impervious to Shaw the dramatist and Shaw the man, even when she constantly tested his kindness by asking favors and read such irresistible messages in reply as "The first coldness Henry dares, we fly together; if Charlotte will let me."[25] "Lena Ashwell will do nothing for *me*," Shaw admitted on one occasion: "perhaps she will for the cause."

From this great struggle, Shaw the fighter and feminist kept himself aloof. ". . . How can you refrain . . . from breaking a lance for us?" Ethel Smyth, suffragist, composer, and creator of the suffragette battle hymn "Shoulder to Shoulder," would write in 1914, "That's my puzzle. . . . I should have thought a brain like yours—unless there's some marring element at work when it's a question of women—should have jumped to the logic, the irresistibility of the whole thing. . . . if you could see your way to some sort of thrust—supposing I am right in feeling you must understand the whole thing as well as I do—it would be very satisfactory—I can't imagine my suggesting such a thing to any other man as no other man could do it. . . ."[26] But he did not take up a lance. Mrs. Pankhurst never forgave him for not taking part in the rally that capped the procession on 13 June 1908 to the Albert Hall. But said Shaw: "If you or anybody else thinks I am going to become the tame Tomcat of the suffrage movement or any other women's movement in this country, you will find yourself mistaken."[27] Yet it was a movement that many distinguished men did not find themselves emasculated in publicly supporting: Keir Hardie, Johnston Forbes-Robertson, Laurence Housman, William Archer, the Bishop of Lincoln, Frederick Pethick-Lawrence. Mrs. Pankhurst was the more baffled because Shaw, of course, had always believed that no social problem could be satisfactorily solved unless women had their due share in solving it.[28] Now Shaw, however, held back, equivocated, and replied to Ethel Smyth that the vote would do no good for women since it had been useless to men, one of the least happy arguments he ever voiced. Privately to Lucy he declared that he did not have time for the suffrage movement. A more plausible reason for his hanging back, however, was his fundamental disagreement with both the guerrilla tactics and the politics of Emmeline and Christabel Pankhurst, who, apart from their militancy for the suffrage, were conservatives.

One issue did at last drive him to public protest. On Tuesday evening, 23 March 1913, at a mass meeting at Kingsway Hall, Shaw took the platform to protest that torture by forcible feeding was illegal. Always adept at disarming opposition, he declared that he had *not* come forward to speak on the behalf of the weaker sex, who, all things considered (*Man and Superman* politics again), had proved themselves hardier than men. No, he had come forward to protest against the crime of force feeding itself: men were also being forcibly fed, and the practice was an illegal as well as a medieval abomination. This was a clever as well as a humane argument; yet Shaw seemed very conscious that he was a tardy comer to the cause, stating defensively at the beginning of his speech that Mr. Forbes-Robertson was the only suffragist gentleman who had not told him he was a dastard for not mounting the platform earlier. He had not come forward, he explained, first, because he had a firm conviction that women could take care of themselves and second, because the sight of some friend of his in the past being "brought forward between petticoats looked so horribly ignominious and performed so very much worse than the women" that personal vanity alone had not permitted him to come forward.[29] While forced feeding shocked many, it is perhaps significant that Shaw stood up at last to protest an act which, by forcing a tube into a woman's body, was the most blatantly rapist of all the varied assaults on the suffragettes.

He had felt uneasy enough about his silence to attempt a play about the movement at the suggestion of Forbes-Robertson; yet "Press Cuttings," the skit he eventually relegated to his *Translations and Tomfooleries,* betrayed his lack of commitment rather than his concern. Jotted down between March and May 1909 on an excursion with Charlotte and her sister Mary Cholmondeley to Algeria and Tunisia, the playlet treated almost everything but the suffrage: the Prime Minister, the war office, the rights of soldiers, the folly of anti-German feeling. The women were three: Mrs. Banger, a baritone war-horse who muscles her way through the war office, and Lady Corinthia, a lewd aesthete—both anti-suffragists —and Mrs. Farrell, a charwoman who refuses marriage because she would have to work just as hard as she does now, only not get paid for it—the only sane voice in the play. "Press Cuttings" is full of jokes about sexual ambiguity (the Prime Minister arrives disguised as a suffragette, and sheds his petticoats to the horror of General Mitchener) and full of uneasy sexual compromises (General Sandstone becomes engaged to Mrs. Banger after she storms his office and "sits on his head"; Mrs. Farrell forfeits her sanity by agreeing to marry General Mitchener). The statement it makes on women is largely negative: whether suffragette or anti-suffragette, Shaw seems to be saying, women are equally unpleasant when they get to fighting.

"Press Cuttings" ran into immediate trouble with the censor, and could only be presented at a private reception at the Court on 9 and 12 July 1909. It was not censored, of course, for its blistering attack on the anti-suffragist government, but was refused a license on the technicality that Shaw had chosen to call his Prime Minister Balsquith (transparently Balfour and Asquith) and his general Mitchener (suggesting the imperialist Kitchener). While headlines about Shaw's "banned play" thus suggested he had taken a strong stand on the vote, the issue in reality was the representation of living persons on the stage. Shaw had struck through the controversy over "Press Cuttings" at a topic far closer to his heart than women's suffrage—the censorship which had plagued him from the writing of *Mrs. Warren's Profession* right up to his most recent play, *The Shewing-Up of Blanco Posnet* (completed March 1909), which Tree had accepted for His Majesty's only promptly to be found guilty of blasphemy by the lord chamberlain and the performance suppressed. As a playwright, Shaw perhaps understandably gave his energies during these years to the problem of the censorship rather than to the fight for political equality for women; yet his brilliance as a fighter made his absence notable. As Yeats reluctantly admitted, Shaw could hit his enemies harder than any man living; as Ethel Smyth had told Shaw, "no other man could do it." The champion had failed to ride forward, like the anti-romanticist he professed to be. Shaw probably rejoiced in his unpredictability.

"Press Cuttings" brought him in contact with a woman from his past. Bertha Newcombe had never married, still lived at Cheyne Walk, Chelsea. As Honorary Secretary of the Civic and Dramatic Guild, she happened to take charge of the play's private production in aid of the London Society for Women's Suffrage. In May she wrote to ask him for a copy. Shaw replied that a copy was not ready, admitted that the only sympathetic woman in it was the char, and suggested that he might read it to her and Forbes-Robertson, except that "really the thing is such a ghastly absurdity, that a reading is hardly bearable." Bertha suggested a meeting; Shaw came in some anxiety to make a good impression, and went home to write: "I did not notice any embarrassment; nor did I expect it after such a barefaced assignation. I expected to find a broken hearted, prematurely aged woman: I found an exceedingly smart lady, not an hour older, noting with a triumphant gleam in her eye my white hairs and lined face. When I think that I allowed those brutal letters to hurt me—ME—Bernard Shaw!! Are you not ashamed?"

Bertha finally secured the Court for a production, but the common cause of Shaw's play did not unite them. After the matinee on 9 July she asked him sharply to stop tipping the employees at the Court since it was unbusinesslike. Shaw wrote what impressed her as a nasty reply, accusing her of spite; and she lost no time in retaliating: "What a villain you are! How I wish I had not written. . . . it is far better that I should again efface myself for another 11 years. Possibly we may all die before then. Your letter seems to me rather out of date. Do you still continue to think of yourself as an idol for adoring women? The idol was shattered for me years ago—even before you married. Inadvertently when you mention the care that has been taken of you, you touch upon the lasting grievance."[30] Obviously Bertha Newcombe had neither forgiven Shaw nor forgotten him.

Shaw had wanted Lena Ashwell for Judith in *The Devil's Disciple*, finding time on his wedding day, in fact, to assure her that he had always had "a tremendous opinion" of her acting and nursed her reputation "with fatherly solicitude." Lena did not play Judith, but in 1910 Shaw secured her for the part of Lina Szczepanowska in *Misalliance* in place of

Lillah McCarthy, who was ill: partly, perhaps, at Charlotte's urging, partly because after a disastrous season at the Kingsway, Charles Frohman had hired most of her company, and it was Frohman who was to produce *Misalliance* in a season of repertory at the Duke of York's Theatre. The role of Lina, the Polish acrobat who drops out of the sky in a crashed plane and astounds a country house party with her daring views of life, seemed fit for Lena, who had excelled at playing female outcasts. Shaw assured her after opening night on 23 February that she had at last achieved the miracle of their art: she had found herself to be Lina "instead of that accidental fiction of christening & circumstances, Lena Ashwell." On 10 March he dropped in at the matinee, where he shared a box with Yeats, who exclaimed over Ashwell's "beautiful gaiety," so rare a quality in the theatre. Shaw rejoiced: yes, Lena should spend the rest of her life in beautiful gaiety "and hear no more of Mrs. Dane and all those other dreadful Mrs'es which foolish people classify as Lena Ashwell parts."[31] Lina Szczepanowska was quintessential Lena.

But Lena did not like her aviator's goggles, tunic, and pants at all. After making her mark in heavily emotional parts which inevitably called upon her to bear an illegitimate child or stab someone to death and then suffer gorgeously for her sins, she could not sympathize with Lina's cool self-assurance, nor be touched by Lina's great speech: "I am an honest women: I earn my living. I am a free woman: I live in my own house. I am a woman of the world: I have thousands of friends: every night crowds of people applaud me, delight in me, buy my picture, pay hard-earned money to see me. I am strong: I am skilful: I am brave: I am independent: I am unbought: I am all that a woman ought to be . . . ." Lina the acrobat could not reconcile love and work and did not feel guilty about choosing the latter; and this—the essence of Shaw's feminism—struck Lena unpleasantly, as though Shaw had robbed the character of dramatic interest. Although widely experienced when she came to *Misalliance*, Shaw's play in general threw her off balance: she declared she felt the rawest amateur in its clear, buoyant medium. But then, she concluded, "No actor can make a real impression in Shaw's plays. Nobody can say that so and so was great in a Shaw character as one would say that he was a great Shylock or Macbeth." Shaw was really an intruder in drama, she thought: he wrote "from outside the theatre, as observer, as critic." His was a "dissecting brain"; his plays "a surgery of life." It was notorious that he disliked and dreaded emotion. He was a mere mechanic. He was a destroyer of tradition on the stage and in life.[32] The outburst came strangely from a feminist who, in Lina Szczepanowska, had been given a feminist part. But then Shaw was skeptical of her progressivism, sizing her up rather as a violent and ungovernable "loyal Canadian Conservative."

Although audiences laughed uproariously at the play (Shaw was moved to a statement in the *Daily Mail* banning applause), critics panned; and Charles Frohman jilted "poor Miss Alliance" after eleven performances to the rage of Shaw, who was touring France by automobile and felt helpless to interfere. Had the play succeeded, perhaps Lena Ashwell would have loved it more. As it was she gave it one line in her autobiography: "The part in Misalliance was small and hardly in my line." Yet Lina's role is the bravura piece that dominates the play. Despite the fact that Lena and her husband Henry Simson became friends of the Shaws, Lena Ashwell proved surprisingly hostile to Shaw in print.

One actress retained her affection for him despite her banishment from the Vedrenne-Barker-Shaw enterprise. And Shaw did not entirely forget Janet in exile at the cottage near Reading. He had suggested Mrs. Clandon in the Court's February 1907 production of *You Never Can Tell;* then had to tell her that Henrietta Watson would play after all. In June that year he had tried to persuade Gilbert Murray to give her the lead in his new translation. This possibility Janet herself seemed destined to frustrate, for she *would* turn up at the Court without teeth. Shaw protested. It was not, he explained to Charrington, that he did not want Janet to be seen, for she was more sylph-like now than she had been since the Australian tour. "What I said is that she must not *speak* to anybody until the teeth are in. When I am trying to persuade Murray & Barker that she is the woman for Medea, which requires the finest diction imaginable, what chance will I have of success if she comes and gnashes her gums at them and goo-goos and ga-gaas like a baby?"[33]

Although the next time Shaw saw Janet she was "clashing a new set of teeth like castanets, and very wild, weird & game for anything," she did not play Medea, but in 1910 returned to the stage in Glasgow as Marete in the violent melodrama *The Witch*.[34] In Glasgow on Fabian business, Shaw went to a matinee performance at the Royalty Theatre expecting the worst, but she acted splendidly. Afterward he hurried backstage to congratulate her, inquiring for the number of her dressing room from someone on the stairs. In a dark room he found three women struggling with their costumes, one of them made up like an old woman. Feeling strange, he went up to her and kissed her hand. But it was not Janet, so redirected, he went up another flight of stairs, knocked at a door, and heard the powerful voice he knew so well call out. He opened the door, and she rushed into his arms. But she was very thin and ill, and he could not help thinking how she would have bowled him over had she rushed him like that in the old days. He felt once again the terrible waste of her genius, which he had always believed in, and yet the miracle that she was still alive and able to storm and rage as powerfully as ever. Janet herself was "awfully jolly" at pleasing him and terribly glad to see him again. And indeed her performance had been a kind of tour de force. Impressed, Shaw would offer £300, as did James M. Barrie, to back

Janet in 1912 in a production of Eden Phillpotts's *The Secret Woman;* but the play failed the censor, and that time he threw his money away.[35]

The Charrington luck did not last long. After *The Witch* closed, Janet went to recover in the mild climate of St. Leonard's on the Sussex coast, but nearly died there instead. Then Nora fell ill. Having grown very lovely and, as Shaw told Barker, worth keeping in mind for the stage, Nora had instead married in 1908 an East Indian exporter named Edward Levetus, a marriage that would end when Nora slammed the door on both husband and child a few months after the birth of a son in September 1911.[36] Now the faithful and harassed Charrington divided his time between his wife at St. Leonard's and his daughter in London, nursing them both back to health.

In November 1910, Shaw opened a letter from Amiens. "I am *not* a deserving case," Charrington began, but went on to plead for a loan of ten pounds. They had gone to Jersey that autumn since Janet had been very ill and they thought they could live more cheaply there. All had gone well until his need for more original material for two books he was writing on the theatre tempted them to cross into Normandy. They had still tried to live cheaply, but then he had gotten sick in a bad third-class hotel, and poor Janet had had to nurse him. Determined to leave the place, but very sick and weak, they had asked for their bill only to find that the Hotel de Normandie had overcharged them fourteen francs. Made obstinate by illness, they refused to pay the overcharge. In that case, they were informed, the hotel refused to release their luggage. Furious, they set out to obtain redress, going from one unsympathetic solicitor's office to another, Janet dealing with the lawyers since she spoke better French than he did. "As usual the lion's share of the work fell to her. . . . About the third time she told the story she was admirably efficient—But before and afterwards—! Especially afterwards when she was tired out—!!!"

One solicitor seemed accommodating until he handed them a bill: "Hotel: 14 francs; Pour mes fois: 30 francs; et transport de bagage = 49 francs." When he saw their money, they would see their baggage. "Ill as I felt," wrote Charrington, "I couldn't help laughing. But Janet never sees any humor on these occasions and I had to get her out of the little ——'s office before she broke down altogether." So here they were at a new hotel with the bill running up by the hour and no money to pay. If they could only get back to England they would be all right. He was expecting £400 next January, and would repay his old friend faithfully. "But the longer we stay the more we shall owe . . . . Janet is very unhappy. . . . Do help!"[37]

"It sounds like a page by Balzac," replied Shaw. Besieged by money requests from Irish cousins, from friends, from acquaintances, from strangers, Shaw nevertheless complied once more:

I have at least the satisfaction of the certainty (as far as one can be certain of anything with so fantastic a man) that the money will be spent on yourself and Janet, and not on your creditors and lawyers. If ever there was a man who lived for others, that man is yourself.

I produce a little play this afternoon, with Barker as Shakespear! Might have had Janet for Queen Elizabeth, I suppose, if she had not been making tragedies with hotel keepers.

Oh Charles and Janet, what a devil of a pair you are! I ask the high gods why—why—why?

Your highly prosperous and
respectable
GBS[38]

The little play was *The Dark Lady of the Sonnets,* suggested by Dame Edith Lyttelton and staged as a charity matinee at the Haymarket Theatre on 24 November by the Committee of the Shakespeare Memorial National Theatre. Shaw wanted Lillah for the Dark Lady and Gertrude Kingston for Queen Elizabeth, but Lillah did not agree. She had been very ill that spring of 1910, and recuperated at Sandgate, H. G. Wells's house overlooking the sea near Folkestone. Having quarreled over Fabian matters with Shaw, Wells had constructed a red-bearded and red-nosed effigy of G.B.S. for an archery target: it stood prominent on the lawn, shot full of as many arrows as St. Sebastian. In this atmosphere, Lillah fell out with Shaw, arguing for the part of Queen Elizabeth, to which Shaw returned, "Here you are, a ready made dark lady; and you want to build up your nose into a hook, stick on a frizzy red wig and ferret's eyebrows, and prance about as Queen Elizabeth, whom you do not in the least resemble." Lillah called the answer Shaw's persuasive wizardry at its worst. Did she even want to play Shaw at the moment?—those strong, sane, supernormal women, those brilliant creatures with their steely brains.[39] In the event, illness prevented her playing either Queen Elizabeth or the Dark Lady; but she rebelled against the supersane heroines of Shaw by considering *The Witch,* although Shaw had assured her that sort of thing was no good for London.

Contrarily, Lillah did it anyway; and the play, which began the last day of January 1911 at the Court, proved it could serve Lillah as well as Janet. But Lillah had grander plans. One morning she left her rooms over the Little Theatre at 5 Adelphi Terrace (she could see the Shaws' flat from hers), went to Lord Howard de Walden in Belgrave Square, proposed that he lend her money for her own theatre venture, and ran back to Adelphi Terrace waving a check for £2,000 and crying, "See! I am going to be an actress-manager, with my own theatre, and here is the beginning of the capital!" She appealed to Shaw for a play; he wrote it.

Leasing the Little Theatre from Gertrude Kingston and with Shaw as producer, Lillah opened in *Fanny's First Play* by Xxxxxxx Xxxx on 19 April 1911. Shaw did not admit authorship until the play was published in 1914, even though it ran successfully for 622 performances and everybody knew it was Shaw. Swelled by crowds for the coronation of George V, London sent regular tides into the Little Theatre. "Is it possible that I am to be connected with a theatrical enterprise and not lose all my money?" marveled art patron Lord Howard. Shaw had taken the idea of suffragettes going to prison, but changed the circumstances of the heroine's assault on a policeman, arrest, and jail sentence from a struggle over the vote to an accidental arrest at a drunken melee following a boat race; the change evidently pleased a London audience weary of causes. The play would not die, said Shaw, apologizing for the fact that *Fanny's First Play* had destroyed the legend that he was an unpopular playwright. "It goes on like Madame Tussaud's. Neither hot weather nor cold can kill it." Lillah was less ecstatic, both over her performance and her profits. According to Shaw, she was not made for the part of a "chump" like Margaret Knox at all. When Shaw directed her—making faces, waving his hands, imitating voice tones—she got it right immediately; when Barker with his perfectionist attention to the production rather than to the performers took over, Lillah went cold and dead. *Fanny's First Play* ran for two and a half years, Shaw's first commercial success. It paid its way, said Lillah temperately, but made no fortunes for anyone.

Arms and the Man was in revival, Ellen O'Malley wanted *Candida*, Gertrude Kingston and Marie Tempest both wanted *Brassbound*, the postman staggered under bags of letters asking him for parts, Shaw told Barker—and Janet wanted to play Shaw again. He replied from Annecy, Haute Savoie, France, where he had gone to meet Charlotte:

Madam,

In answer to your esteemed favor of the 25th May last, I have to point out that the proprietor of a troupe of performing dogs cannot always find a part for an elephant, however talented. That has always been the difficulty. An elephant which not only makes its colleagues look ridiculously small, but kicks its parts round the stage in a superfluity of power, is a beast practicable only in an environment at present hardly attainable. . . .

This is the real story of your exclusion from the Court. It is all over now; and your reappearance in The Witch was a great success, because the old thread had been broken; and the new English school of drama had established itself in complete independence of the Ibsen episode. In 1904, the first condition was, "No Janet, No Ibsen, No Charrington, No Elizabeth Robins, No Florence Farr: the new leaf must have no old names on it." In 1911, it is the Court people who are "the old lot"; and the formerly proscribed can come back with all the splendors of a remote and legendary past if there are parts for them, and they will play them cheaply enough as far as salaries go.

Look at all this personally; and it is heartless. But it isn't really so: if I couldnt do these things I should be no good. My feelings did not change one bit, and have not changed except for the wear and tear of age and absence and one thing and another, all more than counterbalanced by senile sentimentality; for I am pretty *hard work*. Only, ones feelings cannot alter the pieces of the chessboard. What the theatre wanted was the noble Romanity of Barker, not your impulsive genius and devilish thriftlessness, or Charrington's desperate gambling. Your talents were fully blown: I could do no more for you in proclaiming them; but Barker was just beginning his career as possibly a better man than myself—certainly a dramatist of extraordinary gifts both of character and specific literary genius—and I could be of much more use to him than you. And, as you know, I exist to be used.

You observe that I scribble all this to you with less regard to your feelings tha[n] I would have to almost any other woman's; but the real meaning of it is that I am just what I always was; and so are you.[40]

But there was no possibility of Janet coming back "with all the splendors of a remote and legendary past," although Shaw broke down once more and let her have Lady Cicely for the Repertory Theatre in Liverpool. In the spring of 1912, he paid the production a surprise visit, and described it to Charlotte, who was, as usual, traveling. "The performance of Brassbound was ghastly; but Janet pulled it through," he reported from Edstaston, where he was staying with the Cholmondeleys. "She is really still better than anyone else . . . . But the play was not half rehearsed. Brassbound, hopelessly imperfect, managed to cut several pages out of the end of the first act, with disastrous results. . . . In the last scene both the prompter & Janet were making constant and unconcealed efforts to remind Brassbound of his words. In the second act the prompter began prompting Charrington loudly when he was making pauses on purpose as part of the acting; and Janet lost her temper and rushed off the stage to tell him to stop, thereby reducing the scene to absurdity. The American captain floundered helplessly and hardly got a smile. But Janet did enough to save the situation. I refused to appear & make a speech (if I had consented I should have expressed my opinion of the performance pretty frankly) and they yelled for a long time until Charrington came out & said that the house had been searched for me in vain. I saw the Charringtons & Nora afterwards at their hotel. Janet looked almost youthful, but was rackety and without an atom of self-control."[41]

But Janet broke down again after the Liverpool disaster; and once more the Charringtons packed their bags and set out this time for the Tyrolean Alps, hoping that the mountain air would restore her. There Janet fed her hopes on the possibility of playing *Brassbound* at the Little Theatre that autumn, even though Gertrude Kingston had the same plan. She was aching to act, wrote Charlie in October, was much recovered, and after all even the remote possibility of her playing Lady Cicely would keep Gertrude Kingston up to the mark.[42] But that "basket of glass" smashed too: Gertrude Kingston played Lady Cicely in the production that opened 15 October.

"I have a cracky sort of notion of a play," Shaw had written Barker in July 1911, Janet's situation having impressed him again, "—a Superwoman play—with a heroine of 55. My female contemporaries are in great need of it." In great need of a part was Ellen Terry, not so much for her finances as for her morale. With only the Nurse in *Romeo and Juliet* and another grueling tour of one-night stands among "shine-y and brittle" Americans in the offing, Ellen had answered Shaw's query in March 1911: " 'What can you do'? (Thank you for asking.) Why let me play a fine part written by you so I may abide in England!" But although Shaw kept flattering her by pretending he wanted her, his next letter more than a year later was not encouraging. "I now have a grotesque confession to make to you," he wrote from the French Alps, where he was languishing with a broken automobile while Charlotte took the mud bath cure at Kissingen. "I wrote a play for [Sir George] Alexander which was really a play for Mrs. Patrick Campbell. It is almost as wonderful a fit as Brassbound; for I am a good ladies' tailor, whatever my shortcomings may be. . . . And then—and then—oh Ellen; and then? Why, then I went calmly to her house to discuss business with her, as hard as nails, and, as I am a living man, fell head over ears in love with her in thirty seconds."[43]

CHAPTER TWENTY

1912-1913

ON 26 JUNE 1912 Shaw had gone to the house of Dame Edith ("D.D.") Lyttelton to read the play about "a rapscallionly flower girl" he had conceived as far back as 1897, contriving beforehand that Beatrice Stella Campbell should be there. He went to 16 Great College Street, Westminster, with some apprehension, for his heroine was no Tanquerayian beauty but a barbarous-tongued slum girl in desperate need of delousing and a bath; and besides there was no guarantee that the unpredictable actress, currently playing at the St. James's in *Bella Donna*, would appear, or if she did appear, stay to listen.

Yeats was among those unfortunate enough to have read plays to Stella Campbell, having been summoned to Sunday lunch in November 1909 to read her *The Player Queen*. The appointment was for one-fifteen. On toward two Mrs. Campbell and lunch appeared; after lunch she listened with great enthusiasm to Act I, distracted only by the squawkings of the parrot. Yeats had just launched into Act II when a musician arrived. Ten minutes, Stella assured him. An hour and a half later Yeats murmured that perhaps he had better go and cancel a dinner engagement for that evening. "Oh, do," agreed Mrs. Campbell, full of apologies. He returned at six-thirty to find the musician just leaving, but a deaf man ensconced at Mrs. Campbell's side whose sole purpose in life seemed to be the imparting to Mrs. Campbell of irrelevancies. Yeats managed to get through Act II with Mrs. Campbell still enthusiastic until telephone messages and then dinner with relatives interfered. After dinner Mrs. Campbell's dressmaker arrived: would he excuse her for a few minutes? Presently there was a terrible commotion upstairs, and a distraught helper rushed down "like a messenger in a Greek Tragedy" to announce that the dress was a full six inches too short in front. At ten-thirty the group of petitioners in the drawing room consulted: should someone go up and knock at Mrs. Campbell's door? No one seemed to desire the honor. At eleven-thirty she appeared, full of contrition: she would only be a few minutes longer. At half past twelve, leaning on the arm of her daughter Stella, she made a wan entrance into the drawing room. Said Yeats quickly: "This is absurd! You must go to your bed, and I must go home." "No," said she, "I must hear the end of a play the same day as I hear the beginning." Yeats began to read, but she obviously did not understand a word and began to quarrel, complaining, "No, I am *not* a slut and I do *not* like fools," until Yeats gave up and went home to assure her by letter that although his heroine might be a slut who liked fools, he did not mean that she was.[1]

A brilliant reader whose trace of Irish lilt could charm birds off branches, Shaw fared better, as he also had a more attractive play. A letter the next day from 33 Kensington Square thanked him for thinking she could be his "pretty slut," and invited him to come and see her. He went the following day. When she shook his hand she contrived that his fingers brushed her bosom, an "infamous, abandoned trick" that thrilled him. They sat on a sofa with the little dogs Everilda and Georgina in her white-paneled drawing room, they drove in a taxi, they visited a lord. And although he had begun the business "with the most insolent confidence in [his] superiority to a dozen such Dalilas," Shaw told Lillah, "I fell head over ears in love with her—violently and exquisitely in love —before I knew that I was thinking about anything but business. All yesterday I could think of nothing but a thousand scenes of which she was the heroine and I the hero. And I am on the verge of 56. There has never been anything so ridiculous, or so delightful, in the history of the world."[2] "Today," Shaw added, "Richard is himself again," fondly trusting in the hardness of his heart.

But Richard was not quite himself. Suffering acutely from one of his monthly migraine headaches, he nevertheless sat down the next week to cover page after page of the green paper he used when afflicted, though it still "seared his eyes like smoke." He began with business. The single-star system was dead in London, he informed her, and she (Oh, Stella Stellarum and beautifullest of stars) must not choose some twenty-pound-a-week Higgins if *Pygmalion* was to thrive, but a reputable actor like Robert Loraine. But he could not help betraying his intoxication, and at the same time his disgust with his own perennial behavior. Everybody already knew about his infatuation: he could not help speaking her name—to Barker, to Barrie, to Bobbie Loraine. Yet how he hated to drag her into that "brazen atmosphere" which G.B.S. could not help creating and behind which his "poor timid little soul hides and cowers and dreams." He had lived two days without seeing her, and knew now he could endure anything—anything, that is, except forbearing to announce his love far and wide. By the last green sheet, he was almost incoherent: "I know it is all vile, and that I see too far ahead to make any woman happy. But we great people have no need for happiness. Nothing like business, is there, after all? I must now go and read this to Charlotte. My love affairs are her unfailing amusement: all their tenderness recoils finally on herself. Besides, I love an audience. Oh, forgive these blasphemies; but my head is still bad and it makes me naughty."[3] But Shaw's love affairs were not Charlotte's unfailing amusement; and it may be doubted that he went and read her the letter.

He waited for Stella's answer, more curious perhaps about its style than content, for clearly Stella was going to be a great romance like Ellen Terry, who, however, had almost been his match at letter writing and thus could play an equal game with him at love. Surely no two women alive could do that.[4] He had loathed Alice Lockett's slovenly hand, found Jenny Patterson's scrawls offensive, tried to overlook Florence Farr's inadequacies, scolded Erica Cotterill over her failure to paragraph and punctuate, admired Janet for her cleverness with a pen. He received in answer to his effusion a brief erratic scrawl that began by laughing at his "funny green pages" and wishing that he "weren't so early Victorian!" "You must let Loraine have the play if Higgins is more important than Eliza," announced Stella Stellarum coolly. "But he and I cannot be forced into partnership—that would never do." Suggesting Matheson Lang or Aubrey Smith for Higgins, she ended with a veiled threat—"I would be very unhappy if I couldn't feel the very best had been done for your brilliant play—I would far rather lose 'Eliza,'" and a rebuke: "My love to you and to your Charlotte too."[5]

Shaw had tangled with Mrs. Campbell in the past. In the summer of 1908, for example, he had rashly tried to persuade her daughter Stella ("Stellinetta") to abandon her mother's tour with Pinero's *The Thunderbolt* and play his Raina instead. Mrs. Campbell had fallen upon him in her "most governessy mood," calling him names, and scolding him for his lack of good manners, taste, and breeding. So he set himself this time to be charmingly adamant about *Pygmalion*, and to use all his fighting tactics. These included informing Stella immediately that the play would go to Robert Loraine and Cissie Loftus for America, announcing that he would write "SUCH a play for Lena Ashwell, my dear Lena who really loves me," and generally broadcasting an outrageous mixture of truth, exaggeration, and falsehoods calculated to confound everyone. Stella retaliated by rebuking him for foolishness and mischief, and asking him to stop sending her his photographs since she gave them all away on the spot. Her dresser at the theatre had particularly liked the one of him as Jesus Christ at the piano.

And then the battle, which might have reached Wagnerian proportions, was halted abruptly one day when her taxi swerved to avoid a boy on a bicycle and collided with another near the Albert Hall, and her head smashed through the window. It was her second serious accident: touring America in 1904-5 she had been in the act of stepping into her coupé, her arms full of Pinkie, one of the notorious little dogs, when her foot slipped on the frozen step and she fell, striking her knee against the iron bars at the foot of the carriage door. Pinkie was unhurt, but a broken kneecap, an operation, a plaster cast, and a long recovery at the University of Pennsylvania Hospital rewarded Stella for saving her dog.[6] This time, bending to snatch up Georgina, the current griffon, from the taxi floor, she had saved her face; still she was miserable with a mass of aches and bruises and two black eyes, and on 30 July left with Sir Edward and Lady Strachey in their Rolls-Royce for Aix-les-Bains to recover. As a parting shot, she sent Shaw a little verse:

> He's mad, mad, mad,
> He's clean gone off his nut
> He cleans his boots with strawberry jam
> He eats his hat whenever he can
> He's mad, mad, mad—[7]

Her bit of doggerel nearly cost the lives of Charlotte, her sister Mary Cholmondeley, and their chauffeur Kilsby, explained Shaw; for instead of minding his driving (they were again touring the Continent), he wrought himself up to artistic fervor by composing "millions" of additional verses—

> He cleans his boots with strawberry jam;
> He thinks the world of my silly old mam
> Who doesn't value his plays a dam—

as they sped along the road to Bad Kissingen—Charlotte conspicuously unamused under motoring veil and hat, and forming the opinion that Mrs. Campbell was "a middleaged minx." As for Shaw, he could still not quite believe the cataclysm. "I solemnly protest that when I went into that room in Kensington Square I was a man of iron, insolently confident in my impenetrability. Had I not seen you dozens of times, and dissected you professionally as if you were a microscopic specimen? What danger could there possibly be for me? And in thirty seconds—oh Stella, if you had a rag of decency it *couldnt* have happened." And now, all the winds of the north were musical with the thousand letters he had written her on this journey.[8] How hard it would be to turn back at the Stelvio Pass when he knew that by pushing on to Tresenda, skirting Lake Como, hurrying through Milan, dashing through Little St. Bernard, and making through Albertville to Chambéry he could be in her arms in an hour. Oh, he was a dotard, a driveler—like his own brigand, reduced to babbling about Mendoza's Louisa and Louisa's Mendoza. Was it dignified? Was it sensible? He would conquer the weakness or cold-bloodedly trade in it and write a play about his infatuation. Yet he kissed her hands and blessed the Life Force for creating her, for she was a very very wonderful person.

To Lillah McCarthy he wrote that he was plying Mrs. Campbell with letters and photographs; "the deeper fidelities are, however, untouched." To Ellen he made his "grotesque confession." She replied: "It was a joy to get your letter. *I'm* in love with Mrs. Campbell too, or rather I'd like to be, but something tugs me back. She is amusing and was nice to me in America. The flower-girl idea is thrilling."[9]

Ellen Terry and Stella Campbell were indeed unalike; understandably something tugged Ellen back. Born into a prominent stage family, supported by the knowledge that she was her father's favorite child, Ellen had never quarreled with the theatre or doubted it, never believed that players were less than respectable or that there was something compromising about an actress's career. She seemed to have unlimited confidence in herself and her place in the world, and because of that confidence, dared to live and behave very much the way she pleased. Self-centered yet generous, confident that she was loved, strong-willed yet amiable for the sake of harmony, she reigned over her world. She was courted by society, yet chose whom she liked for company, and they were largely people from the arts: Charles Reade, Graham Robertson, Alice Comyns Carr, Lewis Carroll, Oscar Wilde. Next to reigning beneficently in London, she liked best to get away to the country, where Smallhythe, the Tudor farmhouse with its low beamed ceilings, dipping floors, open hearth, and flower-filled rooms, reflected her natural charm. Exerting equal fascination over men and women, she could live well with neither, and perhaps felt most comfortable poised at that delicate edge where friends might turn to lovers and lovers into friends.

Stella Campbell's background was very different. "My father in these early days I do not recall," she writes of her childhood. "I neither remember being caressed by him, nor having any sense of love for me; my whole adoration was for my mother."[10] But the Italian mother, a devout Roman Catholic married to a Darwinian, never laughed or smiled; and though intrigued with her mother's family and past (*was* she a circus rider? she never would tell), Stella thought of her pale, black-clad mother as a woman in whom joy had been silenced by secret sorrow. From her father John Tanner, who had gone through two large fortunes and was ruined by careless speculation by the time she was sixteen, she contracted a sense of social and financial insecurity. Indeed, Mrs. Campbell's account of her childhood is chiefly dark. There was her aunt Stella, who escaped from a locked room up a chimney at sixteen to meet her artist lover, and lived to see him wring the neck of the bird she loved to feed from her lips, before she died at twenty-nine. There was Stella's own sense that she was an alien and difficult child, happiest hiding alone high in a tree and talking to herself, a child who hated dolls and nearly fainted when asked to take a baby in her arms, and wondered miserably whether she was abnormal. Strangers terrified her; schooling oppressed her. She speaks of blankness and misery, tragically depressing effects, morbidity, sinister and tragic memories, miserable hauntings, wretched moments, grave troublings.

She was seventeen when she met Patrick Campbell in 1882, a good-looking, gentle, well-bred young man who passionately loved his dead mother; but marriage four months later did not offer security. Within three years she had a baby son and daughter. A year later in 1887, her husband was ordered abroad for "his health" and went—to Brisbane, Sydney, Mashonaland, Africa. Struggling to make money to send home, seriously weakened by malaria, longing for his wife and babies, pleading "Stella darling, don't get disgusted with me. God knows I have done my best," Patrick was clearly trying to improve his fortune rather than his health; but although many Englishmen came back rich from the mines of Africa, Patrick Campbell was not among them. Even before he left, however, Stella had realized that she could not rely on him. Pacing the garden restlessly one night, nine months pregnant with her second child, she remembered that "with the daylight something entered my soul, and has never since left me—it seemed to cover me like a fine veil of steel, giving me a strange sense of security. Slowly I became conscious that within *myself* lay the strength I needed, and that I must never be afraid." Two months after her daughter Stella was born in September 1886, she made her first stage appearance with one very good speech and some pretty dresses[11]; by 1888, she had decided, with Pat's approval, to go on the stage. A letter from Katherine Bailey, a close friend of her mother's and "aunt" to the young girl who had lived with her in Paris, greeted her decision: "Poor, unfortunate child, may God help you, if, as you say, the die for evil is cast. . . . *How thankful I feel* that it was not whilst with *me* that you took the wrong turning. . . . But your mother!!! I should have thought her the *very last* to allow you to enter on such a path!! . . . Oh, my poor Beatrice, you can form no idea—you have yet to learn—the shame, the humiliation of seeing yourself despised by decent people. . . . Poor, dear child, good-bye. I cannot see for my tears. Oh, Beatrice, how could you?"[12]

When Ellen Terry returned to the stage in February 1874, she had borne two illegitimate children to her lover Godwin and was still married to Watts, who would sue for divorce on the grounds of adultery in 1877. Incredibly these irregularities seemed to bother neither Ellen nor the public. She took to the stage again as though she had never left it: she was a Terry, and her genius was recognized almost at once. Her nod to Victorian convention—marriage to Charles Wardell in 1878—barely interrupted her life. In 1878 she joined Irving at the Lyceum, and from then on ruled the hearts of her subjects who came to pay homage there.

Stella Campbell's decision to become an actress was an act of daring, her chance for success uncertain. No niche was waiting. She tells us of seeking out a theatrical agent in London and, as she was searching for the office number, of catching sight of a mother cat in the gutter licking two drowned kittens and mewing piteously over them. The sight and the reminder of her own two infants so sickened her, that upon the agent's shaking her hand she burst into tears, impressing him inadvertently with her dramatic powers.

She did not cry often again but adopted laughter as a weapon. As a substitute for the private role of wife and mother she had forfeited, she cultivated the public role of the bitch—alternately charming and imperious, generous and demanding, sincere and frivolous, tearful and callous, gracious and wounding, pious and unscrupulous. No one had taught her "the prince's virtues of honor, generosity and panache."[13] People feared her, while her great beauty and success forced them to put up with her. She became a terror to managers and actors at rehearsals. During a performance she could spellbind an audience or, if she did not feel like acting, turn her back on them and amuse herself by pulling faces at the cast, hissing audible insults, or breaking up an actor's speech with a witticism. Her inspiration often depended on who was watching: told there were no titles out front, she would act apathetically. This unpredictability protected a person who was both insecure and self-destructive. She often turned the knife upon herself. "The best thing in this world is to be a useful woman—that's what *I* am not," she believed, "—and the next best to be a kind woman, and I am not even that."[14] Ellen Terry seemed both useful and kind. It was almost as though Stella Campbell, the dark bitch goddess, had created herself in deliberate polarity to Ellen the fair and good.

Mrs. Campbell covered her insecurity another way. Had her mother been a circus rider? Her father ruined? Was her profession despised by decent people? Not if she behaved with governessy respectability and cultivated the right people. She kept her husband's name if not his company (in April 1900 the faithful but shadowy Patrick Campbell died at thirty-six in the South African War). She permitted her portrait in Forbes-Robertson's office but not her name on his lips. Many believed he was her great love. But did they actually have an affair? Of course; yet no one could say for certain. Titles and wealth attracted her. She insulted actors and managers—they were after all only theatre people—and kept her good manners for the social cream. Her memoirs were a silly string of names: the Earl of Pembroke, Sir Hubert and Lady Maud Perry, Lady Horner, The Hon. Mrs. Percy Wyndham, Lady Hamilton, Lady Charles Beresford, Lady Savile, Lady Edward Cavendish, Lady Eden, Viscountess Grey. . . . Affectionate testimonies from these luminaries alternated with tributes to her familial piety from son Beo and daughter Stella, from Patrick, from Uncle Harry—it was all terribly respectable, self-conscious, and dull. And yet she smoked large black cheroots, convulsed people with her "pothouse" humor, and dominated conversation by talking louder and longer than anyone else.

Shaw had a weakness for dark, voluptuous goddesses—Sirens or Calypsos who lured men to destruction against their wills. They complemented his pose as saint with a heart of brass who could only be softened by the deepest wiles. As he told Stella, there was "devilment" and magic at work: she must pray for them both. He also confessed to her his first dark lady: "Once, in my calfish teens, I fell wildly in love with a lady of your complexion; and she, good woman, having a sister to provide for, set to work to marry me to the sister. Whereupon I shot back into the skies from which I had descended, and never saw her again. Nor have I, until this day, ever mentioned that adventure to any mortal; for though dark ladies still fascinated me they half laughed at me, half didn't understand me, and wholly thought me cracked."[15]

Meanwhile he dangled *Pygmalion* temptingly out of reach, pending her capitulation to a first-rate Higgins; while Stella herself hurried back to London at the news of an American tour with a Barrie play. But this was not to materialize, for when she arrived her son Alan—"Beo"—saw that she was very ill. She was put into bed that night, and would not get up for six months, nor walk for nearly nine. "There were whispers of 'brain,' " she remembered; "candles used to be held in front of me, and my eyelids lifted up. My body was the nearest thing to death that life can hold. My living mind grasped the utter futility and weariness of all this business of life, and I dwelt upon the ineffable quiet of death."

Except when Shaw came to talk and tease her into laughter and flirtation. He did not take her illness seriously at first: useless to appeal to him for sympathy: Charlotte was ill, his mother had suffered a stroke, and he was half dead from rehearsing two plays simultaneously. His heart was a nether millstone, for if he ever let himself get tender over serious misfortunes, he should die. "Get up," he commanded; "and console ME." Letters from Beo's American wife Helen and phrases like "if she survives" convinced him, however; and he obeyed her command to come and cheer her by reading his "bellowing, roaring Christian Martyr" play, though he feared it might tire her. He found the Square strewn with straw halfway round to deaden the clattering carriages of the fashionable who came constantly to inquire after Mrs. Campbell, and he found D. D. Lyttelton in the sickroom, and Stella in bed with Georgina in one of her

more perverse humors. He did not want to read *Androcles and the Lion*
to D.D. or even want her there. As shy people will, he talked and read
far too much and too long; and was laughed at for his pains, and not
given any tea nor, when he complained that his hands were cold, allowed
to warm them in Stella's. After he had gone, Stella felt guilty and, although her temperature had shot up to 105.6, scrawled him two little
notes. She and D.D. had been churlish and ungrateful and behaved like
savages—and he so good and gentle. But his talk! A sick woman must not
be stretched on the rack like that. "—Oh dear me—its too late to do anything but *accept* you and *love* you," she complained, "—but when you
were quite a little boy somebody ought to have said 'hush' just once!"

But Shaw would not hush. "O brave high-souled lady and cleanser and
inspirer of my trampled spirit" . . . "O glorious white marble lady" . . .
"My treasure, my darling, my beloved, adored, ensainted friend of my
very soul," he raved during those precarious months of her illness. He
came often to the Square. Her illness seemed to insulate them from the
world: her bedroom became a tomb of love where Shaw could play the
game he feared. And he found that Stella could play with him like a
child in his dream world. They pretended at Tristan and Isolde; she read
to him Poe's "Annabel Lee"—

> And so, all the night-tide, I lie down
>   by the side
> Of my darling—my darling—my life and
>   my bride,
> In the sepulchre there by the sea—
> In her tomb by the sounding sea.[16]

When he was not in raptures he was protesting his absolute callousness. He was "a writing and talking machine," his brains ground as
pitilessly as millstones, he was "a human dredger," "a man of brass,"
"hard as nails." She had might as well press Babbage's Calculating Machine to her bosom. Stella? Who was Stella! "I want no Stella: I want
my brains, my pen, my platform, my audience, my adversary, my mission." Yet, stop. It was all lies. At the mere thought of her the millstones
ceased to grind. She must get well, or he would tear her out of bed and
shake her back into health; and if that failed he would jump into her bed
himself, and, in a spectacular love-death, perish there with her scandal-
ously. Of course, she *must not* fall in love with him; yet she must not
"grudge him the joy he finds in being in love" and "writing all sorts of
wild but heartfelt exquisite lies—lies, lies, lies, lies" to her, "his
adoredest."[17]

Faced with this contradictory man who veered wildly between exaltation and callousness, Stella Campbell kept her equilibrium rather well.

She decided to call him "Joey" after the clown in the pantomime. She adored his "winged words," yet wondered whether he might not be courting her simply for *Pygmalion*. She disliked the self-conscious reminders that his letters were destined for the British Museum. She noted with annoyance that impassioned as he became at her bedside, he always hurried home in time for dinner. And she remembered, and accused him now of the fact, that for years and years he had maligned her in print as an actress. This brought a quick reply from Shaw. Timid soul that he was, he actually believed her, until searching out those old reviews, he looked through them again. "And what a revelation! what a relief! what a triumph! Never did a man paint his infatuation across the heavens as I painted mine for you, rapturously and shamelessly." Why, his love had shone in every line: he, "the greatest critic in the world," had proclaimed her "the most wonderful woman."

This was true. *The Second Mrs. Tanqueray*, Shaw had said, owed its vogue chiefly to the fact that playgoers admired Mrs. Campbell. *The Notorious Mrs. Ebbsmith* left one with nothing except the conviction that Mrs. Patrick Campbell was a wonderful woman. Sardou's *Fedora* was an execrable play, but the moment Mrs. Campbell appeared "our reason collapsed and our judgement fled." As Juliet Mrs. Campbell fit herself into "the hospitable manly heart without effort, simply because she is a wonderful person." Of her Militza in *For the Crown:* "Go and see her move, stand, speak, look, kneel." Of Mrs. Campbell's Rat Wife: "I like being enchanted by Mrs. Patrick Campbell." Of her Lady Hamilton: "Mrs. Patrick Campbell, in a wig so carefully modelled on that head of hair which is one of Miss Elizabeth Robins's most noticeable graces that for a moment I could hardly decide whether I was looking at Miss Robins made up like Mrs. Campbell or Mrs. Campbell made up like Miss Robins, is a charming Lady Hamilton."

An actress may be forgiven, however, for occasionally wanting to be told that she can act. As he had claimed that Elizabeth Robins could be an Ibsen woman but not act one, and that Janet merely gazed into a mirror to create her Nora, so Shaw generally denied that acting had anything to do with Mrs. Campbell's success. The haunted eyes, the parted lips, the fluid play of limb, the low vibrating voice, the smoldering danger like a sleepy tiger's—these qualities had nothing to do with Paula Tanqueray or Agnes Ebbsmith but everything to do with Mrs. Campbell's personal genius. "It is greatly to Mrs. Patrick Campbell's credit," wrote Shaw of *Fedora*, "that, bad as the play was, her acting was worse." Of her Juliet: "Nothing of it is memorable except the dance—the irresistible dance." *Magda:* "Mrs. Campbell has not lived long enough to get as much work crammed into her entire repertory as Duse gets into every ten minutes of her Magda . . . if Mrs. Campbell's irresistible physical gifts and her cunning eye for surface effects had only allowed her to look as silly as she really was in the part . . . her failure would have been as obvious to the greenest novice in the house as it was to me." The Rat Wife was an excellent part, said Shaw, but not an arduous one—that is, anyone could have played it. When Mrs. Campbell changed to Rita Allmers in *Little Eyolf*, Shaw's contempt for her ladylike interpretation knew no bounds. Of Mrs. Campbell's Lady Hamilton: "She even acts occasionally, and that by no means badly." Of her Ophelia, which he admitted was an innovation and seemed to settle her right as Forbes-Robertson's leading lady: "I doubt whether Mrs. Patrick Campbell fully appreciates the dramatic value of her quite simple and original sketch—it is only a sketch—of the part."

Beauty but no brains; instinct without understanding; a surface dexterity in movement and speech, but no depth of interpretation. Beauty is, of course, much; but then Shaw proclaimed his opinion of beauty. "I had rather look at a beautiful picture than be flogged, as a general thing," he wrote, contrasting the Rita Allmers of Janet Achurch and Mrs. Campbell; "but if I were offered my choice between looking at the most beautiful picture in the world continuously for a fortnight and submitting to, say, a dozen, I think I should choose the flogging."

Stella's distrust of Shaw thus had some foundation; but her own middle-class morality curbed her passion as well. She remembered her position as a respectable widow. She had not said "kiss me" yet, she told him, because she would not let any man kiss her unless she were sure of the wedding ring. She began to regret their intimacy. She was going to a nursing home, and when she came out, it was going to be "Mrs. P.C." and "Mr. Bernard Shaw" again, like proper people. And she would be most easy in her mind if Charlotte would send her calling card along with him one day soon as a token of acceptance. Yet she was almost as much of a flirt as Shaw. "All your words are as idle wind—Look into my eyes for two minutes without speaking if you dare," she challenged. "Where would be your 54 years? and my grandmothers heart? and how many hours would you be late for dinner?"

Shaw quailed at the prospect. To stop talking was to have to start acting. "Stella, do not ever bully me," he had protested from the beginning: "you don't know how easily frightened I am. Women never do realise what timid weak creatures men are." He was, he told her, her "knight of the white feather." Besides, he did not believe she really cared for him at all: "I dont like myself well enough—though I admire myself enormously—to expect anyone else to like me." And he could *not* bring her Charlotte's card, because Charlotte knew nothing about her, had no idea that Kensington Square was so often his destination instead of the Kingsway where *John Bull's Other Island* was in rehearsal for Boxing Day.

But there were things he could offer: money, for instance. She was not working and, he knew, had not saved a penny. There were doctor bills, the inevitable Christmas expenses, the rent to pay. How he would love, like Jupiter with Danaë, to turn himself into a shower of gold for her. Fearing a rebuke, he went to her checkbook in hand, prepared to offer her a thousand pounds, and tentatively opened the subject of money. The notion of borrowing was not new to Stella, but she had great pride; and refused in her "high heroic way."[18] He went home to apologize in a letter for his lack of taste. He had known she would refuse; yet he knew her bankers, their interest rate, the friends she could rely on. Had she taken the money he would have felt useful, and more than useful, seraphically blessed in being able to give her what was after all—nothing. For he did love her. He had just come from seeing *Troilus and Cressida*, and as Troilus loved Cressida "in so strain'd a purity" so he loved her. She was going to the nursing home; he knew that their relationship must change; yet just tonight he could shower her with streams of words, if not gold:

> . . . And I love you for ever and ever and ever, Stella. And I agree that when you are well we shall be Mr. Bernard Shaw and Mrs. Patrick Campbell; for Stella means only Stella; but Mrs. Patrick Campbell will mean my treasure, my darling, my beloved, adored, ensainted friend of my very soul.
>
> Oh, before you go, my Stella, I clasp you to my heart "with such a strained purity." A thousand successes, a thousand healings, a thousand braveries, a thousand prayers, a thousand beauties, a thousand hopes and faiths and loves and adorations watch over you and rain upon you. Goodnight, goodnight, goodnight, goodnight, my dearest dearest.

To this orgasm of emotion, Stella Campbell returned one of her ineffably sensitive little notes: "Well not the tureen [operating table] tomorrow—after all—Your letter! Well I never! I never did!!—Sherlock Holmes! he's nowhere—only you did *not* get the name of the Jew. . . . P.S.—— 50%—Stella."[19] Besides, Shaw was not so much on her mind as the husband of the former Lady Randolph Churchill. She and Jennie had become friends when Stella produced her play *His Borrowed Plumes* for a society matinee in 1909, but not such close friends as she had become with Jennie's current husband, George Cornwallis-West. The society playboy had been terribly attracted to her and she, convinced that his wife did not understand him, had "warmly" given him her "friendship and affection." Now divorce and bankruptcy were pending for poor George. This was worrisome, but it also meant that Cornwallis-West might soon be able to offer the wedding ring that would win her kiss. And that prospect left Shaw's "strain'd purity" absolutely nowhere.

Sometime early in 1913, as Charlotte tersely recorded in her Annuary, Shaw told her about Mrs. P.C. Far from being inevitably amused, she was angry, hurt, and contemptuous. Janet Achurch had been a problem, but as a new bride Charlotte had cowed Shaw into refusing the Charringtons their house. Florence Farr had composed her own funeral music on the psaltery. Erica Cotterill had been a worry, but even Shaw had been made to see that the young woman who motor-biked to Ayot and stormed Adelphi Terrace was slightly unbalanced. Ellen Terry had remained reassuringly out of reach. Lillah McCarthy had quickly fallen in love with Granville-Barker and, since Charlotte adored Barker, did not seriously mar the weekends that the four spent together so often during the heyday of the Court. Lena Ashwell had married Henry Simson and become one of her few female friends. But against this siren she seemed to have no weapons at all, except, perhaps, one.

The Campbell affair drove Charlotte to deeper retreat in the mysticism that had increasingly fascinated her. It was a world to which Shaw had already lost in one way or another several women. Lucinda Shaw had been devoted since Dublin days to planchettes and séances ("Do not spend too much on interviews with Oscar Wilde," Shaw had advised two years after Oscar passed over), to spirit drawings, and finally to the spirit photography popularized by Conan Doyle. Annie Besant had deserted the Fabians for theosophy. Janet's morphia and cocaine led to nirvana down the easy path. And Florence Farr had finally abandoned England entirely for the East.

"I go to Ceylon in August about the middle of the month; for five years certain," Florence had written Shaw 22 June 1912. He had continued to be her friend, dispensing advice, recommending her as a journalist to the *New Age* (a periodical his money helped found), and even offering to pay for the spectacles she found she needed as she approached fifty. She in turn never quite gave him up ("Do you want me *for ever*, greedy one?" Shaw had complained in 1896); yet her liking for him was mingled with bitterness. She seldom let an opportunity slip of jabbing at him in the *New Age* and later in another new weekly, *The Mint*. She had launched into journalism immediately upon her return from America in May 1907, and her first article, "G.B.S. and New York," was critical. Like New York, she wrote, Shaw had "a certain delicate brutality." Both had evolved "out of the reach of the influence of a really venerable tradition," both were "feverish devotees at the altar of work," both would collapse if forced to halt their frenetic pace. In May 1908, she had a chance to contrast Pinero and Shaw in a review of *The Thunderbolt* and *Getting Married*. She found that Pinero's play came off better; that Shaw inflicted untold torments on his audience when, after forcing them to attention for three hours, he suddenly "found he had forgotten to mention the customs of Mahomet and country, Henry VIII and church confiscation and turnips"—and hastily dragged them all in.[20] Hits like this bounced off her adversary harmlessly; he preferred Florence fighting to what he described to Stella as "Florence in her most maddeningly good natured aspect." But in spite of her good nature, Florence had always felt exploited by genius. "Once in a dream I stood with the Principalities and Powers before the Tree of Life," Florence wrote in the *New Age*. "One of the branches was dead, with five, ripe and beautiful fruit still hanging to their exhausted stalks. And the Powers whispered to each other, 'Let us cast off the dead branch and cry aloud that we may become a Tree of Life.' And they said those words as they carried the branch away. Then they ate the fruit and threw away the branch. I said: 'Why did you utter those words?' and they replied: 'In order that the other branches may do likewise. The fruit brought forth at the price of the death of the bringer is the fruit we eat with the most relish.'" In this vision was Florence the wasted branch?

Journalism did not satisfy her either. Told that she was more quoted than any other contributor to the *New Age*, she perhaps knew that her contributions lacked weight and coherence, for faced with the social reality of any problem, she inevitably retreated into mystical tangles about the soul's journey. Much of her popularity in 1907 and 1908 reflected the raging interest in women's opinions about the vote, prostitution, marriage, contraception, and divorce; for both the open discussion of these subjects and the notion that women might have opinions about what affects them most were new. Florence commented readily and often intelligently; yet suggestions like the one recommending that the West learn about prostitution from the East where it was practiced in the temples instead of in the gutters of Piccadilly Circus simply caught her supporting the privileges of caste rather than money. Shaw never had been able to interest her in socialist economics. Neither did acting now satisfy her, although she had toured with Mrs. Campbell in 1908, winning good notices as Ann Mortimore in *The Thunderbolt*, and played for Mrs. Pat in a series of matinees after their return. But she was restive under Mrs. Campbell's domination: she could not afford the star's expensive hotels, had no liking for the famous "temperament," and resented playing second fiddle to a younger actress. Her novel *Modern Woman* found a publisher; Shaw footed the publication bill for *The Solemnization of Jacklin:* yet she was intelligent enough to know that she wrote wretchedly.

Her thoughts turned more and more toward the East as both escape and testing ground. She was fifty-two in 1912, and was finding England no country for old women. She had long been tired of life, or so she complained to Yeats—although clad in purple and scarlet scarves and huge hats like straw baskets, her figure slimmed by constant dieting, the eyebrows still crescent, her conversation still lively and good-natured, she did not impress people as despairing. Yet on 5 September, "so happy she was saying Goodbye to the lot of us," as Stella told Shaw, Florence sailed away to end her days "in the society of the wise." It was fifteen years almost to the day that Shaw had written her in 8 September 1897, "Wait fifteen years or so and you will fit yourself in somewhere." To Yeats, who had by now wearied of faeryland and searched for cool, gray reality, Florence's move seemed "upwards out of life." He guessed at her motive, perhaps a little envious that she might find Byzantium before he:

> . . . Florence Emery . . .
> Who finding the first wrinkles on a face
> Admired and beautiful,
> And knowing that the future would be vexed
> With 'minished beauty, multiplied commonplace,
> Preferred to teach a school
> Away from neighbour or friend,
> Among dark skins, and there
> Permit foul years to wear
> Hidden from eyesight to the unnoticed end.

Shaw was himself a religious man. Theosophical thought in some of its aspects did not conflict with his religion of creative evolution.[21] In his renunciation of carnality, his abhorrence of harming living creatures, his hope that life might evolve a human existence of pure thought, he came close to the beliefs of Buddhism. Particularly mystic was his assertion that since suffering ceases with desire, the conquering of desire is the ideal human goal. Charlotte had confronted this indifference to life during the crisis of 1898; Stella confronted the carelessness in lines like "Remember that I am always your saint and that my ecstasy will survive disembodiment," or "My deepest and lastingest happiness beggars all desire." He would express the renunciation best, perhaps, in *Heartbreak House* through Ellie Dunn's "Heartbreak is the end of happiness and the beginning of peace." Yet Shaw did not protect himself from desire through meditation. Curiously, the prophet of a creative, organic evolution thought of himself as a machine: it was "work, work, worry, worry, brains clattering, dating, punctuation, committees, speeches." Endless activity saved him from bothering about happiness; his daily life resembled the millstones grinding rather than the search for peace; and thus Charlotte could not share her quest with him. She shared it instead with her frequent companion, Lena Ashwell, at whose house she met Dr. James Porter Mills.

According to his followers, Dr. Mills was a sincere, powerful, intense, unselfishly devoted man who possessed a key to thinking that could shape life meaningfully. He had begun in Chicago as a doctor; then his wife had proved a more successful healer than himself, even curing him, to his great chagrin. "Being a husband he saw at once that his wife's way couldn't be the right way," Charlotte observed quietly; "being a wife she quite agreed about that." The Millses set out to find the answer in China, Australia, and India. From their mingled experiences they evolved the "Teaching"—a spiritual way of adjusting to life that particularly appealed to Charlotte, who had "everything," yet still felt unsatisfied. Fortified by the Teaching, Charlotte only intermittently lost her self-control over Shaw's behavior with Mrs. Campbell; yet the outbursts were frequent enough to cause him great contrition and alarm.

On Thursday, 30 January 1913, for example, Shaw and Charlotte had lunched with Sylvia Brooke, who "very devilishly" asked him point blank, "How is Mrs. Pat?"—and "watched to see how much damage that shell would do when it exploded." The damage was considerable. Shaw to Stella the next day: "I scribble in great haste—going out with Charlotte to try a car, and darent be an instant late. Oh why, why, why did I fill up this afternoon? If only I could steal a minute before dinner; but I darent, darent, darent: youd make me late and then—" Stella replied scornfully: had Charlotte the "pluck of a mouse," she would treat with charm and sympathy the woman, or women, Mr. Mouse took an interest in; as for him, she adored and at the same time detested his "fears and tremblings and bewitching timidities." Shaw himself was typically divided: "Oh this loathsome but necessary conscience!" he cried. "And oh! this wild happiness that frees me from it!" Either way, he seemed to be the winner.

Winning was important, for the man and woman relation was a duel, exhilarating but dangerous, and one must lose. "The male resumes his predominance," he exulted after one contest with Stella. But gradually he found the ground slipping away from under his feet, for Stella in her better moods did not duel at all, but simply opened her arms. Shaw wrote her in ecstatic terror:

Oh, if only you were alarmed, and could struggle, then I could struggle too. But to be gathered like a flower and stuck in your bosom frankly! to have no provocation to pursue, and no terror to fly! to have no margin of temptation to philander in! to have a woman's love on the same terms as a child's, to have nothing to seize, nothing to refuse, nothing to resist, everything for nothing, the gate of heaven wide open as in my story, to have striven fiercely all my life for trifles and have treasures at last offered for nothing, to miss the resistance that has become to me what water is to a fish, to hear tones in a human voice that I have never heard before, to have it taken for granted that I am a child and want to be happy, to draw the sword for the duel of sex with cunning confidence in practised skill and a brass breastplate, and suddenly find myself in the arms of a mother—a young mother, and with a child in my own arms who is yet a woman; all this plunges me into the wildest terror as if I were suddenly in the air thousands of feet above the rocks or sea. The

measure of that terror is the relief with which I felt the earth yesterday . . . . Yet here I am caught up again, breathless, with no foothold, at
a dizzy height, in an ecstasy which must be delirious and presently end in
my falling headlong to destruction. And yet I am happy, as madmen
are. . . . Oh Stella, Stella, Stella, I no longer regret anything . . . .[22]

Clearly Shaw now surrendered sexually. Or perhaps it was only an
emotional surrender, since the languages of sexual and spiritual exultation
are the same. Shaw's gate of heaven is ambiguous. Marchbanks approached it when he made love to Candida; and was stopped by a
flaming sword and the realization that the gate to that kind of heaven is
the gate to hell. But Candida was married, and the phallic sword prohibi-
tive. With Stella Campbell the gate stood wide open, the treasure lay
there for him to take. Yet that loathsome but necessary conscience! How
to escape it—and yet enjoy? One way is to pretend that they are mother
and child, innocent in their love. As he had told Stella, he was bound to
Charlotte "by all the bonds except the bond of the child to the dark
lady." In Shaw's mind (and in myth) the dark lady stands for sexuality
and dominance. He is fascinated by her, yet fears her power. Yet if he
can change her into a mother, the sexuality will become tenderness and
the dominance a mother's power to bestow comfort and pleasure. Simmering with latent sexuality, the relationship will yet be innocent; for either of them to push it further is taboo. Pleading beautifully with Stella
after she had refused him her room for a few days, Shaw sounds very
much like a willful child:

I want my plaything that I am to throw away. I want my Virgin Mother
enthroned in heaven. I want my Italian peasant woman. I want my rapscallionly fellow vagabond. I want my dark lady. I want my angel—I
want my tempter. I want my Freia with her apples. I want the lighter of
my seven lamps of beauty, honor, laughter, music, love, life and immortality. I want my inspiration, my folly, my happiness, my divinity, my
madness, my selfishness, my final sanity and sanctification, my
transfiguration, my purification, my light across the sea, my palm across
the desert, my garden of lovely flowers, my million nameless joys, my
day's wage, my night's dream, my darling and my star.[23]

He clung more closely to Stella as mother in these months, perhaps,
because he had lost his own. After three strokes and seven months' struggle, Lucinda Shaw died on 18 February 1913 at the age of eighty-three,
having only given up teaching music at the North London School five
years before. For Lucy (her divorce from the unfaithful Charles Butterfield in 1909 encouraged and paid for by Shaw), it was like the end of the

world: "She was the Alpha and Omega of all my hopes, fears and acts," she said. She was cremated four days later. Shaw and Barker took the tube to Golders Green, where they met the violet cloth-draped coffin atop the horsedrawn hearse and an undertaker in a paroxysm of grief. Appalled at this professionalism, Shaw intimated sternly that a display of grief was unnecessary, only to find that the undertaker had known Mrs. Shaw for years and was genuinely affected. For Shaw, however, the occasion was a celebration; and he chose to describe the ceremony to Stella (the beautiful letter would make him infamous for callousness) because she was the only person he knew who didn't consider her mother the Enemy. Imagining all through the service—the entrance of the coffin into the "cool, clean, sunny" chamber where it suddenly burst into "streaming ribbons of garnet coloured lovely flame, smokeless and eager, like pentecostal tongues," the separating in the "kitchen" below of ashes from bone, the scattering of bone dust on a flower bed outside—imagining all through that Mamma was beside him, shaking with laughter at the absurdities of rendering dust to dust, Shaw found the whole process merry and assumed "loyally high spirits" to prove that he indeed rejoiced more in his mother's living memory than grieved for the dead. Stella's rebuke was far gentler than he must have expected (for the letter, though sincere, was surely calculated to shock): she replied that she adored sentiment and adored acrobats—on wires or mental. In seeing in Shaw's merriness a perilous balancing act, she showed much perception.[24]

And so, Shaw continued to berate and congratulate himself over his passion: "I MUSTNT be in love; but I *am*. You have beaten me—my first defeat, and my first success." Meetings of the Society of Authors gave him excuses when he came up to London from Ayot to see her after dinner, although he had to rush for the 10 P.M. train at King's Cross Station. He never missed it, nor caught it by more than a few seconds. If he ever missed it, he would know himself to be an utter brute. A weekend in March on Beachy Head with the Webbs to plan the future of the *New Statesman* gave him the chance to steal away to Brighton, where she had gone from the nursing home for further recovery. Stella was not sure he should come. She had been told terrible things about him—that he did not respect the feelings of those who loved him; that he would certainly hurt her if she gave in. She didn't know whether she was brave enough to face him again. He came anyway, and found her in a dazzling dress and quite well taken care of: oysters and champagne with the dukes and ladies and viscountesses she liked in her train. Nevertheless, his visit vaulted him up to heaven again; to leave her was to be cast down into the mud of the sordid streets once more. Ten days later he spent the night at Leamington, waiting to pick up a new motor bike at Coventry the next morning. She had written nothing for seven days. What did this forebode? He feared that she had perhaps returned to her old hostility to his world. He remembered the velvet dress, the two words she had spoken once when she took him up in her arms. Her silence unmanned him. Begging "Wont you say something to me," he finally admitted, however, the uselessness of words. He had written everything, he had said everything. He did not want to write his love any longer—he wanted to live it.

At the end of March Charlotte roused herself. She had been ailing with severe bouts of asthma and bronchitis; now Sir Horace Plunkett, an old friend, had invited them to Kilteragh, his house in County Dublin. Would G.B.S. accompany her? He would. Away from Ayot, where the tension of waiting to see whether Shaw had indeed caught the ten o'clock from King's Cross must have been severe, Charlotte recovered her poise. She could impress, even in G.B.S.'s shadow: Max Beerbohm had noted the great *charm* of Mrs. Shaw.[25] "Charlotte has suddenly got well, and changed from a fiend into a green-eyed mermaid, smiling and fascinating and dressing in diamonds and generally dispensing charm and childish happiness," Shaw told Stella. "What is more amazing, she actually refers to you without fury, even with raillery. 'Did you go to Brighton that day at Beachy Head?' Boundless contempt for both of us, but no more hatred, almost a joyous contempt. She realizes her superiority now. Quite right too; for you and I see two barefooted playmates on the hills; and she is what you, like a dear ignorant colleen-*contadina* as you are, sum up as a Suffragette. Dont grudge her her contempt; for the difference between that and the sick hatred and fury her illness produced is for me the difference between heaven and hell. She cannot, like you, laugh through her last gasp."[26]

Back at Ayot and London, however, Shaw's indiscretions shattered the domestic peace once more. Accused by Charlotte of having had Mrs. Campbell at Adelphi Terrace, he admitted only to a telephone call; and a call had preceded his visit to Kensington Square, where he had felt beautifully domestic with her—as though they had been married for years—and then ravished when she actually drove with him to King's Cross Station. He conveyed to Charlotte after this meeting Stella's proposal that they should make up a theatre party for Arnold Bennett's *The Great Adventure*. "She cannot understand why you dont love her," said Shaw to Charlotte. "That shows some good in her," said Charlotte grimly to Shaw. Another telephone call was overheard, however. The effect, Shaw reported, was dreadful: he suffered watching Charlotte suffer; evidently he would have to kill either himself or her. The "essential inhumanity" of jealousy appalled him: he never seemed able to escape it. "I throw my desperate hands to heaven," he cried, "and ask why one cannot make one beloved woman happy without sacrificing another."

Then another place of rendezvous presented itself. Lucy was now an invalid, suffering from the tuberculosis that had killed their sister Agnes at twenty-one. Well aware of Charlotte's hostility to Lucy, Stella announced that she would call on her. "Go," said Shaw; "she will tell you lies about my childhood: the relations of great men always do." Stella became a frequent visitor at 8 Park Village West at Gloucester Gate, Regent's Park, the home Shaw had taken for his mother when the lease at Fitzroy Square ran out in 1906. There Stella often met Shaw; and on "dear afternoons" in the house with the pretty garden and the sister with the "delicious brogue," she discovered a new Shaw who surprised her as much as a conjurer had once when, to her childish delight, he had pulled a small soft rabbit out of a hat—"and I feel like that at all the dear tenderness of your nature—struggling about in your heart and eyes and voice—and you holding it hard by the ears but I know it can get away with you in a moment."[27]

"Among my most frequent visitors is Mrs Patrick Campbell," Lucy wrote to her close friend Janey Drysdale. "She is extraordinarily simple, almost childlike in her conversation. She brought Sarah Allgood, the leading lady of the Irish players, one day, and G.B.S. turned up at the same time. They gave quite a good concert. Mrs. plays the piano beautifully, better than many professionals I have heard. Sarah sang plaintive old Irish songs in a tearful contralto, and George sang all sorts of things in a throaty baritone, whilst Mrs. Pat made fun of him. They ended up by dancing a Scotch reel in the hall to the tune of *Wee Macgregor* on the gramophone: such a party of lunatics they looked."[28] Lucy kept track of Shaw's progress, reading his plays and press notices. The Super One she called him, with a mixture of pride and exasperation. "You brought out a nice side of Lucy that I haven't seen since she was a girl," Shaw told Stella. Lucy might have said the same for George.

One day Stella showed up at Lucy's suffering from a splinter driven under her thumbnail at rehearsal. Shaw and Lucy's doctor were there; they took her to a chemist, who found an instrument to remove it. Stella remembered: "Joey exclaimed with enthusiasm—as my nail was being slowly lifted and the splinter withdrawn, the veins in my neck swelling in my efforts to resist the pain—'By jove! what a throat—"Michael Angelo!"' This time I felt Joey's admiration was sincere."[29] A great performance by two accomplished actors.

"My dearest love," Shaw wrote on his return to Adelphi Terrace: "I think all that was good for my soul, because it tore everything that was selfish and imaginary right out of me, and made you a real fellow-creature in real pain (O Lord! my fibres all twist and my heart and bowels torment me when I think of it); and the more real you become the more I discover that I have a real real real kindness for you, and that I am not a mere connoisseur in beauty or a sensualist or a philanderer, but a—but a—a—a—I dont know what, but something that has deep roots in it that you pluck at. Only, why should you have to be hurt to cure me of selfishness and of little fits of acting? Why should it not be an ecstasy of happiness for you: that would move me too, perhaps still more deeply."[30]

Surely Stella could feel that this time too Shaw was being sincere.

1913-1914

MEANWHILE THE QUESTION of *Pygmalion* still hung fire, Shaw and Stella tempting and repulsing, advancing and retreating—making the play as much of a courtship as their romance. J. M. Barrie had also written a play for Stella: *The Adored One*, a one-act drama he had stretched to three acts when he realized that Mrs. Pat needed a success after her costly illness. "Is Barrie going to be faithful to Stella in the matter of that murderess play," Shaw asked Barker (the sexual metaphor was significant), "or will he betray her with Irene [Vanbrugh]? I want to know before I move again in the matter of Pygmalion. I really dont see why Pygmalion should go out of the family. If we cant manage Mrs. Pattikins, whom (of the first order) *can we* manage? 'Love Will Find Out The Way.' "[1] Barrie lived opposite the Shaws in Adelphi Terrace. "He and I live in the weather house with two doors," the shy Scot teased Stella, who alternately knocked at both doors in search of a play, "and you are the figure that smiles on us and turns up its nose at us alternately. However, I would rather see you going in at his door than not see you at all, and as you are on elastic I know that the farther you go with him the farther you will have to bound back."[2] Admiring Mrs. Campbell hugely, Barrie remained cautious of the temperament. To a playwright who complained that his chances had been ruined when, in the midst of reading a first act to Mrs. Campbell in her dressing room, Pinkie had become violently sick, Barrie said thoughtfully, "I shouldn't worry, I've read a play to that dog myself!"

Stella bounded back to the extent of choosing *The Adored One* over *Pygmalion* for the coming September 1913 under Charles Frohman's management at the Duke of York's; but Shaw urged her to it. She had the two best plays and parts in London "in the hollow of her bosom," he told her. She must take Barrie's and wait with *Pygmalion:* first, because Barrie's play was bound to be the surest and most lucrative; second, because although she could offend Barrie by slighting his offer, she could not offend him. If she wanted a sentimental reason for postponing *Pygmalion* (which she wanted to do at the St. James's that summer with Sir George Alexander), she had his word that to rehearse her in *Pygmalion* now would probably kill him. Instead she must agree to a June revival of *The Second Mrs. Tanqueray* with Alexander, who had been masochist enough to offer himself again as her leading man. Chiefly, he did not want *Pygmalion* thrown away in the summer. Protesting that he did not understand her way of doing business, Stella nevertheless took Shaw's advice.

A supper party celebrated the revival at the St. James's. To it Stella maliciously invited Mr. and Mrs. Shaw; from it they quickly declined. A pity, replied Stella: the guests were not a pack of Bohemians, but company quite good enough for Shaw's lady—among them George West. This was the first time Stella named Shaw's rival in a letter; during his next visit to Kensington Square, however, she talked of marrying George Cornwallis-West, whose marriage to Lady Randolph Churchill had been dissolved in April. Back at Ayot, Shaw protested. She must not talk of marrying George, for it brought out the family solicitor in him, the same solicitor who had promoted *The Adored One* before *Pygmalion* for her own good. This solicitor Shaw would perversely drive her into West's arms for the same practical reasons. And if that happened, his heart would turn into rusty iron again, and he would be cut off from what was "common and young" in his humanity. West was young, he was old; West could wait until he had lost his illusions. They could not last much longer now: she could not be what he thought her—a figure from the dreams of his boyhood, all romance and beauty. "I promise to tire as soon as I can so as to leave you free," he urged. "I will produce *Pygmalion* and criticise your acting. I will yawn over your adorable silly sayings and ask myself are they really amusing. I will run after other women in search of a new attachment; I will hurry through my dream as fast as I can; only let me have my dream out."[3]

But Stella did not allow this. Calling on her one day in early June in "a certain importunate mood," Shaw found her impatient and remote, her smile forced. The interview ended with a door slammed in his face. "So it has lasted only a month after all!" thought Shaw; and then remembered that the romance had begun the previous summer and had lasted a whole year, and that not until the year was out had she said: "'Go and love somebody else and dont bother me.'" He had been dreading the event. Ever since her recovery he had watched her "forgetting and coquetting and slipping back to old attitudes and delusions"—drifting back "into suppers and dinners with those dear pleasant spooks of do-nothings" to whom he had been gracious for her sake. He knew that his adoration bored her. How much more interesting was the dilettante lover who diverted himself with suppers, company, operas, outings, races, clubs, and let her alone. Of course, he had been prepared to jump. He possessed a "magnified power of switching off at a moment's notice" when fortune changed: it was his chief protection against heartbreak. And yet he remembered the terrible pang that had rent him when recently, coming upon a Blake drawing, he had read the title, "He shall take from thee the desire of thine eye." Was it really to be so? Amid the pyrotechnics of Shaw's lovemaking, a few phrases ring true. "Wont you say something to me?" he had begged after a silence. "Stella: don't play with me," he pleaded after that door-slamming. They seemed the words of a man deeply affected.

"Why do you go on scolding me because I am the woman I am and not the woman you would have me be?" complained Stella, with justice. The pressure of Shaw's vision—mother of angels, dusty-petticoated gypsy, siren, holiest of holies, adoredest, playmate—crushed her. He did not love her: he loved his creation; and punished her when she failed to com-pete with it. Besides, she was well now, and had George, and Barrie's play. She was going away to the seaside to learn her part for *The Adored One.* She did not want his companionship: she must be alone by the sea so that strength and steadiness could come to her. He had been so kind, so dear lately, she admitted: ". . . Its getting difficult not to love you more than I ought to love you—Offend me again quickly to pull me together—But by the sea I must be alone—you know."[4]

Stella had asked Nigel Playfair, theatrical producer, to lend her his cottage near Ramsgate on the coast of Kent for the second week of Au-gust. Playfair agreed, and privately bet that she would not stand the soli-tude four hours. Stella arrived with Georgina, her chauffeur, her faithful maid Prosser, a mountain of luggage, and Barrie's script. Ordering Prosser to unpack, she settled down to summon strength and steadiness. Twelve sated hours later, she burst out of the cottage, and with Prosser and a train of luggage bearers in her wake, made for the nearest luxury hotel. That evening the Playfairs' housekeeper answered the ring of a tall, slender, silver-bearded, athletic-looking gentleman in stout shoes and knickerbockers who, nevertheless, looked quite done up from his expedi-tion across the sands. Informed that Mrs. Patrick Campbell had removed to the Guildford Hotel at Sandwich, he turned on his heel and strode off into the night.

The territory was familiar to Shaw. Only a few miles north Jenny Pat-terson had lured him to her cottage at Broadstairs long ago with promises of sea air, a vegetarian menu, her favors, and a piano on which to play

Mozart. Fleeing when pursued, Shaw now pursued when evaded: perhaps he reflected upon the irony now. Stella's welcome when she found out Shaw was a fellow guest at the Guildford Hotel lacked enthusiasm. They spent two days together. Shaw radiated zest, adventurousness, romance, productivity, and braggadocio. Stella yawned. On 10 August he opened a note from his belovedest. "Please will you go back to London to-day," wrote Stella, "—or go wherever you like but dont stay here—If you wont go I must—I am very very tired and I oughtn't to go another journey. Please dont make me despise you." George Cornwallis-West might well have been due any day or hour.

Shaw did not take the hint. The day wore away, the letter rested in his pocket. That night he went out to look for her on the sands, but she was not there—being occupied (so she later explained) in a frantic search for Georgina, who had lost herself in the long grass near the hotel. When he finally found her they shared a nightcap, but Shaw failed to catch the meaning of the waiter's "You've paid your bill and ginger beer one shilling." He was terribly sleepy, Stella noted with disgust: hardly a propitious state for lovemaking, had she wanted it. "Let us bathe before breakfast tomorrow at a quarter to eight," said Shaw. "No, at eight," said Stella. "Too late," insisted Shaw. "Please not before eight," begged Stella. The next morning she rose at six; by seven-thirty she and Prosser and Georgina were packed into the motor and headed south along the coastal road for St. Margaret's Bay. At eight Shaw knocked at her door, calling "Come and bathe." A smiling chambermaid emerged. "They've gone, sir," said she. Summoning all his presence of mind, Shaw managed to smile. "What? Today?" he said lightly. "I thought it was tomorrow." Below he found a note waiting: "Goodbye. I am still tired—you were more fit for a journey than I."

Hell hath no fury like a philanderer scorned. Shaw took up pen to pour out his contempt. Had he seemed sleepy? It had been a tactful retreat in the face of her obvious boredom. *He* had been ready enough. "Bah! You have no nerve: you have no brain: you are the caricature of an eighteenth century male sentimentalist, a Hedda Gabler titivated with odds and ends from Burne Jones's ragbag: you know nothing, God help you, except what you know all wrong: daylight blinds you: you run after life furtively and run away or huddle up and scream when it turns and opens its arms to you . . . you are a one-part actress and that one not a real part: you are an owl, sickened by two days of my sunshine. . . . Go then: the Shavian oxygen burns up your little lungs: seek some stuffiness that suits you. You will not marry George! At the last moment you will funk him or be ousted by a bolder soul. You have wounded my vanity: an inconceivable audacity, an unpardonable crime."

As the day turned to darkness, however, and the lights of Ramsgate began to twinkle across the strand, his anger turned to pain; and he wrote again. He had not pressed her into love immediately because, "I said 'There are seven stars and seven sorrows and seven swords in the heart of the Queen of Heaven: and for myself I want seven days.' They began; and I held back: I was not greedy: for I wanted the last to be the best. And you yawned in my face . . . ." He had wanted freedom, frankness, fellowship; she had offered ignorance, sentimentality, fear. But that was nothing compared to the crime of her desertion. "Stella, how could you, how could you? What micrometer could measure the shallowness that prevents you from knowing what you have done. Even if I had been secretly bored to distraction I would have stayed on in fire rather than have dealt you the enormous blow of deserting you." The next day the pain had not gone away. "How could a human heart deal another such a—such a kick? This is what I have to forgive. Stella: why did you do it?" If there was any comfort to be derived from the betrayal, it was this: plainly it was he who cared, and she who did not: order had been restored: it was he who was the mighty spirit, not she.

Borrowing Shaw's style, Stella tried to defend herself against this word magician. "You vagabond you—you blind man. You weaver of words, you—black and purple winged hider of cherubs—you poor thing unable to understand a mere woman. My friend all the same. No daughters to relieve your cravings—no babes to stop your satirical chatterings, why should I pay for all your shortcomings. You in your broom-stick and sheet have crackers and ashes within you—I in my rags and my trimming have a little silver lamp in my soul and to keep its flame burning is all that I ask. That I pray. My friend—my dear friend all the same." Reading his outpourings, she could not help feeling a little pleased, however. "Your two letters—considering," she wrote from Littlestone-on-Sea, "—are very well."

On Wednesday, 13 August, Shaw was back in London from "the land of broken promise." He had finished his play *Great Catherine* punctually at one-thirty that day, in time for lunch. Never neglect work for romance—it had always been his precept. He had constantly thrust work between them for fear he should tire her, and now he had tired her anyway. "Fool!" he cursed himself. "Dupe! Dotard! Crybaby! Useless, these letters; the wound will not heal." He tried desperately to find excuses for her behavior; had seized on the idea that perhaps she had not been able to sleep well at the Guildford Hotel. "You could not argue your case half as well as I have argued it fifty times," he told her. "Did you ever meet so feminine a creature?" He knew he would be weak enough to telephone her when she returned; and he did—but there were disputes and abrupt leave-takings. The world had changed horribly since that Sunday afternoon when he had opened the fatal note; and indeed, the romance was irretrievably broken.

In September Shaw and Charlotte left for the Continent, Charlotte hurt and angry, Shaw subdued. He had intended to stay a week at Sandwich with Stella. What excuse had he given his wife, if any? Nothing that she would have believed. Finally at Valence-sur-Rhône, she exploded; then, as Shaw reported to Stella, "after two perfectly frightful scenes with me, in which she produced such a case against my career and character as made Bluebeard seem an angel in comparison, she quite suddenly and miraculously—at a moment when murder and suicide seemed the only thing left to her—recovered her intellectual balance, her sanity, and her amiability completely, and became once more (after about two years) the happy consort of an easygoing man. Not even the discovery of some telegrams from Barrie about the first night of A.O. has upset her. So I no longer sigh and drift before the storm close reefed, collar up, head bent, and hands in pockets. The relief is enormous: I have such infernal powers of endurance that I never realize the weight of a burden until it is lifted from my shoulders."[5]

Thus Shaw's great romance ended. Stella argued that she behaved like a gentleman in leaving Sandwich and not seducing Charlotte's husband; that she could not have done otherwise. She could, of course, have patiently waited out the seven days to see whether Shaw would finally summon courage to go to bed with her, as he obviously wanted to do. But her taste rather ran to younger, coarser men; and even had she seduced him, she might, after his initial ecstasy and gratitude, have found herself fallen in his esteem and no longer wearing the blue hood of the Mother of Angels. The women Shaw respected were chaste—Elizabeth Robins, Ellen (forced into chastity), Charlotte, or devoted wives like Beatrice Webb and Janet. Or Stella could have responded to his mood: could have played with him for seven holy days on the Celestial Mountains. Holy week over, Shaw would have returned to Charlotte's solicitous care and she to her husbandless house at Kensington Square. In not kissing until she had the wedding ring, Stella behaved in a manner that Shaw outwardly scorned, inwardly did not disapprove. They were both after all cowards: she in failing to recognize the depths of his feeling and his shyness, and flinging off convention to imaginatively satisfy him; he in not leaving Charlotte to frankly pursue her. Both, however, congratulated themselves on their cleverness in preserving their egos almost intact.

Finally, both were terrified of each other. Stella knew her taste for high society, for expensive little suppers and carriage rides, for weekends at country estates; and knew how Shaw despised it. She marveled over his letters, comparing hers to "poor whining beggars," sure that every time she took up her pen she betrayed her inferiority. And then, she knew nothing, really, only six little pieces on the piano and a few lines of Keats. "It will be dreadful when you realize the commonplace witless charwoman I really am! and you with so many 'great women' about you," she deprecated. She had a formidable reputation for wit, yet it could seem insignificant next to the crackling brilliance of G.B.S. His alternate bouts of fantastic adoration and alarming abuse unnerved her. To defend herself, she called him "Joey"; prided herself on her feeling, and amateurism, and her mother's heart—her "born understanding" of things he had to struggle to learn. Poor silly Joey: he might crackle away with all the brilliance in the world, yet he could not understand the simplest human emotion.

Emotion is a much more popular commodity than brain, and something that almost everyone could and did hold over Shaw. Congratulating himself ceaselessly for possessing a heart of brass, Shaw nevertheless felt his deficiency. Part of his woman worship was awe for the emotional depths which even the simplest seemed to possess; his fear of women sprang from a similar source, as well as from fear of the sexuality they seemed to exude. No one had exuded a more powerful *odor di femmina* than Stella Campbell. It excited and terrified him. Masking his fear with the pretense that she was his child, his playmate, his mother, and his Virgin Queen (when he was not desperately protesting that she could not move him), he still had been cast up on Calypso's island. Once there, he trembled lest his deficiencies disgust her—his endless talk, his egotism, his grinding efficiency, his kindness, his modesty, his cowardice. They did, just as her deficiencies were bound to disillusion him. But Shaw was right in one thing: he *had* cared (however self-consciously and selfishly), and she had not.

Whatever the course of their romance, Shaw had warned, he would get a play out of it. In fact Stella Campbell can be found in six or seven plays. At the very beginning of their relationship in early July 1912, he had begun a one-act farce about adultery, inspired, as he told her, by the sign TRESPASSERS WILL BE PROSECUTED on D. D. Lyttelton's gate. Gregory Lunn in *Overruled* is a man who can only love "fully developed" women, and that always plunges him into difficulty since they are inevitably married and bearing a sign posted by their husbands, TRESPASSERS WILL BE PROSECUTED. How delightful it would be if there were no signs: if married couples were free to pursue adventure without the absurd punishments of jealousy or divorce.

The adventure of the two couples in *Overruled* fantasizes his desire for Stella, and teems with a familiar array of Shavian compulsions. Prominent is the fear of satisfaction. "It is so much pleasanter to dance on the edge of a precipice than go over it," announces the Preface. Having succeeded in getting himself on Mrs. Lunn's list of future husbands should her own die, Mr. Juno boasts to Mr. Lunn: "I'm her prospective husband: youre only her actual one. I'm the anticipation: youre the disappointment." Or, Mr. Lunn to Mrs. Juno: "Dont be alarmed: I like wanting you. As long as I have a want, I have a reason for living. Satisfaction is death." "Yes," replies Mrs. Juno; "but the impulse to commit suicide is sometimes irresistible." Gregory Lunn is closest to Shaw, just as Mrs. Juno is clearly Mrs. Campbell; and it is he who is most terrified of the love-death. "Danger is delicious," he says. "But death isnt. We court the danger; but the real delight is in escaping after all." Toppling on the very brink of the precipice, Lunn can only protest the very act he is committing, just as Shaw rejoiced both in his conscience and the impulse that occasionally freed him from it:

MRS. JUNO [*opening her arms to him*]: But you cant resist me.

GREGORY: I must. I ought. [*Throwing himself into her arms*] Oh my darling, my treasure, we shall be sorry for this.

MRS. JUNO: We can forgive ourselves. Could we forgive ourselves if we let this moment slip?

GREGORY: I protest to the last. I'm against this. I have been pushed over a precipice. I'm innocent. This wild joy, this exquisite tenderness, this ascent into heaven can thrill me to the uttermost fibre of my heart [*with a gesture of ecstasy she hides her face on his shoulder*]; but it can't subdue my mind or corrupt my conscience, which still shouts to the skies that I'm not a willing party to this outrageous conduct. I repudiate the bliss with which you are filling me.

Slight as it is, *Overruled* was more than Shavian neurosis, for it discussed the whys and hows of infidelity instead of dramatizing the artificial morality that punishes it. Shaw hoped that his little comedy would be a model for other treatments of this still most popular dramatic subject. He himself did not want to listen to plays about the lies couples tell each other, but about the truths they were forced to tell when they had to face their actions without concealment or excuses. And the truths could be salutary: it was by no means necessary that marital infidelity had to end in tragedy or unhappiness. To make his happy ending, he provided Mr. Lunn's wife with a lover in Mr. Juno (as Charlotte had none), and made the women rather than the men finally declare that there was nothing wrong in married people falling in love with someone besides their own spouses.

Shaw had an obvious preference for unconventional male and female relationships. He had always linked himself to married or attached women, preferring to be "the anticipation" rather than "the disappointment." He had submitted to marriage, but liked long weekends and holidays with other couples such as the Webbs, the Barkers, the Simsons, the Cholmondeleys. He was perhaps only half joking when he proposed a joint ménage with H. G. Wells and his wife Jane. There was, of course, nothing unconventional about adultery; but his claim in *Overruled* that one could love someone else yet still cherish one's husband or wife, and that these multiple relationships could liberate and enrich, was still too radical for the British public. The play, presented in a triple bill at the Duke of York's in October 1912 along with Barrie's *Rosalind* and Pinero's *The Widow of Wasdale Head,* failed conspicuously. An outraged audience could not bear his cheerful solution to something it held dear: the right of every adulterer to be taken seriously. When he sent the play to Stella she found it as odious as *The Philanderer,* and refused to see anything of herself in it at all: "You *blind blind* man."

Besides *Overruled* and still another version of the Shaw-Charlotte-Campbell triangle called *Beauty's Duty,* Shaw had written in this period a new preface and more chapters to *The Quintessence of Ibsenism.* He sent proofs to Stella, asking her to mark anything wrong and say "any silly thing" that came into her head about it, "no matter how crudely." He promised that some of the new stuff was "terrible and wonderful," and instructed her to read his chapter on *Little Eyolf* between the lines.

Between these lines Shaw evidently meant Stella to read his complaint about the misery Rita Allmer's jealous possessiveness of her husband created for both Allmers and herself, just as Charlotte's jealousy was currently causing misery in their household. Having been told to say any silly thing that came into her head, Stella not surprisingly declined with the excuse, "I should write myself an ass on every page." Since she had played both Hedda and Rita as well as the Rat Wife, however, she did venture to object to his explication of those plays:

> . . . your "Hedda" makes me very sad—not one little bit do you understand Hedda—your interpretation of "do it beautifully" positively made me scream—her love—her shame—her physical condition—her agonizing jealousy—even the case of pistols—you're wrong at all points—did you think about it at all—or is it just your adoration for bl—dy plain facts that makes you so indifferent to all the poetry, the universal truths and beauty that lie behind and beyond?—You miss it all dolefully in *Little Eyolf*—the fact is you write carelessly sometimes—And with whom are you quarrelling? Be calm dearest, be gentle with fools. . . . The fact is you have too much brain—you tumble up against it—[6]

Yet many observers felt that Mrs. Campbell had played Hedda Gabler as a far worse person than the Hedda Shaw described in the *Quintessence.* Ralph Richardson, for example, remembered her performance as personified malignancy. Desmond MacCarthy described her Hedda as bored to death like Madame Bovary, envious, power-loving, "in a permanent condition of sulky conceit," inflicting petty humiliations on those in her power, dragging Lövborg down out of a kind of Iago-like malignancy tinged with sexual jealousy. MacCarthy did not even give Campbell's Hedda the credit of cherishing illusions about herself. Shaw did, finding Ibsen's heroine an idealist, engaged in "the monstrous but very common setting-up of wrong doing as an ideal, and of the wrong-doer as a hero." As for Hedda's "Do it beautifully," said Shaw, "she means that Lövborg is to kill himself in some manner that will make his suicide a romantic memory and an imaginative luxury to her for ever." Stella's dislike of Shaw's Hedda, like the audience's dislike of *Overruled*, suggested that she too wanted to make an ideal out of wrongdoing. Surely it was one of Shaw's most infuriating characteristics that he constantly denied murderers, adulterers, cheats, and liars the luxury of heroism and guilt. Shaw's Hedda Gabler was pathetic rather than heroic; and that interpretation was not one that Mrs. Campbell could tolerate.

Although Shaw claimed in his Preface to this 1913 edition not to have tampered with the original, he did make one large omission: the Appendix to the 1891 edition. He may have felt that the question of how actors should play, managers stage, and critics treat Ibsen had been solved: yet the omission served to remove the names of those most influential in establishing Ibsen in England, among them Janet Achurch, Florence Farr, Elizabeth Robins, and Marion Lea. "All four were products of the modern movement for the higher education of women," Shaw had written in 1891, "literate, in touch with advanced thought, and coming by natural predilection on the stage from outside the theatrical class, in contradistinction to the senior generation of inveterately sentimental actresses . . . ." The senior generation had signally failed all around, Shaw pointed out: "Mr Thorne, at the Vaudeville Theatre, was the first leading manager who ventured to put a play of Ibsen's into his evening bill; and he did not do so until Miss Elizabeth Robins and Miss Marion Lea had given ten experimental performances at his theatre at their own risk. Mr Charrington and Miss Janet Achurch, who, long before that, staked their capital and reputation on A Doll's House, had to take a theatre, and go into management themselves for the purpose. The production of Rosmersholm was not a managerial enterprise in the ordinary sense at all: it was an experiment made by Miss Farr, who played Rebecca—an experiment, too, which was considerably hampered by the refusal of the London managers to allow members of their companies to take part in the performance. In short, the senior division would have nothing to say for themselves in the matter of the one really progressive theatrical movement of their time, but for the fact that Mr W. H. Vernon's effort to obtain a hearing for Pillars of Society in 1880 was the occasion of the first appearance of the name of Ibsen on an English playbill."[7] Perhaps Shaw saw no need to repeat these accomplishments in 1913, or felt them too particular to a general study; yet their omission from his influential *Quintessence* certainly helped to hurry the names Robins, Achurch, Charrington, Farr, and Lea into obscurity.

Shaw had carried to Sandwich with him the first pages of another play. *Great Catherine*, however, was written for Gertrude Kingston, actress, feminist, and manager of the Little Theatre in John Street; an actress that exchanged flurries of fond "Little Mother" and "Little Father" letters with him, after the Russian manner of his play. Shaw prefaced this bravura piece with an apology for having made his Catherine not great at all, according to some objectors, but only scandalous. But Shaw actually made no apology for his female sensualist. Byron had said all that there was worth saying about the Russian monarch, and Byron's Catherine was his and everybody's Catherine. Yet Shaw managed an adroit twist away from anti-feminism at the end. "But oh, if I could only have had him for my—for my—" exclaims Catherine. "For your lover?" growls her jealous guard. "No: for my museum," sighs Catherine, naming the project nearest her heart. Writing for Gertrude Kingston, Shaw could not keep Stella out of this play either. The opening scene with Catherine in bed, the courtiers crowded around to do her will, the fastidious Englishman brought in trussed and helpless and thrown ignominiously onto her bed —surely it was a comic version of Shaw's initiation into Stella Campbell's heart via her sickroom.

Despite Shaw's boast that the machine never stopped grinding, his romance with Stella reduced him to two light plays between June 1912 and September 1913, and the beginnings of the even slighter *The Music-Cure*, subtitled "A Piece of Utter Nonsense." Here is Stella again (surely) as Strega Thundridge, a female Paderewski, and Shaw as an infatuated lover who longs to stay at home and wait for his great concert pianist to return in triumph. "Dont laugh at this ridiculous confession," begs Reginald Fitzambey; "but ever since I was a child I have had only one secret longing, and that was to be mercilessly beaten by a splendid, strong, beautiful woman." *The Music-Cure* indicated once again that in his slight pieces Shaw professed openly the attitudes he disciplined with dialectic in his major plays.

On the first of September 1913, however, his *Androcles and the Lion* opened at the St. James's Theatre. Shaw had written the part of Lavinia, the Christian who teaches a Roman captain the meaning of courage, for Lillah McCarthy; but had written the play before the advent of Mrs. Campbell. Beatrissima had since distracted Shaw's attention from the actress who had created Ann Whitefield, Nora, Jennifer Dubedat, and Margaret Knox; at the beginning of his correspondence, in fact, he had announced to Stella: "To Barker I have broken the shattering news that you have captured me for your own theatre, and that Lillah is a widow in a matter of speaking." In this last collaboration with Shaw, Barker and McCarthy gave *Androcles* a handsome production designed by Albert Rutherston. The McCarthy-Barker management were prospering at the moment with a gift from Lord Lucas of £10,000 for Shakespearean productions, Lord Howard de Walden's financial backing, and the 622 performances of *Fanny's First Play*. But their brilliant days with Shaw were over.

Just back from the fiasco at Sandwich, attempting to see Stella between her rehearsals for *The Adored One*, suffering almost constantly from headaches, Shaw turned up for the dress rehearsal at the St. James's to discover that as usual Barker was treating his play with too much restraint. Teased by Stella for having no growl and no claws, Shaw now roared. Then having blown up lines, action, staging, business, and interpretation, he went home to bed, leaving Barker to sweep together the pieces. A distinguished first-night audience included H. G. Wells, Masefield, and Galsworthy. The next day there was outrage from conservatives and/or Christians, praise from the progressives, and from the *Times* a dart of small wit against great humor. It was, of course, the lion's evening, said the critic. "Was ever beast so fortunate? . . . we mean in being the one character in the whole range of Shavian drama who never talks." *Androcles* ran for fifty-two performances; and while Shaw had feared that the play might prove "simply an irritant," Barker, McCarthy, and Shaw himself all expected more from this first-class production.

Ellen Terry was among the first-night audience. Now sixty-six, she wrote Shaw from Smallhythe in October: "It is just a *darling* Play. I saw it again on Thursday & loved it more & more— & most of all *the Lion!*" For herself, there had been two years of "horrible idleness," of thinking of no one but herself when, after all, for years she had pretended to be others. Wistfully she pleaded: did Shaw have a play or know of a play for her? Something "an old Fish like *this* Fish, could swim through with ease & get a little money & give a little pleasure." Two weeks later she wrote more urgently: "*Please* remember me soon—when you can find a spare moment. You don't know how necessary it is that I shall do some work— & I am quite fit now. But—IF I'm not wanted any more on the stage I must turn Nurse or Gardener. *Must* find work. Bless you. Ellen."[8]

You fill me with concern—with dismay [Shaw replied by return post]. What am I to do or say? It's as if Queen Alexandra came to me and asked me to get her a place as cook-housekeeper, except that I'm not in love with Queen Alexandra. Nobody dare have you in a cast: youd knock it all to pieces. A tiny yacht may throw its mast overboard and end its days quietly and serviceably as a ferry boat; but a battleship cant do that; and you are a battleship. . . . Ellen, Ellen, what has become of all the jubilee money?—for you *must* be in difficulties or you would never be content with minor work. You are not wildly extravagant: you dont keep two motor cars and wallow in sables and diamonds. Do you give it all away; or has Teddy a family in every European capital for

you to support? Not my business, isnt it? Then dont harrow my feelings
by telling me that you must get engagements instantly. Must we all sink
with 50 starving parasites clutching our hair? I have three letters just received from unfortunate people, pitiable people, nice people, whose only
refuge is being adopted by me. I *must* turn savage and thrust them from
my plank into the waves or I shall presently be as desperate as they are.
So must you. . . .

O Lord!

Let us tie ourselves together—close—and give some respectable boat-
man our last shilling to row us out and drop us into the sea.[9]

Another love-death. Understandably, Shaw took alarm at Ellen's letter;
but her problem was not lack of money, but lack of work; and her letter
had said nothing about a minor part. Appreciating being called a battleship as little perhaps as Janet had enjoyed being called an elephant or
Elizabeth Robins a Great Western locomotive, Ellen only begged gently
in reply that he not trouble his dear heart about her for a second. She
was not in financial difficulties; indeed his concern had made her see that
she had nothing to complain about. As for the parasite: "Teddy is afloat
now, and my son all along has been my sun. Without the warmth of him
many a time I would have died and died, I know!" Only in thanking
Shaw for turning his "flashlight" on her problems did she rebuke him by
comparison.

As for Stella, she had had a signal failure with *The Adored One*, Barrie
failing in his attempt to write a Campbell play as drastically as Shaw had
succeeded. The fiasco depressed her, as did her reservations about marriage with George Cornwallis-West. Her age was a constant source of
chagrin, although she was only ten years older than George, whereas
Jennie Churchill had been eighteen. Attending a rehearsal of *The Grand
Seigneur*, she had "wept like a baby when the new leading lady slim as a
pin . . . said 'Goodbye' to her silly billy man." To think what she, Beatrice Stella Campbell, had been; to think what she would be ten years
from now, to realize that now was the golden hour, to feel the reality of
life springing shut like a trap. "There are rocks ahead,—you are wise and
clear sighted," she wrote Shaw that November. She wanted him to meet
George, really to meet, and to talk. ". . . be quite serious in your friendship for me," she concluded. "—I am so troubled just now, and must put
aside trimmings and prettiness—"[10]

From the Ilfracombe Hotel in Devon where he watched the old year
out, Shaw composed his last great love letter to Stella, at once a com-
memoration and a goodbye:

New Years Eve. O night of all nights in the year—of my most imme-
morial year! Do you remember last New Years Eve? I am actually asking

you do you remember it? Was it anything to you except that you were ill, and were determined to prevent me from seeing the new year in with Lillah and Barrie? *I* remember it: it tears me all to pieces: I believe we were both well then, and have been ill ever since. . . . On that last New Years Eve and all the eves that went before it, there was Eternity and Beauty, infinite, boundless loveliness and content. I think of it with a frightful yearning, with a tragic despair: for you have wakened the latent tragedy in me, broken through my proud overbearing gaiety that carried all the tragedies of the world like feathers and stuck them in my cap and laughed. And if your part in it was an illusion, then I am as lonely as God. Therefore you must still be the Mother of Angels to me, still from time to time put on your divinity and sit in the heavens with me. For that, with all our assumed cleverness and picked up arts to stave off the world, is all we two are really fit for. Remember this always even when we are grovelling and racketing and drudging; for in this remembrance I am deeply faithful to you—faithful beyond all love. Be faithful to me in it and I will forgive you though you betray me in everything else—forgive you, bless you, honor you, and adore you. *Super hanc Stellam* will I build my Church.

And now let us again hear the bells ring: you on your throne in your blue hood, and I watching and praying, not on my knees, but at my fullest stature. For you I wear my head nearest the skies.

Woman's great art, Shaw had once said, is in lying low and allowing men to imagine things about her. Stella practiced this art now, replying with a few lines. "If I could write letters like you," she concluded, "I would write letters to God—"[11]

The year 1913, rather a failure for Shaw with a collapsed romance, a turbulent domesticity, and less than brilliant London runs for his plays, was nevertheless significant. A key symbol in the campaign for women's suffrage had been Joan of Arc. Embroidered on banners, impersonated in pageants, or mounted on horseback at the head of processions and flourishing the green, white, and purple banner—the figure of the female warrior-saint had crystallized the message of the suffragettes. Traveling on the Continent that September, the Shaws had shopped at Orléans. Why, asked the feminist Charlotte, should he not do a play about Joan of Arc? The idea struck home. "I shall do a Joan play someday," Shaw wrote Stella from Orléans. ". . . Would you like to play Joan and come in on horseback in armour and fight innumerable supers?" On that same continental excursion, the Shaws had joined Lena Ashwell and her husband at Biarritz. There Lena had told about the sea adventures of her father, Captain Pocock, Shaw listening intently. The idea of an old sea captain at the helm of a floundering ship as the central metaphor for a play about Europe poised on the brink of destruction took hold. "When afterwards he read me 'Heartbreak House' he told me that the old sea captain was my father," said Lena, and dismissing her connection with Shavian drama as usual: "but there was no resemblance between that quaint old drunkard and my grand old darling with his power of self-control, of self-denial."[12] And, finally, on 20 November he had met with Herbert Tree, actor-manager of His Majesty's. Wary of "the delightful Stella Campbell," fearful of a rebuff, Tree was nevertheless very much interested in *Pygmalion* with Shaw's Eliza; and negotiations began.[13]

For Charlotte there had been great satisfaction in the performance on 9 December of her translation of Brieux's *La Femme seule* as *Woman on Her Own* with Lena Ashwell in the leading role. More and more she depended on her friendship with Lena, on the daily lectures in the small hall at Logan Place, and on her association with Dr. Mills, whose book on the "Teaching" she was carefully redacting in order to clarify his ponderously obscure message in her own mind. But for her the new year began bleakly. She seldom went to Ayot that winter (she disliked it anyway), and was therefore frequently ill and alone in London, while Shaw migrated between the country and city as usual. As plans for *Pygmalion* crystallized around an April opening and rehearsals became imminent, Charlotte shrank more and more from the event that must have seemed to her like a public exhibition of her husband's infatuation with Mrs. Campbell. The Millses were returning to America; Lena Ashwell was interested in the suffrage movement in the United States; Charlotte had a perennial faith in travel as escape and renewal. On 8 April she sailed on the *Olympic* with the Millses and Lena, leaving G.B.S. to face his fate alone. Among the place-names in her carefully kept travel book she wrote the single word *Pygmalion*. Like Shaw, she was unaware that Stella Campbell had become Mrs. George Cornwallis-West two days before she sailed.

The story of *Pygmalion* has been often told.[14] To no one's surprise, Stella quarreled interminably with Herbert Tree, with Tree's business manager, with Tree's stage manager, with prompters, costumers, stagehands, fellow actors, and with Joey himself—despite her promise that she would be "tame as a mouse and oh so obedient." Difficult now for Shaw to remember that she was his Mother of Angels and he her idolator. Sir Herbert only added to the confusion. Hopelessly unbusinesslike, scatterbrained, gigantically egotistic, often blissfully innocent of lines since he relied on improvisation, the great actor with the foreign-sounding accent drove the precise Shaw wild with frustration. "I like an empty head for my ideas," Shaw had warned Stella: but he found himself confronted instead with two "stars." Desperate, he issued commands and ultimatums, causing Tree finally to raise an eyebrow and remark that plays had actually been produced at His Majesty's once or twice without Shaw. "I will not go so far as to say that all people who write letters of more than

eight pages are mad," mused Tree after one particularly long and vehement directive from the distraught Shaw, "but it is a curious fact that all
madmen write letters of more than eight pages." Between the vague Tree
and Stella the termagant Shaw felt himself martyred.

Stella had been afraid he would discover the charwoman in her. Too
late: he had long ago discovered the guttersnipe. As she lectured him
vigorously on the text that nothing would ever make a gentleman out of
him, Shaw had the satisfaction of watching her play a role that parodied
her basic lack of refinement. For a real lady Shaw created the mother of
Henry Higgins. But this very lack of refinement, Shaw now saw,
prevented Stella from being the Eliza of his play. She attempted the low
accent, the rags, the uncouthness, certainly; but hated to let the social
veneer slip even in pretense, and could not refrain from projecting the
old Campbell fascination into the part. "To let you into an important
professional secret," Shaw would write Cornwallis-West, "Stella is not an
actress at all: she is an enchantress pure and simple. Her magical success
in this capacity involves her being, for Pygmalionic purposes, in the literal sense a complete idiot."[15] All Stella wanted him to do was arrange
"the enchantress's cave" so that she could captivate; Shaw wanted his
Cinderella story to say something realistic about class society.

And even the enchantress, he observed, failed from time to time.
"Dreadfully middleaged moments," he jotted in his rehearsal notes at the
place where Higgins chucks Eliza under the chin and says "Youre not
bad looking." He did not always keep his cruelties to himself. "Good
God," he cried at one point during rehearsal: "you are forty years too
old for Eliza; sit still and it is not so noticeable." He sketched her in his
notebook in hat and feather boa looking all her forty-nine years. Stella
herself veered between adoring the giant in Shaw that put up with her
tantrums, admiring the genius of the playwright, despising the displaced
lover, and loathing the egotism that seemed to her to say that Shaw the
creator was everything, the actors nothing. When not quarreling, she
flirted with him outrageously, grabbing his rehearsal notebook from him
when he came onstage and scribbling "Darling" and "beloved" and "*dear*
DEAR Joey" in the margins.[16] At other times his endless flow of commands, jests, exhortations, and beratings fatigued her to death. "I hope
you will make heaps of money Joey and keep your gay belief that you
and your play alone did it and that without you there would have been
but failure and fools," she wrote coldly as opening night drew near. In
the future, she informed him, he could send his instructions through the
stage manager.

Then on Monday, five days before the 11 April opening, Stella disappeared without a word. It was a childish act, meant to punish and spite;
but it also coincided with a decree granted that Monday morning to

Cornwallis-West and his wife, the former Lady Randolph Churchill. The *Times* notice of 10 April revealed that Stella and George had taken immediate advantage of his freedom:

> The marriage took place at a register office in Kensington on Monday afternoon of Mrs. Patrick Campbell and Mr. George Frederick Myddelton Cornwallis-West. The secret was very closely kept, and the only witness of the ceremony was Mr. Bourchier Hawksley, Mrs. Patrick Campbell's solicitor. The bride, who drove to the office from her residence in Kensington Square, wore black silk, with a black hat. The bride and bridegroom afterwards left for the country by motor-car. Mrs. West is due to appear at His Majesty's Theatre on Saturday, when Sir Herbert Tree is producing Mr. Bernard Shaw's *Pygmalion*.

Stella was due to appear, and she did—in time for six o'clock dress rehearsal on Thursday. Shaw's reception of the prodigal is unrecorded; Tree was incoherent with rage. Over lunch at the Royal Automobile Club, Shaw summed up the amateurism that had afflicted this collaboration of three veterans whose combined ages equaled 166. "Have you noticed that we three people," demanded Shaw, "all of us with established reputations and even eminent ones, and all of us no longer young, have nevertheless been treating one another all through this business as beginners?" They had not; they did now. This recognition did not prevent Shaw from sending round to Tree a last-minute letter meant to "pull him together if it did not kill him"; and to Stella on the day of opening his FINAL ORDERS. "Nepean," he informed her, had two syllables, not three. Her smile on the words "More friendly like" had developed to excess. She must not retreat on "I could kick myself." And at the end when Higgins says "Oh, by the way, Eliza," she must control her fatal propensity to run like Georgina to anyone who called her and forget everything in an affectionate tête-à-tête. "But a good deal will depend on whether you are inspired at the last moment," Shaw conceded. "You are not, like me, a great general. You leave everything to chance, whereas Napoleon and Caesar left nothing to chance except the last inch that is in the hands of destiny. . . . You believe in courage: I say 'God save me from having to fall back on that desperate resource,' though if it must come to that it must. I dont like fighting: I like conquering. You think you like fighting; and now you will have to succeed sword in hand. You have left yourself poorly provided with ideas and expedients; and you must make up for them by dash and brilliancy and resolution. And so, *Avanti!*"[17] Like Tree, Stella might have reminded Shaw that she had actually made rather a mark as an actress without him. Instead, she sent a humble and rather guilty little note: "Dear Joey: All success to you to-night. Its nice to think of your friendship and your genius—I'll obey orders faithfully, I am so thankful you carried through your giant's work to the finish—Stella."

Shaw reported the first night in a letter next day to Charlotte in Boston.[18] The house was packed, but because his old protest against immoderate laughter wrecking his plays had been read aloud from the stage, the audience had tried to restrain itself. At the ends of the first and second acts the applause was long and sincere. In the third act Mrs. Campbell played magnificently, almost exciting the audience to frenzy; but when she said her "Not bloody likely," the roar—after a moment's shocked silence—almost destroyed the play. He had sat aghast as the laughter rocked the theatre; he seriously wondered whether the audience would recover itself enough to let the play go on. It did, after an unparalleled minute and a quarter; and he writhed in torment through the last two acts. Tree's acting descended further and further into absurdity. Intoxicated with the hysterical success of the third act, he forgot all of Shaw's instructions; indeed, he perversely wallowed in doing just the opposite. This outrage, however, had been balanced by Mrs. Campbell, who did almost everything according to orders. But the ending had been sheer travesty. After especially commanding Higgins to engage himself affectionately at the end with his mother, and to toss Eliza the commission to run his errands in the most offhand way, what had he seen to his horror as he fled from the theatre to avoid the final curtain and cries of "Author!" but Higgins abandoning his mother to cuddle with Eliza in the most appalling way.

Rejecting interviews, congratulations, photographs, supper invitations, and the privilege of kissing his leading lady backstage, Shaw went straight home to Adelphi Terrace, where he read Shakespeare for an hour to soothe his nerves.

Brilliant as Shaw's *Pygmalion* indisputably was, not a few of the audience felt that it was Mrs. Campbell's sorcery that had carried the play to its incredible first-night triumph. Of course, she was not Shaw's Eliza: he had given up on Stella's ever understanding Eliza as a social problem, as a human soul with an enormous capacity for feeling that poverty and caste had all but destroyed. Yet no one should have known better than Shaw, who had watched and critiqued her performances for years, that Mrs. Patrick Campbell could not be the Eliza he had in mind. Yet he had wanted her all the same. Perhaps it was his tribute to the inspiration, dash, and courage that he, the perfectionist and reasoner, both deprecated and admired. She was his way of ensuring success and disdaining it.

To atone for deserting on opening night, Shaw invited the new bride and bridegroom down to Ayot St. Lawrence the next day and gave them lunch and tea. Really, he wrote Charlotte, she must drop her hostility to

Stella and consent to receive the Cornwallis-Wests in the country. She would adore (if nothing else) George's black retriever Beppo; and besides Stella and George were both very civil and very happy together, and looked upon him now as some benevolent and eccentric uncle. He ended his long letter to her with an incredible statement: he doubted whether *Pygmalion* could succeed.

Pygmalion succeeded beyond all expectation.[19] Charlotte finally saw it on 23 May; and four days later Lucy saw it for the third time. The first time she had viewed it from a box garlanded with roses from Mrs. Pat, who created a sensation when she brought Tree to the box to meet Lucy. But after all, Lucy (whom Shaw had always called extremely conventional) thought Algernon Grey's Freddy the best thing about the play. Despite pleas from Stella to come and see her Eliza again, Shaw returned to His Majesty's only to watch the one hundredth performance on 15 July. He had had enough: of Stella's temper, of Tree's abominable tom-fooleries, of Eliza's "bloody" completely sweeping away intelligent criticism of his play. Tree, who had enormous respect for Shaw and his play, felt deeply hurt that the author failed to take an interest in the progress of his Higgins and, having made £13,000 out of the run, closed His Majesty's at the end of July after 118 performances and went to Marienbad for a holiday. Stella was furious. But she had also discovered what Shaw kept a dark secret: that the part of Higgins overshadowed that of Eliza. "Your play *goes* each night most wonderfully," she wrote him 20 April. "But Tree's performance is a most original and entertaining affair and most popular with his friends and admirers. Mine is a mere masquerade." She might have made the same complaint about Cleopatra or, in 1929, about Orinthia: certainly Caesar, Higgins, and King Magnus dominate their plays.

Whether or not Tree closed down His Majesty's proved to be irrelevant. Summer had inevitably thinned the houses as the fashionable streamed out of London; and on the fourth of August England declared war against Germany.

1914-1929

ELLEN TERRY WAS AMONG the few who appreciated Shaw's courageous stand against the war. "*Very* strange people are all over the world," she wrote him from New York in December 1914 after his *Common Sense About the War* had raised a cry. ". . . I don't know *them.* I know you!"[1] Shaw's *Common Sense* created many enemies and turned not a few friends sour. Members of the Dramatists' Club intimated that Shaw would not be welcome if he set foot across the threshold, and Arthur Henry Jones, a longtime friend and a playwright Shaw admired, proved a violent enemy: England was his mother, said Jones, and Shaw had kicked his mother on her deathbed.[2] His status as an Irishman and a "privileged lunatic" still protecting him, Shaw was nevertheless regarded in many quarters as a dangerous propagandist and a traitor. He himself felt devastated as the killing mounted and there seemed no end in sight. Particularly appalling was the sight of women, from whom a civilized attitude might have been expected, accosting men not in uniform in the streets and handing them a white feather, the sign of cowardice. Was he the only one who recognized the futility of this slaughter? "The real monstrosity about the war," he wrote Stella, "is that apart from its silly cruelty and destructiveness, it has no true importance and wont settle anything."

As London filled with troops on the move, serious theatre virtually ended for the duration. Leaving George at Kensington Square, Stella sailed for New York 3 October on the *Lusitania*, Shaw having waved her and Wu Pu the Pekinese off at the boat train. "As usual," she noted, "I had to make money." She opened in *Pygmalion* on 12 October 1914 at the Park Theatre in New York, where a letter from Shaw soon followed to enlighten the manager. "You will find that Mrs. Pat Campbell's changes of dress will take longer than the change of scenery," he advised. ". . . If you cannot give her a room on the stage level she will agitate for a tent (she had one at His Majesty's here); and when SHE starts agitating dont argue but surrender at once, even if it involves rebuilding the theatre; you will find it cheaper in the long run." Mr. Tyler would also find that Mrs. Campbell would want to cut the play, "partly because its length hurries her dressing and interferes with the delightful levees she holds in her dressing-room, and partly because she thinks that Mrs. Pearce and Doolittle are insufferable bores and should be cut down to two or three lines apiece." It was no use arguing with her, Shaw advised: "she is clever enough to talk your hair grey." He must simply deplore Shaw's pigheaded insistence on having his play performed without a word omitted, and remain adamant, for Mrs. Pat had "no more judgment than a baby," and would spoil the play if he let her.[3] Delaying the fourth-act curtain on opening night with just such a delightful levee, Stella dispatched a cablegram to Shaw. "From all appearances your play a great success. You are," she added with a straight face, "a made man." And indeed Shaw's gross professional income, March 1914–15, totaled £16,595.

After a successful run, Stella then set out with Eliza and *Tanqueray* across the United States. Shaw did not go across well in Pittsburgh, she thought: the audience felt they were being poked fun at and didn't like it; yet in Chicago, she told him, he was very much loved. Staggering under eight, nine, occasionally eleven performances a week, sick with worry about her son Beo at the front, lonely for George, often ailing, Stella migrated westward in the often sweltering summer of 1915, finding half-empty houses in the small one-night towns, arriving in San Francisco $7,750 out of pocket. A lieutenant colonel commander, Cornwallis-West nevertheless managed to join his wife in America. Trying to find common ground, Stella taught him Orreyed in *Tanqueray* and Doolittle in *Pygmalion*, and thought he played splendidly. But there were money worries, and health worries, and war worries, and behind these the often uncomfortable knowledge that she was the star and the wage earner, as well as the knowledge that at fifty she was too old— thirty years too old for Eliza (although she'd lost weight), and too old for her dilettante husband. She was tired, and had grown plain, she told Shaw, and her hair was quite gray. Ellen Terry might have had much to say to Stella about autumnal marriages to attractive but unstable younger men.

And then toward the end of 1915, Cornwallis-West was forced to return to England to face the igominy of bankruptcy. So terrible for an Englishman, thought Stella, because he had to leave all his clubs. Struggling with her own financial difficulties, Stella now tried to rescue George, booking fourteen weeks of one-night stands in an attempt to rake in the needed £3,000. With any luck, she wrote her California friend, Harriet Carolan, in March 1916, she might have done it, but the people found Shaw "highbrow" (and traitorous about the war) and didn't enjoy themselves at all. And now—it seemed like a wildly mad dream—if there were anyone else in the world with money who cared a straw for her, she would not ask—but since there was not: could Harriet lend her £2,500? George was suffering, and she could not bear to think of her "darling happy George—*crushed*."⁴

Other actors too had fled the insanity of wartime London. Lillah McCarthy and Granville-Barker crossed paths with Stella Campbell in the United States, playing the Greek drama of Gilbert Murray in huge stadiums at New York and Boston, and in New York at Wallack's Theatre getting the audience to laugh a little at *Androcles and the Lion* (no house under £200, Barker reported in February 1915) and watching them get up and walk out of *The Doctor's Dilemma*. In New York Lillah went to hear Ellen Terry give one of her dramatic talks on Shakespeare's women, and saw an old and beautiful woman of sixty-eight. Only recently recovered from an eye operation, her heart "a kicking Donkey," forced to peer at the large type from which she read, Ellen still held her huge audiences spellbound. She had become a legend: a last reminder of the great Lyceum days of Irving and Terry.

From New York, which made him feel like "a chewed string," Barker sent irritable letters to Shaw, who wanted to keep the little Kingsway going with *Fanny's First Play*, and had proposed Lena Ashwell. Losing money steadily, ready to renounce the theatre altogether, Barker viewed this latest proposal as sheer madness. Really, Shaw was getting "fogyish." His notion of throwing in a leading lady, no matter what her age, was ridiculous. Lillah had been too old for Margaret Knox; Lena must be nearly fifteen years older than Lillah. Shaw had "knocked the stuffing" out of *Pygmalion* just that way—having made that blunder, perhaps he felt that *Fanny* didn't matter? Besides, to be sordid, they both knew Lena wouldn't draw a penny. He was as anxious as Shaw to keep people in work if humanly possible, but it was no good going on in this weak way: it was better to shut up altogether.⁵ But Shaw had always been tolerant of maturity, writing Stella reassuringly at one point, ". . . give me a ruined complexion and a lost figure and sixteen chins and a farmyard of crows' feet and an obvious wig. Then you shall see me come out strong."

Undeterred now, Shaw promoted *Fanny's First Play* that February with Lena Ashwell as Margaret Knox. But the six-week revival made only forty-odd pounds a performance—not, as Barker had prophesied, because of its leading lady's age but because of its author's views on the war; and Lena found a better role in her work in the Women's Emergency Corps, the National Food Fund, the Women's Legion, the Women's Volunteer Reserve, and, finally, in promoting entertainment for servicemen in a series of "Concerts at the Front." For this latter effort she was eventually awarded the Order of the British Empire at Buckingham Palace, a ceremony chiefly memorable for the shrieks of the women being honored when the medal-pinners, used to the heavy coats of men, jabbed the pins through the finer material into the flesh.

New York was not wholly unpleasant for Barker, however; for there he met Helen Huntington, a wealthy married woman twelve years his senior, and fell deeply in love as he had never been able to be with Lillah.[6] He returned with Lillah to London in July 1915, but with every intention of returning to New York. After he did, late in the year, he wrote to Lillah on 3 January 1916 asking her to divorce him and sending the letter through Shaw. Lillah ran to Shaw at Adelphi Terrace. "Oh, greatest of all comforters," she cried later in a passage in her memoirs which Shaw prudently cut, "I owe you everlasting thanks." "I went," she explained, "all frozen on a cold January night. I found myself at the flat, climbed painfully the stairs, up which as a girl I had been borne on the wings of youth and hope. Shaw greeted me very tenderly and made me sit by the fire. I was shivering. Shaw sat very still. The fire brought no warmth. My very soul was frozen." Together they went outside to pace up and down the Terrace. "Then how it came about I do not know," said Lillah. "The weight upon me grew a little lighter and released the tears which would never come before. I cried, long and pitifully, and he let me cry. But presently I heard a voice in which all the gentleness and tenderness of the world was speaking. It said: 'Look up, dear, look up to the heavens. There is more in life than this. There is much more.' At that moment, though I did not know it then," concluded Lillah, "hope was born again in me."[7] Fuss about the Barkers, Charlotte noted in her annuary. As friend to both parties, Shaw found himself in the heart of the storm. Convinced that Harley was temporarily insane and still loved her, the devastated Lillah refused to talk divorce; Barker, on the other hand, had engaged Shaw to persuade her. He would spend thousands of words, counseling, arguing, and often infuriating all parties, even Lillah, who resented what she felt to be his light, almost bantering attitude. She did not need a rival genius, he assured her, but someone she could carry in her pocket: she looked five years younger without Harley, who was un-doubtedly unfit for married life at all. It was a difficult position for Shaw; and one of the parties, Helen Huntington, conceived for him a permanent hatred.

Losing Barker meant more to Lillah than losing a husband: it meant losing the "family theatre" after ten splendidly productive years. She was forty now. What would happen to her career? Devoted to Shaw, she had felt suddenly dissatisfied with his parts when, early in 1914, playing

Shakespeare's Helena in a golden wig, she found herself showered with good chocolates, bad verses, flowers, and bracelets—beloved again, as she never was when she played Shaw's heroines. Nor were Shavian parts important enough: after three years, she had decided that Lavinia was mere supering, and had refused to go on tour with it in the United States after the New York run. Nevertheless, she turned to Shaw again: could he help her? But apart from arranging a tense and unsuccessful meeting between Barker and Lillah at his flat in early February 1916, Shaw could not. Advising her to get a good grip on the American star circuit, where there was money to be made, he dismissed her complaint that as an actress she had "never had a chance." Other actresses would give half their toes to have created Ann Whitefield, Jennifer, Margaret, and Lavinia, to say nothing of playing Jocasta, Iphigenia, Hermione, and Viola. She needed a big part now, however, and he did not have one. He seemed to be good for nothing these days but political and religious stuff and, of an evening, sitting down to play highly contrapuntal masses to which he sang the bass. Was he going to die, he wondered. Shakespeare had in 1616, Sheridan in 1816. . . . He recommended a convent.

Shaw was not going to die; but the year ended the life of an actress who had relied on his help time after time, and very often gotten it. Stupefied against the bitterness of a lost career with morphia and cocaine, Janet Achurch had only been jarred into reality two years before by the sudden death of Nora. The tragedy was typical Charrington: rushing to get to their daughter by automobile, they were prevented by a breakdown; and Nora died alone. The shock settled Janet, though for two more years she struggled on. Constance Benson met her briefly in 1916, and was astounded at how terribly the once lovely, blue-eyed actress had aged. Janet died on 11 September 1916 at fifty-two. Charrington's account to Shaw written from the Isle of Wight immediately after her death confirmed the wretchedness of their curiously loyal existence:

We were not to be let off anything that Fate could inflict. . . . At last we had to call in a Ventnor Doctor, an ass in whom she detected a moral judgement against the drugs and consequently loathed him.

She had been operated upon under chloroform, which she enjoyed, at least 6 times. Luckily there was a charmingly kind old feller who insisted on giving it when she wanted her arm, which had swelled terribly, cut. There were I may mention 51 needles in the arms though years ago 15 had been removed. . . .

The ass, a most butcherly person, made seven incisions. Pulse quite steady under the chloroform but from that time the restlessness & torture was out of the question & I gave stronger and stronger doses of morphia to the end. She died in my arms and looked more peaceful than she had

Mrs. Patrick Campbell.

*Caricatures of Mrs. Patrick Campbell
as Eliza Doolittle in* PYGMALION *at His
Majesty's Theatre, 1914.*

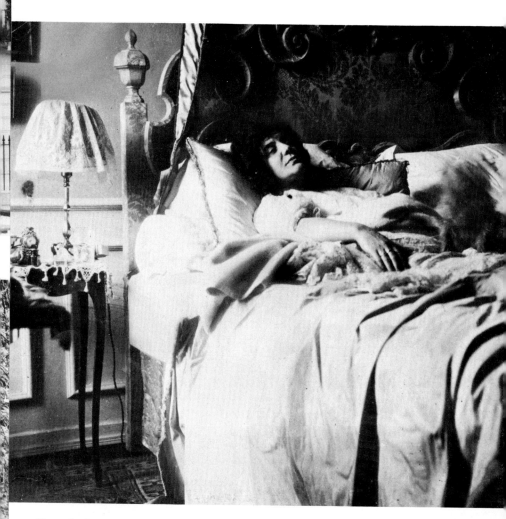

Above, Stella Campbell photographed by Shaw at her Kensington Square house during her illness in the late autumn of 1912.

*Charlotte Shaw's sitting
room, Shaw's Corner.*

*The dining room, Shaw's Corner,
with photographs of Gandhi,
Trotsky, Lenin, Stalin, Harley
Granville-Barker, Shaw's Dublin
birthplace at No. 3 (afterward
33) Synge Street, and Ibsen.*

Hatstand and stick rack, Shaw's Corner.

Bernard Shaw.

done for years. That butcher made me think of the trenches in the end. . . .

Funeral was Wednesday [13 September] at 3. Her grandmother had a catalepsy & was put into her coffin so I made sure she was dead.

The Doctor gave primary cause of death a[s] morphia & cocaine habit Chronic cellulitis & secondary: heart failure.

This of course only for *you*.[8]

A poem on death, Shaw once admitted, could move him more than death itself. Now Shaw chose to view the death of the woman whom he had once really loved not as a defeat but as a victory. Clever Janet: once more she was the Janet of 1889—young, promising, immortal, arrested in that first perfection of his adoration; it was he and Charrington who now had to drag out their weary days. She had always been too big for the fashionable little London stage of the eighties and nineties: she needed a Wagnerian frame, an Ibsen setting. *Candida* had come too late, if indeed it had ever been a suitable vehicle for her talents. So he had always said, and said now, and apparently believed. He sent money to cover the funeral expenses, and forbore reminding Charrington how they had wasted each other's lives; how the debts and the thriftlessness and the drugs had lost them the grip on Ibsen they had achieved in 1889. "Vice is waste of life," Shaw had written in his *Maxims for Revolutionists*. Certainly he had witnessed that vice in Janet. The *Times* notice of 22 September said everything, after all, it was possible to say: "Died: Mrs. Charles Charrington, better known as Miss Janet Achurch, whose wonderful performance as Nora Helmer in the first English production of Ibsen's *A Doll's House* in 1889 was the talk of London for many a day." And yet perhaps not all; for whenever Shaw mentioned Janet's name to serious and aspiring young actresses, he found that a kind of mystique had grown up around her name and her Nora.

Meanwhile, as Lady Principal of Ramanthan College for Girls in Ceylon, Florence Farr still sought a substitute for the values she had lost when, as a New Woman, she had rejected family, marriage, motherhood, and traditional religion. Because she had not replaced the Victorian ethic with the Shavian ethic, Shaw had given her up as spiritually lost. "You have brains and imagination—the means of deceiving yourself," he had told her, "without faith, honor, heart, holiness—the means of saving yourself." Yet Florence persisted in the search for peace, trying to extract from the strange mixture of Buddhist, Hindu, and Christian religions, from the clash of medieval Ceylonese customs with British Colonial rule, from the whining of ragas and the chanting of Tamil and the harping of the vina, from the heat and the languor and the slow rituals, some further clue to the mystery of life. For one accused of lack of grip, Florence proved a surprisingly exemplary disciplinarian and organizer, curbing the noisy and slovenly students, assuming charge of stores, gardens, money, servants, and teachers, and looking quite colonial in her own rickshaw drawn by a coolie. Bespectacled, exotically robed, and tolerant of the strangeness about her, Florence sought her own kind of holiness through Vedantism, and thought to end her days tranquilly in Ceylon.

Just when she had seemed to achieve a kind of permanence, however, she took a vacation at a British hotel in Kandy. There the charms of Western civilization reasserted themselves: British food instead of the interminable curries, freedom of movement, cultural pleasures. After all, she discovered, few roles were as restricting as that of the colonial. A certain ruling-class mentality was required; and she, an admitted eccentric, now felt that playing the typical white European amid Asians unbearably repressed her. She began to think of San Francisco, and returned to her duties at Ramanthan College with little enthusiasm. And she missed her old friend Bernard Shaw a great deal.

Although Shaw was watching her royalty rights for her and in 1913 had bequeathed her £104 per annum in his will (his total profits from *Arms and the Man?*⁹), he had not written since the start of the war. In April 1916, Florence finally applied to him. She was now the Honorable Treasurer, she reported. Her resignation from the duties of Lady Principal had been accompanied by a feast, garlands, songs of praise, testimonies, worship and music in the temple, and a parting gift of a gold silk lace *chelai* and a purse of money. Although never fond of her own sex, she had been loved by the girls and called "Mother" because she respected their religion. Shaw had warned her of moonshees, but through Yoga she had found a state of comparative tranquillity, and had pulled down many of the barriers between herself and liberation. Yet she missed his comradeship, his criticisms, his kindnesses. "You might write me now," she concluded, "—you must have some time to spare, unless you too are making guns or socks!!"

Exactly seven months later, she wrote him again:

At the present moment I am in a private room at the General Hospital at Colombo with my left breast swathed in iodine & cotton wool awaiting an operation tomorrow. I am not writing to tell my people about it until I am well again—but I thought you might be confided in . . . . the greatest specialist here says there is no doubt it is cancer. The peculiar thing is that I have been feeling remarkably well for the last 6 months—never better . . . .

The most tragic moment I think was a fortnight ago when I felt the twinge & became aware of a sort of "dead place"—I said to myself "cancer" & felt the force of doom, but I didnt let anyone see & went and lunched & laughed & talked with the English Principal & teachers. Then when one after the other has confirmed the doom I feel less & less doom-

ful & I now feel full of interest in the experiences. I should like to get a
letter from you someday. . . . Goodbye remember me to your people.

FF Emery.[10]

Registered under the name of her sister-in-law Winifred Emery,
Florence underwent a mastectomy the next day. Back at Ramanthan College, she felt she was making a speedy recovery; but in March 1917, thin-
ner, coughing, and short of breath, she was sent back to Colombo, where
a doctor diagnosed lung cancer too far gone for surgery. Florence
moved into a private room and waited for death, apparently without
great anxiety or regret. She had come to an impasse in her life; always
restless, she had postponed deciding whether to leave Ceylon or stay.
The decision was now made. Her attendant physician was puzzled by
"Mrs. Winifred Emery's" resemblance to Florence Farr, an actress whom
(incredibly) he remembered from her performance as the Nurse in the
Hippolytus of Euripides at the Court in 1906. She finally admitted her
identity, but told him to keep it secret, a request the doctor immediately
interpreted as shame for a wanton and Bohemian life. Cheerful and as
usual giving no trouble, she died on 29 April 1917 and was cremated in
Hindu style the next day. Henrietta Paget read of Florence's death one
day in the Ceylon newspapers. Knowing well Florence's love of a joke,
she thought her sister had sent the notice as a classic example of journalistic inaccuracy. The truth was finally established, however; and on 27
June Henrietta notified Shaw that the woman who had staged his first
success with money from another woman was dead. "Forgive me for
troubling you about this," wrote Henrietta, "but you worked for a long
time together & she was fond of you."[11]

Ezra Pound in his "Portrait d'Une Femme" best expressed the
curiously unfocused quality of Florence, who, in her sampling of
theosophy, occultism, embroidery, psaltery, acting, staging, elocution,
painting, poetry, journalism, novel writing, choral work, musicology,
lecturing, reviewing, and finally administration, had never quite achieved
—unlike far narrower people—a mind of her own:

> Your mind and you are our Sargasso Sea,
> London has swept about you this score years
> And bright ships left you this or that in fee:
> Ideas, old gossip, oddments of all things,
> Strange spars of knowledge and dimmed wares of price.
> Great minds have sought you—lacking someone else.
> You have been second always. Tragical?
> No. You preferred it to the usual thing:
> One dull man, dulling and uxorious,
> One average mind—with one thought less, each year.

> Oh, you are patient, I have seen you sit
> Hours, where something might have floated up.
> And now you pay one. Yes, you richly pay. . . . and yet
> For all this sea-hoard of deciduous things,
> Strange woods half-sodden, and new brighter stuff:
> In the slow float of differing light and deep,
> No! There is nothing! In the whole and all,
> Nothing that's quite your own.
>> Yet this is you.

In the years after her return from America, Stella's letters to Shaw dwelt on two topics: her right to play *Pygmalion* and the increasing woes of age, lack of parts and money. But although Shaw gave her the rights to play *Pygmalion* in six big cities on tour, he was disenchanted—a state of mind Stella only encouraged. In June 1917 he read *Heartbreak House* to her and George, for example; but although Stella granted that it was a fine play, she complained that, after begetting his dramatis personae "like a God," he quickly lost respect for their "bones" so that they became mouthpieces without flesh and blood. This was an error, because Hesione Hushabye, the dark siren with the symbolically false hair, was clearly Mrs. Campbell, and could be played beautifully (still) by Mrs. Campbell. But Shaw was reluctant to let this play, born out of the anger and despair of wartime, be put on the stage. When a London production was finally projected in 1921 after 125 successful performances in New York, Shaw would not have the terrible Mrs. Campbell on any terms, "though nobody," he told her, "could speak the lines as you could or give the quality of the woman as you could if you would." He was through with stars; particularly was he through with Mrs. Campbell. And this was too bad for Mrs. Pat, for she *was* Hesione Hushabye, as well as Mrs. George in *Getting Married*, "which contains the most wonderful of all my serio-tragic woman's parts," said Shaw, describing Stella, "suitable to a female of advanced years with the remains of irresistible beauty"—and could have played Shaw the rest of her career had she been willing to accept the diffuse light of Shavian drama instead of the spotlight. She could not accept it: and now faced the plunge from star to has-been.

Shaw was the more adamant about Stella because he had suffered through the torments of a revival of *Pygmalion* in February 1920. Unlike Herbert Tree, blissfully forgetful of the agonies of the 1914 *Pygmalion* and talking about a revival when Shaw walked home with him from a meeting a few days before the actor's death in July 1917, Shaw remembered. Yet he allowed Viola Tree, Sir Herbert's daughter, to stage the play at the Aldwych with himself as manager. "Now we shall quarrel for the next month," he groaned in January. "Oh Stella, Stella, Stella, why did God afflict us with one another?" "You make a fine mistake if you think I am out for quarrelling!" retorted Stella; and proceeded to turn the rehearsals into chaos.

Addressing her gingerly as "Belovedest," Shaw tried to keep her away from the theatre as long as possible under the pretext that C. Aubrey Smith (Higgins) and the whole cast were still floundering for their lines. He propitiated her with assurances that Viola Tree would be the death of him with her tricks and interference. He reassured her about Marion Terry, engaged for Mrs. Higgins, but refusing to look matronly and—as he feared—showing up Stella's age dreadfully. Marion was all Viola's fault: "Viola is a darling unprofessionally; but as a manageress she is a spoilt child playing with dolls . . . ." He told her that she looked younger than in 1914; he avowed that her voice was better than ever. To Viola, he poured out his contempt for Stella's behavior: she was an anarchist, a shameless clown, a tramp, a fool, a malicious devil, an incompetent, and an idiot. The fourth of February was a kind of highpoint (the show was due to open in six days): Stella surpassed herself, pouring scathing insults upon Shaw and, in a grand exit, dismissing him forever from her affections. On her part, Stella believed that Shaw betrayed her behind her back to Viola by painting her character as black as possible. "Of course I look 60," she cried, unappeased and miserable; "—of course I have a hideous 'gin and misery' voice, and of course I cant give any kind of a performance to compare with a pretty young girl's." It did not seem to occur to her that tractability might be a substitute for youth.

Quite apart from the difficult rehearsals, Shaw disliked what Stella did to his play: insisting on gorgeous dresses that exhibited Mrs. Campbell but killed Eliza; throwing away the third act by showing she knew she was going to say "bloody" and expected laughs; constantly clowning and throwing in pothouse gags about corset stays that drew laughter and wrecked the tempo; reducing the whole play to a vulgar farce by cuddling with Higgins at the end. On 10 May *Pygmalion* moved to the Duke of York's, where Shaw saw it on the fourteenth. In an infinitely insulting letter headed, of course, "Belovedest," Shaw tore her acting to pieces. Some things had improved, certainly: with the elimination of the front spotlight, her face no longer looked like "a kitchen clock covered with make-up" nor was her figure flattened out to twice its normal width. On the other hand, she had finally succeeded in turning the play into "a really good Victorian drawing-room drama, pleasant and sweet" and in what she fondly believed good taste. Charming! and wasn't Higgins the perfect gentleman and didn't she look pretty as a picture postcard and wasn't their courtship just too adorable for words. Only he had just almost fallen asleep over it all. Worse—the receipts, good at the

Aldwych, were appalling, dropping from £1,100 to £800. A procession of sandwich men might help, he concluded wearily—only they couldn't afford one.[12]

Thus they sparred in a love-hate relationship that often disintegrated into mere nastiness. Stella outdid the mild-mannered Shaw with behavior that would have shamed a savage; he easily outdid her verbally, calling her (among other endearments) "a Monster of illiteracy" and a fool, and sending her a diagram of her brain, all black save for one thread of light. She cried out against his brutality; he against being treated by an actress "as no dog was ever treated by the most brutal trainer." Actually it was a difficult period for Stella, for George Cornwallis-West had left her sometime in 1919 when, in her own words, she could no longer reach across "a fundamental gulf of gracelessness" in his heart. She did not tell Shaw about the separation; she did however write him about the death of her charming, irresponsible, beloved son Beo, killed in action in France on 30 December 1917. This personal tragedy reminded Shaw that Stella was a human being with a heart that could be broken. And then Lucy became very ill. Having constantly promised to call and then as constantly begged off, Stella finally visited her on 23 February 1920, and wrote to tell Shaw that she would take him there in her hired car if he would like. "Don't be angry with me any more," she begged, for *Pygmalion* was currently inspiring letters she feared to open. "Life has taken some skins off me and I can't battle with your jibes and jests—though I admit the memory of your golden heart washes all away like waves of the sea—and I do love you."

Most generous with his sister financially, Shaw did not go to Lucy until the twenty-seventh, having first kissed Lillah, who, after a long and traumatic divorce action that ended April 1917, became Mrs. Frederick (later Lady) Keeble that morning, and then his secretary Ann M. Elder at her wedding in the afternoon. After that ceremony he went to Lucy in the pretty little house he had taken for her in Camberwell, and found her either unconscious (according to her companion's testimony) or able to whisper "I am dying" (according to his). "What a day—yesterday!" he reported. "Bride's kisses at 11 (Lillah); bride's kisses at Eliza's church at 3 (my secretary); and at 5 Lucy died in my arms. . . . The disease was no longer active. She died of starvation. The Zeppelins destroyed her appetite. Oh Stella, Stella, Stella!" At a ceremony crowded to Shaw's astonishment with friends of Lucy, she burned "with a steady white light like that of a wax candle." Her will left "Carlotta" a Tara brooch and an ancient silver comb that had belonged to her and Shaw's maternal great-grandmother—though Charlotte's heart had remained unsoftened toward her, said Lucy, even by New Thought. Shaw's astonishment at Lucy's having friends revealed how very little he knew his sister, or for that matter his mother, or for that matter his own wife, who of all the women he had known, he would eventually admit, he knew least.

Toward Mrs. Campbell, Charlotte's heart also remained unsoftened, despite a dream Stella had that Joey's wife had come up to her smiling warmly and saying, "I thought you were a bird of Paradise and you are only a silly goose." Charlotte was the more hardened by an episode that began in 1921: Stella's decision to write her memoirs. The project began innocently enough, Shaw giving her written permission to print extracts from their correspondence, and offering to correct her spelling and punctuation, spot libels, and prune such inevitable little snobberies as "'Darling: come to tea at Marlborough tomorrow: Alexandra: P.S. Edward sends his love.'" Stella refused, too ashamed to submit her "trash" to Shaw's gimlet eye. Then, suddenly wary, Shaw requested to see the correspondence she intended to publish. "Here are the dear letters," Stella replied the day before Christmas. "If I inspired a little of the tenderness of their genius I am proud, not vain. . . . I do not fancy that Charlotte will misjudge me, or that she will see that permitting the letters to be published is other than a *panache* in her bonnet. . . . Don't please misjudge me, or allow others to." Clearly she intended (as she later claimed) that Charlotte might read the letters and cut any bits she did not like; clearly she overlooked the fact that Charlotte might like nothing about the business at all.

Shaw received the packet, read through his old effusions, turned cold:

> Take that terrible wadge of letters, and put it into the hands of any court of honor you can induce your fittest friends to form, or submit it to the judgement of any capable and experienced woman of the world and both will tell you without a moment's hesitation, and with considerable surprise at your having any doubt on the subject, that their public exposure is utterly impossible, except in the physical sense in which it is materially possible for you to undress yourself (or me) in the street. . . .
>
> You say you will behave like a perfect gentleman. Well, a gentleman does not kiss and tell; so that settles *that*.

If Stella wanted a pattern for memoirs, he told her, she might imitate Ellen Terry's. He had sent Ellen a whole string of wonderful love letters, but *The Story of My Life* in 1908 contained not a line that could create mischief in households; and yet Ellen must have bushels of love letters, "for she has kept house with five men, two of them famous, and one very notable, and has married them all when it was possible; and she has been adored by all the poets of her day." Let Stella imitate Ellen's supreme tact. Besides, his letters would play her right off her own stage: her memoirs would become the "Bernard Shaw memoirs"; she only the woman he wrote the letters to.[13] Meanwhile he did not show them to Charlotte. Not only were they filled with the most extravagant declarations, but they contained details about hours and appointments and meeting places that would have pained her deeply and discredited himself.

But Stella refused to take him seriously. She would not mind his publishing her letters; why should he mind her publishing his. If his letters sounded like something out of a breach of promise suit, as he insisted, then he must simply cut the offensive parts. She saw nothing wrong with the whole batch being put in chock-a-block: "That way I think shows you *did* care a little, but of course not enough to sacrifice one hair of your own dear head . . . ."

"Now God defend me from idiots!" Shaw fumed back. ". . . Send me your proofs when you get them. I will then tell you, brutally and dogmatically, what you may say and what you may not. The situation is new to you. You have been before the public for sixty years or so; but during that time you have never uttered a word to it that has not been put into your mouth by somebody else. You have therefore never learnt the rules or acquired the sense of responsibility of authorship. And, owing to abysmal deficiencies in your nature, you never will. So you must do what you are told."[14]

So the battle raged, Shaw protesting that only rotters and courtesans would publish such stuff and demanding the proofs for correction, Stella refusing to let her "twaddle" fall under the unfriendly eyes of Shaw and Charlotte. But finally, Shaw yielded. She might publish some of the letters, but not the portions he now deleted in his small, neat, legible hand. Gone were thus such rhapsodies as "my treasure, my darling, my beloved, adored ensainted friend of my very soul" and replaced with "my adored ensainted friend." "Goodnight, goodnight, goodnight, goodnight, my dearest dearest" yielded up its last three words. Missing from the "Dearest Liar" letter were all the hints that his love for her was not new, all the ecstasy of finding her his "most agitating heart's darling," and all such tactlessnesses as "I am in custody down here." The great New Year's Eve letter was among the missing. The connecting link "Whatever might betide, Charlotte (Mrs. Shaw) must not be kept waiting ten minutes" was one of the touches provided "to set Charlotte right," without which he would have seen the whole creation damned to hell before consenting to publish a line. On 16 January 1922, after two days' work and careful consideration, he sent Stella the edited letters.

> I burn so with blushes at your confounded impudence, that I don't feel the cold [Stella raged back].
> You have spoilt my book.
> You have spoilt the story.

You have hidden from the world the one thing that would have done it good: Lustless Lions at play—
May you freeze in that sea of ice in Dante's Inferno—I dont care.
"Stolen your fig-leaf" indeed! You wear no fig-leaf in your letters. . . .
It is really sad: you creep on the ground, instead of flying in the air—through taking away those delicious letters. . . .[15]

Unused to being crossed, Stella fought back meanly, threatening to publish exactly what she liked since she had his letter of permission, warning "Be *thankful* if I cut enough out, and leave enough in, so that you dare face the public again. Start saying your prayers." She loathed his "epileptic revulsion" from love's truths, despised his timidity. He called himself a Superman, a God? Laughable.

It is perhaps curious that Stella wanted to publish Shaw's letters so badly in the first place. She suppressed a serious love affair completely, referring to Sir Johnston Forbes-Robertson throughout her memoir as "Mr. Robertson" and mentioning him in business connections only. Shaw's letters, moreover, were those of a married man; and she had always been discreet about her private affairs. Nor had she particularly admired Shaw's plays. Unlike Ellen Terry, who read and delighted in Shaw, Stella left Shaw's wedding gift of his works untouched on her shelf, snubbed *Caesar and Cleopatra*, and had serious doubts about *Pygmalion* until its success caused her to reconsider her opinion of Shavian drama. She might have trotted out letters from her other admirers in place of Shaw's, since he violently objected. As Shaw exclaimed in dismay: "You *must* have some more love letters. You cannot appear as a famous beauty who had only one catch: an old idiot of 56. Will there be nobody to keep me in countenance?"

Unfortunately, there seemed not to be. A "well-known London manager" had written her many poems which his wife granted permission to publish; then mysteriously they had disappeared. Stella conscientiously published the remaining poem without a name; had there been others perhaps they too would have been displayed "chock-a-block." But, in fact, despite dozens of testimonies to her beauty, wit, charm, talent, courage, grace, sympathy, hard work, and popularity, Mrs. Campbell managed to emerge from her autobiography as a woman more feared by men than loved. "Everyone" loved Ellen Terry, but Shaw had been among the few who dared to venture into the enchantress's cave and enjoy it there. His letters were after all the most eloquent testimony to her charms: proof that she was an irresistible woman; and somehow, unlike Ellen Terry, Stella seemed to need that proof badly. As she had once told Shaw, "It is better to be loved than to love"; and Shaw's letters, displayed in her book with only the mildest sentiments of her own to accompany them, confirmed this pleasant state. Part of Shaw's reluctance to publish, after all, was the fact that he had not always been playacting. "I felt a great deal more than you did," he wrote in February, still trying to dissuade her; "and I still feel a great deal more about it than you. You are doing—if you only knew it—a dreadful thing; and someday you will say 'I had better have tied a millstone round my neck and cast myself into the sea: why did you not warn me?'"

But still Stella sulked. She was sorry to hear Charlotte was unhappy, but then if Charlotte had only been nice to her (she did not seem to consider it other than a rare treat), they could have chosen the letters together. And if her book was indeed "ignorant, illiterate, ungrammatical, and probably illegal," it was Shaw's fault for crushing her so brutally that she lost all courage to ask him for help. She considered all this talk about saving *her* from scandal the sheerest hypocrisy: she knew perfectly well that he only wanted to save himself. She hoped that when the book appeared he would behave like a gentleman. He was capable—how well she knew it—of behaving in a perfectly disgusting way. She had paid him back in her book for his meanness by not expressing any of her feeling for him; by taking away with one hand all the compliments she gave him with the other; and particularly by inserting after the cropped "wadge" of letters the damning "His wildest letters I do not give." But nothing could repay him for his cowardice in the face of public opinion.

Yet in the event, Stella half got her way. The New York *Herald* published the memoir 10 May 1922 with the letters uncut "despite their promise." How imprudent, really, for Stella to have returned the proofs with the excised material still legible: almost like tempting fate. . . . She was less than repentant, writing, "I feel *very* unhappy because I know how much you will mind—for myself, well. . . ." She jumped at Shaw's despairing "Nothing matters now" as an excuse to publish the rest. She felt, or pretended to feel, triumphant. She was right; he had been wrong: everyone was saying, "You have shown us the real Shaw—the human Shaw—the divine Shaw—" She had turned his Eliza into a living, breathing human being for him; she had immortalized him as a lover with a heart and a soul.

Deciding that Mrs. Campbell had "tilted the shafts of memory's cart and let the contents fall," Desmond MacCarthy found Shaw's letters one of the few treats in her "loose heap of testimonials, compliments, worries and sorrows"; but declined to believe in them as love letters. "They are full of dancing gaiety," said MacCarthy. "They show a most exquisite helpful regard for her. They are full of gratitude to her for having inspired such an excitement in him that, to his immense delight, he can fancy himself in love; the impulse to wild silliness is so strong. But they are not the letters of a man who *wants to be loved*, and therefore they are not love letters. Desire to be loved is itself almost a definition of being 'in love'; without that desire love is indistinguishable from sympathy." If the reader wanted a look at true love, he or she must rake over the heap and extract the letters of Mr. Patrick Campbell to his young wife. In fact, in MacCarthy's opinion, Mr. Patrick Campbell emerged from the autobiography as the only piece of gold in the rubble.[16] But MacCarthy, of course, had read the British version which appeared edited by Shaw's pencil; and even the American version told only half a tale. The Sandwich letters alone testified to Shaw's deep feeling—which is not to claim that had Stella suddenly cried "I love you" he would not have turned and fled.

While this battle between the "Lustless Lions" raged, two typically contradictory events were taking place in Shaw's career. In New York, the Theatre Guild performed Shaw's "metabiological pentateuch" *Back to Methuselah* in February and March of 1922, a play in which Shaw philosophically renounced youth, pleasure, art, love, lust, reproduction, and the body for the ultimate evolution of human existence into a vortex of pure thought.[17] At the same time in his private life Shaw was becoming involved with another enchantress in whose company he sought youth, pleasure, and romance.[18] And this last notable adventure was quintessential Shaw.

The woman was, first of all, married, so that Shaw could take his favorite place in the game of romance between husband and wife. Mary Arthur Tompkins and her husband Laurence were two Americans from Georgia interested in founding a Shavian theatre in the United States. The woman was, secondly, the aggressor. With their two-year-old son Peter, the Tompkinses had come to London in 1921 to find Shaw. Momentarily baffled by not finding his name in the telephone directory, they had coaxed the famous man's address from a clerk at Hatchard's bookstore and descended upon the Shaws at Adelphi Terrace, where the beautiful and imperious Molly soon cast her sculptor husband into the shade (Charlotte's favorite spot). Again, Molly Tompkins was an unconventional woman, a woman already bored with traditional male-female relationships or dissatisfied with marriage—joining in this rebellion such former Shavian interests as Annie Besant, May Morris, Edith Nesbit, Eleanor Marx, Ellen Terry, Florence Farr, Erica Cotterill, Elizabeth Robins, Bertha Newcombe, and Stella Campbell. Like them, she was seeking something "beyond" an ordinary sexual relationship with a man; like them, Shaw's willingness to hover eternally out of reach in that beyond would eventually frustrate and anger her. Then she had the usual qualities that Shaw deplored, yet inwardly admired. He had married what Stella scornfully called a suffragette—a woman with brains, common sense, and an overdeveloped conscience; yet was irresistibly attracted to beautiful, undisciplined, sensual, careless, impulsive, anarchistic, artistic, amateurish, or "illiterate" women whom he would finally rail at for just these qualities. Furthermore, Molly thought she wanted to be an actress so that she could interpret the Shavian drama in America in the theatre her artist husband would design—and Shaw's attraction to women who could make his Word incarnate was strong. And finally Molly's age made her at once desirable and improbable: in 1921 she was twenty-four and he sixty-five.

Shaw seemed to take this charming young adventuress whose acting experience consisted of a twelve-week walk-on in the Ziegfeld Follies as seriously as a young Duse or Sybil Thorndike. He sent her to the Royal Academy of Dramatic Art, an institution he supported financially and directorily. He dispatched her to Professor Daniel Jones, the phonetician on whom he had partially modeled Professor Higgins: Molly's "Amur-ricanisms" were hardly more acceptable than Eliza's "Aaaaaa—ow." He coached her at Adelphi Terrace in the part of Gloria Clandon for an R.A.D.A. performance of *You Never Can Tell.* For physical workouts he devised walks within fifty miles of London which she and Laurence obediently trotted through. He instructed her in dealing with managers. He critiqued her makeup. He changed her stage name from the "charac-terless" Mary Arthur to Molly Tompkins. He deplored her "Sarah of Red Gulch" manners and tried to soften them. And reluctantly at first, then more and more willingly, he began to lace his letters of advice with terms of affection.

It gradually became apparent, however, that Molly Tompkins was far too headstrong to submit to the kind of discipline needed before she could, in Shaw's words, "hit the boy at the back of the gallery in a three hundred pound house." She quarreled incessantly with Kenneth Barnes, the director of the R.A.D.A., over the rule that a neophyte should play a wide variety of roles, particularly comedy: she wanted to play only trag-edy, having evidently forgotten that her intention was to play Shaw. She quarreled incessantly with Claude Rains, director and instructor, who in-formed Barnes that he would rather resign than have her in his class. ("O unmollifiable Molly," Shaw groaned.) Then, discovering that the Ply-mouth Repertory Theatre needed a leading lady, and that Kenneth Barnes had the giving of the job to an R.A.D.A. senior, Molly threw sportsmanship to the winds by taking a train to Plymouth and snapping up the job herself. It was, after all, only the American way of getting things done. Fired after four months because as Lady Teazle her voice was nearly always on top register, she got the lead in a touring produc-tion of Wilde's *A Woman of No Importance;* left the tour, came back to London, met the gray and charming Sir Johnston Forbes-Robertson, who, recognizing another Campbellian siren, fell in love; met the other than charming George Moore, whose opening gambit—"Have you ever slept with a priest? If you haven't, you haven't lived"—shocked her very much; and finally signed on for the provincial trial run of a new comedy called *Blinkers*. Meant for a London success, the play closed after a week just as Shaw had predicted; and although Shaw believed that she had found her stage legs in *Lord o'Creation* afterward at the Savoy, the restless Molly pulled Laurence to Madrid in hopes of discovering there a suitably intense tragic lead to please her.

But by late spring 1924 Molly was losing some of her enthusiasm. "You are in too great a hurry," chided Shaw when she approached him with the notion of playing Eliza. He was fresh from rehearsals of *Saint Joan* with the "hard hammered" Sybil Thorndike, who could do anything he wanted "with a cock of her eye." Molly was five years' hard work away from touching Eliza, five years Shaw doubted she would sacrifice. He predicted that she would gravitate toward literature after a brief reign as a postcard beauty: her letters were delightful. She had better settle down to producing a thousand words a day for the next five years. But whatever she attempted his advice was the same: work, work, work.

Back in London for another play that flopped, Molly was suddenly sick of acting. She had only tried it to please Laurence—or so it seemed in retrospect. She wanted instead to drink deeply of the cup of life. Surprisingly Shaw agreed. With the master's sanction, Molly pleaded with Laurence: they must go away somewhere: she was tired, empty, sick of London. Although he had just set up a studio where he was in the middle of a project, Laurence yielded as usual; only it seemed to him that they were always moving just when he got a little settled. (Shaw would have called Laurence Tompkins a man damned in a fair wife, and perhaps did, privately.) So they set off for Italy, where after much wandering "like lost dogs," Molly saw the island of her dreams in the middle of Lake Maggiore. By great chance at a dinner party she then sat next to a man named Borromeo who happened to be the owner, and with her formidable combination of beauty and persistence, got the renting of it at her price from the Italian prince. "At last an address!" wrote Shaw from Ayot at news of the island. ". . . I must go and have a look at it if I survive my 70th birthday the Monday after next."

To Italy and the island of Calypso came this old Odysseus in the summer of 1926 with the faithful Penelope in tow. The beard had yielded its Mephophelean crackle for a saintly white, but the step was spry, the back straight, the blue eye twinkling with amusement, the vitality high. Yet like all vain people, Shaw was acutely conscious of age. This was not a new obsession, of course: thirty years before he had refused to see Janet after a close haircut had revealed white under the ginger; had been nettled when Florence exclaimed over the white in his beard. But now his seventy years weighed particularly heavily upon him because for at least two years there had been talk between him and Molly of love. Diffident, oppressed with shyness, his self-consciousness was acute.

Forbes-Robertson's advances had given her "the shivers"; Shaw was determined not to expose himself to the same revulsion. Yet surely there might be hope for the very young and the very old? "When David was too old to be interesting to the Bathshebas," he told her, "he had to turn to the Shulamite woman, who was too young not to be flattered into getting over her disgust." He had created such a relationship between the young Ellie Dunn and the old Captain Shotover in *Heartbreak House*. Indeed, if Molly wanted to find out about love, she would find it described as far as it could be in *Heartbreak House*. "It has happened to me twice," he told her. "It does not last, because it does not belong to this earth; and when you clasp the idol it turns out to be a rag doll like yourself; for the immortal part *must* elude you if you grab at it."[19] "To be in love is to create a religion whose god is fallible," said Borges—and believed Shaw.

Shaw did not try therefore to clasp the idol. Instead he placed himself between Molly and Charlotte and offered Molly a chance to clasp him. He had some faith that, like himself, she was a coquette "according to the classical definition"—a person who deliberately excites passions he or she has no intention of gratifying; and thus would not go beyond the proper bounds. Extremely attracted to her, he still behaved with Charlotte like an obedient boy with his mother, allowing her to arrange his mealtimes and his comings and goings. Not used to resistance, Molly's dislike of Charlotte flared. Awful woman: rigid, humorless, smug as a cat, always dressed in black, incorrigibly correct, sweetly polite—and not at all enchanted by Molly. The strain became intense. She and Charlotte must come to some arrangement, Shaw told Molly privately. Couldn't she tell Charlotte to go to hell, just once? They would both feel the better for it. "But I couldn't," said Molly. "She is much too old." As Shaw flinched, she realized that he and Charlotte were the same age. Ah, but there was no comparison: Shaw was so boyish and laughing and full of high spirits: he had no age for her.

And, as summer waned into fall, Shaw found more and more chance to defy Charlotte. There were long intimate walks on the nights that Shaw escorted Molly from Stresa where he and Charlotte were staying to Baveno. There were swims when Shaw and Molly plunged into the water, Shaw displaying his prowess, while Charlotte sat stiffly on the sand in a black taffeta bathing dress with a stuffed canary perched on the shoulder strap. There were picnics with Charlotte sitting with her back to the company and G.B.S.—Charlotte always called him G.B.S.—actually enjoying himself, though she knew he loathed picnics. And while the two women vied for him and hated each other, each in her own way —Charlotte with incorrigible correctness and Molly like Sarah of Red Gulch—there was Shaw: twinkling, good-tempered, charming, and enjoying the tribute to his vanity immensely. Yet there were sober moments, such as when he discovered a pair of powerful binoculars on the balustrade of the terrace outside his and Charlotte's suite at the Hotel Regina.

But Shaw, like Tannhäuser, was constitutionally uneasy in the Venusberg; and after the initial fascination that lured him there, more and more aware of the spiritual darkness of that cavern. Molly's tactlessness eventually forced him to flee; her subsequent inability to settle down to some serious occupation in life alarmed and disillusioned him. She must set her hand to some work; she could not simply prowl the shores of Lake Maggiore, making wives miserable and sulking when the attention of husbands strayed from her one moment. "Laurence works and fences," Shaw lectured in May 1928:

> Troubetskoy sculpts; Albert and Cecil work like negroes and have no use for women who do not work; Basile overworks and has married a gentlewoman who will hold him when he will post policemen to whistle when you are coming so that he may fly; but *you*—what do you do? what will become of you? how will you face old age: With a "lifted" face, with grease paints and an iceball and rouge, with peroxided hair, an old hag desperately pretending to be a young witch. Oh Molly, Molly, Molly, Molly, I must not think about you; for I cannot save you; I have done my best and only made matters worse. . . .
>
> What sort of creature do you suppose I should be now if I had done nothing but exploit my celebrated fascination all my life? Would you have looked twice at so repulsive an object? And yet you thought that when you had secured your Ogygia and lured me to its shores you could play Calypso to m[y] Odysseus and make a hog of me. Aren't you glad you didn't succeed . . . .
>
> Your spiritual values are all wrong.[20]

So he had said to Jenny, to Florence, to Bertha, to Janet, to Erica, to Stella. How to combat the hopeless amateurism in even the most professional of women, and knock into their heads the urgent need to cultivate a talent to the highest pitch, so that no matter what the future they might meet it? Yet Shaw hesitated to renounce Molly, criticizing instead her adventures into painting (good color: but she couldn't paint as well as Bertha Newcombe, who had given up painting); following her adventures in Roman high society after she left the Isolino; claiming, when she found herself pregnant, that he was the spiritual father of the child; sorrowing when she chose abortion; reading of her experiments with love and Veronal more in sorrow than in anger—though from the beginning experience had whispered to him that she must eventually go to the devil. Visiting Italy at the end of 1928, he had again come to her, and again had been forced to leave because she could not manage to behave tactfully with Charlotte. Contrite in the silence that followed, Molly finally wrote to ask whether he was through with her. With his reply, the seventy-two-year-old Shaw shut the door on this last love affair: "At my age one is thru with everybody, and can only beg for a little charitable tolerance from young persons. I hoarded my bodily possessions so penuriously that even at seventy I had some left; but that remnant was stolen from me on the road to Baveno and on other roads to paradise through the same district. Now they are all dusty highways on which I am safe because nobody can rob a beggar. Nothing is left except my eternal genius."[21]

CHAPTER TWENTY-THREE

1916-1950

IN LATER YEARS, Ellen Terry met Shaw several times, and there was always uneasiness between them. Once in June 1916, at the height of the war, they met on the roof of the Coliseum where the stars of a benefit performance for a war charity had assembled to be photographed. Willow-slim now and on the threshold of seventy, she had stirred Shaw to memories of his "blessed darling Ellen." "Why do I make you nervous?" he asked after the event. "I know why *you* make *me* nervous. It is because people are looking on, and the way I want to and ought to behave would be ridiculous and indecorous. But meet me by moonlight alone; and—my word!—you shall see."[1] Blessed Ellen indeed: there had been a ripple of indignation at the appearance of G.B.S. on the roof and protests from some performers against being photographed with the author of *Common Sense About the War*—but only nervousness from loyal Ellen.

There was another chance meeting in the country one summer day when Shaw came across a group of people shooting a film. "Ellen Terry was there, acting the heroine," Shaw remembered. "She was astonishingly beautiful. She had passed through that middle phase, so trying to handsome women, of matronly amplitude, and was again tall and slender, with a new delicacy and intensity in her saddened expression. She was always a little shy in speaking to me; for talking, hampered by material circumstances, is awkward and unsatisfactory after the perfect freedom of writing between people who *can* write."[2] Again Ellen asked Shaw for some work in the theatre—anything: a charwoman's part; again he replied in familiar metaphor that the part of a canal barge can-

385

not be played by a battleship. The film being shot that day marked Ellen's screen debut as a retired actress in *Her Greatest Performance;* but the film was undistinguished, as were three others she made.³ Cinema technique was strange to her—confused, fragmented; the studio, the lights, the camera, the lack of a living audience seemed alien; she took direction badly—or rather, did not take it at all. She still could do no wrong to sympathetic audiences in her infrequent stage performances; yet as the Nurse in *Romeo and Juliet* in 1919, her memory failed sadly.

She continued to take interest in Shaw's work, appearing in a box at the Criterion Theatre for the single performance on 16 December 1917 of *The Inca of Perusalem,* produced by Edith Craig; she met him again at the revival of *Pygmalion* in 1920 when her sister Marion played Mrs. Higgins. And in the autumn of 1921, Shaw received one of her ineffably buoyant notes: "Such 'a Treat' tonight! Just seen 'John Bull's Other Island.' Oh my Dear my Dear—Surely it is the best of your Bunch! Just think—I had neither seen it acted nor read it!!! And now the amazing 'Heartbreak House.' What riches! *What Benefits!*"⁴

Only the postscript—"Queer writing! my right arm full of pain"— hinted at deterioration. But in fact that same year her failing health and precarious financial situation led Edy to insist that her mother give up the Chelsea house at 215 King's Road where she had lived since 1902. Many of Ellen's most precious possessions were sold—the Steinway upright, the Spode supper set, the Kelmscott editions—and she moved into a three-room flat at Burleigh Mansions in dark, narrow St. Martin's Lane. "I am unhinged (*not* unhappy) and comfortable," Ellen recorded in her diary on 26 April 1921. "I wonder where everything is. Cannot remember new things. All is changed. Change at 73 puzzles the will. I live in puzzledom." The grandchildren (fifteen or so of Edward Craig's love children) were grown or gone or out of reach, or dead: Ted and Isadora Duncan's daughter had drowned with her small son in Paris when their unattended car rolled backward into the Seine. Her memory came and went; her health failed. The honor of Dame Grand Cross came in 1925, belatedly. Groping her way out of the reception room at Buckingham Palace with assistance from Edy (she was now seventy-eight) she laughed outright as she realized she had forgotten to walk out of the presence backward; King George V, following within earshot, laughed with her. But she did not care much for the distinction except as it honored women in general, and she declined to be called "Dame."

Although she loved the bustle of the theatre district around St. Martin's Lane and often escaped to wander among the crowds, she retreated finally to Smallhythe. There at night, ghostlike, she prowled the rooms, touching the relics of her past with dreaming fingers: Duse's photograph, the much-worn Globe edition of Shakespeare next to her bed, her silver-backed mirror, Teddy's desk from the old schoolroom. More and more muddled, she still could show flashes of her old humor. "Tell me, Jim," she said to James Carew, who like many of her lovers was now her friend and had come to visit, "I can't quite remember—did I kick you out or did you kick me out?" To Jim's diplomatic suggestion that perhaps they had agreed to separate, she laughed: "Yes, so we did." She paused. "Dam' fools, weren't we!" Slowly, however, her vitality ebbed and her mind clouded over. On 17 July 1928 a stroke paralyzed her. Her son remembered the blind, closed eyes, the twisted face, the still-beautiful motionless hands. On a fresh sunny morning four days later the radiance of Ellen Terry finally went out. A petition to have her buried in Westminster Abbey with Irving was rejected, revealing conclusively that the famous "partnership" of the Lyceum had not been a partnership at all.

Ellen had saved most of Shaw's letters, as he had saved hers; and he now found himself in the midst of another controversy over the publication of his seemingly limitless love letters. By now anything with Shaw's signature had become valuable on the market. "I have been recommending all my friends to sell every scrap of my writing they possess whilst the craze lasts," he told Stella in November 1928. A bookseller named Gabriel Wells had been buying Shaviana right and left, paying £10 for two postcards and snapping up 130 of Shaw's letters to Janet Achurch which had been sold "as waste paper" after Charles Charrington's death in September 1926. He himself had 230 letters from Ellen Terry out of which Edy Craig might make some cash, and as for Stella—

> When I am dead, my dearest,
> Sing no sad songs for me
> But cast my spells on Mister Wells
> And ask a handsome fee.[5]

Shaw turned up at Edy and Christopher St. John's flat at their request, therefore, with Ellen's letters neatly docketed in chronological order. Although there was less chance of hurting Charlotte this time, since she had inherited the correspondence with her marriage, Shaw still demurred, remembering only the affectionate and intimate parts of their letters. But the feminist Edy and Christopher read Ellen's letters quite differently. Here was not the lovable, scatterbrained "little Nell" of contemporary imagination, but the strong, wise, and intelligent woman they had known. Surely Shaw would co-operate to send Ellen down to posterity as she deserved. Shaw reread the letters himself, and agreed. Edy owned the copyright, Christopher St. John would edit them, Shaw might be persuaded to write another preface. There was only one obstacle, and that was Gordon Craig, whose dislike of Shaw had not abated. Both Edy and

Shaw insisted on Craig's consent, knowing that Craig was apt to raise a cry against the undertaking; and Edy forwarded the correspondence to her brother in Italy.

Craig read it through, and wrote to Shaw on 4 April 1929 that in his opinion "what's good in it is too good to allow the public to ever have it." Shaw too hung back until, upon the settling of Ellen's estate, both letters and copyrights were sold, and the new holder of copyright announced that he would publish Ellen Terry's letters by themselves if Shaw could not be persuaded to a joint volume. At this Shaw capitulated, but insisted again that Gordon Craig's consent be obtained in writing. With unfortunate timing, considering he wanted a favor, Shaw chose to criticize Craig's recently finished biography of his idol Henry Irving in a letter about the correspondence. Craig's reply (he had by now read Shaw's Preface) revealed his antipathy:

Dear Mr. Shaw [he wrote from Genoa] . . . I am doing something to make it clear that we of the Lyceum thought [Irving] was a great actor, even as you thought he was a bad one.

What you say in your letter about him, about my mother, my father and myself, is all very interesting, and will be worth something one day, provided you are sure of your facts—I suppose you *are* sure of them? Anyhow, you give them out in such a noisy manner that it is quite likely that they will carry across the footlights of the coming two decades. Personally I should say, from what you have written of it, that you know very little about the Theatre . . . . you seem a little troubled about it, and a little anxious to prove how closely associated you have been with it: I don't know if I am wrong. . . .

Why you go to such lengths to explain to me, not only in this letter, but in the previous letter, that I cannot know about Irving, since I didn't see him fifteen or twenty years earlier, is as incomprehensible to me as it will be to anybody except those funny people who know nothing whatever about the stage or anything else. Why, dear Mr. Shaw, I knew all about the stage—by the grace of God, or instinct, or whatever you like to call it—when I was borne by my mother, whom you seem to forget was Ellen Terry. By jove, you do really seem to forget that, and it is so typical of you, with your powers of observation, that you should fail to note the obvious.

I have read your notes on the letters, of which you were kind enough to send me a copy. I disagree with your conclusions and opinions, and dislike the way you represent us all. Will you excuse my saying that they remind me of some malicious old woman—I really mean no personal offence, but you seem to go nosing around like a cockatrice. You poke your eagerness into the affairs of Irving: you bombard my poor mother with letters (I remember how every night they used to arrive—I was there, she used to talk to me about them): you concern yourself with me, with Edy, with our family in general: and I would not mind a bit of it if you had run off with my mother; but you failed, my dear Mr. Shaw, you failed—and raising my hat, let me assure you this is the last word I shall ever have to say to you.[6]

Craig fumed his way through his copy of the correspondence, penciling contemptuously on the title page "Janet Achurch—Elizabeth Robins—Florence Farr—women—and then *? ? ? ?*" "Actress first & foremost," he jotted after his mother's name; "agitator first & foremost" after Shaw's. Scoring through their names on one of the title pages, he substituted the initials E.T. and G.B.S.: "Essentially the right title as it is a spiritual friendship & a thing of initials—impersonal. Dedicated to the P. M. G. (Post Master General)." Galling were some of his mother's comments about himself, such as "he is a big boy for 7 and that's his age" and "I allow Ted £500 a year"; he amended the letter to "She allowed me £500 for a short time: did not settle a yearly income of £500 on me —which is quite another matter." "Good," he sneered after Shaw's statement on 5 November 1896 that a play reading that night had been "an appalling failure." "Silly," he jibed at Shaw's "No: *I* shall never have a home. But do not be alarmed . . . ." To Shaw's oblique reference to himself on 16 November 1896 as a mere prescription that Charlotte had taken, Craig observed: "This about the future Mrs. GBS strikes me as a bit odd—to say the least of it." To Shaw's "I love you soulfully," he exclaimed "Rats—go & see her—outright rot." "Are you 'a blackmailer,' my precious?" Ellen had once asked in a letter of 18 February 1898 marked "Private—*very*." "Yes he is a 'blackmailer,' " wrote Craig, "& everything else according to HI if he is annoying HI & killing the Lyceum Theatre & all the time writing coo to ET—& she to him. Authority cant exist with people doing this semi-underhand trick all the time." Shaw's tone throughout maddened him: he was everlastingly flattering Ellen Terry's vanity; and as Ellen had no vanity, nothing ever happened. Only once or twice did Craig agree with the man he detested. "Silly Ellen," Shaw had chided when she first decided that Lady Cicely was not for her. "I think he is quite right," noted Craig. And Shaw's rebuke beginning "Oh you lie, Ellen, never was there a part so deeply written for a woman as this for you," Craig conceded to be a "Good letter."[7]

Still angry, he made notes two years later for a letter to the man he vowed he would never give another word to. "You are a sentimentalist but afraid of it being known. Bold as brass apparently you have an astonishing lack of moral courage. . . ." Persuaded by Max Beerbohm, however, that the Shaw-Terry letters had literary value, Gordon Craig finally gave his consent to the publication; then turned and wrote his own version of his mother's life, dedicated significantly to his father, in which he explained:

I had not wished to write this book.

Ellen Terry's name was already one of the most famous names in Dramatic History—no one, by writing, could add to that fame.

But it was possible they could detract from it.

And that is what Mr. Bernard Shaw, through his blind vanity and jealousy has done: first, in permitting the publication of the correspondence between himself and Ellen Terry: secondly, in writing his apologetic Preface . . . a Preface in which he descends here and there not to salute, but to insult the dead.

He cannot help it—it is his unfortunate way.[8]

His mother, Craig argued in his book, had been two women: the successful actress Ellen Terry, and "little Nellie," the golden little mother, his father's loving consort, and a woman unknown to all but her father, mother, sisters and brothers, his father Godwin, and himself. Edy? She had never known "little Nellie": she had looked down on little Nellie's weaknesses and clung to the famous Ellen Terry. As a result, Craig as knight-errant had been forced to come forward and rescue his mother's memory from the unnatural attentions of Edith Craig, Christopher St. John, and Bernard Shaw.

Justifiably, Shaw felt that Craig's attack on him after agreeing to the publication of the letters merited comment; and in *The Observer* of 8 November 1931, he analyzed both Craig's view of Ellen Terry's character and Craig's hostility toward himself. Craig, said Shaw, felt a "psychopathic hatred" of the great Ellen Terry. Fearful of being crushed by her "impetuous, overwhelming, absorbing personality," he had fled from the nest as soon as his wings were fully fledged, recognizing that he must "save his soul alive." His instinct had been sound: a small boy had little chance against a woman who could sweep away an audience of thousands. "What makes this book so tragically moving," said Shaw, "—for if you disregard the rubbish about me, which is neither here nor there, it is a poignant human document—is his desperate denial of the big woman he ran away from, and his assertion of the 'little mother' he loved. He still resents the great Ellen Terry, the woman who would have swallowed him up if he had stayed within her magnetic hold, so intensely that he is furious with me because I did not tear up her letters and stamp them and her into the earth, so that the world would never have known her."

But Craig's hatred of Shaw was more personal than that, and centered in his admission "and I would not mind a bit of it if you had run off with my mother." This was Craig's technique with women: he inflicted his resentment of his mother's domination upon other women by romancing them, impregnating them, and leaving them. He could have admired Shaw, perhaps, had Shaw done the same; he could not respect a man who was content to be something as ambiguous as a woman's friend. With his broad-brimmed hat, flowing cape, wavy locks, and pose as the "Thwarted Genius," Craig was the kind of self-indulgent Bohemian that Shaw deplored. In turn Craig hated the shrewd, self-advertising, seemingly invulnerable public man of affairs. The fact that this "propagandist first & foremost" had invaded little Nellie's life and won her intimate affection seemed to him the most perverse of rapes.

The publication of the Terry-Shaw letters in 1931 and the interest they aroused reawoke the appetite of Stella Campbell, whose own memoirs had brought in a mere £2,500 that had quickly gone the way of all Stella's money. An uneasy truce had existed between her and Shaw for years. "I forgive you the letters," he had written in January 1923, "because there is a star somewhere on which you were right about them; and on that star we two should have been born. I told you you had never learned to live in this one; and the Titanic slavery by which I have learned has separated us."[9] She in turn admitted that he had "loved like a King." Yet Shaw managed to steer very much clear of the actress whose bitchery was now the more formidable since she had lost the beauty that had gone with it. She wanted his plays; he was not going to let her have them. He had created the Serpent in *Methuselah* for her voice, but preferred actresses like Edith Evans and Sybil Thorndike and Ellen Pollock, all of whom believed in him and took his direction—indeed Sybil Thorndike had never let him doubt that she considered him "far superior to the Holy Trinity as producer," and had blessed him for renewing her faith in God. She could not have *Jitta's Atonement*, even though she claimed she could make both their fortunes; she could be no use to him at the Malvern Festival, where Edith Evans was going to play Orinthia in *The Apple Cart* in the coming summer of 1929—even though Orinthia had been inspired by the Stella of Kensington Square. She was a witch—and the spells she cast would interfere with his own.

At mention of Orinthia, Stella sat up. He must come and read her the play immediately, or she would have him up for an illegal act. But Shaw and Charlotte were mercifully off to the Adriatic that April and he could not make it to Pont Street before he left. "Dont go to your grave dearest regretting I didnt play in your Applecart," Stella coaxed in milder mood; but Shaw ignored her. Then in June Stella met Edith Evans at the Selfridge Ball—Edith Evans who gazed eagerly and announced that she was to play Mrs. Campbell at Malvern and Birmingham and London. Indignant, Stella consulted friends, who agreed that it was "infamous" and "a national calamity" and "an insult." She was truly distressed, she told Shaw (still sailing the blue Adriatic): and clearly she intended to create a storm. Back at 4 Whitehall Court, where he and Charlotte had moved in 1927 when their building in Adelphi Terrace was pulled down, Shaw reassured her that the press would never guess that King Magnus, Jemima, and Orinthia were versions of G.B.S., Charlotte, and Mrs. Pat. The first rehearsal was to take place on Monday, 1 July; he had to read the play to the cast, a killing job—and him so old. "You should have sent me your play to read," Stella replied coldly. "You are out of tune with friendship and simple courtesy."

He finally came to 64 Pont Street on 11 July to read her the "Interlude" bit set in the boudoir of King Magnus's mistress. He felt shy about his seventy-three years (though he argued that even the wreck of G.B.S. must be more interesting than a lesser man in his prime), apprehensive of her reaction, and wary of her temper. He was greeted by the magnificent bulk of Stella Campbell—the black hair still luxuriant though bobbed, the chins luxuriant too, the great eyes darkly smoldering, the famous voice throatier than ever, the noxious little dogs yapping at her heels. Thin, pink-cheeked, and irrepressibly youthful, he read to her in his soft, musical voice, over which, once said Rebecca West, the Irish accent shivered like the wind over a lake—and Stella did not like it at all. She did not like the King's criticisms of Orinthia, which were "dreadfully commonplace and vulgar." She did not like the way he had made Orinthia run down the King's wife: jibes such as "Heaven is offering you a rose; and you cling to a cabbage" or "Oh, drown her: shoot her: tell your chauffeur to drive her into the Serpentine and leave her there" were deplorable, while getting him neatly off the hook. As he sat there in her room, reading out what he had done to their beautiful romance, she thought she saw him for the first time. He was nothing but a mountebank—and she had trusted him like a child. What a fool she had been! Some things, of course, were less offensive, lines such as Orinthia's "You are the King of liars and humbugs" and "Since when have you set up a heart? Did you buy that, too, secondhand?" and "Magnus: you are a mollycoddle." No: these had a certain ring of truth. Yet she missed the only truly insulting aspect of the Orinthia episode, and that was its obvious unimportance to King Magnus save as a brief diversion from more important matters.

Shaw remained calm in the storm of her protest. Orinthia was not a portrait but a study; and anyway as an artist he was utterly unscrupulous when it came to using models. He consented to a few changes "to cure the soreness" of her heart, most significantly the alteration from "Orinthia: It is out of the question: your dream of being queen must remain a dream" to "Orinthia: We are only two children at play; and you must be content to be my queen in fairyland." It soon became clear, however, that Stella wanted it both ways: she was furious when he hinted that she was Orinthia and furious when he suggested altering the likeness. She was a fool, SUCH a fool. And yet after all he owed her a great deal:

> . . . Of course we are a pair of mountebanks [he wrote a few weeks be-
> fore *The Apple Cart* opened at Malvern on 19 August 1929]; but why,
> oh why do you get nothing out of me, though I get everything out of
> you? Mrs. Hesione Hushabye in Heartbreak House, the Serpent in
> Methuselah, whom I always hear speaking with your voice, and Orinthia:
> all you, to say nothing of Eliza, who was only a joke. You are the Vamp
> and I the victim; yet it is I who suck your blood and fatten on it whilst
> you lose everything!
> It is ridiculous! There's something wrong somewhere.[10]

Stella wanted very much to get something out of Shaw, however; and her attention finally diverted from *The Apple Cart* (which Charlotte duly witnessed at Malvern), she returned to her pet subject: the letters. It maddened her to think that she could get from £15 to £50 for a single typed sheet initialed G.B.S.; yet she would not bargain with them. Sell copies of his plays he had given her, yes: she had gotten £100 for *Widowers' Houses* in April 1929 and in May took a whole load of volumes to Gabriel Wells. How she *hated* parting with them (Shaw must have smiled: he believed she never read one): the haggling had been a loathsome business. But the books were nothing compared to the value of his letters. In 1931 an American private collector had offered her £3,000 for them; then a publisher valued them at £10,000 and the publishing rights at £20,000. She had behaved like a gentleman over those letters for nineteen years: she could have sold each one of the 125 for $350 or $500 apiece—yet she had clung to them for what they meant to her heart. And now the Terry-Shaw correspondence. Did he realize that his refusal to allow a Campbell-Shaw correspondence had put her in "a strange and not too comfortable position"? And did he realize that she still had his old letter of permission to publish? A little blackmail was permissible against such a heart of stone. Finally she pulled out all the stops. When he wrote those lovely letters, she assured him, something impersonal in her had set his genius on the plane where angels and poets passed the time of day. . . . Their beauty made a golden broom to brush away a little of the worldly dust. . . . They immortalized his youth, and generations would smile joyfully at the Glorious Love Charade and would call his letters a feast for the Gods.[11]

Shaw was not impressed. His and Ellen's letters were literature, he replied, whereas everything meaningful between themselves had been carried on *viva voce*. "You would not come out of it with a halo like Ellen's," he warned. "I should come out better, because, though I amused you handsomely, you kept your head and were never enchanted as I was. Perhaps you have written love letters, but not to me. Ellen, though she came through with me *virgo intacta*, gave herself away heart and soul without a thought of reserve to me as she did to everyone else who invited her confidence. You had no confidence in me; really small blame to you, Stella: do not think I am reproaching you." Besides, *nothing* would make him go through with Charlotte again what he had gone through on the publication of his letters to her back in 1921. The issue was closed.

Then in 1937 she heard from him again. "My antiquity, now extreme at eighty-one, has obliged me to make a clearance among my papers and take measures generally for my probably imminent decease," wrote Shaw. Despite his policy to burn everything not connected with business, he had discovered all her letters: "They *would* not be burnt, I suppose." "With infinite labor and a little heartbreak," he had packed and was now sending her the letters in six sturdy envelopes (his plan of buying a handsome jewel case to hold them had been frustrated by difficulties at the customs house: she must buy one and send him the bill). The correspondence—still not to be published until his and Charlotte's ashes had been scattered among the flower beds of one of the crematoriums in which he held shares—were a valuable literary property, and would mean money eventually to her daughter, if not to herself. "And so, blessed be your days, dear Stella." Stella appeared humbled at last. "God bless us all," replied Stella from New York, "and you most especially, dearest Joey, for all the wit and wisdom and truth and justice, and love of fair dealing; the genius of your work—that you have showered upon the world so bountifully. It is your affection for me that will raise me a little out of the rut and place me somewhere near your side. I am proud and happy that it is so."[12]

For Stella the rut was now deep and the chances of pulling herself out slender. Her last success in England had been *The Matriarch* in the spring of 1929 at the Royalty, where, a generation before, she had reigned as actress-manager. Lillah McCarthy attended and marveled at the "amazing breadth of her genius"; but it was a genius Stella herself seemed bent on destroying. Unmanageable, and still scorning Shaw's advice to re-establish herself in the theatre as "leading Old Woman," she migrated to Hollywood. It was the last place for her. Her bulk, as imposing as a Michelangelo sybil's, her arrogance, her sardonic humor, her age, made her an embarrassing figure among the nymphets that crowded the nightclubs and the studios. She was not photogenic: most of her film footage ended up on the cutting-room floor. "Hollywood and the Camera have taught me humility—deep humility," she wrote Shaw from a hotel on Sunset Boulevard in 1935: "nobody need be afraid of me anymore. Thirteen weeks work *in 16 months*—think of that misery—it has almost broken me up." Calls to her agent were futile: M-G-M was "thinking of her." She was too British, she was too important, she was (nobody said it) too old.

Through the humbling of her pride in the last years, she managed to keep her sense of humor. In a revival of *Tanqueray*, said Mrs. Pat, Duse had made a *tour de force*, but she herself had been forced to tour. Viewing her first screen test, she exclaimed in dismay: she had rather imagined herself looking like the Blessed Damozel leaning out of heaven, but found herself looking more like Mussolini's mother instead. At a gathering of American matrons all exclaiming over their adorable babies at home: "I, too, have the cutest little girlie at home in England— she's sixty!" To a cameraman who greeted her appearance on the set with "Hi, Babe—what's the little dog's name?" her most austere British manner: "Tittie-bottles!" said Mrs. Pat. To Shaw from "a little room in a nice hotel" where she had crept after falling ill in Hollywood, and after the visit of Kate Terry's grandson: "John Gielgud found me there and brought me flowers with tears in his eyes—the Terrys weep easily." Rebecca West met Mrs. Pat from time to time in New York during those last years, and remembered above all the great wit: "one smiled and laughed all the way home."[13]

But her black coat covered with Moonbeam's hair got shabbier, and she trimmed the frayed edge of her felt hat with scissors, and nonchalance cost her more and more. The five hundred pounds a year she received from two benefactors did not provide for many new hats. Having alienated theatre and movieland in America, she sailed for Italy with Moonbeam in 1938, lighting first at the Hotel Sirmione, Lago di Garda, and then moving to a hotel in Paris. There she heard of the huge success of the *Pygmalion* film. "And you on a percentage!" she wrote Shaw enviously in December. "You must be making more money than you know what to do with. I wonder if you remember all the trouble I took—how I took the play to Tree and begged him to ask you to come and read it to him—and said I would play Eliza—How I stood your insults at rehearsals! How I worked day and night over the accent—how loyal I was to you when Tree came to me just before the curtain went up and begged me to 'cut' the bloody . . . how I spilt my heart trying to make Eliza common and beautiful—something about her—to fit into dreams— of course you have forgotten everything or you would send a Christmas box!"[14] From Ayot, Shaw replied that *Pygmalion* was indeed making millions, but that he had not seen the color of them yet. The Jews would get his money this Christmas, and she would get nothing. Did she want to make some money? Then she should write the true story of *Pygmalion* for "the dismal string of lies" in her last letter was "not worth twopence." Better yet a true book entitled *Why, Though I Was a*

Wonderful Actress, No Manager or Author Would Ever Engage Me Twice If He Could Possibly Help It. But she couldn't, even though it would be a best seller, because she didn't know, still. Well, he did.

Stella fought back. What lies! *Six* engagements with Alexander, *nine* with Robertson, *four* with Du Maurier, *two* with Hare, *four* with Tree. "And you dare accuse me of humiliating people! Since you first dipped your pen in the ink-pot what else have you ever done?" But anger was useless; and finally she willed her own fate. Returning to England would have meant putting Moonbeam into quarantine for six months. She had seen the dismal sight of the "little well-bred dogs sobbing softly to themselves" in cages; she decided that it was quite easy for her to put Moonbeam before country and career. Shaw snorted. How he blessed that wretched dog, for it meant she had to stay in France and he would "as soon bring the devil" over to England as Stella Campbell. In his heart, however, he had always rather dreaded that she would *mourir sur la paille*. Gabriel Pascal had thought of her for Mrs. Higgins in *Pygmalion;* and now in 1939 when plans for a film of *Major Barbara* were under way, Shaw unbent to ask her whether she was still "seriously in the field," since Pascal wanted her for the part of Lady Britomart. Stella replied from the Hotel Calais, where she had moved because the Brighton had raised its prices for the Paris summer. She was in the field, she quipped, but "not as cannon fodder." "There is no reception room here, so don't ask Pascal to come & see me. I would be ashamed of my shabby little bedroom," she ended indefinitely.[15] Deciding that Stella would not return to England, Pascal gave Lady Britomart to Marie Löhr. But perhaps after all Moonbeam was only an excuse to save Stella from a last humbling of her pride.

On the eve of the Second World War, she left for the South of France to look for nightingales, orange groves, and sun. Forbes-Robertson was dead, Tree was dead, Barrie was dead; she had heard from a friend, however, that at a recent picture exhibition Shaw had almost skipped down the stairs. On the train she carried with her in a hatbox the precious correspondence that could only be published after his and Charlotte's deaths. She settled in a little *pension* at Pau, and had the sun, and young neighbors, and a girl to run errands for her until in 1940 a cold turned into bronchitis and bronchitis into pulmonary infection. She had always been careless with herself, a kind of perversity driving her to self-destruction. She did not seem to care now, and died insolvent at Pau at the age of seventy-two. "AND IT IS MY DESIRE," read a clause in her will, "should the copyright be free or permission obtained that the Bernard Shaw letters and poems . . . be published in their proper sequence and not cut or altered in any way, that they should be published in an independent volume to be entitled 'The Love Letters of Bernard Shaw to

Mrs. Patrick Campbell' so that all who may read them will realise that the friendship was 'L'amitié amoureuse' . . . ."[16]

Despite endless protestations of dotage and imminent death, Shaw seemed destined to outlast his entire generation. One by one, they had all gone. Kate Salt had died in 1919. Writing to Henry Salt (who would marry a thirty-five-year-old woman at seventy-five), Shaw remembered the sandal-making, the duets on the noisy grand piano, the vegetarianism, the country weekends, and the youthful radicalism as quite Shelleyan and idyllic.

Jenny Patterson had not been able to hold on to Shaw, but she clung to his family even after she left Brompton Square about 1906 and moved to "Bookhams," a pleasant house set in woods and garden at Churt in Surrey. Ann M. Elder, Shaw's secretary, remembered the widow as "a warm hearted and generous lady" who used to invite Shaw's cousins, Georgina (Judy) Gillmore and her brother, to Bookhams during school holidays. Arabella Gillmore and Georgiana Gurly, Shaw's half aunts, also visited Bookhams, and on at least one occasion, Jenny took Judy Gillmore abroad with her. Judy acted as Shaw's secretary from 1907 until Ann M. Elder took over the job in 1912, giving Jenny an indirect line of communication into Shaw's life—had she wanted it. Quite poor after the war, Jenny Patterson died on 15 September 1924. Shaw's aunt Arabella was with her at the end.[17] If she had never quite given up Shaw, he had never quite given her up either: Stella Campbell's dark eyes and violent temper were her reincarnation: the distance between Brompton and Kensington squares was not, after all, great.

"Women have never played an important part in my life," Shaw claimed. "I could always discard them more readily than my friends." Jenny Patterson's death, had he known of it, might not have elicited a second thought. Not so the death of William Archer three months later in December. That friendship, begun so many years before at the British Museum, had demonstrated two characteristics of Shaw's friendships with men: his ability to command their respect despite the most violent disagreement and his sporting way of attacking head on. Archer never feared a stab in the back from Shaw: he got the blows on the chin. The critic had always had mixed admiration for Shaw's "wild and whirling methods of dialectic," just as he had mixed feelings about Shavian drama. "We have never agreed about plays, and we never will," said Archer. "There is not the least reason why we should." Consequently, he always seemed to underrate his friend. "The trouble with you," he told Shaw in 1923, ". . . is that you are incurably credulous. Someone comes along & tells you that wool is the only wear, & instantly you go in for woollen boots, which lead, in due time, to a course of crutches. Then Wagner comes along, & you are a Wagnerite; Ibsen, & you are an Ibsenite (I never was); Nietzsche, & you are a Nietzschean; Bergson, & you are a

Bergsonian. And all the time you are no whit nearer the real secret of things."[18] Archer's last tribute, written in December when he faced a serious operation, was, however, warm: ". . . though I may sometimes have played the part of all-too-candid mentor, I have never waivered in my admiration and affection for you, or ceased to feel that the Fates had treated me kindly in making me your contemporary and friend. I thank you from my heart for forty years of good comradeship." Surely it made Shaw's tribute—"a friend of whom, after more than forty years, I have not a single unpleasant recollection, and whom I was never sorry to see or unready to talk to"—seem curiously lukewarm in its negatives. And yet in 1927, Shaw admitted: "I still feel that when he went he took a piece of me with him."[19]

Annie Besant's last conversion had endured, and her fame and golden oratory had drawn Charlotte to hear her lecture on theosophical thought several times. After Charlotte's return from the *Pygmalion* voyage in 1914, she and G.B.S. entertained Annie at lunch at Adelphi Terrace on 29 May. There was much they could have agreed upon: humanitarianism, vegetarianism, pacifism, anti-vivisection, the cause of international brotherhood. Active till the end for the cause of Indian nationalism, Annie Besant died in India in 1933.

After her beautiful Pre-Raphaelite mother's death, May Morris moved to Kelmscott Manor, the family's old Elizabethan stone house in Oxfordshire close by the Thames. There she lived in this museum to Morris among the tapestries and carpets and vellum manuscripts; and the words "My Father" were always on her lips. Mary Lobb, a large, hearty woman with cropped hair and inevitable Norfolk jacket and knickerbockers, was her devoted companion, though privately considering Morris to have been "an awful old bore." May herself was now masculine and moustached, yet noble and austere, with heavy black brows set tragically like a Greek mask, suggesting some sad and irrevocable pain in her past. If only she could have married the right man, some of her friends thought, how much happier, more effective, and—different—she would have been.[20]

May had approached Shaw in April 1913 for help with a book she was writing about Morris; he had complied, assuring her he was still and always her very special friend, as far as a writing machine could be anything so human. In 1936 she approached him again, this time for an essay on Morris for a two-volume work on her father. Again Shaw obliged; but May was startled upon receiving "Morris As I Knew Him" to find that the irrepressible Shaw had aired the whole story of the "Mystic Betrothal" as well as providing a conclusion:

> Forty years or so later [about 1930] I was motoring one day through Gloster when the spell of Kelmscott Manor came upon me [wrote

Shaw]. I turned off the high road from Lechlade to Oxford and soon found myself in the church with the tempting candlesticks that nobody ever stole, and at the grave of William and Jane Morris, which I had never seen before. I was soon on the garden flagway to the ancient door of the Manor House. It was opened by a young lady whose aspect terrified me. She was obviously strong enough to take me by the scruff of the neck and pitch me neck and crop out of the curtilage; and she looked as if for two pins she would do it as she demanded sternly who I was. I named myself apologetically. The Mystical Betrothal, strong as ever, operated at once, though the athletic lady (Miss Lobb) could have known nothing about it. She threw the door wide open as if I belonged to the place and had been away for ten minutes or so; and presently the beautiful daughter and I, now harmless old folks, met again as if nothing had happened.[21]

With private reservations, May nevertheless thanked Shaw both for his introduction and his kind remarks about her writing. "As to our harmless personal relations I should have been inclined to let them lie 'unsung': on the grounds that no one cares a hang about me, though of course they are interested about you as a public character. But perhaps you are right, and the little toads of story-mongers, who sometimes unexpectedly thrust their heads up will have no mystery there to play with." Shaw replied flatteringly; and May wrote again: "Yes, well, of course Im a remarkable woman—always was, though none of you seemed to think so." Yet her previous letter had expressed some of the pain expressed in those dark, heavy brows: "Yes, I always thought I should have taken seriously to writing; but there it is; I made a mess of things then and always, and only myself to blame for a waste of life. . . ."[22] After the publication of *William Morris: Artist Writer Socialist,* May lived just two more years, until 16 October 1938.

The loss of Harley Granville-Barker after his marriage, both to the theatre and as a personal friend, hit Shaw very hard. Since the time Barker had "blighted" him during rehearsals at the Court by observing that he was just the age of his father, Shaw had conceived a paternal affection for the brilliant young playwright, producer, and actor—even jesting to Stella that future generations would believe she was his mistress and Harley their son. Certainly Barker appreciated Shaw, telling Lillah that he was their best and wisest friend, the one person they could always go to for help and support. During the winter of 1917 when the divorce was pending, a winter of searchlights, air raids, soldier's sheds, and even a gun in the park at Ayot, Barker had come to Ayot every Saturday for that support and counsel. After he married Helen Huntington on 31 July 1918, however, it became clear that his new wife had not forgiven

Shaw for his pro-Lillah stand in the business of the divorce and settlement. Communication between Barker and Shaw gradually broke down. In 1924 Shaw wrote to Archer, asking whether Barker had dropped him as he had dropped himself and Charlotte. Thanks to inhuman marriage laws and the shaky financial state of both parties, Shaw explained, the divorce had been a terrible affair that had finally forced him to blackmail both parties into a reasonable settlement. Faced with Lillah's suffering, which was far greater than either Harley's or Helen's, he had inevitably been forced to "crumple" some of Helen's "roseleaves." He was sure she still hated him for the business. Of course Barker could not impose Shaw on Helen, and of course the difference in their ages had been bound to sever them sooner or later (so Shaw believed); but Barker had stopped writing altogether, and that loss hurt. He could not believe that the young genius of the Court was "an extinct volcano": Helen was certainly sitting on the crater; and if Barker allowed her to stifle his great talents, Shaw was sure he would hate her for it in the end.[23] But Barker had lost his faith in the theatre during the war, and could see no future in it for himself. Nor did he defy his wife and try to maintain his friendship with the Shaws. He died at sixty-eight in Paris in August of 1946. Shaw, ninety then and three years a widower, heard the news over the BBC.

Lillah McCarthy's loyalty to Shaw remained firm: it was, said Sir Herbert Tree, one of her greatest charms. Shaw had written *Annajanska* to cheer her in 1917; but despite its twelve performances and engagements in *The Wandering Jew* and *Blood and Sand* in 1920 and 1921, Lillah's career for all purposes had ended with Barker's defection. She still dreamed of a comeback, however. She was the first to extract a copy of *Heartbreak House*, the play Shaw felt "extraordinarily reluctant" to let go; and she immediately wanted the part of the eighteen-year-old Ellie Dunn. Shaw vetoed the idea promptly. Mrs. Campbell wanted to play Ellie Dunn, Lena Ashwell wanted to play Ellie Dunn, everyone wanted to play Ellie Dunn—and why? Because Ellie played herself. Besides, it was ridiculous—Lillah McCarthy, a ripe Siddonian heavy, left a spiritual bride in the arms of the ancient mariner. But Lillah fought long and hard for Ellie Dunn, feeling that if this part slipped out of her grasp, her long relationship with Shaw in the theatre would be over. And although she became Lady Keeble (every actress's dream) in 1922, she fought for *Saint Joan* too, promising to go into management again if Shaw would let her have it. But Sybil Thorndike was already in management, Lillah saw, and "in the fulness of her powers"; and Lillah failed again. She would have played Joan, she thought, "as a simple girl moved to superhuman strength through inspiration": she neither knew nor cared whether Shaw shared this vision. Shaw did not seem to, writing to Bertha Newcombe that people who attributed Joan's powers to inspiration from above were anti-feminists unwilling to admit that women had the same abilities as men.[24] But Sybil Thorndike was in management, and Shaw this time refused to "knock the stuffing" out of the play with a forty-eight-year-old Saint Joan, friendship or no friendship.

Lillah and Shaw continued to talk about plays, but Shaw was generally discouraging, telling her, for example, that Ann Whitefield and *Androcles* had dated terribly and were unsuitable for comebacks, and that *Too True to Be Good* had only two rowdy girls and a silly old lady—nothing that would interest her. When he did offer her Queen Phillippa in the lively but slight one-act *Six of Calais*, she refused; and Shaw retorted that nothing now would convince him that she meant to desert her fireside for the drudgery of the theatre. And so Lillah had been right about Ellie Dunn, for she never played Shaw again. He often discouraged meetings between them also, pleading that he was not the man he used to be; and of course she scolded him roundly for such a notion. Her autobiography published in 1933 had as its motto "Let us now praise famous men in general and Shaw in particular," for it had been men ("bless their generous spirits") who had helped her to find herself and lead her to the things she loved. Only, perhaps, in stating, "Truth never comes out of the head: if it ever comes out at all, it comes out of the heart" did she reveal a fundamental difference with Shaw.

Eventually Elizabeth Robins discovered that when Shaw was not being provocative he could be a useful person. The extent of her capitulation may be judged by the fact that she not only asked Shaw to criticize the manuscript of her autobiography *Both Sides of the Curtain*, but actually prefaced the book with his letters. Or perhaps it was partly astuteness, since Shaw's name could sell just about anything. She did not follow his advice, of course—or perhaps could not: what Shaw called her "mania for secrecy" made *Both Sides of the Curtain* one of the least revealing autobiographies ever published.

Their early clash had risen, after all, from similarity rather than opposition of character. Both were puritans, contemptuous of material and sensual gratification. After her youthful marriage to George Parks, Elizabeth avoided marriage dexterously; Shaw himself said that had he not found the institution ready-made he never would have invented it. Both were, however, philanderers, provoking emotion which they had no intention of gratifying. Sir Herbert Tree, William Archer, Henry James, and John Masefield were only a few of the beautiful Elizabeth's conquests. Both had primal loyalties which prevented normal relationships with the opposite sex. Elizabeth's attachment to her brother Raymond was overt; Shaw's attachment to a mother image largely subconscious. Both could be cruel, aloof, ascetic. Both feared and resisted sex. Both lived simply—Elizabeth giving away much of her money to young women in want of an education, Shaw, for all his wealth, scorning most self-indulgences. Both were idealists. Both were in the van of causes. Both were propagandists, Elizabeth finding her true voice in the fight for votes for women. Both were moral, as only Victorians deep-dyed with the belief in work, productivity, usefulness, and the triumph of individual will can be. Both, finally, were alike in durability: Elizabeth lived, like Shaw, to ninety-four, maintaining her vitality as successfully as he. Shaw, however, became a world-famous figure; Elizabeth Robins a name known to scholars of the theatre or the woman's movement of 1909–18. Of course, Shaw was a genius. Another factor, however, divides them. Whether propagating the ideas of Marx, Ibsen, Nietzsche, Wagner, Strindberg, or Bergson, Shaw spoke as an original force, whereas Elizabeth wrote under a male pseudonym and thought of herself as a medium for transmitting the ideas of Ibsen, rather than as a creative artist in her own right.[25] As the obscurity of her autobiography indicates, Elizabeth Robins lacked a clear conception of herself as an individual, whereas the ego of G.B.S. (not Shaw) was gigantic.

Bertha Newcombe best illustrated the truth of Shaw's lifelong maxim: satisfaction is death. Never having been satisfied, her feeling for Shaw never died. Unmarried in 1918, she was still attempting assignations, using Charles Charrington as the go-between. At this new eruption of interest, Shaw recognized at last that Bertha, like Flora Finching, had never really adjusted to the fact that he had married. Begging Charrington somehow to rid Bertha of this lunacy, Shaw explained his predicament. Just as Janet had not been an amoeba who could divide herself among a dozen suitors, so he could not divide himself up for all the women who desired, or thought they desired, him. But of all the women Shaw had tantalized, Bertha Newcombe had been the most susceptible, the most hopeful. "Your memories terrify me," Shaw wrote her in 1925, trying to shake off this specter of the past who still haunted him. "Thank God there will be no letters."

In postwar England, where the voice of the phallus, loudly transmitted through the celebrant of "blood," D. H. Lawrence, was heard more and more in the land, Shaw's asceticism seemed more and more out of place. So too in a world of lost values did his insistence upon work and will and evolutionary progress seem dated and unattractive. Like most prophets caught in the trough between the cultural wave that shaped their thought and the wave of the future that might realize it, Shaw began to flounder creatively, and fell back upon repeating his original ideas. Because these ideas had lost much of their vital connection to current thought, however, the characters who realized them in his plays became increasingly bizarre, the landscapes of his dramas more surreal, and his solutions to society's ills more visionary. *Too True to Be Good* in 1931 illustrated these fantastic qualities. Shaw's brave new world is a disintegrated Nowhere of half-naked sunbathers, swearing and obscenity, kissing and cocktails, promiscuity and boredom, cynicism and self-indulgence: a world in which war has shot to hell morals, manners, creeds, purpose, and design. Shaw's answers to this chaos are, as usual, personal organizational genius (in the person of Private Meek, who will perhaps inherit the earth), sexual renunciation (by the Patient, who will found a sisterhood), and the hope that somewhere, someday, there may be a Union of Federated Sensible Societies. Charlotte reported after its performance at Malvern in 1932 that the women loved it and the men loathed it; if true, the women loved it because Shaw once again put his faith in women of action who would eventually help "the lost dogs" home.

Women had had an amazing influence upon Shaw's mind and creativity from the beginning—amazing, because Shaw considered himself a man of action in the sphere of public affairs, an area not notable for its feminine population. This influence can largely be explained by the fact that of the two major social issues confronting Shaw as a young man— the emancipation of the working classes and the emancipation of women —Shaw the artist identified more with the latter. While he never renounced his Marxism, and insisted to the end that equality of income was the only sane social solution, he had little confidence in or empathy for the masses. With the exception of a handful of characters like Doolittle, Drinkwater, and Androcles, the working classes are conspicuously absent from his plays; and Eliza Doolittle, their most prominent representative, is transformed into a genteel young lady. On the other hand, strong or emancipated women are central to Shaw's plays, carrying the burden of Shaw's message of social reform in place of the proletariat. The quintessential Shavian hero—Dick Dudgeon, Marchbanks, Caesar, Blanco Posnet, Don-Juan Tanner—expresses Shaw's preference for disinterested moral vision over mundane gratification. When Shaw has Marchbanks reject Candida to go off into the night, he is approving the artist's need to be selfishly aloof from normal human affairs. When Caesar rejects Cleopatra's wiles, he acts out Shaw's belief that the great leader understands everyone but fraternizes with no one. There is little social realism in these heroes: they illustrate the timeless isolation of the leader, poet, and prophet. But every time Shaw put a strong woman onstage, he was making a politically progressive point, as well as reflecting an actual social struggle. Lady Cicely's rejection of marriage and Joan of Arc's military genius are feministic statements about women's nature and potential.

While actual women had little philosophical influence over Shaw (indeed, there was no feminine philosophy), they exerted a strong pragmatic influence upon his art. He was particularly susceptible to suggestions from women, women of his acquaintance inspired many of his female characters, and he created more roles for particular actresses than for actors.

Jenny Patterson, for example, inspired Blanche Sartorius in his first play, *Widowers' Houses*.

The New Woman of Ibsen, as well as Shaw's relationships with Jenny and Florence Farr, turned into *The Philanderer*, with Florence as Grace Tranfield and Jenny as Julia Craven.

Mrs. Warren's Profession was written in competition with Janet Achurch, who suggested the theme, while Vivie Warren was the result of Beatrice Webb's suggestion that he put a real modern young woman of the ruling classes on the stage, and resembled Beatrice herself. In one mood Shaw could call it "a crude melodrama . . . written to please Beatrice Webb." The role of Vivie would have gone to Janet had the censor not stepped in.

He wrote *Arms and the Man* for Florence's season at the Avenue, based "the enigmatic Louka" on her personality, and later told Archer that Raina was his version of Annie Besant.

Annie encouraged him to expand his Ibsen lectures for the Fabian: the result was *The Quintessence of Ibsenism*.

Although he claimed that the Strange Lady in *The Man of Destiny* was "a confection," his description of her appearance and manner is a description of Ellen Terry, and he meant the play for Ellen and Irving at the Lyceum.

Mrs. Clandon of *You Never Can Tell* was a composite of the advanced woman of George Eliot's day and certain personal traits of his mother.

Candida was created for Janet Achurch, although he gave as his models Ellen Terry, Mrs. H. M. Stanley, and Mrs. Ormiston Chant.

Captain Brassbound's Conversion was Shaw's gift to blessed Ellen. Lady Cicely, however, was in part drawn from Mary Kingsley, the explorer, and Charlotte's sister, Mary Cholmondeley. Shaw also had Mary Cholmondeley in mind when he wrote *The Intelligent Woman's Guide to Socialism and Capitalism*.

He wrote *Major Barbara* for Eleanor Robson.

Lillah McCarthy turned out to be the very Ann Whitefield he had imagined. In turn he created for her Jennifer Dubedat and Lavinia; Lina Szczepanowska and the Dark Lady (neither of which she played); and wrote *Fanny's First Play* and *Annajanska* especially for her. He wrote *The Dark Lady of the Sonnets* at the suggestion of Dame Edith Lyttelton.

Charlotte was responsible for reminding Shaw that there might be a play in the situation of an overworked doctor who has to choose between saving two lives on the basis of each patient's human worth. The doctor might be faced with—a dilemma? Shaw listened without comment; the next afternoon he was writing in his notebook.

Why not do a play about Saint Joan, suggested Charlotte when he was lost for inspiration. He did it.

Lena Ashwell was astonished to hear that Captain Shotover and *Heartbreak House* had evolved from her stories about her sailor father. Written for Ellen O'Malley, surely Ellie Dunn, the young, spiritual bride of the aged Shotover, was a version of the young Erica Cotterill's infatuation for the much older Shaw. And the handsome, haughty Lady Utterword a version of the handsome, haughty Virginia Woolf who visited the Shaws and the Webbs in Sussex when Shaw was at work on the play, and with whom, of course, he fell in love.[26]

Beatrice Webb deplored the frivolity of *Fanny's First Play*. Shaw turned serious and followed it with his Christian fable, *Androcles and the Lion.*

Great Catherine went straight into the hands of Gertrude Kingston, for whom it was written.

Mrs. Patrick Campbell provoked Cleopatra (although Yeats insisted that she was a version of Florence in her Egyptian phase), Eliza Doolittle (patently a joke to force the exquisitely spoken and gowned actress to imitate a working-class cockney), Mrs. Juno in *Overruled*, Hesione Hushabye, the Serpent in *Back to Methuselah*, and Orinthia.

Shaw's daily encounters with the postmistress of Ayot St. Lawrence suggested the delightful *Village Wooing.*

Writing *The Millionaires* Shaw had both Edith Evans and Katharine Hepburn in his eye to play Epifania Ognisanti di Parerga, and based the character of his wealthy "born boss" with a social conscience on Beatrice Webb.

Considering the great influence of women on Shaw and their weight as dramatic characters it is perhaps strange that his attitude toward them is often ambivalent. Audiences walking out of *Man and Superman* today are just as puzzled as they were in 1905. After the laughter and the splendor of the rhetoric has faded, the fact remains that Shaw has presented Ann Whitefield as a very threatening woman. Tanner's capitulation in the last fifteen minutes is not enough to balance the terror with which he has fled Ann through the entire play, nor is it enough to generate real sympathy for Ann. For while Shaw grants that courtship, marriage, and progeny are a woman's business and that women must pursue their business with skill and energy, he fears and dislikes romance, marriage, and sex; and the message we receive is thus contradictory, despite the "happy ending." The message is usually ambivalent when a Shavian character capitulates to passion or marriage. Is Candida really admirable? Did Gloria Clandon do the right thing in forgetting her feminism for Valentine? What does Shaw really think of Cleopatra, Julia Craven, Blanche Sartorius, Jennifer Dubedat, Hesione Hushabye, Lady Utterword, Judith Anderson, Mrs. George, Sweetie, and Z? Does he like them, or doesn't he? Renunciatory characters, on the other hand, whether male or female, are either clearly in Shaw's good graces or generate the energy of their plays: Vivie Warren, Marchbanks, Dick Dudgeon, Caesar, Lady Cicely, Juan Tanner, Undershaft, Lina, Higgins, Ellie Dunn, and Saint Joan— and it was a significant contribution as a playwright that he made women renunciators as well as men. As a reasonable man, Shaw of course granted that sex, marriage, and child-raising were for the present inevitable institutions. He sacrifices many characters to them, while making it clear, however, that his victims are renouncing freedom, tranquillity, and probable greatness. Above all, they are renouncing the possibilities of the unknown: exchanging anticipation for reality, and becoming for satisfaction. Shaw finds it very difficult to integrate love, sex, and marriage with the kind of spiritual aloofness that in his mind generates the superman.

Certainly his life demonstrated this fact. He claimed to divide work and romance into airtight categories, boasting that the first made him all but invulnerable to the second—never really acknowledging the great impact that his various relationships with women had upon his work. He could not integrate mind and passion in his dealings with women. He could neither love nor respect Jenny Patterson, who, because of her passion for him, he branded as little better than a prostitute. He could love but ultimately neither respect nor marry Florence Farr. (It is perhaps significant that he reduced these two women only to initials in his diary.) He adored Ellen Terry, but could not bring himself to know her in the flesh lest somehow their "lower centers" should spoil the higher friendship. He could marry and respect Charlotte, but not maintain a normal sexual relationship with her. He both loved and hated Stella Campbell: loved her as his Mother of Angels, feared her as a siren. Molly Tompkins' ardors both attracted and distressed him. He was the best companion in the world, thought Lillah McCarthy; he could be, because this kind of relationship did not threaten his celibacy: the message was, like his attitude toward his renunciatory characters, unconfused. Certainly he was one of the most frustrating lovers in the world, for faced with passion he veered between the extremes of fear and ecstasy, making his behavior as ambivalent as his attitude toward sex and love in his plays. Shaw does not satisfy, he stimulates, said Lillah wisely of the man who feared that satisfaction was death.

As he grew older, the ecstasy understandably vanished. "I am a man of the most extraordinary hardness of heart," Shaw told an audience in 1927; and this austerity became increasingly apparent in later years. "Heilige Elisabeth: bitte für mich," he had petitioned Elizabeth Robins in Tannhäuserian mood long ago. Dear Sister Laurentia: pray for me, he now begged of the Abbess of Stanbrook, whose spiritual counsel and example refreshed him in the years following their first meeting in April

1924. Although he flourished his cloven hoof conspicuously and had no intention of renouncing his "heresies" for the benefit of the Catholic nun (accusing her typically when she disagreed with him of being heretical herself), he found great solace in writing as "Brother Bernard" to this woman whose unworldly existence touched the chord of unworldliness in his own nature. Eventually her shocked and angry response to his *Adventures of a Black Girl in Her Search for God* disappointed him; yet for a time it seemed as though he had found his Virgin Mother at last.[27]

In his eighties he continued to be strictly regular in his work. Between breakfast and lunch each day he methodically wrote an average of 1,500 words on blocks of green-tinted paper. Unobtrusive, reverent, "like a spring wind around a goat" as Rilke once described her, Charlotte devoted herself to the comfort of G.B.S. She had long ago abandoned any idea of sharing his work or achieving anything important on her own. Conscious of this, Shaw made amends by humoring her in everything. Peace was all. Lillah McCarthy thought that Charlotte always got her way: if she did not want to see people, for example, they did not see them; when she wanted to travel, they traveled; if she did not want G.B.S. to talk politics over lunch, he dropped the subject. Yet there was a sense in which they were strangers.

He had never belonged to literary sets, and did not now; and was considered out-of-date and a crank by the current avant-garde. The number of his intimates dwindled, and he did not attempt to replace them. He was often silent and abstracted. He rarely lost his temper, however, and despite the glare of publicity that attended his every move, did not really care much for his fame. He did not care much for visitors either (though he generously suffered their intrusions), and acquired the habit of conspicuously pulling out his watch and consulting it, or suddenly exhibiting great solicitude lest his guests be caught by the dark.

To Blanche Patch, his secretary, he appeared not to care for anything that other people cared for, and seldom spent an afternoon or evening simply enjoying himself. Miss Patch noted this aloofness with curiosity and, it must be said, disapproval.[28] She watched him dip bits of bread into the vegetable soup that began his lunch, carry them carefully to the French windows, toss them onto the lawn for the birds, and return to the table without waiting to watch the birds swoop down to peck at them. His was a peculiarly cold-blooded kind of philanthropy, she decided; and indeed it seemed the philanthropy of the man who wrote great love letters without particularly caring to be loved. His one indulgence became food, and Mrs. Laden the cook had to scour the countryside for twenty-five miles around in the chauffeur-driven Rolls-Royce in search of the sweetest butter, the thickest cream, the rarest fruits, the finest nuts and cheeses. Meals occupied six and a half hours of the day. He had always loved sweets, and after Charlotte's death indulged more and more in his favorite ices, sundaes, chocolate biscuits, and highly sweetened desserts. Mrs. Laden rarely saw him between meals without a huge piece of thickly iced cake in his hand, and often in the evenings she would discover him sitting alone, spooning up great mouthfuls of sugar or honey from a bowl. At the same time, every calorie in every meal was counted out in the kitchen, and every morning he stepped on the scales to assure himself that his weight had not varied by an ounce.[29]

As the years slipped by more and more swiftly, time became more and more of a luxury. How to hoard precious hours for work? Perhaps if he skipped lunch . . . . Money too seemed to be slipping away. He developed a phobia about the surtax, and was sure that he would be penniless on the morrow. Charlotte's death on 12 September 1943 after a long and debilitating bone disease untied one of the strongest knots that bound him to the world. But still he talked and wrote on.

In 1945, after conquests, disappointments, suicide attempts, financial difficulties, and a divorce from Laurence Tompkins, Molly, now forty-eight, wrote to Shaw from New York offering to come to Ayot for an extended visit. Terrified, Shaw vetoed the idea energetically. "What a monstrous way to misconstrue my letter," Molly raged back. "Come and live with you indeed! Do you think I would give up the serenity of my independence to live with anybody on earth—and be responsible to them for my time and thoughts—even you? Hell no!" She had been thinking, she assured him, of no longer a stay than a month or so. "It would have given you pleasure and satisfaction to have me with you as I am now. It would have been an infinite pleasure to see you and talk to you now that I could talk without being dazed by the violence of my desire for you. . . . I am ashamed of you for being afraid. Only fear could cause such a violent reaction to my modest suggestion. . . . As to the village, darling, you can't think they would suspect me of sleeping with you?"

But Shaw remained adamant, and called her suggestion "inconsidered." It was not the village that worried him, but the insult to Charlotte's memory. Molly wrote to assure him that she had "considered":

> I didn't like Charlotte—she didn't give me much chance to and I never seem to have time to get to know women well enough to know whether I liked them or not. But I do know how very much you cared for Charlotte, and also the slight sense of guilt of the man who is loved more than he loves has, and could not have done anything to hurt her. If I had thought that my visit might by any chance have been mistaken for a readventure I would not have dreamt of coming.

She had wanted to come only because when she could not talk to him, she felt a little lost. "One thing you have never understood is that you are two B Shaws to me," she explained. "It is exciting to know the Great

Man, and bray about it a little. . . . Anyway I have far less interest in him than I have in the B. Shaw that gave my body and my mind and my heart peace when I lay by the side of a river or a lake, with him in Italy, or walked the Baveno Road with him. I don't want either now. The Great Man or my beloved of the Baveno Road. I wanted a short visit with somebody I could be as free as air with . . . . Somebody that you loved and who in spite of themselves loved you. And with the solid background of that love behind you (and me) there would be no awkward snags because one or the other of us wanted (or thought they did) something the other didn't have to give. I don't want the Baveno Road in fact again. I will have it always deep and sweet in my heart."[30]

Shaw was now eighty-nine, but still not taking any chances with sirens. Had their love been consummated? Their letters are as ambiguous as Shaw himself. There were the hoarded bodily possessions that she had stolen from him "on the road to Baveno and on other roads to paradise through the same district." There was Molly's admission that he gave her body peace. There was the violence of her desire for him. Peter Tompkins, Molly's and Laurence's son, remembered Shaw as a wonderfully warm man, and believes that the trunkful of his mother's letters to Shaw he read before his mother burned them offered positive proof that their love had been passionately physical. Yet there was the thing that "the other didn't have to give," and Molly's assurance that she could not have done anything to hurt Charlotte, and Shaw's triumphant, ". . . you thought that when you had secured your Ogygia and lured me to its shores you could play Calypso to my Odysseus and make a hog of me. Arent you glad you didnt succeed?"

"You are talking to a man who is three-quarters a ghost," the ethereally pink and white Shaw joked to a spiritualist at ninety-two. Despite failing eyesight and hearing, however, Shaw remained active until, pruning a dead branch in his garden at Ayot in September 1950, he slipped and fell, fracturing his thigh. He survived that operation and another performed when his prostate gland failed; but decided that at last he had had enough, if only his damnable vitality would let him die. In the dark early morning hours of 2 November he finally willed it to desert him.

Acknowledgments

I WOULD LIKE TO acknowledge the assistance and encouragement I have received in my work from both individuals and organizations, with thanks first of all to the American Council of Learned Societies for a 1976–77 Research Fellowship and to the University of Wisconsin-Whitewater for released time for study. I am grateful also to the staffs of the following libraries and collections for permission to use and quote manuscripts: the British Library; the Humanities Research Center of the University of Texas at Austin; the Enthoven Collection, Victoria and Albert Museum; the Bernard F. Burgunder Collection, Cornell University Library; the Houghton Library, Harvard, and the Harvard Theatre Collection; the Special Collections of the University Libraries, State University of New York at Buffalo; the Ellen Clarke Bertrand Library, Bucknell University; the Mugar Memorial Library, Boston University; the State Historical Library, Madison, Wisconsin; the University of Victoria Library; the Regenstein Library of the University of Chicago; the De Coursey Fales Collection, New York University Library; and the Henry W. and Albert A. Berg Collection of the New York Public Library.

I am also grateful to the following societies or persons for permission to quote from unpublished materials: The Society of Authors on behalf of the Bernard Shaw Estate; the Shaw Academic Advisory Committee; Bischoff and Company (Ellen Terry); the Society of Antiquaries of London (May Morris); Edward Craig, Esquire (Edward Gordon Craig); the National Trust; Peter Tompkins (Molly Tompkins); the Honorable Mrs. Mabel Smith, Trustee of Backsettown (Elizabeth Robins); Curtis Brown, Ltd. and Bartlett & Gluckstein, Crawley & de Reya (Mrs. Patrick Campbell); Francis B. Levetus, O.B.E. (Janet Achurch and Charles Char-

Acknowledgments

rington); Letcher & Son (Dame Ethel Smyth); and Dan H. Laurence, Literary and Dramatic Advisor to the Estate of Bernard Shaw.

Of the many individuals who have corresponded, loaned materials, or submitted to interviews I would particularly like to thank Ellen Pollock, Peter Tompkins, Professor Frederick McDowell, Lois Garcia, Francis B. Levetus, O.B.E., Dame Rebecca West, Raymond Mander and Joe Mitchenson, Mrs. Molly Thomas, Mrs. Ann M. Elder Jackson, Professor Josephine Johnson, and Jane Connor Marcus. My research time in England was brightened by the courtesies and kindnesses of Michael Holroyd; Mrs. Roma Woodnutt of the Society of Authors; playwright Don Taylor; the staffs of the British Library, the Theatre Museum, and the Enthoven Collection; Maureen Risik, editor, and Amanda Hamblin, formerly of Hodder & Stoughton, Ltd.; and the hospitable curators of Shaw's Corners, Ayot St. Lawrence, Beryl and John Whiting. To Ray Ruehl of the American School in London, whose ready camera and readier wit enlivened so many scholarly excursions, my special thanks.

I am indebted to Elsie Merkel McCullough and Donna Lewis for help with proofreading, typing, and Xeroxing.

Very special thanks to Lisa Drew, my editor at Doubleday, for her continued assistance, advice, and encouragement. To the students of my Shaw seminar, fall semester 1978, my thanks for making every session a challenge. And finally, my deep gratitude to Dan H. Laurence, Literary and Dramatic Advisor to the Estate of George Bernard Shaw, who from the beginning contributed materials, information, introductions, advice, and encouragement with truly Shavian generosity.

Bibliography

WORKS BY BERNARD SHAW

Bernard Shaw and Mrs. Patrick Campbell: Their Correspondence. Edited Alan Dent. London: Victor Gollancz, 1952.

Collected Letters: 1874–97, 1898–1910. Edited Dan H. Laurence. London: Max Reinhardt, 1965, 1972.

Collected Plays. 7 vols. Edited Dan H. Laurence. New York: Dodd, Mead, 1975.

Diary. Transcript by Stanley Rypins from the shorthand original. Humanities Research Center, University of Texas at Austin.

Ellen Terry and Bernard Shaw: A Correspondence. Edited Christopher St. John. New York: G. P. Putnam's Sons, 1932.

Florence Farr, Bernard Shaw, W. B. Yeats: Letters. Edited Clifford Bax. New York: Dodd, Mead, 1942.

Immaturity. London: Constable, 1930.

The Irrational Knot. London: Constable, 1930.

Love Among the Artists. London: Constable, 1930.

"Morris As I Knew Him" in May Morris, *William Morris: Artist Writer Socialist.* New York: Russell & Russell, 1966.

My Dear Dorothea: A Practical System of Moral Education for Females Embodied in a Letter to a Young Person of that Sex. New York: Vanguard Press, 1956.

Our Theatres in the Nineties. 3 vols. London: Constable, 1931.

Pen Portraits and Reviews. London: Constable, 1930.

The Perfect Wagnerite. London: Constable, 1930.

Bibliography

Platform and Pulpit. Edited Dan H. Laurence. London: Rupert Hart-Davis, 1962.

The Quintessence of Ibsenism. London: Constable, 1930.

Shaw on Theatre. Edited E. J. West. New York: Hill & Wang, 1958.

Short Stories, Scraps and Shavings. London: Constable, 1932.

Sixteen Self Sketches. New York: Dodd, Mead, 1949.

To a Young Actress: The Letters of Bernard Shaw to Molly Tompkins. Edited Peter Tompkins. New York: Clarkson N. Potter, 1960.

An Unsocial Socialist. London: Constable, 1930.

SELECTED LIST OF BOOKS CONSULTED

Archer, Charles. *William Archer: Life: Work and Friendships*. London: Allen & Unwin, 1931.

Archer, William. *Study and Stage: A Year Book of Criticism*. London: Grant Richards, 1899.

——. *The Theatrical "World" of 1893–1897*. 5 vols. London: Walter Scott, 1894–98.

Ashwell, Lena. *Myself a Player*. London: Michael Joseph, 1936.

Barrie, Sir James M. *Letters of J. M. Barrie*. Edited Viola Meynell. London: Peter Davies, 1942.

Beerbohm, Sir Max. *Around Theatres*. London: Rupert Hart-Davis, 1953.

——. *More Theatres: 1898–1903*. London: Rupert Hart-Davis, 1969.

Behrman, S. N. *Conversations with Max*. London: Hamish Hamilton, 1960.

Benson, Lady Constance. *Mainly Players: Bensonian Memories*. London: Thornton Butterworth, 1926.

Bentley, Eric. *Bernard Shaw: A Reconsideration*. New York: W. W. Norton, 1976.

Besant, Annie. *An Autobiography*. London: T. Fisher Unwin, 1910.

Campbell, Mrs. Patrick. *My Life and Some Letters*. New York: Dodd, Mead, 1922.

Craig, Edward Gordon. *Ellen Terry and Her Secret Self*. London: Sampson Low, Marston, 1931.

——. *Index to the Story of My Days*. New York: Viking, 1957.

Dent, Alan. *Mrs. Patrick Campbell*. London: The Museum Press, 1961.

Dervin, Daniel. *Bernard Shaw: A Psychological Study*. Lewisburg: Bucknell University Press, 1975.

Du Cann, C. G. L. *The Loves of George Bernard Shaw*. New York: Funk & Wagnalls, 1963.

Dukore, Bernard F. *Bernard Shaw, Director*. London: Allen & Unwin, 1971.

Dunbar, Janet. *Mrs. G. B. S.: A Biographical Portrait of Charlotte Shaw*. London: George G. Harrap, 1963.

Edel, Leon. *Henry James: The Treacherous Years*. Philadelphia: Lippincott, 1969.

Farmer, H. G. *Bernard Shaw's Sister and Her Friends*. Leiden: E. J. Brill, 1959.

Franc, Miriam Alice. *Ibsen in England*. Boston: The Four Seas Company, 1919; reprnt. Folcroft Press, 1970.

Henderson, Archibald. *Bernard Shaw: Playboy and Prophet*. New York: D. Appleton, 1932.

——. *George Bernard Shaw: Man of the Century*. New York: Appleton-Century-Crofts, 1956.

Henderson, Philip. *William Morris: His Life, Work and Friends*. London: McGraw-Hill, 1967.

Holroyd, Michael, ed. *The Genius of Shaw*. New York: Holt, Rinehart & Winston, 1979.

Huggett, Richard. *The Truth About Pygmalion*. New York: Random House, 1969.

Irving, Laurence. *Henry Irving: The Actor and His World*. London: Faber & Faber, 1951.

Johnson, Josephine. *Florence Farr: Bernard Shaw's New Woman*. Totowa, N.J.: Rowman & Littlefield, 1975.

Kapp, Yvonne. *Eleanor Marx*. 2 vols. New York: Pantheon Books, 1972, 1976.

MacCarthy, Desmond. *The Court Theatre 1904–1907: A Commentary and Criticism*. London: A. H. Bullen, 1907; Coral Gables, Florida: University of Miami Press, 1966, edited Stanley Weintraub.

——. *Portraits*. London: Putnam, 1931; reprnt. MacGibbon & Kee, 1955.

McCarthy, Lillah. *Myself and My Friends*. New York: E. P. Dutton, 1933.

Mackenzie, Midge. *Shoulder to Shoulder: A Documentary*. New York: Alfred A. Knopf, 1975.

Mander, Raymond, and Joe Mitchenson. *Theatrical Companion to Shaw*. London: Rockliff, 1954.

——. *The Lost Theatres of London*. London: Rupert Hart-Davis, 1968.

Manvell, Roger. *Ellen Terry*. New York: G. P. Putnam's Sons, 1968.

Marcus, Jane Connor. "Elizabeth Robins: A Biography." Doctoral thesis: Northwestern University, 1973.

Meisel, Martin. *Shaw and the Nineteenth-Century Theatre*. Princeton, N.J.: Princeton University Press, 1963.

Mitchell, David. *The Fighting Pankhursts*. New York: Macmillan, 1967.

Moore, George. *Hail and Farewell!* New York: D. Appleton, 1925.

Morris, William. *The Letters of William Morris to His Family and Friends*. Edited Philip Henderson. London: Longmans, Green, 1950.

Nethercot, Arthur H. *The First Five Lives of Annie Besant*. Chicago: University of Chicago Press, 1960.

Pankhurst, E. Sylvia. *The Suffragette*. London: Gay and Hancock, 1911.

Patch, Blanche. *Thirty Years with G.B.S.* New York: Dodd, Mead, 1951.

Bibliography

Pearson, Hesketh. *George Bernard Shaw: His Life and Personality*. New York: Harper, 1942; New York: Atheneum, 1963 (enlarged and revised).

——. *Beerbohm Tree: His Life and Laughter*. London: Methuen, 1956.

Prideaux, Tom. *Love or Nothing: The Life and Times of Ellen Terry*. New York: Charles Scribner's Sons, 1975.

Purdom, C. B., ed. *Bernard Shaw's Letters to Granville Barker*. New York: Theatre Arts Books, 1957.

——. *Harley Granville Barker*. London: Rockliff, 1955.

Robins, Elizabeth. *Ibsen and the Actress*. London: The Hogarth Press, 1928.

——. *Theatre and Friendship*. New York: G. P. Putnam's Sons, 1932.

——. *Both Sides of the Curtain*. London: William Heinemann, 1940.

——. *Raymond and I*. New York: Macmillan, 1956.

Steen, Marguerite. *A Pride of Terrys*. London: Longmans, Green, 1962.

Terry, Ellen. *Memoirs*. Edited by Edith Craig and Christopher St. John. New York: G. P. Putnam's Sons, 1932. Originally published as *The Story of My Life*. London: A. P. Watt and Son, 1908.

Tompkins, Peter. *Shaw and Molly Tompkins*. New York: Clarkson N. Potter, 1961.

Watson, Barbara Bellow. *A Shavian Guide to the Intelligent Woman*. New York: W. W. Norton, 1972.

Webb, Beatrice. *Our Partnership*. Edited Barbara Drake and Margaret I. Cole. London: Longmans, Green, 1948.

Webb, James. *The Flight from Reason*. London: Macdonald, 1971.

Weintraub, Rodelle, ed. *Fabian Feminist: Bernard Shaw and Women*. University Park: Pennsylvania State University Press, 1977.

Weintraub, Stanley. *Journey to Heartbreak: The Crucible Years of Bernard Shaw: 1914–1918*. New York: Weybright and Talley, 1971.

——, ed. *Shaw: An Autobiography: 1856–1898*. Vol. 1. New York: Weybright and Talley, 1961.

——, ed. *Shaw: An Autobiography: 1898–1950*. Vol. 2. New York: Weybright and Talley, 1970.

Winsten, Stephen. *Jesting Apostle: The Life of Bernard Shaw*. London: Hutchinson, 1956.

Yeats, William Butler. *The Autobiography of William Butler Yeats*. New York: Macmillan, 1916; New York: Collier Books, 1971.

——. *The Letters of W. B. Yeats*. Edited Allan Wade. London: Rupert Hart-Davis, 1954.

Notes

CHAPTER ONE (1876 - 1880)

1. The simile of something being as unconscious or natural as the taste of water in his mouth was a favorite of Shaw's: he used it in a letter to Alice Lockett of 8 October 1883 and in a filmed talk at Ayot St. Lawrence when he was ninety. The date of Shaw's leaving Dublin has been disputed. Dan H. Laurence gives it as 31 March 1876, four days after the death of his younger sister Agnes ("Yuppy") of consumption at Ventnor, Isle of Wight. The two events were connected, and it is likely that Mrs. Shaw now felt more able to help her son financially. Although Shaw stated in the 1921 Preface to *Immaturity* that he came to London because he proposed to be "king" of the realm of the English language, this was aftersight.

2. Bernard Shaw, *Sixteen Self Sketches* (New York: Dodd, Mead, 1949): III: 28–29.

3. 24 October [sic] 1875, but probably 24 February 1875. *Collected Letters* (hereafter *CL*), edited by Dan H. Laurence (London: Max Reinhardt, 1965): I: 11–12.

4. *Sixteen Self Sketches:* III: 28.

5. Bernard Shaw, *Immaturity* (London: Constable, 1930): xxvii.

6. *Sixteen Self Sketches:* III: 29.

7. Archibald Henderson, *George Bernard Shaw: Man of the Century* (New York: Appleton-Century-Crofts, 1956): 71. Stephen Winsten in *Jesting Apostle: The Life of Bernard Shaw* (London: Hutchinson, 1956) is negative about Lucy, an attitude countered by H. G. Farmer in *Bernard Shaw's Sister and Her Friends* (Leiden: E. J. Brill, 1959).

8. Diary. Transcript by Stanley Rypins from the shorthand original. Humanities Research Center (hereafter HRC), University of Texas at Austin.

9. 24 February 1875. *CL:* I: 8–11.

10. Bernard Shaw, *My Dear Dorothea* (New York: Vanguard Press, 1956).

Notes

11. The British Library has three volumes of letters from Elinor Huddart, who wrote under various pseudonyms such as Elinor Hume, Elinor Aitch, Louisa Rouile, and anonymously, and published *Via Crucis* (1882), *My Heart and I* (1883), *Commonplace Sinners* (1885), from 21 July 1878 to 8 July 1894. A continual topic of debate between them was the natures of men and women. Huddart argued that women see things differently from men, and that no male writer (except Dickens) had portrayed women realistically. After Shaw had compared women to children (his letters to her apparently do not survive, but much of their content can be deduced), she set him straight: "Women are not grown-up children, nor do they stand in the same relative development to men that children do towards them. The childhood of a man or of a woman means the same thing. A man may remember being a child, but cannot recall being a woman, and a youth cannot have a woman's sensibilities. He is sensitive from youthfulness, which is a different thing" (18 August 1884). Huddart also partially converted Shaw from George Eliot to Charlotte Brontë, whom she admired fervently, calling Eliot "too long in the sentence" and claiming that on "her banner is the name Charlotte Brontë." Shaw had torn *Jane Eyre* apart without having read the book; he did read *Shirley* under her influence in 1881.

12. Bernard Shaw, *Immaturity* (London: Constable, 1930). The novel was not published until the *Collected Edition* of Shaw's works in 1930. *Immaturity* was not his first attempt at a novel, however: he had begun in 1878 to outline *The Legg Papers* (see note, *CL:* I: 21–22).

13. "Woman—Man in Petticoats" in *Platform and Pulpit*, ed. Dan H. Laurence (London: Rupert Hart-Davis, 1962): 172–78. Originally a speech delivered 20 May 1927, and first published in the New York *Times Magazine*, 19 June 1927.

14. 15 January and 5 March 1880. *CL:* I: 26, 29–30.

15. 10 March 1881. Holograph. British Library.

16. Bernard Shaw, *The Irrational Knot* (London: Constable, 1930). Shaw, however, fell out of sympathy with Conolly's "sordid realism," and stated in 1946 that the novel had "carried me as far as I could go in Rationalism and Materialism."

17. Original typescript of an account of George Bernard Shaw and his family written by a friend of his early youth, a woman who, though called Ada Tyrrell Shaw, was no relation. Undated, with no title or heading, and extensive corrections and deletions in the autograph of Shaw. Berg Collection, New York Public Library.

18. Mabel Dolmetsch to H. G. Farmer, quoted from *Bernard Shaw's Sister and Her Friends:* 47.

19. 30 July 1881. Holograph. British Library.

20. Shaw was earning virtually nothing. Mrs. Shaw had £100 a year from a legacy of £1,500. Shaw's father sent from Dublin what he could—a pound to both Shaw and the Mar, 30 shillings, 15 shillings, etc.: letters from George Carr Shaw from 67 Jervis Street, Dublin, to Shaw: 15 and 29 August, 3 September 1884: British Library.

21. Preface to *The Irrational Knot*, dated 26 May 1905: xiv.

22. Preface to *Immaturity*, dated summer 1921: xli.

23. 4 December 1882. 67–8 Jervis Street, Dublin. Holograph. British Library. I have occasionally regularized punctuation and spelling in letters other than Shaw's when they might have interfered with understanding. In the case of Shaw's manuscript letters, I have followed the originals, even when they conflict with his later, preferred usages; in the case of Shaw's printed work, I have followed the publishers' usage.

Notes

CHAPTER TWO (1881 - 1885)

1. Alice Mary Lockett (1858–1942). Alice eventually married Dr. William Salisbury Sharpe, who operated on Shaw's foot in 1898; she remained friendly with Shaw, although they met very infrequently.

2. Quoted in *CL:* I: 62–63. Originally written in shorthand in a notebook.

3. "Woman–Man in Petticoats" in *Platform and Pulpit.* Primrose Hill is located north of Regent's Park, London, near Shaw's Osnaburgh residence; he often walked there.

4. Daniel Dervin's *Bernard Shaw: A Psychological Study* (Lewisburg: Bucknell University Press, 1975) analyzes Shaw's personality at length.

5. 9 September 1883. *CL:* I: 62–64.

6. Quoted in *CL:* I: 65.

7. 11 September 1883. *CL:* I: 65–67.

8. 18 September 1882. Holograph. British Library.

9. 11 September and 19 November 1883. *CL:* I: 65–67, 73.

10. Preface to *Immaturity:* xviii–xix.

11. "Letter to the Author from Mr. Sidney Trefusis" appended to *An Unsocial Socialist* (London: Constable, 1930): 264. Shaw called this "the last of the Novels of My Nonage," but claimed that the opinions of Trefusis anticipated those of Lenin.

12. Letters of 6 November 1883 to 26 September 1884. *CL:* I: 71–96.

13. 11 June 1883. Holograph. British Library.

14. 12 August 1884. *CL:* I: 93–94.

15. 16 October 1884. *CL:* I: 98–100.

16. Ten indignant letters from Alice Lockett to Shaw, dated 15 October to 27 December 1884, chart their final quarrel. Holographs. British Library.

17. 15 May 1885. Holograph. British Library.

18. The *World* (14 December 1892), reprinted in *Bernard Shaw: Collected Plays with Their Prefaces* (hereafter *Collected Plays*), edited by Dan H. Laurence (New York: Dodd, Mead, 1970–74), 7 vols.: I: 37–39.

19. "How William Archer Impressed Bernard Shaw" in *Pen Portraits and Reviews* (London: Constable, 1931): 1–32.

20. *Collected Plays:* I: 38.

21. 27 May 1885. Holograph. British Library.

CHAPTER THREE (1885 - 1887)

1. 3 December 1883. Holograph. British Library. Shaw was currently advocating marriage as a duty to Elinor, a philosophy he used in *An Unsocial Socialist,* which, she told him plainly, she found dull reading.

2. Evidence for Shaw's relationship with Jenny Patterson is derived from 373 letters to Shaw from Patterson (1886–88) in the British Library. Shaw's letters to Jenny apparently do not survive. Judy Musters told Dan H. Laurence that her mother, Arabella Gillmore, Jenny's executor, burned them after Jenny's death, and that Shaw, when informed, approved and agreed to destroy Jenny's. He apparently did destroy all but this cache.

Notes

3. It is interesting to compare here John Stuart Mill's experience as a young man of twenty when, in a state of mental crisis, he happened to read Marmontel's *Mémoires*. Coming to the passage in which Marmontel relates the death of his father, he was moved to tears, and from that moment relieved of much of his mental oppression, having thus participated vicariously in the death of his own father, James Mill, who was largely responsible for his mental state.

4. "Be faithful to me . . ." Patterson to Shaw on 28 May 1886, quoting passage from Shaw's letter to her of 22 September 1885; and letters of 20 August 1885 and Monday, 22 February 1888. Holographs. British Library. Their sexual relationship fluctuated violently, Jenny often promising only "platonics"; yet three years after their meeting, Jenny can talk about his ardor.

5. S. N. Behrman. *Conversations with Max* (London: Hamish Hamilton, 1960): 20.

6. 2 June 1885. 55, Great Russell Street, W.C. Holograph. British Library.

7. *CL:* I: 115.

8. 21 January and 8 June 1885. Kelmscott House, Upper Mall, Hammersmith. Holograph. British Library.

9. 22 September 1885. *CL:* I: 140.

10. Information about Shaw and May Morris in these two paragraphs derived from May's letters to Shaw of 5 May 1886, 12 June 1885, 18 December 1885, 16 February 1886, 21 July 1885, and 25 April 1886. Holographs. British Library.

11. Grace Black to Shaw. 24 and 25 May 1887. Holographs. British Library. Grace Gilchrist to Shaw. 26 March 1888, quoted from *CL:* I: 105–6. Shaw met Gilchrist for the first time on 11 March 1885 when he read an abstract of Marx's chapter on machinery from *Das Kapital* at her home (he had worked at it all day), although her mother was absent. Among those present were Sidney Webb, Sydney Olivier, and Edward R. Pease. Grace Black's name first crops up in Patterson's letters to Shaw in October 1886: on 20 October she says, "Tell Miss Black not to poach on my preserve."

12. Quoted in Arthur H. Nethercot, *The First Five Lives of Annie Besant* (Chicago: The University of Chicago Press, 1960): 213.

13. Annie Besant, *An Autobiography* (London: T. Fisher Unwin, 1910): 303.

14. Archibald Henderson dates their meeting in the spring of 1885, but Shaw's diary says for 21 January 1885: "Wednesday: lectured on 'Socialism' to the Dialectical Society. Made acquaintance of Mrs. Besant who was there with Robertson."

15. Quoted in Nethercot: 221.

16. Letters of 14 and 21 June, 20 July, and 17 December 1886. Holographs. British Library.

17. 14 February 1886. Holograph. British Library.

18. Friday [17 December 1886]. Holograph. British Library.

19. Quoted from Hesketh Pearson, *George Bernard Shaw: His Life and Personality* (New York: Harper & Brothers, 1942; New York: Atheneum, 1963): 112 (1963).

20. Bernard Shaw, *Short Stories, Scraps and Shavings* (London: Constable, 1932): 95–116.

21. Shaw to Stephen Winsten, quoted in C. G. L. DuCann, *The Loves of Bernard Shaw* (New York: Funk & Wagnalls, 1963): 57.

22. Saturday, 20 October 1888. Holograph. British Library. She observes in this

Notes

letter that Shaw her lover is becoming less her love every month; complains about his "deadly tempers"; and claims she won't bother him with many more letters.

CHAPTER FOUR (1887 - 1889)

1. The *Star* (19 September 1889). Reprinted in *London Music in 1888–89* (London: Constable, 1930): 215.

2. Farmer, quoting Hesketh Pearson in a letter to the author: 72.

3. Farmer: 59. The friend was Georgina Sime, who described Lucy in *Brave Spirits* (chapter 8), written with Frank Nicholson (privately printed, 1952).

4. Robert Louis Stevenson to William Archer. March 1886. Holograph. British Library. By April 1890, *Cashel Byron's Profession* had sold only 2,822 copies.

5. A. B. Walkley to Shaw. 7 October 1888. Holograph. British Library.

6. Dan H. Laurence in *CL:* I: 106.

7. "Socialism and Medicine" in *Platform and Pulpit:* 53.

8. Henry Stephens Salt, "Reminiscences of George Bernard Shaw" (March 1929). HRC, University of Texas at Austin. Published as "Salt on Shaw" in Appendix I to Stephen Winsten's *Salt and His Circle* (London: Hutchinson, 1951): 206.

9. "An Aside" in *Shaw on Theatre*, edited by E. J. West (New York: Hill and Wang, 1958): 219.

10. Diary. HRC, University of Texas at Austin.

11. 4 October 1887. *CL:* I: 175–76.

12. 24 February 1888. *CL:* I: 187–88.

13. "Acting, By One Who Does Not Believe in It" in *Platform and Pulpit:* 12–23.

14. 18 April 1889. *CL:* I: 208.

15. In 1884 a travesty called *Breaking a Butterfly, founded on Ibsen's "Nora,"* by Henry Arthur Jones and Henry Herman, had been staged at the Prince's Theatre on 3 March, and in 1885 an amateur performance took place in a hall on Argyle Street. I am indebted to Miriam Alice Franc's *Ibsen in England* (Doctoral thesis: University of Pennsylvania, published Boston: The Four Seas Company, 1919, reprnt. by the Folcroft Press, 1970).

16. Franc: 81.

17. Elizabeth Robins, *Ibsen and the Actress* (London: The Hogarth Press, 1928): 10–12.

18. Franc: 82.

19. "The Author's Apology" to "Still After the Doll's House" in *Short Stories, Scraps and Shavings:* 124.

20. 11 June 1889. *CL:* I: 213–14.

21. Shaw to Achurch. 23 March 1895. *CL:* I: 503–7.

22. Relatively little has been written about the Charringtons. My chief sources here are "A Doll's House and the Open Door" by Ashley Dukes, with two letters from Bernard Shaw, in *Theatre Arts Monthly*, XII (January 1928): 21–38; Charles Charrington's long letter to Shaw describing his wife's career, written after her death in September 1916, at the HRC, University of Texas at Austin; published and unpublished letters from Shaw to the Charringtons, also at Austin.

23. Laurence Irving, *Henry Irving: The Actor and His World* (London: Faber & Faber, 1951): 535.

Notes

24. Ellen Terry to Bernard Shaw. 28 March 1898. Holograph. British Library.

25. 17 June 1889. *CL:* I: 215–16.

26. 21 June 1889. Holograph. HRC, University of Texas at Austin.

27. On 29 June 1889, Shaw began to map out a play inspired by the "Achurch-Archer incident," *The Cassone* (unfinished, included in *Collected Plays*, VII). Shaw felt strongly that marriage had destroyed Archer's possibilities as a playwright; it had been "checkmate for years to come" (Shaw to Archer, 21 August 1893 in *CL:* I: 400–2). The quarrel between Shaw and Frances Archer is also alluded to in "How William Archer Impressed Bernard Shaw" (Ch. 2, note 19). Shaw's unlucky offense was undoubtedly in raving about his love for a married woman; Shaw's reaction was to deplore the limitations and conventions of marriage—and Mrs. Archer.

28. Published in 1889. Shaw severely edited this volume of essays by the seven members of the Fabian Executive, wrote the introduction, and contributed two chapters: "Economic" and "Transition."

29. Charrington to Shaw. September 1916. HRC, University of Texas at Austin. I am also indebted to Francis B. Levetus, O.B.E., F.I. Mech. E., for information about his grandparents, Janet Achurch and Charles Charrington, and his mother, Nora Charrington, and father, Edward Lewis Levetus. The Martins were a respectable family of solicitors; Charrington's marriage to Janet was considered a scandal, and he was cut by his family afterward (although he evidently received money from them from time to time). The subject of the Charringtons was taboo, Francis B. Levetus informs me, after his mother ran away, abandoning his father and himself, an infant.

30. William Archer to his brother Charles. 13 June 1889. In Charles Archer's *William Archer: Life: Work and Friendships* (London: Allen & Unwin, 1931). Archer also said of Janet's Nora: "She is really a delightful Nora—not ideal; her voice and tricks of utterance forbid that—but she *feels* the part right through, and is often very fine and even noble. In short she is *a* Nora and a very beautiful one, though not quite *the* Nora."

CHAPTER FIVE (1890 - 1891)

1. Henry S. Salt, "Reminiscences of George Bernard Shaw" in *Salt and His Circle*. Quotation from Shaw's "A Sunday in the Surrey Hills," *Pall Mall Gazette* (25 April 1888). Kate Salt was the sister of James Leigh Joynes, who had introduced Shaw to Salt.

2. Shaw had visited the Bayreuth Wagner Festival 25 July to 4 August 1889 to write an article for the *English Illustrated Magazine* that appeared in October as "Wagner in Bayreuth."

3. Shaw to Janet Achurch. 23 March 1895. *CL:* I: 503–7.

4. 28 January 1890. *CL:* I: 237–41. The Avelings, according to Shaw, virtually ran the periodical *Time* for E. Belfort Bax.

5. *Time* (February 1890), reprinted in *Short Stories, Scraps and Shavings*: 125–37.

6. Published in *Time* (March 1891). Written with Israel Zangwill and later issued by Eleanor and Zangwill as a 2d. pamphlet.

7. Florence Beatrice Farr was born 7 July 1860 at Bickley (incorporated with Bromley) ten miles from London in Kent. She married Edward Emery of the well-known actor family, whose sister Winifred married Cyril Maude. I am indebted for many facts of Florence Farr's life to Josephine Johnson's *Florence Farr: Bernard Shaw's New Woman* (Totowa, N.J.: Rowman & Littlefield, 1975).

8. *The Autobiography of William Butler Yeats* (New York: Macmillan, 1916; reprinted New York: Collier Books, 1971). References are to the 1971 edition: 93–95.

9. *Autobiography:* 80–81.

10. Shaw to Achurch. 6 January 1891. Typed letter, HRC, University of Texas at Austin. This is certainly the most accurate account of Shaw's meeting with Florence Farr, since closest to the actual time. By October 1890 he was persuading her to play *Rosmersholm* instead of *The Lady from the Sea;* the meeting probably took place in the early fall of that year.

11. "An Explanatory Word from Shaw" in *Florence Farr, Bernard Shaw, W. B. Yeats: Letters,* edited by Clifford Bax (New York: Dodd, Mead, 1942): ix–xii.

12. *Autobiography:* 81.

13. As Shaw told Janet Achurch in a letter of January 1891, Marion Lea had been going to do *Rosmersholm,* but abandoned the idea because she was hurt by a snub from Clement Scott in the *Telegraph.* Shaw later heard that Alma Murray planned to do *Rosmersholm,* but he told her that *The Lady from the Sea* was better. The situation was typical of Shaw's wheeling and dealing.

14. Bernard Shaw, "How William Archer Impressed Bernard Shaw": 21.

15. Wednesday and Thursday [28, 29 December 1886]. Holograph. British Library.

16. Shaw to Janet Achurch. 6 January 1891. Typed letter. HRC, University of Texas at Austin. Pages 3 and 4 are missing. Shaw's diary, not always reliable as to dates, however, gives the date of his writing the letter as 7 January.

CHAPTER SIX (1891)

1. 25 November 1890. *CL:* I: 271–73.

2. Shaw to Farr. 1 May 1891. *CL:* I: 295–97.

3. 30 March 1891. *CL:* I: 286–91.

4. *Autobiography:* 185.

5. *The Quintessence of Ibsenism* (London: Constable, 1930): 17.

6. 30 March 1891.

7. Shaw disliked the word "brilliant" since he felt it suggested "a glittering superficiality" in his criticism which he abhorred. He could not shake off the term then, however; and I use it now without any connotation of superficiality. He protested in *Sixteen Self Sketches,* VII.

8. *The Quintessence of Ibsenism:* 77. Critics used these terms before the *Quintessence,* of course, but Shaw added fuel to the fire.

9. Elizabeth Robins, *Both Sides of the Curtain* (London: William Heinemann, 1940).

10. Shaw to Robins 20 April 1891 and Shaw to Archer 23 April 1891. *CL:* I: 291–92, 294–95.

11. 30 April 1891. Holograph, written on eighteen small slips of paper. Fales Collection, New York University Library.

12. *Ibsen and the Actress:* 18–19.

13. 23 May 1891. Quoted in Laurence Irving's *Henry Irving: The Actor and His World:* 533.

14. "Charles Charrington's Account of His Wife, Janet."

Notes

15. As reported in the *Indian Daily News*. HRC, University of Texas at Austin. Shaw sent a copy to Ashley Dukes, the Charrington specialist, on 14 December 1929.

16. 30 March 1891. Information about the Charrington tour from "Round the World with 'A Doll's House'" in the *Pall Mall Gazette* (14 April 1892): 1–2.

17. 1 May 1891. *CL:* I: 297.

18. 4 May 1891. *CL:* I: 298.

19. 1 May 1891.

20. 20 August 1891. *CL:* I: 306.

21. 7 October 1891. *CL:* I: 313.

22. 25 and 26 October 1891. *CL:* I: 314–19.

23. 7 and 9 November 1891. *CL:* I: 320–23. Shaw sent his letter to Archer to Frank Harris by mistake, and vice versa. "Here let me say, parenthetically, that Archer was incorruptible as a critic," Shaw wrote in 1927 in "How William Archer Impressed Bernard Shaw": 25–27.

24. 9 November 1891. Holograph. Fales Collection, New York University Library.

25. *Both Sides of the Curtain:* Chapter 18. I am also much indebted to Jane Connor Marcus's thesis *Elizabeth Robins* (Northwestern University, 1973), which was lent to me by the author during this writing. Elizabeth Robins was born in Louisville, Kentucky, in 1862, died at Brighton in 1952. She went on stage at sixteen and toured with Edwin Booth and Lawrence Barrett, playing both minor and major roles. After her marriage ended, she went to Norway at the invitation of Mrs. Ole Bull, wife of the famous violinist, where she studied Norwegian intensively; then came to England.

26. 10 November 1891. Holograph. Fales Collection, New York University Library.

Chapter Seven (1892)

1. 28 January 1892. *CL:* I: 331–33.

2. 28 January 1892.

3. Herbert Beerbohm Tree to Shaw. 16 March 1892. Holograph. British Library.

4. *CL:* I: 344–46.

5. 29 June 1892 in *Ellen Terry and Bernard Shaw: A Correspondence* (hereafter *A Correspondence*) (New York: G. P. Putnam's Sons, 1932): 6–7. There must have been still another letter from Shaw to Terry prior to his of 24 June 1892, since in answer to Ellen's letter of 29 June he says, "If the others were really stiff (which I am disposed to deny) your replies were angelic."

6. *A Correspondence:* 8–9.

7. 5 July 1892. *CL:* I: 348–49. Shaw had seen *The Lady from the Sea* in May 1891, in a performance at Terry's Theatre of Eleanor Marx's translation directed by Edward Aveling, and featuring Rose Meller as Ellida—Shaw's "poor ungifted, dowdy, charmless young woman."

8. 21 April 1892. *CL:* I: 337–38.

9. 6 May 1892. *CL:* I: 340.

10. "Charles Charrington's Account of his wife, Janet." Actually the time of Ellen Terry's offer to take Nora is uncertain since Charrington's chronology is vague. He speaks as though it happened in Melbourne, but Terry was not in Melbourne.

11. Johnson: 73.

12. The phrase is James Webb's. See his *The Flight from Reason: Volume 1 of The Age of the Irrational* (London: Macdonald, 1971).

13. Quoted in Arthur H. Nethercot, *The First Five Lives of Annie Besant:* 283. Authentic versions of Annie Besant's conversion were, Nethercot points out, "Shawless," thus suggesting that the Shavian imagination had been active on this occasion.

14. 6 October 1892. Quoted in Elizabeth Robins, *Theatre and Friendship* (New York: G. P. Putnam's Sons, 1932): 72–73. Shaw made a point of explaining this somnambulism in an interview he concocted in the *Daily Chronicle* (27 February 1893) about the Charringtons' season at the Royalty beginning 4 March. The doctor had prescribed a twelfth of a grain. Between scenes Archer kept Charrington awake by talking to him and moving him about.

15. Quoted in *CL:* I: 106–7.

16. An interview drafted by Shaw in the *Star*, 29 November 1892. Reprinted in *Collected Plays:* I: 122–32.

17. March 1893. "The Author's Preface to the 1893 Edition of *Widowers' Houses*" in *Collected Plays:* I: 37–46.

18. 4 May 1893. The *World*.

19. 14 December 1892. *CL:* I: 372.

20. William Morris to J. L. Joynes. 27 December 1892. *The Letters of William Morris to His Family and Friends,* edited by Philip Henderson (London: Longmans, Green, 1950): 353.

21. For a more detailed discussion of Florence's participation in the Golden Dawn, see Josephine Johnson, Chapter 5: 70–99.

CHAPTER EIGHT (1893)

1. "Morris As I Knew Him" in *William Morris: Artist Writer Socialist*, vol. 2 (New York: Russell & Russell, 1966): ix–xl.

2. The content of their interview can be partly deduced from Shaw's and Robins's letters of 5 and 6 February.

3. Dated "Feb. 4 '93 (I mean 5th)." Typed copy. HRC, University of Texas at Austin.

4. 5 February 1893. *CL:* I: 379–81.

5. Typed copy. HRC, University of Texas at Austin.

6. 21 February 1893. Typed letter. HRC, University of Texas at Austin.

7. 22 February 1893. Holograph letter card. HRC, University of Texas at Austin.

8. 9 January 1893. Holograph post card. HRC, University of Texas at Austin.

9. 3 March 1893. *CL:* I: 385–86.

10. 3 March 1893. *CL:* I: 384–85.

11. 5 March 1893. Typed letter. HRC, University of Texas at Austin.

12. 6 April 1893. Holograph letter. HRC, University of Texas at Austin.

13. 27 April 1893. *CL:* I: 391–92.

14. 22 May 1893. Holograph letter. HRC, University of Texas at Austin. For Janet's being too proud to stoop to moneygrubbing, see Ashley Dukes, "A Doll's House and the Open Door," *Theatre Arts Monthly*, 12 (January 1928): 21–38. Other evidence, however, suggests that she "grubbed" for money quite actively.

Notes

15. 7 July 1893. *CL:* I: 397–98.

16. 2 May 1893. Quoted in Mrs. Patrick Campbell, *My Life and Some Letters* (New York: Dodd, Mead, 1922): 85.

17. Alan Dent, *Mrs. Patrick Campbell* (London: The Museum Press, 1961): 57.

18. 5 June 1893. *CL:* I: 396–97.

19. *The Philanderer,* completed 27 June 1893, in Volume I, *Collected Plays.*

20. Florence's novel was eventually accepted out of personal friendship by John Lane, London publisher of the *Yellow Book* and of Oscar Wilde, Richard Le Gallienne, etc., and appeared in the "Key Note" series with a frontispiece by Aubrey Beardsley depicting a faun. Interestingly, Shaw came to be often caricatured as a faun.

21. "Mr. Shaw's Method and Secret," letter to the *Daily Chronicle* (London: 30 April 1898) in *Collected Plays:* I: 267–71.

22. 4 September 1893. *CL:* I: 404.

23. Preface. 1902. *Collected Plays:* I: 231–66.

24. 30 October 1893. Holograph letter card. Fales Collection, New York University Library. Both Shaw and Robins had gone to hear a light opera, *Catarina,* performed at the home of Mrs. W. K. Clifford, the novelist.

25. Shaw later said that both Janet Achurch and Mrs. Theodore Wright were willing: Archibald Henderson: *Playboy and Prophet* (New York: D. Appleton, 1932): 358.

26. 14 November 1893. Holograph letter card. Fales Collection, New York University Library.

27. No date. Typed copy. HRC, University of Texas at Austin. Scrap of paper in William Archer's handwriting written out for Robins to copy. Fales Collection, New York University Library.

28. 20 November 1893. Holograph letter card. Fales Collection, New York University Library.

29. 12 December 1893. *CL:* I: 412–13.

CHAPTER NINE (1893 - 1894)

1. 23 November 1893. Holograph letter card. HRC, University of Texas at Austin. *The Wild Duck* was eventually performed for the first time in England by the Independent Theatre at the Royalty beginning 4 May 1894.

2. 2 December 1893. *CL:* I: 408–9.

3. *Autobiography:* 186.

4. Johnson: 61.

5. George Moore, "Ave" in *Hail and Farewell!* (New York: D. Appleton, 1925): 41–42.

6. Johnson: 62.

7. *Autobiography:* 186–87.

8. 29 March 1894. Holograph. Burgunder Collection. Cornell University Library.

9. *The Theatrical "World" of 1894* (London: Walter Scott, 1895): 91–93.

10. "Arms and the Man" (interview drafted by Shaw for the *Star,* 14 April 1894), in *Collected Plays:* I: 473–80.

11. Written at three fifty-five at the Charringtons' house. n.d. HRC, University of Texas at Austin.

12. 17 April 1894. *CL:* I: 424–25.

13. 1 January 1894. Holograph. HRC, University of Texas at Austin.

14. 15 April 1894. *The Letters of W. B. Yeats*, ed. Allan Wade (London: Rupert Hart-Davis, 1954): 230–31. On another occasion Yeats had called Todhunter's *A Comedy of Sighs* "a rambling story told with a little paradoxical wit."

15. The lone objector was R. Golding Bright, an office clerk aspiring to become a journalist, whom Shaw later made into a friend, entering into an extensive correspondence collected in *Advice to a Young Critic*. Bright had also hissed earlier at what he supposed was an allusion to the Royal Family.

16. Yeats, *Autobiography:* 187–88.

17. 11 May 1894. *CL:* I: 435.

18. *Autobiography:* 188.

19. 12 July 1894. *CL:* I: 451.

20. 2 July 1894. *CL:* I: 447–48.

CHAPTER TEN (1894 - 1895)

1. "A Confession of Their Crimes by Janet Achurch and Charles Charrington from the Cell of Inaction to which They Were Condemned in the Latter Half of the Year of Grace, 1893." From internal evidence, the account was perhaps written in 1900. Shaw sent it to Charrington buff Ashley Dukes 14 December 1929 with the note, "Dear Ashley Dukes—Another find!" HRC, University of Texas at Austin.

2. 24 April 1894. Typed letter. HRC, University of Texas at Austin.

3. 23 March 1895. *CL:* I: 503–7.

4. 4 December 1894. Holograph letter. HRC, University of Texas at Austin.

5. Undated. St. John Ervine dates the letter as 1898, but then says it was written when Lucy was living at Fitzroy Square "about the time when Mansfield was proposing to produce *Candida*." But Mansfield proposed to produce Candida in March of 1895.

6. Mabel Dolmetsch to H. G. Farmer, in *Bernard Shaw's Sister and Her Friends:* 88. The fact that *Arms and the Man*, like the rest of Shaw's plays, was typed at Miss Dickens's Typewriting Office may cast doubt on Lucy's reported effort—or she may have typed one draft.

7. 10 December 1894. Holograph postcard. HRC, University of Texas at Austin.

8. To an unidentified American woman. 1895. *CL:* I: 474–75.

9. 22 December 1894. *CL:* I: 471–72.

10. Shaw to Janet Achurch. 27 December 1894. Folkestone. Holograph letter. HRC, University of Texas at Austin.

11. 3 January 1895. Typed letter. HRC, University of Texas at Austin.

12. 8 January 1895. Typed letter. HRC, University of Texas at Austin.

13. *Our Theatres in the Nineties* (hereafter *OTN*) (London: Constable, 1931) I: 9–12.

14. In J. Comyns Carr's *King Arthur*. Reviewed 19 January 1895. *OTN:* I: 13–19.

15. 26 January 1895. *OTN:* I: 20–25.

16. A copy of the play exists in the British Library. Janet Achurch played it in Manchester at the Theatre Royal in May 1903.

17. 9 February 1895. Typed letter. HRC, University of Texas at Austin.

18. 7 January 1895. 28 Manchester Square Mansions, Dorset Street, W. Typed copy. HRC, University of Texas at Austin.

19. 22 February 1895. *CL:* I: 484–86.

20. 1 March 1895. *CL:* I: 488–93.

21. 6 March 1895. Holograph letter. HRC, University of Texas at Austin.

CHAPTER ELEVEN (1895)

1. Shaw to Janet Achurch. 9 March 1895. Typed letter. HRC, University of Texas at Austin; and Shaw to Mansfield. 9 March 1895. *CL:* I: 494–95.

2. 9 March 1895. 9 Overstrand Mansions. Holograph letter. Cornell University Library.

3. 12 March 1895. *CL:* I: 495–96.

4. Review of 16 March 1895: *OTN:* I: 63–69. Mrs. Campbell, who was quarreling severely with actor-manager George Alexander, left Pinero's play on 11 May to play in Sardou's *Fedora* at the Haymarket with Beerbohm Tree, claiming that Tree had a prior claim on her services.

5. 16 March 1895. *CL:* I: 498–500.

6. 20 March 1895. *CL:* I: 502–3.

7. This letter is dated 10 March 1895 in *A Correspondence:* 14. It is obviously a reply to Shaw, however; and is perhaps the letter he mentions in a letter of 20 March 1895 to Janet Achurch ("–Ellen Terry, who has just written me a letter about another matter"), and should therefore be dated 20 instead of 10 March.

8. *Autobiography:* 81–82. Spillikens was a favorite game of the witty and paradoxical Jane Austen, who had great deftness at it.

9. Shaw to Janet Achurch. 14 April 1896. *CL:* I: 624–27.

10. 23 March 1895. *CL:* I: 503–7.

11. 18 May 1895. New York *Dramatic Mirror.*

12. 27 March 1895. *CL:* I: 507–8.

13. Shaw to Janet Achurch. 3 April 1895. *CL:* I: 513–14.

14. Review of 30 March 1895. *OTN:* I: 76–83.

15. Preface to *The Theatrical "World" of 1894* by William Archer.

16. Dated 14 April 1895 but, as Dan H. Laurence suggests, probably an error since Shaw mentions the letter to Janet on 19 April, before a letter from New York could have reached him. Holograph letter. Quoted in entirety in *CL:* I: 523–24.

17. 5 April 1895. *CL:* I: 515–18.

18. 16 April 1895. *CL:* I: 519–20.

19. 28 April 1895. 104 W. 80th Street, New York. Holograph. British Library.

20. 14 April 1895. See note 16 above.

21. 5 April 1895.

22. Shaw quoted what he had written to Mansfield in a letter to Janet Achurch of 19 April 1895. *CL:* I: 520–22.

23. Janet Achurch sent Shaw a copy of a memorandum from Richard to Felix

Mansfield which stipulated that Richard Mansfield could no longer employ Janet that season, that she would keep the £100 advanced, as well as all amounts paid since, that she would pay her own passage home, and that Mansfield was paying £50 for *Alexandra* on account of royalties and 5 per cent if the play were produced until £1,000 in royalties had been paid. "THIS IS ALL AND EVERYTHING I CAN DO," wrote Mansfield. Shaw sent the memorandum to Charrington on 25 April 1895. HRC, University of Texas at Austin.

24. Quoted from the New York *Dramatic Mirror* of 18 May, and 1, 8, 15, and 22 June 1895.

25. Letters of 19 April and 3 May 1895. *CL:* I: 520–22; 532.

CHAPTER TWELVE (1895 - 1896)

1. Ellen Terry and Henry Irving destroyed almost all their intimate letters. The excerpts here are from letters dated 16 December 1885, 7 June 1887, undated fragment, and 3 June 1891. Quoted in Roger Manvell, *Ellen Terry* (New York: G. P. Putnam's Sons, 1968): 245–46.

2. Blanche Patch became Shaw's secretary in July 1920. See her *Thirty Years with G.B.S.* (New York: Dodd, Mead, 1951).

3. 7 December 1896. *A Correspondence:* 100–1. Wardell acted under the name "Charles Kelly." The marriage lasted about two years.

4. Marguerite Steen, *A Pride of Terrys* (London: Longmans, 1962). Steen believes she has proven that Irving was Ellen's lover. Ellen's biographer Roger Manvell and Irving's grandson, Laurence Irving, do not believe it.

5. I am indebted to Laurence Irving's *Henry Irving: The Actor and His World* for much of my information.

6. Manvell: 210.

7. Ellen Terry, *Memoirs*, edited by Edith Craig and Christopher St. John (New York: G. P. Putnam's Sons, 1932): 268–70. Originally published as *The Story of My Life* in 1908.

8. *CL:* I: 564–65. Shaw finished *The Man of Destiny* 24 August 1895.

9. *A Correspondence:* 16.

10. Shaw told Janet about the Strange Lady, adding: "However I have never seen you in it when writing it: indeed I havent seen anyone in it: it is a pure fantasy." Although he later claimed the same to William Archer, this was obviously tact for Janet's sake, since she badly needed employment.

11. *CL:* I: 608–10.

12. Tuesday, 24 March [1896]. Indianapolis, Indiana. This is one of the letters from the period November 1895 to May 1896 declared in *A Correspondence* to be missing, now in the British Library. As the editors of *A Correspondence* realized, it is impossible to duplicate in type Ellen's letters, which are "orchestrated" with dashes, squiggles, multiple underlinings, and exclamation marks to project her voice on paper. I have retained some of these markings in an attempt to convey the flavor of her style; yet for the sake of uniformity, have generally adopted the policy of *A Correspondence.*

13. Undated: late 1895. *CL:* I: 584–85.

14. 9 March 1896. *CL:* I: 609.

15. 26 March 1896. *CL:* I: 615–18.

16. 31 March 1896. *CL:* I: 618–20.

Notes

17. Bertha Newcombe, "Memories of Janet Achurch." 1928. HRC, University of Texas at Austin.

18. Shaw quoted Bertha's letter in one to Janet of 16 August 1895. *CL:* I: 544–45.

19. Shaw to Janet Achurch. 24 August 1895. *CL:* I: 545–49.

20. Bertha Newcombe to Ashley Dukes in 1928 after reading Shaw's letter of 24 August 1895 included with the Charrington correspondence. HRC, University of Texas at Austin. In *CL:* I: 546.

21. 6 and 8 November 1895. *CL:* I: 568, 568–69.

22. 14 November 1895. HRC, University of Texas at Austin.

23. "Memories of Janet Achurch" in *CL:* I: 568–69.

24. 23 December 1895. *CL:* I: 581–84.

25. To Janet Achurch. 24 May 1895. *CL:* I: 534–38.

26. Shaw to Elizabeth Robins. 2 and 4 December 1894. Holographs. Fales Collection, New York University Library.

27. Shaw to Heinemann about Halkett and Robins. 18 February 1896. *CL:* I: 599–602. Shaw to Charles Charrington. 18 and 27 February 1896. HRC, University of Texas at Austin.

28. To Amy C. Morant. 13 December 1895. *CL:* I: 574–75.

29. 29 January 1896. *CL:* I: 590–92.

30. 19 February 1896. *CL:* I: 602–6.

31. The phrase is Martin Meisel's. *Shaw and the Nineteenth-Century Theatre* (Princeton, N.J.: Princeton University Press, 1963).

32. On 6 April 1896, however, he told Ellen Terry that the clouds had rolled away from the second act of his new play, "leaving the view clear and triumphant right on to the curtain."

33. 14 April 1896. *CL:* I: 624–27.

34. *CL:* I: 624–27.

35. 25 May 1896. Holograph letter card. HRC, University of Texas at Austin. The name "Mimie" occurs several times in Shaw's correspondence with the Charringtons. Dan H. Laurence received information from a Mr. L. M. McLeod in 1972 to the effect that one of Janet's brothers in South Africa had a daughter raised by Janet in England. "This might very well identify the otherwise-unidentified 'Mimie' or 'Mimi' mentioned in Shaw's letter to Janet Achurch on 3rd April 1895," Laurence noted. I am indebted to Dan Laurence for copies of this correspondence, which identified a Captain Samuel Achurch as Janet's brother.

36. 6 April 1896. *CL:* I: 621–24.

CHAPTER THIRTEEN (1896)

1. 7 July 1896. *A Correspondence:* 26.

2. 7 and 10 July 1896. *A Correspondence:* 26–28.

3. N.d. *A Correspondence:* 30–31.

4. 18 September 1896. *A Correspondence:* 50–51.

5. Shaw to Terry. 21 September 1896. *CL:* I: 657–60. Terry to Shaw. 22 September 1896. *A Correspondence:* 55. Shaw to Terry. 22 September 1896. *CL:* I: 661–62.

6. 23 September 1896. *A Correspondence:* 58.

7. 25 September 1896. *CL:* I: 667–69.

8. 26 September 1896. "Blaming the Bard" in *OTN:* II: 204–12.

9. 25 September 1896. *CL:* I: 667–69.

10. 26 September 1896. *A Correspondence:* 63.

11. Terry to Shaw. 2 October 1896. *A Correspondence:* 64–65. Shaw to Terry. 2 October 1896. *CL:* I: 670–72.

12. 26 October 1896. Holograph. British Library. This and other portions of the letter are not printed in *A Correspondence.* In a destroyed letter, Shaw had evidently written mischievously about Kate Gurly. Ellen replied: "Oh, you dearest fellow—about Kate—must I, must I burn it?— There I've done it—quickly—before I'd be tempted—& it only takes a minute to tempt me."

13. Terry to Shaw. 19 October 1896. *A Correspondence:* 80. Shaw to Terry. 12 October 1896. *CL:* I: 675–78.

14. 7 September 1896. Holograph. HRC, University of Texas at Austin.

15. Beatrice Webb, *Our Partnership* (London: Longmans, Green, 1948): 90–91.

16. Itinerary recorded in both Shaw's and Charlotte's diaries for 1896. Shaw to Payne-Townshend. 21 September 1896. *CL:* I: 660. "Words are the counters . . ." from "The Religion of the Pianoforte."

17. 26 and 29 October 1896. *A Correspondence:* 82, 84. Shaw's letters from this period are missing, but on 12 October he had regaled her with a list of his love affairs.

18. 27 October 1896. *CL:* I: 686.

19. 5 November 1896. *CL:* I: 694–96.

20. 5 and 6 November 1896. Holograph. British Library. This portion of the letter is not printed in *A Correspondence.*

21. Saturday, 7 November 1896. Holograph. British Library. This portion of the letter is not printed in *A Correspondence.* Terry's statement about the cousin is oblique: "My cousin has done his duty by it"; but evidently she was trying to analyze Charlotte's character.

22. N.d., but from the contents 11 November 1896. Holograph. British Library. Not printed in *A Correspondence.* The "painter girl" is Nellie Heath, who was doing Shaw's portrait. The name "Lancelot" is a guess, for the word is almost illegible.

23. 16 November 1896. *CL:* I: 701–3.

24. 17 November 1896. *CL:* I: 703.

25. Terry to Shaw. 26 November 1896. Holograph. British Library. Shaw to Terry. 30 November 1896. *CL:* I: 704–6.

26. 24 November 1896. Holograph. British Library.

CHAPTER FOURTEEN (1896)

1. Shaw to Terry. 28 August 1896. *CL:* I: 642–46. Shaw on Janet's pregnancy: letter to Terry of 12 October 1896. *CL:* I: 675–78. A birth record either in the last quarter of 1896 or the first of 1897 does not exist for a Charrington or Achurch infant; a probable assumption is that Janet miscarried. Shaw's concern for her during the *Little Eyolf* run indicates that she was pregnant at that time.

2. 30 October 1896. *CL:* I: 687.

3. Charlotte Shaw to T. E. Lawrence. 17 May 1927. Holograph. HRC, University of Texas at Austin.

Notes

4. Shaw to Robins. 15 July 1896. Typed letter. Fales Collection, New York University Library.

5. *Fedora* by Victorien Sardou at the Haymarket Theatre, opening 25 May 1895; *Romeo and Juliet* at the Lyceum, opening 21 September 1895 (Irving and Terry were on tour in America); *For the Crown*, John Davidson's translation of François Coppée's *Pour la couronne* at the Lyceum, opening 27 February 1896; *Magda* by Hermann Sudermann, translated by Louis N. Parker, at the Lyceum, opening 3 June 1896; *The School for Scandal* by Richard Brinsley Sheridan at the Lyceum, opening 20 June 1896. Except for *Fedora*, Campbell appeared with Sir Johnston Forbes-Robertson, actor-manager.

6. "The Return of Mrs. Pat" (7 March 1896) and "The New Magda and the New Cyprienne" (6 June 1896) in *OTN*: II: 63–70, 152–58.

7. Mrs. Patrick Campbell, *My Life and Some Letters* (New York: Dodd, Mead, 1922): 145–50.

8. 24 November 1896. Holograph. British Library.

9. As Mercy Merrick in a revival of Wilkie Collins's *The New Magdalen* at the Theatre Metropole in suburban Camberwell. The play opened 28 October 1895, but Janet withdrew, ill with typhoid, shortly after. Shaw's review: 2 November 1895, *OTN*: I: 242–50.

10. 28 November 1896. "Little Eyolf" in *OTN*: II: 269–76.

11. 1 December 1896. *CL*: I: 707–8.

12. 12 December 1896 in *OTN*: II: 285–92. Shaw called Achurch the only loser, but said nothing about her alleged private negotiations with the syndicate which irritated Elizabeth Robins.

13. Dated 23 November 1896, but from Ellen's reference in the letter to Violet Vanbrugh in Shaw's review that day, probably 7 November, when he reviewed *Donna Diana* at the Prince of Wales Theatre; Sunday, 29 November 1896. Holographs. British Library.

14. Letters of 1 December 1896, holograph, British Library; 4 December, *A Correspondence*: 98–99; 5 December, *CL*: I: 708–9; 7 December, *A Correspondence*: 100–1; 7 December, *CL*: I: 710–12; 8 December, *A Correspondence*: 103; and 8 December, *CL*: I: 712.

15. 18 December 1896. Holograph letter card. HRC, University of Texas at Austin.

16. 12 October 1896. *CL*: I: 675–78.

17. 12 and 14 October 1896. *CL*: I: 674–75, 679.

18. Johnson: 81.

CHAPTER FIFTEEN (1896 - 1897)

1. Shaw's Preface to his *Three Plays for Puritans* states that in *The Devil's Disciple* he has reversed John Bunyan's proposition that there is a way to hell even from the gates of heaven, Marchbanks' discovery in *Candida*.

2. Letters of 19 October, *A Correspondence*: 80; 5 November 1896, *CL*: I: 694–96; 26 November 1896, *A Correspondence*: 95; 30 November 1896, *CL*: I: 704–6; 7 December 1896, *A Correspondence*: 100–1.

3. Letters of 19 February 1897, holograph, British Library; 23 February 1897, *A Correspondence*: 114.

4. 5 and 15 March 1897. 8 Ackers Street, Manchester. Holographs. University of Victoria Library.

5. 15 March 1897. *CL:* I: 736–37.

6. Shaw to Charrington. 18 March 1897. Holograph. HRC, University of Texas at Austin. "Shakespeare in Manchester" (20 March 1897) in *OTN:* III: 79–86.

7. 29 April 1897. *CL:* I: 750–51.

8. Shaw's amusing account of the *You Never Can Tell* fiasco was published under Cyril Maude's name in his *The Haymarket Theatre*, ch. 16. Also in *CP:* I: 797–803. Aynesworth on Shaw, related to Ellen Terry by her daughter Edy, and relayed by her to Shaw: 9 May 1897. Holograph. British Library. Shaw replied to Ellen that Edy's version was the humane one: that it would have been difficult for Aynesworth to admit the part had beaten him.

9. Shaw to R. Golding Bright. 7 May 1897. *CL:* I: 752–55.

10. Shaw to Terry, 17 April 1897, *CL:* I: 747; Terry to Shaw, 18 April 1897, *A Correspondence:* 139–40.

11. Laurence Irving: 588.

12. 11 and 12 May 1897. *CL:* I: 759–60, 760–1.

13. Letters of 26 December 1896, 5 February, 9 May, 11 May 1897. *A Correspondence:* 104–5, 112–13, 144, 146–47.

14. Shaw to Terry. 13 May 1897. *CL:* I: 762–63. Terry to Shaw. n.d. but probably between 13 and 16 May 1897. *A Correspondence:* 150.

15. 11 May 1897. Holograph. British Library.

16. *My Life and Some Letters:* 154–56.

17. 28 May 1897. *CL:* I: 770–71.

18. Shaw was not elected by popular vote. His friends, Robert and "Lion" (Lucy) Phillimore, members of the St. Pancras Vestry, had negotiated with their non-progressive opponents that certain nominees of theirs would be elected without contest.

19. 28 May 1897. *CL:* I: 770–71.

20. 14-15 June 1897. *CL:* I: 774–76.

21. Shaw to Terry. 5 August 1897. *CL:* I: 790–93. Terry to Shaw. 19 June and Thursday, 1 July 1897: *A Correspondence:* 160, and holograph, British Library. Shaw's letters to Terry circa the end of June about Charlotte's proposal are missing, but their contents can be deduced from Ellen's reply.

22. "A Doll's House Again" (15 May 1897) in *OTN:* III: 136–41.

23. "The New Century Theatre" (10 April 1897) and "Ibsen Triumphant" (22 May 1897) in *OTN:* III: 102–10, 142–51.

24. 20 May 1897. *CL:* I: 765–66.

25. 1 May 1897. Holograph. HRC, University of Texas at Austin.

26. 29 May 1897. *CL:* I: 771–72.

27. Letter dated 15 July 1897, but from content probably 14 June since she responds to Shaw's suggestion made 11 June that Edy could play the Strange Lady, and 9 May 1897 (dated "Shawday" instead of Sunday). Holographs. British Library.

28. 12 September 1929. Via della Corta di Serretto 17, San Martino d'Albaro, Genoa, Italy. Typed letter included with his corrected draft of the Shaw-Terry Correspondence. HRC, University of Texas at Austin.

29. Shaw to Terry. 5 August 1897. *CL:* I: 790–93. Shaw to Achurch. 4 August

Notes

1897. Holograph. HRC, University of Texas at Austin. Shaw to Charrington. 9 and 10 August 1897. Holograph. HRC, University of Texas at Austin.

30. 26 August 1897. *A Correspondence:* 180.

31. 30 August 1897. Holograph. British Library.

32. 17 September 1897. Typed letter. HRC, University of Texas at Austin.

33. Shaw to Achurch, 1 November 1897, and Shaw to Payne-Townshend, 4 November 1897. *CL:* I: 819–20, 821.

34. 1 December 1897. Holograph. British Library.

35. 8 December 1897. *CL:* I: 826–27.

36. 9 December 1897. *CL:* I: 827–28.

CHAPTER SIXTEEN (1897 - 1898)

1. Ellen believed Forbes-Robertson might do it, and suggested Charles Wyndham; Shaw had hopes of an Arthur Bouchier-Herbert Waring combination, Bouchier, actor-manager of the Royalty, playing Burgoyne.

2. Laurence Irving: 613–14. Terriss, of course, had been a member of the Lyceum Company, and had recently asked Irving for a berth again. Once the actor had almost been killed when, standing next to Ellen Terry at Niagara Falls on one of the American tours, his foot slipped, nearly precipitating him over the edge, an incident he tossed off with his usual nonchalance.

3. 20 October, 1 and 4. November 1897. Holographs. British Library.

4. Eliza Aria, *My Sentimental Self* (1922), quoted in Laurence Irving.

5. "Hamlet" (2 October 1897) in *OTN:* III: 210–18.

6. 1 October 1897. *A Correspondence:* 189–90.

7. 31 December 1897. *CL:* I: 838–40. Shaw was vacationing with the Webbs at Sir George Trevelyan's huge estate at Welcombe, Stratford-on-Avon.

8. 5 January 1898. *A Correspondence:* 207–8.

9. 22 January 1898. *CL:* II: 10–11.

10. 7 February 1898. Holograph. HRC, University of Texas at Austin.

11. Robins, *Theatre and Friendship:* 195–96. Robins, Archer, H. W. Massingham, Frederick Pollock, Norman Grosvenor, Gerald Duckworth, Mrs. J. R. Green, and Alfred Sutro made up the N.C.T. committee.

12. "John Gabriel Borkman" (8 May 1897) in *OTN:* III: 128–35.

13. Letter cards of 4 January and 4 March 1898. *CL:* II: 7, 11–12.

14. 12 March 1898. *CL:* II: 14.

15. 12 and 13 March 1898. *A Correspondence:* 220–21.

16. 30 March 1898. *CL:* II: 23–25. The woman who pulled flowers was Beatrice Webb, a habit Shaw's mother also violently objected to.

17. Charlotte Granville. Herbert Waring was planning a production of *The Devil's Disciple;* Granville was financing Waring and expected to play the leading role.

18. Letters to Charlotte of 19, 20, 22, 23, 24, 25, 30, and 31 March, 4, 5, 8, 12, and 14 April 1898. *CL:* II: 19–33.

19. Yvonne Kapp, *Eleanor Marx* (New York: Pantheon Books, 1976): II: 696ff. Aveling himself died four months later; his illness was one of the factors that had depressed Eleanor.

20. Wednesday, 6 April [1898]. Holograph. British Library.

21. 23 April 1898. *A Correspondence:* 225.

22. "Mr. Bernard Shaw's Plays" in *Study and Stage: A Year-Book of Criticism* (London: Grant Richards, 1899): 1–22.

23. Letters and notes of 19, 21, 22, 23, 24, 25, 26, and 27 April, 1 May 1898. *CL:* II: 32–38. Charlotte to Shaw. Holograph. British Library.

24. 12 May 1898. Holograph. British Library. Ellen enclosed a note for Charlotte in her letter. She tried friendship with Charlotte, but was unsuccessful beyond the mere exchange of pleasant formalities in occasional notes. Especially, she offered to help in the foot crisis, but was not needed by the new Mrs. Shaw.

25. Undated, but assigned to 2 May 1898. *CL:* II: 39.

26. "Van Amburgh Revived" (7 May 1898) in *OTN:* III: 394–400.

27. 22 April 1895. *CL:* I: 524–27.

28. Shaw to Beatrice Webb. 21 June 1898. Pitfold, Haslemere. *CL:* II: 49–53.

29. 17 May 1898. *A Correspondence:* 227.

CHAPTER SEVENTEEN (1898 - 1900)

1. 20 June 1898. Holograph. HRC, University of Texas at Austin.

2. Shaw to Charrington. 20 June 1898. Holograph. HRC, University of Texas at Austin. Shaw to Beatrice Webb. 21 June 1898. *CL:* II: 49–53.

3. Shaw to Charrington. 13 August 1898. Holograph. HRC, University of Texas at Austin. 23 October 1898. *CL:* II: 69–70. 13 October 1898. *CL:* II: 64–65. 13 December 1898. Holograph. HRC, University of Texas at Austin. Shaw's letter of 13 October mentions that Charrington has been left money. It was perhaps £2,000, since Shaw says, "Now be praised, Heaven, that he did not leave you a million: you would have sent for £50,000 straight off." Charrington had asked for £100.

4. Lucy Shaw to Janie Crichton Drysdale. 5 October [1898]. Farmer: 7–8.

5. Shaw to Sidney Webb. 18 October 1898. *CL:* II: 65–69.

6. 6 November 1898. Quoted in Janet Dunbar, *Mrs. G.B.S.* (London: George G. Harrap, 1963): 181–82. Both Charlotte and Shaw appealed to the Webbs frequently during this difficult period of adjustment.

7. *The Perfect Wagnerite* (London: Constable, 1930): 230 passim.

8. Gordon Edward Craig, *Index to the Story of My Days* (New York: Viking, 1957): 192–99.

9. 30 August and 21 June 1898. Holographs. British Library.

10. 6 November 1898. *A Correspondence:* 229–30.

11. 13 December 1898. Holograph. HRC, University of Texas at Austin.

12. Ellen Terry, *Memoirs:* 271–72.

13. 15 January and 31 May 1899. Holographs. British Library.

14. *Memoirs:* "H.I.'s arrangement with Syndicate: £11,000 for the remainder of Lyceum lease (£5000 on mortgage still leaves £6000 . . .). Then another £1000 for 'Robespierre.' Every season *both of us* to play at Lyceum from April to July. H.I.'s share, 60 per cent. Then tours in America and the Provinces, also on sharing terms.": 272.

15. In Mrs. Campbell's company were Nutcombe Gould playing Caesar, Courtenay Thorpe, and Harley Granville-Barker as Lucius Septimis.

16. 28 April 1899. *CL:* II: 86.

17. 1 June 1899. *A Correspondence:* 237–38. 1 August 1899. *CL:* II: 95–96.

18. 7 July 1899. *CL:* II: 92–93.

19. 10 July, 12 July, and 3 August 1899. *A Correspondence:* 240, 241, 244–45, and holographs, British Library.

20. 8 August 1899. *CL:* II: 97–99.

21. 9 August 1899. *A Correspondence:* 249–50.

22. 27 September 1899. Glasgow. Holograph. British Library. This is the missing letter about Irving's arrangements with Tennyson mentioned on p. 261 in *A Correspondence.* Irving had produced Tennyson's *The Cup* on 3 January 1881.

23. 11 October 1899. *A Correspondence:* 264–65.

24. 29 September 1899. Off Málaga. *CL:* II: 104–7.

25. With Yorke Stephens as Valentine, Margaret Halstan as Gloria, James Welch as the Waiter, Charrington as Bohun. Shaw mentions the silence of the press in a letter to Charrington of 5 December 1899, HRC, University of Texas at Austin. The play was produced for six matinees at the Strand Theatre on 2 May 1900 by James Welch and Yorke Stephens, was an immediate success with £200 houses, but Shaw, dissatisfied with a cheap, scratch performance, would not let it go past the six matinees.

26. Shaw to Achurch. 12 December 1899. *CL:* II: 117–18. Shaw to Charrington. 30 December 1899. Holograph letter card. HRC, University of Texas at Austin.

27. 7 January 1900. *CL:* II: 129–33.

28. 28 and 29 January 1900. Boody House, Toledo. Holograph. British Library.

29. 9 February 1900. *CL:* II: 147–49.

30. Shaw to Robins. 13 February 1899. *CL:* II: 76–78. A letter from Elizabeth Robins had appeared in the *Daily Chronicle* for 16 December 1898, admitting that she was the author C. E. Raimond. Jane Marcus in her dissertation *Elizabeth Robins: A Biography* (Northwestern University, 1973) calls this "the one letter of Shaw to Elizabeth Robins which seems open, honest, genuinely concerned with just praise and just criticism," but adds, "He could afford it. She was well out of his territory now": 282. Other works of Elizabeth Robins's include *The Magnetic North* (1904), *Come and Find Me* (1908), *A Dark Lantern* (1908), *The Florentine Frame* (1909), *Way Stations* (1913), *Ancilla's Share* (1924, anon.), *Raymond and I* (1956).

31. 24 January 1900. *CL:* II: 136–39.

32. 4 June 1900. Vine Cottage, Kingston Dale, Surrey. Holograph. British Library.

33. 6 and 7 June 1900. *CL:* II: 169–71.

34. 28 October 1900. *CL:* II: 187–88.

35. Diary: October 1900 in *Memoirs:* 274. 2 November 1900. *A Correspondence:* 278–79.

36. 7 November 1900. Holograph. British Library.

37. In a letter of 16 October 1900 (Holograph. HRC, University of Texas at Austin), for example, he tells Charrington that Janet is "no use for this sort of game."

38. Sunday, 2 December 1900, Newcastle-on-Tyne; 5 December 1900 (postmark date), Royal Victoria Station Hotel, Sheffield; and 7 December 1900. Holographs. British Library. The letters of 2 and 5 December are labeled "sometime in December 1900" in *A Correspondence.*

39. Christmas day 1900. *CL:* II: 206–8.

40. Terry to Shaw. Undated, but they met at Marie Corelli's *The Sorrows of Satan*, which opened 9 January 1897, so shortly after that date. Incorrectly dated as the end of January 1898 in *A Correspondence:* 212–13. Shaw to Terry. 25 March 1897. *CL:* I: 737. Terry to Shaw. 25 March 1897. *A Correspondence:* 127.

41. 3 and 8 November 1900. *CL:* II: 191–92, 197–98.

42. "Could not bear her": mentioned in a letter from Terry to Shaw of 10 December 1902. *A Correspondence:* 291. Shaw dismisses the silence of almost a year and a half by pointing out that the correspondence had markedly slacked off before the meeting under the stage (editorial comments: 286–87): the explanation does not seem very satisfactory, since eighteen letters exist or are mentioned in the correspondence from the year 1900, and more are apt to have been written. Ellen refers to Edy's gossiping tongue on several occasions, for example: "Tell Charlotte with my love to take a little salt with Edy's words as a habit. She is the dearest thing, but she does cackle somewhat": 18 December 1902. Holograph. British Library.

43. If Shaw did not make the remark about Ellen, it is possible that he wrote her once or twice after the play, but that she destroyed the letters, as she often had when angry with him in the past. The fact that Shaw initiated the correspondence in April 1902 and not Terry suggests perhaps that she was the one who stopped writing.

CHAPTER EIGHTEEN (1901 - 1906)

1. *The Admirable Bashville or Constancy Unrewarded*, being the novel of *Cashel Byron's Profession* done into a stage play in three acts and in blank verse, preceded *Man and Superman*, Shaw having finished it in February 1901.

2. Julia Neilson in Paul M. Potter's *The Conquerors* (*Saturday Review* 23 April 1898); Lyceum production of J. Comyns Carr's *King Arthur* (*Saturday Review* 19 January 1895); Wilson Barrett's *The Daughters of Babylon* (*Saturday Review* 13 February 1897); Arthur Wing Pinero's *The Notorious Mrs. Ebbsmith* (*Saturday Review* 16 March 1895). See also Shaw to Archer: 22 February 1901 in *CL:* II: 218–19. Women and love as tedious subjects: Shaw to Siegfried Trebitsch: 16 August 1903 in *CL:* II: 344–48.

3. Shaw to Charrington. 12 June 1902. Postcard. HRC, University of Texas at Austin.

4. Both Achurch and Charrington acted in Harold V. Neilson's production of *Captain Brassbound's Conversion* in Manchester, commencing 12 May 1902 for six performances. Shaw's letter to the *Manchester Guardian* appeared 17 May 1902. Janet played in *The Lady from the Sea* for the Stage Society on 4 and 5 May 1902. Shaw to Charrington. 20 May 1902. *CL:* II: 272–74.

5. 4 April 1903 and 8 May 1903. *CL:* II: 320, 322–23. Janet had just played Queen Katherine in *Henry VIII* in Manchester in January 1903, and was planning another tour. In May of that year, she performed her own *Mrs. Daintree's Daughter*, which, the *Manchester Evening News* announced (16 May 1903), was received with considerable interest and approval from the "well-established Manchester favourite," although the critic found the play very uneven and the men's parts weak. Clippings courtesy Dan H. Laurence.

6. August 1903. Holograph. British Library. Reprinted in *CL:* II: 356–57.

7. Shaw to Terry. 12 June 1904. *CL:* II: 42–43.

8. Shaw to Achurch. 6 July 1911. Annecy, Haute-Savoie, France. HRC, University of Texas at Austin.

Notes

9. 28 August 1904. *CL:* II: 445–48.

10. Lillah McCarthy, O.B.E. (Lady Keeble), *Myself and My Friends* (New York: E. P. Dutton, 1933). Preface by Shaw. The material in this chapter derives from *Myself and My Friends,* unless noted otherwise.

11. "A New Lady Macbeth and a New Mrs. Ebbsmith" (25 May 1895) in *OTN:* I: 133–40.

12. 1 March 1905. *CL:* II: 518–19. Shaw had evidently forgotten he gave her the play to read, since he asks her in the same letter whether she had ever read *Man and Superman* and offers her a copy.

13. The feminist Lillah McCarthy's autobiography, interestingly enough, mentions only her mother and Margot Asquith (Lady Oxford) at any length, while it is full of men and their importance to her: Thomas Hardy, Robert Bridges, John Galsworthy, Arnold Bennett, Charles Ricketts, Charles Shannon, William Poel, John Masefield, James Barrie, H. G. Wells, Wilson Barrett, a vast assortment of lords and baronets, and above all, Shaw.

14. Matinees on 23, 25, 26, and 30 May; 1, 2, 6, 8, 9, 13, 15, and 16 June.

15. Desmond MacCarthy, *The Court Theatre: 1904–1907: A Commentary and Criticism* (London: A. H. Bullen, 1907): 84. Future MacCarthy critiques taken from this source.

16. Susan L. Mitchell, *George Moore* (Dublin: Maunsell, 1916), as quoted in the *Daily News* (23 October 1916): 74. Shaw to Josephine Preston Peabody. 29 December 1904. *CL:* II: 474–75.

17. 5 April 1902. *A Correspondence:* 290–91.

18. N.d. 1903. Holograph. British Library. 14 June 1904. *A Correspondence:* 296.

19. 29 June 1904. Typed letter. HRC, University of Texas at Austin. Ada Rehan (1860–1916) played many Shakespearean roles in Daly's company from 1879–99, often co-starring with John Drew.

20. "Mr. Daly Fossilizes" (29 June 1895) in *OTN:* I: 171–78.

21. 26 July 1904. *CL:* II: 436–37. Rehan exclaimed after hearing *Brassbound:* "Oh, the man's part is so good!"

22. Vedrenne apparently went over Shaw's head in this matter. As Shaw wrote to Barker (3 August 1905, holograph, HRC), he had gallantly promised to hold the play until Ada Rehan could act Lady Cicely, and would not go back on his word. But Rehan did "cry off" *Brassbound,* getting Shaw out of a predicament.

23. *Memoirs:* 260–62.

24. Among the cast were Aubrey Smith as Colonel Grey, Irene Vanbrugh as Amy Grey, and Edith Craig as Fanny the maid. The play is collected in *The Plays of J. M. Barrie,* edited by A. E. Wilson (London: Hodder & Stoughton, 1942). Wilson omitted Barrie's play for Mrs. Campbell, *The Adored One,* from this collection, commenting that it was a failure in its original production in London in 1913 and again when it was done in a revised version, and that Barrie evidently only wished it to be preserved in its one-act form, *Seven Women.*

25. 24 October and 1 November 1905. *A Correspondence:* 305–7.

26. 24 December 1905. *CL:* II: 586–90. Shaw called *Major Barbara* "magnificent" and "a summit of dramatic literature" in a letter to William Archer of 1 January 1906 (*CL:* II: 599); Archer had, as usual, announced in the *World* (5 December 1905) that the play was mere discussion, and Shaw was defending himself. Annie Russell finally created the part of Major Barbara and reported her experiences with the play and Shaw in a talk to a New York ladies' club in 1908 called "Bernard Shaw at Rehearsals of 'Major Barbara.'" The manuscript of the talk is in the Theatre

Collection of the New York Public Library; it is printed in *The Shaw Review*, XIX (May 1976): 73–82.

27. 14 March 1906. *CL:* II: 607–8.

28. 14 March 1906. *CL:* II: 609.

29. 16 March 1906. *A Correspondence:* 311.

30. Holograph. British Library.

31. Shaw to J. E. Vedrenne. 16 May 1906. In C. B. Purdom, *Bernard Shaw's Letters to Granville Barker* (New York: Theatre Arts Books, 1957): 60–61. Ada Rehan went to a performance, and wondered how Shaw could want her as Lady Cicely: 1 July 1906, HRC, University of Texas at Austin. In a note on Rehan's letter, Shaw regretted he could not refuse Ellen the play for her fall Jubilee tour. Rehan finally had to decline *Captain Brassbound's Conversion* because of illness.

32. Quoted in *CL:* II: 629.

33. Sources from Shaw's account in his Preface to the Shaw-Terry *Correspondence:* xxvii–xxviii; a note to Ellen of 16 March 1906: *A Correspondence:* 311; and Christopher St. John's biographical supplement to Terry's *Memoirs:* 283ff.

34. Florence Farr also stage-managed an amateur production of *The Philanderer* for the New Stage Club on 20 February 1905.

35. Farr, *The Music of Speech* (London: 1909): 16–17.

36. "Ave" in *Hail and Farewell!:* 81–83. At least one critic found that Florence was "a charming Aleel" when she played in *The Countess Cathleen* in the Antient Concert Rooms, Dublin.

37. 6 June 1902. *CL:* II: 274–75.

38. Quoted in C. B. Purdom, *Harley Granville Barker* (London: Rockliff, 1955): 34, 51.

39. 27 December 1904. *CL:* II: 590–91.

40. 22 September 1904. Holograph. HRC, University of Texas at Austin.

41. Shaw to Achurch. 23 April 1905. *CL:* II: 524–26. Shaw to Charrington. 3 May, 23 July, 23 October 1905. HRC, University of Texas at Austin.

42. "A Confession of Their Crimes by Janet Achurch and Charles Charrington from the Cell of Inaction to which They Were Condemned in the Latter Half of the Year of Grace 1893." The "Confession" was probably written later, after the Stage Society collapsed. Shaw discovered the document, and sent it to Ashley Dukes, a Charrington collector, 14 December 1929. HRC, University of Texas at Austin.

CHAPTER NINETEEN (1906 - 1912)

1. *Myself and My Friends:* 80. Shaw to McCarthy. 1 September 1906. *CL:* II: 644–45. *You Never Can Tell* had been revived at the Court in July 1906.

2. Shaw to Vedrenne. 17 October 1906. Holograph. Enthoven Collection. Victoria and Albert Museum, London.

3. *Myself and My Friends:* 65. *The Doctor's Dilemma* was presented at the Court Theatre beginning 20 November 1906 for nine matinees.

4. 8 November 1907. *CL:* II: 721. *The Philanderer* was Shaw's first failure in Sweden, surviving for only five performances (editor's note).

5. 10 December 1906. *Bernard Shaw and Mrs. Patrick Campbell: Their Correspondence* (London: Victor Gollancz, 1952): 17–18. Hereafter *Their Correspondence*.

6. "Biography" in Terry's *Memoirs:* 286.

Notes

7. 13 September 1907. Holograph. British Library.

8. Terry to Shaw. 13 August [1907?] and 14 March 1908. Holographs. British Library.

9. *A Correspondence* and holograph letters, British Library. Terry wanted to open *Captain Brassbound's Conversion* in the West End, but Vedrenne and Barker objected.

10. 14 March and 13 April 1908, 17 August 1909, 29 September 1910. Holographs. British Library.

11. Lena Ashwell, *Myself a Player* (London: Michael Joseph, 1936): 174.

12. 13 May 1908. Typed letter. HRC, University of Texas at Austin.

13. Beatrice Webb, *Our Partnership:* 359–60. Quotations from the Preface to *Getting Married* from *Collected Plays:* III: 460–63.

14. 12 May 1908. *CL:* II: 779–80.

15. 29 and 22 April 1908, 13 October 1909. *CL:* II: 772, 775–76, 871–72. Shaw eventually drafted a letter for Charlotte to send Erica Cotterill which would "put a stop at once and for ever to any personal intimacy between us"—or more to the point, between Erica and Shaw. Undated, but assigned to 11 October 1910 in *CL:* II: 943–45.

16. Reviewed 15 March and 8 November 1902 in *More Theatres:* 448, 506. *Paolo and Francesca* is by Stephen Phillips.

17. Henry James read the manuscript of *Votes for Women!* and suggested some revisions. The play opened at the Court Theatre on 9 April 1907 for an initial eight matinees, and then ran for another two weeks beginning 21 May. Robins rewrote the play into a novel titled *The Convert*, published in October 1907.

18. John Masefield to Robins. 17 November 1909. 30 Maida Hill West, London, W. Berg Collection, New York Public Library. Masefield had read the play; they met on 26 November and Masefield was deeply impressed, calling it "a white letter day." The Berg Collection has 265 letters from Masefield to Elizabeth Robins: 17 November 1909 to 29 November 1912. Max Beerbohm's review of "Miss Robins' 'Tract'" in *Around Theatres* (13 April 1907): 459–63. Shaw on Robins's play in a letter to J. E. Vedrenne, *Bernard Shaw's Letters to Granville Barker* (New York: Theatre Arts Books, 1957): 77. James O'Donnell Bennett's review for the New York *Times* quoted in Marcus: 314–17. Charlotte Shaw had written to Robins on 25 January 1907, in place of G.B.S., who had counseled Robins to delay production, reassuring her that her "tract" would not date and concluding that Shaw was ready to serve her in any way he could. Holograph. Fales Collection, New York University Library.

19. Robins fictionalized her relationship with her brother in *Raymond and I* (1956) and her Klondike experiences in *The Magnetic North* (1904) and *Come and Find Me* (1908). The papers of Raymond Robins, lawyer, social worker, gold miner, lay preacher, union organizer, are in the archives of the State Historical Library of Madison, Wisconsin, including Robins's cablegram and letters of Raymond Robins to his wife, best described as exalted in their tone. Letters to Elizabeth Robins from Marjorie Hubert, a doctor and colleague of Octavia Wilberforce's, indicate that she was violently in love with Elizabeth (Fales Collection, New York University Library).

20. Elizabeth Robins, *Ibsen and the Actress* (London: The Hogarth Press, 1928). The essay was given as a lecture before the Royal Society of Arts under the auspices of the British Drama League on 12 March 1928. About Shaw, Robins says, "and who could recall Ibsen days without seeing that figure flash across the scene, leaving

a trail of laughter, sometimes of consternation, but always a more vivid sense of our material and our opportunity." She calls him a maker of reputations, and regrets that he did not do more to save the career of Marion Lea. Shaw mentioned two American actresses who disliked him; the second was probably Marion Lea.

21. Terry to Shaw. 8 December 1896. *A Correspondence:* 103. Shaw to Terry. 8 December 1896. *CL:* I: 712. "Richard Himself Again" (26 December 1896) in *OTN:* II: 299–306. Lena Ashwell had appeared in *Her Advocate, The Prude's Progress, The Matchmaker,* and *The Fool of the Family* at the Duke of York's, Shaftesbury, and Comedy theatres.

22. *Myself a Player:* 54. I have drawn on this autobiography for details of Ashwell's early life.

23. Ellen Terry, *The Story of My Life* (London: Hutchinson, 1908): 247–48.

24. E. Sylvia Pankhurst, *The Suffragette* (London: Gay and Hancock, 1911): 242–44 (her description of the procession). Charlotte Shaw recorded in her annuary for 1908 that she walked in both processions. Ellen Terry was a member of the Actresses' Franchise League, but is not on record as having participated in the marches. On 5 April 1912 Elizabeth Robins gave her "Christabel" speech at the Albert Hall and raised £10,000 (Marcus: 335); she dropped her membership in the W.S.P.U. that same year because of its anarchistic politics. Lena Ashwell records marching again on 18 June 1911, and marching with Charlotte in Boston during the spring of 1914. Sylvia, unlike Emmeline and Christabel, did not fault Shaw's patriotism after *Common Sense* appeared, and for her work with the East End women, was the Pankhurst for whom Shaw had most sympathy.

25. 15 December 1912. Holograph letter card. HRC, University of Texas at Austin. There are some twenty letters or so from Shaw to Ashwell at the HRC, and a few from Ashwell to Shaw at the British Library.

26. 2 July 1914. Hôtel du Golf, St. Briac, France. Holograph. British Library.

27. Quoted in David Mitchell, *The Fighting Pankhursts* (New York: Macmillan, 1967): 160–61.

28. "Why All Women Are Peculiarly Fitted to Be Good Voters" in New York *American* (21 April 1907), reprinted in *Fabian Feminist: Bernard Shaw and Women,* edited by Rodelle Weintraub (University Park: The Pennsylvania State University Press, 1977): 248–54. See also Michael Holroyd, "Women and the Body Politic" in *The Genius of Shaw,* ed. Michael Holroyd (New York: Holt, Rinehart & Winston, 1979): 167–83.

29. London *Budget* (23 March 1913).

30. Shaw to Newcombe. 14 May and 9 June 1909. *CL:* II: 843, 845–46. Newcombe to Shaw from Carbery, Sway, Hants on 13 and 22 July 1909. Holographs. British Library.

31. Undated, assigned to 24 February 1910 and 11 March 1910. *CL:* II: 903, 905.

32. *Myself a Player:* 254–56.

33. 30 June 1907. *CL:* II: 695.

34. John Masefield's version of the Norwegian H. Wiers-Jenssen's *Anne Pedersdotter,* produced by Harley Granville-Barker for the Scottish Repertory Theatre, 10 October 1910. Shaw was in Glasgow lecturing on "University Socialism" and, at the Glasgow Repertory Theatre on 27 October, on "Public Enterprise and Dramatic Art": presumably he saw the play during this trip. Beginning 31 January at the Court, Lillah McCarthy took the lead in *The Witch,* very successfully.

35. Shaw's account of meeting Janet after *The Witch* in a letter to Charrington of 17 September 1916, written after he was told of her death. HRC, University of

Notes

Texas at Austin. Janet Achurch played Ann Redvers for two private matinees at Lena Ashwell's Kingsway commencing 20 February 1912. It was generally agreed that Phillpotts's first play was poorly cast as well as undramatic and uneven, however: *Saturday Review*, 2 March 1912.

36. I am indebted to Janet Achurch and Charles Charrington's grandson, Francis Benjamin Levetus, O.B.E., F.I. Mech. E., for information pertaining to his mother, Nora Charrington, and his father, Edward Lewis Levetus. Ashley Dukes stated that Nora married an actor and went on stage (Chapter 4, Note 24), but there is no evidence for this. Charrington wrote Shaw in 1912 that Nora had a "sorting office" in Liverpool.

37. 19 November 1910. Hotel de France et d'Angleterre, Amiens. Holograph. British Library.

38. 24 November 1910. HRC, University of Texas at Austin.

39. *Myself and My Friends:* 127. Shaw to McCarthy. 8 July 1910. *CL:* II: 931–32.

40. 6 July 1911. HRC, University of Texas at Austin. Janet had played Mrs. Linden in a revival of *A Doll's House* at the Court Theatre, 1 April to 20 May 1911, and had played Mrs. Alving in *Ghosts*, a benefit performance for Charing Cross Hospital at the Hotel Cecil on 4 January 1911.

41. 8 May 1912. Holograph. British Library. Actor and producer Basil Dean wrote to Shaw on 4 August 1912 that he quite agreed with him that Charrington's production of *Brassbound* at Liverpool had been "utterly disgraceful," although Dean had seen only one act.

42. 2 October 1912. Hotel Johann[is?], [Murau?], Tirol. Holograph. British Library. Shaw had mentioned a date for Janet's playing Lady Cicely, says Charrington. They had been in the Tyrol for four months and were planning to return that month.

43. 13 August 1912. *A Correspondence:* 326–27.

CHAPTER TWENTY (1912-1913)

1. W. B. Yeats to his father John Butler Yeats. 29 November 1909. *The Letters of W. B. Yeats:* 539–41.

2. 30 June 1912. Holograph. HRC, University of Texas at Austin.

3. 3 July 1912. *Their Correspondence:* 21–25.

4. Letter to Ellen Terry. 13 August 1912. *A Correspondence:* 326–27.

5. N.d. *Their Correspondence:* 25–26.

6. Mrs. Campbell's daughter Stella to her mother's close friend from California, Mrs. Harriet Carolan. Thursday [n.d. but December 1904]. Holograph. Regenstein Library, University of Chicago.

7. Postmarked 29 July 1912. *Their Correspondence:* 31.

8. 9 August 1912. *Their Correspondence:* 32–35.

9. Postcard to Lillah McCarthy from Frankfurt. 26 July 1912. HRC, University of Texas at Austin. And 16 September 1912. *A Correspondence:* 328.

10. Mrs. Patrick Campbell, *My Life and Some Letters:* Chapters I and II.

11. Mrs. Campbell to Harriet Carolan. 27 January 1905. Holograph. Regenstein Library, University of Chicago.

12. *My Life and Some Letters:* 45–48.

13. With a few alterations, I have borrowed this description of the bitch as a neg-

ative female role from Elizabeth Janeway, *Man's World, Woman's Place* (New York: Dell, 1971): 199.

14. Quoted by Alan Dent in *Mrs. Patrick Campbell* from a letter to Elizabeth Young: 222.

15. 19 August 1912, from the Hotel Excelsior, Nancy. *Their Correspondence:* 36–41.

16. References to *Tristan und Isolde* and Poe's "Annabel Lee" can be found in letters of 31 January 1913, 7 February 1913, and 27 March 1924.

17. 27 November 1912 and 8 November 1912. *Their Correspondence:* 57–59, 54–55.

18. Mrs. Campbell had and would ask Mrs. Harriet Carolan for loans. Holograph letters of 25 April 1911 and 13 (or 18) March [1916]. Regenstein Library, University of Chicago. Although Stella was asking for money in 1911, Alan Dent, her biographer, states in *Mrs. Patrick Campbell* that 1911 was one of her good years.

19. Letters of 10 and 11 December 1912. *Their Correspondence:* 65–69, 69.

20. Articles in the *New Age* (London: 6 June 1907): 93; *The Mint* (London: 23 May 1908): 271.

21. See, for example, H. B. Hyams, "Bernard Shaw and Theosophy," *Theosophist* (November 1915).

22. 13 March 1913. *Their Correspondence:* 95–97.

23. 27 February 1913. *Their Correspondence:* 89–90.

24. 22 and 27 February 1913. *Their Correspondence:* 85–88, 89. Shaw's account of his mother's cremation has raised more horror than perhaps any other of his iconoclasms. H. G. Farmer in his book *Bernard Shaw's Sister and Her Friends*, for example, calls Shaw's reaction "diabolic Satanism" and concluded: "How any man could have acted thus at his mother's cremation passes all understanding": 182–83.

25. Max Beerbohm. Holograph notes and fragmentary drafts for projected essays. Unsigned and undated. Berg Collection, New York Public Library.

26. 2 April 1913. *Their Correspondence:* 104–5.

27. 17 June 1913. *Their Correspondence:* 121.

28. 4 September 1913. Quoted in Farmer, *Bernard Shaw's Sister and Her Friends:* 200–1. Sara Allgood (1883–1950), Irish actress associated in her early career with the Abbey Theatre, Dublin.

29. *My Life and Some Letters:* 342.

30. 6 August 1913. *Their Correspondence:* 136–37.

CHAPTER TWENTY-ONE (1913 - 1914)

1. 31 March 1913. Holograph. HRC, University of Texas at Austin.

2. Barrie to Mrs. Campbell. 7 September 1912. *Letters of J. M. Barrie*, ed. Viola Meynell (London: Peter Davies, 1942): 36–37. Shaw must have read Barrie's letter, since he agrees on Mrs. Campbell's elasticity: see *Their Correspondence:* 144.

3. 9 June 1913. *Their Correspondence:* 119–20.

4. 7 August 1913. *Their Correspondence:* 137.

5. Letters of the Sandwich period and aftermath from *Their Correspondence:* 10 August to 25 September 1913: 137–51.

6. 5 February 1913. *Their Correspondence:* 80–81.

7. The 1891 "Appendix" is reprinted in *Shaw on Theatre*, edited by E. J. West (New York: Hill and Wang, 1958): 1–18.

8. 26 October and 7 November 1913. Holograph. British Library.

9. 9 November 1913. Copy. Burgunder Collection, Cornell University.

10. 4 November 1913. *Their Correspondence:* 152.

11. 31 December 1913 and 5 January 1914. *Their Correspondence:* 154–55.

12. *Myself a Player:* 66. "Lena's Father" was Shaw's first working title for *Heartbreak House.*

13. Sir Herbert Beerbohm Tree to Shaw. 19 and 21 November 1913. Holographs. British Library.

14. See, for example, Hesketh Pearson, *Beerbohm Tree: His Life and Laughter* (London: Methuen, 1956); Richard Huggett, *The Truth About Pygmalion* (New York: Random House, 1969); Stanley Weintraub, *Journey to Heartbreak: The Crucible Years of Bernard Shaw: 1914–1918* (New York: Weybright & Talley, 1971).

15. Shaw to George Cornwallis-West. 6 July 1914. Typed letter. British Library. The letter discusses the possibility of Stella and George Cornwallis-West moving *Pygmalion* to the St. James's Theatre, with Cornwallis-West as manager. Shaw was willing to "find capital for this venture"; but the project proved financially impossible.

16. Shaw's rehearsal notes for *Pygmalion*. HRC, University of Texas at Austin.

17. 11 April 1914. *Their Correspondence:* 160–62.

18. Sunday night, 12 April 1914. Holograph letter. British Library.

19. Shaw earned £237.9.4 in royalties for the first seven performances, £286.6.4 the next week, £281.17.9 the next, but dropped to £149.16.8 for the week ending 24 July 1914, when the play closed. At the beginning of the run Tree was grossing more than £2,000 a week.

CHAPTER TWENTY-TWO (1914 - 1929)

1. December 1914. *A Correspondence:* 330. Shaw's *Common Sense About the War* appeared as an eighty-page supplement to the *New Statesman* of 14 November 1914, the periodical his money helped found. Even the Webbs split with Shaw on the war issue.

2. Shaw to Arthur Wing Pinero. 5 and 13 November 1915. Typed letters. HRC, University of Texas at Austin.

3. Shaw to George C. Tyler, quoted in Dent, *Mrs. Patrick Campbell:* 262–63.

4. Mrs. Campbell to Harriet Carolan. [1914] from the Hotel Schenley, Pittsburgh, and 13 March 1916 from Olean House, Olean, New York. Regenstein Library, University of Chicago.

5. Harley Granville-Barker to Shaw. 22 January 1915. British Library. Barker returned to London in June 1915 £5,000 in debt, £2,000 owed to Shaw, who wrote off the debt.

6. Harley Granville-Barker to Lillah McCarthy. New York. 3 January 1916. HRC, University of Texas at Austin. Barker admits in this letter that he had very mixed feelings in marrying Lillah, and despite her assuring him she understood, should not have asked her to marry him—"a very great wrong."

7. *Myself and My Friends.* Emendations by Shaw. HRC, University of Texas at Austin.

8. Charles Charrington's account of his wife, Janet Achurch, bound with Shaw's letters to the Charringtons. HRC, University of Texas at Austin. I am indebted to Dr. Richard Larson for these comments on Charles Charrington's description of his wife's death: "Janet Achurch had cellulitis, as stated, and probably phlebitis, with severe swelling of the arm secondary to the inflammation itself, and probably secondary to venous occlusion from scarring as a result of chronic injections, perhaps with unsterile needles. The arm was undoubtedly cut to relieve the pressure of swelling and/or to drain infection. Death from heart failure was likely secondary to ascending venous infection which, reaching the heart, caused endocarditis. The '51 needles in the arms' are perhaps remnants of needles broken off during injections." Interestingly enough, Dan H. Laurence reports, Janet was buried in the same cemetery as Shaw's sister Agnes; in fact, their graves are quite close.

9. Shaw mentions £90 as his total earnings from *Arms and the Man* in a letter of 12 July 1894 shortly after the run of fifty performances; it is possible he eventually realized another £14.

10. Letters of 7 April and 7 December 1916. Ramanthan College, Chunnakam, N.P., Ceylon. Holographs. British Library. Shaw sent a reply-paid cablegram to Florence in Ceylon on 4 January 1917, motor-biking thirteen miles to do so.

11. Henrietta Paget to Shaw. 76 Parkhill Road, Hampstead N.W. Holograph. British Library.

12. The 1920 *Pygmalion* production: letters from 18 January to May 1920 in *Their Correspondence;* and Shaw to Viola Tree: 16 January; 4, 25, and 27 February; 25 March; and 14 July 1920. HRC, University of Texas at Austin.

13. 24 December 1921. *Their Correspondence:* 234; 30 December 1921. Typed letter: the Special Collections of the University Libraries, State University of New York at Buffalo.

14. 5 January 1922. *Their Correspondence:* 238–39.

15. Undated, but in response to Shaw's letter of 16 January 1922. *Their Correspondence:* 243–44.

16. "Mr. Patrick Campbell" in *Portraits* (London: Douglas Saunders with MacGibbon & Kee, 1955; first published 1931): 59–62. MacCarthy mistakenly calls Mrs. Campbell's autobiography *Myself and Some Letters.*

17. Written between 19 March 1918 and 27 May 1920. First presented in England by Barry Jackson at the Repertory Theatre, Birmingham, in four complete cycles of the five parts in October 1923, and in four complete cycles in London in February 1924.

18. See Peter Tompkins, *Shaw and Molly Tompkins* (New York: Clarkson N. Potter, 1961), and *To a Young Actress: The Letters of Bernard Shaw to Molly Tompkins,* ed. Peter Tompkins (New York: Clarkson N. Potter, 1960). Mr. Tompkins is the son of Laurence and Molly.

19. Shaw to Molly Tompkins. 10 February and 10 June 1924. *To a Young Actress:* 59, 71.

20. 31 May 1928. *To a Young Actress:* 127–28.

21. 2 February 1929. *To a Young Actress:* 131.

CHAPTER TWENTY-THREE (1916 - 1950)

1. 15 June 1916. *A Correspondence:* 330. Ellen stopped at Ayot St. Lawrence that summer of 1916, but typically did not call, only leaving a message at the post office.

Notes

In response, Shaw sent her a photo album with twenty-five of his own captioned photographs of Ayot; it is now at the Terry Museum, Smallhythe, Kent.

2. Preface to *A Correspondence*, written in 1929: xxviii.

3. *The Pillars of Society* (1921), *Potter's Clay* (1922), and *The Bohemian Girl* (1923).

4. Dated only Saturday night. British Library. *John Bull's Other Island* was revived at the Court Theatre beginning 9 September 1921; *Heartbreak House* followed at the Court on 19 October 1921 for sixty-three performances, receiving generally unfavorable reviews.

5. 22 November 1928. *Their Correspondence:* 269–70.

6. 12 September 1929. Via della Costa de Serretto 17, San Martino d'Albaro, Genoa (10), Italy. Holograph. HRC, University of Texas at Austin.

7. HRC, University of Texas at Austin.

8. Gordon Edward Craig. *Ellen Terry and Her Secret Self* (London: Sampson Low, Marston and Co., n.d.).

9. 3 January 1923. *Their Correspondence:* 259.

10. 28 July 1929. *Their Correspondence:* 291.

11. 29 March 1932. *Their Correspondence:* 296–99.

12. Shaw to Stella Campbell: 11 and 14 August 1937, and Stella Campbell to Shaw: 25 August 1937. *Their Correspondence:* 311–12, 313; 313–18.

13. Dame Rebecca West to the author: 19 February 1979.

14. Hotel Brighton, Rue de Rivoli, Paris. 9 December 1938. *Their Correspondence:* 323–24.

15. Postscript to letter of 28 June 1939, not printed in *Their Correspondence*. British Library.

16. Copy of Will in British Library. Agnes Claudius, an Englishwoman who had helped Mrs. Campbell with *My Life and Some Letters*, was with her at the end, and brought the correspondence back to England. Claudius's unfinished memoir is in the Burgunder Collection, Cornell University, signed with her pseudonym "Claude Vincent." George Cornwallis-West, whom Mrs. Campbell never divorced, remarried the day before the memorial service in London for Mrs. Campbell on 17 April 1940. In 1951 he killed himself with his own shotgun.

17. Mrs. Ann M. Elder Jackson to the author: 6 July 1978, Farnham, Surrey. Although Mrs. Jackson stated that Jenny Patterson left "a few little houses" in Newry, Ireland, to Arabella Gillmore, Dan H. Laurence notes that Jenny's will left her heir, Arabella Gillmore, her entire estate, probated in December 1924 at only £573.17.6.

18. 12 June 1923. Typed letter. British Library.

19. Archer's last letter to Shaw of 17 December 1924 is printed in Shaw's essay "How William Archer Impressed Bernard Shaw," from the volume *Three Plays* by William Archer (1927), reprinted in Shaw, *Pen Portraits and Reviews* (London: Constable, 1931), 1–32.

20. Quoted in Philip Henderson, *William Morris: His Life, Work and Friends:* 299–300.

21. "Morris As I Knew Him" in vol. 2 of May Morris's *William Morris: Artist Writer Socialist* (New York: Russell and Russell, 1966; first published 1936): ix–xl.

22. May's reservations about Shaw's essay are hinted at in a letter of 30 June 1936 to Sir Sydney Cockerell. Forster Library, Victoria and Albert Museum. May's letters to Shaw of 23 April and 5 May 1936. HRC, University of Texas at Austin.

23. Shaw to William Archer: 14 December 1924: British Library; and Shaw to Mrs. Thomas Hardy: 15 June 1924: Forster Library, Victoria and Albert Museum.

24. Shaw to Bertha Newcombe. 5 January 1925. HRC, University of Texas at Austin. *Saint Joan* was first presented in England by Mary Moore and Sybil Thorndike at the New Theatre, London, 23 March 1924, for 244 performances.

25. The chief argument of Jane Marcus's doctoral thesis, a biography of Elizabeth Robins (Northwestern, 1973). *Both Sides of the Curtain* (London: William Heinemann, 1940).

26. The suggestion of Stanley Weintraub in *Journey to Heartbreak:* 165.

27. "The Nun and the Dramatist: George Bernard Shaw to the Abbess of Stanbrook," *The Atlantic Monthly* (July and August 1956): 27–34, 69–76.

28. Blanche Patch, *Thirty Years with G.B.S.*

29. Mrs. Alice Laden, *The George Bernard Shaw Vegetarian Cookbook*, edited by R. J. Minney (London: Pan Books, 1972). From the "Introduction" by Minney.

30. Molly Tompkins to Shaw. 51 West 53rd Street, N.Y. [November 1945]. British Library.

Index

Index

Index

Index

455

Index

Index

Index